LANDSCAPE TURNED RED

STEPHEN W. SEARS

LANDSCAPE
TURNED
RED

☆

The Battle of Antietam

TICKNOR & FIELDS

NEW HAVEN AND NEW YORK

Copyright © 1983 by Stephen W. Sears
All rights reserved. No part of this work may be reproduced or transmitted in any form or by any means, electronic or mechanical, including photocopying and recording, or by any information storage or retrieval system, except as may be expressly permitted by the 1976 Copyright Act or in writing by the publisher. Requests for permission should be addressed in writing to
Ticknor & Fields, 383 Orange Street,
New Haven, Connecticut 06511.

Library of Congress Cataloging in Publication Data
Sears, Stephen W.
Landscape turned red.
Bibliography: p.
Includes index.
1. Antietam, Battle of, 1862. Title.
E474.65.S43   1983   973.7'336   82-19519
ISBN 0-89919-172-X

Printed in the United States of America

D 10 9 8 7 6 5 4

Maps by Herbert S. Borst

Acknowledgment is made for permission to quote from the following copyrighted works:

I Rode with Stonewall, by Henry Kyd Douglas. Copyright 1940 The University of North Carolina Press. By permission of the publisher.

A Virginia Yankee in the Civil War: The Diaries of David Hunter Strother, edited by Cecil D. Eby, Jr. Copyright 1961 The University of North Carolina Press. By permission of the publisher.

The General to His Lady: The Civil War Letters of William Dorsey Pender to Fanny Pender, edited by William W. Hassler. Copyright 1965 The University of North Carolina Press. By permission of the publisher.

From the Cannon's Mouth: The Civil War Letters of General Alpheus S. Williams, edited by Milo M. Quaife. Copyright 1959 Wayne State University Press. By permission of the Wayne State University Press.

The Diary of George Templeton Strong: The Civil War, 1860–1865, edited by Allan Nevins and Milton H. Thomas. Copyright 1952 by Macmillan Publishing Co., Inc., renewed 1980 by Milton Halsey Thomas. By permission of the publisher.

Dear Belle: Letters from a Cadet and Officer to His Sweetheart, 1858–1865, narrative and editing by Catherine S. Crary, foreword by Bruce Catton. Copyright 1965 by Wesleyan University. By permission of Wesleyan University Press.

Lincoln and the Civil War in the Diaries and Letters of John Hay, edited by Tyler Dennett. Copyright 1939 Dodd, Mead & Company, Inc. By permission of the publisher.

Civil War Letters of George Washington Whitman, edited by Jerome M. Loving. Copyright 1975 Duke University Press, Durham, N.C. By permission of the publisher.

For Sally T.

CONTENTS

Introduction	xi
Prologue. The Last, Best Hope	1
1. The Limits of Limited War	19
2. Confederate Tide	49
3. Will Send You Trophies	74
4. Fire on the Mountain	114
5. We Will Make Our Stand	150
6. To the Dunker Church	180
7. A Savage Continual Thunder	216
8. The Spires of Sharpsburg	255
9. To Nobly Save or Meanly Lose	298
Epilogue. A Last Farewell	336
Appendix I. The Lost Order	349
Appendix II. Burnside and His Bridge	353
Appendix III. The Armies at Antietam	359
Sources and Acknowledgments	373
Notes	375
Bibliography	405
Index	415

Illustrations follow page 210

MAPS

The Invasion of Maryland September 3–13, 1862	98
McClellan's Offensive at South Mountain September 14, 1862	127
Battle of Turner's Gap September 14, 1862	138
Battle of Crampton's Gap September 14, 1862	138
Battle of Antietam September 17, 1862 Situation at Daybreak	183
Battle of Antietam Attack of the Federal First Corps 6:00–7:30 A.M.	196
Battle of Antietam Attack of the Federal Twelfth Corps 7:30–9:00 A.M.	212
Battle of Antietam Attack of the Federal Second Corps 9:00 A.M.–1:00 P.M.	233
Battle of Antietam Attack of the Federal Ninth Corps 10:00 A.M.–4:30 P.M.	278
Battle of Antietam Situation at Nightfall	295

INTRODUCTION

Of all the days on all the fields where American soldiers have fought, the most terrible by almost any measure was September 17, 1862. The battle waged on that date, close by Antietam Creek at Sharpsburg in western Maryland, took a human toll never exceeded on any other single day in the nation's history. So intense and sustained was the violence, a man recalled, that for a moment in his mind's eye the very landscape around him turned red.

By almost any measure, too, Antietam was pivotal in the history of the Civil War. In September 1862 events across a broad spectrum — military, political, social, diplomatic — were rushing toward a climax. The battle in Maryland would affect all of them radically, turning the course of the war in new directions.

It was a time of opportunity for the South and of peril for the North. Robert E. Lee had carried the war from Richmond to Washington and now led his army northward into Maryland in a bold effort to win independence for the Confederacy. The European powers, closely debating intervention in the American contest, were watching Lee's progress intently. Confederate armies were also on the offensive in the western theater. The Union cause was at its nadir. The Federal army girding to meet Lee, stricken with a crisis of confidence, was entrusted to George B. McClellan, a general many believed to be gravely flawed as a commander. There was growing discontent in the Northern states with the administration's management of the conflict. Abraham Lincoln's political support was divided and wavering even as he grappled with a revolutionary change of purpose, seeking to make this a war against slavery as well as a war for union. When the two armies finally faced one another across the shallow valley of the Antietam and prepared for battle, the sense of crisis was palpable. With his flair for the dramatic, General McClellan announced that the fate of the Republic was at stake, and so indeed it seemed.

This account of the Maryland campaign, of the complex backdrop against which it was played, and of the desperate struggle along the banks of the Antietam is drawn in large part from the testimony of eyewitnesses. There was in this setting — the pastoral Maryland countryside, the rugged terrain at Harper's Ferry and South Mountain, the rolling farmland and open woodlots around Sharpsburg — a particular sense of history being made that set it apart from previous campaigning and inspired men to record their impressions in detail in journals and letters. Their accounts are an invaluable supplement to the official reports and dispatches and battlefield messages.

Beyond providing such primary source materials, Antietam is unique in being the subject of an in-depth nineteenth-century historical research project. In the postwar years two participants in the battle, Colonel Ezra A. Carman of the 13th New Jersey and Major John M. Gould of the 10th Maine, undertook a survey of thousands of Antietam veterans, from both armies, to compile their recollections of the fighting. This material — used here for the first time in a published narrative of the campaign — bears vivid witness to what it was like on that terrible field. In answering the questions posed by Carman and Gould, the veterans repeatedly stressed that no matter how many other battles they endured during the war, there was nothing quite like that bloody seventeenth of September. As one Southerner put it, after the passage of time it might seem "almost impossible to remember with any degree of accuracy, circumstances that took place then. But these things are indelibly impressed upon my memory...." In these recollections is abundant evidence that the struggle along Antietam Creek was the most bitter and savage of the Civil War.

LANDSCAPE TURNED RED

· PROLOGUE ·

THE LAST, BEST HOPE

Charles Francis Adams, Jr., first lieutenant in the 1st Massachusetts cavalry, grandson and great-grandson of presidents, was in Washington to take the national pulse. He was shaken by what he found. At a writing table in one of the parlors in Willard's Hotel he set down his impressions for his father, the American minister to the Court of St. James's in London.

"I think I can give you a little more light than you now have," young Adams wrote under the date August 27, 1862. "Do you know that in the opinion of our leading military men Washington is in more danger than it ever yet has been? Do you know that but for McDowell's jealousy we should have triumphantly marched into Richmond? Do you know that Pope is a humbug and known to be so by those who put him in his present place? Do you know that today he is so completely outgeneraled as to be cut off from Washington?" The Union cause was in deep crisis, he continued. "Our rulers seem to me to be crazy. The air of this city seems thick with treachery; our army seems in danger of utter demoralization. . . . Everything is ripe for a terrible panic, the end of which I cannot see or even imagine." He had looked in vain for a silver lining. "It is my glimpse behind the scenes, the conviction that small men with selfish motives control the war without any central power to keep them in bounds, which terrifies and discourages me."[1]

A lesser mortal might have been content simply to record that day's gloomy mood at Willard's, the central listening post for all rumor and gossip in the capital. An Adams had better connections.

His glimpse behind the scenes was furnished by Colonel J. C. Kelton, a staff officer at the three-story brick building on Seventeenth Street near the White House that housed the War Department. The situation as Colonel Kelton described it was enough to discourage even an eternal optimist.

Viewed from the War Department, the military picture in these last days of August 1862 was badly obscured and thus highly unsettling. At last report, the Army of Virginia under John Pope and his second-in-command, Irvin McDowell — the generals regarded with such disdain by Lieutenant Adams — was being stalked by a shadowy force of armed Confederates in the Virginia countryside just twenty-five or thirty miles to the west. No one in Pope's army or in the capital seemed able to say where these Rebels were or in what strength or what they intended. The one certainty was that things were going very wrong. Only two months earlier Richmond had been under siege and apparently doomed, and with it the Confederacy. Now menace crowded Washington's doorstep, prompting talk of treachery and malfeasance in the high command.

The abrupt reversal had begun late in June with the checkmating of General George B. McClellan's Army of the Potomac on the Virginia peninsula southeast of Richmond. On August 3 McClellan was ordered to give up his balked campaign and return to Washington to combine forces with General Pope's newly formed Army of Virginia. McClellan accepted the order with bad grace, and the evacuation was taking time — too much time, in the opinion of the War Department. For a good part of August most of the Army of the Potomac was off the military chessboard, its troops on the march to embarkation points or aboard transports in Chesapeake Bay and the lower Potomac.

Meanwhile, John Pope reported sudden and alarming pressure from the enemy. "His whole force, as far as can be ascertained, is massed in front of me," he signaled on August 25. He called for reinforcements, for supplies, for guidance. Then, on August 26, the telegraph linking his army with Washington went dead. Within hours the line from Manassas Junction, on the Orange and Alexandria Railroad well to the rear of the Army of Virginia and the site of its main supply base, also went dead. The last news from the

Manassas telegrapher was ominous: "No. 6 train, engine Secretary, was fired into at Bristoe by a party of secesh cavalry — some say 500 strong. . . ."

The clear and sunny weather on Wednesday, August 27, brought no more cheer to official Washington than it did to Lieutenant Adams. News was fragmentary and uniformly bad. Civilian refugees reaching Alexandria, half a dozen miles down the Potomac from the capital, carried tales of the huge supply depot at Manassas Junction looted and in flames and Rebels everywhere. Colonel Herman Haupt, the energetic supervisor of military railroads, had messages from his telegraphers at other stations along the Orange and Alexandria confirming that the enemy was indeed astride the Army of Virginia's supply line, and with more than just cavalry. General Pope remained cut off from communication with Washington. However, one of the Army of the Potomac units already in the field, Fitz John Porter's Fifth Corps, retained a telegraphic link with General Ambrose Burnside at Falmouth, to the south. Porter, waxing sarcastic on Pope's generalship, warned of an imminent battle. He added a personal plea to his friend Burnside: "I wish myself away from it, with all our old Army of the Potomac, and so do our companions. . . . If you can get me away please do so. Make what use of this you choose, so it does good." Burnside forwarded Porter's dispatch to General-in-Chief Henry W. Halleck at the War Department.[2]

General Halleck was a man sorely tried. Porter's commentary was fresh evidence that his task of melding McClellan's Army of the Potomac with Pope's Army of Virginia was a case of mixing oil with water. Part of the trouble was Pope's ill repute among the Potomac army's officer corps. His handling of troops, McClellan angrily wrote his wife, was "infamous conduct & he deserves hanging for it." Porter made no secret of his contempt, calling Pope an ass. General Samuel D. Sturgis, who had served with Pope in the western theater earlier in the war, expressed his opinion more picturesquely. A few days before, Sturgis had tied up Colonel Haupt's railroad by commandeering troop trains for his men at Alexandria. When Haupt stormed into Sturgis's headquarters, he found the general fortified with drink and unrepentant. It would take twenty-four hours to untangle the mess, Haupt complained, and leave Pope out on a limb, a prospect that moved Sturgis to intone, "I don't care for John Pope a pinch of owl dung!" Only by threatening him with arrest on Halleck's authority could Haupt get his railroad back. Yet the problem went far deeper than personal animosity. The greatest of Halleck's trials was proving to be the character and conduct of General McClellan himself.[3]

McClellan and Halleck offered a study in contrasts. The head of the Army of the Potomac was the very image of the fighting general — stocky and martial in bearing, youthful and personable, with a commanding presence that made him greatly admired by his troops. With perfect sincerity his supporters called him the "Young Napoleon." Halleck was called "Old Brains," and seldom admiringly. A dumpy, paunchy figure with staring, fishlike eyes, he was quite without presence; his natural habitat was an office desk rather than a battlefield. Yet in one respect the two men were much alike. Both were versed in the rules of bureaucratic survival: be ever cautious, deflect responsibility whenever possible, protect flanks and rear at all times from the hostile fire of critics. Early that Wednesday, when McClellan reported in from his new headquarters at Alexandria, they began the mutual practice of their art.

Under McClellan's immediate command were two Army of the Potomac corps — William B. Franklin's Sixth and Edwin V. Sumner's Second — not yet in the field with Pope. Halleck wanted Franklin, already at Alexandria, to cover the twenty-five miles to Manassas Junction "by forced marches" to reinforce Pope. McClellan assured the general-in-chief that the necessary orders would go out "at once." "I have no time for details," Halleck wired, explaining that he was busy with recruiting matters and the western theater; "as ranking general in the field, direct as you deem best."

As the day wore on, however, McClellan began urging a prudent second look at the situation. Franklin's corps was short of artillery horses and cavalry and supply wagons. Might it be marching into a trap? Would it not be better to hold it back until reinforced by Sumner's corps? Would it not be best to make the defense of Washington the first priority? He could not approve a proposal by Colonel Haupt for an armed reconnaissance along the Orange and Alexandria; it was too risky an undertaking given the fluid situation. "I am not responsible for the past," he telegraphed Halleck, "and cannot be for the future, unless I receive authority to dispose of the available troops according to my judgment. Please inform me at once what my position is." Halleck sidestepped the question. He had assured McClellan, when ordering him back from the Peninsula, that he would command the joint armies. But events — and the Confederates — were moving too quickly. The general-in-chief now found it neither politic nor possible to displace Pope. McClellan read the politics and the possibilities differently.[4]

Abraham Lincoln was one of those monitoring this McClellan-Halleck byplay. It was the president's habit to cross the White House lawn at least once a day to the side door of the War Department on Seventeenth Street and visit the telegraphers' room on the second floor. In this quiet seclusion he studied copies of all the dispatches, sensing in the flimsy tissues the daily heartbeat of the war. In times of crisis he might stay the night, as he had on the twenty-sixth, when Pope's danger became apparent, dozing on the couch in the adjoining office of Secretary of War Edwin Stanton while awaiting telegrams from the front. It was soon clear to Lincoln that in this particular crisis the most industrious figure on the scene was the railroad man, Colonel Haupt. He began sending Haupt short telegraphic inquiries for the latest news, signed "A. Lincoln."

Haupt believed in direct action, and in any case it was his railroad that was taking a beating and he needed to know the details. McClellan struck him as altogether too cautious, and on his own he hunted up some troops for his reconnaissance scheme. The next day he could report that "The rebel forces at Manassas were large, and several of their best generals were in command." He added that damage to the line was heavy and "the Army of Virginia can receive no more supplies by rail at present...."[5]

By Thursday the twenty-eighth a pattern was evident to readers of McClellan's dispatches. There was assurance of much activity at Alexandria, but no movement. Despite Halleck's repeated orders, Franklin's corps still made no move to march to Pope's support. It was not yet fully equipped, McClellan explained; perhaps tomorrow. Meanwhile, he judged Washington's defenses to be alarmingly undermanned. Worse was to come. In late afternoon he announced to Halleck that "Neither Franklin nor Sumner's corps is now in condition to move and fight a battle. It would be a sacrifice to send them out...." At ten that night he climaxed his day's telegraphing with a doomsday prediction: "Reports numerous, from various sources, ... that the enemy, with 120,000 men, intend advancing on the forts near Arlington and Chain Bridge, with a view to attacking Washington and Baltimore."[6]

There was a familiar ring to all this. In his thirteen months as commander of the Army of the Potomac, the Young Napoleon had furnished Washington with many such carefully constructed castles of logic. The enemy confronting him was invariably a host. Thus every art of war must be perfected, with every man and gun and wagon in place, before risking a move against such odds; thus nothing dared be hurried nor any chances taken. Nothing of what was happening was his fault. He could not be blamed for the crisis, for he had warned of the consequences if his army was withdrawn from the Peninsula. He could not accept responsibility for meeting it, for his troops were being taken from him brigade by brigade, division by division, despite the promise that he would have field command of the joint armies. To certain of Washington's veteran McClellan-watchers, it began to look very much as if the general, maneuvering carefully behind a bureaucratic smokescreen, was manipulating events so as to be in position to pick up the pieces, and in the meantime bending no effort, cutting no corner, to rescue his fellow general.

One of those reaching this conclusion was Secretary of War Stanton, who had long since come to regard George McClellan as a master of cant. Edwin M. Stanton was a man of uncompromising views, virulent suspicions, and vast angry energy. A newspaper reporter who had interviewed him when he took office the previous January remarked that "Force — undaunted Force — Stanton's indisputable characteristic — streamed from the eyes, hair, whiskers, and very garments of the new Secretary of War." The events of the past few days snapped the last frayed strands of the secretary's patience. He vowed that McClellan must be dismissed. His first step was to demand from Halleck an accounting of McClellan's recent stewardship. As if preparing a legal brief of the sort he had produced in civilian life, Stanton called for the point-by-point record, with supporting documents, of the general's actions since the Peninsula campaign, and asked bluntly if these actions were taken "as promptly as the national safety required."[7]

In the continued absence of news from Pope's headquarters, Washington fed on rumor. Halleck had imposed a rigorous newspaper censorship by banning reporters from the Army of Virginia, so newsmen scoured the military camps around the capital and canvassed the public rooms at Willard's for tidbits, however unreliable the source. The Confederate General Lee, it was said, had been seen far behind the supposed Union front lines. Stonewall Jackson had been recognized in half a dozen places and was also believed to be surrounded and his capture imminent. The dreaded Rebel cavalry had been sighted on the very outskirts of Alexandria. The sudden military bustle in the capital seemed significant in itself, with couriers spurring lathered horses along Pennsylvania Avenue and raw new regiments from the North plodding through the streets leading from the depot to the outlying camps.

On Friday morning, August 29, McClellan announced to Halleck that Franklin's corps had marched at 6 A.M., though not "in condition to accomplish much if he meets with serious resistance. I should not have moved him but for your pressing order...." In subsequent signals he continued to urge caution on Franklin's mission, and pressed Halleck to hold Sumner's corps in the Washington fortifications. "I want Franklin's corps to go far enough to find out something about the enemy," Halleck replied with some asperity. "... Our people must move more actively and find out where the enemy is. I am tired of guesses." The president entered the debate with a wire to McClellan calling for a situation report. McClellan confidently spread his cards on the table: "I am clear that one of two courses should be adopted: 1st, to concentrate all our available forces to open communications with Pope; 2nd, to leave Pope to get out of his scrape, and at once use all our means to make the capital perfectly safe."[8]

Lincoln calmly responded that aiding Pope was the proper course, but the phrase "leave Pope to get out of his scrape" deeply angered him. Newspaperman Adams Hill said he had never seen him "so wrathful as last night against George." "The President was very outspoken in regard to McClellan's present conduct," Lincoln's secretary John Hay wrote in his diary. "He said it really seemed to him that McC. wanted Pope defeated."[9]

That day another diarist, George Templeton Strong, a New York lawyer and socialite with good connections in the capital, speculated on the reports from Virginia. The Rebels, he wrote, "have penetrated to Manassas, destroying supply trains and capturing guns, taking us by surprise. Are our generals traitors or imbecile? Why does the Rebellion enjoy the monopoly of audacity and enterprise?" In Washington Secretary Stanton was asking the same questions. He sought reinforcement for his campaign against McClellan by calling on his cabinet ally, Secretary of the Treasury Salmon P. Chase. He found a receptive audience. Chase, whose dedication to making hard war was matched by his ambitions for the White House, was a Pope supporter and thus decidedly unhappy with McClellan's conduct. The two secretaries descended on General Halleck, demanding an explanation for what Chase in his diary described as "McC's disobedience of orders and consequent delay of support to Army of Va." Stanton and Chase then went off to drum up additional cabinet support for their "remonstrance" against the Young Napoleon.[10]

Troubles piled up rapidly on General Halleck's desk during the day. There were reports from the city's outer fortifications of cannon fire from the direction of the old Bull Run battlefield of 1861. Burnside in Falmouth forwarded another pessimistic signal from Fitz John Porter, who remarked on Confederate forces "wandering around loose; but I expect they know what they are doing, which is more than any one here or anywhere knows." That evening Halleck sharply queried McClellan as to why Franklin's corps had halted at Annandale, a village less than ten miles from Alexandria: "This is all contrary to my orders; investigate and report the facts of this disobedience." McClellan replied in a huff: "It is not agreeable to me to be accused of disregarding orders when I have simply exercised the discretion you committed to me." Franklin whiled away his time at Annandale interrogating refugees. They confirmed heavy cannonading to

The Last, Best Hope

the west, he signaled. "All the best witnesses and all of the citizens who have passed consider Jackson in a dangerous position."[11]

"Everything is in the utmost consternation," General John Sedgwick, one of Sumner's division commanders, wrote his sister on Saturday, August 30. "Washington people seem to lose their senses at the most unfounded rumours, but there may be some cause for it now." Franklin's corps took up its march again that morning, and shortly after noon Sumner's corps was also in motion. "They must use their legs and make forced marches," Halleck urged. "Time now is everything." In the three full days since receipt of the order to send troops to Pope's support, McClellan's lead brigades were but fifteen miles west of Alexandria. McClellan blamed the delays on the failure of the quartermaster's department to furnish the necessary wagons. The only role left to him now was that of martyr: "If it is not deemed best to intrust me with the command even of my own army, I simply ask to be permitted to share their fate on the field of battle."[12]

Secretaries Stanton and Chase continued their plotting. They were braced by Halleck's response to their demand for an accounting. McClellan had not obeyed orders, the general-in-chief wrote, "with the promptness I expected and the national safety, in my opinion, required." Chase had no trouble engaging the support of Attorney General Edward Bates. He went on to the War Department, where he inspected a petition calling for McClellan's dismissal that Stanton had drawn up for the cabinet to sign and present to Lincoln. It accused the general of incompetence and disobedience that imperiled Pope's army. After tinkering with the wording, both men signed it. Chase then sought the signature of Navy Secretary Gideon Welles. Welles, one of the cabinet members most respected by the president, "concurred in judgment," Chase wrote, "but thought the paper not exactly right and did not sign it." Chase returned the petition to Stanton for further revision. They intended to confront Lincoln with it no later than the cabinet meeting scheduled for Tuesday. The implied threat was the breakup of the administration unless McClellan was cashiered.[13]

Beginning about noon that Saturday, the muttered sound of artillery could again be heard in the city, and a westerly breeze carried the sharp smell of gunpowder. Listeners thought the sound more distant than the day before, which many took as the sign of a Confederate withdrawal. At last, in midafternoon, General Pope's long silence was broken. A dispatch written at five that morning had finally made its slow way to the War Department. He described a "terrific battle" fought the day before on the site of the 1861 Bull Run contest. "The enemy was driven from the field, which we now occupy," Pope continued. He estimated his casualties at 8,000 and the losses of the "badly used up" Rebels at twice that. The enemy was thought to be in retreat, and he was preparing to follow up his advantage. Secretary Stanton had the good news posted for the crowd gathered around the public bulletin board at the Treasury and released it to the newspapers. It was also flashed to New York, where diarist Strong recorded its arrival. "God grant this may be true and the whole truth," he wrote. "But I am not prepared to crow quite yet. Pope is an imaginative chieftain and ranks next to Cooper as a writer of fiction."[14]

Pope's report of heavy casualties impelled Secretary Stanton to action. He ordered appeals put up in the city's hotels for volunteer surgeons and male nurses and stretcher-bearers, and by late afternoon Washington was jammed with ambulances and hacks and private carriages setting out on errands of mercy. Hundreds of volunteers descended on Colonel Haupt at Alexandria, demanding rail transportation to the front. Haupt was appalled at the prospect. Requested to bring alcoholic stimulants for the wounded, the Good Samaritans were priming themselves instead. He delayed sending this trainload of "rabble" as long as possible, then finally dispatched it with orders to the provost marshal at Fairfax Station up the line to remove everyone he found drunk. The roads leading westward were crowded with similar motley caravans of "excited nurses" and curious sightseers.

Saturday evening brought rain and harsh reality. The turnpike east of the village of Centreville was filled with Federal stragglers and walking wounded. They carried tales of disaster rather than of victory. McClellan's reinforcements finally reached the scene, to discover Pope's army in full retreat. The only role for the 25,000 men of Franklin's and Sumner's corps was deployment to cover the withdrawal. The mood of the battered Army of Virginia was not improved by its reception at Centreville. Captain Charles Walcott of the battleworn 21st Massachusetts remembered that "our hearts leaped with joy" as they approached the Army of the Potomac units that evening. But, he wrote, "they greeted us with mocking laughter, taunts, and jeers on the advantages of the new route to Richmond; while many of them, in plain English, expressed their joy at the downfall of the braggart rival of the great soldier of the Peninsula."[15]

In a dispatch to Halleck, Pope admitted a reverse but put the best face on it: "The troops are in good heart, and marched off the field without the least hurry or confusion. . . . The enemy is badly crippled, and we shall do well enough." A surgeon at the general's field headquarters, however, found no trace of such confidence. He observed Pope sitting slumped in a chair tipped against the wall, head lowered, "seeming to pay no attention to the generals as they arrived but to be wholly wrapped in his own gloomy reflections."[16]

The true reckoning of events did not reach as far as Washington that evening. At a dinner party Secretary Stanton treated his guests to his unsparing view of McClellan, insisting that only "foul play" on the part of the general and his army friends could lose the current campaign and darkly predicting court-martial proceedings. On his way home from the Stantons, John Hay stopped off at the War Department, where he found Halleck confident of Pope's ultimate victory in what the general-in-chief described as the greatest battle of the century. He assured Hay that every available man was in the field.

"Everything seemed to be going well and hilarious on Saturday & we went to bed expecting glad tidings at sunrise," Hay noted in his diary. But at 8 A.M. that wet and gloomy Sunday, Lincoln came to his secretary's room in the White House with ill tidings: "Well, John, we are whipped again, I am afraid." The morning newspapers, in contrast, were cheerful, featuring Pope's optimistic signal of Saturday morning and adding embroidery of their own. A Washington woman wrote in her journal of newsboys crying, "General Jackson and sixty thousand rebels taken!" Later she added, "The papers were rather premature. The latest news is that the Federals are falling back." Thus the truth of Pope's defeat seeped slowly through the capital. It reminded many of the rainy Sunday thirteen months earlier when Washington learned of another defeat at Bull Run. There was growing fear for the capital's safety, and some residents made preparations to flee.[17]

By noon stark evidence of the fighting began to appear as long processions of ambulances packed with wounded clattered through the city's streets. With them came the stragglers, last in battle and first in retreat, peddling their tales to credulous listeners in barrooms and on street corners. The roads leading into Alexandria and Washington were clogged with more ambulances, supply trains, and groups of the would-be nurses and stretcher-bearers, wet and bedraggled and hung over, put off the railroad on Colonel Haupt's order. At Centreville the last of the beaten Army of Virginia filed into the defensive lines. General Sturgis, commanding a brigade of reinforcements, came upon a dispirited John Pope. "Too late, Sammy, too late!" Pope called out. Sturgis was unforgiving: "I always told you that if they gave you rope enough you would hang yourself!"[18]

Pope's forced optimism had sagged into pessimism and doubts about the fighting courage of his men. In a signal to Halleck he promised "as desperate a fight as I can force our men to stand up to. I should like to know whether you feel secure about Washington should this army be destroyed." McClellan added to the general-in-chief's woes with a report that the city's outlying works were inadequately armed, and that 20,000 stragglers from Pope's army were wandering around loose.

Halleck's already limited control over events evaporated entirely. Shortly after ten that Sunday night he wired McClellan, "I beg of you to assist me in this crisis with your ability and experience. I am entirely tired out." McClellan tightened the screws: "I am ready to afford you any assistance in my power, but you will readily perceive how difficult an undefined position, such as I now hold, must be. At what hour in the morning can I see you alone, either at your own house or the office?" He followed this up, an hour later, with a digest of the latest bad news from the front. "To speak frankly — and the occasion requires it — there appears to be a total absence of brains, and I fear the total

The Last, Best Hope

destruction of the army.... The question is the salvation of the country."[19]

The crisis deepened on Monday, September 1. Although the War Department continued to censor the news, insiders picked up enough information to regard the capital's danger as acute. Adams Hill, the well-connected bureau chief of the *New York Tribune*, wrote his managing editor, "For the first time, if I remember, I believe it possible ... that Washington may be taken.... I take my duty to be, being accredited near the Gov't, I stay while it stays and skedaddle when it skedaddles." The arrival of more stragglers and wounded added to the ugly, incendiary talk of treason and treachery on the recent battlefield. To preserve order, provost marshals shut down the city's drinking places.[20]

General McClellan rode into Washington that morning and met with Halleck and the president. McClellan described the conference in a letter to his wife Ellen: "Last night ... I received a dispatch from Halleck begging me to help him out of the scrape & take command here — of course I could not refuse so I came over this morning, mad as a March hare, & had a pretty plain talk with him & Abe.... The result is that I have reluctantly consented to take command here & try to save the Capital.... If when the whole army arrives here (if it ever does) I am not placed in command of all I will either insist upon a leave of absence or resign."[21] At his urging, Halleck sent his aide Colonel Kelton — who, four days before, had given young Lieutenant Adams his behind-the-scenes view of events — to the front for a direct appraisal of the condition of Pope's forces. McClellan hurried back to the fortifications to take up his new duties as garrison commander.

The weekend's news gave fresh urgency to the efforts of Stanton and Chase to remove the general. A toned-down version of their remonstrance was agreed upon and written out by Bates, presumably to give it the force of a recommendation by the attorney general's office. It announced to Lincoln the signers' "painful duty" to declare "our deliberate opinion that, at this time, it is not safe to entrust to Major General McClellan the command of any of the armies of the United States." It was signed by Stanton, Chase, Bates, and a new convert, Interior Secretary Caleb B. Smith. Secretary of State William H. Seward was out of town and unavailable — rather conveniently, the others thought. Postmaster General Montgomery Blair, a McClellan supporter, was not approached. Chase took it upon himself to try once more for Gideon Welles's signature. To his chagrin, he failed. The whole business, Welles said, was improper, disrespectful, and an offense to the president. Chase agreed that the procedure was unusual, "but the case was unusual"; he "deliberately believed McClellan ought to be shot," Welles reported. Although if he could not obtain the navy secretary's signature on the remonstrance, Chase at least won his promise that he "would have no hesitation in saying or agreeing mainly in what was there expressed" at the next day's cabinet meeting.[22]

In the meantime, ruminating on his defeat, General Pope concluded that he was the victim of a treasonous conspiracy. It was his duty, he telegraphed Halleck, to report "the unsoldierly and dangerous conduct" of a number of McClellan's officers in the recent battle. "Every word and act and intention is discouraging, and calculated to break down the spirits of the men and produce disaster.... Their constant talk, indulged in publicly and in promiscuous company, is that the Army of the Potomac will not fight; that they are demoralized by withdrawal from the Peninsula, &c." The only answer for it was to pull back into the Washington fortifications and reorganize. "You may avoid great disaster by doing so," he concluded.[23]

Here at last a leading actor in the drama was giving weight to the swirling rumors of treachery. Pope's charges also gave tongue to a new fear: perhaps some or all of the army's officers and men would refuse to fight should the battle be renewed. McClellan was ordered back to the city that afternoon for another conference with Halleck and the president. By McClellan's account, a distressed Lincoln pleaded with him "as a special favor" to use his influence to persuade the Army of the Potomac's officer corps to support Pope in the crisis. Possibly there was a rather different air about the meeting; John Hay reported the president "in a singularly defiant tone of mind" and determined that the troops must stand and fight. In any event, McClellan sent a dispatch to Fitz John Porter to ask that he and "my friends in the Army of the Potomac ... extend to General Pope the same support they ever

The Last, Best Hope 15

have to me." Porter's response was pious to a fault: "You may rest assured that all your friends . . . will ever give, as they have given, to General Pope their cordial co-operation and constant support. . . ."[24]

Even as McClellan conferred with his superiors, sounds of renewed battle came from the direction of Chantilly, a country estate a few miles north of Centreville and on the flank of Pope's army. At dusk the cannonading was drowned out by a spectacular storm that slashed the darkening sky with lightning and shook the ground with thunder claps. The storm's passing left the battlefield in silence, as if the contestants were stunned by the violent display.

The cool, windswept dawn on Tuesday, September 2, brought with it Pope's latest dispatch. It was a confession of final failure: "We had another pretty severe fight last night. . . . Unless something can be done to restore tone to this army it will melt away before you know it." Colonel Kelton was back at the War Department with a report detailing demoralization and massive straggling at the front.

Lincoln came to a decision. He and Halleck walked the few blocks from the War Department to McClellan's quarters on H Street, where the general had spent the night. McClellan was breakfasting when they arrived. As he later described the meeting, he was magnanimous in victory: the president "regarded Washington as lost, and asked me if I would, under the circumstances, as a favor to him, resume command and do the best that could be done." All the forces under Pope would be ordered back to the Washington fortifications and turned over to him. A few hours later, the Young Napoleon dashed off a note to his wife, telling her that "everything is to come under my command again! . . . I only consent to take it for my country's sake and with the humble hope that God has called me to it. . . ."[25]

Secretary of War Stanton expected September 2 to mark his finest hour. He was a whirlwind of activity. The commandant of the city arsenal was instructed to issue arms and ammunition to government workers for a last-ditch defense of the capital. Any surplus armaments were to be sent to New York to prevent them from falling into Confederate hands. War Department clerks hurriedly bundled up important documents for shipment to safety.

Gunboats steamed up the Potomac to add their powerful batteries to the city's defenses. The steamer *Wachusett* stood by to take off key government officials should it become necessary.[26] In preparation for the scheduled cabinet meeting, the secretary tucked the anti-McClellan remonstrance in his pocket and stopped by Halleck's office for the latest news. What he learned there left him shaking with rage.

While waiting for Stanton and the president, the assembled cabinet members discussed the circumstances of Pope's defeat. There was a consensus, Welles reported, that Pope had "not been seconded and sustained as he should have been by several generals." It was agreed that a change in command was essential, but that McClellan was unfit for the post. Stanton then came in and announced, barely restraining his fury, that McClellan had been appointed to joint command of the two armies defending Washington. "General surprise was expressed," Welles wrote.

The president confirmed the appointment. To Stanton's objection that no such order had been issued by the War Department, Lincoln replied that the decision was his and that he would be responsible for it to the country. Secretary Chase embarked on a long condemnation of the general, concluding that "giving the command to him was equivalent to giving Washington to the rebels." It deeply distressed him to go counter to the opinion of the cabinet, Lincoln said; he would "gladly resign his plan" if there was any other general who could do what needed to be done. But there was none. McClellan's engineering and defensive skills were necessary to prepare and man the capital's fortifications. His organizational ability was vital for the meshing of the two armies. He acknowledged McClellan's "slows" and the criticisms of his recent conduct — privately he had told John Hay that McClellan's actions during the past week were "unpardonable" — yet one factor above all others made the appointment necessary: only McClellan had the confidence of the fighting men.

Thus Lincoln gauged the measure of the crisis — the fear that under Pope the demoralized troops defending Washington would not fight. "There was a more disturbed and desponding feeling than I have ever witnessed in council," Welles observed. The remonstrance remained in Stanton's pocket, its delivery made

The Last, Best Hope

pointless by the president's decision. Stanton returned to the War Department, his secretary remembered, "in the condition of a drooping leaf."[27]

In late afternoon McClellan rode to the headquarters of General Jacob D. Cox in the city's outermost works. Dapper in dress sword and yellow sash, cheerful and animated, he greeted Cox, "Well, General, I am in command again!" Soon the leading element of the Army of Virginia appeared, bound for the fortifications. This division of McDowell's corps, like the rest of the beaten army, was in ill temper; just then there was no man on earth these troops hated more than Irvin McDowell, unless it was John Pope. A bystander watching the retreat described the general attitude as "one of mortification and rage, tempered slightly with disgust."[28]

Pope and McDowell and their staffs were at the head of the column, and McClellan rode out to meet them. After an exchange of formal salutes, he took over command and briefly discussed troop dispositions. General John Hatch was one of those who edged close enough to overhear the conversation. Still smoldering from a recent reprimand and demotion at Pope's hands, Hatch took his revenge. He turned back to the nearby troops, swung his sword above his head, and cried out, "Boys, McClellan is in command again! Three cheers!"

There was a second or two of stunned silence, then the column exploded. For as long as they lived men remembered the moment — how they yelled themselves hoarse and hurled caps and knapsacks high in the air and kicked up their heels in the dusty road. The news flashed along the ranks like summer lightning, sending a continuous thunder of cheering rolling off into the distance. Through the night the tidings spread across the countryside from division to division, corps to corps. Roadside bivouacs were jolted awake as staff officers galloped past, calling out, "Little Mac is back!" Men leaped to their feet and "shout upon shout went out into the stillness of the night," a veteran recalled years later. "The effect of this man's presence upon the Army of the Potomac — in sunshine or rain, in darkness or in daylight, in victory or defeat — was electrical, and too wonderful to make it worth while attempting to give a reason for it." Another man was content with a simpler summary: "A Deliverer had come."[29]

The next day, Halleck dispatched the latest situation report to McClellan. "There is every probability that the enemy, baffled in his intended capture of Washington, will cross the Potomac, and make a raid into Maryland or Pennsylvania," he wrote. "A movable army must be immediately organized to meet him again in the field."[30]

· 1 ·

THE LIMITS OF LIMITED WAR

Washington's week of crisis demonstrated that General George McClellan could dominate the scene even when off-stage. He knew it as well, and accepted it as his due. In writing his wife that he believed it to be God's will that he was called upon to resume high command for the sake of the country, he was not announcing a new revelation.

As early as July 1861, when he was brought to the capital to pick up the pieces after the first Federal rout at Bull Run, he mused to Ellen, "Who would have thought, when we were married, that I should so soon be called upon to save my country?" A week or so later he elaborated the theme: "I feel that God has placed a great work in my hands.... Pray for me, that I may be able to accomplish my task — the greatest, perhaps, that any poor, weak mortal ever had to do." "God will support me and bear me out," he wrote when challenged by those he considered small-minded and incapable; "He could not have placed me here for nothing." McClellan's star and that of the Union waxed and waned in the following months, but his messianic vision burned steadily.

To be sure, it was not uncommon in that era of intense religious fervor for generals to invoke the Deity. Stonewall Jackson, for one, invariably attributed Confederate victories to the blessings of a kind Providence. Yet McClellan alone professed to be the chosen instrument of that Providence rather than simply its grateful servant. This belief formed a vital part of the mental armor he raised against anyone who dared question or dispute his view of the conflict and the way it should be fought. By the late summer of 1862, however, that conception of how to meet the challenge of civil war had carried the Union perilously close to permanent division.[1]

What strength of character George Brinton McClellan brought to his mission was untempered by adversity. He had climbed life's ladder with ease and without pause. The son of a prosperous and socially prominent Philadelphia physician, he entered West Point at age fifteen, receiving special dispensation to do so. He achieved an outstanding record and was graduated second in the class of 1846. Serving as an engineer in the Mexican War, he was twice breveted for gallantry. In 1855 Captain McClellan was awarded a plum — appointment by Secretary of War Jefferson Davis to evaluate the latest military developments in Europe. His tour of Continental defense establishments included two weeks' observation of the siege of Sevastopol during the Crimean War. His report was regarded as a model performance. In 1857 he resigned his commission to enter the railroad business, where he rose rapidly. In April 1861, when Fort Sumter fell, he was head of the eastern division of the Ohio and Mississippi Railroad. Within a month he was a major general in charge of the Department of the Ohio, and was soon conducting in western Virginia one of the war's first campaigns.

He managed the campaign well, producing several small but tidy victories and securing that strategically important region for the Union. His grandiloquent proclamations thrilled the Northern citizenry and inspired the troops. "Soldiers! I have heard there was danger here," he announced. "I have come to place myself at your head and share it with you. I fear now but one thing — that you will not find foemen worthy of your steel." By late July McClellan was in Washington to take command of the dispirited force that would become the Army of the Potomac; by November he was as well general-in-chief of all the Union armies. He would not turn thirty-five for another month. When President Lincoln wondered if the burden might not be too great, he replied, "I can do it all."[2]

McClellan labored with great energy to forge the Army of the Potomac into a fighting machine. The defenses of Washington were strengthened. The troops were organized and equipped and drilled and, most important, given pride in themselves as part of

Little Mac's grand army. He sensed the need of these youthful volunteers to see, to admire, to trust the commander who would lead them to battle. Great reviews were held, with massed bands, uncased flags, everything spit and polish, then the climax of the day's pageantry as the Young Napoleon galloped past the ranks on a great black horse, trailed by his glittering staff. Nathaniel Hawthorne described one of these spectacles for readers of the *Atlantic:* "They received him with loud shouts, by the eager uproar of which — now near, now in the centre, now on the outskirts of the division, and now sweeping back towards us in a great volume of sound — we could trace his progress through the ranks...; they believed in him, and so did I; and had I stood in the ranks, I should have shouted with the lustiest of them...." McClellan spelled out a special quality about this relationship in one of his proclamations. "I am to watch over you as a parent over his children," he promised, "and you know that your General loves you from the depths of his heart." No doubt the emotion was sincere; indeed, perhaps he loved them too well.[3]

The general was less successful in sustaining the admiration of official Washington. At first the cheers were his for the asking. President, cabinet, and legislators deferred to the hero of western Virginia and praised his youthful zeal in organizing the army. "By some strange operation of magic I seem to have become the power of the land," he told his wife. But as the weeks and then the months passed and the army did not advance beyond its drill fields and parade grounds, McClellan faced increasingly sharp questioning. Why were the Rebels still allowed to hold the field they had won at Bull Run? Why were enemy batteries on the lower Potomac still permitted to blockade the water route to Washington? Why was the fine autumn campaigning weather going unused? "The public spirit is beginning to quail ...," Attorney General Bates noted in his diary on September 30. "We absolutely need some dashing expeditions — some victories great or small, to stimulate the zeal of the Country."[4]

The general commanding remained confidently aloof, ignoring what he dismissed as popular clamor. He was preparing for one mighty climactic battle, on ground of his own choosing, at the proper time when everything was finally ready. He could not yet say when that day would come. Autumn turned to winter and "all quiet on the Potomac" continued to sum up the daily situation reports.

Certain character traits surfaced during McClellan's early months of high command. He quickly displayed an imperious arrogance toward anyone he considered in his way, most notably Winfield Scott, the army's general-in-chief, whom he displaced on November 1. Scott was a revered figure, hero of a score of battlefields dating back to the War of 1812. The old warrior was now long past his prime and seriously enfeebled, but McClellan's cavalier pressure to force his retirement won him few friends in Washington. The Young Napoleon also proved to be a thin-skinned messiah. Those who questioned his judgments were without redeeming merit — Abraham Lincoln was "an idiot . . . nothing more than a well meaning baboon"; the cabinet members were geese; Washington's politicians were wretched and despicable triflers; he was disgusted and "perfectly sick" of the entire imbecile administration. "I have a set of scamps to deal with unscrupulous and false," he burst out to Ellen in November. If the army remained inactive over the winter, as he expected, his conscience was clear that "the fault will not be mine."[5]

The element of self-deception in such remarks was coming to dominate McClellan's thinking. The civilian members of the government were unversed in the arts of war and their views contemptible — though useful to excuse whatever might go wrong. The pleas of the newspapers and the citizenry and the civil authorities — what one observer termed "that powerful moving force Public Sentiment" — to take even a limited offensive, to do something about those Rebel forces camped insolently just twenty-five miles from the Capitol steps or those artillerists firing on any vessel that tried to come up the Potomac, made no sense to the general.[6] When his grand campaign got under way in good season, the enemy would have to abandon those advanced posts anyway; there was no point in risking lives against them prematurely. That military strategy was more than a highly professionalized exercise, that it might be intertwined with a need to stimulate public morale and mobilize support for the conflict in a divided North — that, in short, a civil war was a people's war, dominating the thoughts and actions of an entire populace — was something he did not acknowledge.

Another element of McClellan's self-deception was his picture of the enemy. General Joseph E. Johnston's Confederate army around Manassas and Centreville could not be directly challenged, he told the War Department, for the simple reason that it was too powerful. In late October he reported he was facing "a force on the Potomac not less than 150,000 strong, well drilled and equipped, ably commanded and strongly intrenched." He required twice as many men as he had available for "active operations," as well as more than a hundred additional field guns, before he could risk an offensive. "I cannot move without more means," he explained to his wife, "and I do not possess the power to control those means." The fault was not his but the government's. His posture, a fellow general later wrote, was "the inoffensive defensive."[7]

This estimate of Confederate strength was the work of Allan Pinkerton, the well-known Chicago private detective, whom McClellan put in charge of army intelligence. Pinkerton's network of spies and informers throughout Virginia churned out reports of astonishing detail. Rebel infantry, artillery, and cavalry units were identified and assigned manpower strengths; uniforms were described down to the last button; supplies, equipment, and troop morale were evaluated. The reports were models of brisk efficiency and infinite investigative care. The only trouble was that most of them were wrong — not wrong by the reasonable margin of error to be expected in any such intelligence-gathering, but monumentally wrong. This October evaluation, for example, credited General Johnston with more than three times his actual strength.[8]

McClellan had other intelligence sources besides Pinkerton spies, had he chosen to pay attention to them. His own officers in the field painted a very different picture. General James S. Wadsworth, whose brigade was keeping watch on Johnston's army, assessed its strength at only 50,000, based on interrogation of deserters and slave informants. General Daniel E. Sickles, on station along the lower Potomac, furnished useful reports. But neither man was regular army nor in McClellan's inner circle and such military amateurs were ignored. Also largely ignored was the Confederate example of using cavalry forays to collect intelligence. A distinguished foreign visitor, France's Prince Napoleon, inspected both armies and reported (according to *Harper's Weekly*) that the Rebels numbered about 60,000 and were "ragged, dirty, and half starved." McClellan himself, an experienced army administrator and engineer, might have wondered at Richmond's ability to maintain such a vast army as Pinkerton described at the end of a single railroad line more than a hundred miles from its home base, particularly since just then he was detailing the trials of supplying and arming his own forces that had yet to venture beyond sight of their depots.[9]

In any case, McClellan gave his official approval to Pinkerton's report and, in the months to come, to others even more imaginative. In his wartime reports and private letters, even in his postwar writings and memoirs when the facts of Confederate strength were a matter of public record, he insisted he was outnumbered at every turn. In fact these fictions suited his purposes well. The October report, for example, buttressed the strategy he was forming for a waterborne flanking movement against Richmond rather than a direct thrust against the Rebels facing him. Later they justified his incessant calls for reinforcements and strengthened his hold on the loyalty of his men, whom he repeatedly praised for their gallantry in battling great odds. And always his belief in an all-powerful enemy fed his self-fulfilling prophecies and assuaged his self-doubts — victory would be due to the merits of his generalship, delay or defeat to causes beyond his control.

In condemning those pressuring him for action, the general affected the role of an innocent surrounded by scheming, venal politicians. In reality he was himself deeply and deliberately involved in the politics of the Civil War; all his actions, as James Russell Lowell remarked, "were encumbered in every direction by the huge train of political baggage."[10] George McClellan's stance was that of a committed Democratic conservative, a position from which he viewed the Republican administration with growing distrust. He believed a tide was rising in Washington in that first winter of the war that threatened to engulf the very principles he was fighting for. And he further professed to believe that it was deliberately and maliciously aimed at him.

While McClellan was firm in his opposition to secession, he was equally firm in seeking to limit the war. Once the South was taught the error of its ways on the battlefield, which it was his calling to demonstrate, he expected it to rejoin the Union and all would be as before. The instrument of this healing process was to be the Democratic party, the only truly national party. Thus the harsh excesses bred by civil war could be avoided and the Constitution upheld. He dismissed the possibility that there might be those in both North and South unwilling to accept a simple return to the status quo of 1860.[11]

The general was at pains to make his views known where he believed they would do the most good. His disgust with politicians did not extend to congressional Democrats, whom he made welcome in his camp. He actively cultivated newspaper support, particularly from James Gordon Bennett's powerful *New York Herald* and from the *New York World*, whose backing of the administration's war effort was lukewarm at best. Among his correspondents he numbered such prominent conservative New York Democrats as the merchant William H. Aspinwall, the lawyer S. L. M. Barlow, and the financier August Belmont, chairman of the party's national committee. McClellan's closest army friend, Fitz John Porter, added the weight of his political and newspaper connections to his mentor's cause.

On November 8, 1861, a week after replacing Scott as general-in-chief, McClellan spelled out his war aims to his confidant Barlow. "Help me to dodge the nigger — we want nothing to do with him," he wrote. "I am fighting to preserve the integrity of the Union and the power of the Govt — on no other issue. To gain that end we cannot afford to mix up the negro question — it must be incidental and subsidiary." During his western Virginia campaign he had assured slaveholders that their peculiar institution would be "religiously respected," that he would crush with an "iron hand" any attempted slave uprising. Later he would repeat that pledge to the Virginia landowner Hill Carter: "I have not come here to wage war on the defenceless, upon non-combatants, upon private property, nor upon the domestic institutions of the land."[12]

Such views were by no means unique in the North. Indeed, the section of Lincoln's December 3 message to Congress dealing with war aims could as easily have been written by General McClellan: he was most anxious, the president said, not to let the conflict "degenerate into a violent and remorseless revolutionary struggle. I have, therefore, in every case, thought it proper to keep the integrity of the Union prominent as the primary object of the contest...."[13] Yet the rising tide the general sensed was very much in evidence that winter. It was carrying to prominence powerful leaders of the radical wing of the Republican party, to whom the "negro question" was neither incidental nor subsidiary.

Though energized by the slavery issue, the radical Republicans were far from united on how to deal with it. Edward Dicey, an English journalist who arrived in the United States early in 1862 to examine the conflict for readers of *The Spectator* and *Macmillan's Magazine*, explained this division. The more moderate antislavery partisans did not hesitate to condemn the institution and resist its spread, he wrote, but were "not bound by this disapproval to break off all commercial or social relations with slaveholders." In contrast were the abolitionists, the most radical of the radicals. Declaiming from platforms outside the party system as well as from within it, they brooked no compromise at all: "The Abolitionists, pure and simple, have an esoteric creed, more logical perhaps, but less accommodating. With them slavery is an absolute sin . . . a crime." But whatever their internal differences, the antislavery radicals as a group were coming increasingly to affect Northern public opinion, and with it the conduct of the war.[14]

No one was more aware of this than Abraham Lincoln. Confronted with the problem of managing an already unstable coalition in support of his war policies, he was treating sectional politics with the most delicate touch. His own party was split into conservative as well as radical factions. Northern Democrats, too, were divided in the strength of their dedication to the Union cause — there were peace Democrats and war Democrats and even conditional-war Democrats — and Democratic support was essential to the raising of the armies needed to fight the rebellion. He feared that the slaveholding border states still loyal to the Union — Maryland, Kentucky, and Missouri — might shift their allegiance to the South if too roughly handled. Thus the potentially divisive issue of slavery got the most careful executive handling of all. In September, for example, Lincoln repudiated a local emancipation decree issued in Missouri by the radical General John C. Frémont, on the grounds that the matter could be dealt with only from Washington.

The single issue of restoring the Union had been enough to bring half a million volunteers to the colors by the end of 1861. Yet as the contest continued that winter without expectation of a quick end, "all quiet on the Potomac" became a symbol of frustration and disillusion. The president tried hard to make McClellan understand that the nation's patience was waning. The general was unmoved. A bit of doggerel titled "Tardy George" made the rounds. Its closing stanza was pointed:

> Suppose for a moment, George, my friend —
> Just for a moment — you condescend
> To use the means that are in your hands,
> The eager muskets, the guns, and brands;
> Take one bold step on the Southern sod,
> And leave the issue to watchful God!
> For now the Nation raises its gorge,
> Waiting and watching you, tardy George![15]

One immediate and powerful source of radical pressure was the establishment by Congress, on December 10, 1861, of the Joint Committee on the Conduct of the War. It was dominated by radical Republicans, most notably its chairman, the iron-willed, cross-grained senator from Ohio, Benjamin Wade. Wade was quick to spell out his discontent. At a hearing on December 26 he observed that the people of the North were making extraordinary and costly sacrifices to support the war, yet these efforts were not being translated into victories. He laid the blame on McClellan. "All this is hanging upon one man who keeps his counsels entirely to himself," Wade charged. Were the general-in-chief a Napoleon or a Wellington, he would have little cause for concern. "But how can this nation abide the secret counsels that one man carries in his head, when we have no evidence that he is the wisest man in the world?" The committee must know, he continued, "what is to be done, for the country is in jeopardy." General McClellan should consider himself on notice.[16]

For the moment Senator Wade's demand was sidetracked, for McClellan was stricken with typhoid fever. Any movement toward offensive planning came to a halt while he recuperated. The president wondered if the fates were conspiring against him. "What shall I do?" he asked. "The people are impatient; Chase has no money and he tells me he can raise no more; the general of the Army has typhoid fever. The bottom is out of the tub." In desperation, he decided to take the reins himself. If General McClellan was not going to use the army, he remarked, he wanted to borrow it. He pored over textbooks on the military arts from the Library of Congress and in mid-January 1862 called together McClellan's principal lieutenants for a series of strategy meetings.[17]

As it turned out, it did not become necessary for the president of the United States, military textbook in hand, to lead the Army of the Potomac into battle. McClellan learned soon enough of these strategy sessions. "Upon recovering from a severe illness," he wrote in his official report, "I found that excessive anxiety for an immediate movement of the army of the Potomac had taken possession of the minds of the administration."[18] Presumably spurred to action by this revelation, by the end of the month he submitted to the president and the secretary of war plans for what would become the Peninsula campaign against Richmond.

Two other presidential initiatives may have had more to do with McClellan's sudden burst of activity. Lincoln's General War Order No. 1 of January 27 called for a coordinated advance by Federal land and naval forces by February 22, and a supplementary order designated Johnston's army at Manassas as the Army of the Potomac's target. Lincoln's second move was to ease the incompetent Simon Cameron out of the War Department and replace him with Edwin Stanton.

McClellan had been cultivating fellow Democrat Stanton that winter, believing him to be a kindred spirit. He quite misread the man — or, by his own account, was mislead by him. Stanton was the most militant of war Democrats, completely devoted to a vigorous and immediate prosecution of the war. He explained to a friend that he held "many, very many, earnest conversations . . . with General McClellan, to impress him with the absolute necessity of active operations. . . ." He was rather more blunt in a January 24 letter to Charles A. Dana, managing editor of the *New York Tribune*. "Bad passions and little passions and mean passions gather around and hem in the great movements that should deliver the nation," he wrote. ". . . As soon as I can get the machinery of the office working, the rats cleared out, and the rat holes stopped we shall *move*. This army has got to fight or run away; ... the champagne and oysters on the Potomac must be stopped."[19]

Slowly but inexorably, great pressures were building in the North early in 1862, superheated by politics, conflicting war aims, suspicion, and simple frustration. Men of exceedingly strong will were insisting on victory without limits or compromise and threatening dire consequences if it was not forthcoming. Generals in the field would ignore these pressures at their peril.

While General McClellan pushed the merits of his grand campaign, two incidents further damaged his standing with the administration and the country. Before any movement by the army, Lincoln insisted the capital be made safe from a surprise Rebel thrust. Late in February McClellan launched a major expedition to secure the Baltimore and Ohio Railroad, Washington's main link with the Midwest. His plan was to hold the lower Shenandoah Valley in force so that the railroad's Potomac crossing at Harper's Ferry could be reconstructed. A permanent pontoon bridge was to be laid on canal boats floated to the site on the Chesapeake and Ohio Canal paralleling the river. The general-in-chief himself accompanied the 40,000 troops, and all proceeded smoothly and exactly as planned — until it was discovered that the pontoons could not be moved from the canal into the river because they were six inches too wide to fit through the lift locks. Except for a detachment left on the Virginia side of the Potomac, the men had to turn around and tramp back to Washington.

As it happened, the fiasco produced the desired military result, for the railroad's engineers now had at least enough protection to proceed with their bridge-building. The damage was to McClellan's public image. Lincoln was exasperated. A million dollars had been wasted, he snapped at the general's chief of staff; "I am no engineer, but it seems to me that if I wished to know whether a boat would go through a hole, or a lock, common sense would teach me to go and measure it. ... The impression is daily gaining ground that the general does not intend to do anything." Soon a new quip about Tardy George was making the rounds: the Harper's Ferry expedition, said Secretary of the Treasury Chase, normally barren of any sort of wit, had died of lockjaw.[20]

A week or so later, early in March, the Confederate entrenchments around Manassas and Centreville were found to be empty; the enemy had slipped away to the south. The Army of the Potomac again stirred itself into motion. McClellan had no real intention of pursuing, for Pinkerton's latest intelligence estimated the Rebel army at over 115,000 men, but he took this opportunity to give his troops some experience in route marching. Newspaper reporters and artists joined the soldiers wandering through the abandoned defensive positions. The fortifications were imposing enough, but some of the redoubts that had looked so menacing from a distance were found, on closer inspection, to be armed with "Quaker guns" — logs propped on makeshift gun mounts; there was even a smokestack from an old locomotive. Grinning privates posed with these harmless artifacts for Mathew Brady's photographic team, and artists sketched the scene for the Northern illustrated papers.

The Quaker guns were fresh armament for McClellan's detractors in their assault on the general's seven months of inaction. Johnston had "escaped" unharmed; instead of being only twenty-five miles away, he was now out of immediate harm's way behind the barrier of the Rappahannock River to the south. McClellan saw it all differently. Without firing a shot he had won a major victory, forcing his opponent to abandon a powerful and threatening position. It would be judged "the brightest passage of my life," he wrote his friend Barlow.[21]

The Manassas march, like the Harper's Ferry expedition, was the most minor of episodes. Unfortunately for McClellan, however, both took place in public view before a skeptical audience, and neither seemed worthy of a Young Napoleon. The gulf of mistrust and suspicion between the administration and its principal general was widening daily. There was talk, in official circles high and low, that McClellan intended to make only a "soft" Democratic war, seeking a compromise peace to restore the Union with slavery intact. The extreme anti-McClellan faction even suspected him of a treasonous intent to leave Washington undefended and easy prey for capture. That, at least, was McClellan's interpretation of "a very ugly matter" the president brought up in a private interview on March 8. Whatever the facts of the matter — McClellan's account is the only record of the conversation — the general took it as an outrage to his honor rather than as a warning that only vigorous action and victory would silence the rising chorus against him.[22]

McClellan's plan of campaign involved transferring the Army of the Potomac by water to Union-held Fort Monroe, at the tip of the peninsula formed by the James and York rivers, some seventy-five miles southeast of Richmond. From there, with his communications secure, he would march on the Confederate capital. Lincoln was uneasy about the scheme, fearing that it would leave Washington unprotected. The general assured him that the Rebels would have no option but to concentrate all their forces to defend Richmond. In any case, sufficient troops would remain behind to man the capital's defenses. With that promise, Lincoln gave his reluctant approval.

The casual observer watching the massed blue ranks of the Army of the Potomac embarking for the Peninsula on March 17, 1862, had every reason for optimism. For Northerners the war news had turned uniformly good over the past two months. Victories by Generals George Thomas and Samuel Curtis seemed to have secured the key border states of Kentucky and Missouri. An obscure general named U. S. Grant was suddenly famous, toasted as "Unconditional Surrender" Grant after capturing Forts Henry and Donelson in Tennessee and opening that state to further invasion. Nashville was in Federal hands, and an advance down the Mississippi River was proceeding apace. At the mouth of the Mississippi an immense naval force was assembling for an assault on New Orleans, the South's largest city. Other naval-borne forces had seized footholds along the North Carolina coast. On March 9 a strange-looking ironclad warship, the *Monitor*, neutralized the equally strange-looking Confederate ironclad *Merrimack* in Hampton Roads, securing McClellan's line of communications in the Chesapeake. The end of the rebellion was in sight, editorial writers predicted; the Army of the Potomac would provide the finishing stroke.

McClellan could hardly wait to be away from Washington, "that sink of iniquity." To be sure, he would depart only as commander of the Army of the Potomac, having been removed from the post of general-in-chief. No replacement was named, and McClellan accepted it simply as a temporary displacement while he fought his campaign. "I shall soon leave here on the wing for

Richmond — which you may be sure I will take," he wrote Barlow on March 16. *"The President is all right* — he is my strongest friend." The general might have gone far toward cementing that friendship had he sat down with the president and fully spelled out his dispositions for the defense of the capital. Instead, he dispatched a manpower report to Secretary Stanton and departed for the Peninsula without further explanation. The report seemed to Lincoln and Stanton to raise more questions than it answered, leaving them with the distinct impression that, contrary to orders, McClellan was leaving Washington poorly guarded. The march on Richmond thus began on the wrong foot.[23]

It never got back in step. The traits of character that marked McClellan's early months of command burst into full flower on the Peninsula's bloody ground. His arrogant contempt for the administration, his delusions about his enemy and his God-given mission, his incessant search for scapegoats were in daily evidence. All this might have been dismissed as mere eccentricity — a common enough element of generals' mental baggage in that war — had the campaign ended in victory. But McClellan's generalship was also put to the test, and on the battlefield he proved to be paralyzingly cautious. His deep concern for his men, his fixation with avoiding casualties, revealed a sensitivity of nature admirable in most of life's pursuits but crippling when making war. Battle evokes the cruelest probing of the general in command: young men will die and be maimed, win or lose; the hard choice must be made whether to risk attack when opportunity offers, which may (or may not) save many more lives in the long run than will be lost that day. For George McClellan, too often the risk looked too great.

A pattern was established within a day of his arrival on the Peninsula. On April 3 he wired Secretary Stanton that there were 15,000 Rebels entrenched before the historic port of Yorktown; with the 58,000 men and 100 guns already at hand, he would strike forthwith. It was a reasonably close estimate of enemy strength and, as it happened, the last realistic intelligence report issued by McClellan's headquarters during the campaign. The next day caution took command: Yorktown's defenses were formidable, the terrain was difficult and swampy, the weather was bad, an assault would be ill advised. Helping him to reach this conclusion was the

The Limits of Limited War

Confederate commander at Yorktown, General John Magruder. Magruder, known as "Prince John" for his devotion to amateur theatricals, marched his little force this way and that behind the fortifications with great industry and much menacing intent. McClellan ordered up his immense siege train, with which he hoped in due course to blast the Rebels out of their lines.

Having settled on siege warfare, he was then presented with a handy scapegoat for the delay. The president detained General McDowell's corps, ticketed for the Peninsula, to fill the apparent gaps in the capital's defenses. McClellan protested that this threw all his plans into disarray. What role McDowell's men might have played in quickly breaking through the thinly held Confederate lines at Yorktown he did not explain; McDowell had not been scheduled in any case to reach the Peninsula for ten days to two weeks. On April 7 McClellan reported a remarkable feat of Confederate logistics. Yorktown's defenders, estimated to number just 15,000 four days earlier, he now reported to approach 100,000, "and probably more." Because troops had been withheld from him, "my force is possibly less than that of the enemy."[24]

Lincoln found the argument unconvincing. "I think it the precise time for you to strike a blow," he wrote his general on April 9. ". . . Once more let me tell you, it is indispensable to *you* that you strike a blow. *I* am powerless to help this. . . . The country will not fail to note — is now noting — that the present hesitation to move upon an intrenched enemy, is but the story of Manassas repeated. I beg to assure you that I have never written you, or spoken to you, in greater kindness of feeling than now, nor with a fuller purpose to sustain you. . . . *But you must act.*"

The general saw this as continued persecution. "History will present a sad record of these traitors who are willing to sacrifice the country and its army for personal spite and personal aims," he told his wife, and his friend Barlow, the New York Democratic leader, agreed. "The dastardly conduct of those in Washington, who seek to drive you from the Army, or into a defeat, to serve their own selfish ends, is beginning to be understood," he wrote; ". . . the ambitious scoundrels in Washington will wish they had never been born."[25]

McClellan now committed his campaign to a "battle of posts," relying on engineering and artillery to offset what he labeled a severe inferiority in manpower. It took a month to emplace his siege batteries before Yorktown. "Glorious news come borne on every wind but the South Wind," John Hay wrote in exasperation. The day before the bombardment was scheduled to open, Johnston abandoned his lines and withdrew up the Peninsula. A second month was spent in slow pursuit to the defense lines of Richmond. "If I am not re-enforced, it is probable that I will be obliged to fight nearly double my numbers strongly intrenched," McClellan wired Stanton on May 10. "I cannot bring into actual battle against the enemy more than eighty thousand men at the utmost," he told the president four days later, "and with them I must attack in position, probably intrenched, a much larger force, perhaps double my numbers." As evidence of the enemy's strength he cited the vicious assault by Johnston at Fair Oaks on May 31 and June 1, which was repulsed only with great difficulty. On June 25 he gave official status to detective Pinkerton's claim that Confederate manpower before Richmond had reached 200,000, including substantial reinforcements brought east all the way from Mississippi. Should his army be destroyed by this host he was prepared to accept martrydom and "at least die with it and share its fate."

"His own imagination faced him in superior numbers at every turn," James Russell Lowell observed when these dispatches were made public in McClellan's official report of the campaign in 1864. "Since Don Quixote's enumeration of the armies of the Emperor Alifanfaron and King Pentapolin of the Naked Arm, there has been nothing like our General's vision of the Rebel forces, with their ever-lengthening list of leaders, gathered for the defense of Richmond." In his commitment to a world of illusion, McClellan was ripe to be victimized by an opponent whose view of events was entirely without illusion. He now faced such an opponent, for the wounding of Johnston at Fair Oaks brought Robert E. Lee to the command of the Army of Northern Virginia.[26]

Already General Lee, in his capacity as Jefferson Davis's military adviser, had upset Federal plans for the final decisive thrust on Richmond. When he saw that McClellan was settling in to besiege Yorktown, Lee took the gift of time and used it to prey on the Lincoln administration's extreme sensitivity to the safety of Washington. He set Stonewall Jackson loose in the Shenandoah Valley, and Jackson's whirlwind campaign thoroughly befuddled a force more than three times the size of his own. Most important, it caused the movement of 40,000 Yankee reinforcements to the Peninsula to be canceled. By late June, Jackson had slipped southward to join Lee at Richmond. Lee now had some 85,000 men to pit against the Young Napoleon's 105,000. He moved to act promptly, before the odds lengthened.

Lee's relentless offensive in the Seven Days' battles (June 25–July 1) left McClellan's grand campaign in sudden ruin. Stripping the Richmond lines of all but 25,000 troops, the Virginian hammered at the exposed Union right flank with the rest of his army. McClellan tamely surrendered the initiative. Bluffed once again by the threatening play-acting of Prince John Magruder, in charge of the Richmond fortifications, he believed himself assailed simultaneously from front and flank. By the third of the Seven Days his only thought was retreat to a haven on the James River, all the way across the Peninsula.

Although the retreat was conducted with skill and Lee was unable to deliver a final crushing blow, McClellan's mental composure was badly shaken. His vision of events was blinkered by the conviction that the administration had betrayed him. The rancor of months burst out in a bitter dispatch to Stanton written in the early hours of June 28. "I have lost this battle because my force was too small," he wrote. "I again repeat that I am not responsible for this, and I say it with the earnestness of a general who feels in his heart the loss of every brave man who has been needlessly sacrificed to-day.... If, at this instant, I could dispose of ten thousand (10,000) fresh men, I could gain the victory to-morrow." (In fact he could have disposed 60,000 fresh men that day; mesmerized by Prince John's theatrics, they had fired hardly a shot.) In his closing sentences he bluntly indicted the administration for treason: "If I save this army now, I tell you plainly that I owe no thanks to you or to any other persons in Washington. You have done your best to sacrifice this army."

McClellan was surprised that the dispatch did not result in his immediate dismissal from command. "Of course they will never forgive me for that," he wrote his wife. "I knew it when I wrote it; but as I thought it possible that it might be the last I ever wrote, it seemed better to have it exactly true." Possibly it might well have been the last dispatch he ever wrote, but for the fact that neither

Stanton nor Lincoln saw the final incendiary sentences. Shocked by McClellan's charge, the supervisor of military telegrams deleted them before passing the message on. One consequence of this bit of bureaucratic censorship was to poison further McClellan's view of his civilian superiors. To his catalog of their many shortcomings he added guilty cowardice for their refusal to rise to his challenge. His contempt for Stanton in particular now knew no bounds. The secretary of war was an "unmitigated scoundrel," he told Ellen; ". . . the magnificent treachery & rascality of E. M. Stanton would have caused Judas to have raised his arms in holy horror. . . ."[27]

The setback of the Seven Days caused no breach in the Federal soldiers' devotion to their commanding general. He had a ready explanation for what had happened. In a July 4 proclamation he assured them that their valor ranked them among the great armies of history: "Attacked by vastly superior forces, and without hope of re-inforcements, you have succeeded in changing your base of operations by a flank movement, always regarded as the most hazardous of military expedients. . . ." It had been, he assured his wife, "one of the grandest operations in military history." Like the troops, most war correspondents with the army accepted McClellan's assessment. The Democratic press took Secretary Stanton under fire for failing to answer the general's calls for reinforcements. "The only accounts we get are of the multitudes on the other side," Ambassador Charles Francis Adams wrote from London. "Our newspapers and quidnuncs delight in counting them with additions of many ciphers, until I am bound to infer that the census of 1860 is all a northern forgery, and that the slave states have had the fertility of the northern hordes that overran the Romans. . . ."[28]

At Harrison's Landing on the James, while his army rested, McClellan plunged more deeply than ever into partisan politics. For a general, in the harmless privacy of letters to family and friends, to let off steam about the interference and ineptitude of his civilian superiors was hardly unusual, and common enough among both Northern and Southern officers. For the Union's principal army commander to express such sentiments to powerful leaders of the political opposition, with intent to undermine the

The Limits of Limited War

administration in power, was another matter. The messiah's mission was assuming a decidedly political cast.

To Barlow, for example, he wrote that he had lost all respect for the "set of heartless villains" in the administration. His men, he charged, had "fallen victims to the stupidity and wickedness at Washington which have done their best to sacrifice as noble an Army as ever marched to battle." He feared that those in power had no real wish to save the Union but instead "prefer ruling a separate Northern Confederacy," but he hoped that "God will yet foil their abominable designs & mete out to them the terrible punishments they deserve." If he had his way, he added, "my foot will be on their necks." To another prominent New York Democrat, William H. Aspinwall, he explained that "The game apparently is to deprive me of the means of moving, and then to cut my head off for not advancing."

Running through this correspondence was a constant theme: his Peninsula campaign had been frustrated deliberately by withholding reinforcements from him so as to prolong the war until the hated abolitionists grew strong enough to turn the conflict into a revolution against slavery, with all its attendant Jacobin horrors, and thus poison the chances of reunion. His army confidant, Fitz John Porter, helped air the theme publicly. Writing to his friend Manton Marble, editor of the *New York World,* the leading conservative Democratic organ, Porter insisted that the mood of the army was staunchly anti-abolitionist and urged Marble to put an editorial question to the country: "Does the President (controlled by an incompetent Secy) design to cause defeat here for the purpose of prolonging the war?"[29]

It was in this overheated atmosphere of partisan politics that the president was asked to give thought to a paper McClellan offered as his "general views concerning the existing state of the rebellion." These views were handed to Lincoln on July 8, when he arrived at Harrison's Landing to examine the Army of the Potomac for himself. The document could have served as a party platform for conservative Democratic views.

The conflict should be conducted according to the highest principles of Christian civilization, McClellan maintained. "It should not be a war looking to the subjugation of the people of any

State.... Neither confiscation of property, political executions of persons, territorial organization of States, or forcible abolition of slavery should be contemplated for a moment." Southern civilians and their property and their institutions must be strictly protected by the Federal armies. Such a constitutional and Christian policy "would deeply impress the rebel masses and all foreign nations," he predicted. He warned, however, that "a declaration of radical views, especially upon slavery, will rapidly disintegrate our present armies." Lincoln read the paper without comment, McClellan wrote, thanked him, and nothing more was said about it. "I feel that I did my duty in writing it," the general told his wife, "tho' I apprehend it will do no good whatever," for the administration seemed bent on adopting "radical and inhuman views."[30]

Pondering his fate during the scorching July weeks at Harrison's Landing, the general occasionally gave way to shadowy thoughts of taking matters into his own hands. "I have commenced receiving letters from the North urging me to march on Washington & assume the Govt!!" he wrote Ellen on July 11. One such letter urged the Young Napoleon to "turn your army toward Washington, take possession of the city," and serve as provisional president until a national election could be held to reverse the lamentable results of 1860 and "restore harmony to our distracted country.... You can, sir, with your noble, unambitious views, make yourself the savior of this Republic." Another letter writer, signing himself "One of Many," pleaded with him to "disperse this Negro worshipping Congress, give to our Southern brethren all that they are legitimately entitled to under the laws and the Constitution." He could hardly imagine such a course, McClellan told his wife (although he carefully saved the letters for his "archives"), yet he found the thought hard to dismiss. "If they leave me here neglected much longer," he remarked on July 29, "I will feel like taking my rather large military family to Wash. to seek an explanation.... I fancy that under such circumstances I should be treated with rather more politeness than I have been of late."[31]

As the general brooded over the impolite treatment he was receiving, the president was laboring to get the war back on track. If the defeat of the Army of the Potomac before Richmond was his most immediate military problem, it was by no means his only one. Matters in the western theater were also stalled. New Orleans

The Limits of Limited War

and other strategic points were in Federal hands, but further progress did not follow. Lincoln concluded that the day-to-day running of the complex military machine was not a job for him and Secretary Stanton after all, and he brought Henry Halleck east to fill the vacant post of general-in-chief. The western victories in the spring had been won under Halleck's general direction — it was not yet clear in Washington that the recent shift into slow motion there was also Halleck's doing — and he seemed to have earned the promotion.

To put some stiffening into the various commands Stonewall Jackson had handled so roughly in the Shenandoah, General John Pope was also brought east. The captor of Island Number 10 in the Mississippi brimmed with confidence, pleasing the radicals with his promise to make the hardest kind of war on secessionists. He told the men of his newly minted Army of Virginia not to worry about defense and lines of retreat, only about finding the enemy so that he could be attacked.

In urging in his policy paper a conservative war of high principles that would impress "all foreign nations," General McClellan touched a tender nerve. At all times it was necessary for the president to cast a weather eye overseas toward Great Britain and France, where the specter of intervention hung like a thunderhead on the horizon. By midsummer of 1862 that cloud was growing larger and more threatening each day.

How quickly a foreign crisis could escalate had already been demonstrated. In November 1861 the impetuous Captain Charles Wilkes of the Federal cruiser *San Jacinto* stopped the British mail packet *Trent* off Cuba and removed two distinguished Southerners, James M. Mason and John Slidell, who were bound for London and Paris on diplomatic missions. Wilkes's affront to the Union Jack produced great agitation in England. John Bulls in their London clubs sputtered indignantly and demanded vigorous action against the high-handed Yankees. The *Daily Chronicle* raged at "that spirit of senseless egotism which induces the Americans, with their dwarf fleet and shapeless mass of incoherent squads, which they call an army, to fancy themselves the equals of France by land and of Great Britain by sea."[32] Troops were dispatched to Canada and the Royal Navy's North American squadron put on alert. Eventually cooler heads in London and Washington defused the affair, Wilkes's action was disavowed, and Mason and Slidell were released and sent on their way. The diplomatic waters calmed.

The foreign crisis building anew by the summer of 1862, however, was deeper and potentially far more dangerous than the intemperate act of one Yankee sea captain. At issue was the Union blockade of Southern ports and its strangling effect on the cotton textile industries of Lancashire and the lower Seine. In July Parliament was informed that 80,000 textile workers were without jobs and 370,000 were on half-time, and that the cotton famine promised still greater hardships for Britain's largest industry within a matter of weeks. The situation was equally severe in France, leading Napoleon III to instruct his foreign minister to inquire "of the English government if it does not believe that the moment has arrived when the South should be recognized." What the adventuresome emperor envisioned was a powerful Anglo-French fleet stationed at the mouth of the Mississippi to guarantee the reopening of the cotton trade. London was not quite ready to take such a major step, but there was a powerful movement pressing Prime Minister Palmerston's Liberal government in that direction. "The current is against us and is strong," Thomas H. Dudley, the American consul at Liverpool, warned Secretary of State Seward on July 25. "From what I see and hear I am fully persuaded that if we are not successful in some decisive battle within a short period this government will be forced to acknowledge the Confederacy or else be driven from power."[33]

Just what form intervention might take was being closely debated in Parliament and by Lord Palmerston's government. The worst case would be the third Anglo-American war in less than ninety years, with the Confederacy recognized, the Royal Navy forcibly attempting to break the blockade and end the cotton famine, Canada assaulted in retaliation by Federal troops — and the South virtually assured of its independence. The mildest option would be an offer of mediation by the European powers to end the bloodletting, a gesture of noble humanitarian purpose but offering little promise of replenishing British and French cotton stocks in the near future. (Seward instructed Ambassador Adams not to "receive, entertain, or transmit" any British offer of mediation.)[34]

For months Seward had let it be known, in hints too broad to be missed, that the Lincoln government would regard any interference from overseas as an act of war. As Adams observed, this situation presented the British, at least, with the Faustian bargain of trading immediate gratification of their cotton hunger for "the eternal condemnation" of an unforgiving North. Calmly reasoned logic might reject such a bargain, yet logic could be overridden by the heated emotions of the moment. In a letter to Massachusetts Senator Charles Sumner, the liberal English statesman Richard Cobden tried to spell out the real issue. At immediate stake was the welfare of the desperate millions living in the textile districts, Cobden wrote, and "you cannot present the alternative of a greater possible evil to deter a government from attempting to remedy so vast a present danger. I feel quite convinced that unless cotton comes in considerable quantity before the end of the year the governments of Europe will be knocking at your door." Such an economic rationale for intervention would nicely disguise the craving of Europe's ruling classes for permanent disunion and an end to that dangerous American experiment in popular democracy. In Cobden's view, a substantial majority of Parliament "will be glad to find an excuse for voting for the dismemberment of the Great Republic."[35]

The other point on which most overseas observers agreed was that what happened on American battlefields within the next month or so would be decisive. "After pouring forth blood like water and fertilizing the fields of Virginia with thousands of corpses," the pro-Confederate *Times* of London editorialized on July 22, "the North finds itself obliged to begin all over again, with credit destroyed, a ruined revenue, a depreciated currency, and an enormous debt." A month later, on August 24, British Foreign Secretary Lord John Russell sent a coldly cynical note to the prime minister. "I think we must allow the President to spend his second batch of 600,000 men," he wrote, "before we can hope that he and his democracy will listen to reason."[36]

Even as Europe debated intervening in the American conflict, President Lincoln was seeking to come to grips with a change in the war's basic character. The collapse of McClellan's grand campaign marked the last chance to keep the conflict within the chivalrous and prudent limits the general was so vigorously advocating. The prospect of a long, hard, and increasingly bloody struggle now stretched ahead, requiring a fresh commitment in men and treasure and support on the part of Northerners. It had become, said the *Albany Evening Journal*, "a question of pure brute force . . . ; there is no middle ground — no half-way house — between absolute triumph and absolute vassalage."

In calling upon the state governors for a new levy of 300,000 men, Lincoln stated his determination to stay the course "until successful, or till I die, or am conquered, or my term expires, or Congress or the country forsakes me. . . ." The rebellious states, he told Democratic national chairman August Belmont, who had proposed a peace initiative on the basis of the 1860 status quo, "must understand that they cannot experiment for ten years trying to destroy the government, and if they fail still come back into the Union unhurt." The remorseless revolutionary struggle he had told Congress he hoped to avoid could no longer be avoided; if the South was to be defeated, he saw it as essential that the federal government lay hands on the institution of human slavery.

"What would you do in my position?" the president wrote to a Treasury representative in captured New Orleans who had warned that action on slavery would discourage Southerners from returning to the fold. "Would you drop the war where it is? Or, would you prosecute it in future, with elder-stalk squirts, charged with rose water? Would you deal lighter blows rather than heavier ones? Would you give up the contest, leaving any available means unapplied." Clearly he would not. He would play out his hand, he said, and now was the time to make slavery a counter in the game.

Since the time of Fort Sumter abolitionists had argued that slavery was a legitimate target of the war simply because it was an issue of surpassing moral importance, a crime against all humanity. They labored tirelessly to carry this crusade onto the field of battle. The struggle now required far more than just men and money, abolitionist Senator Sumner insisted; "our battalions must be reinforced by ideas." By the summer of 1862 the abolitionists were still a small minority, but a great many other Northerners, war Democrats as well as Republicans, had come to agree that slavery was as much at issue as the restoration of the Union.

Their reasoning, for the most part, was more pragmatic than moral. The terrible losses of a Shiloh or a Seven Days were argu-

The Limits of Limited War

ment enough. Slavery was beginning to be seen as an essential support of those Rebels who were killing Union boys by the thousands. Slaves dug entrenchments and performed other military chores; they raised the food and forage that went to the Confederate armies, and the cotton that was slipped through the blockade to be traded for foreign arms. This growing awareness of the military importance of Southern slavery was the fresh strength Lincoln intended to tap to keep the war going.[37]

The president moved carefully in this tide, seeking to control and guide it to his purposes. If he fell behind, he risked losing control of events to the increasingly vociferous radicals in Congress; if he moved too far ahead, he risked alienating the bipartisan support vital to his leadership. He had to consider as well the slaveholding border states and the sentiments in the army that General McClellan had cautioned him about. Early in July he told Senator Sumner that he would invoke emancipation immediately "if I were not afraid that half the officers would fling down their arms and three more States would rise."

At first Lincoln proceeded cautiously, avoiding any constitutional dispute by proposing to the states a plan for gradual, compensated emancipation. With mathematical care he worked it out that freeing all the slaves in all the border states would cost the government the equivalent of only eighty-seven days of making war at current expenditures. On July 12, in an address to border-state representatives, he appealed to their common sense: "... the institution in your states will be extinguished by mere friction and abrasion — by the mere incidents of the war. It will be gone, and you will have nothing valuable in lieu of it." His listeners, however, could not face such a drastic step, and no state came forward to accept the offer.

If the states would not take the lead, the Republican majorities in Congress would. There was a growing feeling that summer, Senator John Sherman wrote his brother, General William T. Sherman, "that we must treat these Rebels as bitter enemies to be subdued — conquered — by confiscation — by the employment of their slaves — by terror — energy — audacity — rather than by conciliation." Congress abolished slavery in the District of Columbia and in all federal territories. The army was restrained from returning runaway slaves to their masters. The Second Confiscation Act, signed by the president on July 17, took a hard line with the property, including slaves, of those declared in rebellion against the United States, giving Lincoln considerable latitude in the matter if he chose to use it. He doubted the constitutionality of Congress acting on slavery in the states, but it encouraged him to believe the country was moving in the direction he was determined to lead it.[38]

One day in early July the president had paid one of his regular visits to the telegraphers' office in the War Department and, as operator Thomas T. Eckert remembered it, "asked me for some paper, as he wanted to write something special." On that and the following days Lincoln worked periodically on the document. "He would look out the window a while and put his pen to paper," Eckert recalled, "but he did not write much at once. He would study between times and when he made up his mind he would put down a line or two. . . . He would read over each day all the matter he had previously written and revise it, studying carefully each sentence. . . ." On July 13 the president gave Seward and Welles a glimpse of his state of mind, saying that he now regarded emancipation as a military necessity and, Welles wrote, "was earnest in the conviction that something must be done." Secretary Chase also suspected something was in the wind. "The Slavery question perplexes the President almost as much as ever," he wrote a friend on July 20, "and yet I think he is about to emerge from the obscurities where he has been groping into somewhat clearer light. . . . So you see the man moves."[39]

Chase soon discovered that the president had moved farther than even he had hoped. At a cabinet meeting on July 22, Lincoln announced his decision on slavery. He would welcome comment, he said, but his mind was made up. He then read the draft of an emancipation proclamation. He took his lead, he told them, from the recent Second Confiscation Act, and he would continue to press for compensated emancipation. But the heart of the document was its last sentence: "And, as a fit and necessary military measure," based on his authority as commander-in-chief, he declared that on January 1, 1863, "all persons held as slaves within any state or states, wherein the constitutional authority of the United States shall not then be practically recognized, submitted

The Limits of Limited War 45

to, and maintained, shall then, thenceforward, and forever, be free."

This revolutionary document was in fact a carefully crafted political and pragmatic compromise. It would not immediately free a single slave, either in the sensitive border states or in already occupied Confederate territory, and it was couched in purely military terms, as an exercise in presidential war powers; to be of any consequence it required victories by the Federal armies. It would be the "friction and abrasion" of the war itself, as Lincoln had warned the border-state men ten days earlier, that would end the peculiar institution, rather than a simple fiat of the federal government. It was a mailed fist in a velvet glove; unless the eleven seceded states returned to the Union before the year was out, no compromise peace (the sort of outcome so avidly pressed by General McClellan and his backers), no return to the status quo of 1860, would be possible. Thenceforward and forever, the United States would be a very different nation.

The cabinet, though in general agreement with the draft proclamation, had questions. Postmaster General Montgomery Blair, a border-state man, wondered about the political effects on the state and congressional elections in the fall. Secretary Chase had wanted emancipation applied on a local basis by Federal generals in the field; might not this blanket announcement lead to slave insurrections in the South, creating public revulsion at home and abroad? Secretary Seward picked up the theme. With the war going so badly he feared the proclamation "may be viewed as the last measure of an exhausted Government . . . our last shriek on the retreat." The president accepted the point. He would postpone announcement of emancipation until it could be issued from a position of strength. Freedom for the slaves and revitalization of the Northern war effort — like the threat of armed intervention from overseas — was going to hinge on what happened on the field of battle.[40]

The immediate prospects for a victory did not look bright. A few days after the cabinet meeting, General-in-Chief Halleck paid a visit to the Army of the Potomac at Harrison's Landing. McClellan still numbered the enemy before him at 200,000, with more arriving every day, but professed a willingness to resume the game if reinforced. The true defense of Washington, he insisted, was the

Army of the Potomac threatening Richmond. This was sound enough strategic theory, but for the fact that McClellan would now have to play the game without his trump card.

The retreat to the James rendered his siege train — the one weapon he had counted upon since Yorktown to even those long odds against him — all but useless. The only way to transport the great ordnance rifles and siege mortars was by railroad or barge. The Seven Days' battles had driven the Federals from the only available railroad, and at Harrison's Landing there were no waterways to carry the ordnance barges close enough to the Richmond lines to do any good. He talked of moving on Petersburg, the important railroad center south of the Confederate capital, but it was plain to Halleck (who was himself an expert on caution) that when it came down to it McClellan was hardly the general to take such a risk if he really believed the enemy had two men for every one of his.

Halleck went back to Washington with his impressions, and on August 3 McClellan was notified to bring his army home from the Peninsula. The order "has caused me the greatest pain I ever experienced," the general protested; withdrawal "will prove disastrous to our cause. I fear it will be a fatal blow." Possibly Halleck's reply caused him to wince, for it was based squarely on the Pinkerton intelligence reports the Young Napoleon blessed as gospel. "You and your officers . . . ," Halleck wrote, "estimated the enemy's forces in and around Richmond at two hundred thousand men. . . . General Pope's army, covering Washington, is only about forty thousand. Your effective force is only about ninety thousand. You are thirty miles from Richmond, and General Pope eighty or ninety, with the enemy directly between you ready to fall with his superior numbers upon one or the other as he may elect; neither can re-enforce the other in case of such an attack."[41]

Thus the Peninsula campaign ended as it began, with a great gulf between the Army of the Potomac's commander and the administration. During the four-month campaign McClellan's most notable military skills were demonstrated in retreat. The radicals were predictably disgusted. "Place him before an enemy," Senator Ben Wade remarked, "and he will burrow like a wood chuck. His first effort is to get into the ground." Gideon Welles's appraisal was more tempered, and more widely shared in the capital.

The Limits of Limited War

"McClellan is an intelligent engineer but not a commander," he wrote. ". . . The study of military operations interests and amuses him. He likes show, parade and power. Wishes to outgeneral the Rebels, but not to kill and destroy them."

As for McClellan, he abandoned any former kindly thoughts toward the president and consigned him to a rapidly growing list of enemies. "I am confident that he would relieve me tomorrow if he dared do so," he wrote his wife a week before the evacuation order. "His cowardice alone prevents it. I can never regard him with other feelings than those of thorough contempt for his mind, heart, &c." The army alone had remained loyal and devoted, and with it he might still carry out his vision. When his Washington detractors "begin to reap the whirlwind that they have sown I may still be in position to do something to save my country," he told Ellen on August 8. "With all their faults, I *do* love my countrymen, and if I *can* save them I will yet do so. . . ."[42]

That whirlwind was quickly supplied by General Lee. John Pope found that making war on immobile islands in the Mississippi had not prepared him to cope with Stonewall Jackson's swift columns. "The history of Pope's retreat, without a line and without a base, is a military novelty," Lieutenant Colonel Wilder Dwight of the 2nd Massachusetts wrote his family as the dust of the Second Bull Run campaign settled. ". . . Twice cut off by the enemy, — everything in discomfort and confusion. Forced marches, wakeful bivouacs, retreat, retreat. O, it was pitiful!"[43] In the end, Washington survived its crisis and General McClellan survived the efforts of his cabinet detractors to cashier him. Only his personal and paternalistic hold on the Army of the Potomac kept him in command. Once again the chance to save the country would be his.

His burden was larger than he imagined. When the news of Pope's defeat reached London, Prime Minister Palmerston addressed a note to his foreign secretary. The Federals had received "a very complete smashing," he observed, and it seemed to him likely that further such disasters could be expected. "If this should happen," he asked, "would it not be time for us to consider whether in such a state of things England and France might not address the contending parties and recommend an arrangement upon the basis of separation?" Lord Russell concurred, and proposed a cabinet meeting "for the purpose of taking so important a step."[44]

And in President Lincoln's desk was the paper declaring emancipation for the slaves, still requiring a victory in battle to work its revolutionary effect on the war and on the future. A certain irony in the situation could hardly have escaped the president's notice: the most immediate opportunity for effecting this revolution lay in the unknowing hands of the one Union general who above all others was mixing politics and high command to prevent the war from becoming a force for change of any kind.

· 2 ·

CONFEDERATE TIDE

When Robert E. Lee took charge of the Army of Northern Virginia on June 1, 1862, observers might have noted certain striking parallels between his road to high command and that of his opponent, George McClellan. Lee's background was the more distinguished — he was from a first family of the Virginia aristocracy — yet McClellan's upper-caste Philadelphia upbringing did not lack aristocratic flavor. Both attended West Point, both had outstanding records there, both graduated second in their class, both selected the engineering corps. In the Mexican War they served together on Winfield Scott's staff. Scott ranked the Virginian first among his subordinates (at a victory celebration in Mexico City he toasted "Captain Robert E. Lee, without whose aid we should not now be here").[1] McClellan, Lee's junior by twenty years, won a lesser but still substantial glory.

In the Civil War both were first tested in western Virginia in 1861. This time the glory was McClellan's; sent there to reverse the Young Napoleon's campaign, Lee found the task impossible. The two men played roles in shaping the war's early strategy, McClellan as Federal general-in-chief, Lee as military adviser to Jefferson Davis. Both demonstrated the bearing and command presence needed to inspire volunteer soldiers and their officers. When the two finally met in battle before Richmond, however, all the parallels became merely of academic interest. It was soon apparent that Robert E. Lee and George McClellan were not cut from the same bolt after all.

Among the talents Lee applied to his task was a cool, unsparing appraisal of military reality. The South had marched to war — the Second American Revolution, many liked to call it — equally confident in its martial spirit to repel invasion and in the certainty of foreign intervention. The trumpet call of South Carolinian James Hammond's celebrated 1858 Senate speech still echoed: "Without firing a gun, without drawing a sword, should they make war on us we could bring the whole world to our feet," Hammond insisted. "... What would happen if no cotton was furnished for three years? ... England would topple headlong and carry the whole civilized world with her, save the South. No, you dare not make war on cotton. No power on earth dares to make war upon it. Cotton is king!"[2] General Lee fully shared his nation's confidence in the Southern soldier, but he was not so willing to stake everything on King Cotton and the European powers.

The bright but brief international flare-up caused by Captain Wilkes's removal of diplomats Mason and Slidell from the *Trent* confirmed Lee's doubts about intervention. "We must make up our minds to fight our battles ourselves," he wrote his eldest son after the *Trent* crisis had cooled. "Expect to receive aid from no one. Make every necessary sacrifice of Comfort, money and labor to bring the war to a successful issue & then we will Succeed. The cry is too much for help."[3] To his mind, then and later, the Confederacy would live or die only by its armies. In the first winter of the war, while Washington's parade grounds were loud with cheers for the Young Napoleon, Lee pushed for stronger measures to fill the Southern ranks. In so doing he laid his impress on the Army of Northern Virginia before it was his to command.

Over 200,000 men were present for duty throughout the South by the end of 1861. This might be less than half the number of Federals in uniform, but it was nevertheless impressive confirmation of that martial spirit so much applauded. Indeed, there were more men willing to fight than there were arms to give them. While Confederate agents scoured European arsenals and the South's infant arms industry labored to meet Richmond's demands, Lee attacked the immediate problem of keeping the army in being. In the enthusiastic afterglow of Fort Sumter the volunteers had been enlisted for one year only, the Davis government (like the Lincoln government) believing that to be more than enough time to settle the question of secession. Now reality intruded: by the spring of 1862 these enlistments would be up, with no end to the conflict in view.

He was greatly concerned about the army's condition, Lee wrote Virginia's Governor John Letcher on December 26, 1861. "On the plains of Manassas . . . the enemy will resume operations, after a year's preparation and a winter of repose, fresh, vigorous, and completely organized, while we shall be in the confusion and excitement of reorganizing ours." (Along with the radicals in Washington, Lee was puzzled by the Army of the Potomac's inaction. He finally credited General McClellan with shrewdly postponing his campaign so as to strike at the height of the Confederate enlistment crisis. Oddly enough, that was one excuse for delay that McClellan did not press.) Lee's solution to the problem, he told the governor, was "the passage of a law for drafting them 'for the war' unless they volunteer for that period."[4]

The Virginia legislature did move toward a draft on a statewide basis, but at first the Confederate Congress shied away from such a radical plan. The Confederacy, after all, was a compact of sovereign states, and the cornerstone principle of states' rights stood in direct conflict with such things as universal conscription imposed by the central government in Richmond. Instead, it enacted the Furlough and Bounty Act, which promised a fifty-dollar bonus and a two-month furlough for those volunteers who would re-enlist for three years or the duration of the war. In a burst of democratic fervor, the Congress further permitted anyone signing up to transfer from his present company to a different one, or even to a different branch of the service; then, after all this coming and going, new elections would be held for company and regimental officers.

This experiment in grass-roots democracy was noble in purpose but unworkable in practice, producing a tangle of bureaucratic red tape, weakened discipline, and zealous electioneering. Strict disciplinarians found themselves in an uphill competition against crowd-pleasing candidates. Some exasperated officers took matters into their own hands. Lieutenant William Quince of North Carolina, for one, handled a company election with commendable brevity: "Men, there are but two candidates for the office, and there is but one of them worth a damn. I nominate him. All who are in favor of electing Sergeant Blank, come to a shoulder. Company, Shoulder arms. . . ."[5] In spite of such efforts, the "confusion and excitement" Lee feared was much in evidence during the early stages of the Peninsula campaign, and McClellan's glacial movements were received gratefully by the harassed Confederate high command.

Lee's appointment in March 1862 as President Davis's military adviser moved him to press anew for conscription. Returning to his theme that the South must be prepared to stand alone in its struggle, he told Major Charles Marshall, his staff aide, that "since the whole duty of the nation would be war until independence should be secured, the whole nation should for the time be converted into an army, the producers to feed and the soldiers to fight." Only universal conscription would meet the need, and he found Davis in agreement. With Lee's assistance, a bill was drawn up and sent to Congress for the call-up of all men between the ages of eighteen and thirty-five. On April 16, 1862, swallowing its states'-rights pride, the Richmond Congress complied and passed the first conscription act in American history. In addition to calling up additional manpower, it extended the enlistment terms of the current twelve-month men to three years. Even as President Lincoln was seeking to manage a revolutionary change in the way the North viewed the war, the Confederacy had revolutionized itself internally for the struggle ahead.[6]

The immensity of that struggle was beginning to be understood, even if only dimly. The victories in the western theater in the spring of 1862 that cheered Northerners were profoundly disheartening to Southern patriots, who had expected the Federal rout at First Bull Run to set the pattern for later battles. Speaking at the inauguration of his six-year term on February 22, President Davis did not blink the crisis. "A million men, it is estimated, are now standing in hostile array and waging war along a frontier of thousands of miles," he said, indulging in a bit of McClellan-like exaggeration; ". . . the tide for the moment is against us." Although the inauguration was taking place "at the darkest hour of our struggle," he insisted that victory was to be valued whatever its cost, for "nothing could be so bad as failure, and any sacrifice would be cheap as the price of success in such a contest."[7]

Within two months the price was only too clear to the citizens of Richmond. From April onward, as McClellan's army toiled up the Peninsula, ambulances crowded with wounded clogged the streets; after the battle at Fair Oaks they came in an unending stream, day and night. A Virginia private, Alexander Hunter, described an oft-repeated scene: " 'Here one is dead, died on the way,' they say as they lift a corpse from the wagon, while the passer-by, grown rapidly familiar with such fearful sights, glances hastily and passes on." There were wagonloads of the slain, "piled one upon another, their stiffened, rigid feet exposed to view."[8] After a time that spring the people of Richmond — and those of Washington as well — learned to recognize a grim barometer of the war's intensity as periodically the streets and hotels and boarding houses filled with crowds of anxious strangers, simple country folk and well-dressed city dwellers alike, come to seek news of the wounded and the dead from the published casualty lists.

As the battle crept closer, Richmond prepared for the worst. The city was put under martial law, and the files of the War Department were packed for quick evacuation. Mrs. Davis was among the refugees sent to safety. The president, however, did not view the situation as entirely bleak. Davis was a man of solid military background — West Point, service in the Mexican War as commander of the Mississippi Rifles, four years as Franklin Pierce's secretary of war, chairman of the Senate's Committee on Military affairs — and he was taking a hard look at General McClellan's tactics. On May 16 he wrote his wife that "the enemy might be beaten before Richmond or on either flank.... Their army, when reduced to small arms and field pieces I think we can defeat and then a vigorous pursuit will bring the results long wished for." He was seeing exactly what General Lee noticed about his fellow engineer's campaign — its dependence on a siege train. Soon after taking command of the army, Lee remarked, "I think the only way the enemy can get his heavy guns up that way is by the railroad." The Federals' Peninsula supply line became a major objective in Lee's evolving plan for defending Richmond.[9]

Despite his distinguished career in the prewar army, Lee was something of an unknown quantity when he assumed command. Porter Alexander, a promising young engineer and artillerist, questioned Colonel Joseph Ives, who had served under Lee earlier in the war, about the general's fighting spirit. (Lee's first move was to order the strengthening of Richmond's defensive lines, leading some of his troops to grumble at the hard labor involved and to call him the "King of Spades," and the ardent Alexander was wondering just what this foretold.) As Alexander remembered it, Ives's reply was pointed: "Alexander, if there is one man in either army, Confederate or Federal, head and shoulders above every other in *audacity*, it is General Lee! His name might be Audacity. He will take more desperate chances, and take them quicker than any other general in this country, North or South...."[10]

Lee's Seven Days' campaign was nothing if not audacious. On the face of it, its concept was audacious to the point of foolhardiness: dividing his army in the presence of a stronger foe, a tactic condemned by the collective traditional wisdom of military textbook writers; leaving Richmond's front door all but wide open if the Federals discovered what was going on; putting the bulk of his forces well away from their home base and at peril if things did not go as planned. Yet the scheme revealed another aspect of Lee's generalship, one that had the potential of reducing his offensive from a gamble to an acceptable risk — an unsparing and perceptive appraisal of the general who opposed him.

It was becoming clear to Lee that McClellan was the most cautious of commanders — Johnston had told him in April, after inspecting the weak Confederate lines at Yorktown, that "no one but McClellan could have hesitated to attack" — and was very likely to be more concerned about not losing than about staking everything on winning. As a careful reader of the Northern newspapers that passed through the lines, Lee seems to have been aware of the inflated estimates of Confederate strength leaked to the press. He deliberately played on this fixation of McClellan's by dispatching an entire division to reinforce Stonewall Jackson in the Shenandoah Valley in so open a manner that the Pinkerton spies in Richmond could not help but notice. McClellan took the hook. "If ten or fifteen thousand men have left Richmond to reenforce Jackson," he wired Lincoln on June 18, "it illustrates their strength and confidence." Should the Young Napoleon thus be persuaded to believe that any Confederate offensive when it came was backed by a vast reservoir of manpower, that suited Lee perfectly.[11]

As it happened, McClellan's state of mind was the decisive element in the Seven Days. Almost the only aspect of Lee's offensive that worked consistently was its pervasive aggressiveness. Southern troop movements went astray in the Peninsula's swamps and on its miserable roads. Assaults requiring close coordination fell into disarray. Stonewall Jackson, who had gained instant celebrity for the speed and promptness of his moves in the Shenandoah, was surprisingly slow and late on the Peninsula. The last of Lee's attacks that bloody week, at Malvern Hill on July 1, met with decisive defeat. Rebel casualties exceeded those of their opponents by some 25 percent. "Under ordinary circumstances, the Federal army should have been destroyed," Lee summed it up.[12]

Yet in war only victory counts, no matter how raggedly achieved, and the victory was Robert E. Lee's. The Richmond press led the cheering. "The operations of General Lee ... were certainly those of a master," the *Dispatch* announced. He "amazed and confounded his detractors by the brilliancy of his genius, the fertility of his resources, his energy and daring," said the *Whig*. Navy Secretary Stephen Mallory summed up the exultant mood in the Confederate capital when he wrote his wife that "the Great McClelland the young Napoleon now like a whipped cur lies on the banks of the James River crouched under his Gun Boats." Rebel soldiers reacted with predictable derision when they learned of McClellan's description of the week's fighting as simply a "change of base." From then on, any such occurrence as the loser of a dog fight seen scurrying for safety called forth the cry, "Look at him changing his base!" Confidence soared throughout the beleaguered South.[13]

While the two armies rested and re-equipped after the violent struggle of the Seven Days, Lee moved as rapidly to attack the weaknesses in his command structure as he had in striking at McClellan. The half-dozen independent divisional commands he inherited had proved too cumbersome to work together effectively. Since there was as yet no Confederate law allowing him to organize the army into units larger than divisions, he achieved his purpose through two informal "commands," one under Jackson and the other under James Longstreet. Jackson's, the smaller of the two, had as its core the Valley army with which he had inflicted so much damage on the Federals in May and June. If Lee was disappointed with Jackson's record in the Seven Days, he gave no hint of it. By contrast, Longstreet's solid performance in the week of battles was one of the brighter entries in the Army of Northern Virginia's ledger, and Lee advanced him to higher command without hesitation. The commanding general was also quick to weed out officers he considered incompetent. One of those to go was Prince John Magruder, whose talents for play-acting and bluff, so useful at Yorktown and in the Richmond defenses, had proved to be greater than his ability to command in battle.

A winning army tends to acquire a distinctive character more rapidly than a losing one, and by the summer of 1862 this was true of the Army of Northern Virginia. Much of this character derived from the personalities of its generals, whom the public was coming to see as a highly colorful group.

Despite Lee's emergence in the Seven Days, Stonewall Jackson remained the best known. Thomas J. Jackson, former professor of natural philosophy and artillery tactics at the Virginia Military Institute, looking not unlike people's mental image of an Old Testament prophet, had gained both his nickname and the beginnings of his fame at First Bull Run. During the heat of the fighting there he was seen with arm upraised, appearing to his awestruck men to be calling on heaven's bolts to smite the foe. (In fact he was only trying to relieve the pain of a wounded hand, but the tale soon became legend.) Richmond reporter George W. Bagley described him as "a Presbyterian who carries the doctrine of predestination to the borders of positive fatalism — the very man to storm the infernal regions in case of necessity."[14]

The Jackson legend grew during the Valley campaign, where he marched his army twenty-five miles and more a day and in mysterious ways, bewildering his foes and attracting an avid following among Southern newspaper readers. "Down here we sleep securely, with the serenest faith that Stonewall is to flank everybody and never to be flanked himself," wrote the diarist Mary Boykin Chesnut. His aphorisms and eccentricities were remarked. To an officer pleading for a brief rest for his exhausted troops, he replied, "I am obliged to sweat them tonight, that I may save their blood tomorrow." General Richard Ewell, trying to spare the life of a particularly courageous Union officer in one of the Valley battles, earned a Jackson rebuke. "The brave and gallant Federal officers are the very kind that must be killed," he insisted. "Shoot the brave officers and the cowards will run away and take the men

Confederate Tide

with them." His passion for secrecy, his unsparing demands on the hungry and the footsore, his wrath at straggling were at first resented by both officers and men. When it became clear that he possessed the habit of victory, however, the resentment changed to respect and pride to be serving under "Old Jack." Through exchanged newspapers and the stories of prisoners, Jackson's reputation spread also among his foes. "His name was a terror in the Union army," a Massachusetts soldier wrote, "and with us expressed more fear than all the other names put together."[15]

Little lore and few anecdotes attached to James Longstreet. Stolid, untiring, phlegmatic in spirit after a scarlet fever epidemic in Richmond killed three of his four children early in 1862, Longstreet's calm self-assurance made him a balance wheel to the independent opportunism of Jackson. As Lee calculated ways to retain the initiative he had seized during the Seven Days, he revealed his confidence in "Old Pete" by giving him charge of more than three-quarters of the Confederate infantry brigades.

Other generals also attracted notice during the Seven Days. Jackson's brother-in-law, D. H. Hill, outspoken and pessimistic, in frequent pain from a spinal ailment, had exhibited a deliberate and conspicuous bravery under fire in order to inspire his wavering troops. Harvey Hill's hatred of Yankees was long-standing. In a mathematics textbook he compiled before the war, the problems called for such calculations as the relative speeds of two Northern soldiers fleeing a Mexican War battlefield, or the financial gain of a Connecticut purveyor of wooden nutmegs. The Virginian A. P. Hill had led his division in attack with a driving energy that matched his explosive temper. Another relentless attacker was the tall, blond-bearded John Bell Hood, whose Texas Brigade spearheaded the charge that broke McClellan's lines and his spirit and drove him into retreat. The press portrayed the flamboyant cavalryman J. E. B. Stuart as the very exemplar of the Southern cavalier after he led his troopers in a complete circuit of the Federal army in the process of gathering intelligence for the offensive. The Seven Days, for all the mistakes that were made, served notice that the generals of the Army of Northern Virginia made war with single-minded and unrelenting fury.

To be sure, trying to mold this collection of fighting generals into a smoothly functioning military machine tested all of Lee's skill and tact. Their jealousies and hyperactive egos produced sharp intramural warfare after the shooting stopped. A battlefield outburst that Harvey Hill had aimed at one of his brigadiers, the Georgian Robert Toombs, nearly resulted in a duel. A dispute between Longstreet and Powell Hill over credit for some particularly gallant exploit during the fighting spread into the columns of the Richmond papers, leading Longstreet to arrest his division commander and Hill to demand satisfaction on the dueling grounds. Lee transferred Hill to Jackson's command to separate the would-be combatants. Life in the high command of the Army of Northern Virginia was never dull.

The Confederacy's overall military strategy in these summer months of 1862 was lent a new urgency by political and diplomatic developments. The deliverance of Richmond and the slowdown of the Federal offensive in the West provided a welcome breathing space, yet at the same time news from the North was creating disquiet. Clearly, Northern war objectives were shifting. The passage by the Congress in Washington of the strongly worded Second Confiscation Act in mid-July seemed proof that the abolitionists were gaining strength in their campaign against the South's peculiar institution. The astute Mrs. Chesnut detected a certain irony in this shift: "This war was undertaken by us to shake off the yoke of foreign invaders. So we consider our cause righteous. The Yankees, since the war has begun, have discovered it is to free the slaves they are fighting — so their cause is noble."[16] Equally alarming was a new and rougher tone to the conduct of the Union armies themselves. It first emerged during the Peninsula campaign. Despite General McClellan's pledge to direct military affairs according to the highest Christian principles, discipline in his Army of the Potomac left much to be desired, and civilians on the Peninsula were the victims of extensive foraging and pillage and destruction. Now came General John Pope, who seemed prepared to give official license to this sort of conduct.

In July a series of draconian proclamations issued over Pope's signature promised to visit the harshest of measures on Southerners living within the area occupied by his Army of Virginia. The army was allowed to confiscate any food or forage that might be needed; civilians were to be held responsible for the actions of guerrilla bands operating against Federal troops and communications, and anyone aiding these raiders was liable to summary execution; those refusing to sign a loyalty oath could be driven from their homes in the occupied territory and shot as spies if they returned. As it happened, the severest of these measures were never carried out, yet it was also true that from that time on no chicken coop or smokehouse or kitchen pantry in northern Virginia was safe from marauding Yankee foragers.[17]

Howell Cobb, the Georgian who had done much to bring the Confederate States into being and who was now a brigadier in Lee's army, took a long look at these various measures and pronounced his verdict to Secretary of War George Randolph. "This war must close in a few months, perhaps weeks, or else will be fought with increased energy and malignity on the part of our enemies," he wrote. "I look for the latter result."[18] The chilling truth of Cobb's prophesy was settling across the South in these summer weeks. The enemy was demonstrating a grim determination to turn a war for Southern independence into a revolution against Southern institutions. The dream of simply beating off the Northern invaders until they went home and division was assured began to fade. Fighting spirit might remain as strong as ever, but the resources needed to fuel that spirit were in distressingly short supply. The Confederacy's financial structure was tottering and its war economy beginning to groan and crack alarmingly under the pressure of the all-out struggle. Conscription was not producing the expected new armies to take the field; in Lee's army, for example, reinforcements scraped up from Charleston and the flow of new recruits together did not even make good all the losses of the Seven Days. But most disillusioning of all was the failure of King Cotton to guarantee early foreign intervention.

The major difficulty with the King Cotton theory was that its timing had gone wrong. The bumper crops of Southern cotton in the last two years of peace had created a glut in Europe. Great Britain's textile mills still had over 700,000 bales on hand at the end of 1861, some 160,000 more than a year earlier. Southerners had refrained from shipping their cotton through the leaky Federal blockade during the first year of the war, but because of the glut this unofficial embargo failed to pressure the great powers into action. The textile manufacturers were happy enough to reduce their inventories, particularly since they did not expect the

American conflict to last long enough to inflict hardship on the industry. In any case, the Davis government was having second thoughts about the wisdom of an embargo, even an informal one, for it was liable to be regarded abroad as a form of diplomatic blackmail. As a British official warned, "I wonder the South do not see that our recognition *because* they keep cotton from us would be ignominious beyond measure, & that no English Parlt. could do so base a thing." In the spring of 1862, by circumstance and by choice, the Confederacy's cotton strategy changed. "White gold" was now its only healthy medium of foreign exchange, and cotton-laden blockade runners began to risk the Federal navy to trade overseas for arms and medicines and other war materiel.[19]

The arrival of even a few cargoes of British Enfield rifles or Blakely fieldpieces was certainly welcome, but Richmond's first diplomatic goal remained active foreign intervention. The long-anticipated cotton famine finally took effect in Britain and France during the summer, and although Confederate statesmen regretted that it had not struck six or eight months sooner, they did their best to exploit it. However, what had seemed so simple in those hopeful days of 1861 — recognition and intervention in direct exchange for unlimited cotton — proved not to be simple at all.

"Nothing can exceed the selfishness of the English statesmen except their wretched hypocrisy," John Slidell wrote in exasperation from Europe on August 24. "They are continually casting about their disinterested magnanimity and ... high-toned morality, while their entire policy is marked by egotism and duplicity." The British aristocracy might rage at Yankee barbarity toward Southern civilians, and the lordly *Times* might praise the South's gallant struggle and pray for a disunited United States, and shipowners and merchants might mourn the loss of the Southern market, yet for the moment the Palmerston government was content to wait and watch. To Slidell this policy was wretched hypocrisy, yet when all the nuances of the international balance of power were weighed and all the growing miseries of the Lancashire cotton workers and their families taken into account, one clear fact emerged — the great powers, individually or collectively, had no intention of backing a loser. Like Lord Palmerston, the frustrated Confederate diplomats could only wait and watch military events in America. "We are still hard and fast aground here," Slidell concluded. "Nothing will float us off but a strong and continued current of important successes in the field."[20]

Thus both at home and abroad the remorseless logic of the conflict was pushing the Confederacy, in the summer of 1862, toward the offensive as its best hope to gain independence. It had in General Lee — whose name, said Colonel Ives, might be Audacity — a commander perfectly attuned to that strategy. Lee had seized the initiative in the Seven Days and had no intention of giving it up. To be sure, no grand campaign on the McClellan model suggested itself. The South had not the slightest prospect of assembling the manpower and heavy weaponry necessary to bludgeon its enemies into submission in one great "battle of posts." Instead, speed and maneuver would have to serve as Lee's weapons, and opportunism be his watchword.

As General Halleck was at pains to point out to McClellan, the Army of Northern Virginia held the enviable interior position between the two widely separated Union armies. Yet until the Federals' intentions were clearer — Would reinforcements go to Pope or McClellan? Would either move to support the other? — Lee could make no definite move on his interior line. He positioned his forces — Longstreet before Richmond to confront McClellan on the Peninsula, Jackson to the north to harass Pope — and watched carefully for the Federals to reveal their hand. By early August it was clear that Pope was being strengthened for active operations. Within forty-eight hours of the first shifting of McClellan's troops away from Harrison's Landing, Lee concluded that he had nothing to fear from a renewed offensive against Richmond by the Young Napoleon. He set his sights on Pope's Army of Virginia.

No doubt it was a decision he took with a sense of personal satisfaction. Pope's repressive orders had aroused Lee's enmity, a quality he would rarely exhibit toward any general facing him. Labeling his opponent a "miscreant," Lee told Jackson bluntly, "I want Pope to be suppressed. The course indicated in his orders, if the newspapers report them correctly, cannot be permitted...."[21]

Lee's Second Bull Run campaign, from first to last, evoked the quality of hairsbreadth Victorian melodrama. Challenging the converging Federal armies, which when combined would outnumber him overwhelmingly, he won the race (by the slimmest of margins) to beat the one before the other arrived in decisive force.

Confidently he gauged a whole series of risks against the blundering Pope and the cautious McClellan and took each one without hesitation. When a matter of hours promised to be the difference between victory and defeat, the Rebels were always there first. By the time the curtain fell on the drama, Lee had completely shifted the focus of the conflict in the East. It was audacity of a kind not before seen in the war.

Lee could take encouragement from the fact that during these two weeks of complex maneuvering there was seldom a trace of the fumbling and mistiming by his subordinates that had marked the Seven Days. Both he and his lieutenants were learning the art of handling large bodies of troops. The largest misstep occurred at the opening of the campaign, when Pope evaded the first concentration against him along the line of the Rappahannock. His respite was only temporary. Once again Lee divided his forces in the face of the enemy. Freezing the Union army in place with Longstreet's command, he dispatched Jackson to turn Pope's flank with one of those forced marches he had executed so successfully in the Valley. "Close up, men, close up! Push on, push on!" Old Jack exhorted his "foot cavalry," and they responded by covering fifty-four miles in two days. Their reward was a gargantuan feast on the commissary riches of the Army of Virginia's supply depot at Manassas Junction. Jackson continued to befuddle the pursuing Federal columns before taking a strong defensive position on the field of the 1861 Bull Run battle. Pope attacked him there on August 29, was beaten back, and boasted to Washington that victory was in his grasp. The frailty of his grasp on events was fully demonstrated the next day, when Longstreet — whose troops had made a forced march to rival the foot cavalry's — crushed the Federal flank and completed the suppression of General John Pope.

Within three months to the day of assuming command, Lee had carried the battle from Richmond's suburbs to Washington's and now stood on the threshold of new opportunities. With the exception of Fort Monroe and nearby Norfolk, nearly all of Virginia was, or was about to be, free from Yankee occupation. The promising Federal second front along the North Carolina coast went unexploited in favor of reinforcing Pope's operations. After more than a year of command, General McClellan found himself back at square one.

In the western theater, too, the fortunes of war turned abruptly. On August 28, as Jackson's troops recovered from their spectacular banquet at "Commissary" Pope's expense, Confederate General Braxton Bragg sidestepped his opponent and drove northward from Chattanooga, with a goal no less ambitious than the reclaiming of all Tennessee and Kentucky. In his train he carried wagonloads of rifles to begin arming the swarms of new recruits expected once Kentucky was liberated. Marching on a parallel course was a second Rebel army, under General Edmund Kirby Smith, and Bragg spoke confidently of uniting the western forces "upon the Ohio" for further adventures. Ohio's governor hastened to call out the militia and all able-bodied citizens to rally in the emergency and defend Cincinnati and the Ohio Valley from the invaders.

For the Army of Northern Virginia, the withdrawal of the Federals into their Washington lines meant a blessed pause after two harrowing weeks of nonstop marching and fighting. Men found a moment to dash off a letter to let their families know they were still alive. "I tell you a soldier in Jackson's Army has got no time to write," one complained. ". . . If he can only address his wife he is satisfied to close and return to bed immediately." Troops policed the blasted fields around Bull Run, burying at least the Confederate dead, caring for the wounded, scavenging equipment, and searching for food in abandoned Yankee knapsacks. "The night after the battle we drank a gallon of real coffee per man," recalled Private Alexander Hunter of the 17th Virginia, "and filled up on salt pork, boiled beef and canned vegetables, and groups of soldiers sat by the camp fires, and boiled, stewed, and fried, and ate off and on all night." There was a particular hunt among the Union dead for shoes to replace those worn and broken down from the prodigious marching of the past weeks. But however hungry and ragged and bone-weary Lee's men might be, their morale was raised high by victory. "I hope you have preserved my letters in which I have spoken of my faith in Lee," Lieutenant John Chamberlayne wrote his mother. "He and his round-table of generals are worthy the immortality of Napoleon and his Marshals." Rear-rank strategists speculated on their general's next move.[22]

His victory over Pope did not reward General Lee with the luxury of mature reflection upon that next move. The hard reality was that his army could not remain where it was for long. This part of northern Virginia was picked clean of food for the men and forage for the animals, and his supply line southward was too rickety to make up the difference. The railroad that had enabled the Confederates to hold the field after their first victory at Bull Run was now a shambles, with the bridges over the Rappahannock and Rapidan rivers destroyed. Although the initiative remained in his hands, Lee was forced to make an immediate choice of moving in one of four directions. Each choice involved a major strategic decision.

He could drive on eastward and attack Washington, as the Lincoln administration and a great many alarmed Washingtonians feared he would do. That course, however, was promptly rejected out of hand. As Lee explained to President Davis, he lacked the means to invest the Federals once they were safe behind their fortifications. "If I possessed the necessary munitions," he wrote, "I should be unable to supply provisions for the troops." Alternatively, he could pull back westward into the agriculturally rich Shenandoah Valley to feed his men and gain access to a rail connection with Richmond, but that was a short-term solution only. At that distance he would be giving up his hard-won control of events. Returning southward to the vicinity of the Rappahannock would shorten his communications and allow him to recruit the army's thinned ranks, but there is no evidence that Lee considered this except as an emergency measure. Such a withdrawal would reduce the fruits of the recent victory to little more than the 16,000 casualties he had inflicted; worse, it would surrender the initiative, once again expose northern Virginia and its fall harvest to the untender mercies of a Yankee occupation, and grant the beaten Federals the time to regroup and prepare yet another grand campaign against Richmond.

East, west, south — all appeared barren of military profit. That left only an advance northward. And to the north, Lee concluded, lay manifold opportunities.

The decision to cross the Potomac was made with necessary promptness, and on September 3, two days after the clash at Chantilly that ended the Bull Run fighting, Lee explained his reasoning in a dispatch to Davis. "The present seems to be the most propitious time since the commencement of the war for the Confederate Army to enter Maryland," he wrote. The Federal forces defending Washington were "much weakened and demoralized" and the new recruits arriving from the North, whom he estimated at 60,000, were not yet trained or organized. He admitted that exploiting this situation involved a major risk: "The army is not properly equipped for an invasion of an enemy's territory. It lacks much of the material of war, is feeble in transportation, the animals being much reduced, and the men are poorly provided with clothes, and in thousands of instances are destitute of shoes." Still, he could not afford to be idle. "Though weaker than our opponents in men and military equipments," he would "endeavor to harass if we cannot destroy them. . . . I do not consider success impossible. . . ."

Shifting the war north of the Potomac, he assured the president, would occupy the full attention of the enemy and keep Richmond safe from attack. As added security, however, he proposed that should Braxton Bragg "find it impracticable to operate to advantage on his present frontier" in Kentucky, that general might bring his army east to defend Virginia. He added that if the Confederacy wanted to give material aid to Maryland to enable it to throw off the Yankee yoke, this was the opportunity to do so.

There was the suggestion here of a limited offensive for limited goals — lifting the pressure on Richmond and war-torn Virginia, aiding Marylanders sympathetic to the Confederate cause, harassing the Federals to keep them off balance. Should the "expedition," as Lee called it, run into trouble, he could always slip off westward to the safety of the Shenandoah. Yet in fact there was nothing at all limited about Lee's ambitions. In subsequent dispatches to Davis he spelled out his plans in growing — though not complete — detail.[23]

It was his intention, he told the president, to support the army in the rich Northern countryside as yet untouched by war. Supplies would be obtained by purchase rather than by the confiscations of the despised General Pope, but as it was likely that "many individuals will hesitate to receive Confederate currency" he would issue certificates of indebtedness on the Confederacy for "future adjustment." As for ammunition and other military necessities, he anticipated that his drive northward would force the Federals to evacuate their outposts at Winchester and Martinsburg and Harper's Ferry in the Shenandoah, opening up a secure supply route from Richmond through the Valley into western Maryland — and beyond. "Should the results of the expedition justify it, I propose to enter Pennsylvania," he wrote, "unless you should deem it unadvisable upon political or other grounds." Meanwhile, he would continue to threaten Washington and Baltimore openly, so as to "annoy and harass the enemy." Learning of McClellan's reappointment to command, he was confident that time was on his side. He had yet to see that general move with anything but the utmost deliberation.

While Lee continued to outline his military objectives in cautious generalities, he laid before President Davis a political analysis that was considerably more bold. Now was the moment, he wrote, for the Confederacy to propose an end to hostilities in exchange for its independence. "Such a proposition, coming from us at this time, could in no way be regarded as suing for peace; but, being made when it is in our power to inflict injury upon our adversary, would show conclusively to the world that our sole object is the establishment of our independence and the attainment of an honorable peace." Even if the offer was rejected, Lee saw profit in making it. A proposal for peace, he concluded, would present Northern voters in the impending fall elections with the choice to "support those who favor a prolongation of the war, or those who wish to bring it to a termination...."

This political proposal is the most revealing of Lee's dispatches to Davis explaining his decision to turn the Rebel columns into Maryland. Only here did he hint at what high stakes he was willing to play for. To force acceptance of Southern independence or to exploit Lincoln's unstable political coalition, the "power to inflict injury upon our adversary" would necessarily involve a good deal more than just helping oppressed Marylanders or provisioning the army in Northern territory or distracting the foe from a new invasion of Virginia. Lee was pushing to a new level the opportunism that had marked his operations since he took command. There was little doubt that if by a direct challenge he could lure General McClellan out of his fortifications and bring him to a finish fight north of the Potomac, on some field where the Army of Northern Virginia's demonstrated talents for speed and maneuver could be put to use, he would do so without hesitation. Behind the

Confederate Tide

cool, calm, dignified face he presented to the world, Robert E. Lee had the calculating instincts of a riverboat gambler.

To be sure, nowhere in these early September dispatches to Davis did Lee put it in so many words that above all else he was marching north to force the Army of the Potomac into an all-out fight. Perhaps he believed that he and the president were naturally of one mind on the subject — one military man speaking to another — and it was hardly necessary to belabor the obvious truth that the Confederacy might never have a better chance to go for the enemy's jugular. (After the fact, Lee did not equivocate. "I went into Maryland to give battle" was how he summed it up to an interviewer in 1868, and went on to elaborate the point in a conversation with his former wartime aide, Colonel William Allan. According to Allan's notes, the general spoke of his determination to have "all my troops reconcentrated on Md. side, stragglers up, men rested and *intended then to attack McClellan,* hoping the best results from state of my troops and those of enemy.")[24] Perhaps he did not want to raise undue expectations in Richmond. Or perhaps he simply did not want to risk being overruled in this deviation from accepted Confederate defensive strategy. However that may be, he was keeping the lid on his ambitions when he told Davis that his intention of advancing beyond Maryland into Pennsylvania was simply "for the purpose of opening our line of communication through the valley, in order to procure sufficient supplies of flour."

Lee was considerably more explicit in a conversation with General John G. Walker when that officer reported to him with two brigades of reinforcements from Richmond. As Walker recalled the scene, Lee stood at a large map and pointed to Harrisburg, Pennsylvania, some seventy miles north of the Maryland line, and told him, "That is the objective point of the campaign." He reminded Walker of the major bridge that carried the Pennsylvania Railroad across the Susquehanna River near Harrisburg. "Well, I wish effectually to destroy that bridge, which will disable the Pennsylvania railroad for a long time. With the Baltimore and Ohio in our possession" — that much-beleaguered line would be squarely on the Confederate line of march in Maryland — "and the Pennsylvania railroad broken up, there will remain to the enemy but one route of communication with the West, and that very circuitous, by way of the Lakes. After that I can turn my attention to Philadelphia, Baltimore, or Washington, as may seem best for our interests."

Walker could not conceal his astonishment. Noticing this, Lee asked, "Are you acquainted with General McClellan?" He had known him only during the Mexican War, Walker replied. "He is an able general but a very cautious one," Lee continued. "His enemies among his own people think him too much so. His army is in a very demoralized and chaotic condition, and will not be prepared for offensive operations — or he will not think so — for three or four weeks. Before that time I hope to be on the Susquehanna."[25] Once again, Lee was relying on his perception of how his opponent played his hand to reduce gamble to acceptable risk.

With Confederate armies on the march east and west, President Davis hastened to send his generals the draft of a public proclamation, with spaces left blank for them to insert the name of whatever state their invading forces might reach. While issuing such proclamations accorded with traditional usage, Davis wrote, his real purpose was to explain to the public (and, no doubt, to the European powers as well) why the South seemed suddenly to be abandoning an article of faith in its secession argument. Until now, the Confederacy had taken the principled position that it was the victim of aggression and merely defending itself against "foreign" invasion. Davis argued that in fact nothing had changed. The South was still waging a war of self-defense; there was "no design of conquest" in the dual invasions, but only an all-out effort to force the Lincoln government to let the South go in peace. "We are driven to protect our own country by transferring the seat of war to that of an enemy who pursues us with a relentless and apparently aimless hostility." He spoke of desolated Southern fields and homes, of murder and rapine resulting from this "unjust and oppressive warfare." He pointed out that the citizens of the invaded states — and, by implication, other Northerners as well — had it in their power to bring all this destruction to an end. If they could not persuade the national government in Washington to act, they could at least initiate peace on the hallowed basis of states' rights, with separate state-by-state peace treaties, which Rich-

Confederate Tide

mond "will ever be ready to conclude on the most just and liberal basis."[26]

In the event, Davis's draft proclamation did not reach his commanders until after they had issued proclamations of their own. All three generals — Lee in Maryland, Bragg and Smith in Kentucky — stressed that they had come not as conquerors but as liberators to these border states oppressed by the tyrannies of the Lincoln administration. None, however, addressed the larger issue of the Confederacy's shift in strategy, and possibly the president regretted that this chance to make a more lasting impression on public opinion was missed.

Like General Lee, Davis had his eyes fixed on the Northern political scene. Throughout the summer, newspapers had carried any number of rumors of a growing antiwar sentiment in the states of the Old Northwest, where ties to the South were still strong. Just how much of this was fact and how much windy talk was not yet clear, nor was it clear whether wavering Northerners might be persuaded by the issuance of proclamations, no matter how noble in intent. Like so many other Southern hopes that September — of clearing Confederate soil of invaders, of peace treaties that would bring the pivotal border states into the fold, of vigorous military intervention from abroad — any exploitation of a Northern peace movement was going to depend finally on the armies. Only victories could sustain the Confederate tide.

On September 3, the day he wrote Davis of his decision to cross into Maryland, Lee began shifting his army north and west from Chantilly toward Leesburg, near the shallow fords of the upper Potomac. Reinforcements from Richmond — the divisions of D. H. Hill and Lafayette McLaws and two brigades under John Walker — were at hand or on the way, but they barely made good the 9,000 men lost at Bull Run and Chantilly. On this date Lee could count perhaps 50,000 troops with which to undertake his expedition beyond the Confederacy's northern frontier. They left behind them a ghastly field of victory. A brigade of South Carolinians crossed Bull Run past hundreds of unburied corpses, blackened and putrid in the hot sun, and the unit's historian wrote, "the harrowing sights that were met with were in places too sickening to admit of description."[27]

The routes of march to Leesburg covered only some twenty-five or thirty miles, but even that was too much for thousands of shoeless men tortured by bruised and bleeding feet and other thousands enervated by diarrhea resulting from the steady diet of green corn and apples. Private Hunter of Longstreet's command wrote that his regiment had not seen a commissary wagon in almost a week; each day companies had to send out details to forage in the countryside for whatever food they could find. "The ambulances were full, and the whole route was marked by a sick, lame, limping lot...."[28] Many hobbled on as best they could, slipping farther and farther behind their units, hoping to catch up when the army halted. Others, by necessity or by choice, did not keep up at all, and the Army of Northern Virginia shed strength with every mile.

Spirits revived in Leesburg, where there was a brief chance to rest and savor the last Virginia hospitality before they crossed the river. "The doorways and curb stones are like living bouquets of beauty," war correspondent Felix G. de Fontaine reported to the *Charleston Daily Courier*. "Everything that wears crinoline or a pretty face is out, and such shouts and wavings of handkerchiefs and hurrahs by the overjoyed gender never emanated from human lips...." One of Harvey Hill's North Carolinians, Sergeant James W. Shinn, noted in his diary that most of these women must have been baking all day, for before long they were "giving bread, honey & fruit pies & throwing open their springhouses" to the famished troops. Another man remembered an elderly woman with upraised arms and tears in her eyes, crying out, "The Lord bless your dirty ragged souls!" He added that his company was certainly no dirtier than the rest of the army, "but it was our luck to get the blessing."[29]

On September 4 General Lee took stock of the alarming manpower drain and issued stern orders to his brigade commanders to sweep up anyone "leaving the ranks, right, left, front, or rear" and return them summarily to their units. (The iron-handed Jackson issued orders of his own that any man in his command leaving the column without excuse was to be shot.) Straggling was nothing new in the Army of Northern Virginia, or for that matter in any of the Union or Confederate armies. Every regiment had its "skulks" and "coffee-coolers," as the troops called them, those who could be relied on to be present only on paydays or when rations were issued. But this was different. The faint-hearted in uncounted numbers were taking refuge among the truly ill and footsore, defying the efforts of the provost marshals to root them out.[30]

As word of the impending march into Maryland spread through the army, another and quite unexpected defection took place. "There were two opinions in the army as to the propriety of the move," wrote the Reverend Joseph Stiles, who was traveling with Lee as a kind of unofficial headquarters chaplain. "A minority believed that as a matter of *prudence* at least we should not leave our own soil: that it looked a little like *invasion*. The consequence was a large number hung back & would not cross the river...." This principled opposition seems to have centered mostly among men enlisted from the westernmost counties of North and South Carolina, where Unionist feeling was strong at the time of the secession referendums. They had volunteered willingly enough to defend their homes, a regimental historian explained, but "some did not believe it right to invade Northern territory." With their numbers added to those already fallen out of the ranks, it became painfully clear to Lee that when he took his army north he would be leaving behind a second army of stragglers.

Orders went out to the provost guard to collect this ragtag band and escort it to the Shenandoah, from where he hoped at least some portion of it might be sent to him later when the expedition secured its communications through the Valley. Losing these men was bad enough; he did not want to compound his problems by leaving them to wander around loose, scavenging for food in the larders and springhouses of loyal Virginians and supposedly loyal Marylanders.[31]

In keeping with its growing reputation for intramural scuffling, the army was about to embark on its great adventure with two of its best fighting generals under arrest. The tempestuous Powell Hill discovered that life with Stonewall Jackson was even thornier than it had been with James Longstreet. During the recent campaign, Jackson had got the idea that Hill was careless about enforcing the strict marching regimen expected of any general under his orders, and on the move to Leesburg the dispute boiled over. As a result, Hill was relieved of command of his division and went stumping along in high dudgeon at the rear of the column. Another division commander, John Bell Hood, was also sentenced to the rear ranks. Hood had become embroiled in nothing more weighty than a dispute over who was entitled to several fancy new Federal ambulances captured at Bull Run. Personal honor ranked high with officers of this army, however, and Lee had to yield to the formalities of military protocol. Yet he made sure that these two combative generals remained with their commands, at hand in case of emergency.

If these were not annoyances enough, Lee himself was suffering the effects of a freak accident. A few days before, while standing with his aides, he had stumbled and fallen heavily trying to restrain his horse Traveller when it shied. Both hands were incapacitated, the right one with a broken bone, the left with a severe sprain. Splints were applied, and he would be forced to make a somewhat inglorious entry into Northern territory riding in an ambulance. Nor did Longstreet present a very martial appearance. A badly blistered heel required him to give up his boot in favor of an old carpet slipper, to the amusement of his troops. (A few days later, the third of the army's top commanders would be incapacitated as well. Jackson was presented with a new horse by a proud Marylander, but Old Jack was no sooner mounted than the beast reared and threw him. Stunned and bruised, he too was confined to an ambulance for a time.)[32]

Undeterred by these various developments, Lee brooked no change in his schedule. On Thursday, September 4, advance elements of the Army of Northern Virginia pushed on to White's Ford on the Potomac and began crossing into Maryland, an operation that continued through the weekend. There was a universal sense that here was a historic moment. Men long remembered the glowing pastoral scene. The Potomac, shallow and a half mile wide, flowed gently under the golden autumn sun past richly wooded green banks. The sunrise, Sergeant Shinn wrote in his diary, "caused the rippled surface to sparkle with the brilliancy of a sea of silver studded with diamonds set in dancing beds of burnished gold.... The scene was one of grand & magnificent interest." Bands played "Maryland, My Maryland," and the men were cheerful, splashing through the waist-deep water, yipping the Rebel yell. The only thing Lieutenant William Johnson, of the 2nd South Carolina, found wrong with the crossing was that it was too brief. "We needed a good washing of our bodies," he wrote, "but wading in the water did us no good in that direction."[33]

Even Stonewall Jackson unbent, sitting his horse in the middle of the river and tipping his battered forage cap to the cheers of his men. When one of the wagon trains got into a tangle in midstream and Jackson's quartermaster, Major John Harman, untangled it with a spectacular exhibition of profanity — "There's only one language that will make mules understand on a hot day that they must get out of the water," Harman explained — pious Stonewall forgave him his blasphemy with a smile and said mildly, "Thank you, major." A canal boat was overturned in the Chesapeake and Ohio Canal paralleling the northern bank to provide the columns passage. As welcome as anything else was the discovery of a barge full of melons, providentially tied up on its journey to Washington. It was promptly picked clean, the first of the rich provender the troops hoped to find on Northern soil. All things considered, wrote Heros Von Borcke, a gaudy cavalryman who had left the Prussian service to fight for the Confederacy, "There were few moments, perhaps, from the beginning to the close of the war, of excitement more intense, of exhilaration more delightful. . . ."[34]

Richmond's *Southern Illustrated News*, in an editorial headed "The Invasion of Maryland," considered it a great moment as well: "Mighty events — mightier than any that have yet occurred — are evidently on the wing. Before another issue of this paper, a great battle may have been fought, and the fate of Washington, possibly the war, have been determined. We wait with anxiety, yet without the smallest fear, for the result. Our brave boys are not to be beaten by any force the Yankees can bring against them."[35]

· 3 ·

WILL SEND YOU TROPHIES

Newspaper accounts of General Pope's defeat and of the Confederate advances into Maryland and Kentucky cast a pall across the Northern states, made all the more ominous by the War Department's imperfect efforts at censorship. "The morning papers and an extra at mid-day turned us livid and blue," wrote the New York diarist George Templeton Strong. ". . . Stonewall Jackson (our national bugaboo) about to invade Maryland, 40,000 strong. . . . Cincinnati in danger. A rebel army within forty miles of the Queen City of the West. Martial law proclaimed in her pork shops. . . . Rebellion is on its legs again, East and West, rampant and aggressive at every point." A New York editor described the city's mood to a friend as "rife with rumors of Cabinet changes and army jealousies. We feel very much as if this was a national crisis. . . ." Pope's official report charging the leadership of the Army of the Potomac with deliberate delay in coming to his aid at Bull Run was leaked to the press, creating further national dismay. A newly commissioned lieutenant assigned to a Rhode Island regiment arrived in Washington early in September and was surprised to find the morale of the defeated army actually higher than that of the dispirited civilians he left back home.[1]

Some war correspondents were beginning to balk at the handouts fed them at McClellan's headquarters describing the overwhelming Confederate numbers. On September 8 the *New York Tribune* ran a dispatch from one of its reporters who had interrogated paroled Federal troops and Southern prisoners. Under the headline "A Glimpse Behind the Rebel Lines," he wrote bluntly,

"The enemy has had no more men, not so much ordnance, nor provisions, nor transportation facilities, nor nearly so much encumbering baggage but he has outgeneraled us from Slaughter Mountain to Edward's Ferry, and God knows but he will do so hereafter.... This is the plain, unvarnished truth; we have been whipped by an inferior force of inferior men, better handled than our own." The pro-McClellan *New York Herald*, however, would not buy the Republican *Tribune's* line. The next day the *Herald* reported that the Confederate army was "at least 150,000 strong." How much weight readers gave such conflicting reports no doubt depended on the strength of their political convictions.[2]

In the days immediately following the Second Bull Run battle, Yankee soldiers also put down their views of events for the people at home. The tone of these letters was angry and bitter, and not a few of them received wider circulation by being printed in hometown papers. A New Yorker in Fitz John Porter's corps was disturbed by the Rebels' determination: "... all the prisoners we take seem to be confident of success in the end; they still persist that the *South will never give in;* some of the Texans drawled out in a conversation, 'We will fight you until we are all dead, Yanks, and I reckon then the women will fight you.' " General John Sedgwick also thought the enemy more dedicated. "On our part it has been a war of politicians; on theirs it has been one conducted by a despot and carried out by able Generals," he wrote his sister on September 4. "I look upon a division as certain; the only question is where the line is to run." Captain William Lusk was unreservedly bitter in a letter to his mother: "The battle comes — there is no head on the field — the men are handed over to be butchered — to die on inglorious fields. Lying reports are written. Political Generals receive praises where they deserve execration. Old Abe makes a joke.... Alas, my poor country!" Many letter writers took aim at hapless Pope and McDowell, but it was generally agreed that there was more than enough blame to go around.[3]

The radical Republicans in particular found events hard to swallow. An editor at the Democratic *New York Journal of Commerce* reported with satisfaction to a friend that the radicals were "indignant, outraged, and sullen or violent ... and they denounce the *President* with ferocity." A case in point was Zachariah Chandler, Republican senator from Michigan and a member of the Joint

Committee on the Conduct of the War. For Chandler, *"treason, rank treason"* was the root cause of General Pope's defeat. "Are imbecility *and treason* to be retained and promoted to the End of the Chapter," he raged to Secretary Stanton in a letter written on September 10; "under the belief that traitors in the army would be punished & the enemy yet be exterminated, the people of the North West were hopeful, but the restoration of McLelland Porter & Franklin to command without trial has cast a hopeless gloom over our entire community. . . ." The same day, his temper still at white heat, Chandler told his fellow Republican senator from Illinois, Lyman Trumbull, "Your President is unstable as water. If he has as I suspect, been bullied by those traitor Generals, how long must it be before he will by them be set aside & a Military Dictator set up. . . . For God & country's sakes, send some one to *stay* with the President who will control & hold him."[4]

Zach Chandler was an uncommonly suspicious man, and his dislike of McClellan was so intense that he disdained to learn to spell his name, yet his conviction that the war was spinning out of control was by no means unique. The struggle had gone on now for almost a year and a half. The Union had nearly two-thirds of a million men under arms, with the new call-up of 300,000 only partially filled. As the president pointed out, to run the war was costing Northerners about $2 million a day. Important gains had been made, certainly — the blockade tightened, footholds gained on the Confederate coasts, New Orleans captured, much of the Mississippi Valley under Federal control — yet at the center of things, where it mattered most, the large and expensive war machine was moving in reverse. The South's two principal field armies had shifted from the defensive to the offensive, and a great many people throughout the Northern states were wondering where it had all gone wrong.

Abraham Lincoln was wondering as well, and searching for some deeper meaning. He was moved to commit his musings to paper at about this time and to confess his perplexity. Both Northerners and Southerners believed they were acting in accordance with God's will, he wrote. "I am almost ready to say this is probably true — that God wills this contest, and wills that it shall not end yet. By his mere quiet power, on the minds of the now contestants, He could have either *saved* or *destroyed* the Union without a human contest. Yet the contest began. And having begun He could give the final victory to either side any day. Yet the contest proceeds."[5]

The president's principal commander did not share any such perplexity. General McClellan's messianic vision was reinvigorated by his recall to high command. Clearly, here was evidence of God's will. "The case is desperate," he wrote his wife on September 5, "but with God's help I will try unselfishly to do my best, and, if He wills it, accomplish the salvation of the nation.... Truly, God is trying me in the fire...." Two days later his mood was up, and he brimmed with self-assurance. "I have now the entire confidence of the Govt & the love of the army — my enemies are silent & disarmed" — a judgment that Zach Chandler, for one, would have disputed — "if I defeat the rebels I shall be master of the situation."[6]

Evidence accumulated rapidly that General Halleck was right in supposing, on September 3, that the Confederate army intended to cross the Potomac and "make a raid" into Maryland and possibly Pennsylvania. Although Jeb Stuart's squadrons kept the Federal cavalry at arm's length, Lee made no effort to restrain the civilians who witnessed the crossing. Indeed, it suited his purposes for the Federals to learn that his army was on the loose on Northern soil — if not in what strength — and that they would have to react to his moves. On the afternoon of September 4 a rustic Paul Revere spurred his horse down Pennsylvania Avenue, shouting that Rebel troops "by the thousand" were crossing the river. On the sixth the War Department finally made it official and released the news to the papers. "The newsboys are now crying, 'General Jackson has crossed into Maryland,' " Mrs. Elizabeth Lomax, a Southern sympathizer living in Washington, noted in her journal. "That young man usually does the thing he starts out to do. Now we shall have fighting in good earnest."[7]

In later years, General McClellan liked to send chills up his listeners' spines by relating that when he led the Army of the Potomac into the field after Lee in these early days of September he was overstepping orders limiting him to the defense of Washington, risking court-martial and a probable death sentence. His brave confrontation with martyrdom made a good story, but in fact it was another of the fictions he spun so effortlessly.[8] Halleck told another story. "The assignment of General McClellan to the command of the army in the field, just prior to the Maryland campaign, was made verbally by the President at General McClellan's own house, in my presence," he explained to Senator Wade's Joint Committee on the Conduct of the War. "He said to him, 'General, you will take command of the forces in the field.'" Halleck added that Lincoln had been debating the question "for two or three days." Diarist Gideon Welles put a different light on the assignment. The president told him on September 8, he wrote, that "Halleck selected McClellan to command troops against the Maryland invasion. I could not have done it, said he, for I can never feel confident that he will do anything."[9]

Whoever took the decision, the assignment was made, and by September 5 military routine in the army and the War Department was operating on the clear assumption that McClellan was preparing to march. Halleck notified him of certain command changes contemplated at the corps level "so that you may act accordingly in putting forces in the field." Orders were issued to corps commanders to be ready to march with three days' rations; the general commanding "expects to take the field himself tomorrow." Writing to his wife on the morning of the fifth, McClellan left no doubt that his calling did not restrict him to guarding the capital: "It is probable that our communications will be cut off in a day or two, but don't be worried. You may rest assured that I am doing all I can for my country...."[10]

The president, to be sure, accepted this decision only with the gravest misgivings and after struggling with the whole command question. First General Pope had to be dispensed with, which was done promptly enough by sending him west to the frontier to fight Indians. Pope departed in bitterness, and spent a good deal of his time in this military exile writing angry letters to various authorities defending himself and blaming his defeat on the "praetorian system" of McClellan and his army cohorts. Lincoln believed the public feeling against McClellan made a change necessary, and he called in General Ambrose Burnside and offered him the command of the Army of the Potomac.[11]

On paper Burnside seemed a reasonable choice. He was the only one of the army's corps commanders with any experience of independent command, having directed the successful amphibious operation against Confederate posts on the North Carolina coast earlier in the year. He was a large and impressive man with spectacular muttonchop whiskers and an open, friendly manner. It was hard not to like Ambrose Burnside. It was considered a point in his favor that in this highly politicized army, and despite a long-standing personal friendship with McClellan, he was thought to be without political taint or ambition. Once before, after the Seven Days, these traits led Lincoln to offer him the army command, but he had turned it down. Now he did so again, revealing another unusual characteristic — a candid admission of his limited grasp of the military arts. "I had always unreservedly expressed that I was not competent to command such a large army as this," he later told Senator Wade's committee, adding that he assured the president there was no one as capable of handling the job as General McClellan.[12]

The list of candidates after Burnside was short. Among the other corps commanders only Fitz John Porter had turned in a solid fighting record on the Peninsula. But Lincoln considered Porter to be as deeply embroiled in opposition politics as McClellan, and in any case he was under a cloud of suspicion for allegedly disobeying Pope's orders at Second Bull Run. Only the impending campaign postponed a court of inquiry on the matter. Leading a division on the Peninsula, Joseph Hooker had met the test of combat and been christened "Fighting Joe" by the newspapers (in fact the epithet was a typographer's error, the label "Fighting — Joe Hooker" on a piece of telegraphed news copy having been mistaken for the story's headline), earning him promotion to corps command in place of McDowell. Hooker, however, had a somewhat unsavory personal reputation and was widely mistrusted as an intriguer. Lee's rapid movements allowed the president no time to reach farther afield, leaving him no real choice but to tolerate McClellan in field command once again. "We must use what tools we have," he told John Hay.[13]

One rationale for his expedition, Lee wrote President Davis, was the disorganized and demoralized condition of the Federal forces at Washington. Initially at least, he was entirely correct in his appraisal of the disorganization. McClellan was confronted with the task of patching together two separate armies in the wake of a resounding defeat, and doing so in a very short time. The capital and its environs were overrun with stragglers — officers without commands, commands without officers, bewildered individuals knocked loose from their units by the shock of battle and wandering about aimlessly in search of something to eat and somewhere to sleep. In addition, there were thousands of new recruits whose initiation into the mysteries of military life was taking place just when the army itself was in a state of high confusion.

A certain number of these rookie troops were replacements slated for regiments that had sent recruiting officers back home to try to fill ranks depleted by combat and disease. For the most part, however, Northern governors and leading local citizens preferred to display their patriotism and turn a political profit by organizing entirely new regiments. As a consequence, the Army of the Potomac and the Washington garrison had to absorb no fewer than thirty-five brand-new regiments, with more on the way. (Although the paperwork would take a week or so, Pope's Army of Virginia, for all practical purposes, ceased to exist when McClellan took over.) There was simply no time to do the job properly. The case of the 16th Connecticut was typical. Less than two weeks after taking the oath in Hartford, these green troops went on campaign having received, the regimental historian wrote, "no drill, no discipline, few instructions even in marching. It was little more than a crowd of earnest Connecticut boys."[14]

An important beginning in creating order from confusion was the sense of security provided by the Washington lines. Once free of Confederate pursuit, the troops found time to get food and some sleep, and the command structure soon took hold. The defenses were put in shape and manned. Cavalry detachments took on the job of clearing the capital's streets and taverns of stragglers, lost units were tracked down and dispatched to their proper places, and the quartermaster and commissary organizations began to restore the sense of military routine that an army of necessity lives by. The new replacements and the new regiments were sorted out and assigned. General McClellan, whose talents as an organizer were admitted by even his harshest critics, was "working like a beaver" (in Lincoln's approving phrase) during these early days of September.[15] Much remained to be done, and the sorting out continued even after the army took the field, yet the transformation was remarkable for all that.

Lee's estimate of the Federals' demoralization also proved to be an overstatement. The Yankees who had been beaten at Second Bull Run were more angry than disheartened. Normally, the ordinary soldier's view was decidedly limited, a combination of his own narrow vision, army rumor, and what he read in the newspapers. In that campaign, however, even the lowliest private was witness to the command confusion, the fruitless marching and countermarching, and found in Generals Pope and McDowell a handy outlet for his anger.

Rather than being outfought the army believed almost to a man that it had been outthought. "The force brought against us was not larger than our own, was equally fatigued, and, still more, without food," Wilder Dwight of the 2nd Massachusetts observed. "But we allowed them, — impotently and with fatal blindness, allowed them to outgeneral us." In a letter home, General Alpheus Williams wrote of Pope, "It can with truth be said of him that he had not a friend in his command from the smallest drummer boy to the highest general officer. All *hated* him. McDowell was his only companion and McDowell is disliked almost as much. . . ." The relief at having McClellan back in command was all but universal. Even Joe Hooker, who was by no means a McClellan admirer, was heard to say that if the Young Napoleon had been left in command the Second Bull Run disaster would never have happened.[16]

McClellan spent long hours in the saddle, visiting the camps, letting himself be seen, acknowledging the enthusiastic cheers with his special salute, a jaunty twirl of his cap, giving the unmistakable impression that now that he was in command again all was right with the world. "I hear them calling out to me as I ride among them, 'George, don't leave us again!' " he wrote Ellen. Even a cynical reporter for the Republican *Chicago Tribune* was disarmed. "I have disbelieved the reports of the army's affection for McClellan, being entirely unable to account for the phenomenon," he wrote. "I cannot account for it to my satisfaction now, but I accept it as a fact."[17]

On Sunday, September 7, the general began shifting his headquarters from Washington to the field. Before he left the capital, however, he could not resist a final theatrical flourish. At the White House, the War Department, and the home of Secretary of State Seward he left his calling card on which he had written the initials P.P.C., the French military idiom "Pour Prendre Congé" that formally notified the government of his departure. That evening Navy Secretary Welles, out for a walk, encountered McClellan and his staff cantering along Pennsylvania Avenue. He hoped all the activity indicated an advance, the secretary said; "the country will expect you to go forward." McClellan assured him that the campaign was under way. "Success to you, then, General, with all my heart," Welles replied, and with that blessing the Young Napoleon hurried on his way.[18]

If Lee's appraisal of the condition of the Federal army was somewhat imperfect, there was no question that his grip on the initiative remained unchallenged. To force McClellan to march to his tune, he intended to take full advantage of what was for his purposes the highly favorable geography of western Maryland. The primary terrain feature was a series of parallel ranges running almost due north and south. In order to lure the Army of the Potomac out of the Washington fortifications, he began his campaign very much in the open, keeping to the east of the low ridgeline of Catoctin Mountain, the extension of the Bull Run Mountains of Virginia. With his army at Frederick, Maryland, twenty-three miles north of the Potomac crossing at White's Ford, he would appear to the Federals to be poised for a thrust at either Washington or Baltimore.

It was to the west, however, that Lee intended to conduct his war of movement, leading the Army of the Potomac ever farther from its Washington supply base even as he began drawing his own supplies via the Shenandoah Valley. A half dozen or so miles west of the Catoctin range is the considerably more rugged and imposing ridge called South Mountain, running some fifty miles northward from the Potomac. Separated from South Mountain by Pleasant Valley is the third of the parallel ranges, another extension of Virginia's Blue Ridge, called Elk Mountain. Beyond it to the west is the broad Cumberland Valley, the northward continuation of the Shenandoah.

Militarily, the most important of these three ranges was 1,300-foot South Mountain, for between the Potomac and Frederick it could be crossed by an army at only a handful of passes. Once behind this concealing curtain, screened from prying eyes by Stuart's cavalry holding the gaps, Lee was confident he would have the time to rest and recruit his forces and plot the kind of battle of maneuver, somewhere in the Cumberland Valley of Maryland or Pennsylvania, that had been so successful at Second Bull Run. This was good campaigning country, with bountiful supplies of food and an extensive road network. The primary artery was the historic National Road, which ran through Frederick, crossed South Mountain at Turner's Gap, angled northward to Hagerstown, Maryland, and turned westward toward Ohio. With the advance of the Rebel army outflanking the Federal posts in the lower Shenandoah, Winchester was quickly evacuated, and Lee expected the Martinsburg and Harper's Ferry garrisons to follow suit. His Shenandoah supply line would then be secure.

The Confederate force that began crossing into Maryland on September 4 hardly looked the part of a conquering army. The long and tortuous supply line from Richmond was hard pressed to furnish even such essentials as ammunition, and in any case the quartermaster and commissary departments were the weakest links in the Confederate administration. The hard summer's campaigning had completed their breakdown. Those who recorded their impressions in letters and diaries during these days, including the Rebel soldiers themselves, agreed that this was the most ragtag of armies.

Uniforms were in rags and tatters, described as "multiforms"; faces were unshaven, unkempt hair stuck through torn slouch hats, and the dusty roads added new layers of dirt. In many infantry regiments the barefooted seemed to outnumber those with shoes. From generals to privates the army was lousy, and the marching columns, it was said with only slight exaggeration, could be smelled before they could be seen. "They were the dirtiest men I ever saw," a young civilian remembered, "a most ragged, lean, and hungry set of wolves." It was noted, however, that rifles were clean and cartridge boxes full. Alfred R. Waud, a *Harper's Weekly* war artist who was picked up and briefly detained by some of Jeb Stuart's troopers, described his captors as homespun in dress but well mounted and well armed with carbines "mostly captured from our own cavalry, for whom they expressed utter contempt." The artillery batteries, too, were patchworks, liberally sprinkled with captured Yankee guns.[19]

The overriding topic of conversation in this invading army was food — where to find it, and how to get it without running afoul of Lee's orders against inflicting excesses on the good citizens of Maryland. Officers were authorized to "buy" cornfields and apple orchards, but that provided a diet guaranteed to be debilitating. Foraging became a necessity. The standard explanation for unauthorized foraging (in this or any other Civil War army) was that the innocent soldier had been assaulted by an unpatriotic cow or pig or chicken, and it was kill or be killed. "Some of the men came into camp one morning with a pig, and declared that the pig attacked them, and they were obliged to kill it in self defense," one of Stuart's horse artillerists explained. "It was keenly enjoyed for breakfast and no questions asked." Individual foraging by purchase was more common. Diarist J. R. Boulware, a surgeon in the 6th South Carolina, found good pickings: "I bought some apple butter, bread, etc., got as many apples as I could carry, had a long chat with a pretty nice cross-eyed girl.... I never saw apple butter until I came to Maryland. I am fond of it."

There was also sanctioned organized foraging, with company details sent out to comb the countryside to purchase anything edible. Virginia Private Alexander Hunter described one such expedition. His squad came upon a prosperous farm whose owners had fled. At first the men were content to fill their canteens with cold spring water, until someone investigated the dairy and temptation took over; milk replaced water in the canteens. The storeroom above the dairy was checked, a barrel of cider found, and the milk emptied out in favor of cider. Then came a discovery of major proportions — a barrel of apple brandy. The canteens soon brimmed with applejack. An animated debate followed, Hunter wrote. "The whole squad, except the sergeant, wanted to carry the barrel and leave everything else behind, but then came the difficulty about obeying orders. The discussion waxed high...." Finally the sergeant stove in the brandy barrel (which held enough to make a whole brigade "glad," Hunter noted ruefully) and the company had to be satisfied with the contents of the canteens and half a dozen crocks of apple butter. "The owner's health was honestly drunk, however, none asking or caring whether he was Yank or Reb."[20]

Maryland was a border state divided in its loyalties, with Unionist sentiment strongest west of the tidewater region. North

Carolinian James Shinn wrote admiringly of the "fine thickly settled country, splendid farms & houses with plenty" in western Maryland, but detected "little symptoms of 'secesh' "; in Buckeystown, indeed, "the houses were all shut up & nearly all the people we saw looked as if they had lost a dear friend." Lieutenant William Johnson agreed: "We were not received with cheers or songs or other evidences of approbation, but instead they looked on us in self-evident pity." There were frequent instances of individual kindnesses, with citizens putting out buckets of cold water for the parched marchers, and here and there a bystander handed over his shoes to a barefooted infantryman, but on September 7 Lee had to admit to President Davis, "I do not anticipate any general rising of the people in our behalf." He added that he hoped for some additions to the ranks, but in that too he was largely disappointed. Marylanders moved to enlist in the Southern cause may have had second thoughts when they took a good look at the condition of the army they would be joining. The total of new recruits probably did not exceed 200.[21]

Frederick was alive with rumors and alarms as the Southern army approached. Supplies were removed from a local military hospital, and Captain William T. Faithful of the state home guard collected cars and a switching engine from the Baltimore and Ohio and was able to send a trainload of stores safely off to Baltimore. Bank deposits were spirited away. The roads leading northward were filled with frightened residents in carriages and on horseback. "Impressment into the ranks as common soldiers, or immurement in a *Southern* prison — these were not attractive prospects for quiet, Union-loving citizens!" Dr. Lewis H. Steiner noted in his journal. "Every mouth was full of rumors as to the numbers, whereabouts, and whatabouts of the Confederate force."

On Saturday morning, September 6, Dr. Steiner, a Frederick native who was an inspector for the U.S. Sanitary Commission, a civilian agency dedicated to the welfare of Union soldiers, watched the arrival of Stonewall Jackson's vanguard. "These were received with feeble shouts from some secession-sympathizers," he wrote sourly. ". . . A dirtier, filthier, more unsavory set of human beings never *strolled* through a town — marching it could not be called without doing violence to the word. . . . But *these* were the chivalry — the deliverers of Maryland from Lincoln's oppressive yoke." Another witness, writing to a friend in Baltimore, said she "felt humiliated at the thought that this horde of ragamuffins could set our grand army of the Union at defiance." She admitted to being surprised at how cheerful this motley army was, "on the broad grin all the time," and confessed that she felt a certain sympathy "for the poor, misguided wretches, for some were limping along so painfully, trying to keep with their comrades."[22]

The awful fears of Frederick's Unionists did not materialize, for the Army of Northern Virginia proved to look a great deal worse than it acted. There was no impressment into the ranks, and respectable women were able to appear in public after all. Lee's provost guard patrolled the streets, enforcing discipline with the flat of a saber when necessary. The troops purchased rather than confiscated, although some storekeepers, highly dubious of the value of Confederate currency, wondered if this was a difference in principle only. The one recorded act of violence during the five-day occupation was the attempted sack of two local Unionist newspapers by a mob of secessionist-minded residents. Confederate troops quickly restored order, jailed the attackers, and helped the newspaper staffs clean up the mess. Once the town's stocks of shoes and foodstuffs were sold out — Jackson's men got most of what was available, to the disgust of later arrivals — Lee confined the troops to their outlying camps, with no one permitted in town without a pass. On September 8 he issued a proclamation to the people of Maryland, pledging aid "to enable you again to enjoy the inalienable rights of freemen.... No constraint upon your free will is intended; no intimidation will be allowed.... This army will respect your choice, whatever it may be...." Marylanders, regardless of their loyalties, were going to be handled with kid gloves.

While the good Union patriot Dr. Steiner could not resign himself to the disgrace of Rebel feet pressing upon Northern soil and was "not disposed to bow the knee to Baal," his curiosity got the best of him. Engaging the invaders in conversation, he found no lack of morale or confidence. "The movement they have now made is believed by them to be a desperate one, and they must 'see it through,'" he wrote. "They all believe in *themselves* as well as in their generals, and are terribly in earnest. They assert that they have never been whipped, but have driven the Yankees before them whenever they could find them." Their next move, he was told, would be an advance into Pennsylvania, "and they speak freely of their intention to treat Pennsylvania very differently from Maryland. I fear there will be great destruction of property...."[23]

For most of the men in Lee's army, the stay in Frederick was the first extended breathing spell in as much as a month of ceaseless marching and fighting. Instead of gulping down raw corn, they had the chance to boil or roast the fresh-picked ears that still made up the largest part of their diets. There was leisure to bathe and to wash clothes, and the army began to look slightly better and to smell a great deal better. Inveterate foragers evaded the camp pickets and bought or cadged enough in town for an occasional decent meal. "The ragged were clad, the shoeless shod, and the inner man rejoiced by a number and variety of delicacies," one of Jackson's officers wrote, with pardonable hyperbole. Spirits were further raised by the announcement of a resounding victory by Kirby Smith's army in Kentucky that resulted in the capture of 3,000 Yankees. In writing to his wife on September 7, Dorsey Pender, a brigadier in Powell Hill's division, reflected a mood of optimism tempered by the realities of the army's condition: "Md. is rising, we have a victorious army, and no troops in our front. Gen. Lee has shown great Generalship and the greatest boldness. There never was such a campaign, not even by Napoleon. Our men march and fight without provisions, living on green corn when nothing better can be had. But all this kills up our men. Jackson would kill up an army the way he marches and the bad management in the subsistence Dept. — Gen. Lee is my man."[24]

Lee, Longstreet, and Jackson made their headquarters in a grove of handsome oaks two miles south of town, where Southern sympathizers thronged in the hope of a glimpse of their heroes. Still troubled by his injured hands, Lee kept to his tent, dictating dispatches to Richmond. Jackson, too, was recuperating after the fall from his gift horse and was seldom to be seen. By the Sabbath, however, he was feeling well enough to attend church, where the Reverend Daniel Zacharias held steadfast to his Union principles and offered a prayer to President Lincoln. To the amusement of the general's staff, however, this act of moral courage fell on deaf ears. As was his custom, Old Jack fell asleep during the sermon and was awakened only at the end of the service by the voices of the choir and the resounding tones of the organ.

Jeb Stuart took advantage of this pause in the affairs of war to host a grand ball at Urbana, the cavalry's headquarters a few miles southeast of Frederick. The local female academy was taken over and decorated with roses and regimental flags, the band of the 18th Mississippi was rounded up, and invitations went out to all the young ladies in the vicinity, regardless of political preference. It was a gay triumph for Southern chivalry. At the height of the festivities, a breathless courier arrived to announce a clash with the Yankees. Stuart's cavaliers galloped off to the rescue, then returned to dance the night away. A few troopers slightly wounded in the skirmish were cared for by ministering angels in ball gowns, and confessed that the wounding was well worth it. All things considered, the Army of Northern Virginia would look back on these days at Frederick as an interlude to be treasured.[25]

By September 9, however, Lee could no longer postpone a major decision. Matters were not going entirely according to plan. As far as the Army of the Potomac was concerned, he was satisfied that his calculations were correct. Stuart's intelligence reports indicated that McClellan had moved into Maryland, but only very slowly and without aggressive intent, with his columns that day still some twenty-five miles southeast of Frederick and spread out to cover both Washington and Baltimore. But in the lower Shenandoah Valley the enemy was not acting as predicted. Though now completely outflanked and isolated, the garrisons at Harper's Ferry and Martinsburg remained in place. This defied traditional military wisdom, which Lee had come to depend on and to exploit in Federal high-command thinking.

No doubt he would have taken comfort had he known that McClellan's mind was actually working in the predicted channels. As soon as it was clear that the Confederates were invading Maryland, he had urged the evacuation of the 10,400 men at Harper's Ferry and the 2,500 at Martinsburg, insisting that they were nothing but fair game if they remained. General-in-Chief Halleck, however, rejected the suggestion ("with ill-concealed contempt," as McClellan later recalled the conversation). Halleck believed Harper's Ferry should and could be defended, that indeed it was a goc place to make a fight.

The situation there was somewhat odd. Like the troops at Martinsburg, the Harper's Ferry garrison was little more than a glorified railroad guard, responsible for protecting the Baltimore and Ohio from Confederate raiders, with its commander reporting to General John E. Wool at the area departmental headquarters in Baltimore. Wool, a crusty old-timer and contemporary of Winfield Scott's whose career dated back to the War of 1812, was responsible for keeping military routine running smoothly in divided Maryland. Now that his Valley garrisons were suddenly thrust into the middle of an active campaign, he still had the responsibility but lacked the means to command effectively. McClellan, on the scene and with access to field intelligence, had the means but not the responsibility. Halleck, as was his habit, sidestepped nimbly. "Harper's Ferry may be attacked and overwhelmed," he warned Wool on September 5. "I leave all dispositions there to your experience and local knowledge." Harper's Ferry was thus consigned to military limbo.[26]

The Valley garrisons were decidedly short on combat experience. Only two regiments, the 32nd and 60th Ohio, had seen any fighting, against Stonewall Jackson in the Shenandoah that spring. Seven other regiments were brand new, and there were various militia and Maryland home-guard detachments of doubtful value; indeed, the 12th New York militia, its tour of duty expiring, was agitating loudly to go home. The capability of the Harper's Ferry commander, Colonel Dixon S. Miles, was also suspect. A year earlier, a court of inquiry had affirmed the charge that Miles was drunk while leading a division in the First Bull Run battle, but he escaped being cashiered. Quietly shuffled off to a backwater command at Harper's Ferry, he had until now watched the war pass him by.

As if Colonel Miles did not have enough problems already, he was being ordered to defend one of the most indefensible spots imaginable. The town of Harper's Ferry, fifty miles from Washington, was tucked into a narrow angle of land where the Shenandoah River enters the Potomac and was dominated by high ground on every side. To hold the place required the defense of these encircling ridges — towering Maryland Heights to the north, Bolivar Heights to the west, and Loudoun Heights to the south and east. There were men and guns and fortifications enough to protect against enemy raiders, but meeting a full-scale and fully manned assault was another matter. "Be energetic and active, and defend all places to the last extremity," General Wool telegraphed Miles on September 5. "There must be no abandoning of a post, and shoot the first man that thinks of it, whether officer or soldier."[27] These brave words were all well and good, and designed to brace a possibly unsteady subordinate to his task, but there was no promise that help was on the way.

The suspicion that Harper's Ferry was in danger was well founded. Lee might be able to provision his troops north of the Potomac, but unless he shifted his munitions supply line westward into the Shenandoah and cleared that route of Federal troops, his campaign would end before it was fairly begun. Characteristically, the plan he evolved was more opportunistic than simply masking the posts or applying pressure to force their evacuation. He wanted to capture the garrisons entire, including their substantial stock of ordnance and supplies, and he assigned the task to Stonewall Jackson.

It was a plan to Jackson's liking; he had been entirely too neglectful of his friends in the Valley, he observed with a smile. Longstreet happened by as Lee and Jackson discussed the operation, and listened with growing dismay as it was explained to him. Old Pete had a conservative turn of mind, and dividing the army in the present situation did not strike him as sound military practice. But, he later wrote, "They had gone so far that it seemed useless for me to offer any further opposition."[28]

The operational plan for the movement, dated September 9 and designated Special Orders No. 191, was to take effect the following day. It was Lee's intention to fall swiftly and without warning on Harper's Ferry from three directions, cutting off all escape routes simultaneously. General John Walker with his small two-brigade division was to retrace the army's invasion route, recross the Potomac into Virginia, and come up on Loudoun Heights from the south. Lafayette McLaws, with his own division and that of Richard H. Anderson, would cross South Mountain and seize the commanding position of Maryland Heights. The three divisions under Jackson had the longest march. From Frederick he would follow the National Road across South Mountain at Turner's Gap, turn off westward beyond Boonsboro, and cross the Potomac into the Shenandoah Valley. Capturing the Martinsburg garrison or driving it before him, he was to seal off Harper's Ferry from the west by taking Bolivar Heights. The schedule called for springing the trap on Friday morning, September 12. The remainder of the army, with the reserve artillery and the supply trains, would meanwhile cross South Mountain and assume a holding position at Boonsboro. After taking Harper's Ferry, the army would reassemble at Boonsboro or at Hagerstown, thirteen miles to the north on the National Road, as circumstances dictated.[29]

Once again, as he had done when facing McClellan before Richmond and Pope along the Rappahannock, Lee chose to meet a pressing tactical problem by doing the unexpected and dividing his army, this time into four parts. And once again, he judged the risk worth taking. Twenty-six of the army's forty brigades were assigned to the Harper's Ferry objective, a force of such strength as to make resistance hopeless once the Federal garrison was penned in. To be sure, for however long this took, the balance of the army would be isolated, with most of Jackson's troops on the far side of the Potomac and beyond practical supporting distance. The entire plan depended on speed and on General McClellan continuing to do exactly as he had been doing for the past week: moving blindly and with the consequent caution that Lee firmly believed was the dominant factor in his military character. The opposing armies would be separated by the substantial barrier of South Mountain, with its gaps sealed off from probing Yankee scouts by Stuart's cavalry. By the time the Union general sorted out what was happening, Lee reasoned, the Army of Northern Virginia would be reunited, its supply line secure, at least some of its stragglers back in the ranks, and preparations begun for the next and decisive phase of the campaign.

During the day of September 9, Lee's adjutant, R. H. Chilton, busied himself at army headquarters making copies of Order 191 for delivery to the generals involved. It was a simple and routine operation for the dispatch couriers, for almost the entire army was then encamped in the immediate vicinity of Frederick. When Jackson received his copy of Order 191, he transcribed another copy and sent it to D. H. Hill, whose division had been under his command entering Maryland but was now being detached for duty with Longstreet. All divisions were duly informed, and that evening marching orders went down the chain of command to prepare to move out the next day, with Jackson leading off at his customary starting time of earliest dawn.

"At four o'clock this morning, the rebel army began to move from our town, Jackson's force taking the advance," Dr. Steiner wrote in his journal on September 10. He detected no "genuine enthusiasm" for the marchers among his fellow townspeople. "Their friends were anxious to get rid of them and of the penetrating ammoniacal smell they brought with them." With some bitterness he remarked on the considerable number of artillery pieces he saw bearing the initials U.S., and added, "This rebel army seemed to have been largely supplied with transportation by some United States Quartermaster."

However the staunchly Unionist doctor may have viewed the scene, the troops made their departure in high good humor, with regimental bands playing "The Girl I Left Behind Me." "Saw a number of pretty ladies and amid waving of Secession flags by the ladies and cheering by the soldiers had a lively time," surgeon Boulware recorded in his diary; ". . . I was caught lifting my cap, and not a few times either." William Owen, a Louisiana artillerist, passed what he described as a "buxom young lady" with a small Union flag pinned to her dress. "Look h'yar, miss, better take that flag down," one of his fellow marchers called out; "we're awful fond of charging breast-works!" This produced great amusement in the ranks, Owen recorded, and the lady in question blushed and smiled "but stuck to her colors."

Howell Cobb, one-time secretary of the treasury under James Buchanan and a founding father of the Confederacy, now a brigadier in Longstreet's corps, was the target of a good deal of jeering and shouted insults from Unionists in the crowd, which he returned in kind. According to Lieutenant William Johnson of the 2nd South Carolina, "He told them we would whip the Yankees and secure our independence, and that we were not leaving Frederick for good, but that we would return, and then he would take time to put the last one of them in jail." Cobb rode on and finally spotted a friendly face, a young girl waving a Confederate flag from her window. "Sissy, you're the gal I'm looking for!" he cried, and launched into a burst of oratory of such grandiloquence that he soon had the crowd cheering good-naturedly. (Dr. Steiner was not amused, calling the Georgian "a drunken, bloated blackguard.") By nightfall, except for Stuart's screening cavalry, Frederick was free of occupation. If there was general relief, there was also agreement that the experience had been relatively painless.[30]

In the annals of American literature, the singular consequence of the Confederate occupation of Frederick was the inspiration it furnished the poet John Greenleaf Whittier, whose "Barbara Frietchie" would swell patriotic spirits across the North when it appeared in the *Atlantic* in October 1863. At the time, however, no one in Frederick made note of any rifle blast unleashed by a Rebel horde at any national flag, particularly one held by an elderly lady in an attic window. Mrs. Frietchie, ninety-six and in frail health, did indeed live in Frederick, and she did wave a flag, although she was on her front porch and the occasion was the subsequent arrival of Federal troops. A Mrs. Mary Quantrell was seen to wave the Stars and Stripes at a passing Confederate column, which ignored her, and Dr. Steiner told of "an aged crone" (worthy of Sir Walter Scott's Meg Merrilies, he thought) who shouted defiance at the occupying troops. Stonewall Jackson no doubt saw a flag or two waved in Frederick, but made no recorded comment. Somehow a gallant tale was woven from these insubstantial threads and passed on to Whittier by a Washington lady novelist, and Barbara Frietchie became a national heroine. In vain did Jackson's staff point out that the general never came within sight of Mrs. Frietchie or her house; fruitlessly did the *Richmond Examiner* debunk the poet's handiwork. "The uncultivated may pronounce the poem so much unadulterated and self-evident nonsense, but the wise, the gifted, the good, know that it will outlive and disprove all histories, however well authenticated," the *Examiner* concluded sarcastically.[31]

Although the Confederates had now been in Maryland for a week, the news was slow to reach the people back home. Two of the South's best war correspondents, Felix G. de Fontaine and Peter W. Alexander, were traveling with the army, but they had no means of getting dispatches back to their home papers. Lee was already leaving Frederick by the time the Richmond papers picked up enough from contacts within the War Department to announce the invasion of Maryland. The *Dispatch* felt constrained to explain this shift in basic military policy from the defensive to the offensive: "The movement which Gen. Lee has now made is bold, but it is sagacious, and justified by the highest military authorities." Like many of his fellow Southerners, the young poet Sidney Lanier, serving on garrison duty in Petersburg, was electrified by the news. "Events have followed each other in such rapid succession, here, that I am dazzled, and under the influence of exultant feelings, can hardly form a sober opinion in regard to the future," he wrote on September 10. If the reports in the Richmond papers were true, he continued, "the fall of Washington is inevitable — and after the fall of Washington — ? Perhaps Peace!"[32]

Jackson's first day's advance from Frederick took him across South Mountain to Boonsboro, where he learned from scouts that his march route would have to be lengthened to more than sixty miles. Martinsburg was still occupied, which meant abandoning the most direct line to the objective through the village of Sharpsburg and the nearby Potomac crossing at Shepherdstown in favor of a wider swing to come down on the Martinsburg garrison from the north and west to prevent its escape. September 11 saw Jackson's three divisions cross the Potomac at Williamsport. The regimental bands played "Carry Me Back to Ole Virginny." Jackson made an important addition to his fighting strength that day by releasing A. P. Hill from arrest, and Hill rode once again at the head of his Light Division. As the columns approached Martinsburg, Brigadier Julius White and his 2,500 Federal troops beat a hasty retreat to Harper's Ferry. Jackson was well pleased; the more Yankees shut up there, the easier it would be to bag them all. "I expect this will be the last you will hear of me until this affair is over," Colonel Miles wrote Halleck from Harper's Ferry on the eleventh. "All are cheerful and hopeful."

In Martinsburg the Confederates were welcomed as deliverers, and the foot cavalry continued their habit of feasting happily on captured Union commissary stores. Old Jack settled into a parlor at the Everett House to write dispatches, but admirers slid the windows open and tossed in bouquets of roses. Finally he agreed to admit the throng, and they swarmed around him, everyone talking at once, his aide Colonel Kyd Douglas wrote, "with the disjointed eloquence of a devotion that scorned all coherent language." Autographs were demanded, and buttons snipped off his coat as souvenirs. Finally extricating himself and his men from their admirers, Jackson pushed ahead on the road to Harper's Ferry, sealing off the enemy's western escape route.[33]

Meanwhile, General Walker was encountering complications in carrying out his part of the plan. Before setting off, he had been ordered to destroy the aqueduct carrying the Chesapeake and Ohio Canal across the Monocacy River where it empties into the Potomac, but the sturdy granite span resisted the best efforts of his engineers. With both his timetable and the enemy pressing him, he abandoned the demolition project and withdrew westward to cross the Potomac. On Friday morning, the twelfth, about the time Jackson was setting off from Martinsburg, Walker approached his objective, Loudoun Heights.

Lafayette McLaws, with the third arm of the encircling forces, had the shortest distance to travel but the most demanding task. Maryland Heights, as the southernmost promontory of Elk Mountain was called, was the key to the entire operation. From its crest Confederate artillery would command every foot of the Federal positions at Harper's Ferry, but the heights could prove difficult to capture if vigorously defended. McLaws crossed South Mountain into Pleasant Valley and pondered how to get from the valley to the mountaintop. He decided to split his force. Two of his best brigades, Joseph Kershaw's South Carolinians and William Barksdale's Mississippians, were sent to scale Elk Mountain at a pass called Solomon's Gap four miles north of Maryland Heights and then advance along the rocky spine of the ridge. With the balance of his troops McLaws secured his communications and moved down Pleasant Valley to the Potomac to shut the eastern exit from Harper's Ferry. Kershaw and Barksdale found Solomon's Gap undefended, and by nightfall on the twelfth they were on the ridge and poised to attack the Maryland Heights defenders. The entire operation — Jackson, Walker, McLaws — was now running about twenty-four hours behind the schedule called for in Order 191.

At the same time, the part of the operational plan relating to Longstreet's command was undergoing a change. His two divisions, plus Harvey Hill's division on detached service, had followed Jackson along the National Road over South Mountain to

Boonsboro on September 10. There Lee received a report — the source of which he did not specify — that a Federal force of unknown strength was approaching Hagerstown from the direction of Chambersburg, Pennsylvania. Since Hagerstown was a road center and a supply depot Lee considered vital to any advance into Pennsylvania, and since an enemy force there could interrupt his communications with the Harper's Ferry operation, he determined to counter the threat promptly. Hill was to remain at Boonsboro with his division, the army's supply trains, and half the reserve artillery, perhaps 5,000 men in all. His primary assignment was to prevent any Yankees who might evade the Harper's Ferry trap from escaping to the north. Lee and Longstreet with the two remaining divisions would march the thirteen miles to Hagerstown.

Longstreet was unhappy with this further dispersal of the army. It would now be in five separate pieces rather than four, and more widely scattered than ever. It was exactly what he had feared when the Harper's Ferry scheme was laid out. "General, I wish we could stand still and let the damned Yankees come to us!" he said.[34] Lee would not be swayed; Hagerstown had been in his campaign plans from the beginning, and taking it now was simply a change of schedule, not a change of plan. If it meant reducing the watch on the South Mountain barrier to Jeb Stuart's cavalry and Harvey Hill's single division for a few days, it was a risk he would accept. His confidence in General McClellan's inbred caution was unshaken.

War correspondent Peter Alexander joined the advance to Hagerstown on September 11 and wrote of "the quiet valleys, the clear rocky streams, the white farm houses and immense barns, wheat stacks and hayricks, . . . the clusters of simple country people who have gathered along the road side or in front of their houses to witness the passing spectacle." Surgeon Boulware found few Southern sympathizers among these rural Marylanders, but no lack of kindness. "The ladies would have buckets of water at their doors to give to the thirsty soldiers as they marched by," he wrote in his journal. "One said *remember a Union lady* is giving you water.' " He concluded that "Maryland is the finest state I have been in." The many barefooted men in the ranks viewed matters rather less cheerfully; marching on the macadamized National Road was a painful experience.[35]

Ever since learning of the Confederate occupation of Frederick, the citizens of Hagerstown had been preparing for the worst. Town records and specie from the banks were sent off to safety. Refugees, including the mayor and the sheriff, filled the cars of the Cumberland Valley Railroad, which evacuated its rolling stock northward to Chambersburg. There was not a single Federal detachment in the town or on the way, however. As Lee discovered when he entered Hagerstown on the afternoon of September 11, the report that had brought him there was false.

The troops met a mixed welcome, although William Owen of the Washington Artillery thought it more demonstrative than the one in Frederick, with young girls presenting bouquets of flowers to the marchers. The local merchants were quickly sold out of shoes, clothing, and food. In a dry-goods store Owen and his comrades discovered a large stock of old-fashioned bell-crowned beaver hats, "just the style our fathers wore," and took a shine to them. In an army noted for the diversity of its headgear, the men of the Washington Artillery could make the proud claim that their tall beavers were unique.

The next day, in a letter to President Davis, Lee summed up the results of the expedition so far. Hagerstown had furnished 1,500 barrels of flour but little beef and no bacon, he wrote. The 400 pairs of shoes purchased there brought the total so far found in Maryland to less than 1,700 pairs, far too few "to cover the bare feet of the army." He had picketed the roads as far north as the Pennsylvania line, and would remain at Hagerstown to await news of the Harper's Ferry operation. His first objective, to draw the Federal army out of its Washington fortifications and north of the Potomac, had been accomplished, he told the president.[36]

"Lord, what a scare they are having in the North!" John B. Jones, a clerk in the Confederate War Department, wrote in his diary on September 9. "They are calling everybody to arms for the defense of *Philadelphia,* and they are removing specie, arms, etc., from Harrisburg and all the intervening towns." It was a fair enough appraisal, for readers of Northern newspapers (like clerk Jones) faced a daunting task sorting out fact from the welter of

THE INVASION OF MARYLAND
September 3-13, 1862

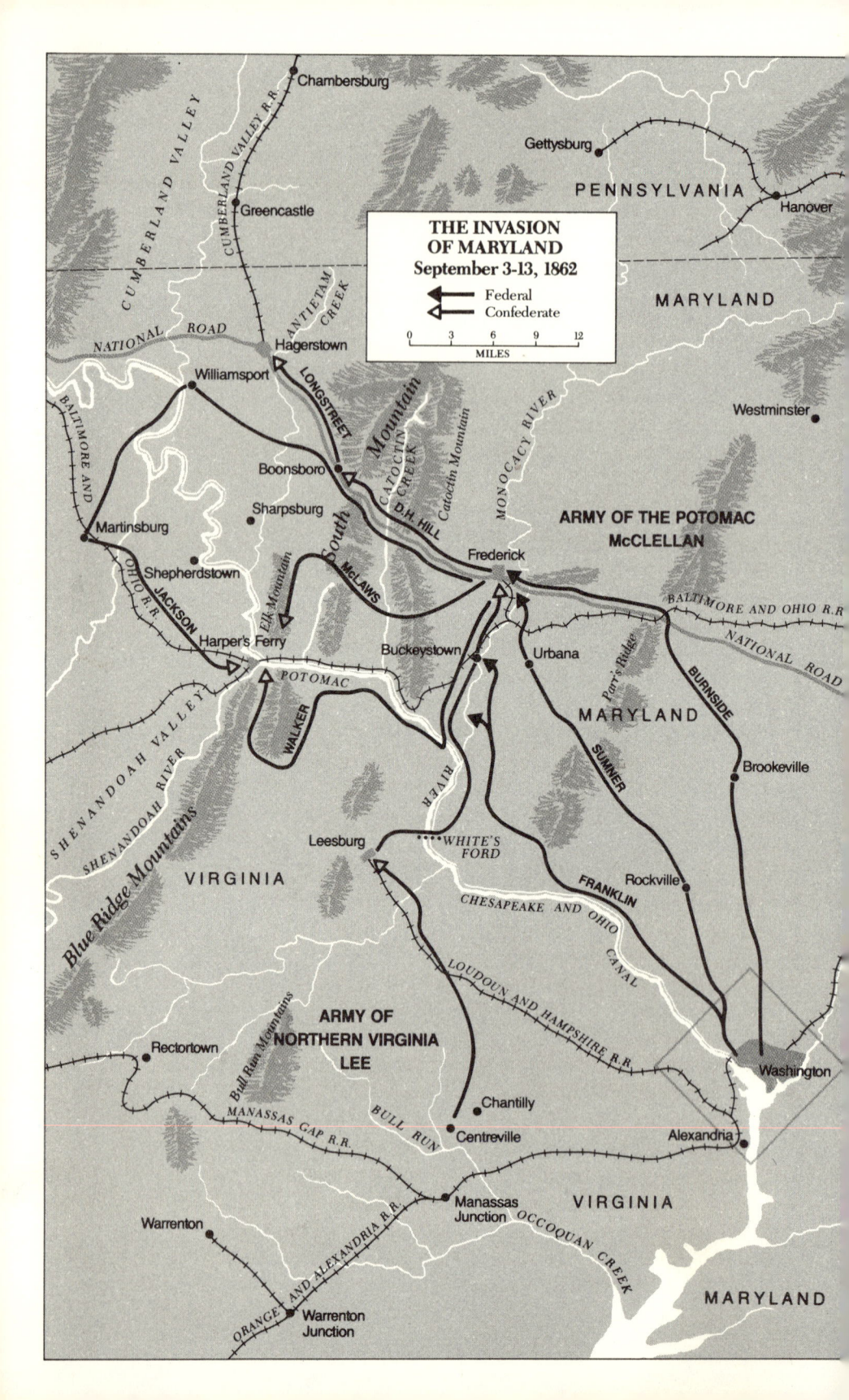

rumor and speculation that filled the pages. The worst was imagined, and found its way into print. "No one knows the strength of the invading column," diarist Strong complained. "Some say 30,000, and others five times that.... Newspapers tell us little or nothing about the situation in Maryland.... I suppose we shall soon hear that McClellan has commenced a series of masterly fieldworks and is engaged on an irrefrangible first parallel from the Potomac to the Susquehanna, with a series of dashing and brilliant zig-zags toward the enemy." One rumor making the rounds, Strong reported, was that the leading generals in the opposing armies, with their background of common beliefs and drawing on their comradeship in the old army, would soon "all come together and agree on some compromise or adjustment, turn out Lincoln and his 'Black Republicans' and use their respective armies to enforce their decisions North and South...."

Admittedly, the war correspondents and their editors were working under constraints. General Halleck had banned reporters from the Army of the Potomac, though with limited success. The *New York Tribune*'s George Smalley wrangled a staff appointment with General John Sedgwick in Sumner's corps, and his fellow correspondent Albert Richardson doctored an old military pass to attach himself to Burnside's staff. Other reporters worked similar ploys, taking advantage of the fact that officers with an affinity for press coverage found ways to wink at Halleck's ban. (The same was true for the newspaper artists; Alfred Waud of *Harper's Weekly* and Edwin Forbes and Frank Schell of *Leslie's Illustrated* had no trouble finding places with the army as it moved north.) The reporters' most troublesome problem was getting stories to their papers, for they were barred from using the War Department-controlled telegraph lines. With the government furnishing almost nothing in the way of news about the campaign, the alarmists held sway.[37]

The alarm in Baltimore was considerable. Since the first days of the war, when a mob attacked Federal troops passing through the city, Baltimore had been regarded as a hotbed of secession, waiting only the appearance of a Confederate army to revolt. The Lincoln government had come down hard on supposed dissidents, suspending the writ of habeas corpus and initiating wholesale arrests. ("The government of your chief city has been usurped by armed strangers," General Lee wrote in his September 8 proclamation to the people of Maryland, and he went on to outline the various offenses committed under "this foreign yoke.") As reports and rumors of the invasion spread, crowds milled in the streets outside the newspaper offices, waiting for the latest bulletins. The sale of liquor was halted to restrain the excitable. Citizens fearful of a siege stocked up on food and other essentials, and appeals went out to local Union men to organize companies for defense.

Baltimore at least had defenses to man, assuming the necessary manpower could be raised. Philadelphia, so its leading citizens insisted, was utterly defenseless, an invitation to sack and pillage. A committee drafted a resolution to the president spelling out what was needed to meet the threat, and prominent bankers added the considerable weight of their positions to the appeal. Lincoln tried to soothe the city fathers, tactfully pointing out that Philadelphia was 150 miles from Hagerstown and in no immediate danger, and in any event the best way to counter the Rebel army was to pursue and fight it rather than dispersing strength to guard every city and town that might feel threatened.[38]

Such problems seemed likely to resolve themselves. General Wool, for all his years, was full of fight and could be relied on to defend Baltimore if it came to that, and the nervous Philadelphians needed reassurance more than anything else. The governor of Pennsylvania, Andrew G. Curtin, required more special handling. The continued strong political support of Republican Curtin was essential to the administration. For one thing, his state was furnishing a great many soldiers to the cause; when the Army of the Potomac advanced into Maryland, forty-eight of its regiments consisted of Pennsylvania troops — outnumbered only by those from New York — and there were a dozen more in reserve at the capital. Governor Curtin believed his state was about to be invaded, and as a figure with many strings to pull in Washington, he began pulling all of them.

A barrage of telegrams went out to Generals Wool and McClellan, to General-in-Chief Halleck, to Secretary of War Stanton, to President Lincoln. The governor wanted the latest information on Lee's movements, and he passed along what his own increasingly active intelligence network was finding out. He wanted munitions from the government's arsenals, and he urged that new regiments

Will Send You Trophies

on their way to Washington be halted and assigned to guard threatened areas in his state. He wanted authority to call out 50,000 state militia and nominated as their commander a native son, John F. Reynolds, who was then heading a division of Pennsylvania troops in the Potomac army. McClellan and Joe Hooker, Reynolds's corps commander, protested — "a scared Governor ought not to be permitted to destroy the usefulness of an entire division," Hooker agued — but Halleck brusquely told them that someone else could command the division and ordered General Reynolds to Harrisburg posthaste.

The Washington authorities seem to have found Governor Curtin something of a trial in this time of many trials, and on occasion they tried to sidetrack him in bureaucratic paper-shuffling. But Curtin was persistent and got most of what he wanted. The militia was called out, and plans were made to block, or at least delay, the Confederates if they tried to set foot in the Keystone State. What these Sunday soldiers would actually do should they come face to face with Lee's veterans was a prospect no one cared to dwell on. At least it was hoped their presence might reassure nervous civilians, for Rebel threats to lay waste Pennsylvania, of the sort Dr. Steiner had heard in Frederick, were beginning to gain circulation.

One of the militia officers called up was the unwarlike newspaper editor Alexander K. McClure, who was posted with a small detail of amateur cavalrymen to guard the Hagerstown–Chambersburg turnpike. Thaddeus Stevens, one of the most outspoken Republican radicals in Congress, found a certain grim amusement in the editor's assignment. He was confident that McClure would do something, he told Governor Curtin: ". . . if he couldn't do anything else he would instruct the old lady who kept the toll gate not to let Lee's soldiers pass through." And then he added, "God only knows what McClellan would do."[39]

What General McClellan was doing just then was moving with extreme caution, for he had only the sketchiest information on Confederate strength and dispositions, and no information at all about the enemy's intentions. In addition, the Army of the Potomac was still undergoing a command shakeup as it began to fan out slowly into Maryland. He hastily devised a new triad structure for the movement.

The army's left wing was commanded by William Franklin and consisted of his own Sixth Corps plus the division of Darius Couch. The center was put under Edwin Sumner and contained his Second Corps and Alpheus Williams's Twelfth Corps, formerly an Army of Virginia unit under Nathaniel P. Banks. Ambrose Burnside's right wing included his Ninth Corps, now under Jesse L. Reno, and Joe Hooker's First Corps, another transplant from the Army of Virginia where it had been led by Irvin McDowell. It was of necessity a patchwork organization and still incomplete. Just five of the fifteen divisions had fought under McClellan on the Peninsula.

Seniority dictated the choice of the three subcommanders, and only his old friend Burnside had McClellan's full confidence. At sixty-five Sumner was the oldest of the army's corps commanders, and any military imagination he once possessed had ossified after four decades of frontier service in the old army. Reviewing one of the Peninsula battles for his wife, McClellan wrote that "Sumner has proved he was even a greater fool than I supposed & had come within an ace of having us defeated." Franklin he considered slow and lacking in energy, he told Ellen. "I do not at all doubt Franklin's loyalty now" — that general was one of those whom Lincoln had called into his strategy sessions when McClellan was on his sickbed the previous January, arousing the Young Napoleon's suspicions — "but his efficiency is very little." He was also dubious about the two luckless corps inherited from Pope's army. General Williams's position was temporary, and the Twelfth Corps was due to get another old regular, Joseph K. F. Mansfield, as its commander. Hooker had been put in charge of McDowell's former corps to "bring them out of the kinks" and "make them fight if anyone can."[40]

When McClellan shifted his headquarters to Rockville, Maryland, on September 7, he had some 85,000 men under arms. Another 72,500 troops manned the Washington defenses under General Banks, including three corps — one of them led by McClellan's favorite, Fitz John Porter — with the training and experience to serve in the field.[41] Continued straggling and sickness had further reduced the Army of Northern Virginia by the time it entered Frederick, giving the Federals at the moment nearly a two-to-one superiority in manpower. Depending on how many reinforcements might be called up from Washington, that ratio could rise to as high as three to one. General McClellan, however, proved quite unable to discern this reality, or anything close to it. His management of military intelligence produced the same results in Maryland that it had at Manassas and on the Peninsula.

McClellan embarked on the Maryland campaign with two statistics at hand against which to measure fresh intelligence. An analysis by Allan Pinkerton, dated August 10, assessed the total available Confederate manpower in Virginia at 200,000. Then, on the eve of the Second Bull Run battle, the general gave credence to reports that 120,000 Rebels threatened Washington.[42] Detective Pinkerton was caught short by Lee's invasion — setting up a new spy network takes time — and contributed little to the intelligence-gathering in Maryland. McClellan had therefore to rely heavily on his cavalry for information, plus any number of reports from patriotic citizens eager to help. Indeed, the Federal high command suddenly found itself with a very considerable volume of intelligence to evaluate.

One of General Pope's failings in the Second Bull Run campaign was his mishandling of the cavalry arm, and McClellan had moved quickly to institute a reform. He gave the job to Alfred Pleasonton, a veteran of frontier service in the old army who had impressed him with his work on the Peninsula, and Pleasonton reorganized the cavalry into five brigades under his central direction. His patrols were soon probing for information in a widening arc in advance of the army. On every road they encountered Jeb Stuart's troopers, who were not disposed to let the Yankees get past them for a look at the movements of the Army of Northern Virginia. The skirmishing was sharp and often bloody, but Stuart's cavalry screen remained unbroken. Pleasonton's men had to be content with interrogating any captives taken in these clashes, as well as a number of deserters and stragglers they swept up in the wake of Lee's army. They also searched out Union men in towns through which the Rebel columns had passed and questioned them as to what they had seen and heard.

By September 6 a picture of the Confederate army began to form in faint outline. That day Pleasonton reported that A. P. Hill was across the Potomac with 30,000 men. Stonewall Jackson was leading 60,000 toward Baltimore, a civilian told the cavalry;

whether that included Hill's men he did not say. "The rebel soldiers are running over the country, hunting something to eat, and are a hard-looking set, with a large number of stragglers," the dispatch continued. A Baltimore and Ohio telegrapher confirmed that "many barefoot and clothes much worn out." The next day, Governor Curtin forwarded a report from one of his informants detailing the occupation of Frederick. "Jackson told an intimate friend of mine . . . ," the informant wrote, "he designed crossing into Pennsylvania, through Adams, York, and Lancaster, to Philadelphia." Pleasonton continued to believe that Baltimore was the enemy's target. Halleck was nervous and warned McClellan to move cautiously; the Confederate invasion might be a feint to draw him northward, leaving Washington exposed to a surprise attack. General Wool telegraphed a report from one of his sources that Braxton Bragg had crossed from Kentucky into the Shenandoah Valley with 40,000 Rebels. This startling news was questioned by President Lincoln, who as usual was monitoring dispatches at the War Department. Wool replied that the information was secondhand.[43]

On the evening of September 8 McClellan summed up the situation for Halleck: "I am by no means satisfied yet that the enemy has crossed the river in any large force. Our information is still entirely too indefinite to justify definite action. . . . As soon as I find out where to strike, I will be after them without an hour's delay." Later that night, fresh but conflicting evidence began to accumulate. General Wool forwarded two reports to Washington, one stating the Confederates had 75,000 men at Frederick, the other estimating their strength at 30,000 to 50,000. Cavalryman Pleasonton had a very different story to tell: "Most reliable information has been obtained that the enemy has crossed the river in force over one hundred thousand (100,000) strong. They are to march to *Frederick* thence to *Gettysburg* thence to *York* & thence to *Baltimore*."

Tuesday, September 9, the day Lee decided upon the Harper's Ferry operation and composed Order 191, was also a pivotal day in the evolution of McClellan's mental picture of his enemy. That morning the situation was still clouded. A query to Pleasonton produced the explanation that the previous night's figure of 100,000 had come from "a strong Union man who was told it by Capt.

White, a noted Secessionist who is guide to the Rebel army." White was "drinking a little when he described these facts and they are firmly believed to be true by those best acquainted with him." McClellan telegraphed Halleck that Captain White was "notorious" and he considered the report unreliable. In a cheerful note to his wife, he thought it "worthy of a triumph that my enemies have been put down so completely" — he was referring to his detractors in Washington — "and if to that, if I can add the defeat of secesh I think I ought to be entitled to fall back into private life...."

By late afternoon, however, the picture as he saw it suddenly became clear and ominous. Another dispatch arrived from Pleasonton: "Jackson crossed with eighty thousand (80,000) men and Longstreet with about thirty thousand (30,000)...." When questioned, Pleasonton confirmed his figures with assurance, adding that his information came from "rebel officers & men to citizens as they passed through." A Pennsylvania Railroad executive contributed a report, from local citizens and a Confederate deserter, that the enemy at Frederick was "believed to be over 100,000 strong." For General McClellan, the indefinite was now definite. He passed Pleasonton's findings on to Halleck without qualification, and added, "I am pretty well prepared for anything except overwhelming numbers." He assured Fitz John Porter that he was prepared to punish the enemy "if he commits a blunder." Staff aide David Strother recorded in his diary a conversation he had that evening with the general: "He had information which, he said, he could not reject — that the enemy lay behind Monocacy a hundred thousand strong."[44]

The intelligence that arrived at McClellan's headquarters over the next three days only strengthened this delusion. Pleasonton forwarded more "reliable" and "trustworthy" interrogations of captured stragglers and of civilian eyewitnesses. Other solid citizens, including at least one church elder, managed to visit the Confederate encampments and passed on their impressions of vast numbers and impending advances. Cavalry scouts south of the Potomac estimated Rebel strength in Maryland as high as 200,000. On the afternoon of Thursday, September 11, McClellan composed a long telegram to Halleck that outlined the daunting prospect before him. It was a litany entirely familiar to those in Washington who had been reading the general's dispatches for a year and more.

"All the evidence that has been accumulated from various sources since we left Washington goes to prove most conclusively that almost the entire rebel army in Virginia, amounting to not less than 120,000 men, is in the vicinity of Frederick City," he wrote. These were veteran troops, made confident by their recent victories and commanded by their best generals, and they intended "to hazard all upon the issue of the coming battle. They are probably aware that their forces are numerically superior to ours by at least 25 per cent." Considering these odds, he thought the issue to be in doubt, "and if we should be defeated the consequences to the country would be disastrous in the extreme." It was imperative that he be reinforced immediately by at least one of the army corps in reserve in Washington, as well as by Colonel Miles's troops at Harper's Ferry. He believed the capital to be safe from any sudden Confederate thrust, but even if it should be taken that would be of small import compared to the catastrophe to follow if, for want of reinforcements, the Army of the Potomac should be defeated by "the gigantic rebel army before us."[45]

The president spent most of these tense, waiting days in the War Department telegraphers' room. However discouraging he may have found this latest example of self-fulfilling prophecy, he patiently continued to promise his cautious captain full support. Just ten minutes after McClellan's telegram reached the War Department, Lincoln replied that Fitz John Porter's corps would take the field immediately. "I am for sending you all that can be spared, and I hope others can follow Porter very soon." Halleck, however, did not share the Young Napoleon's analysis of events. The Army of the Potomac must move to the aid of Harper's Ferry, and to that end he finally made Miles subject to McClellan's orders. Halleck had it fixed in his mind that the enemy's real target was Washington; all else was bluff, he thought. "You attach too little importance to the capital," he complained. "I assure you that you are wrong. The capture of this place will throw us back six months, if it should not destroy us. Beware of the evils I now point out to you."[46]

From September 9 on, George McClellan's vision of an opposing army triple its actual strength was fixed immutably in his thinking. To be sure, he did not reach this conclusion without help. From the situation reports he sent to Washington it is clear that he relied mostly on Pleasonton's cavalry for intelligence-gathering. And from the results, it is equally clear that when it came to evaluating that intelligence General Pleasonton was remarkably gullible.

It seems not to have occurred to him, for example, that even the best-intentioned small-town civilian, when exposed for the first time to long and crowded columns of marching troops, might find it easy to exaggerate their numbers. Entirely typical was the reaction of a villager who watched Harvey Hill's division stream past and exclaimed that she did not think there were so many men in all the world. Stonewall Jackson and Jeb Stuart did their skillful best to muddy the waters by planting rumors and false trails among the civilians they encountered. Nor, apparently, did Pleasonton suspect that the Rebel stragglers he collected or the prisoners he took in the skirmishes with Stuart's patrols might enjoy stringing along their Yankee captors. "Bragging is a favorite game with them, and they do it well," Dr. Steiner observed of the Confederates he talked to in Frederick. Union officers were less perceptive. As the interrogation reports flowed into army headquarters, the enemy divisions grew and multiplied until they became a host.[47]

In the end, of course, responsibility for the evaluation of all this intelligence rested with General McClellan. Its contents could not have come as any real surprise to him; conditioned by more than a year of such fictions, he was fully prepared to accept that once again he was outnumbered. If those reports of numerous stragglers and of ragged, barefooted Rebels scrambling for whatever food they could find raised any nagging suspicion in his mind that perhaps Richmond was incapable of supporting such a massive force on Northern soil, he left no record of it. In any case, it was hardly credible that General Lee was now daring to invite battle in command of an inferior force; by McClellan's reckoning, he had never done so before. Nor was it credible that God would call the commander of the Army of the Potomac to save his country from an outnumbered foe. Consequently, the Young Napoleon advanced his army slowly and with elaborate caution, making no attempt to seize control of events.

The Yankee veterans found the march into Maryland a happy contrast to their previous campaigning in the unfriendly Virginia countryside. "The women and young ladies opened their doors and windows to give us bread and butter, meat, apples, peaches and preserves!" Major John M. Gould of the 10th Maine noted in his diary. "I tell you it was cheering to see their pleasant faces, clean, white and beautiful, after we had been so long in the Virginia wilderness, where the few women have ruined their faces by looking sour." There were washtubs of cold water and lemonade at front gates along the roadsides, and in Rockville the jubilant boys of the 5th Connecticut lined up with their tin cups when they discovered a bucket of whiskey put out for their benefit. "Like the Israelites of old, we looked upon the land, and it was good," the 7th Maine's Major Thomas W. Hyde wrote.[48]

This was the first exposure to route marching for most of the new regiments, and the eager young recruits were anxious to make a good showing. "I noticed that they kept closed up better than we did," Major Gould wrote of the three new regiments in his brigade, "but they are harrahing or yelling all the time, and on the march they try to out-run each other as all green troops will." One of these outfits campaigning for the first time, the 118th Pennsylvania, had gone off to war splendidly outfitted through the generosity of the brokers of Philadelphia's Corn Exchange. The rookies quickly discovered all these camp comforts to be an unendurable burden on the march. A passing soldier recorded their dilemma: "In many a convenient fence corner could be seen a council of war, deliberating, while overhauling their loads, as to whether the Jamaica ginger, soap, writing (patent) desks, blacking, tactics, emery powder, cholera powder, pills, paper collars, extra shirts, etc., should be dropped." Veterans took sardonic pleasure in such sights, and were soon pawing through heaps of disgarded gear for anything useful.[49]

For all its prowess on the drill field, the Army of the Potomac was considerably deficient in march discipline. Even at the undemanding pace set by McClellan's advance it trailed thousands of stragglers and hard-handed foragers. "Discipline slack and nerveless; swarms of stragglers marauding, or making up select card-parties by the road side," diarist Strong noted after talking to a Sanitary Commission official just back from Maryland. "We cover

Will Send You Trophies

the whole face of the country round about like a cloud of locusts, as thick and as destructive," wrote Samuel Fiske, a transplanted Massachusetts clergyman whose letters from the ranks of the 14th Connecticut, signed "Dunn Browne," appeared in the *Springfield Republican*. "Acres and acres of soldiers, but not an acre of corn or potatoes or fruit, or anything else eatable within a circle of miles. . . . I am sorry to acknowledge it, and yet more sorry to see and believe, that our soldiers very generally are, or soon become, a set of lawless plunderers. . . ." Maryland loyalists sadly concluded that the proportion of larcenous foragers among the Union troops was a good deal higher than among the Confederates who had passed through earlier. McClellan issued a strongly worded general order against straggling and unauthorized foraging on September 9, but it had little effect. The Army of the Potomac continued to take a heavy toll of this land of milk and honey.[50]

On September 11, the day he informed Halleck that he was confronting a "gigantic rebel army" and called for reinforcements, General McClellan had his forces arrayed in a twenty-five-mile arc ranging northeastward from the Potomac, with the head of each of the three main columns some fifteen miles from Frederick. He had by now convinced himself of two facts: the Confederate army outnumbered him substantially, and it was on the move again. Where it was bound, however, he was not at all certain. A report forwarded that morning by Governor Curtin placed Stonewall Jackson on his way to Martinsburg, in the Shenandoah Valley; that evening another of the governor's informants had Jackson in Hagerstown, and threatening Pennsylvania. A substantial Confederate force was said to be in Boonsboro. It was thought that yet another Rebel column was recrossing the Potomac into Virginia near Harper's Ferry, helping to raise General Halleck's alarm for the capital's safety.

On Friday, the twelfth, as the Confederates began closing the ring on Harper's Ferry, McClellan's grasp of Confederate intentions continued uncertain. At 10 A.M. he telegraphed Washington that the Rebel army had left Frederick, "moving in two directions, viz, on the Hagerstown and Harper's Ferry roads." He would push on toward Frederick. He wrote his wife of his anxiety for the Harper's Ferry garrison and of his concern that the enemy might escape back across the Potomac "before I can catch him." General

Burnside, in command of the right wing, could not fathom the enemy's moves at all: "If they are going into Pennsylvania they would hardly be moving upon the Harper's Ferry road, and if they are going to recross, how could they be moving upon Gettysburg?" General Hooker was sure at least of one thing: "It is satisfactory to my mind that the rebels have no more intention of going to Harrisburg than they have of going to heaven." It was the general opinion at headquarters, staff aide David Strother wrote in his diary, that the Confederate army had met a cool welcome and gained few recruits in Maryland and was retreating into the Shenandoah Valley, possibly intending to scoop up the hapless Harper's Ferry garrison in the process.

Before dawn that day President Lincoln telegraphed his general the brief query, "How does it look now?" In his reply that evening, the Young Napoleon made it clear that he would continue to wait for the enemy to reveal his hand more fully before risking an advance beyond South Mountain: "If Harper's Ferry is still in our possession, I think I can save the garrison, if they fight at all. If the rebels are really marching into Pennsylvania, I shall soon be up with them. My apprehension is that they may make for Williamsport, and get across the river before I can catch them." The general's caution was proving to be every bit as great as his opponent had predicted.[51]

There was rising excitement in Frederick that day as rumors of the approaching Federal army filtered into town. A rear guard of Wade Hampton's Rebel troopers rode in from the east and took up station in the main street. Shortly after noon the advance of the Ninth Corps, General Jacob Cox's Kanawha Division, came in sight. The commander of one of the Kanawha brigades, Colonel Augustus Moor, decided he would personally sweep Frederick clear of any remaining enemy. Leading a headquarters cavalry troop and a single gun, he galloped into the center of town, driving the Rebel cavalry pickets before him. Moor had not reckoned on any serious opposition and was surprised by a countercharge "made in grand style" (as Dr. Steiner described it) by Hampton's squadrons. As Frederick's fascinated citizens peered out from between their window shutters, the two columns crashed together. Carbines cracked, saddles were emptied, and the cannon fired once, wounding men and horses, before being tipped into a ditch.

Colonel Moor was one of those ridden down and captured in the melee. As Yankee infantry entered one end of town at the double-quick, Hampton's troopers trotted out the other with their prisoners. Frederick was back in Union hands.[52]

The town jubilantly welcomed the liberators. "Handkerchiefs are waved, flags are thrown from Union houses, and a new life appears infused into the people," Dr. Steiner noted in his journal. The troops responded with volleys of cheering, and regimental bands blared out martial music. David L. Thompson of the 9th New York wrote his family that by evening "the place was alive with girls going around the streets in squads waving flags, singing songs & inviting the soldiers in for hot suppers." The townspeople did not restrict their welcome to these early arrivals. When the Second Corps marched in the next day, a Massachusetts man wrote, "the Stars and Stripes were flung from many places, and happy homelike faces beamed on us. . . . The people began to cook for us, bringing out as we passed, cake, pie and bread." General McClellan was all but overwhelmed that morning by well-wishers. People crowded forward to shake his hand and present their babies to be kissed, and girls decorated his horse with garlands of flowers. It was like a gigantic Fourth of July celebration, and the Army of the Potomac had its spirits up.[53]

As Nathaniel Paige of the *New York Tribune* remembered it, however, at least part of McClellan's military household was not in such a lighthearted mood during the stay in Frederick. Paige had it from Colonel Thomas M. Key, acting judge advocate on the headquarters staff, that a proposal was making the rounds for the army to countermarch on Washington and intimidate the government. According to these disaffected officers, the direction of the war by the "old women" of the administration was producing only folly and defeat; any interference with slavery would make it impossible to achieve an end to the fighting and an honorable peace with the South. Colonel Key assured Paige that he had put a stop to such talk and that General McClellan was not a party to the scheme, but he saw it as evidence that in certain quarters in the army "they were fighting for a boundary line and not for the Union." Paige "did not doubt the entire accuracy" of Key's account.[54]

Among the Federal units arriving at Frederick on Saturday

morning, September 13, was the First Division of the Twelfth Corps. Bivouac sites were assigned, and the 27th Indiana was one of the regiments that drew a meadow on the outskirts of town, where a division of Confederates had encamped during their occupation a few days before. Making camp where other troops had stayed any length of time was usually unpleasant, for soldiers were notoriously careless about such things as sanitation, but the Indiana boys found a comparatively unspoiled section of meadow alongside a rail fence and settled down to boil their coffee and relax.

Sergeant John M. Bloss and Corporal Barton W. Mitchell of Company F were chatting idly when Mitchell noticed a bulky envelope in the tall grass nearby and picked it up. Inside was a sheet of paper wrapped around three cigars. The cigars were a major discovery, a considerable cut above the usual debris found in an abandoned encampment, and out of curiosity Mitchell and Bloss scanned the official-looking document with them. It was headed "Headquarters, Army of Northern Virginia, Special Orders, No. 191," and was dated September 9. Scattered through the text were names the Yankee soldiers knew only too well — Jackson, Longstreet, Stuart. It concluded, "By command of Gen. R. E. Lee" and was signed, "R. H. Chilton, Assist. Adj.-Gen." It was addressed to Major General D. H. Hill. Sergeant Bloss and Corporal Mitchell began to suspect that the piece of paper might be a discovery even more important than the cigars.

The two men delivered the find to their company commander, Captain Peter Kop, who took one look at it and hurried them off to regimental headquarters and Colonel Silas Colgrove. Colgrove did not stop at brigade and division, the next links in the chain of command, but took the document straight to corps. Mitchell and Bloss went back to their regiment, apparently without even the reward of the cigars; indeed, who finally smoked them is lost to history.

General Alpheus Williams was still commanding the Twelfth Corps until General Mansfield arrived to take over, and he and his aide, Colonel Samuel E. Pittman, examined the paper closely. Its implications were stunning. If it was authentic, here, spelled out in complete detail, was the current operational plan of the entire Rebel army, including the location of every one of its commands.

Will Send You Trophies

And there was every reason to believe it was authentic. It just so happened, Colonel Pittman explained, that he had been stationed with Chilton on a tour of duty in the prewar army and knew him well — and knew his handwriting. He would vouch for the fact that the writer of the document was General Lee's adjutant.

Williams rushed the find on to General McClellan's headquarters, along with a covering note: "I enclose a Special Order of Gen. Lee commanding Rebel forces which was found on the field where my corps is encamped. It is a document of interest & is also thought genuine." In a footnote he wrote, "The Document was found by a corporal of 27 Ind. Rgt, Col. Colgrove, Gordon's Brigade." It was late morning when the copy of Order 191 was handed to McClellan. At his headquarters just then was a delegation of local citizens come to discuss the army's stay in Frederick. He broke off his discussion with them to study the dispatch and Williams's covering note. Suddenly he threw up his hands and exclaimed, "Now I know what to do!"[55]

The general no doubt ushered his visitors out with the explanation that he had pressing army business to attend to. At hand were two telegrams from President Lincoln sent late the previous afternoon — telegraphic service to Frederick had not yet been restored, and communications with Washington were erratic — one asking again, "How does it look now?" and the other reporting that it seemed certain that Jackson was recrossing the Potomac upstream at Williamsport. "Please do not let him get off without being hurt," he added. McClellan promptly addressed a reply to the president.

Dateline "Frederick, September 13, 1862 — 12 m." (12 meridian, or noon), it contained a sense of elation quite unlike any other dispatch he had sent Lincoln: "I have the whole rebel force in front of me, but am confident, and no time shall be lost. I have a difficult task to perform, but with God's blessing will accomplish it. I think Lee has made a gross mistake, and that he will be severely punished for it.... I have all the plans of the rebels, and will catch them in their own trap if my men are equal to the emergency. I now feel that I can count on them as of old.... My respects to Mrs. Lincoln. Received most enthusiastically by the ladies. Will send you trophies."[56]

· 4 ·

FIRE ON THE MOUNTAIN

How the famous Lost Order was lost is one of the Civil War's enduring mysteries. It was not until the spring of 1863, when the Joint Committee on the Conduct of the War made public McClellan's testimony that "at Frederick we found the original order issued to General D. H. Hill by direction of General Lee, which gave the orders of march for their whole army," that questions were asked. Southern journalists were quick to take Harvey Hill under fire. The prickly Hill was not one to view such charges lightly, then or later. He insisted with considerable heat that no copy of Order 191 had ever reached him from adjutant Chilton of Lee's staff on September 9, and supported his defense with an affidavit to that effect from his own staff adjutant. What he did receive that day — and carefully saved — was the copy made for him by Stonewall Jackson. This was entirely proper procedure, Hill said, for up to that point in the campaign he was under Jackson's command and received all orders through him. He maintained that he did not even learn of the Lost Order until McClellan made the news public months later.

For his part, Chilton insisted that his courier must have returned with the required receipt of delivery from Hill's headquarters, or there would have been a follow-up to verify that so important an order had been received. Thus nowhere in the chain of command of September 9 was an alarm raised. Hill had his marching orders, and from Jackson as expected. Army headquarters, hearing nothing to the contrary, assumed that the full set of orders had been safely delivered. Chilton could be faulted for de-

Fire on the Mountain

parting from command channels in issuing Order 191 directly to Hill — another division commander, Richard Anderson, recalled that his orders for the Harper's Ferry operation reached him through his superior, Lafayette McLaws — or at least for not notifying Jackson of that fact. Beyond that slip-up the trail dies out. No investigation of the matter was undertaken by the Confederate high command. No contrite courier or staff man came forward to confess his carelessness. No memories were jogged when, in the 1880s, the curious detail of the three cigars was revealed.

In the postwar years Harvey Hill raised the specter of a traitor in the ranks as the answer to the mystery. That seems a highly improbable theory. Any turncoat courier or staff officer who deliberately tossed D. H. Hill's copy of Order 191 into a meadow near Frederick with the expectation that the Yankees might come along and somehow stumble on it, recognize it for what it was, and get it to McClellan's headquarters must rank as the war's most naively optimistic spy. As it was, the actual circumstances of Corporal Mitchell's discovery stretch the workings of chance to their limits.[1]

However it happened, the loss of Order 191 threatened unreserved disaster for the Army of Northern Virginia. McClellan himself put the case with perfect clarity in a conversation that September 13 with an old army friend, Brigadier John Gibbon. "Here is a paper," he said, waving the Lost Order and revealing to Gibbon adjutant Chilton's signature, "with which if I cannot whip Bobbie Lee, I will be willing to go home." He was cheerful and confident, Gibbon remembered, and thinking in Napoleonic parallels. "Tomorrow we will pitch into his centre and if you people will only do two good, hard days' marching I will put Lee in a position he will find hard to get out of." And he added, "Castiglione will be nothing to it," a reference to Bonaparte's victory over the Austrian army in 1796, a classic example of beating in detail an overextended opponent.[2]

It must have seemed to General McClellan that his prayers had been answered. Four days earlier he had told Fitz John Porter that the enemy would find it hard to escape "if he commits a blunder." Now Lee had done exactly that, to McClellan's way of thinking, by dividing his army and spreading it all across the map. Order 191 could hardly be an elaborate ruse; not only was it certainly in

Chilton's handwriting, but, clinching the matter, it explained in exact detail what up to that point was a bewildering tangle of conflicting Federal intelligence reports. Suddenly the scales fell from the Young Napoleon's eyes. Stonewall Jackson was not trying to escape back into Virginia but was instead descending on Harper's Ferry from the west. Those Rebels reported on the National Road beyond South Mountain were Longstreet's. That column on the Harper's Ferry road was McLaws's, bound for Maryland Heights. The force said to be across the Potomac east of Harper's Ferry, which so alarmed General Halleck, was in fact Walker's division aiming for Loudoun Heights to complete the encirclement of Colonel Miles's garrison. It was all spelled out, including a timetable, and the Army of the Potomac was in a perfect position to divide and conquer. George McClellan could now truly save his country. Even the great Napoleon himself had never been presented with such an opportunity; Castiglione would indeed be nothing to it.

In fact McClellan's remarkable good fortune was even greater than he imagined. Lee's overly optimistic timetable for the capture of Harper's Ferry was hourly falling further behind schedule, prolonging the separation of the various commands. With Longstreet at Hagerstown instead of Boonsboro as specified in Order 191, the army was divided into five parts rather than four, leaving only Stuart's cavalry and D. H. Hill's single division to confront any Federal thrust at Turner's Gap in South Mountain. Thus the two major segments of the Confederate army, Longstreet's two divisions and Jackson's three, were a river crossing and more than twenty-five miles apart by the shortest route. Walker's division was isolated between the Potomac and Shenandoah rivers. McLaws and Anderson at Maryland Heights were at risk of being ground between the upper stone of the Army of the Potomac and the nether stone of the Harper's Ferry garrison. At Boonsboro the division of D. H. Hill, along with the Rebel trains and reserve artillery, was equally vulnerable to a sudden surprise attack. The door to a spectacular military coup was not merely ajar; it was wide open.

Even before Corporal Mitchell's find, McClellan had unwittingly taken a first step toward exploiting his opportunity. Early on the morning of September 13 the Federals began probing beyond Frederick. By midafternoon Pleasonton's cavalry, backed by Ninth Corps infantry, had chased the Confederate cavalry screen away from the low ridgeline of Catoctin Mountain to the west and pushed on along the National Road toward Middletown, a pleasant little village of white clapboard houses just four miles from the foot of South Mountain. Jacob Cox's Kanawha Division led additional Ninth Corps forces moving up in support. Jeb Stuart reported this development to Harvey Hill, assessing the enemy infantry strength at the point of advance at two brigades. As a precaution, Hill posted one of his brigades at Turner's Gap to keep an eye on the Federals.[3]

By noon that day, when he sent his exuberant telegram to President Lincoln promising to punish the foe severely, McClellan could count four full army corps, plus the lead division of Porter's corps from Washington, within his immediate command in the vicinity of Frederick. A half-dozen miles to the south, at Buckeystown, was William Franklin's Sixth Corps, with Darius Couch's attached division five miles farther south.[4] The total force came to some 87,000 men. This was almost exactly double Lee's strength, although to be sure that fact did not enter into McClellan's calculations; in his mind's eye he continued to multiply each of the Rebel soldiers by three.

The record is clear that the Young Napoleon readily enough grasped the opportunity beckoning to him. He knew too that Harper's Ferry still held out — his flag-signal stations to the south reported the sound of firing from that direction during the afternoon — and that consequently Lee's army remained divided. "No time shall be lost," he promised in his noon wire to the president. But like the pledges of similar prompt action before Yorktown on the Peninsula, or at Alexandria during the Second Bull Run battle, or to Halleck just five days earlier that he would strike "without an hour's delay" as soon as he located the enemy, this was empty posturing. A full eighteen hours would pass before the first Yankee soldiers marched in response to the discovery of "all the plans of the rebels." And when they did march, it was in obedience to a plan of action remarkable for its misapprehensions.

Once McClellan was satisfied that the Lost Order was genuine, he clung to its every sentence as revealed gospel, including the now out-of-date placement of Longstreet's troops along with

D. H. Hill's at Boonsboro, just across South Mountain from the bulk of the Federal army. During the previous forty-eight hours, however, intelligence had been reaching him from a variety of sources — cavalry reports, civilian informants, General Wool, Governor Curtin — that located a substantial Rebel force in Hagerstown. That day, in fact, a telegram from Curtin confidently placed Longstreet in Hagerstown and Jackson across the Potomac and moving on Martinsburg and Harper's Ferry. If the strength estimates included in this intelligence ranged from exaggerated to improbable, here at least was a body of solid eyewitness testimony that an enemy force of some considerable size had moved northward from Boonsboro since the writing of Order 191. The general refused to credit this possibility. He geared his plans to finding Longstreet with Hill at Boonsboro.

One thing Order 191 did not supply was any clue to the Rebel numbers. It merely mentioned the divisions of McLaws, Anderson, Walker, and D. H. Hill and the commands of Jackson and Longstreet. Combining this information with what he had already deduced, McClellan arrived at a Confederate order of battle comprising eight "commands," as he described them to General Halleck in a dispatch sent at eleven that night. To square this assessment with the "120,000 men or more" he assured Halleck were facing him, McClellan selectively assigned them an average of 15,000 men apiece. He was equally liberal in the matter of Lee's table of organization, using the terms "command" and "corps" interchangeably. In this manner he promoted D. H. Hill to corps commander. (The Army of Northern Virginia actually consisted of nine infantry divisions, five grouped nominally under Longstreet and four under Jackson, averaging at most 4,500 men.) By the Young Napoleon's arithmetic, he calculated that on his immediate front, beyond Turner's Gap, he would encounter at least 30,000 Rebels.[5]

Such a prospect called forth his usual prudence; tomorrow would be soon enough to begin any advance. In midafternoon Pleasonton was told to try to confirm the enemy dispositions as spelled out in Order 191, but to approach Turner's Gap "with great caution." He did so, was chased off by Rebel skirmishers, and learned nothing. The corps of Reno, Hooker, Sumner, and Williams and George Sykes's division of regulars were alerted only

Fire on the Mountain

late that evening. They were not to leave their camps at Frederick before daylight on September 14. There is nothing on the record to indicate that the senior commanders were alerted to the secrets revealed by the Lost Order. In any event, it seems to have been McClellan's plan to spend the fourteenth getting the bulk of his army up to South Mountain and across Turner's Gap in tidy preparation for a big fight on the fifteenth. No effort was made to preserve the advantage of surprise. The divisions of Reno's Ninth Corps around Middletown enjoyed their campfires that cool evening, a fact reported to Harvey Hill by his brigade commander at Turner's Gap. Hill alerted Lee in Hagerstown that the Yankees were close by in far more force than Stuart had thought.[6]

Having determined to throw the main weight of his advance through Turner's Gap, General McClellan turned his attention to Harper's Ferry and its besiegers. William Franklin's left wing — three divisions, totaling 19,500 men — would undertake that mission without reinforcement. McClellan thus established his priorities: fewer than 20,000 men assigned to relieve Harper's Ferry and to contend with whatever Confederates they might encounter in the process; and almost 70,000 men to remain under his direction to do battle with what he calculated to be less than half that number at Boonsboro, two days hence. General Lee, if he obligingly made no moves in the meantime, might then be "severely punished" and his army reduced to parity with the Army of the Potomac.

McClellan's instructions to Franklin were lengthy and detailed. Following an explanation of Confederate dispositions as revealed by Order 191, he was given the task of breaking through Crampton's Gap, six miles south of Turner's, to put his corps in Pleasant Valley and in the rear of McLaws's two divisions at Maryland Heights. "Having gained the pass," McClellan wrote, "your duty will be first to cut off, destroy, or capture McLaws' command and relieve Colonel Miles. . . . My general idea is to cut the enemy in two and beat him in detail. . . . I ask of you, at this important moment, all your intellect and the utmost activity that a general can exercise." Franklin was granted the latitude "to change any of the details of this order as circumstances may change, provided the purpose is carried out." He was assured that his force, if well managed, would be "sufficient for the end in view."

There was a notable contrast between the appraisal of the foe confronting Franklin and that confronting the general commanding. The Rebel divisions of McLaws and Anderson were presumably of such a size that they could be dealt with by Franklin's three divisions without reinforcement. The commands of Longstreet and D. H. Hill, however, were of greater magnitude, not to be challenged by McClellan without every man he could lay hands on.

McClellan went to some effort to tailor Franklin's instructions for a subordinate he considered (as he had told his wife) of "so little energy" whose "efficiency is very little." Yet, like the orders to the corps commanders at Frederick, there was nothing said of any advance earlier than "daybreak in the morning," and as if to underscore that timetable Franklin's orders were not sent until 6:20 P.M. on the thirteenth. Orders to Darius Couch's attached division were sent a few minutes later. Franklin was bivouacked that day twelve miles from Crampton's Gap. There is no evidence that McClellan thought to have him march those dozen miles on the afternoon and evening of the thirteenth so as to be in position to break through Crampton's at first light. If after receiving his instructions Franklin contemplated a night march for that purpose, he left no record of it. Independence of mind was not his forte.[7]

So the afternoon hours of September 13 slipped away, and then the evening hours. Except for the advance to Middletown, begun before Order 191 reached McClellan's hands, no Federal troops stirred from their camps that day. It could not be said they needed the rest; the farthest any of them had marched the previous day was ten miles. No doubt had the situation been reversed and a Lost Order presented to Robert E. Lee, that general would have had Jackson's foot cavalry on the march within the hour and every other man in his army who could carry a rifle moving after them within two. But George McClellan marched to a very different drum. Within his illusionary world he forever faced a superior foe — "I have the mass of their troops to contend with," he wired Halleck that night, "and they outnumber me when united" — with the self-imposed and crushing weight of responsibility for the fate of the Union preying on his mind.[8] As a result, he geared all his plans to reducing the risk to his own army to a minimum; he hoped for a victory, but if nothing else he should at least be able to

Fire on the Mountain

force this divided enemy host from Northern soil. Surely the country would see that as accomplishment enough. To do more, to strike ruthlessly and suddenly for the jugular, to seek to win it all at a stroke — and with it most likely the war — would be to gamble, and a messiah could not afford to be a gambler.

McClellan would maintain that he acted with commendable speed that September 13, and by his lights perhaps he had. In any case, for all his delay in acting on his good fortune, he still held a winning hand. With a vigorously directed offensive the next day, he might yet realize his dream of casting Napoleon's Castiglione into the shadows of history.

They could not know it, but the finding of the Lost Order meant a gleam of hope for the nearly 13,000 Federals at Harper's Ferry. What rescue efforts McClellan might have undertaken had he never seen Order 191 can only be guessed, yet his cautious movements up to that point suggest that Lee's appraisal of his opponent was accurate enough. The failure to advance Franklin as far as Crampton's Gap on September 13 was not going to make that general's rescue attempt any easier, but now at least there was some chance for the garrison where there had been none before. Certainly General-in-Chief Halleck must have been heartened to read McClellan's dispatch announcing the finding of the Rebel plans. Among its other benefits, perhaps this would get Old Brains off the hook — a place that careful man seldom allowed himself to be — for ordering the defense of a place that was looking more indefensible with each passing hour.

The beleaguered garrison was just then in need of good news. Harper's Ferry was a dismal enough assignment to begin with. Nathaniel Hawthorne, who had visited there in the spring, found an "inexpressible forlornness resulting from the devastation of war and its occupation by both armies alternately." Another visitor, David Strother, wrote in his diary that "charred ruins were all that remain of the splendid public works, arsenals, workshops and railroads, stores, hotels, and dwelling houses all mingled in one common destruction." The town had already changed hands twice since the war began, and the Yankees there were beginning to suspect that a third change was about to occur.[9]

The rumors of Rebels approaching in force were confirmed on September 12 with the arrival of Brigadier Julius White and his

Martinsburg garrison. Close on their heels, they reported, was the dreaded Stonewall Jackson. At the same time, the outpost atop Maryland Heights sent word that there were Rebel troops on the ridgeline to the north. Learning that the enemy was at the back door was as alarming as the prospect of meeting Jackson at the front door.

One reason for the troops' low morale was a general lack of confidence in the garrison commander, Dixon Miles. (White outranked Miles, but he followed military protocol by putting himself under the officer commanding on the scene in a crisis.) By all accounts, Colonel Miles had sworn off liquor after being nearly cashiered for drunkenness at First Bull Run, but his long-standing alcoholism evidently left permanent aftereffects. His officers noted a mental dullness, a lack of decision, a mulish stubbornness; "It seemed as though everything was mixed up in his mind," one regimental commander said. Though a West Pointer with almost forty years' military experience, Miles displayed little initiative in planning to meet an attack, and none when it came. General Halleck's premise that Harper's Ferry could be defended may have been faulty, but Miles's obtuseness was making that decision look even worse than it was.

The primary example of his laxness was Maryland Heights. One of the keys to any defense of Harper's Ferry was a powerful battery — two 9-inch naval Dahlgren rifles, one 50-pounder Parrott rifle, and four 12-pounder smoothbores — halfway up the heights and sited to cover the approaches to the town from the south and west. These guns, however, were useless for the defense of Maryland Heights itself, and Miles had done nothing to fortify either the crest or Solomon's Gap, the only practicable approach to the crest from the north. There was a last-minute attempt to throw up a crude log breastwork on the heights, but this was hardly any barrier to a determined attack.

Both Halleck and McClellan had proposed that the entire Harper's Ferry garrison withdraw to Maryland Heights to hold out to the last ditch, but there was a catch to that: there was no water on the mountain, and no one had thought to build cisterns. As a consequence, Maryland Heights and Harper's Ferry were mutually dependent; neither could survive an assault without the other. Early on the morning of September 13 the Confederate bri-

Fire on the Mountain

gades of Joseph Kershaw and William Barksdale set themselves the task of seizing Maryland Heights.[10]

Miles had assigned only some 1,600 troops to defend the mountain, all or parts of four regiments under the command of Colonel Thomas H. Ford of the 32nd Ohio. His Ohioans, veterans of the Valley campaign, were the only ones with any combat experience. The men of the 126th New York had been in the army exactly twenty-one days when they were sent up to the crest the previous afternoon, and most of them were still trying to grasp such essentials as the complicated nine-step drill for loading their rifles. At first light they were put into a line of battle about a quarter mile in advance of the makeshift breastwork. Ahead of them, in the thick woods, they could hear the enemy talking and moving in the underbrush and forming up to shouted orders.

The battle opened with a spatter of skirmishing fire, and the Yankee pickets came running back, shouting the alarm. Suddenly there was the crash of heavy volleys and the unnerving sound of Rebel yells, and smoke roiled up from the woods. The rookies of the 126th had not imagined it would be anything like this, facing unseen foes in a dark and smoky woodland who seemed to know a great deal more about fighting than they did. They managed to get off some ragged return fire and then someone gave the order to fall back, and they ran pell-mell for the breastwork behind them.

The 126th's Colonel Eliakim Sherrill was as new to battle as his men, but he did not lack courage. Shouting orders and waving his pistol, he managed to halt the flight and get the men back into some semblance of a battle line. There was a pause while the Rebels got themselves sorted out, and then they came on again. They delivered another withering volley, and one of the bullets caught Colonel Sherrill in the face, inflicting a ghastly wound. Seeing their colonel writhing on the ground was too much for the green troops, and the 126th broke again, this time in complete rout. Officers of other regiments tried to rally them, but it was hopeless. "They were in wild confusion and dismay," a lieutenant of the 32nd Ohio testified. ". . . Nobody could possibly hold them." Soon they were scattered in their hundreds down the mountainside, hiding behind rocks and bushes and in patches of woods; the regiment's adjutant saw three men trying to conceal themselves behind a single tree.

Colonel Ford did what he could to patch together a new line with the troops remaining, and sent a dispatch to Miles in Harper's Ferry. "I cannot hold my men," he wrote. "The One hundred and twenty-sixth all run, and the Thirty-second are out of ammunition. I must leave the hill unless you direct otherwise." Miles hurried to the scene to see for himself, raging furiously at the routed men he encountered. Ford pleaded with him for reinforcements. "You can't have another damned man," Miles told him. "If you can't hold it, leave it."

Ford tried to continue the fight, but he was badly outnumbered and the Confederates were crowding in on him from front and flank. Believing he had discretionary power from Miles, he ordered an evacuation. The guns in the mountainside battery were spiked or tumbled into the river below, and the defenders made their way across the pontoon bridge over the Potomac at the foot of the mountain and into Harper's Ferry. Kershaw and Barksdale had Maryland Heights all to themselves.

In the meantime, Jackson had reached the scene and drawn up his divisions opposite the Federal positions on Bolivar Heights. To the south, John Walker's two brigades arrived at the foot of Loudoun Heights. His patrols cautiously made their way up the slope and to their surprise found the crest unoccupied. Of the three areas of high ground commanding Harper's Ferry, only Bolivar Heights now remained in Federal hands.

That evening Colonel Miles called Captain Charles H. Russell of the 1st Maryland cavalry to headquarters. He wanted Russell and a few of his troopers to break out and, as Russell recalled the conversation, "try to reach somebody that had ever heard of the United States Army, or any general of the United States Army, or anybody that knew anything about the United States Army, and report the condition of Harper's Ferry." He was to say that Miles believed he could hold out for forty-eight hours, "but if he was not relieved in that time he would have to surrender the place."[11]

For most of September 13, at his headquarters in Hagerstown, General Lee was isolated from the day's rush of events. The last dispatch from Jackson, written in Martinsburg, indicated that the Harper's Ferry operation was running about a day behind schedule. Even the foot cavalry could not cover sixty miles in two days. There had been no word at all from McLaws or Walker. From

Fire on the Mountain 125

Stuart's reports he imagined that by now McClellan was occupying Frederick. He sent a politely prodding message to McLaws expressing his hope "that the enemy about Harper's Ferry will be speedily disposed of, and the various detachments returned to the main body of the army."[12] He was no doubt aware that his margin of safety was being worn very thin by the delay, but that was no particular cause for alarm so long as his opponent continued to leave him in control of events.

During the evening, however, dispatches arrived at Hagerstown that abruptly altered the picture. A message from Stuart announced that his cavalry screen had been pushed back from Catoctin Mountain. D. H. Hill reported that the numerous campfires around Middletown, visible from Turner's Gap, indicated the presence of Yankees in considerable numbers at the base of South Mountain. Then the element of chance that had so favored McClellan earlier in the day tipped briefly toward Lee. A second Stuart dispatch presented him with a rare glimpse inside enemy headquarters.[13]

Among the delegation of local citizens visiting McClellan in Frederick that morning when he was handed the copy of Order 191 was a Confederate sympathizer. He was witness to McClellan's exuberance when he realized his good fortune, and to the subsequent bustle of staff officers. The general was surely not so careless of security as to reveal to his visitors the exact nature of the find, but even so, from the reaction it was clearly a dispatch or intelligence report of no little importance. The Marylander — his name is lost to history — may also have witnessed the departure from camp shortly after noon of Cox's Kanawha Division on its support mission to Middletown, and understandably (if wrongly) connected it with what he had just seen at headquarters. However that may be, he was soon on his way through the lines, and about dusk he managed to locate Jeb Stuart near Turner's Gap. He explained what he had seen and offered his surmise that the Federal army was embarking on some sort of offensive operation. This was solid enough intelligence for Stuart to forward it promptly to Hagerstown.

The dispatch probably reached Lee about 10 P.M. He and Longstreet discussed how to react to what appeared from the evidence to be a major — and puzzling — shift in McClellan's tactics. Since there was as yet no certainty of Federal intentions for the next day, Lee was unwilling to give up the Harper's Ferry operation when it seemed so near success. To do so would be to give up his entire plan of campaign to secure his supply line and draw the Army of the Potomac into battle somewhere to the west in the Cumberland Valley in circumstances of his own choosing. Instead, he would seek to buy time by holding the South Mountain passes, should that become necessary. He told Longstreet to prepare to march at dawn for Boonsboro to support Harvey Hill.[14]

Longstreet protested. His men would arrive too late and too tired from the hard march to be effective if there was a fight. He urged a more conservative course: withdraw his and Hill's divisions, with the army's trains and reserve artillery, to the most convenient central location, the town of Sharpsburg near the Potomac, where there was good defensive ground and better opportunity to reunite the army. From there, he argued, they could operate against McClellan's flank should he attempt to lift the siege of Harper's Ferry. "Lee listened patiently enough," Longstreet later wrote, "but did not change his plans...." Old Pete was so troubled by the decision that he could not sleep. He got up, put his thoughts on paper, and sent them to the commanding general. "To that note I got no answer," he wrote.[15]

Lee meanwhile was sending off a string of couriers with fresh orders. McLaws's position at Maryland Heights was the most exposed, and he was warned that the enemy was believed to be planning an advance against his rear to relieve Harper's Ferry. "You will see, therefore, the necessity of expediting your operations as much as possible." Jackson too was apprised of McClellan's activity and asked to speed his movements. Harvey Hill was told that any advance by the Federals on his front must be blocked, and that he was to go himself to Turner's Gap in the morning and plan its defense with Stuart. Stuart's orders were simple and direct: "The gap must be held at all hazards until the operations at Harper's Ferry are finished. You must keep me informed of the strength of the enemy's forces...."[16]

So ended a day crowded with melodramatic intensity. In the most unlikely way imaginable, an Indiana corporal had presented George McClellan with a dazzling opportunity to smash the Confederacy's most important army. Listening to the niggling inner

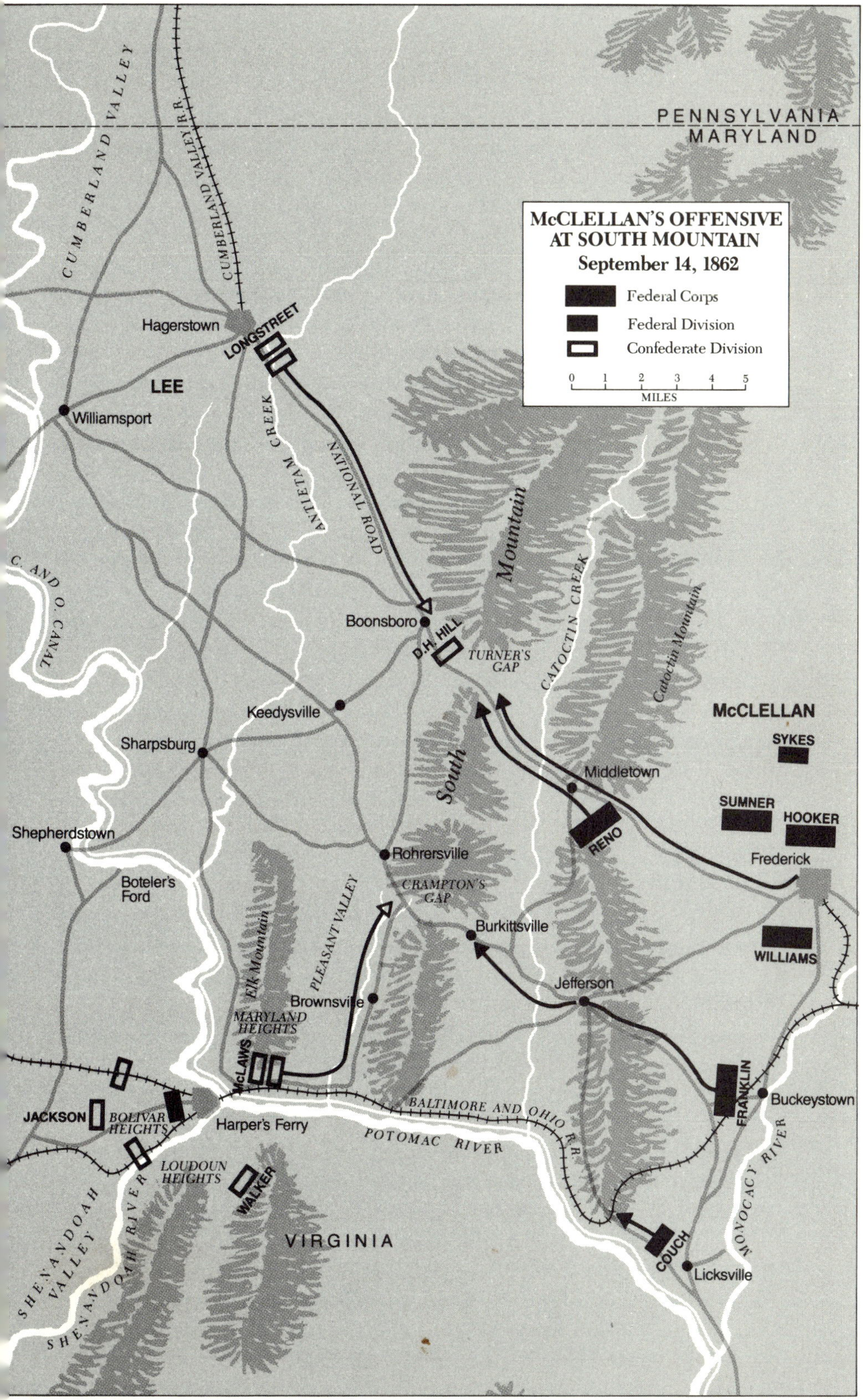

McCLELLAN'S OFFENSIVE AT SOUTH MOUNTAIN
September 14, 1862
Federal Corps
Federal Division
Confederate Division
0 1 2 3 4 5
MILES
PENNSYLVANIA
MARYLAND
CUMBERLAND VALLEY
CUMBERLAND VALLEY R.R.
Hagerstown
LONGSTREET
LEE
Williamsport
ANTIETAM CREEK
NATIONAL ROAD
South Mountain
CATOCTIN CREEK
Catoctin Mountain
C. AND O. CANAL
Boonsboro
D.H. HILL
TURNER'S GAP
Keedysville
Sharpsburg
McCLELLAN
SYKES
Middletown
SUMNER
HOOKER
RENO
Frederick
Shepherdstown
Boteler's Ford
Rohrersville
CRAMPTON'S GAP
PLEASANT VALLEY
Burkittsville
WILLIAMS
Elk Mountain
Jefferson
Brownsville
MARYLAND HEIGHTS
McLAWS
FRANKLIN
Buckeystown
JACKSON
BOLIVAR HEIGHTS
Harper's Ferry
BALTIMORE AND OHIO R.R.
POTOMAC RIVER
MONOCACY RIVER
LOUDOUN HEIGHTS
WALKER
VIRGINIA
COUCH
Licksville
SHENANDOAH VALLEY
SHENANDOAH RIVER

voice of caution, he let that opportunity start to slip away, but it was not yet beyond his grasp. On Maryland Heights a regiment of Yankees pathetic in their inexperience fled their first test of battle, putting the 13,000-man Harper's Ferry garrison a large step closer to capture. And in a final bizarre twist, an anonymous civilian gave General Lee warning that his entire campaign plan, which depended heavily on his opponent's caution, might be in jeopardy. For both armies, as for the troops at Harper's Ferry, the day marked the start of a race against time.

The next morning, Sunday, September 14, the sky was just beginning to brighten when D. H. Hill rode up to Turner's Gap in response to Lee's orders to prepare a defense should the Yankees try to break through the South Mountain barrier along the National Road. Since reaching Boonsboro, Hill had occupied himself with watching for a breakout to the north by the Harper's Ferry garrison, leaving the guarding of South Mountain to Jeb Stuart. He soon discovered he had much to learn about his new assignment.

For one thing, he found that Stuart had gone south to Crampton's Gap, where he judged the danger to be most immediate, leaving behind only a 200-man cavalry regiment under Thomas Rosser and a battery of horse artillery. Hill then found that Alfred Colquitt's infantry brigade, sent the previous day to keep an eye on things, had moved down the east face of the mountain. He brought Colquitt back to the crest and hurried along Samuel Garland's brigade in support. But Hill's most alarming discovery was that Turner's Gap was going to be far more difficult to defend than he had first thought.

There was good enough defensive ground around the defile where the National Road crossed the mountain, and even a small force there could make it very hot for an attacking column. The problem was that the position was vulnerable on both flanks. Two roads branched off the National Road near the eastern base of the mountain. One, called the Old Sharpsburg Road, angled to the south and crossed the range at Fox's Gap, a little less than a mile from Turner's Gap. A rough farm road left the Sharpsburg road part way up the slope and made a loop farther to the south before turning back and continuing along the top of the ridge through Fox's Gap to Turner's. The second branch, the Old Hagerstown Road, made a circuit to the north, rejoining the National Road at

Fire on the Mountain

the crest. From it, too, there ran a wide-looping farm road, presenting the enemy with still another flanking route. All told, to hold Turner's Gap meant spreading defenders across a good three miles to cover all five roads.

The terrain of South Mountain was irregular, marked by ravines and hollows and rounded peaks. The slopes were heavily wooded and thick with undergrowth and tangles of mountain laurel. Where the ground leveled off near the crest, a number of hard-scrabble farms had been carved from the forest, their fields and pastures marked out by snake-rail fences and stone walls. It promised to be a difficult place to maneuver troops and manage a battle — and General Hill now had no doubts that a battle was imminent. After posting Colquitt's brigade at Turner's Gap and ordering Garland to Fox's Gap to the south, Hill climbed a lookout at the mountain's summit and encountered a sight that left him breathless. Spread across the valley before him were Federal troops in all their array. "It was a grand and glorious spectacle," Hill later wrote, "and it was impossible to look at it without admiration."[17] Many other soldiers, North and South, would speak of spectacle and military pageantry and the like that day, for never before in the war had a battle been staged in so spectacular a fashion.

Hill was far from prepared to fight that morning, with only a cavalry regiment and two of his five brigades yet on hand — perhaps 2,300 men in all — but fortunately for him the Yankees were not prepared either. Having persuaded himself that the Confederates on his front were all in Boonsboro in accordance with Order 191, McClellan considered Pleasonton's cavalry plus a single infantry brigade adequate to clear the way through Turner's Gap. Within supporting distance were three of the four divisions of Jesse Reno's Ninth Corps, whose serried ranks so impressed General Hill. Additional manpower would be a long time coming, however. First in line in McClellan's march schedule for the day was Joe Hooker's First Corps. From their camps east of Frederick, Hooker's men had the longest way to go to reach the scene, a dozen miles or so, and could not arrive before midafternoon. If there was going to be any rapid breakthrough at Turner's Gap, it would have to be made by the Ninth Corps.

Jacob Cox's Kanawha Division was camped closest to South

Mountain, and Cox assigned Eliakim Scammon's brigade of Ohioans to support Pleasonton. They set off at 6 A.M., with Cox riding along to observe the proceedings. To his astonishment, he came upon Colonel Augustus Moor, his brigade commander who had been captured in the cavalry clash in Frederick two days before, standing by the roadside. Moor explained that he had been paroled by the Rebels and was on his way back to sit out the war until there was a prisoner exchange. He asked where Scammon's brigade was bound, and Cox told him it was backing up a cavalry reconnaissance toward Turner's Gap. "My God! Be careful!" Moor exclaimed; then, realizing he was honor-bound to abide by the terms of his parole, he turned away and said nothing more. For Cox he had said enough. He sent back for his second brigade, informed Reno that he thought they were going to have a fight on their hands, and warned his regimental commanders to expect trouble on the mountain.[18]

After consulting with Pleasonton, Cox decided on an indirect approach to Turner's Gap. He had Scammon's brigade turn off to the left on the Old Sharpsburg Road leading up to Fox's Gap. His second brigade, under George Crook, toiled along behind on the steep mountain road. When a Rebel battery lobbed a few shells at them from the ridgeline, Scammon increased the radius of the turning movement by shifting to the farm road that circled off through the trees to the south. Before long they came to an open pasture near the crest with a stone wall at the far end and behind the wall they saw a Rebel line of battle. It was now nine o'clock. Scammon got his men deployed, with Crook's brigade in close support — six Ohio regiments in all, some 3,000 men — and the scattered skirmishing fire grew into long ripping volleys.

The troops blocking the Federals' path were North Carolinians under Samuel Garland, five thin regiments totaling perhaps a thousand men. Garland was one of the most promising young officers in the Confederate army; like D. H. Hill, his division commander, he led by example and had displayed conspicuous bravery under fire during the fighting on the Peninsula. He was in a difficult spot. In this alternating pattern of field and woodland there was nothing much on which to anchor his flanks, he could see that he was badly outnumbered, and except for Tom Rosser's dismounted cavalrymen and a single battery under Captain J. W.

Fire on the Mountain

Bondurant, he could expect no help until Hill got his other brigades up from Boonsboro.

The firing grew in intensity as the Federals began to push hard along the whole line. Lieutenant George Crome and his gun crew manhandled a section of the Ohio Light Artillery close enough to open with canister, but Rebel sharpshooters picked off the lieutenant and most of his gunners until there was no one left to man the guns. Garland hurried to his left flank, where the threat seemed greatest. He found Colonel Thomas Ruffin, commander of the 13th North Carolina, behind the firing line. "General," Ruffin exclaimed, "why do you stay here? You are in great danger." Garland was unruffled. "I may as well be here as yourself," he replied. Ruffin told him it was his place to be at the front with his regiment and the general's place to be where he could command the brigade in safety. Almost immediately Ruffin was wounded in the hip, and moments later a bullet struck Garland. Those who rushed to his aid saw that the wound was mortal.

Scammon ordered his men to fix bayonets and charge the stone wall. The attack unnerved the green troops of the 12th North Carolina. Their commander, a young captain as inexperienced as his men, gave the order to "fire and fall back," but the Yankees returned the fire so rapidly that the withdrawal collapsed in confusion. Like the troops of the 126th New York on Maryland Heights the day before, these North Carolina boys had neither the experience nor the leadership to cope with their sudden crisis, and they broke and ran.

The veteran regiments on each side of the break tried to stand their ground, and there was a melee of slashing bayonets and clubbed rifles, but the weight of numbers was against them. Scores surrendered as Crook's brigade pitched in to overlap both flanks, and Bondurant's battery had to pull back hastily to avoid being overrun. Leading the assault on the Confederate right was the 23rd Ohio, its colonel, Rutherford B. Hayes, shouting, "Give 'em hell! Give the sons of bitches hell!" Hayes went down with a bullet in the arm, but his men drove on and sent the enemy flying. (The 23rd Ohio was uniquely rich in presidential timber; in addition to Hayes, there was a supply sergeant on the roster named William McKinley.)[19]

The remnants of Garland's brigade, demoralized by the loss of their commander, were soon scattering in every direction, some of the survivors fleeing down the western face of the mountain. One 20th North Carolina straggler was trapped in a tangle of branches as a Yankee solid shot splintered the tree he was sheltering behind. As he struggled to free himself, the regiment's terrier mascot, driven frantic by the din, began snapping and biting at him. "He suffered more than he would have had he gone into the fight," the 20th's historian tartly remarked. Harvey Hill estimated that almost a third of the brigade had been shot down or captured and "was too roughly handled to be of any further use that day." He resorted to bluff by running forward two guns from Turner's Gap and backing them up with a "support force" of staff aides and cooks and teamsters. With the rest of his division still on the march from Boonsboro and with only stragglers, a handful of guns, and Colquitt's single brigade remaining on the mountaintop, Hill's overwhelming emotion just then was loneliness.

The Ohioans of the Kanawha Division turned north and reached Fox's Gap and the open fields of the Daniel Wise homestead, where the farm road crossed the Old Sharpsburg Road. Turner's Gap was less than a mile away. As far as General Cox could tell, however, the Rebels in the woods ahead were still full of fight and their artillery had dead aim on Wise's fields, plowing furrows in the ground "with a noise like the cutting of a melon rind." His casualties were heavy, particularly in Scammon's brigade, ammunition was running low, and the men were badly winded from their long climb and the hard fight. He had them pull back from their exposed position at Wise's and consolidate their gains. It was getting on toward noon and past time for the rest of the Ninth Corps to take over the advance. But the remaining three divisions of the corps were nowhere to be seen.[20]

Little sense of urgency impelled the Federal high command that morning. General McClellan remained in Frederick, immersing himself in the details of the army's movements. He found time to send off the latest news to his wife. "It is probable that we shall have a serious engagement to-day, and perhaps a general battle," he wrote, but was content to leave its direction to others. At about 9 A.M. Captain Russell of the 1st Maryland cavalry arrived at his headquarters with news from Harper's Ferry. It had been a night of high adventure for the captain. Accompanied by nine troopers,

Fire on the Mountain

he had slipped past Jackson's pickets in the darkness and made his way on back roads and through fields to cross the Potomac at an upstream ford. Dodging Rebel patrols, he found an unguarded path across South Mountain, reached the Union lines at Middletown, and on a fresh horse galloped on to Frederick. He gave McClellan Colonel Miles's estimate that the garrison could hold out through the fifteenth and recounted the evacuation of Maryland Heights. The general received this news, Russell recalled, with surprise and dismay. He wrote out a dispatch to Miles assuring him that every effort was being made to relieve him: "Hold out to the last extremity. If it is possible, reoccupy the Maryland heights with your whole force." The staff was put to the task of locating volunteers to slip through the lines, and three couriers were soon on their separate ways with the message. None of them would reach Harper's Ferry.[21]

Ambrose Burnside, whose command of the army's right wing included both the First and Ninth corps, was not at the front that morning either, which left Jesse Reno of the Ninth in immediate control. Reno, a Virginian by birth and a West Point classmate of McClellan's, had led a division with distinction at Second Bull Run, helping to prevent Pope's defeat from becoming rout. He was a stocky and determined no-nonsense regular; when one of his brigades had tied up traffic during the triumphal entry into Frederick two days before by halting to dress ranks and go through the evolution of presenting arms in salute to the cheering crowds, he rode up and ordered a stop to the foolishness and told everybody to get on with it. But for some reason on this morning he was not acting with his usual resolution.

By at least 8 A.M. Reno had received Cox's warning to expect a stiff fight on the mountain, and he promised Cox the support of the rest of the Ninth Corps. Yet the first of these supports, Orlando Willcox's division, did not set off much before 10:30 or 11, was misdirected, and did not reach Cox's position until 2 P.M., a full five hours after the fighting began. The other two divisions, under Samuel Sturgis and Isaac Rodman, were even later in starting to the front. When Burnside appeared on the scene, he compounded the delay by holding back Sturgis and Rodman until Joe Hooker's First Corps arrived and was in position for a coordinated attack against both Confederate flanks.[22]

So the lull in the fighting dragged on and the chance to exploit Cox's solid victory and quickly sweep D. H. Hill's handful off the mountaintop faded and then was gone entirely. By the time Willcox's reinforcements finally arrived, Hill no longer felt so lonely. His remaining three brigades were at hand — George B. Anderson's North Carolinians filling the gap left by the destruction of Garland's brigade, Roswell Ripley's Georgians and North Carolinians close behind, and Robert Rodes's Alabamians moving into place north of Turner's Gap. Longstreet was approaching with his two divisions from Hagerstown and was expected to be on the scene in an hour or two. Hill knew his problems were by no means over, but at least he now had something to fight with.

When the first of Longstreet's units, the brigades of Thomas Drayton and George T. Anderson, came rushing up the mountain from Boonsboro, Hill steered them toward Fox's Gap. With the four brigades of Ripley, Drayton, and the two Andersons now manning his southern flank, he mounted a counterattack to try to gain some time and breathing space. It was a fiasco. Ripley as the senior brigadier was put in charge, but he apparently lost his sense of direction and led his whole brigade somewhere off into the laurel thickets and missed the action entirely. The rest of the attack was piecemeal and confused as it hit Cox's and Willcox's troops. One Tarheel remembered fighting "in so many directions that no one knew which was front."

However badly it was managed, there was some very severe fighting around Fox's Gap in these afternoon hours. A pair of untried regiments in Willcox's division, posted by the Old Sharpsburg Road, had an especially tough time of it. The rookies of the 17th Michigan, who had been with the army barely two weeks and were dressed in their best uniforms for their first battle, found themselves sharing a stretch of split-rail fence with the 45th Pennsylvania, an outfit that had experienced war only at a distance during a long stay on the South Carolina coast. Across a pasture were the Rebels behind another of those stone walls, and as the firing grew heavier the Yankees discovered that a rail fence furnished the most dubious kind of shelter against bullets and artillery. When Willcox ordered the line forward, these green troops responded with a courage born of desperation. "We rushed into

Fire on the Mountain 135

them . . . ," one of the Michigan men wrote his father, "and all the time every man shouting as loud as he could — I got rather more excited than I wish to again." The Rebels had to give up their wall and withdraw into the forest, leaving behind a considerable number of dead and wounded. When they were relieved, the rookies from Michigan and Pennsylvania were proud of the way they had met the test, but theirs was a costly initiation; 266 of them had been killed or wounded in those few minutes.[23]

As the struggle swept back and forth through the woodlots and pastures and cornfields around Fox's Gap, the two rival army commanders arrived at the eastern and western bases of South Mountain to feed men into the spreading conflict. Although his injured hands were still splinted, Lee had found riding to war in an ambulance intolerable and was mounted on Traveller again. Near Boonsboro he was sitting his horse by the roadside when John B. Hood's Texas Brigade marched past. Hood, still under arrest in the contretemps over the Yankee ambulances captured at Second Bull Run, was confined to the rear of the column. His men considered the whole business silly and wanted the best leadership they could get for the coming battle, and they began to yell, "Give us Hood!" These were Lee's sentiments as well, and he raised his hat and told them, "You shall have him, gentlemen." He called Hood out of the column and offered him his command back in exchange for a simple statement of regret. Hood refused, insisting that his soldier's honor would not permit an apology. Lee brushed the explanation aside and said the arrest was suspended while there was fighting to be done, and sent him to the head of his division. The Texans greeted the news with a great shout and hurried on toward the mountain.

A few miles away on the other side of the mountain, on a knoll alongside the National Road, George McClellan was also watching his army march past on its way to the fight. The troops of Hooker's First Corps raised cheer upon cheer when they saw the martial figure on his great black horse, Dan Webster. It was the kind of setting the Young Napoleon loved above all others, and he embraced the drama of it, raising his arm and pointing steadily toward the smoke-wreathed mountain ahead. The men redoubled their cheers at the sight. "It was like a great scene in a play, with the roar of the guns for an accompaniment," one of Hooker's men recalled, and he ranked it as one of the unforgettable moments of the war.[24]

At about the same time, the men of the 9th New York, in the last of Reno's divisions to reach the battle, were taking a breather halfway up the Old Sharpsburg Road. Private David L. Thompson looked back across the valley at the advance of Hooker's corps and an indelible picture formed in his mind, as he later wrote, of "a monstrous, crawling, blue-black snake, miles long, quilled with the silver slant of muskets at a 'shoulder,' its sluggish tail writhing slowly up over the distant eastern ridge, its bruised head weltering in the roar and smoke upon the crest above...." At the summit D. H. Hill was also watching. "From the top of the mountain the sight was grand and sublime," he recalled, "but the elements of the pretty and the picturesque did not enter into it." He decided that the Hebrew poet's simile "terrible as an army with banners" must have been inspired by just such a sight.

The Yankees in the ranks of this army with banners knew little of their general's plans and nothing at all of the glittering opportunity he was wasting. All they saw was the great army in purposeful motion at last and their beloved Little Mac pointing them ahead to the battle on the mountain. "All thoughts of our recent defeats was for the moment forgotten," wrote Corporal Austin Stearns of Hooker's corps, "for in our front were the enemies of our country, and the old thoughts and feelings, and love of country, flag, and home came back, and how eager we all were to again measure our strength with the enemy, and wipe the stain of defeat away.... So we marched on down the ridge, across the valley and through the village of Middletown on that sabbath day."[25]

As Hooker's three divisions arrived they were directed off to the right on the Old Hagerstown Road for a turning movement against the Confederate northern flank. At the hamlet of Frosttown, where a farm road circled farther to the north, the corps was deployed for the advance up the mountain, John P. Hatch's division on the left, George Gordon Meade's on the right along the farm road, James B. Ricketts's in reserve. It was now about 4 P.M.; seven hours after the battle opened the Federals were finally ready to begin a coordinated attack against both flanks of the Turner's Gap position.

Fire on the Mountain 137

As the 21st New York, the lead regiment in Hatch's division, started forward, it encountered an elderly woman who had fled her cabin on the mountaintop when the shelling began. She wanted to know where the Yankees were going. They were just going up the hill, an officer told her. "Don't you go there," she insisted, waving them back. "There are hundreds of 'em up there. Don't you go. *Some of you will get hurt!*" The boys laughed and assured her they would be fine and sent her along to the rear, and then they headed into the heavy timber on the slope and discovered that the woman knew exactly what she was talking about.[26]

Robert Rodes had only 1,200 Alabamians in his brigade to meet this new Federal threat, and he needed to win as much time as he could until help arrived from Longstreet. He had ordered the 12th Alabama to advance a skirmish line into the woods, and the best shots in the regiment were assigned the job. Dodging Indian style from tree to tree, they made life miserable for Hatch's men struggling through the underbrush. Eventually the skirmishers were cleared out and the winded Yankees reached the open ground in front of Rodes's main line posted on the heights. Like Garland, Rodes was considered one of the rising stars in the Southern army; and like Garland earlier in the day, he was facing the problem of defending too wide a front with too few men.

The First Corps's attack was well coordinated and relentless. George Meade, who had taken over John Reynolds's all-Pennsylvania division when Reynolds was sent north to soothe Governor Curtin and command the state militia, continually pressed for the Rebel left flank and the high ground overlooking Turner's Gap, forcing Rodes to keep stretching his line ever farther to the north. At the eleventh hour help finally reached him from Longstreet's command, with Old Pete himself on hand to take charge of the defense, but these men arrived exhausted and in poor shape to fight. Through bad staff work, three of the four brigades were somehow shunted off to the south of the National Road beyond Boonsboro and had to backtrack cross-lots and climb rough farm tracks to get where they were needed, in the process leaving a trail of stragglers all the way down the mountain. As a result, Rodes's Alabamians had to do most of the work, and it was four hours of the hardest fighting they had ever imagined.[27]

McClellan had his chief of staff, Randolph Marcy, traveling

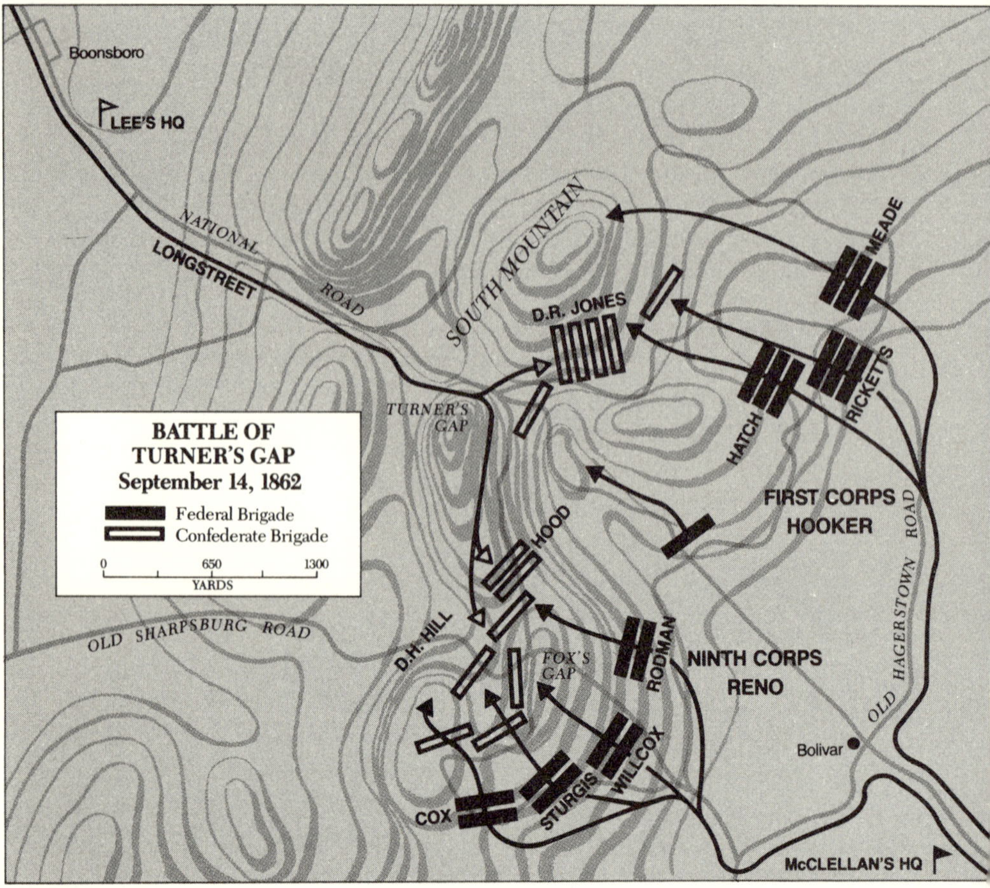

BATTLE OF
TURNER'S GAP
September 14, 1862
Federal Brigade
Confederate Brigade
0
650
1300
YARDS
Boonsboro
LEE'S HQ
NATIONAL
ROAD
LONGSTREET
SOUTH MOUNTAIN
D.R. JONES
MEADE
RICKETTS
HATCH
TURNER'S GAP
FIRST CORPS
HOOKER
OLD HAGERSTOWN ROAD
HOOD
D.H. HILL
OLD SHARPSBURG ROAD
FOX'S GAP
RODMAN
NINTH CORPS
RENO
WILLCOX
STURGIS
COX
Bolivar
McCLELLAN'S HQ

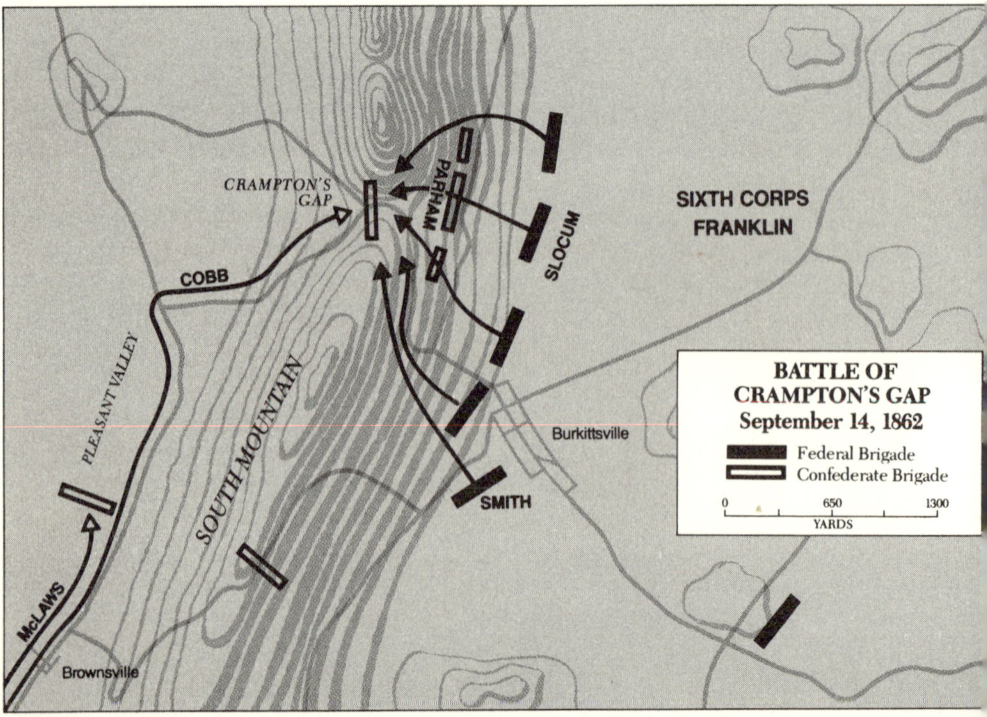

BATTLE OF
CRAMPTON'S GAP
September 14, 1862
Federal Brigade
Confederate Brigade
0
650
1300
YARDS
CRAMPTON'S GAP
PARHAM
SLOCUM
SIXTH CORPS
FRANKLIN
COBB
PLEASANT VALLEY
SOUTH MOUNTAIN
Burkittsville
SMITH
McLAWS
Brownsville

Fire on the Mountain

with Hooker, and at 5:20 P.M. Marcy signaled that there did not seem to be much enemy infantry in front of them and "Hooker will have the top of the Mt. in an hour." His optimism was premature. The 6th Alabama under Colonel John B. Gordon, who may have been the best regimental commander in the Army of Northern Virginia, repeatedly bore the weight of Meade's flanking assaults and somehow fought them off. Firing downhill from the crest, the Rebels were tending to shoot somewhat high, often enough missing their targets — the color-bearer of the 107th Pennsylvania was untouched, but reported his flag shot to ribbons — yet of the hits they did make an unusual number were fatal head wounds. The color-bearer of the 76th New York, Sergeant Charlie Stamp, was not so lucky as his counterpart in the 107th Pennsylvania. Dashing out in front of the battle line he planted his flag, turned to his comrades, and shouted, "There, come up to that!" At that instant a Confederate bullet smashed through his head. The gallant Charlie Stamp, wrote the unit's historian sadly, "was mustered out of the army militant and mustered into the army triumphant."

Hatch's men climbed up a ravine between two spurs of high ground in an attempt to split the Confederate line and got into a terrific firefight for possession of a cornfield fence. Hatch was wounded as he spurred on his troops in a charge that gained the fence and drove the defenders back into the corn. The Rebels counterattacked and were stopped by a killing volley delivered at virtual pointblank range, leaving their dead within thirty feet of the fence. Rodes was now being steadily pushed back and taking heavy losses — his brigade would suffer 218 men killed and wounded and a nearly equal number captured — but at the cost of a third of the force he took into the battle he was winning precious time. When at last Hatch and Meade wrested the high ground from the defenders it was too dark to drive on to Turner's Gap.[28]

At the same time, two or three miles to the south, the Ninth Corps was making a concerted effort of its own to break through to Turner's. Reno had his remaining divisions, under Sturgis and Rodman, in action now, and as the afternoon shadows lengthened, the entire crest of the mountain was crowned in battle smoke and thunderous noise. "We barely held our own," Southern war correspondent Felix de Fontaine wrote. "Advance we could not. The enemy in numbers were like a solid wall.... Retreat, we would not, and thus we fought, doggedly giving and taking the fearful blows of battle...." Another correspondent, the *New York Tribune*'s George Smalley, was at Federal headquarters in the valley below. McClellan seemed strangely divorced from what was going on, Smalley thought: "It was, in fact, from a military point of view, a very critical moment, but this general commanding had a singular air of detachment; almost that of a disinterested spectator; or of a general watching maneuvers."[29]

The Ninth Corps found the going hard. The Confederates put up a stubborn and aggressive defense, and Hood was on the scene with two brigades of veterans to support D. H. Hill's tired troops. As bad as anything else was the difficulty seeing or understanding what was going on. Up on the firing line the 46th New York had used up most of its cartridges and was ordered to make way for the 9th New Hampshire, another untrained regiment going into action for the first time. Just then, Rebels hidden in the woods ahead unleashed a volley, and the jittery New Hampshire boys began firing back before the New Yorkers could get out of their way, "thereby greatly endangering the lives of our soldiers, who only saved themselves by throwing themselves down on the ground," the 46th's colonel wrote angrily. Fortunately, the rookies' aim was so bad that nobody was hurt in the mix-up.

General Reno himself was up on the mountain by now, and he went forward to see what was holding up the advance. He reached Sturgis's position about sunset and rode ahead to get a better view. He was near the spot where Rebel General Garland had fallen that morning when a Rebel sharpshooter put a bullet through his body. He was brought back to Sturgis's command post on a stretcher. "Hallo, Sam, I'm dead!" he called out in a voice so natural that Sturgis thought he must be joking. He said he hoped it was not as bad as all that. "Yes, yes, I'm dead — good-by!" Reno repeated, and minutes later he died.

Cox took command of the corps and continued the advance, managing to push beyond Wise's to within perhaps a half mile of Turner's Gap, but that was as far as the Yankees got that day. Rebel artillery posted around the gap continued to rake the fields where the Federals tried to form up, and sharp counterattacks kept them off balance. At dusk two North Carolina regiments tried

Fire on the Mountain

to storm a battery and stumbled into a deadly trap. There were three regiments of New Yorkers positioned to support the guns but out of sight of the attackers. The 89th New York was lying in a cornfield off to one side, a situation, Private David Thompson wrote, "ideally, cruelly advantageous to us. The Confederates stood before us not twenty feet away, the full intention of destruction on their faces — but helpless, with empty muskets. The 89th simply rose up and shot them down." The stunned survivors fled back into the woods. When he came to describe his experiences that day to his family, Thompson wrote feelingly of the fearful slaughter he had seen and of the many wounded, "their beards clotted with thick blood, groaning & cursing on all sides — these made me wish myself back at home."[30]

As the First and Ninth corps were pressing the Confederate flanks, General Burnside devised a diversion by sending a column straight up the National Road to attack Turner's Gap head-on. For this unenviable task he selected John Gibbon's brigade from the First Corps. Gibbon was a veteran artillerist from the old army with a talent for handling volunteers. His troops were Westerners — three regiments from Wisconsin, one from Indiana — and he had found in training them that the martinet ways of the regulars were far less effective than the promise of reward for good performance. He granted the men time off for such things as blackberrying and outfitted them with nonregulation but distinctive black slouch hats. The proof of his methods had been demonstrated at Groveton, just before Second Bull Run, when the brigade met its first test by standing up to Stonewall Jackson's veterans and slugging it out, giving as good as it got. Jackson's men called them "those damned black-hat fellers" and said it with grudging respect. Gibbon himself was an example of why this was called a war of brothers. A native North Carolinian, he had three brothers in the Confederate army. And when D. H. Hill, the man he would fight this day, was married, John Gibbon had been his best man.[31]

The sun was dipping behind South Mountain when the Black Hat Brigade was ordered forward. The 7th Wisconsin and the 19th Indiana were out front, marching in column along both sides of the road, skirmishers out front, the 2nd and 6th Wisconsin in rank behind. Two guns of Gibbon's old regular army outfit, Battery B,

4th U.S., were along to provide artillery support. From headquarters on the knoll behind them McClellan and the rest of the high command watched, the general remarking favorably on the precision of the march.

Soon Rebel skirmishers began blazing away, and the parade-ground look disappeared. These were Alfred Colquitt's men, most of them Georgians, who had been posted all day at Turner's Gap without seeing much action. They seemed to the Yankees to be everywhere, behind trees and rocks and fences, concealed in barns and outbuildings on both sides of the road. Battery B came up, unlimbered, and put "several splendid shots" into the upper story of a house, "causing a general stampede of their forces from that point," as the colonel of the 19th Indiana described it. Colquitt's guns up on the ridgeline opened fire, one shell striking in the midst of the 2nd Wisconsin and killing or wounding seven men. General Gibbon, wrote Major Rufus Dawes of the 6th Wisconsin, was "always on the highest ground, where he could see the whole line, giving his orders in a voice so loud and clear as to be heard throughout."

Gibbon pushed his men on doggedly until they reached Colquitt's main line, deployed securely behind stone walls on the high ground ahead. As the Yankees maneuvered into line of battle the Georgians began taunting them: "Oh you damned black hats, we gave you hell at Bull Run!" One of Gibbon's boys yelled back, "You thieving scoundrels, no McDowell after you now!" and then the heavy volleys drowned out the shouting.

Burnside had given Gibbon nowhere nearly enough strength either to break through this solid position or to turn it, and the Yankees could do no more than hold their ground and keep up the firefight. It was growing dark now, and at McClellan's headquarters in the valley one of the staff officers thought it looked as if the mountainside was lit by thousands of fireflies, with the artillery adding flashes of lightning. Finally it grew too dark to see anything to shoot at, and both Gibbon's and Colquitt's men, almost out of ammunition, stayed where they were with bayonets fixed. The firing flickered out all along the mountaintop, and in the sudden silence the cries of the wounded could be heard.[32]

Fortune had smiled on D. H. Hill in the long day's struggle for

Fire on the Mountain 143

Turner's Gap. When he was slow getting all his troops into action, Reno and Burnside were even slower; when he had no one to defend his northern flank, McClellan had no one in position to attack it. The Federals lost just over 1,800 men, the Confederates perhaps 2,300. Lee met with Longstreet and Hill and agreed that they would have to abandon Turner's before daylight. But what they had gained was just then more important — time. McClellan was content with the outcome. "It has been a glorious victory," he telegraphed Washington.[33]

For the garrison at Harper's Ferry, that Sunday began peacefully enough but with a sense of foreboding. The Yankees were on alert in their rifle pits, and the batteries were manned for any assault that Jackson might attempt, but he made no immediately threatening moves. On paper, the opposing forces were evenly matched: if it came to an infantry struggle for Bolivar Heights or an attempted breakout to the west, Jackson and Miles could count about the same number of troops, and each side had just over seventy artillery pieces. But that was on paper. There was no comparison in quality between Jackson's veterans and Miles's green regiments; the fearsome reputation of Stonewall Jackson was by itself worth at least a division; and the Rebel gunners had all the advantages of the high ground on Maryland Heights and Loudoun Heights.

In any case, Dixon Miles had it fixed in his mind that his orders to hold Harper's Ferry meant literally that. The evening before, when one of his officers suggested they abandon the town and try to recapture Maryland Heights, Miles rejected the idea out of hand. "I am ordered by General Wool to hold this place," he insisted, "and God damn my soul to hell if I don't hold it against the enemy." Colonel Miles was not giving thought to breaking out in any direction.

Unaware of events to the north at Turner's Gap, Jackson was in a deliberate frame of mind that day, planning a big-gun assault on the garrison with all the skills of a former professor of artillery tactics. Although he had exasperating problems communicating with Generals Walker and McLaws by flag signals, the work of placing the batteries went on without delay. By afternoon he had seized ground from which to enfilade Bolivar Heights. Federal resistance was feeble. On Loudoun Heights, Walker had five rifled pieces in place by noon and in range of any target around and within Harper's Ferry.

McLaws once again had the most difficult job. The rough track along the ridgeline of Elk Mountain that the Rebels had used in their attack on Maryland Heights could not accommodate artillery, so he put everybody to work hacking a path up the mountainside from Pleasant Valley. Ropes were tied to fieldpieces and as many as 200 men assigned the task of dragging each one up to the crest. Not long after Walker announced his readiness to open fire, McLaws had four guns sighted on the Federal defenses below.[34]

To achieve maximum effect it was Jackson's intention to open fire from all the encircling guns simultaneously, but at 1 P.M. the Federals spotted Walker's battery on Loudoun Heights and began shelling it. Walker returned the fire, and a short time later McLaws's guns on Maryland Heights and some of Jackson's joined in. "Their shells at first fell far wide of the mark and we laughed at them," a Yankee cavalryman in the garrison recalled, "but they soon got the range and plumped shell after shell among us, killing a few horses and causing a rush for cover."

This was the first time most of these Federals had ever been under fire, and whether or not the shells hit their targets, the overall effect was terrifying. "The *infernal screech owls* came hissing and singing, then bursting, plowing great holes in the earth, filling our eyes with dust, and tearing many giant trees to atoms," one of the men wrote. The Yankee gunners returned fire gamely, but hitting anything high up on the crest of Loudoun Heights involved more luck than gunnery science, and Walker suffered only four casualties. The battery on Maryland Heights was out of their reach entirely. The cannonade continued after nightfall, creating a spectacular show of deadly fireworks that further demoralized the garrison. Under cover of darkness, Jackson moved up batteries to within a thousand yards of the Bolivar Heights defenses and placed to take them in flank and rear.[35]

From the beginning of the operation against Harper's Ferry, Lafayette McLaws consistently faced the most difficult assignments. He was a short, square-built Georgian with a full curling beard and a careful, conscientious military mind. He had seized

Maryland Heights and found a way to put a battery on the crest with commendable dispatch, meanwhile shutting off the eastern exit from Harper's Ferry. He also posted the various roads and passes leading into Pleasant Valley in his rear, well aware of his vulnerability until Harper's Ferry should fall. Beginning about noon on the fourteenth, McLaws confronted his greatest challenge yet, one that grew rapidly into a full-blown crisis.

In addition to the Crampton's Gap road, a second road crossed South Mountain into Pleasant Valley through Brownsville Gap, not quite two miles to the south. These roads forked left and right from the village of Burkittsville at the eastern foot of the mountain. McLaws had two brigades watching the passes, and that morning Jeb Stuart dropped off two regiments of cavalry and a battery of horse artillery under Thomas Munford to support the infantry. Scouting reports, and perhaps the arrival of Lee's warning dispatch sent the night before from Hagerstown, persuaded McLaws to order Howell Cobb's brigade to march back to Crampton's to stiffen the defenses further. He felt no particular sense of alarm. Three of his ten brigades and Munford's cavalry were on guard, and he was reassured when Stuart arrived at 2 P.M. with a report that Federals he had seen in Burkittsville appeared to be in only single-brigade strength.

The usually reliable Stuart was either off his form or suffering a patch of bad luck. The afternoon before, he had assured Harvey Hill that there were but two brigades of Yankees around Middletown, and then left Turner's Gap before the bulk of the Ninth Corps appeared on the scene in late afternoon and early evening. This morning, he left Crampton's Gap without waiting to find out what might be behind that single enemy brigade. What he missed seeing was William Franklin's Sixth Corps.

In obedience to McClellan's orders, Franklin had broken camp at Buckeystown early that morning and put his two divisions on the road by 6 A.M. At midmorning, in the village of Jefferson, he paused to wait for Darius Couch's attached division, which was supposed to be coming up from the south to join him, but Couch never appeared. (General Couch's activities that day are something of a mystery; he did not catch up until ten that night, despite repeated messages from Franklin to speed his march.) Franklin pressed on for Burkittsville, arriving about noon. As his advance units chased Rebel cavalry pickets out of the town, enemy batteries on the slopes ahead began shelling his columns. Franklin turned his men off into the fields to rest for an hour and a half while he pondered the situation.[36]

Off to the left, the Brownsville Gap road slanted across South Mountain on a long diagonal to the village of Brownsville in Pleasant Valley, a half-dozen miles from Harper's Ferry. To the right, the Crampton's Gap road followed a northerly course up the mountainside before turning west to cross the pass. Below this road and running parallel to it was a second road serving a succession of farms laid out along the base of the mountain, and along this farm road was a stone fence that Franklin's skirmishers soon discovered sheltered a Confederate battle line. On both the Brownsville and Crampton's Gap roads, halfway up the mountain, enemy batteries continued their show of defiance.

In his orders to Franklin, General McClellan had asked of him his best efforts of intellect and activity but omitted any summons to act with all speed. Franklin had much to consider. As well as seizing Crampton's Gap, cutting off McLaws's command, and relieving Harper's Ferry, he had as a fourth objective the village of Rohrersville, located in Pleasant Valley a mile and a half or so to the north of Crampton's. Rohrersville was important militarily, for it lay near the mouth of Pleasant Valley from where roads led north to Boonsboro and west to Sharpsburg and the Potomac crossing. The shortest route to Rohrersville was through Crampton's Gap; McClellan had said nothing in his orders about Brownsville Gap; and initiative did not come easily to William Franklin. He put the Brownsville road out of his mind — along with its flanking opportunities — and let the hours slip by as he focused his intellect and activity on the problem of seizing Crampton's Gap.

Franklin had 12,300 men under command in the divisions of Henry W. Slocum and William F. "Baldy" Smith, all seasoned veterans of the Peninsula fighting. Confronting them across open pastures and fields of corn were three slim Virginia regiments under Colonel William Parham and Colonel Munford's two regiments of dismounted cavalrymen, who had sent their horses back up the mountain for safekeeping. A regiment of Georgians soon hurried over the mountain from a posting in Pleasant Valley to join in the defense. There were in all fewer than a thousand men. Up on the Crampton's Gap road behind them was Munford's horse artillery, with two rifled guns that were effective enough but also several little naval howitzers that proved too short-ranged to be of much use. There was a battery to the south on the Brownsville road within range of the contest, and in Pleasant Valley Cobb's brigade was on the march but could not arrive until late afternoon. That was all, and, like D. H. Hill a half-dozen miles to the north at Turner's Gap, these Rebels felt exceedingly lonely. One of Munford's artillerists later wrote that there were Yankees as far as he could see, "so numerous that it looked as if they were creeping up out of the ground."[37]

Shortly after 2 P.M. Slocum's division was deployed in line of battle facing the stone wall, and the firing grew rapid as the Yankees took what shelter they could find and exchanged volleys with the well-protected enemy. Two of Baldy Smith's brigades were placed off to the left, watching the Brownsville road and waiting to exploit whatever gains Slocum's men might make; Smith's third brigade was in reserve a mile or so to the rear. Franklin was in communication by flag signal with McClellan, who told him that if he should encounter the enemy "in very great force at any of these passes let me know at once, and amuse them as best you can so as to retain them there." By this time Franklin had devoted a good three hours to assessing the situation and calculating the strength of the enemy, and he came to the conclusion that he was stalled for the day and in need of reinforcement.

In his reply to McClellan written at 3:20 P.M., Franklin reported, "I have been severely engaged with the enemy for the last hour. I have two brigades in action with musketry & two others just going in. Of course I have no troops but my reserves, and Gen. Couch has not come up. I have sent to hurry him. The force of the enemy is too great for us to take the pass to-night, I am afraid. Shall await further orders here & shall attack again in the morning without further orders."[38]

Franklin's astonishingly myopic view of the situation was apparently not shared by Slocum and his officers, and at about 4 P.M., impatient with the stalemate, they massed their regiments for a head-on charge. With a yell the Yankees went rushing through the corn and across the stubbled fields, clambering over fences and pausing to realign their formations, then driving on. Parham's infantry and Munford's troopers fired as fast as they could, but it was plain to every one of them that they were about to be overwhelmed by a blue wave. Before it reached them they turned and ran for the woods behind them and scrambled up the steep mountainside, dropping knapsacks and canteens and everything else that would slow them down.

The race for the crest was on, but some of the Rebels went stubbornly, pausing to get off a shot or two at their pursuers. "I can safely say that I brought one fellow down, sure, that day," Confederate John Sale wrote his family. "I was behind a tree . . . and when they charged us I loaded my gun and took aim at an officer who was as large as Pa, and who was behaving very bravely bringing his men up cheering and talking to them all the while. I waited until they were about 75 or 100 yds from where I was. I let fly at him and he threw his arms up in the air and fell. . . ."[39]

Howell Cobb's two leading regiments arrived on the scene only in time to be caught up in the rush for the rear. There was a brief stand at the crest of the pass, but Cobb's remaining troops did not get into position promptly and, in Colonel Munford's opinion, "behaved badly." Slocum's men were on them relentlessly, supported now by one of Baldy Smith's brigades, and the Rebels broke again, this time in such disorder and confusion that they lost an artillery piece. Cobb and his officers tried desperately to rally the fugitives, with the general waving a regimental flag as a rallying point until the flagstaff was shot out of his hand, but the men streamed past unheeding and raced down the mountainside toward Pleasant Valley. They reminded the disgusted Munford of a flock of frightened sheep.

Back on Maryland Heights the rising sound of the battle had alerted McLaws to the crisis, and with Stuart he was hurrying toward Crampton's for a firsthand look. On the way he encountered a courier carrying a plea for reinforcements, and he sent back for another of his brigades. Before long the party came upon a distraught General Cobb. Cobb's background was far more political than military — indeed, he could be considered the highest-ranking political figure in the Confederate service — and he was plainly beyond his depth. The enemy was close on his heels, he cried. "That I should live to experience such a disaster! What can

Fire on the Mountain 149

be done? What can save us?" Stuart sent one of his staff galloping ahead to find out what was happening, and he returned to report that the Federals were halted on the mountaintop.

By now the survivors from Crampton's had outrun their panic, there were some fresh troops at hand, and a battle line was patched together stretching across Pleasant Valley about a mile and a half south of Crampton's. It was not much of a line, but it proved to be enough for the moment. General Franklin took a look and decided that it was too much to ask of his troops to keep up the attack. In any case, it was getting late, and enough had been done for one day. Crampton's Gap, the first of the four objectives, was his.[40]

Certainly his troops were well satisfied with their afternoon's work. The charge on the stone wall and the pursuit up the mountainside had been a rare and exhilarating experience. The service of some of Slocum's veterans went back to First Bull Run, and this was the first time they had ever seen their enemy in a rout; it was a moment to savor. They had taken four Confederate battle flags, and there were any number of abandoned knapsacks and other possessions to pick over. Opportunists in the 4th New Jersey went over the field collecting good rifled Springfields to replace their antiquated smoothbore muskets, and their colonel reported with pride that his whole command was thus re-equipped, at no cost to the government.

Federal losses in the fight for Crampton's Gap totaled 531, nearly all of them from Slocum's division. Except for supporting the final stages of the rout, Baldy Smith's men had been spectators, losing just 1 man killed and 18 wounded. The Confederate losses in killed and wounded were probably about equal to the Federals', but they also had 400 men taken prisoner.[41]

The management of General Franklin's battle was strikingly similar to McClellan's handling of the fight for Turner's Gap — the same glacial pace, the same fumbled opportunities, the same satisfaction with limited achievement. South Mountain was won, to be sure, but won half a day too late. The Army of Northern Virginia remained alive and dangerous to fight another day.

· 5 ·

WE WILL MAKE OUR STAND

For a few hours on the evening of September 14, 1862, it appeared that General McClellan, almost in spite of himself, had achieved his hope of delivering Maryland from the Confederate invaders. Even before learning of the setback at Crampton's Gap, General Lee decided not to risk another battle north of the Potomac.

Whatever had so abruptly impelled McClellan to attack the South Mountain passes, Lee was forced to acknowledge that it was a highly effective tactic; the Federals had captured the initiative and put the Army of Northern Virginia in peril. The campaign seemed to be in ruins, and he must now work with all speed to get the commands of McLaws, D. H. Hill, and Longstreet back across the river and reunited with the rest of the army. At eight that Sunday night a dispatch went by courier to McLaws. "The day has gone against us and this army will go by Sharpsburg to cross the river," it read. McLaws was to abandon his position immediately and find some way to return to Virginia. Hill and Longstreet would pull their troops quietly out of Turner's Gap during the night and march for Sharpsburg and the nearby Potomac crossing at Shepherdstown.

Then the pendulum swung back. A dispatch from Jackson suddenly brightened the dull prospect of confessing the Maryland expedition a failure. "Through God's blessing, the advance, which commenced this evening, has been successful thus far, and I look to Him for complete success to-morrow," Jackson wrote. "The advance has been directed to be resumed at dawn...." Should Harper's Ferry be taken the next day, as Jackson was promising, the situation might yet be retrieved. Fresh orders went out to McLaws: he was now to make his best effort to join the army north of the Potomac, at Sharpsburg, whether he had to detour back into Virginia, or even find a way across Maryland Heights, to do so. Hill and Longstreet would continue on toward Sharpsburg. As a precaution, part of the reserve artillery was ordered to post the Virginia side of the Potomac fords to furnish covering fire if a retreat became necessary after all. But Robert E. Lee was now thinking aggressively again, looking to follow up the capture of Harper's Ferry with a challenge to his opponent to give battle on Northern soil.[1]

Of all the Federals penned up in Harper's Ferry that Sunday, the 1,300 cavalrymen were probably the most restive. An artillery siege was no place for them; they could contribute little to the defense, and they discovered that trying to protect their horses from the shelling was both thankless and dangerous. Colonel Benjamin Franklin Davis of the 8th New York cavalry determined to do something about it, and he went to Colonel Miles with a plan for a breakout that night. "Grimes" Davis was a Mississippian, a hard-bitten veteran of Indian fighting on the frontier, and to him any escape attempt, even if it meant a bloody running fight with the Rebels, was preferable to staying where they were and suffering the humiliation of surrender, along with all their mounts and equipment. The two men got into a hot argument about it, but when Davis made it plain that the cavalry would go with or without Miles's consent, the garrison commander gave in. Some of the infantry and artillery officers heard about the scheme and wanted their units to join in, but Miles insisted that Harper's Ferry had to be held to the last cartridge and artillery round and sent them back to the lines.

Davis recruited two local men to act as scouts. The line of march they chose would take them across the Harper's Ferry pontoon bridge spanning the Potomac, swing west around the base of Maryland Heights, then north on an obscure winding road that ran between the river and Elk Mountain toward Sharpsburg. When it grew dark the troopers saddled up and set off, Davis and the scouts in the lead. It was a pitch-black night; often they were guided only by sparks struck by the horses' shoes on the rocky road. Once across the river Davis picked up the pace, and by the time the last horseman trotted over the bridge the column was strung out over ten miles. One Confederate picket post was overrun and scattered, and another was evaded by going cross-lots. Whenever a horse gave out, the rider doubled up with a comrade and the column kept moving.

It was a clean breakout, blessed with a touch of good fortune. This happened to be the same road old John Brown had taken when he descended on Harper's Ferry back in 1859 to incite the slaves to rise, and Jeb Stuart, who was then a lieutenant in the U.S. 1st Cavalry and helped to capture Brown, knew it well. He had cautioned McLaws that afternoon to make sure it was blocked securely to prevent any Yankees from getting away. But then came Franklin's attack at Crampton's Gap, and McLaws had all he could handle and more, and Stuart's warning slipped his mind.

The column pushed along steadily through the night, detoured around Sharpsburg, and shortly before dawn reached the turnpike linking Williamsport, on the upper Potomac, with Hagerstown. Just then a Rebel wagon train was detected approaching from the direction of Hagerstown. As the lead wagon reached him, Davis called up his rich Mississippi accent and ordered the driver to take the next turning; there was enemy cavalry up ahead, he said. The turning was made smoothly, each wagon following obediently, and by the time it was light enough for the sleepy teamsters to suspect anything they found an escort of Yankee cavalrymen riding alongside with pistols cocked. The 12th Illinois brought up the rear, fending off the Rebel cavalry escort that discovered too late that the train it was supposed to be guarding was headed off to the north. By nine that morning Grimes Davis and his troopers were in Greencastle, Pennsylvania, proudly displaying General Longstreet's forty-wagon reserve ordnance train. Governor Curtin hastened to telegraph news of the bold exploit to Secretary of War Stanton, but ended his wire on a sobering note: "Colonel Davis says he thinks Colonel Miles will surrender this morning."[2]

Break of day that Monday morning, September 15, revealed a shrouding mist over Harper's Ferry. Almost immediately the quiet was shattered by a tremendous bombardment, the thunder of the guns reverberating through the valleys. The Rebel batteries on Maryland Heights and Loudoun Heights poured in shells from above, but the heaviest and most destructive cannonading came from Jackson's guns taking the Federal lines on Bolivar Heights under fire from front, flank, and rear. The return fire was erratic and ineffective, and sputtered out shortly before eight o'clock. Jackson's infantry was preparing to storm the works when a horseman appeared within the lines, waving a white flag.

Confederate officers quickly called for a cease-fire, but it took time for the word to reach all the batteries and not everyone could see the white flag in the drifting mist and battle smoke, and scattered shelling continued for some minutes. One battery commander sent word that his guns were still loaded; what should he do? "Tell him to fire them off the way they are pointed," Colonel Andrew J. Grigsby of the Stonewall Brigade replied. "He won't kill more of the damn Yankees than he ought to!" As the firing died down, Colonel Miles stood talking with his aide. "Well, Mr. Binney," he said, "we have done our duty, but where can McClellan be?" Just then one of these final shots struck nearby, tearing a great wound in Miles's leg. He died the next day, a commander who had foundered haplessly in a situation far beyond his depth.

Brigadier White, wearing his best dress uniform and mounted on a handsome black horse, rode out to meet Jackson and complete the formalities of surrender. White, wrote Old Jack's aide, Kyd Douglas, "must have been somewhat astonished to find in General Jackson the worst dressed, worst mounted, most faded and dingy looking general he had ever seen anyone surrender to." The Federals were to be paroled, Jackson directed, with their officers allowed to keep side arms and baggage. The total count of prisoners came to just over 11,500. Captured materiel included 13,000 small arms, some 200 wagons, abundant supplies, and, most important, 73 pieces of artillery. Casualties in the siege were about 200 on each side, mostly in the fight for Maryland Heights. The only Rebels unhappy with the outcome were the cavalrymen, who had looked forward to resupplying themselves with fresh mounts and new equipment. The breakout by Grimes Davis, one of Stuart's men wrote, "was enough to vex a saint."[3]

Jackson was quick to send a courier off to Lee with the news. "Through God's blessing, Harper's Ferry and its garrison are to be surrendered," he wrote. A. P. Hill's division would remain to handle details of the surrender and to see the booty safely off to Richmond; "The other forces can move off this evening so soon as they get their rations."

Needy Rebels were soon pawing through the Federal supply depots and sutlers' wagons for anything to eat and wear. By the time the troops from Maryland Heights and Loudoun Heights reached the town it was picked clean, a circumstance greeted with considerable bitterness; they had done all the fighting, they claimed, and Jackson's men had got all the plunder. Regiments armed with old smoothbores were re-equipped with new rifled Springfields, and a draft of conscripts was finally issued rifles after having marched unarmed all over Maryland. Altogether it was a notable occasion, and Heros Von Borcke, the Prussian soldier of fortune serving on Stuart's staff, congratulated Jackson on his success. "Ah, this is all very well, Major," Jackson replied, "but we have yet much hard work before us."

Later that morning, Jackson rode into Harper's Ferry to supervise the movement of his forces. Federals lined the roadside, eager for a glimpse of the famous Stonewall. "Boys," one of them observed after he rode past, "he isn't much for looks, but if we'd had him we wouldn't have been caught in this trap," and there was general agreement to the truth of that. A *New York Times* correspondent, however, was singularly unimpressed with everything he saw of the conquering army and its commander. Jackson, he wrote, "was dressed in the coarsest kind of homespun, seedy and dirty at that; wore an old hat which any Northern beggar would consider an insult to have offered him, and in general appearance was in no respect to be distinguished from the mongrel, barefooted crew who follow his fortunes . . . and yet they glory in their shame." The Rebels he talked to were cheerful and confident, joking about all the "On to Richmond" talk in the Northern papers and derisive of McClellan's skill at changing his base. "Cincinnati is ours," one of them boasted, "and so will Washington soon be."[4]

A few miles away at Crampton's Gap, General Franklin had received his orders for the day before dawn. McClellan directed him to seize control of Pleasant Valley, "attacking and destroying such of the enemy as you may find"; to press on to relieve Harper's Ferry; then to move north to Boonsboro where the rest of the army expected to be fighting. Should the enemy flee Boonsboro, he

We Will Make Our Stand

was to turn toward Sharpsburg "to fall upon him and cut off his retreat." But there was an important caution to all this. Franklin must place sufficient force at Rohrersville in case the enemy somehow got loose from McClellan's grip and came pouring into Pleasant Valley to fall on the Sixth Corps's rear. General Franklin, in short, had a good deal to think about.

He began early to get his three divisions — Couch was on hand at last — down off the mountaintop and into Pleasant Valley. The cannonading from the direction of Harper's Ferry was easily heard. A few minutes before 9 A.M. Franklin sent McClellan a situation report. It was written by a general in an advanced stage of perplexity.

Two miles to the south, he reported, the Confederates were drawn up in line of battle across the valley, and as soon as one of Couch's brigades and a battery of artillery reached Rohrersville to guard his rear — that would take another two hours — he would be ready to attack. But it was beginning to seem to him that the hunter might become the hunted. "If Harper's Ferry has fallen — and the cessation of firing makes me fear that it has — it is my opinion that I should be strongly re-enforced." Already Franklin had to worry that the enemy might attack him from the north; with Harper's Ferry in Rebel hands, their forces there would be freed to attack him from the south as well. McClellan's reply did nothing to galvanize him into action: "It is important to drive in the enemy in your front, but be cautious in doing it until you have some idea of his force.... Thus far our success is complete, but let us follow it up closely, but warily."[5]

The force confronting Franklin was the best that McLaws could scrape up — six brigades, in whole or in part, including what was left of the Crampton's Gap defenders, some 5,000 men in all. There were almost four times that many Federals on the field, but only Baldy Smith's division was positioned to go into action. Franklin considered Slocum's division, which had suffered 500 casualties the day before, unfit to fight again so soon; the balance of Couch's division was also put in reserve. Not long after Franklin sent off his situation report, the incongruous sound of cheering came rolling down Pleasant Valley from the direction of Harper's Ferry. Then the men in McLaws's battle line began cheering too. One of the Yankees climbed up on a stone wall and shouted,

"What the hell are you fellows cheering for?" A Rebel yelled back, "Because Harper's Ferry is gone up, God damn you!" "I thought that was it," the Yankee said in disgust as he jumped down from the wall.

This news was enough to induce a final paralysis of will on Franklin's part. His 11 A.M. report included the information that "They outnumber me two to one. It will of course not answer to pursue the enemy under these circumstances." At 3 P.M. his tale of stalemate was the same, with the addition of the remarkable postscript that Baldy Smith had just reported the enemy withdrawing up the valley "too fast for him." Thus Lafayette McLaws marched into captured Harper's Ferry with his entire command while the Federals watched quietly from a distance. With the exception of the winning of Crampton's Gap — in which Slocum's veterans demonstrated their physical courage to be greater than their corps commander's mental courage — the offensive of the Sixth Corps had come up empty of military profit.[6]

During these early morning hours of September 15, while the Harper's Ferry garrison was being bombarded into submission and a bemused General Franklin idled away his time in Pleasant Valley, in Turner's Gap and on the roads to the west the Army of the Potomac was on the march. At first light Federal pickets advancing cautiously on the mountaintop discovered that the enemy had slipped away in the darkness. Orders for a pursuit were issued, the First, Second, and Twelfth corps to use the National Road, the Ninth and Sykes's division of the Fifth Corps to follow the Old Sharpsburg Road through Fox's Gap.

These routes took the troops past the positions held by the Confederates in the previous day's fighting. It was a rare look at a field abandoned by the enemy, and many men recorded their impressions in journals and letters home. "I awoke about five o'clock on the battle-field of yesterday and went out to see what war was without romance," a sergeant in the 14th Connecticut, one of the new regiments, wrote his family. "I cannot describe my feelings, but I hope to God never to see the like again." Lieutenant George Washington Whitman, the poet's younger brother, wrote his mother that "in some parts of the field the enemys dead lay in heaps and in a road for nearly a quarter of a mile they lay so thick that I had to pick my way carefully to avoid stepping on them."

Some felt a morbid curiosity to look on the faces of the dead. "They had a portion of blanket — or some covering over their face," one man wrote in his journal; "removing this, sometimes you were surprised by a smile yet on the cold features and then horrified by some ghastly wound, and the look of agony, fear still to be seen.... It was a sad sight, and in the woods they could be counted by hundreds." Burial details were put to work, and at Fox's Gap one party hit on the laborsaving scheme of throwing the bodies down farmer Wise's well. Wise, seeing that his well was ruined, made the best of a bad bargain. He arranged to take over the job for a dollar a body, and before the day was out had filled his well, sealed it, and earned himself sixty dollars.[7]

General McClellan remained at his headquarters east of the mountain, reading and sending dispatches. It was not his habit to lead or observe from up front, leaving that to his lieutenants — indeed, he had never been on the field when his army went into a major action — and in any case it appeared that the enemy was now in full flight, heading for safety across the Potomac. "Some citizens from Boonsboro are just in & report to me that the rebel army is in a perfect panic," Joe Hooker reported. "... They tell me that Lee said publicly last night that they must admit that they had been shockingly whipped.... You may be assured that they are heading for the Potomac fords and Williamsport as rapidly as possible." Captain George Armstrong Custer of McClellan's staff was with the First Corps, and he too had been interrogating civilians. "Gen. Lee (Rebel) is wounded and Garland killed," he told headquarters. "Lee reports he lost fifteen thousand men yesterday. Gen. Hooker says the rebel army is completely demoralized. The rebels are moving towards Shepherdstown. Boonsboro is full of rebel stragglers.... Everything is as we wish."

Joe Hooker was in fine form, cheerful and full of confidence. As his men marched through Turner's Gap, one of them saw him "in the saddle taking his brandy and water, looking as clean and trim as though he had just made his morning toilet at Willard's." The cavalry was out front, scooping up stragglers. There was a rear guard of Confederate troopers putting up a stiff fight to delay the pursuit, but all the prospects looked good. He told Custer "to inform the General that we can capture the entire rebel army."[8]

McClellan promptly telegraphed all this good news in full detail to Washington. "I am hurrying everything forward to endeavor to press their retreat to the utmost," he assured General Halleck, adding that "the *morale* of our men is now restored." He telegraphed his wife, "Have just learned that the enemy are retreating in a panic and that our victory is complete," and followed up his wire with a letter. "How glad I am for my country that it is delivered from immediate peril!" he wrote. " . . . If I can believe one-tenth of what is reported, God has seldom given an army a greater victory than this." President Lincoln was at the War Department following events closely. "Your dispatch of to-day received," he wired his general. "God bless you, and all with you; destroy the rebel army if possible."

Navy Secretary Gideon Welles also read McClellan's telegrams reporting Lee's confession that he had lost 15,000 men and been "shockingly whipped." In his diary he remarked that the whole business sounded suspiciously familiar: "A tale like this from Pope would have been classed as one of his lies." While he did not doubt there had been a victory at South Mountain, he wrote, "I am afraid it is not as decisive as it should be, and as is the current belief. I shall rejoice if McC. has actually overtaken the Rebels which is not altogether clear."[9]

In fact some of the euphoria was beginning to wear off at Army of the Potomac headquarters. By midday word arrived that perhaps the triumph was not quite so signal as it had first seemed and that the country was not yet delivered from its peril. At 12:40 there was a report from an observation post near Turner's Gap: "A line of battle — or an arrangement of troops which looks very much like it — is formed on the other side of Antietam creek and this side of Sharpsburg. It is four times longer on the west than on the east side of the road. . . . " A message arrived from Captain Custer confirming the report. "They are in full view," Custer wrote. "Their line is a perfect one about a mile and a half long. We can have equally good position as they now occupy. . . . We can employ all the troops you can send us." The Young Napoleon decided it was time for him to go to the front.[10]

The Army of the Potomac was in high spirits that morning. For the first time in its history it had a victory that put the Rebels on the run, and no one was minding the hot and dusty marching very much. Rumors ran through the ranks that such famous Confederate generals as Lee and Longstreet and D. H. Hill were dead or wounded. As they tramped along they passed captured Rebel stragglers being herded to the rear, and a man in the new 130th Pennsylvania called out to one of these groups to ask if there were any more Rebels left. A Southerner fixed the brash rookie with a hard look and assured him that soon enough he would encounter all the Rebels he ever cared to see.

The passage through Boonsboro was a triumph, with good Unionists lining the streets to cheer and wave flags. A "respectable old gentleman" came up to Major Rufus Dawes of the 6th Wisconsin and exclaimed, "We have watched for you, Sir, and we have prayed for you and now thank God you have come!" So when General McClellan came cantering past on Dan Webster, the troops were ready to cheer him to the echo. "The welcome that he Received from his ole Army of the Potomac must have done his heart good," a man in Sumner's corps wrote in his journal. "God bless General Mc Clellan. Long may he lead...."[11]

Two miles beyond the village of Keedysville, McClellan caught up with the troops of the advance — Israel B. Richardson's division of the Second Corps and Sykes's regulars under Fitz John Porter — deployed to the right and left of the turnpike running from Boonsboro to Sharpsburg, awaiting futher orders. The First Corps and the rest of the Second Corps were halted along the road to the rear, also awaiting instructions. Ahead was Antietam Creek, and beyond the creek valley was the Rebel army, no longer retreating but instead arrayed in line of battle.

It was not until 3 P.M. that McClellan, with his staff and generals, began what he described as a "rapid examination" of the Confederate position. When the large party attracted the attention of a Rebel battery, the order was given to disperse, and McClellan and his confidant Porter continued the reconnaissance alone. What they discussed is not on record. In his official report McClellan said only, "I found that it was too late to attack that day...."[12]

Nothing much in the way of hard marching had ever been demanded of the Army of the Potomac, and nothing much was demanded of it that September 15. Sharpsburg is hardly eight miles from Turner's Gap, yet beyond skirmishing with a cavalry rear guard and collecting several hundred footsore stragglers, the army passed the day without further event. Until midday McClellan had remained at headquarters far to the rear, basking in the reflected glory of his army's first offensive victory over the foe since he had assumed command, satisfied to leave it to his lieutenants to see the panicked Rebels off in their flight from Northern soil. Then General Lee once again did the unexpected and turned to offer battle.

George McClellan was invariably nonplussed by the unexpected. He had fallen victim to bluff before Yorktown on the Peninsula and again before Richmond during the Seven Days. Now he was confronted with a bluff that he could calculate was just that, thanks to the Lost Order. Even counting by his own inflated arithmetic, he knew the force before him, after the fight at Turner's Gap, could not be much more than 25,000 men (or only about 15,000 if he credited the new intelligence reports from Hooker and Custer). He knew it was beyond immediate help from the commands of Jackson, Walker, McLaws, and Anderson still at Harper's Ferry, which Franklin reported had surrendered only that morning. By all logic, he should be seeing a mere rear guard, left behind to protect the main body as it hurried to get across the Potomac.

Yet there was General Lee, standing defiantly and in apparent force on the far side of Antietam Creek, his guns taking aim at any Federals who showed themselves. It was a surprising development, the sort of thing to prompt pangs of self-doubt and to require careful further study and perhaps recalculation. It was his intention, McClellan told Franklin at 4:30 that afternoon, "to concentrate everything this evening on the force at or near Sharpsburg"; the Sixth Corps should "keep the enemy in your front without anything decisive until the Sharpsburg affair is settled...."[13] Tomorrow — it was always tomorrow — would be soon enough for a next step. Meanwhile, there were batteries to place and bivouacs to assign and supplies to bring up, all the administrative chores the general commanding liked to supervise personally.

By Lee's reckoning, bluff worked well against McClellan, and he employed it that day with a certain cool contempt for his opponent's military competence. When they reached Sharpsburg Longstreet told his battery commanders, "Put them all in, every gun you have, long range and short range." The gunners kept up a

We Will Make Our Stand

harassing fire, and the infantry was ordered to spread out along a wide front. There was no knowing what had caused McClellan to take the offensive so suddenly (Stonewall Jackson was as mystified as Lee, remarking, "I thought I knew McClellan, but this movement of his puzzles me"), but to Lee it looked out of character. Before admitting he had made an error in judgment, he was going to put his conviction that his opponent was the most timid of generals to the test once more.

At the moment there was hardly any strength behind his bluff. Lee had with him, including artillery and cavalry, perhaps 15,000 men. Twenty-six of the army's forty brigades were still at Harper's Ferry, a hard day's march by the most direct roads. At about noon the arrival of Jackson's courier confirmed Lee in his decision to brazen it out against the pursuing Federals. He had the news of the capture of Harper's Ferry announced to the troops, providing a much-needed boost to morale. Most important, the surrender meant that Jackson and a good part of the army ought to be up the next day. Unless McClellan called the bluff and pressed him too hard that afternoon, he would remain where he was. Here on these hills, he told his officers, "We will make our stand...."[14]

To be sure, there was more to his decision to stand at Sharpsburg than simply a low opinion of the opposing general. Robert E. Lee was supremely confident of his own abilities and judgments. He found it intolerable to see his ambitious campaign end in ignominious retreat, with only the capture of the Harper's Ferry garrison and its arms as compensation. Too much was at stake to accept such an outcome with equanimity. Surely the country would not think well of it, or of him. Furthermore, Lee had confidence in the ability of his men to beat just about any number of Yankees; a few days earlier he had told Jefferson Davis they were "the best in the world."[15] He had marched north primarily to fight and win a battle he believed would be decisive for the Confederacy, and if Sharpsburg did not promise the contest of thrust and maneuver he would have preferred, he would fight defensively instead. Indeed, for an army so weakened by illness and straggling, that might now be the better choice. What counted was the battle, and the winning.

That afternoon he was on high ground along the Boonsboro turnpike studying the Federal positions across the Antietam when

Stuart arrived with more details of the surrender of Harper's Ferry and the stores and munitions captured. "General, did they have many shoes?" Lee wanted to know. "These good men are barefoot." His good men were also hungry. The troops were happy enough to learn that Harper's Ferry had fallen and that the army was to be reunited, but their more immediate interest was finding something to eat. They were chewing straws, one of Longstreet's men wrote, "merely to keep their jaws from rusting and stiffening entirely."

The commissary trains had taken roundabout routes during the withdrawal and were not yet on the scene, so details went about collecting pumpkins and apples and green corn and anything else they could find. "They nearly worried us to death asking for something to eat," a Sharpsburg woman remembered. "They were half famished and they looked like tramps...." A company of the 27th Georgia, one of D. H. Hill's regiments, made camp near a farmhouse whose residents had fled at the first sight of the arriving armies. An exploration of the pantry turned up no food, but in the cellar they discovered several barrels of prime hard cider. Eagerly they knocked off the barrel heads and dipped in their tin cups, Captain Ben Milliken recalled, and "drank until some of them was drunk or very near it. I know I was the drunkest I ever was. It was all I could do to get up the hill to camp."[16]

A heavy mist lay in the valleys and hollows around Sharpsburg at dawn on Tuesday, September 16. McClellan was quick to strike a note of confidence. At 7 A.M. he wired his wife, "Have reached thus far and have no doubt delivered Penna. and Maryland. Am well and in excellent spirits." At the same hour he sent a situation report to General Halleck in Washington: "This morning a heavy fog has thus far prevented us doing more than to ascertain that some of the enemy are still there. Do not know in what force. Will attack as soon as situation of enemy is developed." A scout reported that the Rebels at Harper's Ferry were rapidly crossing the Potomac into Virginia, he informed General Franklin in Pleasant Valley forty-five minutes later. "I think the enemy has abandoned the position in front of us, but the fog is too dense that I have not yet been enabled to determine. If the enemy is in force here, I shall attack him this morning."[17]

These were empty promises. Only sporadic shelling broke the

quiet as the hours passed, and the thousands in both armies who had steeled themselves for combat began to relax. The Young Napoleon had no intention of fighting a battle on September 16. He was not yet ready. No orders had been issued and no troops moved into attacking positions. Some eighteen hours had passed since his army reached the field, but he had as yet no clear picture of the Confederates' positions. Additional time was required for reconnoitering, McClellan would explain in his official report, for "examining the ground, finding fords, clearing the approaches, and hurrying up the ammunition and supply trains...."

Perhaps he needed more time as well to nerve himself for the test against Robert E. Lee. Except for a minor engagement on the Peninsula, McClellan had never planned and directed a battle. Certainly he had never been so boldly challenged to initiate one, and he was intent on having everything just right. The delay came as no surprise to Lee. The previous afternoon he had told one of his artillerists that there would be no battle that day, or the next day either. He expected to have the time to reunite his army.

Three days before, with the Lost Order at his elbow, McClellan had described to General Franklin his plan "to cut the enemy in two and beat him in detail." With the good fortune of an Aladdin, he had been granted the first wish of any general, and four golden opportunities to realize it — at Turner's and Crampton's gaps on September 14, and at Sharpsburg on the afternoon of September 15 and the morning of September 16. He had let the first three opportunities go begging, but the fourth was perhaps the best chance of all: no Rebel cavalry screen to block his view, no mountain range to fight his way through, no necessity for bringing fresh troops up to the front. He had some 60,000 fighting men at his command at dawn on September 16, odds of four to one in reality and almost two and a half to one even by his system of phantom calculation. Yet McClellan plodded through the day as if the copy of Order 191 had never been found, leaving history to judge him (as Abraham Lincoln had judged him) as the general with the "slows," the captain who would not dare.[18]

There is evidence, however, that the Young Napoleon followed his own unique line of reasoning to the conclusion that by now the Confederate army before him was no longer divided; thus Order 191 was out of date, and time was not a factor. Pennsylvania's

Governor Curtin telegraphed the president a report sent him that day by Captain William J. Palmer, one of the governor's most reliable scouts. Palmer had been at McClellan's headquarters at Keedysville during the night of the 15th. "The general believes that Harper's Ferry surrendered yesterday morning," Palmer reported, "and that Jackson re-enforced Lee at Sharpsburg last night.... Rebels appear encouraged at arrival of their re-enforcements."[19]

If that indeed was the general's mental picture of the enemy, it fitted into the pattern of his thinking that invariably credited the Rebels with feats quite beyond what his own army could perform. Franklin had told him on the morning of the fifteenth that Harper's Ferry was believed lost; Sharpsburg was seventeen miles from Harper's Ferry; Jackson's troops were known to be prodigious marchers; thus the Army of the Potomac was once more outnumbered, a situation calling for the usual full measure of caution.

In that event, Stonewall Jackson's reputation served him well that critical day, for even Old Jack could no longer bend the troops to his iron will. They were ill and footsore and worn far beyond simple exhaustion, and the condition of the animals was as bad. A Louisiana colonel in one of his divisions wrote home from Harper's Ferry on September 15th that as much as he would like to go along on an invasion of Pennsylvania, he would "like it better to get a leave of absence, as I am completely tired out with our constant marching.... It is too much as the state of our ranks show, and if Jackson keeps on at it, there will be no army for him to command." It was not until the afternoon of the fifteenth that the first of Jackson's and Walker's men were provisioned and started on the roads for Sharpsburg. The march continued on through the night, and even Jackson admitted that it was "severe."[20]

It was noon on September 16 when he rode up to find Lee and Longstreet studying the Federals across the valley. His troops and those of Walker continued trailing into the lines all afternoon. As the three conferred, one of Longstreet's soldiers went up to Kyd Douglas, Jackson's aide, and asked if Stonewall had really arrived.

"That's he, talking to your General, 'Old Pete' — the man with the big boots on," Douglas told him.

We Will Make Our Stand 165

"Is it? Well, bless my eyes! Thankee, Captain," the soldier replied, and turned back to his comrades, waved his hat, and yelled, "Boys, it's all right!"

It was not quite all right yet, but Lee could breathe easier. Six of his nine divisions were at hand. Those of McLaws and Anderson were on the march from Harper's Ferry. A. P. Hill's division was completing arrangements for paroling the captured Federals and for getting the guns and stores off to the south and would march for Sharpsburg the next morning. As the batteries continued their sporadic long-range dueling, Lee warned his gunners to conserve their ammunition; they were soon going to need it for the enemy's infantry.

Positions were assigned to the newly arrived artillery and infantry. Jackson made a careful reconnaissance of the ground he would have to defend. Longstreet, too, was studying the terrain and the enemy dispositions taking shape across the creek. He rode slowly along behind the lines, glasses to his eyes, reins slack on his horse's neck, rider and mount indifferent to the harassing fire of the Federal guns.[21]

There was a strong current of tension in Washington that Tuesday. The Army of the Potomac had outrun its telegraphic communications, and dispatches were slow to reach the capital. A worried Lincoln wired Governor Curtin, "What do you hear from General McClellan's army? We have nothing from him to-day." General Halleck remained preoccupied with the idea that the invasion of Maryland was simply a smokescreen behind which the Rebels were maneuvering for a surprise attack on Washington. "I think . . . you will find that the whole force of the enemy in your front has crossed the river," he fussed at McClellan. "I fear now more than ever that they will re-cross at Harper's Ferry, or below, and turn your left, thus cutting you off from Washington. This has appeared to me to be a part of their plan, and hence my anxiety on the subject. . . . " The general-in-chief was encountering crises wherever he looked. In Kentucky the Confederate flag flew over Frankfort, the state capital, and at Munfordville 4,000 Federals were closely besieged by Braxton Bragg's army and apparently beyond help. (They would surrender the next day.) The citizens of Cincinnati were feverishly digging entrenchments to repel the invaders.

A chief topic of conversation all over town was what was already being called the Harper's Ferry fiasco. Diarist George Templeton Strong was in Washington at the War Department that day on U.S. Sanitary Commission business, and reported Secretary of War Stanton to be in a towering rage. "Stanton could not be seen but was heard cussing frightfully in an adjoining apartment," he wrote. Strong met General Halleck for the first time, an interview that left him in consternation. He thought him weak and shallow and wondered if he was "a little flustered with wine, an inadmissible apology for a commander-in-chief at a crisis like this." The news of the Harper's Ferry surrender was released to the press that evening, but War Department censors reduced the number of prisoners lost by half to soften the blow.[22]

There was as well in the capital an undercurrent of continuing rumor that Lincoln had prepared an emancipation plan for the slaves but that his administration was divided on the question. The president had been addressing the slavery issue frequently since the July cabinet meeting, keeping it before the public eye. In a reply to a demand for immediate emancipation by Horace Greeley, editor of the *New York Tribune*, he wrote that beyond all else his policy was to restore the Union: "If I could save the Union without freeing *any* slave I would do it, and if I could save it by freeing *all* the slaves I would do it; and if I could save it by freeing some and leaving others alone I would also do that." Meanwhile slavery, the views of the radical Republicans, and the lagging military fortunes were subjects of intense politicking throughout the North, where the first of the fall elections was less than a month away. Strong-willed Andrew Curtin of Pennsylvania and John Andrew of Massachusetts were organizing a Northern governors' conference scheduled for Altoona, Pennsylvania, a week hence, where it was widely believed the president would be challenged on his war leadership.[23]

In Great Britain, too, there was a sense of crisis. Unemployment and hardship in the textile districts were daily growing worse, and a strong anti-Northern tide was running in the nation's centers of power. News from America arrived a week or two after the event, and in a September 16 editorial the *Times* of London expressed unreserved pleasure at the outcome of the Second Bull Run campaign: "If the renown of brilliant courage, stern devotion to a

We Will Make Our Stand

cause, and military achievement almost without a parallel can compensate men for the toil and privations of the hour, then the countrymen of Lee and Jackson may be consoled amid their sufferings. From all parts of Europe ... comes the tribute of admiration." The next day Foreign Secretary Lord Russell wrote to Prime Minister Palmerston, suggesting an October cabinet to debate the matter of recognition of the Confederacy. It was clear to him that the Federal army "has made no progress in subduing the insurgent States." If recognition was agreed upon, as he believed it would be, the next step should be a proposal for concerted action by Britain, France, Russia, and the other powers.[24]

As General Lee anticipated, his campaign in Maryland had become a pivot on which events of incalculable importance turned. By every indication a crisis in the affairs of both North and South was at hand. At about noon on September 16 General McClellan came at last to a decision. Orders went down the chain of command. He would bring Lee's army to battle the next day.

Before the armies came, Sharpsburg, Maryland, was a quiet place, an entirely ordinary little rural community where the roads came together. In September 1862 it was just a year short of being a century old, having been founded a dozen years before the Revolution and named in honor of Maryland colonial governor Horatio Sharpe.[25] Its main street was called Main Street, and there was the usual proportion of churches and taverns and stores, with the 1,300 residents living in unprepossessing frame houses scattered along side streets and lanes. Some of them worked on the nearby Chesapeake and Ohio Canal or at the ironworks a few miles away at the mouth of Antietam Creek, but mostly they made their living as shopkeepers and blacksmiths and gristmill hands serving the farming trade. A good many of the local farmers were of sturdy German stock, with names like Rohrbach and Mumma and Otto and Poffenberger, and they had made the land bloom. In neatly fenced fields the corn stood tall, the orchards were heavy with fruit, and the haylofts in the big barns were full. Life in Sharpsburg might have continued on in its pleasant, uneventful way, unremarked by history like a thousand other little towns dotting the American landscape, except for that suddenly all-important fact that it was the place where the roads came together.

Three miles or so west of Sharpsburg the Potomac makes its

way southward in a series of sweeping bends, and a mile east of the town the little Antietam meanders along, also on a generally north–south axis, to enter the Potomac some three miles to the south. From Sharpsburg a turnpike ran due north to Hagerstown and on into Pennsylvania. A second turnpike ran northeast to Boonsboro — the route followed by both armies on September 15 — and a junction with the National Road. Lesser roads went east to Rohrersville in Pleasant Valley and south along the Maryland side of the Potomac to Harper's Ferry. Before the war, traffic on the two turnpikes had funneled through Sharpsburg and crossed the Potomac into Virginia's Shenandoah Valley at nearby Shepherdstown, but the bridge there had been burned in 1861, and now the only practicable Potomac crossing for an army between Harper's Ferry and Williamsport well upstream was Boteler's Ford, just below Shepherdstown. In mid-September 1862 the three-mile stretch of road leading to Boteler's was the most important of all Sharpsburg's highways. It was General Lee's lifeline to Virginia and, should the impending battle go against him, his only escape route.

The terrain around Sharpsburg presented a picture seemingly as ordinary as the town itself. A low north–south ridgeline, along which the Hagerstown turnpike ran, crowned the irregularly shaped peninsula between the Potomac and the Antietam, with the ground falling away in most places in gentle folds east and west to the two streams. To Federal observers scanning the field from across the Antietam, the variations in the texture of the landscape looked most pronounced south of the town, where broken and wooded hills and ravines climbed fairly steeply 150 feet or so from the creek to the crest of the ridge. Sharpsburg lay beyond the ridge, with only its church spires visible.

North of town the ground seemed flatter and more inviting for maneuver, but the impression was deceptive. The terrain there, wrote a Northern war correspondent, was "completely deceitful," full of little hollows and rises and stone outcroppings — mostly invisible to McClellan and his generals from their vantage points a mile or two away — and the patchwork pattern of fields and woodlots made it uncommonly hard to calculate what might await an attack. It was harvest time, and while some of the crops had already been gathered, other fields were still thick with corn at its full growth, standing head-high. Autumn had not yet touched the Maryland countryside, and the foliage was thick and green. General Cox called it "as pleasing and prosperous a landscape as can easily be imagined," but that was a judgment more aesthetic than military. With his careful engineer's eye General Lee had chosen his ground well.[26]

Antietam Creek was not so much a barrier to the Federal army as it was a nuisance, limiting troop movements and hampering a close look at the enemy's positions. It was spanned by four arched stone bridges, one to the south at the mouth of the creek; the second on the Sharpsburg–Rohrersville road, known locally as the Rohrbach Bridge but soon to be better known as the Burnside Bridge; the third, called the Middle Bridge, where the Boonsboro turnpike crossed the creek; and, farthest to the north, the Upper Bridge, near Samuel Pry's gristmill, where a road from Keedysville to Williamsport crossed the stream.

The Antietam was neither very wide nor very deep, but it was just enough of both that a Federal offensive in any strength would need an uncontested crossing at one of these bridges, particularly for the artillery and the ammunition trains. Difficult terrain and a limited field of maneuver ruled out the southernmost bridge at the creek mouth, and Lee had drawn his lines so as to contest any crossing attempt at the Rohrbach and Middle bridges. Only the Upper Bridge seemed to fill the bill.

Consequently, as McClellan described it in his preliminary report on the campaign written a month later, his "design" was to throw the main weight of his attack against the Confederate left or northern flank. Beyond that certainty, there is no clear statement of the rest of his plan for the coming battle. He issued no written general orders on September 16. He called no conference of his corps commanders to outline his intentions. The explanations in his preliminary report, in his official report written in 1863, and in his postwar memoirs are at variance one with another and heavily embroidered with hindsight.

In any case, it was his intention also to force a crossing at the Rohrbach Bridge against the Confederate right — whether in conjunction with the assault against the left or only after it developed, whether as a diversion or a full-scale attack, was never made clear. When "one or both of the flank movements were fully successful," he wrote, he intended to attack the enemy's center "with any reserve I might then have on hand." The effect on Lee, staff aide David Strother heard McClellan predict, would be comparable to "pinching him up in a vice." Considering the circumstances and what was known of the ground on September 16, it was a sound enough general plan. McClellan's command assignments and the distribution of his forces, however, were a recipe for potential confusion and discord, reflecting as they did his doubts about some of his lieutenants and his misconceptions about the enemy.[27]

McClellan had found it convenient to divide his army into three subcommands, under Franklin, Sumner, and Burnside, when he marched into Maryland. He continued that arrangement for the battles at South Mountain, assigning Crampton's Gap to Franklin's wing and Turner's Gap to the First and Ninth corps under Burnside. Now, on the eve of what looked like a showdown fight, he abruptly — and without explanation to the generals concerned — abandoned the triad command structure. Perhaps he considered it too unwieldy for the task at hand. An equally likely reason was his appraisal of the abilities of the generals involved.

Fighting Joe Hooker had lived up to his nickname at Turner's Gap, demonstrating that the kinks were out of the command he inherited from the hapless McDowell, and his First Corps was McClellan's choice to spearhead the main attack on the Confederate left. Hooker would no longer be under Burnside's direction, however, which rankled that normally genial and uncomplaining officer.

Relations between "Burn" and "Mac," as they called each other, had cooled in the last day or so. Their acquaintance dated back to West Point days. Burnside had resigned from the army in 1853 to manufacture a breech-loading carbine of his own invention, but when the company later failed, McClellan, then an executive with the Illinois Central, found his friend a position with the railroad. Whatever strain was put on their friendship by Lincoln's offers of the army command to Burnside, McClellan was manifestly irritated on September 15 when his subordinate was slow to put the Ninth Corps on the road in pursuit of the retreating Confederates, blocking Porter's Fifth Corps in the bargain. McClellan called him to account with unaccustomed sharpness. Possibly it was beginning to dawn on him that the man's often-expressed modest view of his military abilities was in fact the truth of the matter.

The second of Burnside's two corps, the Ninth, was posted at the opposite end of the Federal line from the First Corps and given the task of confronting the Confederate right overlooking the Rohrbach Bridge. Burnside regarded this as a humiliating demotion and blamed the whole business on the devious machinations of Joe Hooker to win independent command for himself. Jacob Cox, promoted to temporary command of the Ninth Corps after Reno's death at Fox's Gap, offered to step down in favor of Burnside and return to his Kanawha Division, but Burnside would have none of it; that would appear, he said, as if he was accepting the slight. As a result, orders to the First Corps went directly from McClellan to Hooker, but orders to the Ninth Corps went to the sulking Burnside, who did no more than pass them on to Cox. It was an awkward diffusion of command responsibility, made all the worse by McClellan's failure to smooth his old friend's ruffled feathers or to clarify just what was expected of him in the coming fight.[28]

McClellan visited a more subtle demotion on Sumner, whom he had characterized to his wife during the Peninsula fighting as "even a greater fool than I had supposed." When Hooker received his orders on the afternoon of September 16 to cross the Antietam at the Upper Bridge near the Pry mill and take position opposite the Confederate left flank, he was told (according to his report) that he was "at liberty to call for re-enforcements if I should need them, and that on their arrival they would be placed under my command...." These reinforcements would come from the Second and Twelfth corps, nominally under Sumner's command but now no longer subject to his initiative. On Hooker's warning that "the rebels would eat me up" if his First Corps was left alone on the enemy flank without support, McClellan ordered Mansfield's Twelfth Corps to cross the Antietam late that night to back him up. Sumner was told to prepare to cross the Second Corps early the following morning, where he would go into battle as Hooker directed, ranking general giving way to subordinate on the scene.[29]

At 7:30 P.M. on the sixteenth, McClellan finally ordered up Franklin from his empty vigil in Pleasant Valley, where he was on guard against any flanking movement by the enemy; McClellan had taken care not to be surprised as John Pope had been. Franklin would only set off for the battlefield the next morning. When he arrived, his troops and those of Fitz John Porter's Fifth Corps were to act as a general reserve. Alongside Porter at the center of the Federal line was Pleasonton's entire 4,300-man cavalry division, perhaps the strangest of McClellan's troop placements.

Positioning the cavalry to deliver the coup de grâce against the center of the enemy's battle line was an archaic tactic out of the picture-book wars of the past, a Napoleonic gesture by the Young Napoleon. Of all the effects wrought on military tactics by the introduction of the rifled musket, none was more dramatic than the change forced on the cavalry arm. To order a mass cavalry charge on Civil War infantry — unless that infantry was in the final stages of rout — was to invite a mass slaughter. Yet such a cavalry charge was very much a part of McClellan's thinking, and he would in fact propose one during the coming battle. Whatever the pros and cons of holding the cavalry for such an eventuality, there was one certain consequence: it would be unavailable for scouting and intelligence-gathering.[30]

This checkrein on the cavalry was typical of the Federal reconnaissance efforts. What was known about tomorrow's battlefield was learned only at long range and with a minimum of initiative. On September 16, while McClellan rode back and forth along the lines pondering the situation, *New York Tribune* correspondent Albert Richardson came upon two key corps commanders, Sumner and Hooker, whiling away the hours back at headquarters awaiting their orders, Sumner sitting idly under a tree and Hooker dozing on the ground nearby. General Mansfield, who had arrived only the day before from Washington to take over the Twelfth Corps, was too busy trying to get acquainted with his new command to discover what he might soon have to face. Burnside and his officers seem to have gained no clear idea of the terrain even on their own side of the Rohrbach Bridge. According to local citizens there was a usable ford downstream from the bridge and outflanking it, but no one in the Ninth Corps was sent to locate it. For one reason or another, the Federal high command was going into battle with blinkered eyes.

We Will Make Our Stand

By the roster counts, General McClellan had just under 75,000 troops, of all arms and all services, at his immediate call. There were 19,000 more in the three divisions under William Franklin in Pleasant Valley, some four hours' marching time away. Of those 94,000 men, however, a sizable number were unlikely ever to see the firing line, for the Army of the Potomac was hardly a lean organization — there were cooks and teamsters and excessive numbers of other detailed men, as well as the ill and the shirkers and the stragglers. His army's total effective strength of all arms came to about 71,500, backed by 300 pieces of artillery. A division of Porter's Fifth Corps, 6,600 men, was twenty-three miles away at Frederick.[31]

Of the troops earmarked for the leading offensive role in his plan of battle, none were from what General McClellan liked to think of as his old battle-tested Peninsula army. Hooker's First Corps and Mansfield's Twelfth, positioned for the initial attack on the Confederate left, were from John Pope's ill-fated Army of Virginia; the Burnside-Cox Ninth Corps, assigned to the vaguely defined mission against the Rebel right, had not seen combat with the Army of the Potomac before South Mountain. If all went as planned, however, it would be the Peninsula troops who would supply the final crushing blows — Sumner's Second Corps and perhaps Franklin's Sixth against the enemy left, Porter's Fifth Corps and the cavalry against the center. If all did not go well — indeed, if it should be General Lee who took the offensive — these trusted veterans would be the army's last line of defense.

As always, caution was a dominant element in General McClellan's planning: the most careful balance must be struck between offense and defense; thoughts of ambush and an enemy counteroffensive preoccupied him. He was not alone in his apprehensions. His corps commanders were equally persuaded that behind that ridgeline and concealed in those woodlots across the creek were Rebels in vast numbers. Joe Hooker would testify that Lee took his stand at Sharpsburg on September 15 with 50,000 men, subsequently reinforced by Jackson's command from Harper's Ferry. Sumner thought each side had about 80,000 troops. A similar myopia afflicted the headquarters staffs. Aide David Strother noted in his diary on September 17 that the enemy was 100,000 strong "in round numbers." Colonel Alexander S. Webb, Porter's chief of staff, wrote a few days later of the 100,000 to 130,000 Confederates who defended Sharpsburg.

McClellan's grip on the underdog's role was as firm as ever, and would never waver. In testimony before the Joint Committee on the Conduct of the War some six months later, for example, he explained that the Rebel army that confronted him at Sharpsburg was "pretty close upon 100,000 men." His sense of mission also ran as strongly and as deeply as ever. On the evening of September 16 he assured his staff that "to-morrow we fight the battle that will decide the fate of the republic."[32]

The Sharpsburg landscape did indeed offer numerous places of concealment, which was one reason Lee decided to make his bluff there, but just then most of the hiding places were going unused. Even after the arrival of Jackson's and Walker's troops on the sixteenth, Lee could count fewer than 26,500 men, including cavalry and artillery. He was increasingly concerned over the whereabouts of Lafayette McLaws, in command of his own and Richard Anderson's divisions. Along with A. P. Hill, winding up the surrender affairs at Harper's Ferry, it meant that fully a third of the Army of Northern Virginia was not yet on the field. And by now the bluff had worn thin. It was apparent that even McClellan would not present the Confederates with any more gifts of time.

Although McLaws was ordered to follow behind Jackson and Walker, nothing had gone right. His men were hungry and tired and worn from the fighting they had done, there were thousands of paroled Yankees eager to get out of Harper's Ferry just as his troops were trying to pass through the town, and no one could find anything to eat. He got his columns on the road at last, a half a day and more late, and bivouacked them for the night of September 16 a few miles short of Boteler's Ford on the Potomac. Lee's courier found him there and delivered orders for a forced march to Sharpsburg. A second courier carried orders to Powell Hill at Harper's Ferry, directing him to put his division on the road as early as possible in the morning. Every man and every rifle were going to be needed.

These problems remained General Lee's secret, however, thanks to the lack of aggressive Federal reconnaissance. No hint reached McClellan that the Army of Northern Virginia was still not yet fully united. No cavalry was posted to observe Confederate movements between Harper's Ferry and Sharpsburg. General Pleasonton's best efforts on September 16 served only to muddy the waters. So far as he could discover, the Rebels were in full retreat. "The greater portion of the forces of the enemy have gone towards Williamsport," he reported at noon. "Some have gone towards Shepherdstown.... Arty. & infan. of the enemy on both these roads."[33]

As Lee filled it out on September 16, the Confederate battle line was some four miles long, paralleling the Hagerstown turnpike north of Sharpsburg and extending southward past the town to the bluffs overlooking Antietam Creek a mile below the Rohrbach Bridge. Longstreet's command held the right, Jackson's the left. Thomas Munford's cavalry guarded the lower Antietam to the point where it entered the Potomac. Jeb Stuart, with Fitzhugh Lee's cavalry brigade, tied the northern flank to the Potomac as well, with his horse artillery and three regular batteries posted on a modest ridge called Nicodemus Hill. The area covered by the infantry and artillery — Lee would have some 200 guns available for the battle — lay generally on the eastern or forward slope of the ridge, but the line twisted and turned and bunched to take advantage of the terrain.

For the most part this was good defensive ground, with the infantry well placed and clear fields of fire for the guns. The Hagerstown turnpike and the country roads and lanes on the western slope of the ridge provided routes for shifting troops wherever they might be needed. The major disadvantage of the battlefield as far as the Confederates were concerned was the restricted Potomac crossing at Boteler's Ford in their rear should they be broken and have to retreat; defeat could easily turn into disastrous rout on the riverbank. Lee apparently gave little thought to such a prospect beyond posting five batteries of his reserve artillery on the Virginia side of the ford. He was not being forced into battle against his will. He chose his ground deliberately, throwing down the challenge to his opponent.

What did trouble him was the fearful toll straggling had taken of his army. The wastage of sick and footsore and faint-hearted men since the campaign began exceeded 20 percent; "none but heroes are left" was how one of A. P. Hill's officers put it. When every man was finally in place the next morning — and until Hill could reach the field late in the afternoon, at the earliest — there would be fewer than 35,000 of them. In numbers and condition this was a far cry from the command Lee had inherited three and a half months earlier. (The Army of Northern Virginia would not again be so diminished until it made its final march, toward Appomattox Court House.) To Lee's way of thinking, however, these men were, as he had told President Davis, the best soldiers in the world, and unlike McClellan he had full confidence in the fighting abilities of his lieutenants.[34]

It was four in the afternoon on the sixteenth when Hooker's men began to move. The columns crossed the Antietam at the Upper Bridge and nearby shallows and swung north and west through the fields and woodlots to strike the Hagerstown turnpike north of the Confederate flank. Lee's scouts reported the crossing, and Hood's division was moved quickly to the left to meet the threat. George Meade's Pennsylvanians were in the lead, furnishing flank protection for the main column, and at sunset they got into a sharp fight with Hood's men in a patch of woods. Artillery on both sides joined in as the light faded. But Hooker was not looking for battle just then, only position. "The fight flashed, and glimmered, and faded, and finally went out in the dark," the *New York Tribune*'s George Smalley wrote. The First Corps bivouacked behind a concealing ridge on the farm of Joseph Poffenberger, and Hooker notified headquarters that he would open the battle at dawn. As the generals spread their blankets in the Poffenberger barn, Smalley heard Hooker mutter, "If they had let us start earlier, we might have finished tonight."[35]

There was in fact more to McClellan's late start on September 16 than granting the enemy yet another day's respite. Whatever he gained by putting Hooker into position for the assault on the seventeenth he more than lost by throwing away any chance of surprise. Knowing now exactly what to expect, Lee had the time to broaden and thicken his left until it was a solid front. Rather than a flank attack to roll up the enemy line, Hooker would be making a frontal attack on a position drawn squarely across his line of advance. Once again, as he had done when he made no secret of his advance toward Turner's Gap, General McClellan was telegraphing his punch.

Shortly before midnight, Mansfield's Twelfth Corps crossed the Antietam in Hooker's wake to take a supporting position a mile or so to his left and rear. It had started to rain gently but steadily, and the men stumbled along in the dripping darkness as best they could. The movement was something of a nightmare for the recruits in the new regiments, who had enough trouble trying to keep together on a route march in the daylight. Finally, about 2 A.M., the officers told them they were more or less where they were supposed to be, and to get some sleep. The men of a brigade that was halted on the George Line farm wondered what ill fate had directed them to be bivouacked on a freshly manured field. They could only shrug, roll up in their blankets, and hope the rain would stop.[36]

It apparently did not occur to McClellan that in ordering Hooker's march he had given away the only surprise in his battle plan, for that night he suddenly became security conscious and banned all fires. In their wet and cheerless camps the Yankees chewed hardtack and handfuls of dry ground coffee and speculated on what daylight would bring. Their enemies would have envied them even the dry coffee. A good many of the Rebels were still living on green corn and apples, a diet they were heartily sick of by now. Hood persuaded Jackson to let him pull his two brigades back from their advanced positions to cook something hot for the first time in days. Jackson allowed them to go into reserve, moving up two other brigades in their place, but told Hood that he must bring his men to the front on the double if he called for them in the morning.

An undercurrent of nervous energy was running through the two armies that night. On Hooker's front there were spatterings of shots on the picket lines, and sudden bursts of artillery fire that achieved nothing except to keep men awake. A New Yorker in Burnside's Ninth Corps was prowling restlessly through the dark camp when he tripped over someone's pet dog, knocked down a stand of stacked rifles as he fell, and in a matter of moments had two entire regiments awake in alarm. Jeb Stuart was also on the prowl that night, reconnoitering the new Federal positions to the north on the Hagerstown road. Riding back to the Confederate lines, he found Major John Pelham, the commander of his horse artillery, asleep in a fence corner. Shaking him awake, he remarked, "My dear fellow, don't you know that the cornfield at the foot of the hill is full of Yankees?" Pelham and his gunners made haste to find safer quarters.

Union General Alpheus Williams wrote his family that it was a night he would never forget, "so dark, so obscure, so mysterious, so uncertain; with the occasional rapid volleys of pickets and outposts, the low, solemn sound of the command as troops came into position, and withal so sleepy that there was a half-dreamy sensation about it all; but with a certain impression that the morrow was to be great with the future fate of our country. So much responsibility, so much intense, future anxiety!"[37]

That intense anxiety gripped many minds. The two armies had been staring at one another across the Antietam's shallow valley for the better part of two days now, and from the noisy clash at dusk every man could calculate that a big fight — perhaps the biggest they had ever seen — was about to take place. In one respect at least, these armies were very much alike. Except for the scattering of conscripts recently brought into Lee's ranks and some in the new Federal regiments who had signed up for the sake of sizable bounties to avoid the threat of conscription in their home states, these men were all volunteers. They had enlisted for a variety of reasons perhaps, but devotion to a cause was their common coin. It had not taken long for the hard realities of army life to rub most of the gloss from innocent illusions, but a solid core of conviction remained. They were there because of what they believed, and when it came down to it they would face the test of battle with a certain extra resolution inspired by these beliefs. "When I was a boy I never thought I should be called upon to fight for my country," one Yankee soldier wrote. "But I am no better to die for liberty than any one else. If I lose my life, I shall be missed by but few; but if the Union be lost, it will be missed by many." A man in Lee's army might change the words but not the sentiments. Neither army would ever entirely lose this spirit, but it was never higher nor more widespread than in September of 1862.

Some men claimed they slept the sleep of exhaustion that night; more recalled dozing and waking and dozing again, with the half-dreamy sensations General Williams described. They prepared themselves to die and convinced themselves they would not. By evening's last light and dawn's first light they scribbled letters they knew might be their last. "I don't talk seriously for you know all my last words if I come to grief — You know my devoted love for you . . . ," Captain Oliver Wendell Holmes, Jr. of the 20th Massachusetts wrote his parents. "It's rank folly pulling a long mug every time one may fight or may be killed — Very probably we shall in a few days and if we do why I shall go into it not trying to shirk the responsibility of my past life. . . . "[38]

· 6 ·

TO THE DUNKER CHURCH

The Antietam battlefield, as it gradually emerged in the foggy half-light of dawn on Wednesday, September 17, 1862, was a largely anonymous landscape, except for such casual everyday designations as this farmer's woodlot or that farmer's lane or someone else's cornfield. The war would change all that, imprinting names of its own for the historical record — names like the East Woods, the West Woods, the Cornfield, the Sunken Road. The new names were every bit as mundane as what the local people had called these places. But for the thousands of men who would fight desperately there that day, and for the countless others, North and South, who were touched at second hand by the struggle, they would echo forever in the mind, terrible and heroic and melancholy.

For the moment, in that first gray light of morning, the names were just names, without echoes to them. Shortly after five, as the sky began to lighten, Joe Hooker rode up to the picket line to inspect the ground in front of his First Corps. His objective was easily chosen — a raised, open plateau just to the east of the Hagerstown turnpike and a mile from where he was standing. It was thickly ranked with Confederate guns, and visible just across the turnpike from it was a small, plain, whitewashed brick building set into a patch of woods. Many of the soldiers took it for a schoolhouse, but it was in fact a church of the German Baptist Brethren, a gentle and pacifist sect that shunned such vanities of the world as church steeples and whose baptism by total immersion led people to call them Dunkers. If General Hooker could seize the plateau and the area around the Dunker church, it would mean a break-

To the Dunker Church 181

through and the opportunity to destroy the Army of Northern Virginia.

That woodlot on the west side of the turnpike — the West Woods, it would be called — ran from the church northward along the turnpike some 300 yards, where it was cut back to make room for two roadside fields planted in clover. Behind these fields the woods continued to the north in an irregular strip to a point halfway between the church and the First Corps's jumping-off position on the Joseph Poffenberger farm. At that halfway point, the prosperous farmstead of David R. Miller straddled the Hagerstown road, barn and haystacks to the west, house and kitchen garden and orchard to the east. Just beyond the house and orchard Hooker could see Mr. Miller's thirty-acre cornfield, the corn tall and ripe and ready for harvest. There were a half-dozen other cornfields in the vicinity of Sharpsburg where men would fight that day, but only this one earned a grim fame as *the* Cornfield. It extended eastward from the turnpike to the edge of another woodlot — the East Woods — where Hood's men and Meade's had clashed the evening before and where nervous pickets exchanged shots throughout the night.

Hooker's plan was to attack due south toward the Dunker church along the axis of the Hagerstown turnpike. The division of Abner Doubleday — Doubleday had replaced John Hatch, wounded in the fight at Turner's Gap — would advance on the right along the pike and through the Miller farm toward the West Woods, the division of James Ricketts on the left through the Cornfield and the East Woods. George Meade's division would back them up in the center. Since no specific orders from McClellan are on record, it is uncertain just how much initiative Joe Hooker was exercising that morning. In any event, there was no provision for a joint attack along with Mansfield's Twelfth Corps, bivouacked a mile away. The 8,600 infantrymen of the First Corps would open the battle on their own, against a foe whose positions and strength were largely unknown.[1]

Stonewall Jackson could muster some 7,700 men to meet the expected attack. The better part of two divisions were placed in defensive positions — Ewell's division, put in charge of Alexander R. Lawton after Richard Ewell lost a leg at Second Bull Run; and Jackson's old division, now under John R. Jones. Jones's four brigades were in and close to the West Woods, a quarter mile or so north of the Dunker church. Lawton had one brigade in a pasture immediately south of the Cornfield, and another in line farther to the east on the farm of Samuel Mumma and extending across a little country road that angled off the Hagerstown turnpike at the church and turned northward through the East Woods toward the hamlet of Smoketown. The Mumma homestead was already a battlefield landmark of sorts, for some of D. H. Hill's men had put it to the torch so it would not be used as a strongpoint by Yankee sharpshooters, and a tall pillar of black smoke smudged the morning sky.

This irregular battle line facing north was altogether some three-quarters of a mile long. Wherever they could, the Confederates sheltered in the hollows and behind the little rises and the limestone ledges that dotted the fields and woods; the only man-made defense was a rough breastwork of fence rails thrown up in the pasture south of the Cornfield. Lawton's two remaining brigades, plus the two brigades of Hood's division, were in reserve in the West Woods. Skirmishers were posted well to the front on the Miller farm and in the East Woods, but except for a few skirmishers at its southern edge the Cornfield was empty of Rebels.

Colonel Stephen D. Lee had crowded four batteries from his artillery battalion onto the plateau near the Dunker church, with a clear line of fire to the north and east. The most commanding high ground in the northern part of the field, however, was Nicodemus Hill, where Jeb Stuart and his artillerist John Pelham had fourteen guns in position to hit the Yankees in the flank as they advanced. Jackson soon sent a brigade from his thin reserve to protect this key spot. Although Union officers would complain repeatedly about the killing fire delivered from the hill, nothing was done about it beyond counterbattery fire. Jackson could be grateful that neither Hooker nor anyone else in the Federal high command gave thought to seizing Nicodemus Hill, from where their guns could have taken most of his positions under a deadly enfilade.[2]

Lieutenant A. W. Garber, commanding one of Stuart's batteries on Nicodemus Hill, would lay claim to firing the opening shot of the Battle of Antietam. However that may be, Stuart's guns and Doubleday's were blazing away at each other as soon as it was light enough to see anything. The rain had stopped, but a patchy

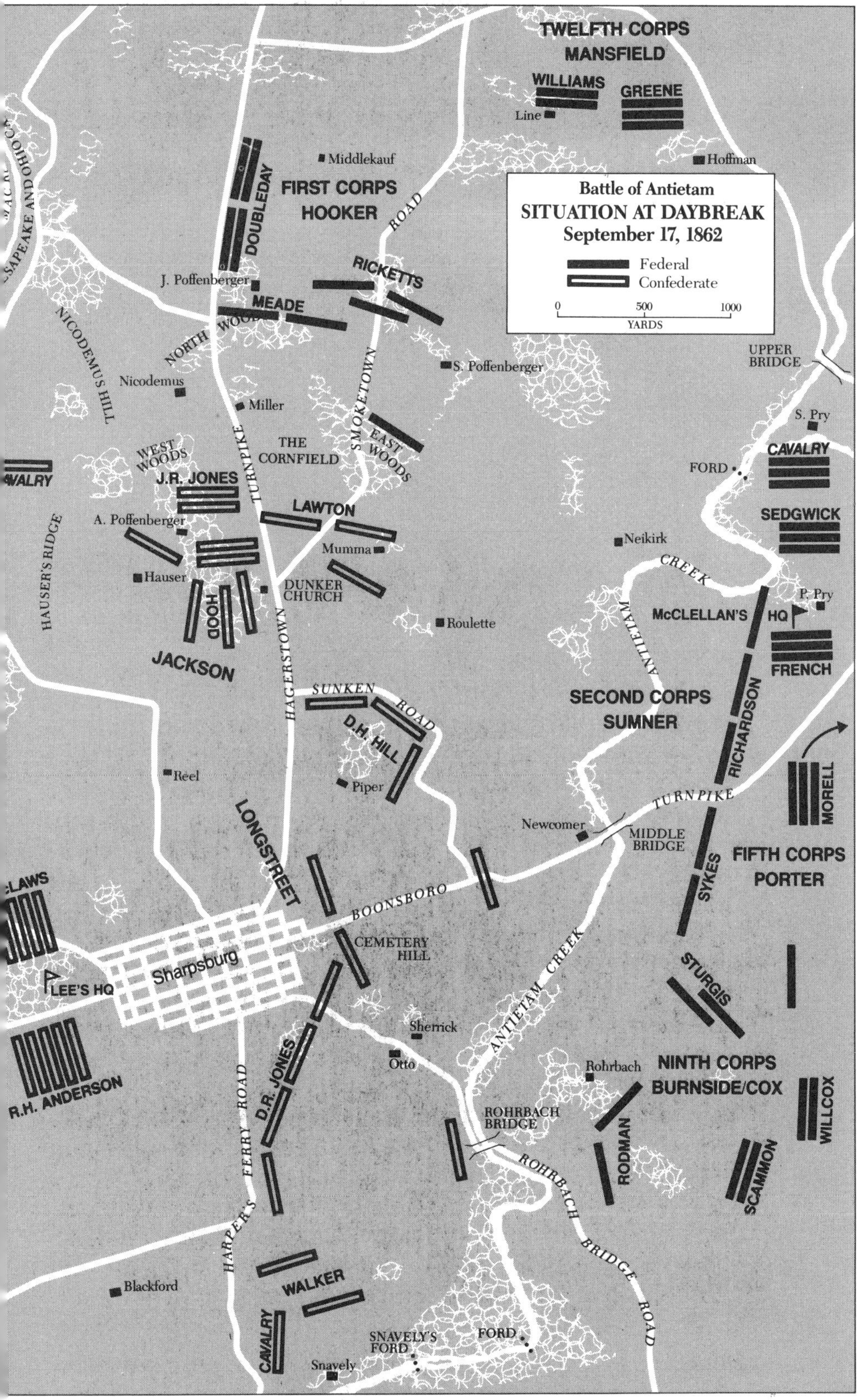

Battle of Antietam
SITUATION AT DAYBREAK
September 17, 1862
Federal
Confederate
0
500
1000
YARDS
TWELFTH CORPS
MANSFIELD
WILLIAMS
GREENE
Line
Hoffman
Middlekauf
FIRST CORPS
HOOKER
DOUBLEDAY
RICKETTS
MEADE
J. Poffenberger
NORTH WOODS
SMOKETOWN ROAD
S. Poffenberger
NICODEMUS HILL
Nicodemus
Miller
WEST WOODS
THE CORNFIELD
EAST WOODS
TURNPIKE
J.R. JONES
LAWTON
A. Poffenberger
Mumma
Hauser
DUNKER CHURCH
HOOD
HAUSER'S RIDGE
Roulette
JACKSON
HAGERSTOWN
SUNKEN ROAD
D.H. HILL
Reel
Piper
LONGSTREET
UPPER BRIDGE
S. Pry
CAVALRY
FORD
SEDGWICK
Neikirk
CREEK
ANTIETAM
P. Pry
McCLELLAN'S HQ
FRENCH
SECOND CORPS
SUMNER
RICHARDSON
MORELL
TURNPIKE
Newcomer
MIDDLE BRIDGE
FIFTH CORPS
PORTER
SYKES
BOONSBORO
CEMETERY HILL
Sharpsburg
LEE'S HQ
STURGIS
ANTIETAM CREEK
Sherrick
Otto
R.H. ANDERSON
D.R. JONES
Rohrbach
NINTH CORPS
BURNSIDE/COX
WILLCOX
ROHRBACH BRIDGE
RODMAN
SCAMMON
HARPER'S FERRY ROAD
ROHRBACH BRIDGE ROAD
Blackford
WALKER
CAVALRY
SNAVELY'S FORD
FORD
Snavely

ground fog still lay in the valleys and hollows. Stephen Lee's batteries in front of the Dunker church soon joined in, and the long-range 20-pounder Parrott rifles of McClellan's reserve artillery east of the Antietam added their deep clanging reverberations to the din.

A score of women and children of the neighborhood had taken refuge in the sturdy stone country house on the Nicodemus farm, and the crash of the cannonading and the scream of the shells flying overhead threw them into a panic. Rebel cavalryman William Blackford saw the door fly open and the terrified women rush out "like a flock of birds . . . , hair streaming in the wind and children of all ages stretched out behind." They stumbled through a plowed field toward the Confederate lines, and "every time one would fall, the rest thought it was the result of a cannon shot and ran the faster." Captain Blackford could not help laughing at the spectacle, but with proper Southern chivalry he galloped into the field, swung several children up behind him, and escorted the rest of the refugees to safety. He noted with approval that the Yankee gunners held their fire during the rescue.[3]

There was no truce in the East Woods, where Meade's Pennsylvanians under Brigadier Truman Seymour picked up the fight where they had left it the night before. Three of his regiments pushed ahead the moment it was light, driving the Rebel pickets ahead of them, until they reached the Smoketown road and the southern edge of the woods. From behind trees and a snake-rail fence they opened a sharp fire on a Confederate line in a plowed field on the Mumma farm. The 13th Pennsylvania, known as the "Bucktails," had a particular score to settle, for its colonel had been killed in the firefight the evening before. These men were woodsmen and hunters from mountain country who had taken to wearing the tails of bucks pinned to their caps to advertise their prowess as marksmen. They were specially equipped with Sharps rifles, single-shot breechloaders, and they proceeded to lay down a rapid and deadly fire from behind the Smoketown road fence.

The Rebels they were shooting at were from Isaac Trimble's brigade, now led by Colonel James Walker, and they had to suffer fire not only from the Pennsylvanians on their front but also from the big guns across the Antietam. The effect of the crossfire was at first demoralizing, but it was soon evident that the long-range

To the Dunker Church 185

shelling was more disquieting than accurate. "As my command was exposed to full view of their gunners and had no shelter," Colonel Walker reported, "this fire was very annoying, but less destructive than I at first apprehended it would be."[4] His men ignored the shelling as best they could and crouched in the dirt or took cover behind the Mumma family graveyard to return the Pennsylvanians' fire.

The fast-firing Bucktails began to run short of ammunition and were ordered to pull back. The colonel of the regiment alongside them, seeing the Bucktails withdraw but not seeing their replacements move up — in fact unable to see hardly anything through the trees and the pall of battle smoke — thought he was about to be outflanked and quickly marched his men to the rear and out of the fight. It was the kind of mix-up that would be repeated often on this day of smoky and chaotic confusion. Trimble's brigade drove back the third of Seymour's regiments and won a respite, but only a brief one. Within a matter of minutes, a fresh Federal battle line came swinging south, through farmer Miller's corn.

As Seymour's men battled in the East Woods, Hooker had been getting the divisions of Doubleday and Ricketts into attacking positions. Ricketts moved up his three brigades from their bivouac at dawn to form the left wing of the First Corps assault. The moment his columns cleared the cover of Joseph Poffenberger's woodlot — soon to be better known as the North Woods — Colonel Lee's gunners spotted them and opened fire with shell and solid shot. The 107th Pennsylvania was moving across a plowed field when a precisely aimed solid shot fell a few yards in front of the column; miraculously, it ricocheted off a rock outcropping and in one spectacular bound cleared all ten companies without harming a man. Other regiments were not so fortunate. Scores of Yankees were knocked out of the ranks before they were on the battlefield five minutes.

Ricketts's lead brigade, under New Yorker Abram Duryea, deployed in line of battle at the northern edge of the Cornfield, and the divisional artillery was hurried forward to take up supporting positions in the field east of the Miller orchard. These two Pennsylvania batteries, under Captains Ezra Matthews and James Thompson, promptly began a duel with Lee's guns near the church. A Rebel shell exploded almost under the muzzle of one of

Thompson's guns, the blast somehow sparing the gun crew but by freakish chance igniting the fuse of a shell the loader was holding. With remarkable presence of mind, he smothered the burning fuse with his bare hand, saving himself and no doubt most of his crew. The Yankee batteries switched to canister and threw a few precautionary rounds into the Cornfield, and at 6 A.M. Duryea's 1,100 men started through the head-high corn.[5]

General Lawton's old brigade, now under Colonel Marcellus Douglass, was posted in the rolling pasture south of the Cornfield, some of them behind the piles of fence rails. These Georgians had been told to lie down, pick out a row of corn as an aiming point, and await the order to fire. When Duryea's brigade — three regiments of New Yorkers and one of Pennsylvanians — broke out of the corn, the Georgians rose up and, as one Northerner described it, "poured into us a terrible fire."[6] More Yankees crowded forward over the dead and wounded of their first line to return the volley, and the two battle lines, disdaining cover, stood 250 yards apart in plain sight of each other and blazed away, loading and firing with feverish haste. Shouted commands went unheard in the din, and ragged sheets of dirty white smoke hung low in the windless air over the pasture and in the corn. Finally, as if by mutual consent, the two lines could take it no longer and lay down behind whatever cover they could find and continued the fight.

Three regiments of Trimble's brigade — 12th Georgia, 21st Georgia, 21st North Carolina — moved up across the Smoketown road to the shelter of a low rock ledge and poured fresh volleys into Duryea's decimated ranks. But the Rebels were taking terrible losses in return. When some of Colonel Walker's men tried to advance farther and outflank the Yankees, they were themselves hit in the flank by the remnants of Seymour's Pennsylvanians still holding on in the East Woods. Walker noticed that when he gave the order to advance, only a few men of the 12th Georgia, battle-tested veterans of the Valley and the Peninsula and Second Bull Run, responded. The rest remained on the ground behind the ledge. He rode up for a closer look and found only dead men; the regiment had taken 100 men into battle and barely 40 were left.

The reinforcements he supposed were following him, Duryea discovered, were nowhere to be seen. Ammunition was running low, his men were outnumbered and taking fearful losses, and it was reported that Rebels were edging into the East Woods on his left. He ordered a withdrawal back through the Cornfield. The color-bearer of the 107th Pennsylvania was down, but Private John Delancey, the youngest man in the regiment — he had somehow managed to enlist when he was fourteen — scooped up the regimental flag and helped rally the men at the northern edge of the field. One of his comrades paused to fire off a last defiant shot, but in his haste forgot to remove the ramrod and it went whirring off through the corn. Duryea's brigade completed its retirement in good enough order, but it would fight no more that day. In thirty minutes almost a third of the men had been shot.[7]

General Ricketts had in fact intended his other two brigades, under George L. Hartsuff and William A. Christian, to follow in successive close support of Duryea, but there was a command breakdown in both outfits. Brigadier Hartsuff went forward to reconnoiter and was badly wounded by a shell fragment, and between the confusion of the command change and a mix-up in orders, the entire brigade remained standing under arms back in Poffenberger's meadow while Duryea's lines were broken and driven back. Finally everything was straightened out and Colonel Richard Coulter hurried the brigade forward.

The situation in Christian's brigade was even unhappier, for its commander unexpectedly went to pieces. As their columns approached the East Woods they were put through what a veteran described as "an unnecessary amount of drilling.... First it was 'forward,' then by the 'left flank,' then 'forward,' then by the 'right flank,' 'forward,' 'left oblique,' etc. until we thought they were making a show of us for the benefit of the Rebel artillery. Many of our men fell...." Stuart's and Colonel Lee's gunners had them in a crossfire now, and suddenly Colonel Christian dismounted and hurried to the rear, muttering that he had a great horror of such shelling. "He would duck and dodge his head, and go crouching along," one of the men recalled. Those in the ranks might feel a certain toleration for one of their own who fled the field, overcome by "cowardly legs," perhaps because at one time or another most of them experienced that same unreasoning fear when going into battle, but their tolerance seldom extended to officers who broke and ran. Veterans of the brigade remained unforgiving in recalling the incident years later. The unfortunate colonel would resign his commission two days after the battle.[8]

While Christian's brigade was trying to sort itself out, Hartsuff's troops under Colonel Coulter emerged from the Cornfield and the East Woods to meet a blizzard of fire. "Just in front of us a house was burning," a man in the 83rd New York wrote his family, "and the fire and smoke, flashing of muskets and whizzing of bullets, yells of men, etc., were perfectly horrible." Colonel Lee's guns had the exact range, and men were knocked sprawling at every step. "I do not see how any of us got out alive," a Massachusetts private told a friend. "The shot and shell fell about us thick and fast, I can tell you, but I did not think much about getting shot after the first volley. . . ."[9]

The battered Confederate regiments in this part of the field were barely hanging on, the survivors scrambling among the dead and wounded looking for cartridges, and General Lawton rushed a fresh brigade to their relief, Harry Hays's famous (or infamous) Louisiana Tigers. The Tigers had adopted the name and at least some of the raffish reputation of a unit recruited in the early days of the war from among the denizens of the New Orleans waterfront, and the brigade as a whole was a mixture of nationalities ranging from Irishmen to French Creoles. That strict Presbyterian Stonewall Jackson always regarded the habits and pleasures of the Louisiana "foreigners" with some suspicion, but there was no question of their worth in battle.[10] As they charged across the pasture toward the Cornfield they were riddled by shells from Thompson's and Matthews's batteries, and then they collided head-on with Coulter's men.

One of the regiments the Tigers faced, the 12th Massachusetts, was a world apart in reputation. It had gone off to war soon after Fort Sumter to the cheers of blue-blooded Bostonians, with Colonel Fletcher Webster, son of Daniel Webster, riding at its head. The 12th included a good many staunch abolitionists in its ranks, and it had popularized an old revivalist hymn with new words set to it that told how John Brown's body lay a-mouldering in the grave but his soul was marching on. It was a superb marching song, and became widely popular in the Army of the Potomac. (General McClellan found the lyrics objectionable and tried to ban

To the Dunker Church

it, but the men, especially the New Englanders, sang it anyway.) One day in Washington the poet Julia Ward Howe heard the soldiers singing it and was inspired to put new words to the measured cadence and create the greatest of all American war songs, "The Battle Hymn of the Republic." Those bright days of 1861 were only memories, Colonel Webster was dead, killed at Second Bull Run, and now the 12th Massachusetts came out of the Cornfield to encounter what the regimental historian called "the most deadly fire of the war."[11]

The charge of the Louisiana Tigers, joined by some of Colonel Douglass's Georgians, drove Coulter's men back into the corn and the fringes of the East Woods, but they rallied there and stubbornly held on. "Never did I see more rebs to fire at than at that moment presented themselves," one of the Federals wrote. Corporal Lewis Reed of the 12th Massachusetts saw men fall all around him when suddenly to his surprise he was sprawled on the ground as well, "with a strange feeling covering my body. I found my shirt and blouse filled with blood and I supposed it was my last day on earth. I had the usual feelings of home and friends." Then his senses returned enough for him to realize that he had been shot through the shoulder. He managed to get to his feet and make his way, staggering and half fainting, to the shelter of the East Woods. On all sides among the trees were stunned and wounded men streaming to the rear. "It was a hot time for us," Reed added, "and most all of our Regt. were used up in a very short time."

Captain Thompson aggressively pushed his Federal battery right into the Cornfield and found a position on a little hillock in the center from which he could direct fire at the enemy. At the same time, the Rebel batteries near the church were pouring case shot — fused shells filled with marble-sized balls — into the Cornfield and solid shot into the East Woods, where they seemed to the Yankees there to "drop down cords of wood at a time." It appeared that neither side could hold the initiative for long. The advancing Louisianians and Georgians were caught in a converging arc of fire from the corn in their front and the woods on their right, Colonel Douglass was killed, and finally they drifted back to the cover of the hollows and outcroppings in the pasture. From there they kept up a steady and murderous fire on the thinning Federal ranks.[12]

By now the battle in this part of the field was something over an hour old. At 7 A.M. Christian's brigade, put in charge of Colonel Peter Lyle of the 90th Pennsylvania after Colonel Christian's flight, finally advanced through the East Woods. Coulter hurried back from the front line, found Lyle, and called out, "For God's sake, come and help us out!" Coulter's wrecked formations were pulled back and Lyle's men took their places.

When the order was given to withdraw, there were only 32 men of the 12th Massachusetts left to escort the regimental colors to the rear. A few score more would eventually turn up — stragglers, men knocked loose from the unit in the heat of the fighting, others who had helped wounded comrades off the field — but when a final count was made the proud 12th was little more than a shell. Its commanding officer was mortally wounded, and it had lost 224 of the 334 men it took into battle, earning the terrible distinction of suffering the highest casualty rate (67 percent) of any Federal regiment on that bloody day. Losses among the Louisiana Tigers were very nearly as great — 61 percent — and every one of its regimental commanders was killed or wounded.[13]

For the moment, although the firing hardly slackened, the battle in the eastern part of the Cornfield and the East Woods was stalemated. Through a sequence of misfortunes, the attacks of Ricketts's three brigades were made piecemeal, without any coordination, and the Confederates were able to meet each with roughly equal or (in the case of Duryea's brigade) superior forces. Nor had the Federals been able to make their overall superiority in artillery felt, and from their commanding position near the Dunker church Colonel Lee's batteries played a major role in blunting Ricketts's assault.

While Hooker's left wing was making its fight, Doubleday's division took the offensive on the right in the area of the Hagerstown turnpike. Even as Hooker looked south toward the Dunker church, he had to be concerned for his open flank to the west. There was no knowing how many divisions Lee might have concealed in the lower ground toward the Potomac or behind the West Woods. Hooker placed four of his nine batteries to cover this flank and to contend with Stuart's guns on Nicodemus Hill, guarding them with a brigade of infantry. By his decision or McClellan's, the Twelfth Corps remained in reserve. This left but

To the Dunker Church

twenty-four of the First Corps guns to support the infantry, one more consequence of the Federals' cautious opening gambit. With three divisional batteries, Colonel Lee's batteries at the church, and Stuart's guns on Nicodemus Hill, Jackson had a substantial edge in field artillery for his fight with Hooker, an edge that the big Federal guns across the creek were unable to counter.

This long-range gunnery was not without effect, to be sure, and the shells took a toll among General Jones's men massed near the West Woods awaiting the assault of the Yankee infantry. An air burst stunned Jones so badly that Brigadier William E. Starke had to take over the divisional command. Starke had the men lie down behind whatever cover was handy. This shelling was a particular frustration to the Confederate artillerists, for they had just six 20-pounder Parrott rifles to reply to the twenty across the Antietam. The disparity would be evident in the casualty figures. The Federal reserve artillery suffered only eleven killed and wounded, compared with eighty-six in Stephen Lee's battalion, a favorite target of the Yankee gunners. It was this mismatch that led Colonel Lee to remember Antietam as "artillery Hell."[14]

Joe Hooker was a tall, florid, handsome man, clean-shaven in an army where beards were the rule, and he was mounted this morning on a large milk-white charger that caught the eye of everyone on the field. Hooker claimed to object to the nickname "Fighting Joe," saying it made him sound like a hotheaded bandit, although he had no objection to the laudatory newspaper publicity it brought him; he was always careful to cultivate reporters, and in fact the *New York Tribune*'s George Smalley was with him that day and acting as an unofficial courier. Yet Fighting Joe was a fair enough label, for Hooker was not a general to command from headquarters in the rear. He liked to lead from up front, encouraging his men by example, and now he was out in the open beyond the North Woods, pushing troops forward, personally placing batteries, seeking a firsthand view of the developing battle. John Gibbon's brigade moved out to spearhead Doubleday's attack, with two more brigades in close support — 2,200 men in all. "Hooker's men were fully up to their work," Smalley wrote. "They saw their General every where in the front, never away from the fire, and all the troops believed in their commander, and fought with a will."

The men of the First Corps were out to prove something on this field (perhaps to themselves as well as to the enemy), and if General Lee still believed the Yankees he was facing were disheartened and demoralized from past defeats, he would soon learn otherwise. Some of these troops had suffered through the Valley campaign against Jackson, and most of them had fought at Second Bull Run, and they knew only too well what it was to serve under poor generals; as the men of Gibbon's Black Hat Brigade had yelled at the taunting Rebels at Turner's Gap, this was not McDowell's command any more, and they had better watch out. McClellan thought the corps was "in bad condition as to discipline & everything else" when he took it into Maryland, but whether it was the assignment of Hooker to lead them, or their morale-boosting fight at Turner's Gap, or something else, the First Corps would fight, as one regimental historian wrote, with "clear grit."[15]

The Black Hat Brigade pushed southward astride the turnpike, with the 6th Wisconsin in the lead. Gibbon's men seemed to attract uncannily accurate artillery fire. At Turner's three days before, a single enemy shell had caused seven casualties in the marching ranks of the 2nd Wisconsin; now the men of the 6th had scarcely been ordered forward when a shell exploded squarely in their midst, killing two and wounding eleven. One man had his foot blown off, another lost both arms. The shaken regiment pushed on to the Miller farm and ran into a blaze of skirmishers' fire.

The Wisconsin skirmishers finally chased the Rebels out of Mr. Miller's garden and orchard and the Federal advance continued on both sides of the turnpike, entering the Cornfield at the same time Colonel Coulter was leading Hartsuff's brigade into the corn to their left. A two-gun section of Battery B, 4th U.S., General Gibbon's old regular army outfit, moved up to a supporting position near the Miller barn west of the turnpike, and close behind came the brigades of Walter Phelps and Marsena R. Patrick. There would be no delay in reinforcing this wing of Hooker's assault.

Off to its right beyond the turnpike the 6th Wisconsin had two companies detailed as skirmishers to protect its flank, but they entered a patch of drifting battle smoke and the last tatters of the morning ground fog, and in this hazy obscurity their regiment mistook them for the enemy and opened fire, sending them scattering for the rear. The suddenly exposed Federal flank was hit hard by a strong force of Confederate skirmishers hiding behind a rock ledge in the Miller pasture. Moments later, a battle line in two-brigade strength — Virginians under Colonel Andrew Grigsby of the Stonewall Brigade — rose up in the clover field in front of the West Woods and delivered a surprise volley that tore into the Wisconsin regiment, killing and wounding dozens of men.

To meet this threat, Gibbon pushed the 7th Wisconsin and the 19th Indiana into the fields west of the turnpike, and Doubleday moved Patrick's brigade up in support, and their steady volleys pressed the Virginians back toward the woods. Grigsby sent his aide pelting off to General Starke with word that he had to have help to hold the flank. Just as the aide arrived to deliver the message, he saw the Virginians break and run for cover. "There they are, coming back now, General," he announced. The remnants of Grigsby's two brigades, reduced to barely 250 men, were rallied and took shelter behind the numerous limestone ledges that marked the woodlot, but the Federals had a solid foothold in the West Woods that advanced them to a point opposite the Cornfield.[16]

Freed from the pressure on his flank, General Gibbon sent the 2nd and 6th Wisconsin, with Phelps's brigade close behind, on through the Cornfield. They reached the southern edge to encounter the same deadly fire that had greeted Duryea's brigade when it burst out of the corn a half hour earlier. A long Rebel battle line rose from the pasture where it had been lying unseen and unleashed a killing volley. "Men, I can not say fell; they were knocked out of the ranks by dozens," recalled Major Rufus Dawes, who had taken command of the 6th Wisconsin when its colonel was wounded. The Wisconsin regiments closed ranks and began to fire back, supported now by the men of the 84th New York, distinctive in baggy red zouave pants that were a holdover from their Sunday-soldier days as militiamen.

In the choking smoke and ceaseless noise Major Dawes found his men yelling incoherently, overcome with a wild, hysterical excitement. "Men and officers of New York and Wisconsin are fused into a common mass, in the frantic struggle to shoot fast," he wrote. "Every body tears cartridges, loads, passes guns, or shoots. Men are falling in their places or running back into the corn." In the line of battle facing them, three Georgia regiments of Lawton's brigade, there was the same furious, desperate energy. Farther to the east in the pasture and the corn the battle was raging between the Louisiana Tigers and the New York and Massachusetts men of Hartsuff's brigade. "The fire now became fearful and incessant," Southern war correspondent Felix de Fontaine wrote, " . . . merged into a tumultuous chorus that made the earth tremble. The discharge of musketry sounded upon the ear like the rolling of a thousand distant drums. . . . "[17]

Pressed hard by Gibbon's spearhead, the Georgians were giving way when suddenly a new Rebel line rushed out of the West Woods and came slanting across the clover field. These were the 1,150 men of General Starke's two remaining brigades, led by the general himself. Their charge carried them to the stout post-and-rail fence along the turnpike, where they lay down and blazed away at the Yankees in the pasture beyond the road. At one point the battle lines were scarcely thirty yards apart.

Starke's counterattack succeeded in halting Doubleday's offensive, but — like Hays's Louisiana Tigers — only at the cost of being trapped in a murderous converging fire. His men were hit by musketry from the pasture and the Cornfield, by case shot rained on them from Battery B in the Miller barnyard to the north, and by sharpshooting skirmishers advancing on their flank and rear from the Federal foothold in the West Woods. General Starke was struck by three bullets and carried from the field; he would die within the hour. The Stonewall Brigade's Grigsby took over, a colonel in command of a division. The order was given to pull back to their starting point.

Captain R. P. Jennings of the 23rd Virginia, wounded in the hip by the burst of a Federal case shot, found himself the lone survivor of his company. Another wounded man urged him not to risk the gauntlet of fire to reach the rear. "I may as well be killed running as lying still," Jennings replied. To his amazement, he "ran like a deer" to the safety of the woods, and credited fear with overcoming his crippling wound. As the 1st Louisiana pulled back, its color-bearer was hit and the regimental flag toppled over the turnpike fence into the roadway. Lewis C. Parmelee, adjutant of the 2nd U.S. Sharpshooters, dashed out into the road, picked up the flag and tried to jam the broken staff on the point of his sword,

To the Dunker Church

and was cut down by seven bullets. Another Yankee picked up the colors and escaped safely. What was left of Starke's brigades sheltered in the West Woods to continue the fight.[18]

General McClellan had established his headquarters tents on the lawns of Philip Pry, whose large brick house was on the high ground east of the Antietam, not quite two miles from where Hooker opened the battle. A little redan of fence rails had been erected for protection against enemy shells, and easy chairs were brought from Mr. Pry's parlor for the comfort of the high command. Stakes were driven into the ground as telescope rests, and a local man was on hand to help plot the action on the headquarters maps.

The general was intent on the battle panorama unfolding before him. At his side was Fitz John Porter, resting a telescope on the top rail of the redan. "His observations he communicated to the commander by nods, signs, or in words so low-toned and brief that the nearest by-standers had but little benefit with them," wrote Colonel Strother of the headquarters staff. Strother noted McClellan's extreme calm as he sat smoking a cigar, talking quietly with the staff, and receiving and sending messages. As the clamor of the guns intensified on the Confederate left, a flag-signal report from the First Corps was relayed to headquarters, and McClellan was heard to remark, "All goes well; Hooker is driving them." As yet he had issued no orders to Burnside's Ninth Corps, posted opposite the Confederate right, or to Sumner's Second Corps, bivouacked near army headquarters. The fight remained Hooker's alone, with Mansfield's Twelfth Corps still in reserve.[19]

At his headquarters in a grove of trees just west of Sharpsburg, General Lee was equally intent on events. The divisions of McLaws and Richard Anderson had resumed their march from Harper's Ferry about midnight, and by sunrise the exhausted troops were filing into the fields near headquarters, where Lee ordered them to be rested before being put in the line. While the battle intensified in Jackson's sector, the Federals opposite the Rohrbach Bridge were seen to be inactive except for desultory shelling. At about 7:15 A.M. Lee sent orders to one of Longstreet's brigades posted on the right, George T. Anderson's Georgians, to march to the other flank to support Jackson.

Fifteen minutes later, at Harper's Ferry, A. P. Hill's Light Divi-

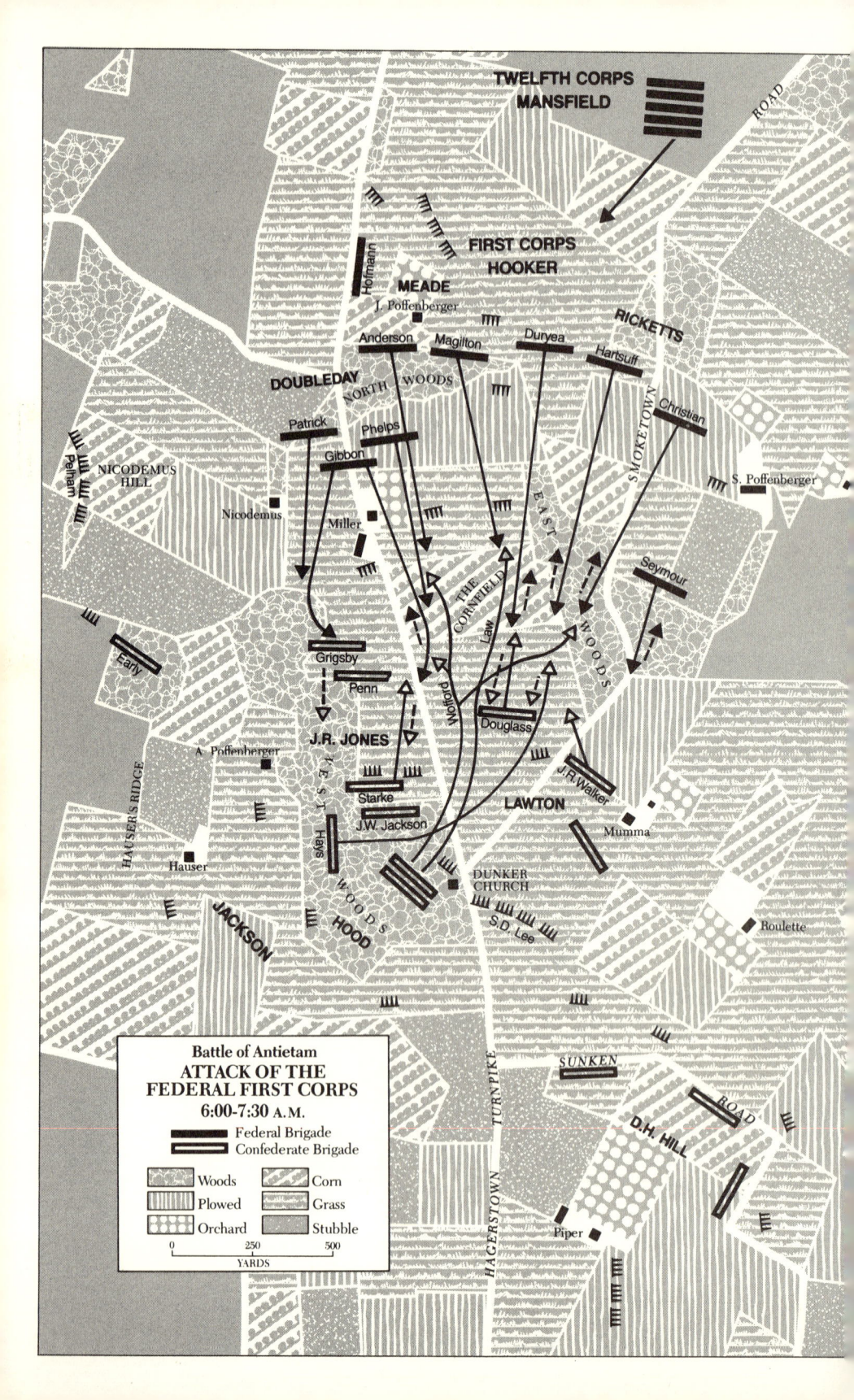

Battle of Antietam
ATTACK OF THE FEDERAL FIRST CORPS
6:00-7:30 A.M.

- ▬ Federal Brigade
- ▭ Confederate Brigade
- Woods
- Plowed
- Orchard
- Corn
- Grass
- Stubble

0 — 250 — 500 YARDS

sion set off for Sharpsburg, seventeen miles away. Lee's courier had reached Hill at 6:30, and he had his men on the road within the hour. The pace was fast, and the march regulation of a ten-minute rest every hour that Jackson prescribed for his foot cavalry was ignored. Hill rode back and forth along the column exhorting his men. The veterans noticed that he was wearing the distinctive red shirt he favored when going into battle.[20]

As the struggle against Hooker's attack grew more desperate, a staff aide searched out General Hood at his bivouac in the West Woods behind the Dunker church with an appeal from the hard-pressed Lawton. "General Lawton sends his compliments with the request that you come at once to his support," the aide said, and added that Lawton had been wounded. Hood, his fighting blood up, was expecting the summons and promptly called his division to arms.

John Bell Hood had a positive taste for war, and a way of inspiring his troops to look on combat as he did. He was thirty-one, an imposing figure over six feet tall with a full tawny beard and (wrote the diarist Mrs. Chesnut) a "sad Quixote face, the face of an old crusader who believed in his cause, his cross, his crown." A West Pointer from Kentucky, Hood had linked himself with the Texas troops in the army when his state did not secede, and on the Peninsula the men of his Texas Brigade won a reputation as superb shock troops. Led now by Colonel William T. Wofford, the brigade included the three Texas regiments, plus the 18th Georgia and Hampton's Legion from South Carolina. Hood's second brigade, under Evander Law — 2nd and 11th Mississippi, 4th Alabama, 6th North Carolina — contained fighters just as determined. Following the previous night's clash with Meade's Pennsylvanians, the division was back in reserve trying to get something to eat. The commissary wagons did not appear until shortly before daylight, and then the only issue was flour. When the call to arms sounded, the men were baking hoecakes on their ramrods, and they bolted what they could of the half-baked dough as they snatched up their rifles and fell into line.[21]

It was 7 A.M. when Hood's division, 2,300 strong, came pouring out of the woods, crossed the turnpike at the gap in the fences near the church, and pushed on into the pasture south of the Cornfield. Pausing only long enough to let the remnants of Lawton's command through their ranks, they raised the Rebel yell and delivered a volley that, said Major Dawes, was "like a scythe running through our line." The Yankee spearhead was knocked almost bodily back into the Cornfield. Dawes snatched up the regimental flag and swung it back and forth over his head to try and rally his men. "When I took that color in my hand, I gave up all hope of life," he later wrote his sweetheart. "It did not occur to me as possible that I could carry that flag into the deadly storm and live (four men had fallen under it). I felt all that burning throng of thoughts and emotions that always come with the presence of Death."

Hood rushed his troops into a line stretching from the Hagerstown turnpike across the pasture to the East Woods and ordered a general advance. One of Jackson's aides reached him just then with a request for an appraisal of the situation. "Tell General Jackson," he replied, "unless I get reinforcements I must be forced back, but I am going on while I can!" Wofford's and Law's men drove forward through the bloody wreckage of dead and wounded from the earlier fighting. They lay so thickly, Hood said, that he had to guide his horse's every step so as not to trample the injured.[22]

The Federal artillery in and beyond the Cornfield redoubled its efforts. The gunners in Thompson's Pennsylvania battery in the corn could not fire canister, the most effective weapon against infantry at short range, because of the scores of wounded lying in front of the guns. They turned to case shot, progressively shortening the range until the shells were fused to explode just a second and a half after leaving the muzzles. Rebel sharpshooters had the range as well. "My men and horses were dropping fast," Thompson said, and he gave the order to pull back. So many of the battery horses were hit that the guns had to be abandoned during the withdrawal.

The right of the Rebel line pitched into Christian's brigade, the last of General Ricketts's units still on the field. These Yankees had been assailed by an accurate fire from the Mumma farm from the moment they reached the front, and the ominous sight of Hood's veterans, yelling and firing as they came, seemed to unnerve some of the officers. Three of the four regiments were ordered back through the East Woods, leaving the 90th Pennsylvania to bear the brunt of the counterattack. Shelling and musketry, wrote a diarist in the 90th, were "flying around like hail, cutting down trees or any thing in the way." Finally the 90th, with half its men dead or wounded, could hold no longer, but it withdrew slowly and defiantly, the color-bearer walking backward all the way, believing that to be found on the field with a wound in the back was the ultimate disgrace. Ricketts's entire division was now out of the fight, with more than a third of his men casualties and most of the survivors far to the rear and under no effective command.

The 4th Alabama and 5th Texas, accompanied by the remaining men of the 21st Georgia who had been fighting stubbornly on the Mumma farm since dawn, swept into the East Woods on the heels of the retreating Federals. Their counterattack accelerated the stream of stragglers and walking wounded pouring out of the woods toward refuge in the fields and farms to the north. A man in Hartsuff's brigade who had stayed behind to help a wounded friend wrote that "fear gave us wings, and strength as well," and somehow he and his injured charge outdistanced their pursuers. The more seriously wounded could only curse bitterly as the battle swept over them once more, knowing that help was now farther away than ever. A captain in the 4th Alabama saw a wounded Union officer lying behind a log painfully crawl to the other side of his shelter as the Rebels passed him so he would not be hit by the shots of his retreating comrades.[23]

The rest of Hood's division stormed into the Cornfield and up to the fence bordering the turnpike on their left. "In ten minutes the fortune of the day seemed to have changed," wrote the *Tribune*'s Smalley. Hooker, calling at last for support from Mansfield's Twelfth Corps, moved up his last uncommitted troops, two brigades of Meade's Pennsylvania division, and threw two more batteries into the battle. The Cornfield again became a seething, smoking caldron.

Three of Evander Law's regiments on the right pushed all the way through the corn to the rail fence at its northern boundary and opened fire on the flank of one of Meade's brigades as it was hurrying toward the East Woods to stem the breakthrough there. The two regiments in the center splintered and broke under the assault, but the other two held their ground stubbornly. One of Meade's men remembered being stampeded and not expecting to stop running "this side of the Pennsylvania line," only to be brought up short by a boyish soldier swinging his hat and crying, "Rally, boys, rally! Die like men; don't run like dogs!" Law's Mississippians, the fury of battle on them, leaped the fence and ran into the open field beyond to blaze away at the Pennsylvanians to left and right and at the batteries on their front that were firing double-shotted canister at a range of less than 200 yards. Unprotected artillery could not last long against infantry fire at that distance, and there was carnage among the gunners and battery horses. One battery was abandoned, a second silenced, and a third driven off before it could unlimber and open fire.

The contest in the western half of the Cornfield and along the turnpike was if possible even bloodier. Three of Wofford's regiments — 4th Texas, 18th Georgia, and Hampton's Legion — wheeled into line of battle facing almost due west and became locked in a murderous exchange with Gibbon's and Patrick's men across the road and with Lieutenant James Stewart's two-gun section of Battery B. A pickup force from Starke's battered command moved up along the fence on the western side of the road. In a matter of minutes fourteen of Stewart's gunners were shot down. The battle smoke was now so thick that hardly anything could be seen but waving flags. Three of the Hampton Legion's color-bearers were shot down in succession. Major J. H. Dingle seized the flag, shouted, "Legion, follow your colors!" and rushed to the turnpike fence only fifty yards from the Yankee ranks, and then he too was killed.[24]

The other four Napoleons of Battery B came forward in a rush and went into battery alongside Lieutenant Stewart's guns near the Miller barnyard west of the turnpike. As they opened with canister, former artillerist Gibbon noticed that in the frantic routine of loading and firing one of the gunners had allowed the elevating screw to run down until his gun was firing high and harmlessly over the heads of the attackers. Gibbon's shouts went unheard in the tornado of sound, and he dashed over to the piece, ran up the screw until the barrel was pointing well below the horizontal — canister was most deadly when it struck in front of charging troops and ricocheted upward — and the next shot splintered the turnpike fence and carried away the whole front rank of the nearest Confederates.

Still Hood's men came on. Battery B went to double charges of canister. Regulations called for the powder cartridge of the extra round to be knocked off so as not to risk a burst barrel, but that was a technique beyond the skills of one of the infantry volunteers serving the battery in the crisis, and he kept loading full double charges; somehow the Napoleon withstood the strain. Men were literally torn apart by this storm of fire. A Union officer saw a shot strike home and "an arm go 30 feet into the air and fall back again.... It was just awful." "Whole ranks went down," Gibbon wrote, "and after we got possession of the field, dead men were found piled on top of each other." The Rebel drive along the turnpike was stymied.[25]

Meanwhile, the 1st Texas had "slipped the bridle" and recklessly pursued the retreating Federals almost to the fence at the northern edge of the Cornfield, 150 yards ahead of the rest of the brigade. Their aggressiveness was their undoing. General Meade was working hard to dam the break, and he had Colonel Robert Anderson's brigade posted along the fence line. The Pennsylvanians rested their rifles on the lower rails and waited until they could see the Texans' legs beneath the obscuring curtain of smoke; then, at thirty yards, they unleashed a volley that had the savage impact of double rounds of canister. Without support, smashed from front and flank by musketry and artillery, the Texans fell back — the few that were left. Eight color-bearers were down and the regimental flag lost in the confusion; two companies were completely wiped out. All in all, four of every five men in the 1st Texas were killed or wounded in perhaps twenty minutes.

As new forces from both armies appeared on the blasted field, the strong tide of Hood's counterattack began to recede, leaving only a beachhead in the East Woods. It was now 7:30 A.M., and in an hour and a half of fighting Hooker's command and Jackson's had been reduced to mutual shambles. Jackson had held back one brigade to protect Stuart's batteries on Nicodemus Hill, and Hooker had posted a brigade with his batteries that were dueling Stuart, but they had pushed every other unit they commanded into the struggle. Jackson had been able to meet force with equal force in the successive attacks, and the two sides were about where they had been when the killing began at dawn.

Of the three Confederate brigades under General Lawton that

made their fight on the Mumma farm and in the pasture south of the Cornfield, one of every two men had been hit. Lawton was wounded, one brigade commander was dead and a second wounded, and eleven of the fifteen regimental commanders were casualties. A third of the troops in Jackson's old division, commanded in the fight for the West Woods by General Starke, had been shot down. Starke was mortally wounded, and the toll of officers was nearly as severe as in Lawton's division. Hood's division was simply shot to pieces; when he was asked where his command was, Hood replied, "Dead on the field." In his seven regiments that fought in the Cornfield and along the turnpike, nearly 60 percent were killed or wounded.

Casualties in Hooker's First Corps came to almost 2,600, close to a third of those engaged. General Ricketts had gone into action with just over 3,150 men; now, between casualties and heavy straggling, he counted barely 300 answering the colors. The situation in the divisions of Meade and Doubleday was better — they seem to have applied a firmer hand to straggling than did Ricketts — but neither was in any condition to renew its advance when Mansfield's Twelfth Corps came on the scene. The First Corps had indeed fought with "clear grit," but without support from the rest of the Army of the Potomac.

There had been an awful frenzy to the combat, and Rebel and Yankee veterans of the Seven Days' battles and the struggle at Second Bull Run would remember this as quite simply the worst fighting they had ever experienced. Perhaps in part it was the nature of the battlefield. In previous battles it was rare for men actually to see their foes, but repeatedly on this open ground the battle lines had been a hundred yards apart or fifty or even thirty, and the struggle became personal and somehow savage beyond all reckoning. One officer had even urged his men not to fire until they saw the whites of their opponents' eyes, an anachronism in the era of the rifled musket that was effectively accurate at 300 yards and more and could kill at half a mile. The survivors were stunned and unutterably weary; for most of those who had been at the center of the firestorms in the East Woods or the West Woods or the Cornfield in these early morning hours, it was quite beyond reason that they could return to the contest any time soon.[26]

Whatever role Hooker and McClellan had originally intended

To the Dunker Church

for the Twelfth Corps — to exploit a breakthrough by the First, to guard against some unexpected offensive by the supposed Rebel host — its mission now was to shore up Hooker's wrecked formations. These Yankees were from Nathaniel Banks's old command, bearing a catalog of unhappy encounters with Stonewall Jackson in the Valley and the campaign of Second Bull Run, and they were badly thinned as a result. Three Ohio regiments in one of its brigades were so sparse that there was headquarters talk of combining them, but the Ohio boys objected to this loss of identity, and the idea was shelved. Bringing the brigade up to strength was the 28th Pennsylvania, going into action for the first time and mustering almost twice the total manpower of the Ohio regiments. The same disparity marked the entire corps. There were five other big regiments, hardly a month from home, that would have to endure their baptism of fire with only the sketchiest of training. The Twelfth Corps carried some 7,200 infantrymen into action, half of whom had never before fired their rifles in anger.

Their commander, Joseph K. F. Mansfield, was new on the job as well. He was a forty-year army man, white-haired and white-bearded but with a vigorous manner, who had arrived only on September 15 to take over the corps. He had been an engineer in the old army and this was his first combat command, and his officers thought him nervous and somewhat fussy. The men liked him well enough, however, as he bustled about the camps displaying enthusiasm and fatherly assurance. His effort to build confidence was deliberate, for General Mansfield had an old regular's mistrust of the staying power of volunteers.

His men were roused from their bivouacs a mile or so to the rear of the First Corps as soon as the battle opened, and immediately ordered to arms. They formed columns and started to march to the sound of the firing, but no one seemed to know what was going on, and there were long halts. Officers would let the men break ranks to make breakfast and boil coffee, but they no sooner got their fires kindled than the order came to move out; a few hundred yards' advance and the whole scene was repeated. In later years, when veterans of the corps put down their recollections of Antietam, a number made a point of noting how many times they were frustrated that day trying to make morning coffee.

During one of these halts Lieutenant Colonel Wilder Dwight of the 2nd Massachusetts, like a good many other men, started a letter home. "Dear Mother," he wrote, "It is a misty, moisty morning; we are engaging the enemy, and are drawn up in support of Hooker, who is now banging away most briskly. I write in the saddle, to send you my love, and to say that I am very well so far...."

Mansfield rode on ahead to get his orders from Hooker. As the Twelfth Corps's lead brigade moved through an open field to the east of the Miller farmstead, the Confederate gunners took them under fire. It was a bad moment for the rookies. At the scream of a shell "most men ducked and then would straighten up with a sickly kind of grin," wrote a man in the new 125th Pennsylvania. They were also unnerved by the grim debris of battle beginning to appear. The walking wounded were coming back, bloody and dazed. "Go in, boys," a man with a shattered wrist kept repeating; "give 'em hell, give 'em hell!" They passed an artilleryman with both legs terribly mangled, screaming in agony and pleading for someone to shoot him.[27]

The troops were still in their compact marching formation, and officers ordered deployment in open battle lines to lessen the risk as the shelling intensified. On his return Mansfield countermanded the order, insisting they stay in column. If spread out beyond the immediate control of their officers, he said, the men would break and run. General Alpheus Williams, back in command of a division after his temporary stint as corps commander, protested, but Mansfield was deaf to his arguments. The orders were to move immediately to Hooker's relief. They were to form in an arc behind the hard-pressed First Corps, extending from the Hagerstown turnpike on the west across the Miller farm and into the East Woods.

The immediate problem was maneuvering and deploying the big new regiments — there were three of them in Brigadier Samuel Crawford's leading brigade — which had only the slightest experience in such matters. General Williams himself took the green 124th Pennsylvania over to the turnpike and prodded it into a line of battle facing south. "I got mine in line pretty well by having a fence to align it on," he wrote his family. These new men were willing enough and certainly courageous enough, he went on, but neither they nor their officers knew the first thing about drilling, and "in attempting to move them forward or back or to make any maneuver they fell into inextricable confusion and fell to the rear, where they were easily rallied.... Standing still, they fought bravely."

Mansfield, meanwhile, was personally leading part of Crawford's brigade to the other flank, in the East Woods. He insisted that even the old regiments remain in column. He placed the veteran 10th Maine where he wanted it and went back for another regiment, and as soon as he was out of sight the eminently sensible Maine colonel promptly deployed his men in line of battle. Yet however outdated Mansfield's tactics may have been, the arrival of these massed formations was not without effect. The sight of the 125th Pennsylvania marching toward their flank, and looking big enough to be an entire brigade, was enough to persuade Hood's embattled troops in the eastern part of the Cornfield to pull back.[28]

While the Twelfth Corps was maneuvering into position, the Rebels too were pushing fresh forces into the fight. D. H. Hill, in charge of the center of the Confederate line, had stationed Roswell Ripley's brigade on the Mumma farm, and when Hood launched his doomed counterattack Hill himself led Ripley's men at the double-quick toward the pasture south of the Cornfield. It was a timely move, although Hood would complain that it was not timely enough, that his division was decimated for lack of support. It is more likely that his attack was pressed with such suddenness — and repelled with such ferocity — that it was over before help could get there. In any case, when Wofford's men and Law's were driven out of the corn, Ripley's brigade was at hand to deliver smashing volleys at their Yankee pursuers and drive them in turn back to their starting places. The Rebels advanced to the southern edge of the corn to link up with Hood's men still hanging on in the East Woods, and Hill called up two more of his brigades.

Hood's men in the East Woods — 4th Alabama, 5th Texas, and the adventuresome Georgians they had picked up on the way — were engaged in Indian-style bushwhacking and giving a good account of themselves. The woodlot was fairly open, with little underbrush, but it was full of rock ledges and fallen logs and stacks of cordwood that farmers had cut, and from behind this cover they kept up a sharp fire at the Yankees still in the Cornfield and at the

10th Maine at the northern edge of the woods. In testimony to the effectiveness of these tactics, a Maine man wrote that he expended his forty rounds as conscientiously as possible, but he could not be certain that he had actually seen a live Rebel the whole time.

When General Mansfield returned, leading another regiment, he saw the 10th Maine firing into the woods. Someone on Hooker's staff had told him there were still First Corps men in there, and he rode down the regimental line crying out, "You are firing into our own men!" There was a chorus of disagreement. As Sergeant E. J. Libby recalled it, "Thomas Wait and myself told him we were not firing at our own men for those that were firing at us from behind the trees had been firing at us from the first." Others pointed to suddenly visible Rebels leveling their rifles at them — and at him; mounted officers were prime targets.

"Yes, yes, you are right," Mansfield replied, and just then his horse was hit and a bullet caught him squarely in the chest. He managed to dismount and lead his horse to the rear before collapsing. He was carried to an ambulance and delivered to a field hospital, where a flustered young surgeon gave him a drink of whiskey that nearly choked him. He clung to life through the night, and died the next day. For months the earnest old regular had pulled strings in Washington to win the field command that would crown his career, and it had lasted barely two days.[29]

The regiment General Mansfield led to the front just before his mortal wounding was the 128th Pennsylvania, another of the new formations in Crawford's brigade. The 128th was one of the nine-month levies that the indefatigable Governor Curtin assembled in answer to President Lincoln's July call for 300,000 new troops. It reached Washington in the midst of General Pope's crisis and spent most of its time there laboring on the city's fortifications. On this morning its lack of drill was tragically apparent.

Mansfield had ordered the regiment to deploy from its marching column into a line of battle partly in the East Woods and partly in the pasture just short of the no-man's land of the Cornfield. The maneuver had hardly begun when Hood's men in the woods and Ripley's on the far edge of the Cornfield sent a hail of bullets into the ranks, killing the regiment's colonel and wounding his second-in-command. The bewildered and leaderless rookies promptly got themselves into a terrible tangle. Whatever rudiments of drill they

To the Dunker Church

had learned were immediately forgotten under the killing fire. They stumbled off to the right and left where they thought they were supposed to go, nobody could hear any orders in all the racket, and when they tried to shoot back at their tormentors there always seemed to be comrades in the way.

Colonel Joseph Knipe of the 46th Pennsylvania hurried up and began sorting things out, and the 28th New York sent several sergeants "to help to untie the knot," and finally they were horsed into a rough line of battle. No one told them what to do next, however. Mansfield had been hit and the other general officers were off somewhere else. Colonel Knipe suggested to the 128th's major that an advance was better than just standing there taking losses. The order was given and the rookies did their best to atone for the fumbling by charging straight into the Cornfield "in gallant style, cheering as they moved," as the major reported. Then they reached the southern edge of the corn and Ripley's men simply mowed them down. The shocked survivors fled back through the Cornfield and the East Woods and out of the battle, having achieved nothing but the addition of 118 names to the casualty rolls.[30]

Mansfield's wounding put General Williams back in command of the Twelfth Corps, and he held a hurried conference with Hooker in front of the North Woods "amidst a very unpleasant shower of bullets," as Williams recalled the scene. Gibbon and Meade were there to call urgently for reinforcements. Hooker had Williams direct one of his trailing brigades off to the right to brace Gibbon's position near the West Woods, and then George H. Gordon's brigade arrived at the double-quick to plug the hole Hood's men had punched in the center of the First Corps line. Their greeting was a bloody one. As Gordon's 2nd Massachusetts, 3rd Wisconsin, and 27th Indiana approached the Cornfield, they had to endure the enemy's fire for maddeningly long minutes without being able to reply until the Pennsylvania rookies milling about in the corn in front of them got out of the way. Then the vicious battle for the Cornfield was renewed.

"Very soon our Reg was under fire the balls whisin over us," Private Calvin Leach of the 1st North Carolina recorded in his diary. " . . . I commenced loading and shooting with all my might but my gun got chooked the first round, and I picked up a gun of one of my comrades who fell by my side and continued to fire.... I do not know whether I killed any one or not." A good number of Ripley's men were still equipped with old smoothbores firing "buck and ball" — a cartridge containing three buckshot in addition to the standard ball — that at this close range had the effect of miniature shotgun loads. The deadly spray from the smoothbores of the 3rd North Carolina inflicted an extraordinarily high ratio of wounds (eleven wounded for every man killed) in the 27th Indiana facing it. The 27th's toll of casualties included Corporal Barton Mitchell, who had discovered the lost copy of Lee's Order 191 four days before, and his friend Sergeant John Bloss, both wounded; the company commander to whom they had taken their find, Captain Peter Kop, was killed.[31]

Harvey Hill was furiously busy pushing more men into the fight. Alfred Colquitt's brigade came hurrying up from the Confederate center, and as the men crossed the Mumma farm they were startled by the incongruous sight of half a dozen cows, panicked by the roar of the artillery, bearing down on them. "I remember I was more afraid just then of being run over by a cow than of being hit by a bullet," a man in the 6th Georgia wrote. They avoided the stampede and advanced into the Cornfield to reinforce Ripley's brigade. Hill ordered Garland's brigade, put under D. K. McRae after General Garland's death at Fox's Gap, into the East Woods to hold the flank. This infusion of over 2,000 fresh troops once again threatened to crack open the Union lines.

Gordon's Yankees from Massachusetts and Wisconsin and Indiana would not break, however. The Miller pasture north of the Cornfield was on slightly higher ground, and their line "crowned the hill and stood out darkly against the sky, but lighted and shrouded over in flame and smoke," correspondent Smalley wrote. "... There was no more gallant, determined, heroic fighting in all this desperate day." Whenever they could find a clear field of fire, the Federal artillery poured canister into the Rebels in the corn and long-range fire from across the creek. For his part, Stephen Lee ordered two sections of his guns into close support, firing over the heads of his own men into the Yankee troops and guns beyond. "The roar of the infantry was beyond anything conceivable to the uninitiated," General Williams told his family. "... If all the stone and brick houses of Broadway should tumble at once the roar and rattle could hardly be greater, and amidst this, hundreds of pieces of artillery, right and left, were thundering as a sort of bass to the infernal music." The cannon could be heard as far away as Hagerstown, sounding like the muttered rumble of a summer storm on the horizon.

Both battle lines were soon blanketed in choking smoke. An officer of the 3rd North Carolina came upon one of the regiment's new conscripts walking distractedly back and forth behind the firing line, complaining that he could not see anything to shoot at and hated to waste his ammunition. He was instructed to lie down and "look for blue britches under the smoke." At this the conscript's face lit up in comprehension, and he went to work. A Pennsylvanian in Gordon's brigade, also going into battle for the first time, told how under fire he "lost all fear and thought of Home and friends, and a Reckless don't care disposition Seemed to take possession of me. Then was two of our Company Shot down near me and Even their Shrieks and yells did not affect me in the least. This is the way I felt and I have heard other Soldiers Say the Same...."[32]

Garland's brigade of North Carolinians had been in a state of shock since its rout at Fox's Gap and the death there of its much-admired commander. The task of restoring morale was complicated by the lack of time and the large leavening of ill-trained conscripts in the ranks, and it was not under very firm control when it entered the bloody battleground of the East Woods. No one could say where friend or foe might be encountered, producing nervous alarms and scattered shots at the remnants of Hood's division still stubbornly holding their ground among the trees. Just as a battle line was formed, an excitable young officer of the 5th North Carolina spotted what seemed to be a brigade-sized body of Federals angling toward the right of their line. He cried out loudly that they were about to be flanked. Suddenly all anyone could think of was Fox's Gap, and the result was mass panic. "The most unutterable stampede occurred," brigade commander McRae recalled. "It was one of those marvelous flights that beggar explanation or description."

The 5th North Carolina, containing seventy-five or eighty conscripts, was apparently the first to break, carrying most of the other regiments with it. The men in Hood's 5th Texas watched the flight in amazement and mounting fury. They had been calling repeatedly for reinforcement as they hung on in the East Woods by their fingernails, help was finally at hand, and then it was gone almost before firing a shot. One Texas captain told his company to open fire on the fleeing men, then in disgust countermanded the order. With blood in his eye he collared one of the conscript's officers and demanded to know the man's name and regiment. The North Carolinian took one look at the enraged Texan confronting him, exclaimed, "I'll be damned if I will tell you!" and dashed off after the fugitives. Some did not stop running until they reached Sharpsburg and beyond; some stood their ground and others were rallied and fought well enough later in the day. As an effective command, however, Garland's brigade was out of the battle.[33]

The "brigade" of Yankees that set the North Carolinians off on their flight was the 28th Pennsylvania regiment, coming into battle for the first time almost 800 strong. It was the spearhead of the Twelfth Corps's Second Division, commanded by Brigadier George Sears Greene, and its flanking move on the Rebels fighting in the Cornfield was exactly what Garland's brigade had been sent into the East Woods to prevent. General Greene, related to the famous Revolutionary War general Nathanael Greene and father of Lieutenant Dana Greene, executive officer of the *Monitor* in her historic fight with the *Merrimack,* was a tough old warhorse who believed in hard drill and discipline in camp and hard driving on the battlefield. He was just the sort to exploit the opportunity opening before him.

The Pennsylvanians were brigaded with the three small Ohio regiments, under Colonel Hector Tyndale, and as they entered the East Woods Tyndale swung them around until they were facing almost due west. When the Ohioans on the right of the line reached the edge of the woods, they could see not thirty yards away a line of Colquitt's men along the fence marking the northern boundary of the Cornfield, intent on their fight with Gordon's Yankees in the pasture beyond. The Ohioans quickly unleashed a murderous volley on the unsuspecting Rebels, taking them squarely in the flank at pointblank range. Coming up alongside, the 28th Pennsylvania added a volley delivered with such precision that it sounded like a single thunderous explosion. "The sight at the fence, where the enemy was standing when we gave

The Maryland campaign opened on September 4, 1862, as Lee's Army of Northern Virginia began crossing the Potomac at White's Ford near Leesburg, Virginia. Northern war artist Alfred R. Waud sketched this moonlit scene from the Maryland shore. In the foreground are Union scouts.

Robert E. Lee

James Longstreet

Thomas J. Jackson

A. P. Hill

D. H. Hill

John B. Hood

Lafayette McLaws

George B. McClellan

Joseph Hooker

Ambrose Burnside

Edwin V. Sumner

Israel B. Richardson

William B. Franklin

Harper's Ferry, photographed in late 1861 from the foot of Maryland Heights. In September 1862 a pontoon footbridge spanned the Potomac to the right of the piers of the burned-out Baltimore and Ohio railroad bridge.

Alfred Waud sketched the crest of Maryland Heights, overlooking Harper's Ferry, where the 126th New York was routed by the Confederates.

An 1864 lithograph of the 23rd Ohio attacking at Fox's Gap on South Mountain on September 14. At far left is the wounded Rutherford Hayes.

The Lutheran church in Sharpsburg, photographed shortly after the battle by Alexander Gardner, was heavily damaged by Federal artillery fire. Rebel flag signalmen were stationed in the tower during the fighting.

Gardner's general view of Sharpsburg looks westward along Main Street. Some residents remained on September 17, sheltering in basements.

The Boonsboro turnpike and the Middle Bridge over Antietam Creek, a mile from Sharpsburg, taken by Gardner from the Union lines.

A painting by Union soldier James Hope shows Stephen Lee's Rebel batteries in action. At left are the Dunker church and the West Woods.

A close-up of the scene depicted by Hope, photographed by Gardner after the battle, now strewn with Southern dead and an artillery limber.

Human wreckage from the struggle north of the Dunker church between Hooker's First Corps and Stonewall Jackson. These are Louisianians of Starke's brigade. At right is the Hagerstown turnpike; at left is a farm lane.

The assault on Lee's center, by combat artist Frank H. Schell. In the distance, beyond the burning Mumma farmhouse, smoke clouds rise from the Sunken Road fighting. A Rhode Island battery moves up in support.

These Northerners of the Irish Brigade, killed in storming the Sunken Road, were gathered for burial when Gardner photographed them.

The heaped dead in the section of the Sunken Road defended by George B. Anderson's North Carolinians. Beyond is the trampled Piper cornfield.

The triumphant charge across the Burnside Bridge by the 51st Pennsylvania and the 51st New York. Edwin Forbes did this sketch and the one below.

High tide of the Ninth Corps's advance toward Sharpsburg, led by the zouaves of the 9th New York. A. P. Hill's counterattack drove them back.

Alfred Waud visited a field hospital behind the Union lines during the fighting and sketched surgeons at work, assisted by civilian volunteers.

On September 18 a truce was declared to exchange wounded and to begin burial of the dead. Waud drew Rebels and Yankees at the Dunker church.

On October 3, during his visit to the Antietam battlefield to confer with General McClellan, President Lincoln posed facing McClellan for Alexander Gardner's camera. The scene is Fifth Corps headquarters; corps commander Fitz John Porter, hand on sword, is to the right of the president.

our first fire, was awful beyond description," Colonel Eugene Powell of the 66th Ohio wrote; "dead men were literally piled upon and across each other...."

The Pennsylvanians and Ohioans followed up their fire with a charge into the corn, and there were a few moments of savage hand-to-hand combat among the trampled cornstalks, with men swinging clubbed muskets and stabbing at each other with bayonets. Colquitt's men stood it as long as they could, but the weight of the flank assault overwhelmed them and they began running back through the corn. Private B. H. Witcher of the 6th Georgia urged a comrade to stand fast with him, pointing to the neatly aligned ranks still lying to their right and left. They were all dead men, his companion yelled at him, and to prove it he fired a shot into a man on the ground a few yards away; the body did not twitch. Private Witcher was convinced and joined the retreat. More than half of Colquitt's men, and every one of his field officers, had been shot down. The 6th Georgia, the immediate target of Tyndale's charge, was all but wiped out. Of the 250 men it brought into the Cornfield, 24 survived unhurt.[34]

D. H. Hill, who had personally spurred his troops into action, was now working with equal energy to pull them out of the Cornfield before they were annihilated by Greene's flank attack. He managed to get what was left of Ripley's brigade on the way to the West Woods in time, but Colquitt's retreat was more disordered. Greene continued to drive hard, pushing another brigade, under Henry J. Stainrook, in a wider arc through the East Woods so that it came out of the trees near the Smoketown road and the Mumma farm. It drove before it the remnants of Hood's division. The 4th Alabama and the 5th Texas, plus the Georgians who had joined them, went back stubbornly, firing off their last rounds before they gave up the woods. The artillery Colonel Lee had sent forward to support Hill had to come back too, but one two-gun section on the Mumma farm did not act quickly enough and was overrun.

With aggressive leadership at the divisional and brigade levels — and aided immeasurably by the flight of Garland's brigade — the Twelfth Corps had made its edge in manpower count at every turn. That they were not called into action earlier to turn the Confederate flank during Hooker's assault failed to dim the exuberance of the Yankees in the ranks as they chased Hill's men to-

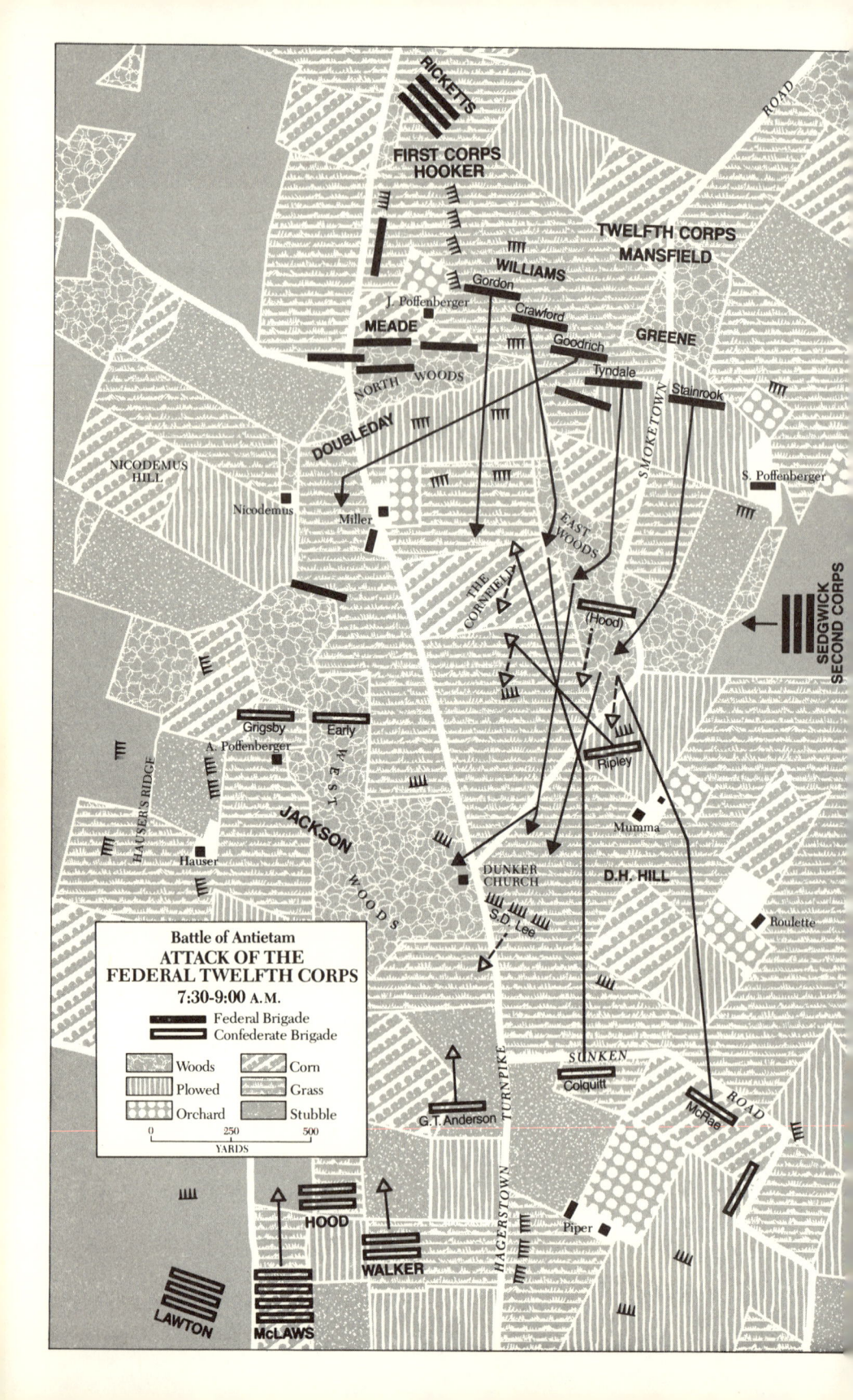

Battle of Antietam
ATTACK OF THE FEDERAL TWELFTH CORPS
7:30-9:00 A.M.

ward the West Woods. General Greene even had to dampen their enthusiasm for a time. He rode after the 102nd New York shouting, "Halt, 102nd, you are bully boys but don't go any farther! Halt where you are! I will have a battery here to help you."[35]

The morning's battlefield east of the Hagerstown turnpike — Cornfield, East Woods, the Miller and Mumma farms, the pastures along the Smoketown road south of the corn — was now in Union hands. It was a hellish landscape. "It was never my fortune to witness a more bloody, dismal battle-field," General Hooker commented in his report. A man in the 6th Wisconsin who was in the desperate struggle in the Cornfield wrote home that the fighting was "a great tumbling together of all heaven and earth — the slaughter on both sides was enormous." Something over 8,000 men had been killed or wounded in three hours, Northerners and Southerners in nearly equal measure.

The dead lay everywhere in the East Woods and the open pastures, but the toll was greatest in the Cornfield and along the Hagerstown road. The northern border of the corn was marked by a long, precise row of Evander Law's Mississippians, struck down where they stood by one terrible fire. It was the same at the southern edge of the field where Hooker's men had emerged into a hail of bullets. Bodies were in heaps amid the broken cornstalks near the turnpike; dead men were draped over the high post-and-rail fences, killed in the act of climbing in pursuit or retreat. Stretcher-bearers were able to reach some of the injured in the East Woods, but in the Cornfield and by the pike thousands of wounded lay helpless, still under fire and beyond immediate help.

In the West Woods, Jackson and his lieutenants were working desperately amidst chaos, regrouping broken commands, finding officers for leaderless formations, posting artillery in new positions, bringing up ammunition from the ordnance trains. Jackson put some of Stuart's cavalry to rounding up stragglers and driving them back to their regiments. He gave quiet orders to the troopers, however, that any of Hood's men they found were to be left alone; they had done enough fighting for one day, even by Old Jack's iron standards. Half-wrecked batteries were hurried to the rear for refitting and to refill ammunition chests. Cavalryman Blackford saw one section limp back from the front, wounded horses cut loose from the traces but following along behind in pathetic obedience. One horse was trailing what Blackford at first took to be a rider caught in a stirrup, "but to my horror discovered that the horse was dragging his own entrails from the gaping wound of a cannonball." As he rode up to put the animal out of its misery, "the poor brute fell dead with a piercing scream."[36]

At the time Hood made his counterattack, about 7 A.M., Jackson had sent an aide to find Lee and request reinforcements; Hood's advance meant that his last reserves, save Jubal Early's brigade guarding the artillery on Nicodemus Hill, were committed. Lee responded that he was sending for another of Longstreet's formations on the right, John Walker's division, to march to Jackson's support, and he promised to order up Lafayette McLaws's division as well. Now, as the new crisis boiled up with the repulse of Ripley's and Colquitt's brigades, Hood took it upon himself to order Stephen Lee to go to the commanding general and say that without immediate reinforcement the day would be lost.

The artillerist was halfway to Sharpsburg when he encountered Lee, who was on his way to the scene to see the situation for himself and to assemble a back-up line of guns on a piece of high ground due west of the West Woods called Hauser's Ridge. An aide was leading Traveller, for Lee's splinted and bandaged hands made it difficult to manage the horse. Colonel Lee delivered Hood's call for help. "Don't be excited about it, Colonel," Lee replied calmly; "go tell General Hood to hold his ground, reinforcements are now rapidly approaching between Sharpsburg and the ford. Tell him that I am now coming to his support." As the colonel started to ride off, Lee called out to him and pointed to the head of McLaws's column, advancing at the double-quick toward the fighting.[37]

These reinforcements, however, were three-quarters of a mile from where Jackson's thinned ranks were confronting disaster. A fresh brigade of the Twelfth Corps was with Doubleday's men holding the Miller farm and the nearby section of the West Woods, threatening an attack from the north. To the east, Greene boldly pushed the brigades of Tyndale and Stainrook up to the plateau only 200 yards from the Dunker church, driving Colonel Lee's guns back beyond the woods. Hooker ordered two of his First Corps batteries to exploit Greene's breakthrough, and they

To the Dunker Church

came galloping up to take position to support a further advance. The big new 125th Pennsylvania of Crawford's brigade, which so far had been trailing along behind the hardest fighting, suddenly found itself at center stage, ordered forward right up to the church itself. The rookies crossed the Hagerstown turnpike and formed up in the woods around and to the north of the little building, nervous but determined to make a good showing in their first battle.

It was close to nine o'clock now and Joe Hooker was on the scene, riding into the pasture south of the Cornfield on his white charger to direct events personally. The ground around the Dunker church he had contended for since dawn was finally within his grasp. Then a Rebel sharpshooter put a bullet through his foot. He tried to stay on the field but could not; weak and faint from loss of blood, he was taken to the rear. Hooker left the field, he later testified, thinking there were forces enough at hand "to drive the rebel army into the Potomac, or to destroy it.... I supposed that we had everything in our own hands."

At 9 A.M. General Williams of the Twelfth Corps sent a message by flag signal to McClellan at his headquarters at the Pry house. "Genl Mansfield is dangerously wounded," he reported. "Genl Hooker wounded severely in foot. Genl Sumner I hear is advancing. We hold the field at present. Please give us all the aid you can...."[38]

· 7 ·

A SAVAGE CONTINUAL THUNDER

At age sixty-five Major General Edwin Vose Sumner, commander of the Second Corps, was the oldest of the old-army general officers in the Army of the Potomac. Before George McClellan was born he was fighting Indians on the frontier, where he was known as "Bull" for his great booming voice. Behind his back he was also called "Bull Head," allegedly because musket balls bounced harmlessly off his thick skull. Sumner was tough and brave and full of martial spirit, and afflicted with the narrowest of military minds. His one notable wartime achievement had been perfectly characteristic: at Fair Oaks on the Peninsula he was ordered to take his command to the front with all speed, and he had done so, driving the men across a tottering military bridge awash in the turbulent Chickahominy River in disregard of his engineers' warnings, roaring that orders were orders and by God he would obey them. He blamed the failure of the Peninsula campaign on all the entrenching; put troops behind fieldworks, he said, and they became timid. Left to find his natural level, Bull Sumner might have achieved brigade command. Now through seniority he was leading the largest Federal corps and, nominally at least, a third of the army.[1]

McClellan was well aware of the old man's limitations, and doing his best to keep him on a tight rein. The night before the battle, when Mansfield's Twelfth Corps was sent across the Antietam to support Hooker, Sumner assumed that he and the Second Corps would go as well, and that he would continue to command the two corps. McClellan restrained him. He was to stay where he

A Savage Continual Thunder 217

was; further orders would be forthcoming the first thing in the morning. Sumner got his men up early, and by first light they were breakfasted and ready to march. Six A.M. came and the battle began, and he and his son Samuel, his aide-de-camp, went to headquarters at the Pry house to straighten out the delay. (The general's former aide, his son-in-law Armistead Long, went south in 1861 and was serving that day as General Lee's military secretary.) According to young Sumner, the general commanding would not see them. Staff officers he talked to dismissed the gunfire as merely a rearguard action, insisting that Lee was too good a general to give battle with a river at his back. The fighting ran its bloody course through the East Woods and the West Woods and the Cornfield, and still no orders came. Sumner paced impatiently.

His men were waiting nervously. Many units had received a double issue of ammunition, eighty rounds, a hint of what they might be facing. Some took the opportunity to write home, giving their letters to noncombatants to mail. "It looks now as though there will be a battle before Jackson can get across the river on his retreat," Captain Richard Derby of the 15th Massachusetts wrote his mother in Boston. "This is beautiful country, and we have fared quite comfortably.... We have very bad news from Harper's Ferry, but get no reliable particulars; yet prospects are bright with us for giving the rebs a good whipping at this point."[2]

Whatever his shortcomings, Bull Sumner believed in direct action. By his lights, the proper way to assault the enemy's flank was for the 15,200 infantrymen of the Second Corps to attack in concert with Hooker's and Mansfield's 15,800 — not, as he later testified, "sending these troops into that action in driblets...." Headquarters was seeing it differently, and Sumner was left to cool his heels. When it actually came down to fighting the great battle to decide the fate of the Republic (as he had described it to his staff), General McClellan threw boldness to the winds.

Certainly those phantom Confederate battalions, concealed and poised for counterattack, induced McClellan to think in terms of a highly defensive offense. In addition, he was having difficulty in these early morning hours understanding what was happening on the field of battle two miles away. From the Pry house he and General Porter and their staffs could see the central portion of the field across the Antietam well enough, but they were blind to events on both flanks. Burnside's Ninth Corps and the Rohrbach Bridge to the south were blocked from their view by trees and high ground; much of the contest to the north, on the Miller farm and in the Cornfield, was shielded by the East Woods. Captain George Noyes of Doubleday's staff, sent on a mission to headquarters, described the view from the Pry house. "Smoke-clouds leaped in sudden fury from ridges crowned with cannon, or lay thick and dim upon the valleys, or rose lazily up over the trees," he wrote; "all else was concealed; only the volleyed thunder was eloquent." Until the situation was clarified, McClellan thought it entirely too risky to commit the Second Corps.[3]

Hooker's message that he was driving the enemy was gratifying, but within a matter of minutes it was clear that events were taking a turn for the worse. The battle line in ragged butternut that stormed out of the West Woods near the Dunker church at 7 A.M. — Hood's division — was clearly visible from headquarters. At 7:20 Sumner was ordered to the rescue. He had two miles to march to reach the scene, but even then McClellan's commitment was cautious. One of Sumner's three divisions, under Israel B. Richardson, was ordered to remain east of the creek until George W. Morell's division of Porter's corps was brought up to take its place in the tactical reserve. No matter that Morell was then bivouacked just a mile to the rear; no matter that for some reason it took him an hour and a half to march that distance. General Richardson would not be released for action until nine o'clock.

By that time Sumner was on the field and preparing to join the fight. He had moved promptly in calling to arms his other two divisions, commanded by John Sedgwick and William H. French, and rather than looping off to the north to the Upper Bridge, where Hooker and Mansfield had crossed the Antietam, he used a ford almost due east of the Dunker church. Sedgwick's lead division was an imposing sight as it marched up the slopes and across the pastures. "With flags flying and the long unfaltering lines rising and falling as they crossed the rolling fields, it looked as though nothing could stop them," wrote an observer at headquarters. The division reached the East Woods and was readied for action. Like the veteran dragoon he was, Bull Sumner would take it into battle personally.

A sudden and unexpected silence had fallen over the battlefield, broken only by the occasional crack of a rifle or the clang of a cannon shot, and by the moans and screams of thousands of wounded men. "Not an enemy appeared," General Williams recalled. "The woods in front" — the West Woods, he meant — "were as quiet as any sylvan shade could be." There was something ominous about it all, and men looked about them uneasily. As if by mutual consent, both sides appeared to be trying to catch a second wind before renewing the struggle. The weather had turned sunny, and the day was warming.

The Yankees of the First and Twelfth corps were holding their ground and awaiting reinforcement. Except for Patrick's brigade in the West Woods near the Miller barnyard and Gibbon's Black Hat men and other scattered commands in the North Woods, what was left of Hooker's corps was off to the north on the Joseph Poffenberger farm, back where it had been at dawn. Williams's Twelfth Corps was spread from one end of the field to the other — one brigade backing up Patrick on the Miller farm, Gordon's brigade in the East Woods, isolated regiments here and there in support of batteries, the new 125th Pennsylvania in the West Woods around the Dunker church, and George Greene's two brigades at the edge of the plateau opposite the church from which it had driven Colonel Lee's Rebel artillery. All these lodgments were well and good, Williams thought, but he wondered how he could ever get his forces back under any unified command. Greene sent back word that his men were badly in need of ammunition. He also warned that the woods in front of him were still full of Rebels, who had demonstrated their presence by shooting up a battery sent too far to the front; it had to withdraw hastily, one of the guns being dragged off by infantry volunteers after every one of the battery horses was shot down.[4]

The Rebels who sent the Yankee battery to the rear were Virginians from Jubal Early's brigade, just then Jackson's only uncommitted unit in the West Woods. Like D. H. Hill, Early was an abrasive, uncompromising sort more admired for his bravery than for his personality. He was grizzled and stooped beyond his forty-five years by rheumatism, and his men called him "Old Jube" and feared his wrath as Jackson's men feared his. Jackson had ordered him to hold on at whatever cost until reinforcements arrived, and Early was doing so with much activity and aggressiveness. His

1,200 men and the 200-odd survivors of Jackson's old division, rallied by the equally aggressive Colonel Grigsby of the Stonewall Brigade, were virtually all that remained of the Confederate left flank, but they were spared a last-ditch stand. Early and Grigsby would have been sorely pressed by a determined attack by the Second Corps an hour or even a half hour earlier; now when it came they would have substantial help.

Once again Robert E. Lee was demonstrating a particular talent for exploiting his opponent's mistakes and hesitations. He pushed reinforcements into the center of the conflict just when they were most needed. First on the scene was the brigade of George T. Anderson — called "Tige" to distinguish him from the numerous other Andersons in the army — which had been pulled out of Longstreet's lines before Sharpsburg. McLaws's division was close behind.

There was hardly a man in the Army of Northern Virginia that morning who could boast of being well fed, well rested, and well shod, but certainly none were more hungry, tired, and footsore than McLaws's. They had endured the heaviest fighting in the Harper's Ferry operation, at Maryland Heights and Crampton's Gap, much of the hardest labor, and they had been on the march for most of the previous twenty-four hours. Even the crash of battle was not enough to disturb the brief rest Lee granted them after they reached the battlefield earlier in the morning. McLaws himself fell asleep in a meadow near Lee's headquarters and no one could immediately find him in the tall grass when the division was called to the front, and he had to ride hard to catch up with his troops as they were marched at the double-quick toward the West Woods.[5]

It was clearly General McClellan's intention to have Sumner go into action under Hooker's orders, as the officer commanding on the scene, and indeed had the Young Napoleon brought himself to push the Second Corps into the fight early and decisively, Joe Hooker might well have realized his ambition of driving Lee's army into the Potomac. McClellan's irresolution cost more than the failure to exploit what the men of the First and Twelfth corps had gained at such terrible cost. The Rebel marksman who wounded Hooker put Bull Sumner precisely where McClellan did not want him — in the field in an independent command.

A Savage Continual Thunder

Sumner called a brief halt in the East Woods to appraise matters. He had set off with the same imperfect understanding of the situation that prevailed at headquarters. On the march he met Hooker being carried to the rear in an ambulance, but that general was semiconscious and unable to give him a briefing. The only other First Corps officer who could be found was General Ricketts, and from him Sumner got the impression (as he later testified) that beyond a doubt the entire corps was "dispersed and routed." Alpheus Williams of the Twelfth Corps met Sumner in the East Woods and attempted to brief him, but without apparent result. When Williams began to explain the disposition of his forces and what he knew of the enemy, Sumner brushed him off. In a letter written a few days later to a friend, Williams made bitter reference to Sumner when he told of "generals who would come up with their commands and pitch in at the first point without consultation with those who knew the ground or without reconnoitering or looking for the effective points of attack."

It was an apt summary of Sumner's actions. He got it into his head that the two Federal corps that had preceded him to the field were completely used up and swept away; all he could see of them were some Twelfth Corps men lying down in a field off to his left, obviously not preparing to join his advance. If they marked the Union flank (clearly very little that General Williams told him had registered), then he must be beyond the enemy's flank as well. In that event, he had simply to march straight ahead — due west — and then make a wheel to the left to bring him in behind the Rebels. He would then drive them southward before him, into the arms of Burnside's Ninth Corps and Fitz John Porter's Fifth Corps. The lull must mean the enemy was fought out; he would strike immediately before they could regroup.[6]

At some point in this formulation his trailing division, under General French, was lost sight of. It was marching about twenty minutes or so behind Sedgwick, and when it reached the East Woods Sedgwick was gone — and French had no idea where. Later there would be much heated debate about the lack of communication between the two divisions. Whoever was at fault — Sumner or his staff, French or his — the upshot was that French looked around, saw those Twelfth Corps troops to the left, decided they could use his support, and went slanting off to the southwest toward the center of the Confederate line. Sedgwick's division, with Bull Sumner riding in the van and never looking back, marched straight ahead in isolation. He was not on hand to receive a belated warning from headquarters: "General McClellan desires you to be very careful how you advance, as he fears our right is suffering."

Having devised a plan of action based almost entirely on misapprehension, General Sumner had Sedgwick's division deployed in three parallel brigade-wide battle lines, some 500 yards wide and scarcely 50 yards apart. In this formation it could effectively contend with an enemy met head-on, and when the division gained a point beyond the Confederate flank, as Sumner intended, all that was required to sweep southward was for every man to make a simple left-face. If his assumptions about the Confederate positions should turn out to be wrong, however, there could be unrelieved disaster; if attacked from the flank the Yankee battle lines would be quite helpless. This danger did not go unnoticed in the ranks. "The total disregard of all ordinary military precaution in their swift and solitary advance was so manifest that it was observed and criticised as the devoted band moved on," wrote Lieutenant Colonel Francis W. Palfrey of the 20th Massachusetts. If there were any protests by his general officers, Sumner ignored them.[7]

John Sedgwick was one of the more solid and dependable Union divisional commanders, a West Pointer (where he was a classmate of Jubal Early's) with wide experience in the old army. He made it a point to take good care of his men, and they liked him for it and called him "Uncle John." By an odd coincidence, two of his brigade commanders, Willis A. Gorman and N. J. T. Dana, were both formerly colonels of the 1st Minnesota, the only regiment from that state in the Army of the Potomac. Gorman, a lawyer and onetime governor of Minnesota Territory, led the brigade spearheading the advance. Close behind came the command of Napoleon Jackson Tecumseh Dana, whose name apparently had almost obliged him to pursue a military calling. The third brigadier, Oliver Otis Howard, had been with the division only three weeks, and his men did not know quite what to make of him. Howard was well known as a twenty-four-hours-a-day Christian soldier; at West Point, so the story went, he had invariably asked any new female acquaintance "if she had reflected on the goodness of God during the past night."[8] He lacked the knack for inspiring troops, but it was not for want of personal bravery; he had lost his right arm leading a charge on the Peninsula. Altogether there were just over 5,400 men in the division, nearly all of them tested veterans, and Sumner was full of confidence as he took them into action.

The advance was signaled a few minutes after nine o'clock. The line of march took them through the blasted Cornfield, where the wounded of both armies waved their arms and cried out in fear of being trampled. Mounted officers had to be careful that their horses did not tread on the injured lying half-hidden in the corn. Some of the marchers broke ranks for a moment to offer their canteens to wounded men pleading for water. Colonel Norman J. Hall of the 7th Michigan paused to commiserate with one of Evander Law's Mississippians. "You fought and stood well," Hall told him. "Yes," the Mississippian replied grimly, "and here we lie."

No musketry as yet greeted the advance, but as Gorman's lead brigade climbed the fences along the Hagerstown turnpike and passed into the meadow beyond, aiming toward the cut-back portion of the woods north of the Dunker church, artillery fire began to strike the tightly massed lines. The resourceful John Pelham had shifted his horse artillery southward from Nicodemus Hill to Hauser's Ridge behind the West Woods, and his gunners could hardly miss. Their shot and shell were plainly seen arching above the trees, Colonel Palfrey wrote, and "the projectile that went over the heads of the first line was likely to find its billet in the second or third." The Yankees took their losses and bent their heads as if they were in a hailstorm and pushed on. Old Sumner rode along with the 1st Minnesota at the point of the advance, indifferent to the shelling. Suddenly he noticed that the regiment's colors were cased. "In God's name, what are you fighting for?" he bellowed. "Unfurl those colors!"[9]

Gorman pressed on all the way through the West Woods and came out at a farm lane that ran along its far edge. Beyond lay open fields. He was now a quarter mile or so west of the Hagerstown turnpike. Pelham's guns opened up once again, at closer range now, and there was a sharp firefight with Colonel Grigsby's pickup force that had survived the earlier struggle with Hooker.

Grigby's men were posted behind the cover of the house and outbuildings and haystacks on the Alfred Poffenberger farm, but there were only a few hundred of them. Gorman had lost one of his regiments along the way, the 34th New York on the extreme left of his line having drifted away when it crossed the turnpike and halted near the rookies of the 125th Pennsylvania at the Dunker church, but he still had sufficient firepower in his three remaining regiments to handle what looked like only a delaying force in front of him. Dana came up behind Gorman with three of his four regiments, his 7th Michigan also having paused back at the church. Howard, bringing up the rear of the division, noticed a rising clatter of musketry in the woods off to his left, but his orders were to stay up with the brigades ahead, and he did so.

When Sedgwick's division began its advance, the 125th Pennsylvania had been in the West Woods twenty minutes or so, and its commander, Colonel Jacob Higgins, was wondering what was going on. So far as he could see, no other Twelfth Corps units were coming up to support him. He had pushed some skirmishers deeper into the woods, but bursts of gunfire soon sent them scampering back. The ground here was sloping and uneven, broken by little ravines and rock outcroppings among the trees, and it was hard to see very much, but he thought there were troop movements in front and off to his left, west and south of the little brick church. It looked like a bad spot to be in, especially for a brand-new regiment, and Higgins gave his horse to his aide and told him to ride back to the brigade commander, Brigadier Crawford of the Twelfth Corps, and ask for help immediately.[10]

Colonel Higgins had reason for alarm. Lee's reinforcements were coming on the scene — Tige Anderson's brigade and McLaws's division — and Jackson was not wasting a moment preparing a counterstroke. He would have preferred more time to coordinate the new arrivals with Early's and Grigsby's men, but these fresh Yankee forces were incautiously leaving themselves open to a flank attack and he was not going to miss his opportunity. One of McLaws's brigades went astray on the march to the front (the Federals had no monopoly on misplacing units this confusing day), but that still left 3,000 troops to add to the 1,400 or so that Early and Grigsby could muster. Sedgwick's division plus the 125th Pennsylvania substantially outnumbered them, but the Confederates had all the advantage of position and an uncontested artillery edge as well. As important as anything else, they had the advantage of surprise.

Shrilling their yip-yip Rebel yell, the Confederates opened a sudden and murderous fire on the Pennsylvania rookies near the church. A Yankee veteran recalled that these "jerky, canine cries" had an unsettling effect even on older troops; new men, he observed, were liable to be quite demoralized by the sound. The attackers were McLaws's men, South Carolinians under Joseph Kershaw and Mississippians under William Barksdale, the same veterans who had shattered the green 126th New York at Harper's Ferry four days before.

At first the Yankees stood up bravely to the volleys, but then Jubal Early's troops and Tige Anderson's joined the fray and they were being hit simultaneously from front and flank, and abruptly the Pennsylvania boys gave it up and ran. "Had I remained in my position two minutes longer," Colonel Higgins reported, "I would have lost my whole command." The two strayed regiments from Sedgwick's division, the 34th New York and 7th Michigan, arrived in the woods just in time to catch the brunt of the next Confederate volleys. Five bullets struck down the 34th's color-bearer. "You could hear laughing, cursing, yelling and the groans of the wounded and dying, while the awful roar of musketry was appalling," Sergeant William Andrews of the 1st Georgia recalled. "Where the line stood the ground was covered in blue, and I believe I could have walked on them without putting my feet on the ground."[11]

The routed Yankees burst out of the woods and ran across the turnpike and into the meadow south of the Cornfield. A man in the 125th Pennsylvania remembered that every time the winded men slowed to a walk to catch a breath, a fresh volley from the rear sent them running again. One of the Second Corps batteries, Lieutenant George A. Woodruff's Battery I, 1st U.S., came dashing out of the East Woods and unlimbered in the middle of the field to challenge the Confederate pursuit. The six Napoleons were loaded with canister, "but our men persisted in running before the guns, in spite of all our endeavors to get them to get from before the battery . . . ," artillerist Tully McCrea wrote his sweetheart. "At last our cannoneers became so impatient to fire that it was impossible to restrain them any longer, and the battery opened. Some of our men, I have no doubt, were killed but it was better to sacrifice a few of their lives than to allow the rebels to capture our battery."[12]

The fire of Woodruff's guns and a stand east of the turnpike by survivors of the veteran 7th Michigan and 34th New York regiments halted Kershaw's pursuit, but in any case the main weight of Jackson's counterattack was now being aimed at Sedgwick's division packed into the West Woods. Driving northward from the church, Barksdale's Mississippians and Early's Virginians reached the open field along the turnpike and smashed first into the unprotected flank of Howard's brigade. Farther to the west, on the Alfred Poffenberger farm, the third of McLaws's brigades, under Paul Semmes, struck at Gorman and Dana.

For some minutes General Sumner was quite unaware of the avalanche sweeping down on him. When the flank attack began, he was up with Gorman's lead brigade watching the action in front of him, a quarter of a mile from where his left and rear were coming under fire. At first he could not believe what was happening, but when the danger finally dawned on him he cried out, "By God, we must get out of this!" and went galloping off to the rear to try to save his command.

The troops he encountered in the second and third brigade lines were standing idly, leaning on their rifles, and some of the officers had lit up their pipes as they waited for orders. When Sumner rode up, waving his hat and gesturing violently, his white hair streaming in the wind, no one could hear anything he said in the din, and they thought he was calling for a charge. With a cheer they fixed bayonets. Finally he could be heard shouting, "Back, boys, for God's sake, move back! You are in a bad fix!"[13]

Howard and Dana were already trying to get their men on the endangered flank turned to meet the onslaught, but there was little room to maneuver and everything was in an infernal tangle. Howard's Pennsylvanians, known as the Philadelphia Brigade, were hit first and broke first. The regiments collapsed left to right like a stand of dominoes and streamed off to the north, toward the Miller farm. Some companies hardly had a chance to fire a shot before they were overrun by their comrades and swept along in the tide of fugitives. Howard would blame it on lack of time to properly drill his new command, but even the best-drilled troops could not have withstood an attack aligned as they were. The brigade lost almost 550 men in perhaps ten minutes.

The left of Dana's brigade collapsed as well. The veteran 42nd New York, called the Tammany Regiment for its sponsorship by New York's social and political club, had experienced heavy fires before, but nothing like this. It tried manfully to face left to meet the assault, but it was hit by three successive withering volleys that killed or wounded 181 of its numbers, more than half the regiment, and drove it from the field. By now the Rebels were well into the meadow and wheeling to face west and strike the rear of the Federals still in the woods. Dana was wounded but refused to go to the rear, wherever the rear might be in this fearful confusion. Sedgwick was hit three times and had to be carried off. Sumner was at his best now, the fearless old warrior riding slowly back and forth encouraging his men by calm example. "We were completely flanked on the left and in two minutes more could have been prisoners of war if Gen Sumner himself had not road in through a terrific fire of the enemy and brought us off," a man in Dana's command wrote home. "... My men fell around me like dead flies on a frosty morning."[14]

Fully half of Sedgwick's division was wrecked and in retreat now, and the remainder was being hit from three directions. The smoke hanging thick among the trees and in the fields bordering the West Woods was laced with continuous flashes of musketry, and additional Rebel batteries were coming into action from Hauser's Ridge to the west to add a rain of shell and canister to the deadly crossfire. Some Federal regiments in Dana's second line were able to about-face to meet their attackers — indeed, the only volleys delivered by the 20th Massachusetts in those desperate minutes were to the rear, in the direction from which it had come — but the brigade lines were so close together that it was impossible for regiments to wheel to meet the flanking assault without overlapping. General Williams recorded that one of Dana's colonels later complained to him that he had lost sixty of his men before they could fire a single shot in return.

This was the first combat for the 59th New York, and it got into such a panic that when it opened fire in the smoke and confusion its volleys tore into the backs of the men of the 15th Massachusetts. The frantic yells of the Massachusetts men went unheard, and it was not until Sumner rode up and bellowed for the New Yorkers to cease firing that the slaughter was halted. The men of the 59th long remembered how the general "cussed them out by the right flank" in his booming voice. Between the fire of friend and foe, the 15th Massachusetts would suffer 318 casualties, more than half the regiment and in numbers the highest regimental loss in either army that day. One of the dead was Captain Richard Derby, who had written his mother an hour or two earlier that the prospects looked bright for giving the Rebels a whipping.[15]

The confusion was as great among veterans as among the men under fire for the first time. Captain Oliver Wendell Holmes, Jr. of the 20th Massachusetts saw an Irishman of his company down on one knee, methodically firing to the rear where Holmes assumed Howard's brigade to be. When the Irishman paid no attention to his demand to stop firing, Holmes cursed him and knocked him over with the flat of his sword. Suddenly he heard the cry, "The enemy is behind us!" and realized that the Irishman had known exactly what he was doing. He had hardly given his company the order to face about than he was cut down by a bullet in the neck. As he drifted in and out of consciousness, he was aware of the regimental chaplain bending over him, asking urgently, "You're a Christian, aren't you?" Holmes managed to nod. "Well then, *that's all right!*" the chaplain said and left to join the retreat.

"Again and again, and at every command of the officers we formed," a lieutenant in the 19th Massachusetts wrote, "but the fire was so hot." The only way out of the closing trap was to the north, and some regiments broke and ran in wild retreat. Others went in good order and more stubbornly, stopping to rally around the regimental flags at fence lines or behind rock ledges. For a time their resistance, along with the fire of the Federal batteries south of the Cornfield, managed to halt the pursuit of the jubilant Rebels, but the check was only temporary. Once more the cry went through the Yankee ranks that they were being outflanked.[16]

This new flanking movement came from the west, spearheaded by Paul Semmes's brigade of Georgians and Viginians from McLaws's division and strongly supported by the aggressive artillery tactics of Jeb Stuart. Stuart now had four batteries, plus

Pelham's horse artillery, under his command — nineteen guns in all — and he leapfrogged them from Hauser's Ridge northward to keep pace with Semmes's men. This combination of musketry and shelling became too much for Sedgwick's battered division, and what remained of it fled through farmer Miller's meadows and barnyard, past the Nicodemus house, and on to the shelter of the North Woods. Borne along in the rout were the advance elements of the First and Twelfth corps defending the foothold in the West Woods gained during Hooker's initial attack.

The tide of retreat was finally dammed by a makeshift line of artillery and First Corps troops in the North Woods. John Gibbon's Black Hat Brigade took this opportunity to settle a grudge with fellow Yankees from Gorman's brigade. After the bloody evening's fight at Turner's Gap three days earlier, Gibbon's command was supposed to be relieved by Gorman's fresh brigade, but the relief never showed up, leaving the Black Hat men to spend a cold and hungry and sleepless night on the mountaintop. The word went around that General Gorman had rejected the plea for aid with the remark that it was too dangerous to send his brigade forward because "all men are cowards in the dark." Now, as Gorman's desperate troops reached their lines, Gibbon's men greeted them with jeers and called them skulkers, as cowardly in daylight as they were in the darkness.[17]

The Confederates made one last effort to continue the momentum of their pursuit, and there was a vicious firefight on the Nicodemus and Miller farms. One Southerner stuck his head in the parlor window of the Nicodemus house, which was filled with Federal casualties. Moved by their calls for water, he tossed his canteen to them and went back to the fight. "In about fifteen minutes," one of the wounded Yankees recalled, "that good-hearted fellow came back to the window all out of breath, saying: 'Hurry up there! Hand me my canteen! I am on the double-quick myself now!' Someone twirled the canteen to him, and away he went."[18]

In the face of the stiffening resistance, the Rebel pursuers finally fell back into the West Woods to reorganize and replenish ammunition. Their attack on Sumner's isolated and mishandled lead division had taken a devastating toll. Sedgwick's command and the rookie 125th Pennsylvania together lost more than 2,300 men, the largest share of them falling in the first ten or fifteen minutes of the surprise assault. The attackers suffered hardly a thousand casualties. Flag-signal stations relayed the news to McClellan's headquarters. "Things look blue," one message read. "Re-inforcements are badly wanted. Our troops are giving way," Sumner reported. Among the support he hoped could be located, he went on almost plaintively, was his own Second Corps division under General French. He also sent back to General Williams for any help he could furnish from the Twelfth Corps. To those around him the old man seemed to be in a state of shock.[19]

It was about 9:45 A.M. when Williams received the call to reinforce Sumner. He sent the first troops he could lay hands on, the veteran 2nd Massachusetts and the raw new 13th New Jersey. "For the first time in their soldier experience the men loaded their muskets," the 13th's Colonel Ezra A. Carman reported, and the two regiments made their way through the Cornfield. As they reached the fence bordering the Hagerstown turnpike they came under a deadly fire from a line of Rebels sheltered behind a low ridge of limestone in front of the West Woods, some 200 yards away. "The men were being shot by a foe they could not see, so perfectly did the ledge protect them," Carman wrote.

Once again General Lee had fresh troops at hand where they were needed. An hour earlier he had called up John Walker's division from the extreme right of his line, and Walker's lead brigade, North Carolinians under Robert Ransom, came up through the West Woods just in time to meet this new Federal advance. To sixteen-year-old Walter Clark, newly appointed adjutant of the 35th North Carolina, the din of the musketry sounded like "a shower of hail-stones on an enormous tin roof." Young Clark was sitting his horse behind the firing line when a big private from his regiment reached up and grabbed his coat, yelling, "Git off'n this horse, you darned little fool, you'll get killed!" and jerked him to the ground just as a bullet nicked his hand grasping the pommel of the saddle.[20]

The Yankees along the turnpike fence were in a nasty spot. Sumner's men whom they were supposed to support were nowhere in sight, they could make no headway against the well-protected Confederates on their front, and losses were rising alarmingly. "The flag-staff was shot almost in two in two places, the socket shot off the sergeant's belt, and twenty new holes were put in the flag," a man in the 2nd Massachusetts wrote in a letter home. "It was impossible to advance and a useless sacrifice of life to keep my position," the colonel of the Massachusetts regiment explained in his report. The two regiments about-faced and marched back the way they had come — in perfect order, their officers noted proudly. Among the wounded left behind at the turnpike fence was Lieutenant Colonel Wilder Dwight of the 2nd Massachusetts. As he lay between the lines with a shattered leg, he pulled out the letter he had begun at dawn while waiting to go into action. "Dearest Mother," he wrote in a labored postscript. "I am wounded so as to be helpless. Good by, if so it must be. I think I die in victory. God defend our country...." His men would come back for him at the first opportunity, but his wound was mortal and he died two days later.[21]

Additional Federal batteries were coming into action now, blasting the woods north of the Dunker church in a "horrid concert" of sound. A Georgian in Tige Anderson's brigade remarked that the industrious Yankee gunners must have a contract to turn the woodlot into stove wood. The barrage did no particular harm to the Confederates under cover of the numerous rock outcroppings, but it was an ordeal for the many wounded lying unprotected in the woods. "Battle Oh horrid battle," one of Sumner's men wrote in his pocket diary. "... I am wounded! And am afraid shall be again as shells fly past me every few seconds carrying away limbs from the trees and scattering limbs around. Am in severe pain. How the shells fly.... Oh I cannot write...."[22]

The one bright spot in the abruptly dismal Union picture was the performance of General George Greene's two Twelfth Corps brigades that had advanced earlier to the plateau opposite the Dunker church. With empty cartridge boxes and fixed bayonets they held this key spot for half an hour. Finally their ammunition was replenished and they received the welcome support of a six-gun Rhode Island battery boldly pushed to the front by Captain John A. Tompkins. The cannon and the cartridges arrived just in time. After helping to clear the West Woods in Jackson's counterattack, Joseph Kershaw turned part of his South Carolina brigade against Greene and Tompkins, only to be driven back with heavy losses.

At 10 A.M. they were tested again, this time by the second of

John Walker's brigades, under Colonel Van H. Manning, that had marched all the way from the Confederate right. Three of Manning's regiments dashed out of the West Woods "in gallant style" (as Walker described it) and crossed the turnpike. Concealed behind the rim of the plateau, Greene's men let them approach within seventy yards, then rose up and delivered a killing volley. Their fire and the canister from Tompkins's guns tore the Rebel line to shreds. "The enemy fell like grass before the mower," reported Major Orrin Crane of the 7th Ohio, and a man in the 102nd New York remembered it as the worst slaughter he witnessed in the entire course of the war: "It seemed as if whole companies were wiped out of existence." Colonel Manning was severely wounded and the survivors ran back across the turnpike and all the way through the West Woods before they could be rallied. The 30th Virginia was devastated, losing 160 of the 236 men it had taken into battle.[23]

With a cheer, the Yankees went storming into the woods after the fleeing Confederates. Greene aggressively pushed a battle line 200 yards beyond the Dunker church and posted a regiment along the fence at the southern edge of the woodlot. Once more the Federals had a lodgment in the West Woods, potentially the most dangerous one yet for Lee's army. Greene sent back an urgent call for reinforcements.

While it was not General Lee's habit to look over the shoulders of his lieutenants in battle, he was nevertheless keeping in close and active touch with the pulse of the fighting that morning. McLaws had found him waiting with orders at army headquarters near Sharpsburg when he arrived with his command from Harper's Ferry at dawn. Colonel Stephen Lee, seeking reinforcements for the embattled left, came on the general already riding to the scene of the crisis. Lee personally supervised the posting of the fall-back gunnery line on Hauser's Ridge. General Walker, leading his division to reinforce the left, saw him far to the front closely observing the Federals' movements from the high ground near the Boonsboro turnpike. Lee even took a moment to collar a straggler from Jackson's command making for the rear with a stolen pig. In a rare burst of temper he had the man sent back to Jackson with orders to have him executed for desertion. Old Jack thought it

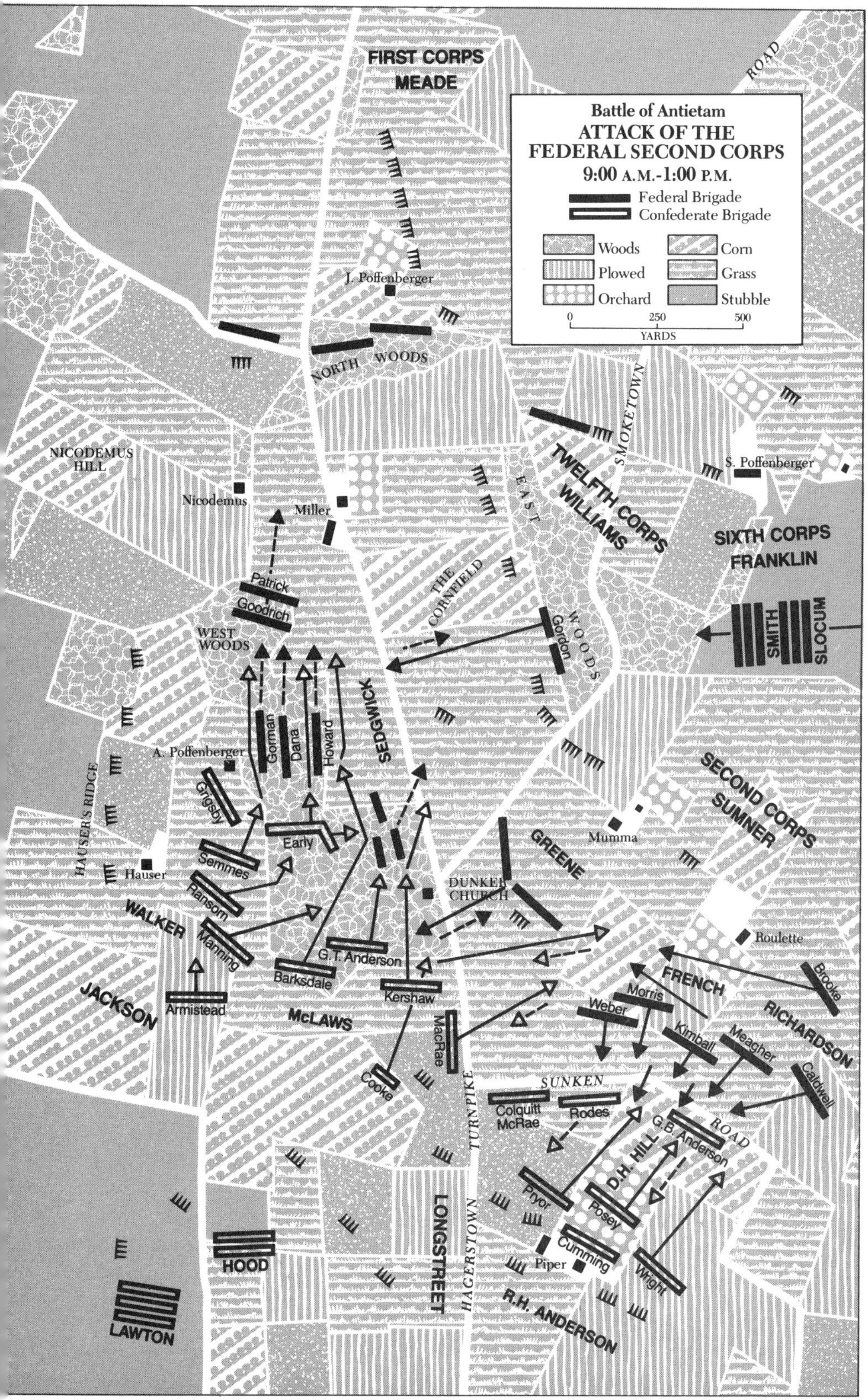
Battle of Antietam
ATTACK OF THE FEDERAL SECOND CORPS
9:00 A.M.-1:00 P.M.
Federal Brigade
Confederate Brigade
Woods
Corn
Plowed
Grass
Orchard
Stubble
0
250
500
YARDS
FIRST CORPS
MEADE
ROAD
J. Poffenberger
NORTH WOODS
SMOKETOWN
NICODEMUS HILL
Nicodemus
Miller
TWELFTH CORPS
WILLIAMS
EAST
WOODS
S. Poffenberger
SIXTH CORPS
FRANKLIN
SMITH
SLOCUM
THE CORNFIELD
Patrick
Goodrich
WEST WOODS
Gordon
SEDGWICK
Gorman
Dana
Howard
A. Poffenberger
HAUSER'S RIDGE
Grigsby
Early
Semmes
Hauser
Ransom
WALKER
Manning
Armistead
JACKSON
Barksdale
G.T. Anderson
Kershaw
McLAWS
DUNKER CHURCH
GREENE
Mumma
SECOND CORPS
SUMNER
Roulette
FRENCH
Brooke
Morris
Weber
RICHARDSON
Kimball
Meagher
Caldwell
MacRae
Cooke
SUNKEN
ROAD
Colquitt
McRae
Rodes
G.B. Anderson
D.H. HILL
TURNPIKE
HAGERSTOWN
LONGSTREET
Pryor
Posey
Cumming
Piper
Wright
R.H. ANDERSON
HOOD
LAWTON

more practical to let the Yankees carry out the sentence and put the straggler into the hottest front-line fire; he stood to the task, however, and earned a reprieve.[24]

Lee, in short, was fighting defensively with the same boldness displayed when he had seized the initiative on the Peninsula and in the Second Bull Run campaign. Gauging the continued inactivity of the Yankees elsewhere on the field — gauging, that is, the familiar timidity of his opponent — he had committed McLaws's division from his reserve and three brigades from his right to meet the crisis in Jackson's sector. The Southerners' aggressiveness in counterattack achieved a double result. It succeeded, narrowly, in blunting the main thrust of the Federal effort to turn the Army of Northern Virginia's flank. And it played on General McClellan's worst fear: surely there could be no doubt now that he was contending against great odds.

The hot pulse of battle beat only faintly at Union headquarters far to the rear. "Every thing was as quiet and punctilious as a drawing-room ceremony," Colonel Strother wrote.[25] Like Lee, it was McClellan's policy to delegate battlefield responsibility to his lieutenants; unlike Lee, he was proving quite unable to exercise the essential command corollary — incisive overall control. The Army of the Potomac was being maneuvered in disjointed, slow-motion fits and starts.

In consequence of his hoarding of forces behind the Antietam, any decision to commit fresh troops to the battle on the northern flank meant a delay of an hour and a half or more before they could reach the fighting. And these decisions were being taken without apparent attempt to control events there but rather only in response to them. The combat was at fever pitch in the East Woods and the West Woods and the Cornfield for nearly three and a half hours before McClellan put more than 15,800 men into the critical opening of his battle plan. When Sumner's big Second Corps — by itself half the size of Lee's entire infantry force then on the field — was finally ordered into action, it arrived piecemeal: one of its divisions was wrecked while the second was three-quarters of a mile away looking for an enemy to fight and the third was held by McClellan's order east of the creek until its place in the army's reserve was filled. "Destroy the rebel army if possible," President Lincoln had urged his general two days earlier; that was

A Savage Continual Thunder

all well and good, but first he must take every precaution to ensure that his own army was not destroyed.

This preoccupation with guarding against an enemy counterstroke was evident as well in his handling of the Ninth Corps posted on the Union left. By 7 A.M. General Burnside was alerted to expect the order to open his attack at the Rohrbach Bridge. As in General Sumner's case, however, that order was a long time coming. From Ninth Corps's headquarters overlooking the bridge Confederate troops on the other side of the creek could be seen marching off to the north to reinforce Lee's threatened left flank. It was not until after nine o'clock that McClellan deemed it safe to commit the Ninth Corps; only at that hour was he notified that William Franklin's Sixth Corps was approaching the battlefield from Pleasant Valley with two divisions to replenish the tactical reserve.

At 9:10, as Sumner launched his offensive, army headquarters drafted orders for Burnside. "General Franklin's command is within one mile and a half of here," the dispatch read. "General McClellan desires you to open your attack.... So far all is going well."[26] By the time the dispatch reached Burnside at ten o'clock, however, all was not going well. Sedgwick's division was routed and Sumner was calling urgently for help. And more by accident than by design, the battle was spreading like a brush fire out of control.

The new battle front was the center of the Rebel line, taken under attack by French's division of the Second Corps that had found itself alone on the field after Sumner marched off on his doomed attack. French was without orders, either for an advance or for cooperation with the remaining Second Corps division, under Israel Richardson, just then starting across the Antietam. At 9:30, as Sedgwick's routed men were being pursued through the West Woods and the Miller barnyard, French decided to direct his command southward to come in on the left of George Greene's brigades then holding the plateau in front of the Dunker church.

General Lee was now with D. H. Hill behind the Confederate center, watching French's advancing lines. As Lee spoke words of encouragement to some of Hill's men, Colonel John B. Gordon of the 6th Alabama called out to him, "The men are going to stay here, General, till the sun goes down or victory is won!" Acknowledging the pledge, Lee and Hill moved on to continue their reconnaissance. On an exposed knoll near the Hagerstown turnpike they were joined by Longstreet, in command of the Confederate right, and he and Lee dismounted to scan the field. Hill remained in the saddle. "If you insist on riding up there and drawing the fire, give us a little interval," Longstreet suggested. Only moments later a Federal shell severed the forelegs of Hill's horse, and the animal plunged forward but did not fall. "Hill was in a most ludicrous position," Longstreet wrote. "With one foot in the stirrup he made several efforts to get the other leg over the croup, but failed. Finally we prevailed upon him to try the other end of the horse, and he got down." Old Pete considered the near miss one of the most remarkable pieces of shooting he had ever seen.[27]

Harvey Hill's position was one of considerable natural strength. Some 600 yards south of the Dunker church a little farm road turned off the Hagerstown turnpike to the east, angled southeasterly, and then zigzagged southward to reach the Boonsboro turnpike halfway between Sharpsburg and Antietam Creek. For generations local farmers had driven their heavily loaded wagons along the lane to a gristmill on the Antietam, and the heavy travel combined with erosion had worn down the road surface until it was several feet below ground level. On the military maps it would be labeled the Sunken Road or, more aptly, Bloody Lane.

In this natural trench Hill had posted the brigades of Robert Rodes and George B. Anderson, Rodes on the left in the part of the lane running east from the turnpike, Anderson on the right in the section that turned to the southeast. Rodes was supported by fragments of Colquitt's and Garland's brigades that Hill had been able to collect after they were routed out of the Cornfield and the East Woods earlier. A late addition to the defenses was Howell Cobb's small brigade, which had strayed from McLaws's division when it was ordered to the front. Political general Cobb was "necessarily absent" (as he phrased it) after the Crampton's Gap fight, and the brigade was now led by a lieutenant colonel. In all Hill could count perhaps 2,500 men to confront French's 5,700. These Rebels were first-class troops, however, and well led. On the Peninsula George Anderson had won the praise of Harvey Hill, a man hard enough to please, and Rodes and his Alabamians had demonstrated their mettle in the fight at Turner's Gap. The men strengthened

A Savage Continual Thunder

the position with a rough breastwork of fence rails and waited, resting their rifles atop the rails.

William French was a tough enough customer in his own right. When Texas seceded he had defied his Southern commanding officer and led his frontier garrison 300 miles down the Rio Grande to the Gulf and embarked it for Union country. He was red-faced and choleric of temper, and his men called him "Old Blinky" because of his disconcerting habit of blinking furiously when he talked. His division was an oddly mismatched one and only recently assembled. One brigade was made up entirely of raw troops, and another had seen only garrison duty; of his ten regiments, just three had seen any combat before. A dispatch from Sumner reporting he was "being severely handled" now reached him, and urged him to press his attack with full force.

As French's Yankees advanced across the Mumma fields and through the pastures and apple orchard of a farmer named William Roulette, they made a good show. They came on, Hill wrote, "with all the precision of a parade day," and Colonel Gordon of the 6th Alabama remarked that "the banners above them had apparently never been discolored by the smoke and dust of battle." Rebel skirmishers were chased out of the Roulette buildings and regimental surgeons took over Mr. Roulette's big barn, fashioning their operating tables from planks and ordering straw to be laid out for the wounded.[28]

Leading the Federal advance was the brigade of former garrison troops under Brigadier Max Weber, 1st Delaware on the right, 5th Maryland in the center, 4th New York on the left. There were a good many soldiers of German descent in the Maryland regiment, including the color-bearer, an enormous man over six feet tall and weighing 300 pounds. He marched at a pace so measured and stately that the flank regiments began gradually moving ahead until the line was shaped in a great crescent. Beyond the Roulette farmstead the ground rose steadily to a low ridge running along in front of the Sunken Road. Except for a twenty-acre cornfield owned by Samuel Mumma, the meadows and plowed fields offered no cover for the attackers. As they neared the crest of the ridgeline the order was given to fix bayonets and charge. The officers' commands rang out loudly across the suddenly hushed battlefield.

Colonel F. M. Parker of the 30th North Carolina had warned his men that he would not give the order to fire until the Yankees crossed the ridge and they could see the belts of their cartridge boxes "and to aim at these." They obeyed his order so precisely, he added, that their first volley "brought down the enemy as grain falls before a reaper." It was a grimly accurate simile. That volley and those of George Anderson's other North Carolina regiments knocked down 150 men of the 4th New York in one sweep. The fire of Rodes's Alabamians on the left, also delivered at a range of less than eighty yards, did similar execution in the Maryland and Delaware regiments. "The effect was appalling," Colonel Gordon wrote. "The entire front line, with few exceptions, went down in the consuming blast." In five minutes Weber's brigade suffered more than 450 casualties. The Yankees recoiled and fell back over the crest. They held there and lay down to return the fire. The 5th Maryland's flag-bearer, as brave as he was ponderous, moved up to within fifty yards of the Rebel line, calling his regiment to rally on the colors.[29]

French's second brigade, commanded by Colonel Dwight Morris, soon came up the slope behind Weber's men. These raw troops of the 14th Connecticut, 108th New York, and 130th Pennsylvania had been in the army hardly a month. In this frontal attack they were not called on to do the kind of maneuvering that so bewildered other new regiments in the earlier fighting, yet there was confusion enough when they came under the deadly fire from the Sunken Road. "Troops didn't know what they were expected to do," wrote Samuel Fiske of the 14th Connecticut, "and sometimes, in the excitement, fired at their own men." The victims of the flustered rookies were the men of Weber's 1st Delaware; caught between a hail of bullets from front and rear, some of them broke and ran back into the Mumma cornfield. The stragglers rushed through his regiment, Fiske wrote, "crying 'skedaddle, skedaddle!' Some of our men tried to stop them; and a few of them, it must be confessed, joined in their flight." The rest of the Connecticut boys did their best to continue the advance, but the Rebel fire was too much for them and they fell back into the corn. For green troops, Fiske thought, they had behaved as well as could be expected, "the men firing with precision and deliberation, though some shut their eyes, and fired up in the air." He added that veteran officers he talked to later said the musketry was the worst they had ever experienced.

Morris's Pennsylvanians and New Yorkers came up to the brow of the ridge to join those of Weber's brigade still holding their ground, and Hill's men redoubled their efforts, firing and loading and firing with frantic speed, yelling and cursing wildly. In their new dark-blue uniforms, their faces smeared with powder soot, the Yankee rookies looked like fearful dark apparitions as they appeared silhouetted against the sky on the ridgeline, and the Rebels screamed at them, "Go back there, you black devils!" Some of Anderson's men leaped over the fence-rail breastworks in ragged, spontaneous charges, only to be driven back. Seeing the apparent disorder in the enemy ranks, General Longstreet ordered a counterattack by the left of the line under Rodes. On the grassy slope beyond the road it was the Rebels' turn to be cut down by the score. Captain Tompkins's rifled guns a quarter of a mile to the north took them under a devastating enfilading fire of shell and case shot and they fell back to the Sunken Road.[30]

Old Blinky relentlessly drove the last of his Federal brigades into the savage battle. Riding along his lines, Brigadier Nathan Kimball called out, "Now boys, we are going, and we'll stay with them all day if they want us to!" Under his command were the only veteran regiments in the division, the 8th Ohio, 14th Indiana, and 7th West Virginia. The Ohio and Indiana boys, in fact, could make the singular boast that back in March, at Kernstown in the Shenandoah Valley, they had taken on Stonewall Jackson and actually beaten him. Brigaded with the veterans was the new 132nd Pennsylvania, another of Governor Curtin's nine-month regiments, and the rookies were visibly apprehensive. "An occasional shell whizzed by or over, reminding us that we were rapidly approaching the 'debatable ground,'" one of them wrote. "... The compressed lip and set teeth showed that nerve and resolution had been summoned to the discharge of duty. A few temporarily fell out, unable to endure the nervous strain, which was simply awful. ..." Their first shock of war, however, came from a totally unexpected direction. A Rebel solid shot crashed through Mr. Roulette's row of beehives, and swarms of angry bees threw the

Pennsylvania boys into the wildest disorder. It was some minutes before their officers and Kimball and his staff could get them back into line and moving forward again.

Kimball sent his brigade in at the double-quick with bayonets fixed, and the musketry flashed in the Sunken Road like a quarter-mile-long bolt of lightning and slaughtered them. Rebels in the rear of the firing line passed loaded rifles to the front to speed the execution. The dead and wounded formed a blue carpet in the meadow grass. Sergeant Thomas Galwey of the veteran 8th Ohio wrote in his journal that while his regiment had seen a good deal of combat before, "our fighting had been mostly of the desultory, skirmishing sort. What we see now looks to us like systematic killing." As the brigade staggered back over the crest of the ridge and tried to regroup, Galwey saw Kimball pass by and heard him mutter, "God save my poor boys!" Although a good many of French's men would hang on stubbornly and continue the fight, the division's offensive power was spent. When its losses were totaled for the day they came to 1,750, second only to Sedgwick's casualties. The Confederate center was not dented.[31]

It was now 10:30 A.M., and the Bloody Lane struggle became a great whirlpool, sucking more thousands into its vortex. General Greene had gained his foothold in the West Woods and was calling for reinforcements, but the fresh Union troops on the field were directed instead toward this new crisis a half mile to the south. The last of Sumner's Second Corps divisions, 4,000 men under Israel Richardson, came swinging up from the Antietam crossing through the backwash of stragglers and walking wounded, too late to attack in concert with French's division but in time to try anew where French had failed. On the Confederate side the last of Lee's reserves, Richard Anderson's division, was moved up to support D. H. Hill.

Rebel officers were pushing every available gun into the sector between Sharpsburg and the West Woods. Stonewall Jackson came on a six-gun battery standing idle behind the lines and demanded to know why it was not engaged. "No orders and no support," the battery commander told him. "Go in at once," Old Jack ordered curtly. "You artillery men are too much afraid of losing your guns." The Federal gunners across the Antietam and Tompkins's battery to the north could not aim much direct fire at the close-in fighting for the Sunken Road itself for fear of hitting their own men, but the Rebel artillery coming up from the rear offered better targets. A South Carolina battery was taking position when a shell scored a direct hit on one of its caissons and exploded it with a tremendous roar and a belching column of flame and smoke. "On the great field," the *New York Tribune*'s Albert Richardson wrote, "were riderless horses and scattering men, clouds of dirt from solid shot and exploding shells, long dark lines of infantry swaying to and fro, with columns of smoke rising from their muskets, red flashes and white puffs from the batteries — with the sun shining brightly on all this scene of tumult. . . ." The uproar was not simply noise, a New Yorker wrote in his journal, "but a savage continual thunder that cannot compare to any sound I ever heard."[32]

The prosperous farm of Henry Piper occupied most of the rising ground between Hill's position and the Hagerstown turnpike to his rear. Most of Mr. Piper's gently rolling fields were freshly plowed for winter wheat, but he had not yet harvested the twenty-five-acre cornfield that lay behind George Anderson's brigade in the Sunken Road, and the corn stood head-high. Farther to the rear was a fifteen-acre apple orchard and beyond that, in a little hollow, were the Piper house and outbuildings. In bringing up his division Dick Anderson sought the cover of the orchard and the cornfield, but the advance could not be entirely masked and his casualties were numerous. French's men, frustrated in their efforts to break Hill's line, turned their fire on the infantry reinforcements beyond the lane. The reserve artillery across the creek did the same. The Southern batteries, Hill complained, "could not cope with the superior weight, caliber, range, and number of the Yankee guns." A private in the 9th Alabama was beheaded by a solid shot, a grisly incident that stunned the men of his company. Another shot mangled the horse of Brigadier Ambrose Wright; somehow he was unharmed and led his brigade on foot into the Piper cornfield, only to be wounded by a bullet. The most serious loss, however, was division commander Anderson, down with a severe wound before he could put his men into action alongside Hill's.

He had brought 3,400 men in four brigades onto the field — Wilcox's under Colonel Alfred Cumming, Featherston's under

Colonel Carnot Posey, and the brigades of Wright and Brigadier Roger A. Pryor. A fifth brigade was detached for service with McLaws, and Colonel William Parham's brigade, reduced now to just eighty-two men after its punishing fight at Crampton's Gap, was consolidated with Pryor's command. Anderson's wounding elevated Roger Pryor to the divisional command. The youthful Virginian, a vehement secessionist and former newspaper editor and congressman, was (like Howell Cobb) an officer with talents more political than military. He quickly demonstrated that directing a division under fire was beyond his skill.

The Federals were taking a rapid toll of Harvey Hill's officers as well. Brigadier George Anderson was hit in the ankle, a wound that would eventually prove fatal, and his successor was shot through the head even as he was acknowledging the command change. The stalwart Colonel Gordon of the 6th Alabama was hit in the face, his fifth wound of the day. He fell unconscious with his face in his cap, and only the fact that yet another Yankee bullet had ripped through the cap saved him from smothering in his own blood. The Confederate command was in growing disarray as Richardson's Federal division joined battle.[33]

Israel Richardson was one of those uncommon old-army types (along with John Gibbon and John Sedgwick) who trained his men hard for the test they would have to meet in battle but understood that volunteers required a different kind of handling than regulars. He had an informal, common-sense attitude toward military routine — he came originally from Vermont — that his men greatly admired. Richardson was nicknamed "Fighting Dick" and it was no newspaper invention but earned in full measure in the Mexican War. He often assured his men that he would never take them where he was not willing to go himself.

His division contained veterans with solid reputations of their own. Of the three brigades, under Thomas F. Meagher, John C. Caldwell, and John R. Brooke, Meagher's was the most famous. It was celebrated as the Irish Brigade, 63rd, 69th, and 88th New York, all recruited in New York City, who went into combat under emerald battle flags bearing gold shamrocks and harps. Meagher was a hardcase Irish revolutionary who had escaped from internment in Tasmania, and he was as colorful as his reputation promised. (His brigade was in fact only three-quarters Irish, for during the Peninsula campaign the army in its wisdom assigned to it the 29th Massachusetts, an outfit so rich in colonial stock that it would have been at home aboard the *Mayflower*. Somehow the oil and water mixed and the four regiments fought together through the Seven Days without event.) The division had other officers of fighting reputation as well, notably Colonels Edward E. Cross and Francis C. Barlow of Caldwell's brigade. Cross was typically blunt in addressing his New Hampshire troops: "You have never disgraced your state; I hope you won't this time. If any man runs I want the file closers to shoot him; if they don't, I shall myself. That's all I have to say."[34] All in all, Richardson's command was as formidable as any in the Army of the Potomac.

With the Irish Brigade in the lead the division came up on the left of French's men. Waiting for it were George Anderson's North Carolinians, now under Colonel R. T. Bennett, supported by Wright's newly arrived brigade of Alabamians and Georgians. It was Meagher's idea to pause at the crest of the ridge to deliver two volleys — the brigade was armed with smoothbores firing buck-and-ball cartridges, highly effective at this close range — and then rush the Confederates with the bayonet, "relying on the impetuosity and recklessness of Irish soldiers in the charge." A thunderclap of gunfire greeted them as they reached the ridgeline, in volume the greatest yet delivered from the Sunken Road. "Boys, raise the colors and follow me!" Meagher shouted as his shattered line recoiled. Captain James McGee of the "Fighting 69th" picked up the emerald banner from the wounded color-bearer and waved it in response. A bullet clipped the staff in two. As McGee ducked down to retrieve the flag, another bullet went through his cap. Continuing to lead a charmed life, he waved the colors defiantly. But the fire was more than anyone could stand and the charge collapsed. The 63rd and 69th New York each lost some 60 percent of their numbers, most of them in these first minutes of combat. Like French's men beside them, they could do no more than hug the ground and return the fire. Officers searched out the cartridge boxes of the dead and wounded, filling their pockets and hats with ammunition to carry to the firing line.[35]

Meagher concluded his official report by noting that during the assault his horse was shot from under him and he was stunned in the fall and had to be carried from the field. Army rumor had it that in fact whiskey was the cause of his fall. "Meagher was not killed as reported, but drunk, and fell from his horse," Colonel Strother of the headquarters staff wrote in his journal the next day, and the story would be circulated in the newspapers. Whatever the facts of Meagher's case, reports of drunken officers, both Northern and Southern, were not uncommon that day. Generals with whiskey courage were in evidence in every battle, a Yankee soldier wrote bitterly, and "the officers who did not drink more or less were too scarce in the service...."[36]

Since Dick Anderson's wounding, only Wright's brigade of his division had advanced as far as the Sunken Road to get into the fight, helping to repel the Irish Brigade. His other brigades remained scattered through Mr. Piper's cornfield and apple orchard, apparently without orders. Robert Rodes took in the situation and went off to hunt up General Pryor and urge him to move the reinforcements forward. But Anderson's sure hand was missing, and the advance was disjointed and without plan.

Pryor's own brigade finally reached the road and pushed in among the North Carolinians there, creating considerable confusion. Casualties mounted rapidly in the tangled ranks behind the firing line. Colonel Carnot Posey took Featherston's brigade of Mississippians right on across the lane in a counterattack that was wrecked before it fairly began. Posey's men charged through his command, Colonel Bennett wrote, and "flowed over and out of the road and many of them were killed in this overflow. The 16th Mississippi disappeared as if it had gone into the earth." Wilcox's brigade, under Colonel Cumming, never even got as far as the firing line. It was close to noon by now, and with startling suddenness the entire Confederate position in the Sunken Road came apart at the seams.[37]

What triggered the collapse, at least on the Confederate right, was the arrival of fresh Federal troops on the scene. As it advanced, Richardson's second brigade under John Caldwell swung off to the south, beyond the Irish Brigade, a course that would have outflanked the Sunken Road position. The movement was very cautious, however, and Colonel Barlow and other officers who could see Meagher's men under a severe fire chafed impatiently at the delay. General Richardson was equally impatient. Lieutenant Thomas Livermore of the 5th New Hampshire saw

Richardson come up and yell, "Where's General Caldwell?" Richardson was on foot, Livermore noted, "with his bare sword in his hand, and his face was as black as a thunder cloud." Caldwell was off to the rear, he was told, behind a haystack. "God damn the field officers!" Fighting Dick roared, and sent the brigade in at the double-quick to relieve Meagher's beleaguered force.[38]

As the Rebels watched Caldwell's approach with concern, Colonel Joseph Barnes of the 29th Massachusetts, the establishment regiment in the Irish Brigade, took it upon himself to relieve the pressure on his lines with an attack. "The shouts of our men, and their sudden dash toward the sunken road, so startled the enemy that their fire visibly slackened, their line wavered, and squads of two and three began leaving the road and running into the corn," the regimental historian wrote. At the same time, Colonel Posey made the mistake of trying to extricate his Mississippians from the lane to relieve the crowding that was making it all but impossible to maintain a battle line. The move was soon out of his control, and word spread quickly through the ranks that a general retreat was on.

"The minnie balls, shot & shell rained upon us from every direction except the rear," Sergeant James Shinn of the 4th North Carolina wrote in his diary. When the withdrawal began, he added, "many men took this chance (from all regts') to leave the field entirely.... Many officers were killed & wounded, & I am sorry & ashamed to say, left the field unhurt...." One minute his brigade "appeared perfectly self-possessed," Colonel Bennett wrote in his report; the next minute a stampede was on, "if we may so term it."

The three brigades of reinforcements from Dick Anderson's division — Pryor's, Featherston's, and Wright's — that had advanced into or near the Sunken Road all broke for the rear through the Piper cornfield and orchard. "The slaughter was terrible!" one of Wright's Georgians wrote. "When ordered to retreat I could scarcely extricate myself from the dead and wounded around me." Wilcox's brigade, posted behind them, was carried along in the tide in great disorder. "We had either to run or surrender," recalled one of the fugitives; "we ran *rapidly* through a large orchard...." Half of George Anderson's brigade from Hill's division, which had beaten off the repeated Federal assaults for more than two hours, went back as well, leaving only the 2nd and 14th North Carolina regiments in this section of the Sunken Road.[39]

At almost the same moment, and after a remarkably similar chain of events, the Confederate left under Robert Rodes collapsed. The most dangerous spot for the Rebels in the Sunken Road was the shallow salient where the farm lane turned from its easterly course toward the southeast. Not only did the road rise here almost to ground level, leaving the defenders with little protection, but it was subject to an enfilading fire by the Yankees holding the crest of the ridge in front. As Meagher's men crowded in with French's, this fire became very destructive. The 6th Alabama was particularly hard hit. Lieutenant Colonel J. N. Lightfoot, now in command after Colonel Gordon's wounds finally took him out of the fight, hurried off to find Rodes and explain the situation. He was told to pull the right wing of his regiment back down the lane, away from the salient, to a more sheltered position. Lightfoot somehow got the intent of the order completely wrong. He returned to the front and called out, "Sixth Alabama, about face; forward march." The commander of the neighboring regiment demanded to know if the order was meant for the entire brigade. Lightfoot assured him that it was. The word was passed rapidly down the line, and suddenly all five of Rodes's regiments abandoned the Sunken Road and ran for the rear. Men were shot down by the score as they left the shelter of the fence-rail breastworks and scrambled up the steep road bank.

Rodes meanwhile had been preoccupied with seeing a wounded aide off the field. When he returned he was horror-struck to discover his men retreating in disorder, "without visible cause to me." He worked desperately to form a new line near the Hagerstown turnpike and managed to rally a few hundred troops there. But the entire center of Lee's line was cracked wide open.[40]

McClellan's headquarters at the Pry house offered a panoramic view of the breakthrough. "Up the slope moves the line to the top of a knoll," Charles Coffin of the *Boston Journal* wrote. "Ah! what a crash! A white cloud, gleams of lightning, a yell, a hurrah, and then up in the corn-field a great commotion, men firing into each other's faces, the Confederate line breaking, the ground strewn with prostrate forms." General McClellan was exultant. "It is the most beautiful field I ever saw, and the grandest battle!" he exclaimed to Colonel Strother. "If we whip them today it will wipe out Bull Run forever."[41]

The Federals pressed the advantage hard. Caldwell's direction of his brigade continued to be lax, but his officers resolutely took up the slack. Francis Barlow, in joint command of the 61st and 64th New York regiments, was quick to exploit the opportunity opening up before him. Barlow was something of an unlikely warrior. Twenty-seven, a Harvard man and a lawyer, he had enlisted as a private five days after Fort Sumter, leaving his bride of a day to go off to war. He proved as competent on the battlefield as at the bar, and was a colonel within a year. There was a ruthless driving energy to his leadership. It was his habit to carry a big cavalryman's saber, and any straggler he whacked with the flat of the heavy blade remembered it. Barlow swung his men into a position where they could take the remaining North Carolinians in the Sunken Road under a vicious enfilading fire. They soon broke and ran, and the New Yorkers swept up some 300 prisoners.

Richardson himself was right up in the front lines now, driving every man within his reach into the fight without regard to formation, French's troops as well as his own. With a shout the Yankees poured across the Sunken Road and into the Piper cornfield after the fleeing enemy. "In this road there lay so many dead rebels that they formed a line which one might have walked upon as far as I could see . . . ," Lieutenant Livermore of the 5th New Hampshire remembered; "they lay just as they had been killed apparently, amid the blood which was soaking the earth." The pursuers overran and captured several stands of Rebel colors. A triumphant rookie of the 108th New York was running to the rear with one of these prizes when he was stopped by an officer from another regiment and told that he had better give up that flag before he was shot by his own men. "Not knowing any better," his colonel wrote with some asperity, the rookie turned over the trophy.[42]

As Richardson's men stormed into the Piper cornfield, there was a startling explosion of noise and furious action to the north, in the woods around the Dunker church. Suddenly, across a half mile of battlefield, everything seemed to be happening at once. This new eruption began partly by design and partly by accident.

When Richardson first put in his attack, with the Irish Brigade in the van, Longstreet had thought to relieve the growing pressure on Hill by striking at the opposite end of the enemy's line, in the area of the Mumma cornfield. He could round up fewer than a thousand men for the mission, however — Cobb's little brigade from McLaws's division and the 3rd Arkansas and 27th North Carolina regiments from John Walker's division, jointly commanded by Colonel John R. Cooke — but in the emergency he concluded they would have to do. Cooke was one of those ardent young officers labeled as promising by the army high command, and Longstreet apparently had no qualms about putting his counterattack in the charge of a very junior twenty-nine-year-old colonel. (Cooke's background was yet another example of a family rent by civil war. He and his sister, the wife of Jeb Stuart, stood with Virginia in 1861; their father, the veteran cavalry officer Philip St. George Cooke, remained with the Union. His father-in-law, Stuart wrote, "will regret it but once and that will be continually.")[43]

When they arrived on the field, Cooke had put his two regiments to skirmishing aggressively with George Greene's men holding the West Woods near the Dunker church. A few reinforcements from the Twelfth Corps had been scraped up for Greene, including the rookie 13th New Jersey and two pieces of artillery, to bring his force to 1,350 men. An appeal to Sumner for help was refused. No one having told him otherwise, Greene assumed that Sedgwick's division of Sumner's corps was off in the woods to his right, and he was impatient to get on with it. He had penetrated deeper into the Confederate lines than any other Union force, and he thought it was time, and past time, to exploit what he had won.

General Greene's disillusionment came abruptly. It was about noon when one of Sumner's staff finally appeared and, under questioning, mentioned that Sedgwick's entire command was routed and driven from the field. "Didn't you know it?" he asked. Greene's reply, the 13th New Jersey's Colonel Ezra Carman recalled, "was more picturesquely sulphurious than polite." Greene had hardly digested this disturbing news when he was suddenly assailed on both flanks. Acting quite independently, two Confederate units a quarter mile apart achieved a nice coordination.

One of John Walker's officers, Colonel Matthew W. Ransom, sent the 49th North Carolina toward the church, striking from the area of the West Woods where Greene had presumed Sedgwick to be. In fact Greene had warned his men not to fire in that direction for fear of hitting their comrades in arms. The Rebels surprised a small unit of Maryland troops called the Purnell Legion and caught the raw 13th New Jersey in the flank and sent them all flying for their lives out of the woods and across the Hagerstown turnpike toward the safety of the East Woods. The uproar of battle on their right and rear was enough to stampede the rest of Greene's command; in a matter of minutes the hard-won Union foothold in the West Woods was wiped out.

Meanwhile, south of the woods, Colonel Cooke was ordering his North Carolina and Arkansas regiments to charge the two Federal guns just then going into battery near the church to support Greene. As they were forming up, Cooke's men were startled to see an officer, reeling drunkenly in the saddle, ride up waving his hat and announcing, "Come on, boys: I'm leading the charge!" Who he was or where he came from they had no idea. One of Cooke's aides went up to him and said indignantly, "You are a liar, sir! We lead our own charges!" With that the tipsy stranger wandered off to the rear and the troops drove forward.[44]

Their charge quickly overran and captured one of the Yankee guns, and alongside Ransom they joined the pursuit of Greene's troops. "His men came scampering to the rear in great confusion," General Alpheus Williams wrote. "The Rebels followed with a yell but three or four of our batteries being in position they were received with a tornado of canister...." Williams was with one of these batteries, directing its fire, and he described the effects of canister fired at short range: "Each canister contains several hundred balls. They fell in the very front of the line and all along it apparently, stirring up a dust like a thick cloud. When the dust blew away no regiment and not a living man was to be seen." Colonel Ransom's men, the victims of this carnage, fell back to the West Woods carrying their wounded, leaving scores more dead in the blood-soaked meadow south of the Cornfield.[45]

Longstreet's order for the counterstroke now reached Colonel Cooke, and he turned his two regiments from the pursuit of the fleeing Yankees to their new objective. In preparing his attack, Old Pete had intended Robert Rodes's men in the Sunken Road to advance in cooperation with Cooke. The abrupt collapse of

Rodes's brigade, however, meant that the assault was now little more than a forlorn hope.

Cooke led his 675 men at a run over the plateau in front of the church, across the fences bordering the lane leading to the Mumma farm, and into Mr. Mumma's cornfield. Cooke cautioned the color-bearer of the 27th North Carolina, Private William Campbell, that the men could not keep up with him. "Colonel, I can't let that Arkansas fellow get ahead of me!" Campbell protested. The left of the attacking line made a dash at several score Yankee stragglers hiding behind the Mumma haystacks and forced their surrender. The 250 men of Cobb's brigade, now under Lieutenant Colonel William MacRae, moved forward on the right of Cooke's troops.

The sudden assault penetrated deeply into the flank of the Yankee lines facing the Sunken Road, catching them unprepared. There was no panic to sweep away their ranks, however. Brigadier Kimball of French's division swung around two of his veteran regiments, the 8th Ohio and 14th Indiana, to take the charge, and collected a part of the rookie 130th Pennsylvania to help out. The opportunistic Colonel Barlow saw what was happening and double-quicked his New Yorkers to the threatened flank to meet Cobb's brigade. Cooke drove his men into the cornfield until the two battle lines were slugging it out less than 200 yards apart. Federal reinforcements were coming up fast now, turning the cornfield into a killing ground. The Rebels ran short of ammunition, no reinforcements were at hand, and Cooke finally had to break off the unequal contest and order a retreat.

"This, of course, was done at double-quick," Captain James A. Graham of the 27th North Carolina recalled. "As we returned we experienced the perfidy of those who had previously surrendered to us and whom we had not taken time to disarm.... We had to pass between two fires.... Many a brave man lost his life in that retreat." More than half of Cooke's men were shot down in the charge, and Colonel MacRae brought back only 50 of the 250 men he had set out with. The survivors reformed behind the Hagerstown turnpike, and Longstreet sent Major Moxley Sorrel of his staff to commend Cooke for his splendid fight and to tell him he must hold his position at any cost. "Major, thank General Longstreet for his good words, but say, by God almighty, he needn't doubt me!" Cooke replied. "We will stay here, by J. C., if we must go to hell together!"[46]

Cooke soon had the chance to make good his pledge, if not at the stated price. Baldy Smith's division of the Sixth Corps had reached the field from Pleasant Valley, and Smith ordered William H. Irwin's brigade to take a holding position beyond the Mumma farm to prevent any repetition of Cooke's counterattack. Irwin, another of those officers who found courage in a flask, took it upon himself to send three of his regiments straight for the Dunker church. From behind good cover Cooke's men and those of Colonel Ransom shot this unsupported and ill-conceived assault to pieces, adding 224 more names to the Federal casualty lists.[47]

In the meanwhile, the Piper farm had become a maelstrom of battle smoke and shot and shell and zipping bullets. Longstreet pushed Captain M. B. Miller's battery of the crack Washington Artillery of New Orleans into the middle of the apple orchard to brace his broken line, and it poured a rapid fire into the cornfield, smashing the advancing enemy ranks and kicking up great clouds of dust. Miller's cannoneers, however, were soon being picked off by Yankee sharpshooters, and their fire began to slacken. Longstreet rode up and put his staff to work manning the guns, with Old Pete, wearing his carpet slipper and clinching an unlighted cigar between his teeth, holding their horses and calmly directing the fire. Miller went to double charges of canister, and the Napoleons leaped a foot in the air with each discharge.

Harvey Hill and his officers worked desperately to rally the scattered infantry. They managed to collect a mixed force, mostly from Dick Anderson's division, with the idea of swinging it around to the right to take the enemy in the flank. "At this point Genl. D. H. Hill was with us in person walking up and down our lines and speaking words of encouragement . . . ," a man in the 9th Alabama recalled. "Genl. Hill in a clear loud voice gave the order — *Attention — Charge!*"[48]

Colonel Cross of the 5th New Hampshire saw them coming and swiftly faced his men to the flank to take the attack. The Confederates came on "in line of battle yelling awfully," the regimental historian wrote, and the two lines blazed away at each other, the Rebels in the corn, the Federals kneeling amid the dead in the Sunken Road. Lieutenant Livermore saw one of Hill's color-bearers rush forward to within fifteen yards of the lane. "Our men fairly roared, 'Shoot the man with the flag!' and he went down in a twinkling...." Cross was an awesome figure, tall and red-bearded, a red bandanna tied around a shrapnel wound in his bald head, his face caked with blood and black with gunpowder. The Rebel yell seemed to irritate him. He shouted, "Put on the war paint!" and his men got the idea and smeared their faces with powder from torn cartridges. "Give 'em the war whoop!" Cross yelled. "All of us joined him in the Indian war whoop until it must have rung out above the thunder of the ordnance," Livermore wrote. "I have sometimes thought it helped to repel the enemy by alarming him ... ," he went on, "and at any rate, it reanimated us and let him know we were unterrified." Some Pennsylvanians from the brigade came over to help, and the counterattack faltered and the Rebels fell back to the Piper orchard. The 5th New Hampshire would earn the distinction of suffering more combat losses in the course of the war than any other Union regiment, and Antietam furnished more than a third of that somber record.[49]

The savage battle for the Sunken Road was almost three hours old now, reducing Lee's center to a shadow. Defiantly Harvey Hill took up a rifle and personally led a counterattack with 200 men, most of them Rodes's Alabamians. "We met, however, with a warm reception, and the little command was broken and dispersed," Hill admitted. Yet his charge, like Colonel Cooke's, won a few more precious minutes for the artillery to come up. Some of Tige Anderson's infantrymen found a light 6-pounder smoothbore on the Hagerstown road that had been abandoned after the battery horses were killed, wheeled it into position, and with a makeshift crew began firing case shot at the enemy. It was one of some twenty guns pouring a storm of shell and canister into the Piper cornfield. Colonel Barlow was severely wounded, and casualties in the Federal ranks began to mount.

The last-ditch Confederate line contained these batteries and very little else. "We were already badly whipped and were only holding our ground by sheer force of desperation," Longstreet would write. Nearly 2,600 Rebels had been killed and wounded defending the Sunken Road, 30 percent of those engaged, and the infantry that remained was in great disorder, with commands intermixed and short of officers and leaking swarms of stragglers to the rear. Some regiments reported they were entirely out of ammunition. "I have not a cartridge in my command," Colonel Cooke notified Longstreet, "but will hold my position at the point of the bayonet."[50]

For the moment the line of guns proved to be enough. Shortly before 1 P.M., seeing his attack stalling in the face of the lethal barrage, Richardson ordered his men to pull back across Bloody Lane to the shelter of the ridgeline. As far as he was concerned, this was a temporary expedient; as soon as his division and French's were sorted out and resupplied with ammunition, and as soon as he received effective artillery support to clear the way, the assault would be renewed. No doubt he expected headquarters to order reinforcements from the army's reserve to advance alongside him.

Although this entire fight was taking place within sight of observers at the Pry house, with General McClellan regarding it as the grandest battle he had ever seen, it apparently occurred to no one there to ask why there was so little artillery support for the attackers. Richardson's two divisional batteries had been held back by Sumner's chief of artillery and posted in the area of the East Woods. Captain Tompkins's Rhode Island battery provided strong fire support until noon, expending more than a thousand rounds, but its replacement battery had to withdraw hastily when Colonel Cooke attacked. The long-range Parrotts east of the Antietam were very active, yet often they fired blindly into the obscurity of battle smoke and were unable to suppress the Rebel gunners. There was much admiration expressed at headquarters for the gallantry of Captain William Graham's battery, the only one sent forward in response to Richardson's plea for more artillery, but it was a gallantry without profit: the fire of Graham's smoothbores fell far short of the enemy guns.

What General Richardson wanted was a battery or two of rifled guns to supply on-the-spot counterbattery fire, but he was informed that none could be spared. The Army of the Potomac had 300 guns on the field, but it seemed that all the pieces were assigned to other duties of supposedly higher priority. There were, for example, no less than seven batteries, containing forty-four guns, just a mile or so to the north, ranked hub to hub along the front of the East Woods in case Lee should launch a counterattack in that sector with his presumed vast reserves. All the First Corps artillery was massed on the Joseph Poffenberger farm, farther to the north, for the same purpose.

The furious struggle for the Sunken Road had not begun by plan, and it had cost the Yankees just under 3,000 casualties, but it promised to break the battle wide open. If that truth did not yet reach as far as army headquarters, Israel Richardson had not given up hope that his superiors would see the light. He went to Captain Graham to tell him to put his battery under cover so that (as Graham remembered the conversation) "it might advance with his division at a signal then expected from Major General Sumner." Any further action Richardson might have taken was cut short when a Rebel case shot exploded nearby and struck him down. He left the battlefield with a wound that six weeks later would kill him, believing — as Joe Hooker had believed four hours before — that one more hard push would shatter the Army of Northern Virginia.[51]

· 8 ·

THE SPIRES OF SHARPSBURG

The Battle of Antietam was something over seven hours old when the mortally wounded General Richardson was carried from the field. Neither army had ever experienced so fearful and concentrated a slaughter. "We are having a terrible battle," a man in McClellan's headquarters guard wrote home; "it commenced at daylight this morning and has been raging furiously all day. All other battles in this country are merely skirmishes compared to it." In the fields and woods north of Sharpsburg almost 18,500 Northerners and Southerners were dead, wounded, or missing, close to one of every three of the 60,000 who struggled there during the hot morning hours. It seemed to the Confederate diarist James Shinn that only "mutual extermination would put a stop to the carnage."[1]

Now, shortly after one o'clock, there was a sudden lull in the tempest of gunfire. On the northern flank, in the East Woods and the West Woods and the Cornfield, the weary, bloodied antagonists had fought themselves out. The savage thunder from the Sunken Road diminished. Rifle and artillery fire along the banks of Antietam Creek to the south became sporadic. At his headquarters at the Pry house General McClellan took this moment of comparative peace to compose a telegram to General Halleck in Washington. The dispatch, marked "September 17, 1862 — 1.20 p.m.," revealed a commander caught in the toils of uncertainty.

He began prosaically enough by calling for ammunition and supplies to be rushed to him. Then he announced, "We are in the midst of the most terrible battle of the war — perhaps of history.

Thus far it looks well, but I have great odds against me. Hurry up all the troops possible. Our loss has been terrific, but we have gained much ground. I have thrown the mass of the army on the left flank. Burnside is now attacking the right, and I hold my small reserve, consisting of Porter's (Fifth) corps ready to attack the center as soon as the flank movements are developed. It will be either a great defeat or a most glorious victory. I think & hope that God will give us a glorious victory." He reflected a moment, thought better of his forecast, and crossed out the final two sentences, concluding the dispatch with the "hope that God will give us a glorious victory."[2]

In spite of this better face he put on events for Washington's benefit, the specter of "a great defeat" was very much on his mind. The battle had spun out of control, beyond his feeble attempts to manage it. The three army corps he had intended to turn the enemy's flank were badly mauled, with two of the three corps commanders wounded and out of the fight. Without his conscious design the fighting had shifted prematurely to the Confederate center. Bull Sumner, left to command the northern part of the field, was pleading for reinforcements simply to hold his ground. In the face of this check to his plans, McClellan became preoccupied not with winning that glorious victory but with saving his army.

At 10 A.M. Baldy Smith, leading the first of Franklin's Sixth Corps divisions to reach the battlefield from Pleasant Valley, had presented himself at the Pry house for orders. In McClellan's original design the Sixth Corps would be thrown into the battle offensively, where opportunity offered. From their vantage point east of the Antietam the general and his advisers could see only crisis, however, and Smith was ordered to the right to shore up the demoralized Sumner. When he reported to Sumner at his field headquarters, Smith recalled, "I was told to close my division in mass facing a certain way from which point he expected an attack." Only the brigade of the impetuous William Irwin was engaged. Upon the arrival of Franklin's second division, under Henry Slocum, it too was ordered to the defense of the right, along with two of Porter's brigades. However much he may have regretted seeing Sumner in field command, McClellan made no effort to intervene

The Spires of Sharpsburg

or to investigate matters at first hand. He was content to remain at his headquarters, communicating by courier and flag signals.

He did act quickly to replace the wounded Richardson, calling on Winfield Scott Hancock, a brigade commander in Franklin's corps. Hancock was as determined a fighter as Richardson, and he made a dramatic appearance on the battlefield, galloping with his staff along the lines held by the Second Corps facing the Sunken Road and the thin rank of defiant Rebels beyond. The Yankee troops nerved themselves to renew the offensive. Hancock carried different orders, however. "Now, men, stay there until you are ordered away," a veteran remembered him shouting as he positioned one of his regiments; "this place must be held at all hazards!" The Confederate center was to be spared further attack.[3]

Meanwhile, Darius Couch's division was tramping back and forth in Pleasant Valley to no purpose. The instructions McClellan had sent Franklin the previous evening included an order to occupy Maryland Heights overlooking Harper's Ferry, and early in the morning, when Smith's and Slocum's divisions marched toward the battlefield, Couch dutifully set off in the opposite direction. Whatever McClellan had intended of this strange errand, he changed his mind when the battle began and sent out a recall order. The message caught up with Couch after he had marched five miles or so toward Maryland Heights. If there was a sense of urgency in this summons, if thought was given to bringing his division with all speed by the shortest route — a dozen miles from where he was halted in Pleasant Valley — to reinforce the Federal left under Burnside, it is not on record. While A. P. Hill drove his Light Division at a killing pace west of the Potomac toward the sound of the guns, the plodding Couch was setting an undemanding pace east of the river. His division did not approach the field until that evening, four or five hours too late to be of any use.[4]

Other calls were going out for every fighting man within reach. Shortly after 7 A.M. the first of a string of couriers was sent galloping off toward Frederick, where the third of Fitz John Porter's divisions, under Andrew A. Humphreys, had arrived from Washington the previous afternoon. "Hasten your command," one of these messages read. "Much depends upon our getting re-inforcements at once."[5] And as the morning wore on, the headquarters glasses were trained with increasing frequency to the south, where Ambrose Burnside was making his fight.

For most of the morning, the officers and men of the Ninth Corps were idle spectators to the struggle raging back and forth across the farms and woodlots to the north. For some four hours the only disturbances on the Federal left were periodic artillery exchanges and a flurry of firing on the picket lines at dawn that chased off a handful of Southern sharpshooters who had ventured across the Rohrbach Bridge in the darkness. Some of the men in the new regiments edged forward to peer across the Antietam in the hope of catching their first glimpse of live Rebels, but most of the troops remained sheltered from the probing fire of the guns. "The whirring of the shells above us had a drowsing effect, and some of our men dozed," a regimental historian wrote. The 21st Massachusetts had the particular good fortune of a mail call, and the men hunched down in the hollows and behind trees to read their letters from home.[6]

Generals Burnside and Cox spent these hours waiting for orders at Burnside's headquarters on a high knoll on the Henry Rohrbach farm, a half mile back from the creek. Both men were only too aware of their awkward command situation. Burnside was a general with responsibility but without troops. The First Corps had been taken from him to open the battle against the Confederate left, and the Ninth Corps was under Cox's direction for the proposed attack on the enemy right. Cox's orders came to him through Burnside, however, and he would be executing them with his superior at his elbow, lacking any real responsibility of his own.

Jacob Cox was a newcomer to the Army of the Potomac. A thirty-three-year-old lawyer and former Republican state legislator from Ohio, he was one of those uncommon political generals who demonstrated a natural talent for the military. He had performed well in the western Virginia campaign back in 1861, and three days earlier at South Mountain only a lack of support by the rest of the Ninth Corps prevented him from driving D. H. Hill off the mountaintop. In the present delicate situation he saw little room for exercising initiative; he was simply in tactical command of the corps, carrying out whatever orders Burnside (and, through him, McClellan) might issue. His task was made no easier by the fact that exercising initiative was the furthest thing from General Burnside's mind.

McClellan was making little effort to hide his displeasure with his old friend. On September 16, once his plans were formulated, he had inspected the Ninth Corps's position and redirected the placement of the troops. He brought along his headquarters engineering officers to examine the creek for fording sites to outflank the Rebels at the Rohrbach Bridge, and they selected a ford two-thirds of a mile downstream from the bridge, notified Burnside of his objectives, and told him where to put his men. The whole business seems to have been handled rather officiously, doing nothing to persuade Burnside that he had the confidence of the general commanding. That evening McClellan decided there was unnecessary delay in getting the Ninth Corps into the new positions. A sharp rebuke from headquarters, the second one in two days, called on Burnside to account for this lapse — as well as for the delay in organizing the pursuit of the Rebels after the fight at Turner's Gap — and closed with the warning that "the commanding general cannot lightly regard such marked departure from the tenor of his instructions." The censorious message was delivered in the morning as Burnside awaited his attack orders.

General Cox, for one, detected the insidious hand of Fitz John Porter in all this. During the recent crisis at Second Bull Run, Porter's dispatches belittling John Pope's generalship were forwarded by Burnside to Washington, where they were read by Halleck and Secretary Stanton and the president. Porter, Cox thought, blamed his pending court-martial on charges of dereliction of duty on this indiscretion and in the manner of an Iago took his revenge by poisoning McClellan's mind against his old friend. However that may be, these various reproofs did not put Burnside in the best of temper. He dictated a defense of his conduct, concluding stiffly that he was "sorry to have received so severe a rebuke" but assuring McClellan that he would heartily cooperate "in any movement the general commanding may direct."

Obeying the letter of his orders was all he would do, however. He initiated no reconnaissances and made no evaluation of the tasks laid out for him by headquarters. Evidently General Cox felt he had no leave to do so either. Had he been in a position of responsible command, Cox later observed, he would certainly have done his own reconnoitering; apparently in the Army of the Potomac they did things differently.[7]

One thing that was entirely clear at Ninth Corps headquarters was the difficulty of the task immediately at hand. The Rohrbach Bridge, a triple-arched stone span 125 feet long and a dozen feet wide, soon to be more famous as the Burnside Bridge, was one of the most defensible spots on the battlefield. The valley of the Antietam is narrow here, flanked on both sides by steep hills. The road from Rohrersville in Pleasant Valley wound across the ridges to the east, dipped into the valley a quarter mile or so downstream from the bridge, and ran close to the creek bank before turning at right angles to cross the bridge. At the west end of the bridge a farm lane angled up the slope to the left, while the main road turned sharply right to follow the creek bank again before climbing the bluff through a ravine and entering Sharpsburg.

The Confederates could hardly have asked for better terrain to defend. The wooded heights west of the creek slanted steeply to the water's edge and on the hillside overlooking the bridge there was a stone wall and an old quarry, and the Rebels had strengthened these natural strongpoints with piled fence rails and fallen trees. On higher ground to the rear were three batteries with a dozen guns for close support, and on a plateau in front of Sharpsburg — to be known as Cemetery Hill — were two more batteries whose guns commanded the bridge area. The only real weakness of the position was the small number of infantrymen available to hold it.

Lee had originally assigned the defense of his right flank to the divisions of David R. Jones and John Walker, but by 9 A.M. Walker's division and Tige Anderson's brigade from Jones's command had been pulled out to help stem the Federal push into the West Woods. This left Jones with about 3,000 infantry to cover Sharpsburg and the entire field south of the town. Posted at the bridge itself were 400 men of the 2nd and 20th Georgia regiments under Colonel Henry L. Benning, a former justice of the Georgia supreme court, who was known as "Old Rock" for his determination in combat. However thin this line, every rifleman in it was behind good cover and able to draw a bead on the bridge and the road leading to it at a killing range of a hundred yards or less. Farther downstream, in what amounted to an extended skirmish line,

The Spires of Sharpsburg 261

were the 50th Georgia and a company of South Carolinians, perhaps another 120 men in all. The force was under the overall command of Brigadier Robert Toombs.

On the eastern side of Antietam Creek the Federals had little cover from which to mount an attack. The hillsides facing the creek were open and under cultivation, planted in corn or newly harvested or plowed. The only comparatively sheltered approach to the creek was the Rohrbach farm lane, which ran down from the high ground through a ravine to reach the road some 250 yards below the bridge. Although there were 12,500 infantrymen in the Ninth Corps, the narrow bottleneck at the bridge crossing and on the road leading to it severely limited the size and firepower of any storming party, and the creek here was four or five feet deep, a daunting prospect to try to wade under fire. General Cox called the Confederate position "virtually impregnable to a direct attack over the bridge." Consequently, it was the Federals' plan to pin down the bridge defenders while forcing a crossing at a downstream ford to take them in flank and rear.[8]

It was close to 10 A.M., and Burnside and Cox were watching General French begin the fight for the Sunken Road — looking "down between the opposing lines as if they had been the sides of a street," Cox wrote — when Lieutenant John M. Wilson of McClellan's staff rode up with the 9:10 order to open the attack at the bridge. "As soon as you shall have uncovered the upper Stone bridge" — the Middle Bridge on the Boonsboro turnpike — "you will be supported, and, if necessary, on your own line of attack," the dispatch continued. In other words, once he had won a foothold on the west bank of the stream, General Burnside was promised help in his offensive from reinforcements advancing over the Middle Bridge. Burnside passed the order along to Cox, who rode off to the front to put things in motion.[9]

It seems that when this order was written, shortly after nine o'clock, McClellan saw Burnside's movement as a support for the main offensive, a diversion to prevent Lee from shifting troops to meet the Federal drive on the northern flank. Having inspected the terrain the day before, he was well aware of the natural strength of the defenses there; Burnside faced a "difficult task," he wrote a month later in his preliminary report. When McClellan finally decided to open this phase of the battle, however, it was much too late to serve any diversionary purpose. Lee had long since stripped his right to the bone to counter the early morning attacks north of the Dunker church. Nor did anything happening in Burnside's sector persuade him to delay committing his reserves under McLaws and Dick Anderson to meet the Second Corps's assaults. And by the time the attack of the Ninth Corps was actually launched, the Young Napoleon had come to see it in a new and very different light: at any risk, a new front must be opened south of Sharpsburg to distract Lee from throwing his concealed thousands into a massive counterstroke elsewhere on the field. "Tell him if it costs 10,000 men he must go on now," a staff aide heard him say urgently to one of the messengers he hurried off to Burnside's headquarters in late morning.[10]

The Ninth Corps contained four divisions, under Brigadiers Orlando Willcox, Samuel Sturgis, and Isaac Rodman, and Colonel Eliakim Scammon, moved up to command Cox's Kanawha Division. All had seen action at Fox's Gap on South Mountain. It was planned to lead off the attack on the bridge with George Crook's brigade of Ohioans from the Kanawha Division, preceded by the 11th Connecticut acting as a skirmishing force and backed up by Sturgis's division to exploit the crossing once the bridge was won. Meanwhile, Rodman's division and the other Kanawha brigade — 3,200 men in all — were to cross the Antietam at the downstream ford McClellan's engineers had selected for them, to take Toombs's line in flank. Willcox would remain in reserve. Everything had been readied since McClellan's 7 A.M. alert, and by ten o'clock or a few minutes after the offensive was under way.

The 11th Connecticut, under Colonel Henry W. Kingsbury, had the unenviable task of feeling out the enemy strength across the Antietam. After a brief artillery bombardment, Kingsbury got his men down to the creek, using the cover of the Rohrbach lane. The Connecticut boys managed to form a skirmish line well spread out along the bank, but the Rebels had them in easy range and losses mounted rapidly. Captain John Griswold led his company in an attempt to wade the creek below the bridge, but one man after another, including the captain, were shot down in the water. Then Colonel Kingsbury was hit four times in quick succession and the enemy fire became too much to stand any longer and the regiment

The Spires of Sharpsburg

fell back, a third of its men dead or wounded. Kingsbury was carried back to the Rohrbach farmhouse, where presently he died.[11]

It was intended that Colonel Crook, under the covering fire of the Connecticut skirmishers and part of his own brigade, would lead a storming party straight down the hillside facing the bridge to seize it in a coup de main. His attack was a fiasco. Crook had made no examination of the terrain, nor did he ask for a guide, and he proceeded to lead his troops off into the woods behind the front and soon became quite lost. Eventually he found his way to the creek, but 350 yards above the bridge, where his men took cover behind a snake-rail fence and spent the next few hours sniping at Confederate skirmishers across the stream. He reported to Cox that he had his hands full and could not reach the bridge. The rest of his brigade had no better fortune and was driven back to the cover of Mr. Rohrbach's orchard.

It was soon apparent that Colonel Crook was not the only Federal officer unable to fathom the geography of this part of the battlefield. By now Cox expected to be hearing the sound of gunfire from downstream, indicating that Rodman had his division across the creek and in position to break the stalemate at the bridge. He was disappointed; Isaac Rodman and a quarter of the Ninth Corps seemed to have simply disappeared.

General Rodman's troubles began with the discovery that those bright young engineers on McClellan's staff did not know their business very well. The ford they had selected for him, two-thirds of a mile below the bridge where the Antietam makes a sharp bend to the west, was unusable. The creek banks there were high, and on the Federal side was a bluff that rose steeply 160 feet from the water's edge. How this unhappy fact escaped everyone's notice until that moment was never explained; General Burnside's sulky determination to restrain any trace of initiative unless it came in direct orders from army headquarters seems to have infected the entire Ninth Corps high command that day.

Rodman did the best he could. In the nearly forty-eight hours since the Federals first arrived in front of Sharpsburg, information had been picked up from local farmers of a good crossing somewhere downstream — a place called Snavely's Ford — but no one in the entire Army of the Potomac had bothered to go find it. Normally this was a job for the cavalry, but McClellan's insistence on keeping Pleasonton's troopers by his side at army headquarters ruled out such reconnaissances. Possibly it was Snavely's that McClellan's engineers thought they had found, or possibly Burnside and his officers accepted it as such. In any event, Rodman sent two companies of the 8th Connecticut to look for a better crossing, and they struggled along the creek bank through the woods and thick underbrush, all the while being sniped at by sharpshooters of the 50th Georgia across the stream. Apparently this fire was enough to discourage any attempt by the flanking force to wade the creek. When Snavely's Ford was finally located, it proved to be a two-mile march, most of it cross-lots and hard going, from the Federals' starting point. Rodman's command was going to be out of the battle for some little time.[12]

General Sturgis was given the next turn at the Burnside Bridge, and he called on James Nagle's brigade. No one could get lost this time, for the assault was to be made at the double-quick on the Rohrersville road that ran alongside the creek straight to the target. The 2nd Maryland was picked to lead the charge in a column of fours, followed by the 6th New Hampshire. The rest of the brigade was positioned to provide covering fire in the hope of keeping the Rebels' heads down. There would be more artillery preparation this time, too, and every Federal gun that would bear opened a thunderous barrage on the bridge defenders. The 300 men in the assaulting column were lined up in the plowed field next to the Rohrbach lane, and as the barrage lifted the order was given to fix bayonets and advance.

With the Marylanders' Lieutenant Colonel Jacob Duryea at its head, the column charged onto the road and toward the bridge 250 yards away. It was immediately hit in flank and front by a withering fire from across the creek and by a hail of shells from the Confederate batteries on the high ground beyond. Dr. Theodore Dimon, a surgeon with the 2nd Maryland, was watching the charge. Colonel Duryea looked back, Dimon wrote, and "saw the Regiment shrinking and elbowing out under this tremendous fire and just ready to break.... He demanded, 'What the hell are you doing there? Straighten that line there! Forward!' "[13] Under this spur they kept going, but dozens of men were now being knocked down at every step by the scything volleys, particularly from the Georgians crowded into the old quarry on the hillside. Finally the

The Spires of Sharpsburg

Yankees could take no more of it and the column disintegrated, the men ducking and running for whatever cover they could find. In these few minutes the 2nd Maryland suffered casualties of 44 percent.

It was close to noon by now, and an observer on Fitz John Porter's staff reported to headquarters that he could not see "that Burnside has done a thing. He sent two rgts to cross the bridge, & were driven back like sheep by enemies' artillery." Several couriers had already been dispatched to the Ninth Corps to hurry things along. McClellan increased the pressure by sending his inspector general, Colonel Delos B. Sackett, to Burnside with firm instructions to press the assault at whatever cost. As Sackett remembered it, Burnside reacted with some heat: "McClellan appears to think I am not trying my best to carry this bridge; you are the third or fourth one who has been to me this morning with similar orders." Sturgis was told to renew the attack on the bridge with fresh troops.[14]

Sturgis ordered his other brigade, under Brigadier Edward Ferrero, to make the advance on a two-regiment front. Ferrero, a dapper little officer who had run a dancing school in New York before the war, chose what he considered the toughest of his troops to lead the charge — the 51st New York, his former outfit, and the 51st Pennsylvania — and delivered a little speech. According to Lieutenant George Whitman, the poet's brother, he told them that they were General Burnside's personal choice for the job, "saying (so the story goes) that he knew we would take it." However much these veterans may have been moved by such sentiments, the Pennsylvanians thought that at least there ought to be some reward involved. One of them called out to Ferrero to ask if they would get their whiskey ration back if they took the bridge. The 51st Pennsylvania was something of a fractious, hardcase outfit, and as punishment for some misconduct or other Ferrero had cut off the liquor ration often issued to the troops after a battle or a hard march. "Yes, by God!" he assured them, and that earned him a cheer.

It was all too obvious by now that any advance along the road paralleling the creek exposed an attacking column to a lethal flanking fire, so Cox went back to the original idea of charging straight down the hill facing the bridge. All the officers were briefed and shown the proper attacking positions, and two batteries were pushed up close to the creek above the bridge to take the enemy line under an enfilading fire. The guns began banging away with case shot and canister and Ferrero's other two regiments laid down a heavy covering fire, and at about 12:30 the storming party, 670 strong, set off down the hill toward the bridge.

The Yankees had 300 yards of open ground to cross, and the Confederates hit them hard before they were halfway to the little meadow at the foot of the hill. The column, New Yorkers on the left and Pennsylvanians on the right, began to falter and the officers saw they would never make it across the bridge in one rush, and instead swung them off to the left and right. The New Yorkers found some cover by the post-and-rail fence that bordered the road below the bridge, and the Pennsylvanians ducked behind a stone wall running along the creek bank upstream. "We were then ordered to halt and commence fireing, and the way we showered the lead across that creek was noboddys buisness," Lieutenant Whitman wrote.

The Georgians under Colonel Benning had been fighting off repeated assaults for close to three hours, and their ammunition was almost gone. "The combined fire of infantry and artillery was terrific," Benning reported of this latest attack, and it was finally more than his men could stand. After the firefight had gone on for some minutes, the Yankees noticed the musketry across the creek begin to slacken, and they could see Rebels in twos and threes leaving their positions and running back up the hillside.

Colonel Robert B. Potter of the 51st New York acted quickly to exploit the situation. With the color-bearer in the lead, he rushed his men onto the bridge. The Pennsylvanians from the right joined them, and in a solid column under the two regimental flags carried side by side, they poured across. Some of the men raised the cry, "Remember Reno!" Colonel John F. Hartranft of the 51st Pennsylvania, his voice gone, stood by the stone coping and urged them on, waving his hat and croaking, "Come on boys, for I can't haloo any more!" From the hills east of the creek there was a chorus of cheering.

Benning passed the word to withdraw, and his men hurried up the steep slope, with snipers jumping down from their perches in the trees and joining the retreat. A few did not get away quickly

The Spires of Sharpsburg

enough and were overrun and captured. Sword in hand, a defiant Lieutenant Colonel William R. Holmes of the 2nd Georgia tried to lead a doomed counterattack and went down in a hail of bullets. It was one o'clock now, and General Burnside had his bridge — and a few days later the 51st Pennsylvania had its reward, a full keg of it.[15]

If McClellan's decision to put the Ninth Corps into action was taken too late to ease the way for the rest of the Army of the Potomac in its morning attacks, and if matters were then so mismanaged that three precious hours were devoted to finding a way across the twelve-foot-wide Burnside Bridge bottleneck, that took nothing away from the men who did the fighting there. No spot on the Antietam battlefield was assaulted — and defended — with more raw courage, and in proportion to the forces engaged, the 500 Yankees and 120 Rebels killed and wounded there rank it among the bloodier contests of that bloody day.

The rest of Sturgis's division was soon sent across the bridge, and the Yankees formed in line of battle on the heights west of the Antietam. Once the enemy skirmishers withdrew, Colonel Crook discovered that from his position upstream the creek could be waded, and he brought his men into line with Sturgis's. Two batteries pounded across the bridge and up the farm lane to provide fire support. And, at long last, off to the south, General Rodman's command splashed across Snavely's Ford, losing only a handful of men to sniper fire, to link up with the troops in the bridgehead. The Federal line, in nearly three-division strength, ran in a long arc from Snavely's to the bridge road leading into Sharpsburg. Toombs's Confederates had fallen back to a stone wall a half mile west of the bridge, and the only opposition to the Federal buildup was the harassing fire of the Rebel batteries.

Colonel Thomas M. Key of McClellan's staff rode back to the Pry house with Burnside's assurance that he was across the Antietam in good strength and thought he could hold the bridge. "He should be able to do that with five thousand men," David Strother heard McClellan say; "if he can do no more I must take the remainder of his troops and use them elsewhere on the field." Colonel Key was sent back to Burnside with a bluntly worded message that everything depended on his continuing the advance. McClellan was silent on his earlier promise to support the drive with reinforcements sent across the Middle Bridge. Key also carried with him an order relieving Burnside and replacing him with General George Morell from Porter's corps, to be used if the Ninth Corps did not push ahead immediately.[16]

Burnside was willing enough, but it presently developed that there were going to be problems meeting McClellan's demand. General Sturgis made the belated discovery that the important matter of ammunition resupply had been overlooked when mounting the assault on the bridge, and most of the troops in his division had empty cartridge boxes. Simply hurrying forward the ammunition train would not answer for it; his men were exhausted from their recent efforts, he announced, and in no shape to make any further advance anyway. The impulse for hard driving, for asking something extra of troops, was apparently not in General Sturgis's nature, nor did General Cox press the matter. He accepted the appraisal without comment and called on Burnside for ammunition and for Willcox's division to be brought across the Antietam to relieve Sturgis's command.

That would mean some considerable additional delay, for Burnside's mental pattern that day was limited to thinking about just one thing at a time. Instead of being positioned for rapid deployment in case of need, Willcox was fully three-quarters of a mile to the rear, where he had been waiting patiently for orders since ten that morning. It was two o'clock before the first of his troops could even reach the bridge. Burnside himself was on hand to direct traffic, for there was a sizable tie-up as the men waited their turn to cross the narrow span. None of the regiments was ordered to wade the creek to speed up the movement. It was three o'clock by the time Willcox was in place and Sturgis's division pulled back to the hills overlooking the stream to rest and refill cartridge boxes.

During the two hours required to sort out the Ninth Corps after its capture of the bridge, the lull in the fighting on the rest of the battlefield continued. There were sporadic exchanges between batteries and a scattering of musketry on the skirmish lines, where men fought deadly individual combats from behind fences and haystacks and rock ledges, but the steady thunder of the morning hours was stilled.

Yet men were killed seemingly at random in this desultory firing. A shell fragment took the life of thirteen-year-old Charlie

King, a drummer boy in the 49th Pennsylvania, no doubt the youngest soldier to die at Antietam. A civilian boatman for the Chesapeake and Ohio Canal remembered seeing a shell from one of the long-range Federal guns explode at the feet of a Rebel straggler in Sharpsburg and "turn him over and over like a wagon wheel." A man in reserve in Porter's corps watched horrified as one of the walking wounded paused to remove the boot from his wounded foot and was crushed to a bloody pulp by a Rebel solid shot that came bounding along the ground in an aimless, deadly trajectory.

There were other, less grim incidents to catch the attention. A high ridge off to the east called Red Hill was crowded with civilian spectators, and a few of these country people ventured forward to the Pry house during the lull, where Colonel Strother was amused to find them as anxious to catch a glimpse of General McClellan's famous horse, Dan Webster, as to see the general himself. The men in Captain William Graham's Federal battery, ordered back to a more sheltered position by General Richardson but still under fire, were astonished to see a civilian drive a carriage right up to their guns west of the creek and hand around biscuits and ham from a hamper. After inspecting a wound one of his horses had received, he calmly drove back over the Middle Bridge, taking with him several wounded gunners to deliver them to a field hospital, then returned for a second load of wounded. Captain Graham was too surprised to think to ask the Good Samaritan his name, but according to local tradition he was Martin Eakle, a miller from nearby Keedysville.[17]

Among the men who had survived the morning's slaughter, most could imagine nothing worse than to have to face the call to action once again. "The sun seemed almost to go backwards," a North Carolinian wrote, "and it appeared as if night would never come." An Alabamian in Dick Anderson's division who fought at the Bloody Lane wrote simply, "We were praying for night to come." A Yankee in the 10th Maine remembered hoping against hope "that we might not be called upon again, and lo the luck of the 10th Me. was with us and we were undisturbed." As for the two commanding generals, they responded to the stalemate in perfectly characteristic fashion.[18]

General McClellan continued to devote his energies to meeting or deflecting the Confederate counterstroke he believed was heralded by the destruction of Sedgwick's division in the West Woods. His staff and most of his lieutenants were of the same mind. "All wore a serious air," Colonel Strother wrote in his diary. "From the signs of the day and the report of prisoners" — captured Rebels, it seems, were boasting as convincingly as ever — "it was evident the enemy was before us in full power, and the fact that he had risked a battle in his present position showed that he felt great confidence in his power." From what he could learn, Colonel Charles S. Wainwright wrote the next day, "nearly if not quite all our . . . generals expected Lee would make an attack on us. . . ."

The threat to Sumner's command appeared the most immediate, but McClellan also expressed a concern for his center along the Boonsboro turnpike, where Porter's Fifth Corps and Pleasonton's cavalry were stationed. "It was necessary to watch this part of our line with the utmost vigilance," he wrote, "lest the enemy should take advantage of the first exhibition of weakness here to push upon us a vigorous assault, for the purpose of piercing our centre and turning our rear, as well as to capture or destroy our supply trains." (One of John Pope's failings, after all, had been to suffer his supply line to be severed by the resourceful Rebels.) Porter shared this concern for the army's trains.[19]

Taken at their word, the commander of the Army of the Potomac and his principal adviser thus professed to believe they were at risk of an enemy attacking column that would have to cross a mile of open ground toward the narrow defile where the Middle Bridge spanned the Antietam, exposing its flank in doing so, against three brigades of infantry and a division of cavalry and the concentrated fire of 80 to 100 guns positioned on commanding ground behind and on both sides of the bridge. If these statements reflect a true concern and not after-the-fact rationalizing, perhaps nothing so well demonstrates Robert E. Lee's dominance over his opponents' minds that September 17.

Shortly before noon, McClellan had ventured to push several batteries across the Middle Bridge, supported by Pleasonton's cavalry and a force of regulars from George Sykes's Fifth Corps division. He was nervous about the move — it was taken against the advice of Porter and Sykes — and he cautioned Pleasonton not to

The Spires of Sharpsburg

risk the batteries unduly. As an afterthought, he asked, "Can you do any good by a cavalry charge?" Pleasonton wisely ignored the suggestion. He asked instead for more infantry to support the guns. Headquarters replied that there was "no infantry to spare," and if he could not guard his guns with the men he had he was to withdraw them. There would be no compromise in protecting the Union center.[20]

Thus the entire Federal cavalry division, except for a few details tracking down infantry stragglers, idled away the hours in the valley west of the creek, taking cover from the shells shrieking overhead. Lieutenant Charles Francis Adams, Jr. of the 1st Massachusetts cavalry found the situation "unmistakenly trying." But as time passed the shelling became hypnotically monotonous. "I was very tired," Adams remembered; "the noise was deadening; gradually it had on me a lulling effect; and so I dropped quietly asleep — asleep in the height of the battle and between the contending armies! ... Such is my recollection of that veritable charnel-house, Antietam...."[21]

The timidity that had marked William Franklin's generalship at Crampton's Gap and in Pleasant Valley evaporated when he rejoined the main army that day; shedding the responsibility of independent command apparently restored his confidence. At about one o'clock, as the Bloody Lane fighting died out and General Burnside captured his bridge, both of Franklin's Sixth Corps divisions were at the front. He proposed an immediate attack on the West Woods by Smith's and Slocum's 10,500 fresh men and notified Sumner of his plan. Sumner was appalled at the thought. "General Sumner rode up and directed me not to make the attack," Franklin wrote, "giving as a reason for his order, that if I were defeated the right would be entirely routed, mine being the only troops left on the right that had any life in them." The two men argued the question with some heat, and Franklin sent a staff man hurrying off to the general commanding to plead his case.

Franklin remarked that he found Sumner "much depressed," an appraisal shared by others who were with the old man after the disastrous rout of Sedgwick's division. The historian of the Second Corps thought he had simply lost courage — "not the courage which would have borne him calmly up a ravine swept by canister at the head of the old First Dragoons, but the courage which, in the crash and clamor of action, amid disaster and repulse, enables the commander coolly to calculate the chances of success or failure." Perhaps Bull Sumner had seen too much in those terrible minutes in the West Woods, with his helpless men swept away all about him by what seemed in irresistible enemy tide. No doubt there was considerable demoralization among Sedgwick's troops, but George Meade and Abner Doubleday and Alpheus Williams would have disputed any contention that their men too had no life left in them. Despite the heavy casualties and the straggling, they could still muster between them 10,000 to 12,000 infantrymen of the First and Twelfth Corps with enough fight left at least to hold a line, and there were also Porter's two brigades on the way to back them up.

In any event, soon after this meeting Lieutenant James Wilson of the headquarters staff rode up to Sumner with McClellan's instructions "to get up his men and hold his position at all hazards." Sumner's reply to this summons was grim: "Go back, young man, and ask General McClellan if I shall make a simultaneous advance with my whole line at the risk of not being able to rally a man on this side of the creek if I am driven back." Wilson tried to explain that the instructions he had just delivered said nothing about any general advance. "Go back, young man, and bring me an answer to my question," Sumner repeated.

Wilson galloped back to the Pry house to find McClellan suddenly energized by the report of Franklin's plan for a renewed offensive. As Wilson recalled the conversation, he was instructed to tell Sumner "to crowd every man and gun into ranks, and if he thinks it practicable, he may advance Franklin to carry the woods in front, holding the rest of the line with his own command, assisted by those of Banks" — that is, the Twelfth Corps — "and Hooker." Once more Wilson spurred back to Second Corps headquarters behind the East Woods. He delivered his message, but old Sumner was adamant: "Go back, young man, and tell General McClellan I have no command. Tell him my command, Banks' command and Hooker's command are all cut up and demoralized. Tell him General Franklin has the only organized command on this part of the field!"

On hearing this, shortly after two o'clock, the Young Napoleon

The Spires of Sharpsburg

concluded it was time for him to go to the front to settle the matter in person. Perhaps here was the opportunity for the dramatic gesture he managed so well, the launching of an attack with the same inspirational presence he had displayed three days before at Turner's Gap when he pointed his cheering men into the battle. That thought, if he entertained it, did not last long. The picture Sumner painted for him was gloomy, and it carried the day. "General Sumner expressed the most decided opinion against another attempt during that day," McClellan wrote. However he may have felt privately about his subordinate's competence, he did not overrule him or replace him as he was ready to do with Burnside. His reasoning, Franklin testified, was that matters had gone well enough elsewhere on the field and "that he was afraid to risk the day by an attack there on the right at that time."

After telling his generals to hold their ground at any cost and deciding that those two brigades of Porter's were not needed on the right after all, McClellan returned to headquarters. He appeared satisfied that his reserves — the 20,500 men of the Fifth and Sixth corps — were in position for a last-ditch stand to save the army should the fortunes of battle require it. However, the centerpiece of his battle plan, to turn the Confederate northern flank, was abandoned. He rested content with the few acres of savaged and bloody ground won by the First, Second, and Twelfth corps.[22]

Lieutenant Wilson thought he saw a great victory being thrown away. Twenty-five-year-old James Wilson, West Point '60, was headstrong and hot-tempered, and he decided not to let the matter rest there. He came upon the *Tribune*'s George Smalley at army headquarters and began questioning him closely on the condition of the wounded Joe Hooker. "Most of us think that this battle is only half fought and half won," Smalley recalled him saying. "There is still time to finish it. But McClellan will do no more." He wanted Smalley to visit Hooker, find out if he could mount his horse, "and if he can, ask him whether he will take command of this army and drive Lee into the Potomac or force him to surrender."

That smacked of out-and-out mutiny, Smalley pointed out. "I know that as well as you do," Wilson said. "We all know it, but we know also that it is the only way to crush Lee and end the rebellion and save the country." He did not indicate who else he might be speaking for. Smalley finally agreed to go to Hooker, but only to see if he would resume command of his own corps. Perhaps that would be enough, Wilson said. Let him enter the battlefield in an ambulance or even on a stretcher, with bugles blowing and the corps flag flying over him; the men would rally to him.

Smalley went to Hooker's bedside in the Pry house and heard Fighting Joe denounce in a "copious vocabulary" the army's slow progress since his wounding. He then tried to sound out the general about resuming command of the First Corps. He could not, Hooker assured him. "No, no; I cannot move. I am perfectly helpless." He began to become suspicious, and the reporter backed off. The whole business was impossible, Smalley told the disappointed Lieutenant Wilson. Bull Sumner's view of the situation would prevail.[23]

There was one calculation General McClellan made in these midday hours that was quite correct. His opponent was indeed looking for a way to seize the initiative — although to be sure without being able to call on those phantom battalions of McClellan's invention. At about noon, General Lee asked Stonewall Jackson to devise a counterstroke to relieve the growing pressure on D. H. Hill's center and to try to take control of events.

Jackson had already concluded that the Federal offensive against his flank was stalled. Dr. Hunter McGuire of the medical staff reported to him that the field hospitals were swamped with casualties. In view of the apparently critical situation, he wondered if the wounded should be transferred back across the Potomac immediately in anticipation of a general retreat. Old Jack saw no need for concern. "Dr. McGuire," he said, "they have done their worst."

He outlined his plan to General John Walker, who found him in the West Woods about 12:30, sitting his horse and foraging a meal from an apple tree. After listening to Walker's situation report without comment, Jackson asked him abruptly, "Can you spare me a regiment and a battery?" Walker replied that the 48th North Carolina was available, as were his two divisional batteries. He wanted to assemble a force of some 5,000 men, Jackson continued, under Stuart's command and including most of the cavalry, to swing around the Federals' northern flank and take them in the

The Spires of Sharpsburg

rear. Simultaneously with Stuart's attack, Walker was to advance from the West Woods to put the Yankee flank between two fires. Walker remembered Jackson saying, with great emphasis, "We'll drive McClellan into the Potomac!"

To support the counterattack, General Lee sought out any batteries refitting in the rear areas that still had a serviceable gun or two. Captain William Poague's Rockbridge Artillery, which had been in the thick of the morning's fight north of the Dunker church, could supply horses and ammunition and men enough for a single gun. One of Poague's gunners was the commanding general's son, twenty-year-old Robert. The young man, his face blackened with powder and battle smoke, approached his father and asked, "General, are you going to send us in again?" It took a moment for Lee to recognize him, and then he said quietly, "Yes, my son. You all must do what you can to help drive these people back."

Jackson meanwhile went forward to the 35th North Carolina, posted on the edge of the West Woods where Sedgwick's division had come to grief earlier. The enemy forces fronting the East Woods were concealed by a rise in the ground, and he called for a volunteer to climb a tall hickory nearby to reconnoiter. Barefooted Private William Hood of the 35th stepped forward and quickly scrambled to the top of the hickory.

"How many troops are over there?" Jackson called to him.

"Who-e-e! There are oceans of them, General!" the young private yelled down.

"Count the flags, sir," Old Jack told him sternly.

Dutifully Hood called out his count as Jackson listened patiently and Yankee sharpshooters took aim at the treetop. The number had reached thirty-nine when Jackson interrupted, "That will do, come down, sir." With two flags to a regiment, national and regimental, that meant four or perhaps five brigades. It was a daunting prospect — what Private Hood saw were elements of the newly arrived Sixth Corps — but Jackson nevertheless warned his commanders to be ready to advance as soon as the sound of Stuart's guns was heard in the enemy's rear. (Some days later, at an army review, young Hood's comrades saw him riding proudly with the staff, promoted to brigade courier and wearing a pair of spurs on his bare ankles.)[24]

As Jeb Stuart set about assembling his cavalry brigades and the regiment of infantry and artillery from various batteries for his movement, Jackson revealed no apparent concern at the fact that there were hardly 6,500 fighting men left under his command in the West Woods to hold the Confederate flank. The myth of overwhelming Rebel numbers was serving the Army of Northern Virginia very well.

General Lee displayed a similar calm toward the situation on his right flank. Burnside's capture of the Rohrbach Bridge did not persuade him to shift any troops from the left — Hood, for example, had collected 800 men and returned to the West Woods — or to halt preparations for Stuart's expedition. He seemed confident that David Jones would cope with any renewed Federal offensive south of Sharpsburg, and that in any case A. P. Hill would soon be up with his Light Division from Harper's Ferry. His confidence in Hill was quickly justified. At 2:30 Hill rode up to the army commander to report that his column was crossing the Potomac at Boteler's Ford. Lee directed him to put the men as they arrived in support of Jones on the right. No hint of the march of Powell Hill's division had reached the Federal high command. Rather than posting them to watch his flanks, General McClellan had directed the eyes of the army, Pleasonton's troopers, in another direction, toward the improbable prospect of a grand cavalry charge.

It was three o'clock or a few minutes after when General Cox gave the order for the Ninth Corps to advance. There were 5,500 fresh troops in the lead divisions of Rodman and Willcox, backed up by another 3,000 or so in the two brigades of the Kanawha Division; Sturgis's division was in reserve a short distance to the rear. In addition to the long-range guns east of the creek, four batteries, with twenty-two guns, had been brought across the bridge for fire support. This part of the field was easily visible from the Pry house — the earlier fight for the bridge down in the creek valley had not been — and as the Yankee battle lines started forward they were a striking sight. "Burnside made his grand effort," Colonel Strother wrote in his diary. "His advancing rush was in full view and magnificently done."[25]

David R. Jones was a general in the mold of Lafayette McLaws, lacking color or flair but competent and reliable for all that. A courtly South Carolinian, he had been at West Point with McClellan and had served in the Mexican War. Although he was only thirty-seven, he suffered from chronic heart disease, which would kill him four months later. Longstreet had assigned him the considerable responsibility of defending Sharpsburg, all the ground south of it, and the vital road to Boteler's Ford. Confronted by the Ninth Corps now advancing on a front three-quarters of a mile wide, he had also to consider the threat of a supporting push directly on Sharpsburg by Yankees crossing at the Middle Bridge.

Jones now had fewer than 2,800 men in his division to meet this challenge, and until Powell Hill came up there was no expectation of any infantry reinforcements. On his left he had posted the brigades of Richard B. Garnett and Micah Jenkins (led that day by Joseph Walker) on Cemetery Hill in front of Sharpsburg, to cover the town and the Boonsboro turnpike, plus a mixed command acting as advanced skirmishers. On his right, south of the town, the terrain was steeply rolling and broken by hollows and ravines but generally rising toward the north–south ridgeline along which ran a country highway known as the Harper's Ferry road. Most of this ground was cultivated and divided by stone or rail fences, and in the middle of it was another of those cornfields, this one of forty acres owned by a farmer named John Otto. Defending the right were the brigades of Thomas F. Drayton, James L. Kemper, and Robert Toombs. Toombs had relieved the weary troops who fought at the bridge with two of his regiments newly arrived on the field. Jones had twenty-eight guns under command when the fight began, and Lee promised him whatever additional artillery he could round up elsewhere on the field.

The plan worked out by Burnside and Cox was to send Orlando Willcox's division, supported by George Crook's Kanawha brigade, due west, straight toward Sharpsburg. Isaac Rodman's division, backed by the other Kanawha brigade under Colonel Hugh Ewing, was to keep pace on Willcox's left and then converge on the town from the south, the idea being to roll up the Confederate flank and get astride the Boteler's Ford road, Lee's lifeline to the Potomac crossing. Burnside assumed that once his offensive was under way McClellan would reinforce him with the army's reserves advancing across the Middle Bridge, as promised in the

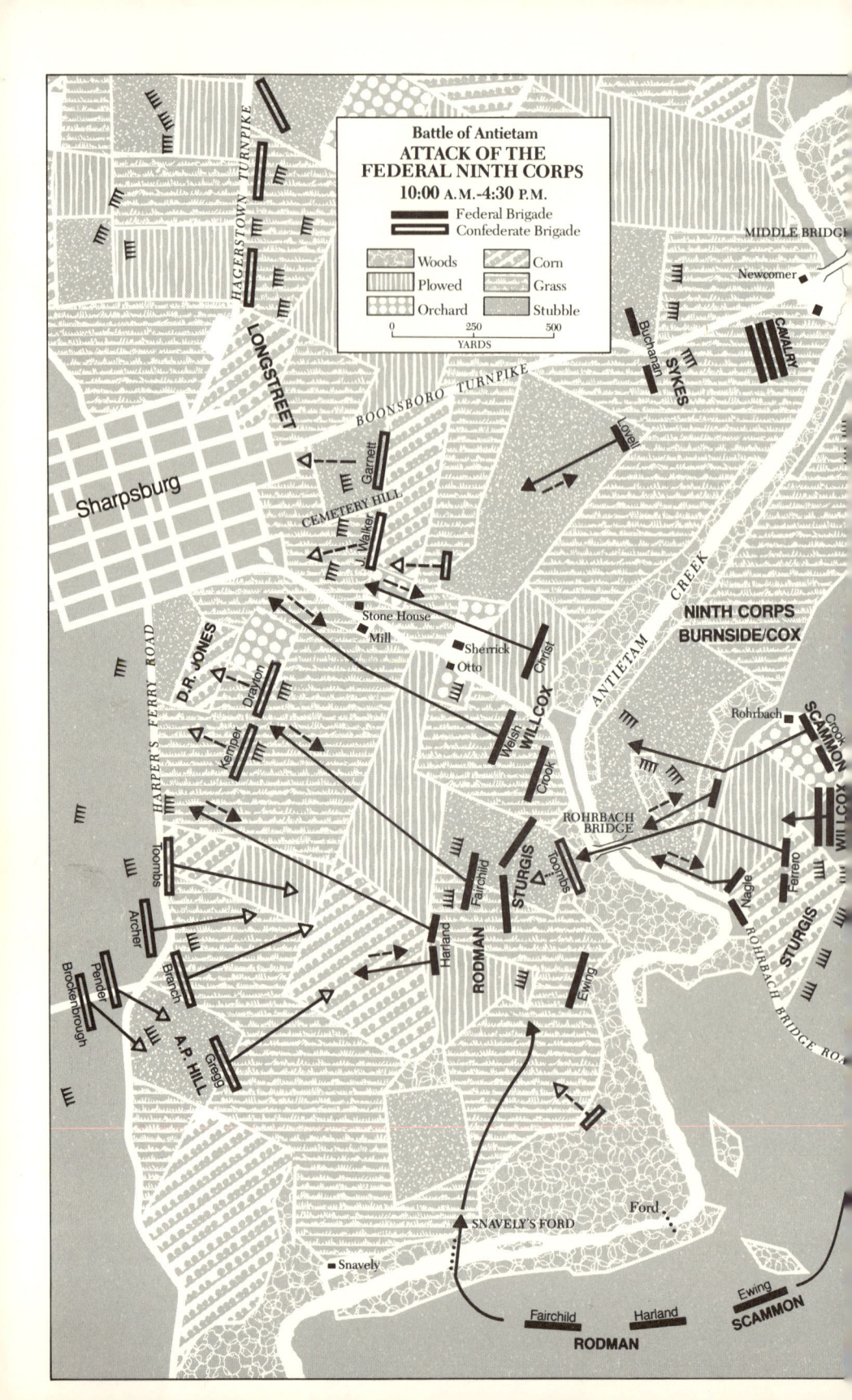

Battle of Antietam
ATTACK OF THE FEDERAL NINTH CORPS
10:00 A.M.–4:30 P.M.

The Spires of Sharpsburg

original attack order sent him that morning. Some four hours of daylight remained in which to bring the day-long battle to a decisive climax.

Willcox's division had the farthest to go, and set off first. The two brigades were deployed on each side of the Rohrbach Bridge road that climbed through a hollow from the creek into Sharpsburg, the four regiments under Colonel Benjamin C. Christ to the right of the road and the four under Colonel Thomas Welsh to the left. The ground here was steep and broken, forming a checkerboard of plowed and stubbled fields and orchards and stands of corn, and there were Rebel skirmishers concealed along every fence line and behind the house and outbuildings of the Joseph Sherrick farm. There were not in fact very many of these Southerners — it was a small detachment of South Carolinians and Georgians under Colonel F. W. McMaster — but they used cover skillfully and inflicted many casualties. From the high ground in front and to the south of the town came a nasty crossfire of musketry and artillery.

In Colonel Christ's brigade was the 79th New York, known as the Highlanders, a fancy-Dan militia outfit that went off to war after Fort Sumter wearing Scottish kilts. The army proved unsympathetic to their attire and their distinguished lineage, which led the Highlanders one day to stack arms and demand an adjustment of their grievances. McClellan's response was to surround them with hardbitten regulars with orders to shoot if the volunteers did not promptly return to duty, and that was the end of the brief mutiny. McClellan took away the regimental colors and said they would have to earn them back. The Highlanders had long since done so and it was all past history (including the kilts), and today Christ gave them the tough assignment of leading the advance.

The regiment pushed ahead resolutely through the curtain of fire and eventually chased McMaster's Rebels back into an apple orchard on the slopes of Cemetery Hill and a nearby stone house and mill. They rallied there and got some reinforcements, and the Highlanders could only hang on until the rest of the brigade came up. For a time the advance was supported on the right by part of Sykes's division of the Fifth Corps, spearheaded by Captain John S. Poland's two regiments of regulars. Word came back to General Sykes from the firing line that the Confederate position in front of

Sharpsburg appeared thin and wavering, and asking leave to charge it. "Fall in, you men," one of the regulars' officers called out. "Our turn has come at last." Instead, Poland was recalled to the Middle Bridge. The regulars' job was to protect the batteries there, and until anything different was heard from army headquarters, that was where they would stay. And so they did, notwithstanding McClellan's earlier promise to Burnside to reinforce him. The Ninth Corps — like every other Federal army corps that day — would launch its offensive unsupported.[26]

The rest of Christ's brigade was pinned down on the Sherrick farm by a vicious fire from the Rebels posted on their commanding high ground. The new 17th Michigan had received its baptism of fire at Fox's Gap on South Mountain, and on that day and this one the rookies were rapidly being disabused of any illusions about the reality of war. "I have heard and seen pictures of battles," sixteen-year-old Private William Brearley wrote his father, " — they would all be in line, all standing in a nice level field fighting, a number of ladies taking care of the wounded, &c &c. but it isent so." He discovered that the sound of battle "was rather Strange music.... I had a bullett strike me on the top of the head just as I was going to fire and a piece of Shell struck my foot — a ball hit my finger and another hit my thumb," and he added, "I concluded they ment me."[27]

The Confederate batteries on Cemetery Hill and on the ridgeline south of Sharpsburg were repeating the pattern established earlier in the day north of the town — firing with great effect on the Yankee infantry, but at the price of suffering without reply the counterbattery fire of the Yankee guns east of the creek. A Rebel officer wrote that the long-range Parrott guns across the Antietam "had the range perfectly, as they had been practicing all day." In Captain Hugh R. Garden's South Carolina battery on Cemetery Hill, one gun was disabled by a direct hit on the muzzle and a second knocked out when a shell smashed its carriage. Presently Garden's ammunition ran out and the guns were hauled off the hill by hand, the horses hitched up, and the battery went clattering back through the streets of Sharpsburg under the lash of the drivers, the gun with the splintered wheels dragged along in a great dust cloud by its straining team.

Advancing in short rushes across the hills and through the ra-

The Spires of Sharpsburg

vines south of the bridge road, Thomas Welsh's brigade threatened the flank of the Rebels blocking Christ's men. Colonel Walker had brought Jenkins's South Carolina brigade down off Cemetery Hill to join his skirmishers in the orchard, and there was a savage firefight among the apple trees. A two-gun section of a Massachusetts battery was pushed forward into John Otto's barnyard and began shelling the orchard at a range of 400 yards. The South Carolinians made a determined stand for a time in the stone house and mill alongside the road until the Yankees finally stormed the strongpoints at bayonet point and drove them out. Walker pulled what was left of his command back behind a stone wall on the outskirts of town. Cemetery Hill was under a severe fire from two directions now, and the last of the Rebel guns and their infantry supports had to abandon that commanding high ground. A young girl from one of the Unionist families in Sharpsburg was watching all this from her attic window. "On all the distant hills around were the blue uniforms and shining bayonets of our men," she recalled, "and I thought it was the prettiest sight I ever saw in my life."[28]

As Willcox's division pressed ahead toward the town, Isaac Rodman's division was going into action on the rolling open fields to the south. Of Rodman's two brigades, under Harrison S. Fairchild and Edward Harland, Fairchild's New Yorkers had found the waiting particularly trying. They had been put into line of battle behind two batteries that were dueling with the Rebel guns on the ridge to the west, and whenever the enemy gunners overshot their targets their fire plowed into the infantry. "They dropped shot and shell right into our line repeatedly," a man in the 9th New York recalled; especially nerve-racking were the solid shot that skittered along the ground or bounded overhead to knock limbs off the trees behind them.

Of the three New York regiments in Fairchild's command, the 9th was literally the most colorful. It was still outfitted in the baggy red trousers and short blue jackets and tasseled fezzes widely popular early in the war, modeled on the gaudy uniforms worn by the Algerian zouaves of the French colonial service. The men of the 9th had a reputation for the unusual anyway. When time had hung heavy on their hands during service with Burnside's North Carolina expedition back in the spring, they organized what they called the Zouave Minstrel and Dramatic Club and staged musical extravaganzas and comic farces, complete with elaborately painted backdrops and stage props. General Burnside joined the audience applauding their efforts. Recalled to Falmouth in Virginia, they had somehow wrangled space in the transports for their scenery and props, but then Falmouth was abandoned and with it all the theatrical paraphernalia. The would-be dramatists often wondered what the Rebels must have thought when they came on this strange example of Yankee ingenuity.[29]

Although the zouaves and the rest of Fairchild's brigade were well enough drilled and led, their limited action on the North Carolina coast and at South Mountain hardly prepared them for what they now faced. It was clear enough to every man in the ranks that they would have to charge straight into a storm of artillery fire from those Southern batteries plainly visible on the ridgeline a half mile away. Private David Thompson of the 9th New York recalled that the waiting was almost unendurable. So intense was the fearful anticipation that when the order was finally given to charge and they leaped up with a shout and began running forward, he was reminded of Goethe's description of a similar incident in the Napoleonic Wars and it seemed to him that "the whole landscape for an instant turned slightly red."

The New Yorkers rushed across a plowed field and clambered over the snake-rail fences of a lane that ran to the Otto farm. A dozen Confederate guns had them under fire at every step, and shell and canister tore wide gaps in the charging blue lines. A single shell killed eight of the zouaves, tossing knapsacks and blanket rolls and parts of bodies into the air. Private Thompson saw the man directly in front of him throw up his arms and drop his rifle and shout an oath as he was hit. Beyond the lane there was a shallow depression in a meadow, and the officers halted the men there briefly to realign their ranks. Fully a quarter of Fairchild's 940 men had been hit in those brief moments. Colonel Edgar A. Kimball of the 9th New York went up and down the line shouting encouragement: "Bully, Ninth! Bully, Ninth! Boys, I'm proud of you! Every one of you!"

Then they were on their feet again, yelling and cursing as they ran through the meadow sloping up toward the line of guns on the summit of the low ridge. They came on, a Rebel gunner recalled,

The Spires of Sharpsburg

as thick "as Pharaoh's locusts." It was clear now that artillery alone was not going to stop this determined charge, and the order was passed to the two forward batteries to withdraw before they were overrun. The guns were hastily limbered up and driven back to the Harper's Ferry road and then through the streets of Sharpsburg to the rear. As they left, the brigades of Kemper and Drayton, which had been lying concealed beyond the ridge, moved up to a stone wall and a post-and-rail fence on the crest to meet the Yankee attack.[30]

The roar of the guns was stilled as the opposing artillerists ceased fire for fear of hitting their own men. The Confederates rested their rifles on the wall and the fence rails, waiting for the enemy to appear over the crest of the ridge. In the sudden silence they could hear the tramp of feet and the shouted commands of the officers. It was close to four o'clock now, and for a moment it seemed as if the whole great battle had come to a single sharp focus on the impending collision between these 590 Virginians and Georgians and South Carolinians and the 700 or so New Yorkers that remained of Fairchild's brigade.

"The first thing we saw appear," wrote Private Alexander Hunter of the 17th Virginia, "was the gilt eagle that surmounted the pole, then the top of the flag, next the flutter of the stars and stripes itself, slowly mounting, up it rose, then their hats came in sight, still rising the faces emerged, next a range of curious eyes appeared, then such a hurrah as only the Yankee troops could give, broke the stillness, and they surged against us." The two battle lines, scarcely fifty yards apart, erupted in sheets of flame and smoke.

In an instant the color guard of the 9th New York was down, the colors tumbling to the ground. Dozens of others rushed forward to raise them again, only to be shot down in their turn. Whole ranks on each side were struck by the sweeping volleys, some men falling without a sound, others shrieking in their agony. Bullets splattered against the stone wall and splintered the fence rails and posts. To desperate men the fifteen or twenty seconds it took to reload seemed an eternity.

The struggle continued for perhaps ten minutes, then the New Yorkers, with their company officers in the lead, rushed straight for the fence line. The Rebels stood to meet them, and there were brief swirls of hand-to-hand combat with bayonets and swinging muskets. Finally the superior Yankee numbers tipped the balance, and Kemper's and Drayton's men ran for the rear. "I was afraid of being struck in the *back*," the 1st Virginia's Private John Dooley wrote, "and I frequently turned half around in running, so as to avoid if possible so disgraceful a wound." He kept pace with his long-legged captain only because that officer was running backward facing the enemy, "and managed not to come out ahead in this our anything but creditable race." The victorious Yankees began cheering in unison, "as if they had gained a game of base ball."[31]

Some of Fairchild's men rushed on in pursuit of the fleeing Rebels, going even into the streets of Sharpsburg. Their officers yelled at them to get back in line, so that as soon as support came up they could exploit what they had won. Their charge had been bravely made and very costly. The brigade as a whole lost 455 of its 940 men, with the heaviest casualties — 63 percent — suffered by the zouaves of the 9th New York.

The collapsing Confederate flank produced chaos in Sharpsburg. Guns and caissons careened through the narrow streets on their way to refit and replenish ammuniton. A slave woman remembered ambulances rolling past and trailing rivulets of blood through their floorboards; from one the keening cry, "O Lord! O Lord! O Lord!" continued steadily until the vehicle was out of hearing. For a time General Lee joined his officers attempting to rally their broken and disorganized commands, calling the men to stand to their regimental colors. Federal shells came over in steady parade, smashing through roofs and walls, setting fires and tumbling timber and bricks and broken glass into the streets. The Lutheran church on Main Street near Cemetery Hill was struck repeatedly and great swatches of its plastered exterior torn off. "I never was so tired of shelling in my life before," surgeon J. R. Boulware of the 6th South Carolina wrote in his diary. *"I hate cannons."* The unending racket sent flocks of pigeons fluttering into the sky.

Less visible were the hundreds of Rebel stragglers hiding in barns and stables and cellars all over town. A Sharpsburg woman remembered the day as one long nightmare. She and her neighbors had crowded into the cellar of a sturdy stone house as the bom-

The Spires of Sharpsburg 285

bardment grew in intensity, and they were soon joined by a half-dozen stragglers numbed by the fighting they had seen. "A number of babies were there, and several dogs, and every time the firing began extra hard the babies would cry and the dogs would bark," she recalled. Federal shells exploded so close that the walls shook, leaving some of the women unnerved and hysterical, "and some of those old aged men would break out in prayer." Among Sharpsburg's residents who elected to remain during the battle, at least one, a young girl, was killed.[32]

General Lee rode back to a knoll near his headquarters, where he watched intently the rapidly worsening situation on the flank. Of Jones's division, only the thin brigade of Robert Toombs was still in place. Yankee skirmishers were prowling the streets and dodging among the houses on the edge of town. Looking beyond the struggle taking place near the Harper's Ferry road, Lee could see columns of other troops off to the south. In a passing battery he noticed an officer, Lieutenant John Ramsay, with a telescope. Calling him over, he asked, "What troops are those?"

The lieutenant offered him the telescope, but Lee held up his bandaged hands and said, "Can't use it." Ramsay focused on the nearest column for a moment and said, "They are flying the United States flag."

What about the other column, Lee asked. After another pause, the lieutenant announced, "They are flying the Virginia and Confederate flags."

Lee nodded and observed, "It is A. P. Hill from Harper's Ferry." As he expected, Powell Hill was bringing up his men from Boteler's Ford with all speed and in the proper place. Lee directed Ramsay to open on the Federal column with his two rifled guns until Hill engaged, then to shift to other targets.[33]

A. P. Hill was a general with an impetuous streak and a fiery temperament that matched his red beard, traits that at times had brought him trouble on the battlefield and off. On this day they served him well. His Light Division's remarkable march from Harper's Ferry — seventeen miles in less than eight hours — rivaled the best marks of Jackson's famous foot cavalry. That along the way Hill actually prodded laggards with the point of his sword is possibly apocryphal — probably the troops' two days of rest following the capture of Harper's Ferry had more to do with their achievement — but however he did it, "Little Powell" inspired a sense of desperate urgency in all ranks.

To be sure, uncounted hundreds were left by the roadside exhausted, and Hill then rushed his brigades into action piecemeal, without that pause for reorganizing and realigning that other generals (particularly Army of the Potomac generals) regarded as essential before going into battle. Hill's reward for boldness was having enough of the 3,300 of his men who finally reached the field in the right place at the right time. His good fortune — and that of the Army of Northern Virginia — was the gift of time presented by the Federal high command. The hours squandered on Burnside's front were the last of exactly forty-eight hours that General McClellan, since he arrived before Sharpsburg, had granted General Lee to reassemble the scattered pieces of his army.

Hill's arrival did not completely escape the Federals' notice. At three o'clock, as the Ninth Corps's offensive got under way, a flag signalman on Red Hill, the ridgeline behind the Union front, warned Burnside, "Look out well on your left; the enemy are moving a strong force in that direction." The message took probably less than ten minutes to send, but when it was received at the signal station near Burnside's headquarters a half mile east of the Antietam, the general was not there. He had crossed the bridge to press his attack, and if the warning reached him at all, it arrived too late to be of any use.[34]

This was the first of a series of misfortunes beginning to plague the Ninth Corps's offensive. Willcox's drive on Sharpsburg was well directed and resolutely pressed, and the charge of Fairchild's brigade was as gallant an exploit as any that day. But meanwhile nothing was going right for the second of Rodman's brigades, under Colonel Edward Harland, making up the left wing of the Federal advance. The trouble began with a mix-up in orders. The 8th Connecticut went forward alone while the two regiments on its left, the 16th Connecticut and the 4th Rhode Island, remained at their starting lines on the edge of the Otto cornfield. Their orders to advance were finally delivered, but by that time all three regiments were marching into ambushes.

Both Rodman and Harland were with the 8th Connecticut as it moved up toward Fairchild's brigade to go into action alongside it.

The Spires of Sharpsburg

It was during this march, at about 3:30, that they first sighted enemy troops off to the south, moving toward the Ninth Corps's open flank. Rodman sent an aide to warn the 16th Connecticut and the 4th Rhode Island then entering the cornfield, and spurred ahead to alert Fairchild. As Rodman galloped across an open meadow, a Rebel sharpshooter knocked him off his horse with a mortal wound in the chest. He was the ninth Union general to be hit that day. Harland had turned back to bring up the two lagging regiments, had his horse shot out from under him, and hurried toward the endangered flank on foot.

The 8th Connecticut pushed straight ahead, aiming for three Confederate guns that had gone into battery on the ridge in front of the Harper's Ferry road. This was one of the Light Division's batteries, under Captain D. G. McIntosh, sent on ahead by Hill from Boteler's Ford. As the range closed, McIntosh went to double loads of canister, the guns bounding backward with each discharge. Gaps were torn in the charging lines, but still the Yankees came on. They were only sixty yards away now, nearly all the battery horses were down, and McIntosh ordered his gunners to leave the pieces and save themselves. One of the Connecticut boys ran forward, leaped atop a cannon barrel, and waved his arms in triumph.

The elation was short-lived, for suddenly these Yankees realized they were half a mile ahead of the rest of their brigade and there was not another Federal soldier anywhere in sight. And they were coming under an increasingly severe converging fire as Toombs's Georgians and some of A. P. Hill's North Carolinians counterattacked from front and flank. The Connecticut regiment stood up to the volleys for some minutes; "even the chaplain snatches the rifle and cartridge-box of a dead man, and fights for life," the regimental historian wrote. Finally it had to retreat back across the meadow, leaving 173 of its 350 men on the grassy slope.[35]

The isolation of the 8th Connecticut left only the 4th Rhode Island and the 16th Connecticut to hold the Ninth Corps's flank against Powell Hill's attack. The Rhode Islanders had seen some action with Burnside on the North Carolina coast, but the Connecticut regiment was as raw as any in the Army of the Potomac. Just three weeks before, the men were experiencing their first taste of army life at a place called Oyster Point at New Haven, a favorite spot, the unit's historian reported, "for patriotic and tender-hearted young women, who rode down to distribute needle-books, sweet pickles, bouquets, and smiles." It would be their fate — as it had been the fate of numerous other brand-new Federal regiments that day — to undergo their baptism of fire at a critical moment in the battle.

Mr. Otto's cornfield was a particularly nasty place to make a fight. There was hardly a level spot anywhere in it. A hollow that was forty feet deep in places slanted all the way across it, and jutting up like an island in a sea of corn was a large rock outcropping surrounded by a grove of trees. At its southern and western boundaries were stone walls several hundred yards long. The two Yankee regiments were advancing down into the hollow when Maxcy Gregg's veteran South Carolina brigade approached the corn from the south and west. The Federals had the edge in manpower, about 1,000 to 750, but the Confederates had the critical advantages of position and experience.

The 16th Connecticut's Lieutenant B. G. Blakeslee wrote in his diary that the order to move on had just been given "when a terrible volley was fired into us from behind a stone wall about five rods in front of us. ... In a moment we were riddled with shot." He added that "orders were given which were not understood. Neither the line-officers nor the men had any knowledge of regimental movements."

As the rookies milled about in the corn, the South Carolinians continued to pour a murderous fire into them from higher ground. The Connecticut boys did their best in the smoky confusion, and for a time they even drove back some of their attackers. Brigadier Gregg was hit by a bullet and knocked off his horse. Stretcher-bearers came up and he ordered his second-in-command to take over. A medical orderly examining him suddenly exclaimed, "General, you aren't *wounded,* you are only *bruised!*" Gregg jumped to his feet and went back to the fight.

The Rhode Islanders too were putting up a desperate fight, but in the tall corn it was hard to tell friend from foe. A flag in their front looked very much like the national colors, and they were ordered to cease firing while their own color-bearer and two company officers went forward to investigate. They were within twenty feet of the other line when a volley cracked out and the

The Spires of Sharpsburg

color-bearer fell dead. The officers snatched up the fallen flag and ran back through the corn and gave the order to resume firing. What they had seen, it turned out, was the colors of the 1st South Carolina. During the pause, however, Gregg worked another regiment farther around to the right to take the Rhode Islanders in flank, and their line began to waver and break.

Colonel Harland reached the scene and tried to regain control of his shattered command, but it was too late. The colonel of the 16th told him that his troops had virtually no drilling "and hardly knew how to form in line of battle." The Connecticut boys broke and ran in "irretrievable disorder" (as one of Gregg's men described it), carrying the Rhode Islanders with them. The entire Federal flank brigade was gone now.

Seeing the men rushing back out of the cornfield, General Cox had to order Willcox and Fairchild to withdraw from their suddenly exposed positions on the outskirts of Sharpsburg; without the Fifth Corps's troops to cover his right flank, forming a new front facing south to cope with this sudden counterattack on his left would be too perilous a venture. The men received the order with curses, furious at having to surrender ground so hard-won. It was close to 4:30, and the Ninth Corps was on the defensive and falling back.[36]

Colonel Hugh Ewing brought up his Ohio regiments of the Kanawha Division to try to mend the break, and they made a hard fight of it for possession of a stone wall near the Otto cornfield. A. P. Hill had three of his five brigades in the fight by now, perhaps 2,000 men — Gregg's South Carolinians, James J. Archer's Tennesseans and Georgians, and L. O'Brien Branch's North Carolinians — and the fiery Robert Toombs had strengthened his own command with fragments collected from various broken brigades and announced that he was going to drive the Yankees into Antietam Creek. Toombs, a prominent Georgia political figure and for a time the Confederacy's secretary of state, had told his wife it was his ambition to distinguish himself in a great battle and then retire "if I live through it," and he was doing his best to realize his hopes.

The Ohioans, like the Rhode Islanders before them, were having difficulty making out who was who in the confusion, and they held their fire as some of Gregg's men advanced toward them through the cornfield, thinking they were Yankees. (It seems that some of

Hill's needy troops had supplemented their ragged uniforms from the Federal stores captured at Harper's Ferry.) They discovered their mistake too late, were outflanked, and had to join the retreat. General Branch rode to the front to press the pursuit and was killed instantly by a bullet through the head. His death raised the casualty toll among the Confederate generals to nine, matching the Federal army in that grim statistical category.[37]

By now the Southerners had more than forty guns bracing their lines, collected from no less than fifteen batteries, and they were putting down a killing barrage. The Yankee batteries were outgunned and began pulling back. The long-range Parrotts across the creek ran short of ammunition trying to suppress the enemy fire; on Burnside's order, one battery continued to put up a brave show by firing blank powder charges. Once again, as it had done so often during the day, the well-handled Confederate artillery gained superiority at the point where the two armies joined battle.

Cox was working hard to build a new line covering the bridge and the heights west of the creek, calling up some of Sturgis's regiments from the reserve. The rookies of the 35th Massachusetts were put up front, suffered severely from artillery and musketry, and lost more than 200 men. So great was the volume of fire that the meadows appeared to be alive with bullets, riffling through the tall grass like a summer breeze. A Pennsylvania gunner delivering a message to another battery was seen to run on tiptoe and jerk his knees high with each step as he crossed an open field, looking as if he was dashing through a nest of angry yellow jackets. "Things began to look rather squally," Lieutenant Whitman of the 51st New York wrote, "and although our Brigade was nearly out of ammunition we were ordered to the front again.... Our Regt fired every round of ammunition we had, and took from all the dead and wounded on the field and then we lay down as we would not leave the field untill we were ordered."[38]

General McClellan had not returned to the Pry house after meeting with Bull Sumner in time to see much of Burnside's initially promising advance. And shortly after he reached his headquarters, he heard a tremendous eruption of cannon fire from the extreme northern flank of the army. It seemed a matter of grave concern; surely the long-expected Confederate counterattack was at hand.

The Spires of Sharpsburg 291

The cannonading did indeed herald Lee's planned flanking movement — and also signaled its collapse. Jeb Stuart had assembled seven regiments of cavalry, the infantry of the 48th North Carolina, and a mixed collection of twenty-one guns and moved them to a point due west of the Joseph Poffenberger farm where the First Corps, now under General Meade, was posted. Stuart would have to pass his command through a corridor less than a mile wide, between Meade's position and the Potomac, to reach the Federal rear. He advanced his guns to Nicodemus Hill and some high ground to the north to open the way, and found the enemy waiting. Meade had thirty-four guns massed on high ground near the Poffenberger homestead, ranked hub to hub pointing west. Captain Poague of the Rockbridge Artillery concisely described what happened next: "an attempt was made to dislodge the enemy's batteries, but failed completely, being silenced in fifteen or twenty minutes by a most terrific fire...."[39] After mulling the situation for an hour or so, Stuart turned his little command back to its starting point. The aborted attack did achieve one benefit, however: it gave General McClellan one more thing to worry about.

McClellan already had reason for concern as he witnessed A. P. Hill's counterattack and the turnabout on Burnside's front. "He sees clearly enough that Burnside is pressed — needs no messenger to tell him that. His face grows darker with anxious thought," reported the *Tribune*'s Smalley, who had stationed himself at headquarters. Smalley saw McClellan glance at Fitz John Porter's Fifth Corps arrayed before them, and then turn to Porter with a questioning look. "But Porter slowly shakes his head, and one may believe that the same thought is passing through the minds of both generals," Smalley wrote. " 'They are the only reserves of the army; they cannot be spared.' "

McClellan and Porter called for their horses and rode toward the left flank, and had reached the Boonsboro turnpike when a Ninth Corps courier intercepted them. Correspondent Smalley heard him deliver Burnside's warning: if he did not receive more men and guns immediately, he could not hold his position half an hour. McClellan contemplated the western sky for a moment and replied, "Tell General Burnside this is the battle of the war. He must hold his ground till dark at any cost. I will send him Miller's battery. I can do nothing more. I have no infantry." The courier started to turn his horse away but McClellan called him back. "Tell him if he *cannot* hold his ground, then the bridge, to the last man! — always the bridge! If the bridge is lost, all is lost!"[40]

On that histrionic note, George McClellan revealed the final dimension of his own loss of courage, every bit as great as that suffered by Bull Sumner. On hand just then, by Porter's count, were 4,000 of his men who had yet to fire a shot. Some 1,500 of Sykes's regulars who had crossed the Middle Bridge earlier were also available; in their afternoon of skirmishing they had suffered only 95 casualties. Thus it was not so much that the general commanding had no infantry to answer Burnside's call for help, but that he had none he cared to risk. To do so would leave the army's center and its trains to the protection of Pleasonton's 4,000 or so cavalry, Porter's two brigades then returning from Sumner's front, and those long ranks of guns. He apparently concluded that committing his reserves would be a fatal sign of weakness, an open invitation to the enemy to attack and cut the Army of the Potomac in two. General Burnside (like General Pope on an earlier occasion) would have to get out of his scrape as best he could.[41]

As it happened, Burnside eventually did get out of his scrape unaided, although he was driven nearly all the way back to the Rohrbach Bridge. The Ninth Corps suffered 2,350 casualties but it was not in danger of final rout after all. The Rebels were content to pin the Federals in their bridgehead on the hills west of the creek. The combined losses in Jones's and A. P. Hill's divisions came to just over a thousand men, substantially less than what they had inflicted but still too large in proportion to those engaged to think of trying to drive the Yankees into Antietam Creek before nightfall. Lee's right flank and the vital Boteler's Ford road were secure.

Even as the fighting south of Sharpsburg was winding down, there was a brief flare-up near the Sunken Road. It was a small fight as such things went, but it stands as a symbol of much that happened that long day; of all the individual battles, great and small, that made up the larger battle of Antietam, none was more senseless.

During the afternoon's lull, Harvey Hill had advanced sharpshooters through the Piper farm and orchard to harass the Yankee

The Spires of Sharpsburg

positions beyond the Sunken Road. The Sixth Corps's Colonel William Irwin, who earlier had directed an ill-advised charge toward the Dunker church, decided to clear them out. He rode up to Major Thomas W. Hyde of the 7th Maine and ordered him to take his regiment and do the job. Hyde was appalled at the prospect and convinced that his commanding officer was drunk. Having detected substantial numbers of Rebels on the Piper farm, he suggested that a full brigade rather than a single regiment would be needed.

"Are you afraid to go, Sir? Those are your orders, Sir," Irwin blustered.

"Give the order so the regiment can hear it and we are ready, Sir," Hyde replied. Irwin did so, and the 181 men of the 7th Maine set off.

They had got as far as the Piper barn and haystacks when a savage fire was opened on them from three sides. Hyde rode through the orchard looking for a way out of the trap. Above the apple trees he could see four Confederate battle flags closing in on his little regiment, and the hail of enemy fire was knocking men down all around him and showering the survivors with branches and twigs. They finally made their way to safety, to the cheers of their watching comrades, but only after half the men were killed or wounded. When he later found out that the expedition had been mounted on no higher authority than Irwin's, that it was "from an inspiration of John Barleycorn in our brigade commander alone," Hyde wrote, "I wished I had been old enough, or distinguished enough, to have dared to disobey orders."[42]

The sun, a great blood-red disk in the smoky late-afternoon light, went down at last and the light faded and the bloodiest day of the Civil War — indeed of all American history — was finally done. "Gradually the thunder dies away," Charles Coffin of the *Boston Journal* wrote. "The flashes are fewer. The musketry ceases and silence comes on, broken only by an occasional volley, and single shots, like the last drops of a shower."

But the field did not remain silent. The din of armies at battle was replaced by the sound of armies of wounded, a mournful and unceasing dirge of pain. Within the opposing lines lanterns winked and bobbed like bright fireflies in the woodlots and fields as medical orderlies and stretcher-bearers searched for the injured.

Thousands more lay beyond aid in the no-man's land between the lines. "This was a miserable night to me...," wrote a Federal artilleryman posted near the Cornfield; "groans and cries for water could be heard the whole night. We could not help them...."

Survivors wandered about seeking missing comrades — it seemed to Kyd Douglas of Jackson's staff that "half of Lee's army was hunting the other half" — starting or ending their search at the field hospitals. These were nightmarish places, churches and farmhouses and barns and sheds packed with wounded men in numbers far too great for the medical staffs to handle. Hour after hour blood-spattered surgeons worked by lantern light at their crude operating tables, yet it seemed that for each man treated two more were delivered by the stretcher-bearers. Those who died before the surgeons could take them, or afterward, were laid in growing ranks outside the hospitals, and hastily dug pits contained heaps of amputated hands and feet and limbs.[43]

Some men presumed killed were found alive. One such was Captain Holmes of the 20th Massachusetts, left for dead during Sedgwick's fight in the West Woods. A friend, Captain William G. LaDuc, came on Holmes that evening wandering aimlessly behind Sumner's lines. He took him in charge and asked where he was wounded. "Shot in the neck," Holmes muttered. LaDuc was momentarily taken aback, for the phrase was army argot for being drunk, but upon inspection he found the description precisely right and wondered how Holmes could still be alive. Unable to find an available surgeon, LaDuc cleaned and bandaged the wound as best he could. "The Captain squirmed a little under my surgery, and said I'm glad LaDuc it aint a case for amputation for I have duced little confidence in your surgery," he recalled. At the first opportunity LaDuc sent a telegram to Holmes's famous father, "The Autocrat of the Breakfast Table," in Boston: "Capt. Holmes wounded shot through the neck thought not mortal at Keedysville."[44]

At that point, no one really knew how bad the day had been, and officers hoped decimated commands would fill out once stragglers turned up and the men who had helped wounded comrades to the rear rejoined their units. When the counts were eventually tallied, they were as bad as could be imagined. The toll in the Army of the Potomac came to 2,108 dead, 9,540 wounded, and 753

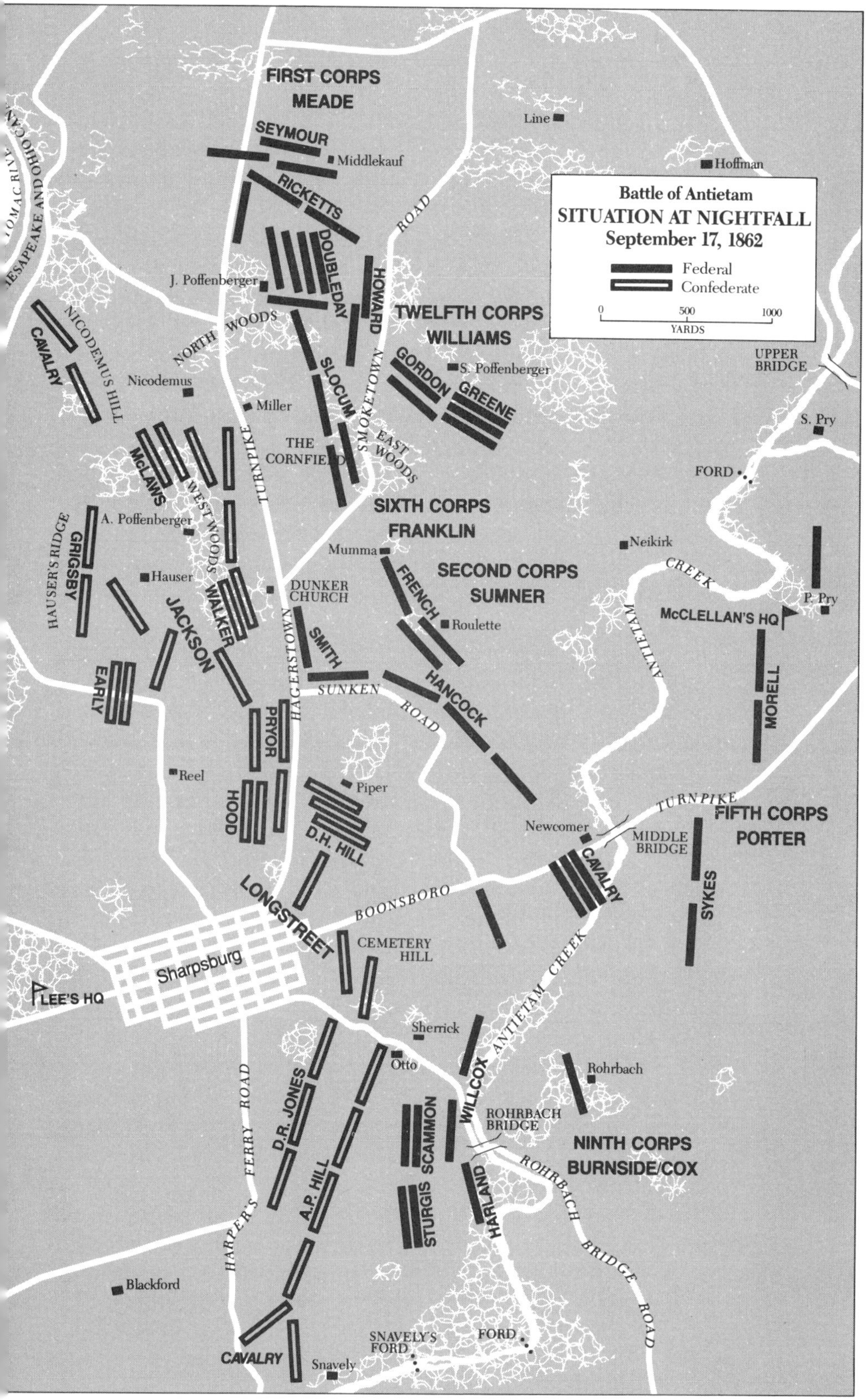
Battle of Antietam
SITUATION AT NIGHTFALL
September 17, 1862
Federal
Confederate
0
500
1000
YARDS
FIRST CORPS
MEADE
SEYMOUR
RICKETTS
DOUBLEDAY
HOWARD
TWELFTH CORPS
WILLIAMS
GORDON
GREENE
SLOCUM
SIXTH CORPS
FRANKLIN
SECOND CORPS
SUMNER
FRENCH
SMITH
HANCOCK
McCLELLAN'S HQ
MORELL
FIFTH CORPS
PORTER
SYKES
CAVALRY
NINTH CORPS
BURNSIDE/COX
WILLCOX
SCAMMON
STURGIS
HARLAND
A.P. HILL
D.R. JONES
LONGSTREET
D.H. HILL
HOOD
PRYOR
WALKER
JACKSON
EARLY
GRIGSBY
McLAWS
LEE'S HQ
Sharpsburg
Line
Hoffman
Middlekauf
J. Poffenberger
S. Poffenberger
Nicodemus
Miller
A. Poffenberger
Hauser
Mumma
Roulette
Neikirk
S. Pry
P. Pry
Reel
Piper
Newcomer
Sherrick
Otto
Rohrbach
Blackford
Snavely
NICODEMUS HILL
HAUSER'S RIDGE
NORTH WOODS
WEST WOODS
EAST WOODS
THE CORNFIELD
DUNKER CHURCH
CEMETERY HILL
TURNPIKE
HAGERSTOWN
SMOKETOWN
ROAD
SUNKEN
BOONSBORO
HARPER'S FERRY ROAD
ROHRBACH BRIDGE ROAD
ANTIETAM CREEK
UPPER BRIDGE
MIDDLE BRIDGE
ROHRBACH BRIDGE
FORD
SNAVELY'S FORD
CHESAPEAKE AND OHIO CANAL
POTOMAC RIVER

missing, 12,401 men in all, 25 percent of those who went into action. Confederate casualties would never be precisely reckoned, but the best estimate of Lee's losses on September 17 is 1,546 dead, 7,752 wounded, and 1,018 missing, for a total of 10,318, 31 percent of those on the firing lines. The combined casualties for those twelve hours of combat came to 22,719. No single day of this or any other American war would surpass that fearful record.

Nor do these figures reflect a true count of the dead and wounded. There is no doubt that a good many of the 1,771 men listed as missing were in fact dead, buried uncounted in unmarked graves where they fell. Civilians returning to their farms around Sharpsburg in the following days told of numerous corpses they discovered under haystacks or in cellars or hidden in thickets and which they buried unrecorded. Certainly many others among the missing were wounded, for it appears that comparatively few men on either side in this battle were captured unhurt. In addition, a substantial number of those tallied as wounded would die weeks and months later of their injuries.[45]

The Federals' losses were concentrated almost entirely in the corps of Hooker, Mansfield, Sumner, and Burnside. Porter's Fifth Corps lost but 109 men, all from the detachments of gunners and regulars sent across the Middle Bridge. Casualties in Franklin's Sixth Corps came to 439, most due to Colonel Irwin's hapless adventuring. General Couch's division spent the day marching uselessly back and forth in Pleasant Valley. In making his battle against great odds to save the Republic, General McClellan had committed barely 50,000 infantry and artillerymen to the contest. A third of his army did not fire a shot. Even at that, his men repeatedly drove the Army of Northern Virginia to the brink of disaster, feats of valor entirely lost on a commander thinking of little beyond staving off his own defeat.

It was clear enough to General Lee that his army was grievously hurt. Every unit had been thrown into the day's struggle except Jeb Stuart's cavalry and two of A. P. Hill's late-arriving brigades. He could call on no fresh reserves to mend his lines. The nearest Confederate troops were in the small brigade Hill had left behind to hold Harper's Ferry.

That evening his lieutenants assembled at army headquarters west of Sharpsburg to make their reports. Lee's only outward concern was the whereabouts of Longstreet. Finally Old Pete rode up, having stopped in town to assist a family whose house had been set afire in the shelling. "Ah, here is Longstreet; here is my old war horse," Lee greeted him, and the two conversed briefly. Lee then issued orders for the movement of some artillery and called for the rounding up of stragglers from the rear areas. Rations were to be cooked and delivered to the men in the forward lines. That was all. He said nothing about a withdrawal across the Potomac. September 18 would find the Army of Northern Virginia again standing at its guns before Sharpsburg.[46]

The slave woman who had witnessed the chaos in the town during the afternoon's crisis now found that calm had been restored. Troops and guns and wagons went past in purposeful order. She saw a Rebel soldier standing nearby and asked him, "Did you have a hard fight to-day?"

"Yes, Aunty," he replied, "the Yankees gave us the devil, and they'll give us hell next."[47]

TO NOBLY SAVE OR MEANLY LOSE

When Dame Fortune smiled on General McClellan, she blessed him beyond all logical workings of the laws of probability that operate in war. During the Maryland campaign he was presented with not just one but six highly favorable opportunities to crush the rebellion's principal army. At the two battles on South Mountain on September 14, thanks to the Lost Order, he was invited to divide and conquer Lee's forces. At Sharpsburg on September 15 and again on September 16 came opportunities to force the enemy into battle against overwhelming numbers. In the great struggle on September 17 he had the chance (though by then at somewhat less favorable odds) to break the Army of Northern Virginia and drive it into the Potomac. Finally, on Thursday, September 18, it was within his power to finish what had been so bloodily begun at dawn the previous day. However these chances may be measured one against the other, this last one was as good as any of them.

When the *Tribune*'s George Smalley left the field on the evening of the battle to get his story to New York, it was his impression that everything "was favorable for a renewal of the fight in the morning. If the plan of the battle is sound, there is every reason why McClellan should win it." At army headquarters Colonel Strother was of a like mind, and he went to sleep that night confidently expecting the contest to resume at dawn. The comings and goings of staff couriers awakened him in the early hours of the morning, and he overheard McClellan tell someone, "They are to hold the ground they occupy, but are not to attack without further orders." Strother was so upset by this that he could not get back to sleep, he recalled; "I feared we would thus lose the fruits of a victory already achieved."[1]

At 8 A.M. on September 18, General McClellan wired a situation report to General-in-Chief Halleck in Washington: "The battle of yesterday continued for fourteen hours, and until after dark. We held all we gained, except a portion of the extreme left.... Our losses very heavy, especially in general officers. The battle will probably be renewed to-day." At the same hour he telegraphed Mrs. McClellan: "The battle of yesterday was a desperate one. We hold all we gained. The contest will probably be renewed to day," and then set down his more private impressions in a letter to her. "The spectacle yesterday was the grandest I could conceive of; nothing could be more sublime," he wrote. "Those in whose judgment I rely tell me that I fought the battle splendidly and that it was a masterpiece of art." He did not specify who volunteered that remarkable analysis.

In reporting that he expected the battle to be renewed on Thursday, McClellan neglected to add an important qualification: any fighting done that day was not going to be initiated by him. "A careful and anxious survey of the condition of my command, and my knowledge of the enemy's forces and position," he wrote on October 15 in his preliminary report, "failed to impress me with any reasonable certainty of success if I renewed the attack without re-enforcing columns."

The Young Napoleon's inactivity on September 18 would draw heavy fire from his critics — one Northern paper labeled the day "fatal Thursday" — and he felt compelled to construct an elaborate defense of his decision when he came to write his official report of the campaign some months later. It was an argument buttressed by misstatements and half-truths, yet perhaps it should come as no real surprise that a general laboring under so great a weight of self-deception (ranking his management of Wednesday's battle as a masterpiece of art, for one example) could not find it within himself to renew the fight that day.[2]

As McClellan explained it, all the information available to him indicated that the Yankee soldiers who fought on September 17 had been too roughly handled to resume the battle. They were exhausted by the combat and the "long day and night marches" (he gave no examples of such exhausting marches) and many of them were demoralized. He pointed to a field return for the First Corps showing only 6,729 men present for duty, compared with a roster strength of about twice that number. In fact the real wastage in Hooker's corps had come from straggling before the battle began. That day's return (as later corrected) counted the infantry strength at 5,327; subtracting casualties from the 8,600 who actually went into action left some 800 stragglers from Wednesday's fighting unaccounted for. This was a serious enough problem, to be sure, and it made hot-tempered General Meade very angry, but it was hardly cause to write off the corps. The efficiency of the men, Meade reported on the eighteenth, was good "so far as it goes, ... although I do not think their morale is as good for an offensive as a defensive movement."[3]

McClellan's disparaging appraisal of the Ninth Corps in his official report is also suspect, and was not shared by Generals Burnside and Cox. On the previous evening, Burnside testified to the Joint Committee on the Conduct of the War, he went to McClellan's headquarters and proposed that if reinforced by 5,000 fresh men he would reopen the attack on the Confederate right at dawn. Colonel Delos Sackett, McClellan's aide, remembered the conversation quite differently. According to him, Burnside insisted his own men were so dispirited that the 5,000 reinforcements were needed simply to hold his position.

General Cox, in tactical command of the corps, vigorously denied the allegation that Burnside or anyone else had claimed "the 9th Corps except part of Rodman's division was not in good condition & heart on the evening of the 17th." The figures, at least, support Cox. Rodman's division had suffered almost half the corps's casualties. Losses among the men engaged in the divisions of Sturgis, Willcox, and Scammon were 21 percent, 10 percent, and 8 percent, respectively. All factors considered, including straggling, it is likely that the Ninth Corps had between 9,000 and 9,500 infantrymen at hand on September 18.[4]

No field returns for September 18 are on record for the other two corps involved in the battle, the Second and Twelfth. If the condition of the First Corps is taken as a fair example, however, they had between them, after Wednesday's casualties and straggling, perhaps 14,500 infantrymen available for duty. Facing the Dunker church and the West Woods, then, the three Federal corps that had fought there the previous day could furnish a total of nearly 20,000 troops capable of at least holding their positions in support of an offensive by fresher troops. McClellan reported the shortage of shells for the long-range Parrott rifles in the reserve artillery; he did not mention that there was sufficient ammunition for the long ranks of field guns — some eighty of them, with others in immediate reserve — massed in battery from the Mumma farmstead on the Smoketown road to the Joseph Poffenberger farm on the northern flank.

Another matter McClellan did not go into was the number of fresh troops he had that day. Only one of Franklin's Sixth Corps brigades had done any serious fighting on the seventeenth; in his other five brigades, losses in the afternoon's shelling and sniping came to just 80 men. The situation in Porter's Fifth Corps was comparable. Casualties among the infantrymen in his six brigades totaled 95, all among the regulars who had crossed the Middle Bridge. These two corps, favorites of McClellan's from the Peninsula campaign, could put at least 20,300 effectives on the firing line.

Then there was the matter of the reinforcing columns the general commanding was waiting for. Darius Couch's division, McClellan wrote, did not come into position until late morning after "marching with commendable rapidity." That statement obscured his own shortcomings as well as Couch's. General Couch must rank as the slowest general officer in either army during the Maryland campaign. At Crampton's Gap on September 14 he was twelve hours late in linking up with Franklin's Sixth Corps. On the seventeenth, once McClellan had belatedly recalled him to the main army, his rate of march from Pleasant Valley was scarcely commendable, even by Army of the Potomac standards. A message from headquarters, sent at midnight on September 17, ordered him to march "with your command to-morrow morning in time to report with it to Major General Franklin, as soon after daylight as you can possibly do so." Couch was a good four to five hours late in meeting that summons. In any event, he brought with him another 6,000 or so effectives.[5]

The Federal troops who deserved the praise for commendable rapidity were the Pennsylvanians of Brigadier Andrew A. Humphreys's Fifth Corps division. This was a brand-new outfit, with seven of its eight regiments made up of raw troops, and General Humphreys had been having a terrible time with it. When he took command in Washington on September 12 he found, among other problems, that half the men were equipped with defective Austrian rifles that would not fire. Famous throughout the army for his command of profane invective, a talent he put to good use, Humphreys finally got things sorted out and reached Frederick on September 16. The call to join the main army reached him shortly after two o'clock on the afternoon of the battle, and in the fashion of A. P. Hill he had his men on the road within the hour. Early that evening he notified McClellan, "We will march all night — slowly and resting at intervals, and come in in the morning fit for something." He promised to be in Keedysville, a mile behind the Union lines, by 9 A.M. on the eighteenth, "unless you order us to hurry up faster."

Humphreys was as good as his word. Before ten o'clock that morning, after a hard night march of twenty-three miles, his division was in place in the army's reserve. More than that, he had lost only 600 of his 6,600 men to straggling. It was with understandable outrage, then, that he read in McClellan's preliminary report a month later that one reason no attack was made on September 18 was that "Humphreys' division of new troops, fatigued with forced marches, were arriving throughout the day, but were not available until near its close." Humphreys made an issue of it, demanding from Secretary of War Stanton a court of inquiry to defend his reputation, and McClellan was forced to correct the record.[6]

The upshot of all this counting of heads and bringing up of troops was that George McClellan had at hand by late morning on September 18 close to 30,000 men in the positions gained in Wednesday's battle; another 26,300 fresh troops, nearly all of them veterans, available to renew the offensive if he so chose; and Humphreys's 6,000 rookies. (Humphreys's men might have been used in an attack as well, although if McClellan learned anything from events on the seventeenth it was that new troops were likely to be terribly cut up. Stark figures were lesson enough: just over a tenth of the 136 Yankee regiments that saw combat were made up of troops going into battle for the first time, and they suffered 20 percent of the army's total casualties.)

To Nobly Save or Meanly Lose

In several important respects, the position of the Army of the Potomac on Thursday was more promising than it had been at dawn on Wednesday. On the south flank the Ninth Corps was across the barrier of the Antietam and ready (by Burnside's and Cox's testimony, at any rate) to pin down a sizable portion of Lee's army if nothing more. To the north, a renewal of the offensive against the Confederate left could now begin with all forces across the creek and solidly supported by field artillery. The coordination between units that was so lacking on Wednesday would no doubt be easier to achieve from this advanced starting line. The number of troops available for combat exceeded 62,000. Hooker and Mansfield and Richardson were out of the fight and Bull Sumner continued to counsel caution, but George Meade and Alpheus Williams were considered reliable and competent, Winfield Scott Hancock was a driver, and Fitz John Porter retained McClellan's confidence. And William Franklin of the Sixth Corps was still ready and willing to fight. At 10 A.M. Franklin proposed to headquarters an assault by his corps on the high ground of Nicodemus Hill, behind and on the flank of the Confederate positions in the West Woods.

General McClellan, however, remained in character, so fearful of losing that he would not risk winning. What it came down to finally was his conviction that on September 17 he had saved his country by saving its most important army, and that was not a risk he cared to repeat just then. "One battle lost, and almost all would have been lost," he insisted. "Lee's army might then have marched as it pleased on Washington, Baltimore, Philadelphia, or New York."[7]

Perhaps the one man on the field that day who best understood the workings of General McClellan's mind was Robert E. Lee. Lee was standing his ground at Sharpsburg on September 18 for certain practical reasons — to care for the wounded and start as many of them as could be moved across the Potomac into Virginia; to feed and rest his battle-weary men; to gain time to evacuate the last of the captured ordnance and supplies from Harper's Ferry. But contempt for his opponent was evident in his decision as well. He knew from his scouts that the Federals were receiving reinforcements and that he would have to return to Virginia, but he was refusing to be driven there by the Young Napoleon. The decision would be his, taken deliberately in his own good time. If there was a moral victory to be claimed at Sharpsburg, General Lee was determined to claim it.

The Confederate lines were straightened and made more compact. Some 5,000 footsore stragglers had come up during the night and were put into place along the front. Thus strengthened, the Army of Northern Virginia — the army General McClellan dared not challenge lest it defeat him and then fall upon the great cities of the North — consisted of about 28,300 infantry and artillerymen and Stuart's 4,500 cavalry. "Though still too weak to assume the offensive, we awaited without apprehension the renewal of the attack," Lee reported, and added, "The day passed without any demonstration on the part of the enemy...."[8]

It is doubtful that many of his men were sharing Lee's confidence that day. Captain Alex Chisholm of the 9th Alabama, who counted it a miracle that he had survived the terrible fire at the Sunken Road, recalled that he and his comrades "passed the 18th in dread of another advance from McClellan." D. H. Hill went along his thin lines trying to brace his troops and calling them his "Faithful Few." They took encouragement when the Federals granted a truce to collect the wounded and begin burying the dead, knowing that no attack would be made so long as it remained in effect. Rebels and Yankees met between the lines to exchange wounded, a sight a diarist in Harvey Hill's division found incongruous. "It seemed very curious to see the men on both sides come together and talk to each other when the day before were fireing at each other," he wrote. During the truce a Federal gunner near the Cornfield saw scores of injured Confederates dragging themselves toward his battery, "wounded in all imaginable ways and crying piteously for help. One poor fellow had one leg shot off and was hobbling along with two guns for crutches."[9]

Burial details began their grim work. Some companies made up their own parties to search out fallen comrades, digging individual graves and marking them with rude little headboards scavenged from hardtack boxes or ammunition cases, scratching in the name and unit of the dead men. Colonel Strother rode forward to the East Woods to look over the field of battle. "In the midst of all this carrion," he noted in his diary, "our troops sat cooking, eating, jabbering, and smoking; sleeping among the corpses so that but for

To Nobly Save or Meanly Lose

the color of the skin it was difficult to distinguish the living from the dead."[10]

Men took advantage of the truce to let their people at home know they had survived the battle and to record their impressions of the fighting. "I have lived through my first battle, and I am well," a rookie in the 107th New York assured his family. "But when I think of the brave boys who lost their lives yesterday in defence of their country, I feel sad to think that Jeff. Davis did not die in their stead." A Wisconsin man, a new replacement in John Gibbon's Black Hat Brigade, wrote, "I suppose the great fight of the Rebellion was fought on the 17 at least I hope so for none of us ever wants to see another such, but we whiped them bad. They are lying by thousands on the field of battle but we to suffered terribly." For others there were letters of a different sort to write. "It gives me intensest pain to tell you of death of my dear brother, your devoted husband Andrew," a Texan in Hood's division wrote his sister-in-law. " . . . He was killed on yesterday morning in the fight at Sharpsburg. Of the conflict being undesided, his body has not yet been recovered, but Maj. George has promised to attend to his interment. I am too badly wounded to return to look after him. . . . To God I commend you. . . . "[11]

The desperate work at the field hospitals continued through the day. Southern newspaperman Peter Alexander looked in on one of these places and was sickened at the piles of amputated limbs and the gaping wounds. "There is a smell of death in the air," he wrote, "and the laboring surgeons are literally covered from head to foot with the blood of the sufferers." A steady parade of wagons carrying wounded Rebels crossed Boteler's Ford and entered Shepherdstown on the Virginia side of the Potomac. Casualties had been arriving there since the South Mountain battles on Sunday, and by now the townspeople were numbed at the sight. "They filled every building and overflowed into the country round, into farm-houses, barns, corn-cribs, cabins, — wherever four walls and a roof were found together," a local woman recalled. "Those able to travel were sent on to Winchester and other towns back from the river, but their departure seemed to make no appreciable difference."

Behind the Union lines there were similar scenes. Clara Barton, the former Washington Patent Office clerk who had appointed herself unofficial ministering angel to the Army of the Potomac's wounded — and conscience to the army's medical department — was dressing wounds and comforting the dying and finding food for the living at the Sam Poffenberger farmhouse. Following the sound of the guns, Miss Barton had reached the field with her wagonload of medical supplies in the midst of the battle and gone to work. Once a stray bullet clipped her sleeve and killed the patient she was caring for. She would remain on duty there for three days, until all her supplies were exhausted. Other civilian volunteers were arriving as well, serving as nurses and helping evacuate casualties to more permanent hospitals in nearby towns. In Hagerstown the Ladies Union Relief Association organized nursing care and collected supplies and made bandages from donated sheets and tablecloths and the like. In spite of everyone's best efforts, however, the sheer volume of wounded — more than 17,000 all told — continued to overwhelm the medical personnel and facilities of both armies for days. When the diarist George Templeton Strong reached Sharpsburg on September 22 to represent the U.S. Sanitary Commission, he would find hideous scenes at the hospitals he visited. "It was fearful to see," he wrote; "Gustave Doré's pictures embodied in shivering, agonizing, suppurating flesh and blood."[12]

So the hours slowly passed and fatal Thursday ended, and after dark the Federals could hear the steady cadence of marching men and the rumble of artillery wheels that continued through the night. The Army of Northern Virginia was leaving the field. Only the dead and the critically wounded remained behind. At Boteler's Ford cavalrymen were stationed with flaring torches to mark the crossing. "The trees and overhanging cliffs and the majestic Blue Ridge loomed up in dim but enlarged and fantastic proportions," newspaperman Alexander wrote, "and made one feel as if he were in some strange and weird land of grotesque forms, visited only in the hour of dreams." It is recorded that at sunrise, when the regimental band of the 18th Mississippi — the same outfit that had furnished the music for Jeb Stuart's grand cavalry ball at Urbana ten days earlier — sought to cheer up the troops with a rendition of "Maryland, My Maryland," it was shouted down.

General McClellan would claim that it was his intention all along to renew the battle on September 19, but except for a message to Franklin to be prepared to advance, no general orders for such an attack are on record. What is recorded suggests instead that he was waiting for General Lee to make the first move. At 4 A.M. orders went out to General Sumner: "The commanding general directs you, if the enemy appears to be retiring, to mass your troops in readiness to move in any direction. The other corps commanders are directed to push forward their pickets, and if the enemy is retreating, to mass their commands." That the Confederate army was gone was soon confirmed. "I have been in my 'barn window' for half an hour and cannot see a Rebel," a Federal signalman reported at 6:30 A.M. "... I have scanned the whole ground from right to left & at this moment there is not a Rebel in sight."[13]

Lee started his army toward Martinsburg, eight miles to the west in the Shenandoah Valley, leaving his reserve artillery and a small force of infantry to discourage any pursuit. Fitz John Porter pushed a detachment of the Fifth Corps across the Potomac and succeeded in capturing four artillery pieces, but early on the morning of September 20 his bridgehead was counterattacked by A. P. Hill and driven back across the river. In this sharp clash yet another of the new Yankees regiments was severely mauled. The 118th Pennsylvania, the Corn Exchange Regiment from Philadelphia, came under fire for the first time, discovered among its other problems that half its rifles were defective, and suffered 269 casualties before it could escape. On that unhappy note the Maryland campaign came to an end.[14]

Robert E. Lee was not easily persuaded that the campaign was in fact over. To his mind, the battle at Sharpsburg was merely a brief check to his plan to maintain the war on what he liked to call the Confederacy's northern frontier. After a short halt to fill his ranks by collecting stragglers, he intended to recross the Potomac upstream at Williamsport and again invade Maryland to force McClellan into another battle, this time on his own terms.

He discovered soon enough that it was not that simple. Among the thousands of stragglers were a considerable number of men who had simply had enough. One of the army's division commanders, John R. Jones, was sent to Winchester in the Valley to round up these absentees, and found the task impossible. "It is disgusting and heartsickening to witness this army of stragglers," he wrote.

They evaded his infantry picket lines, he said, and only a full-fledged effort by the cavalry would get them back into the ranks. Lee concluded that many in this army of stragglers were nothing better than deserters. Such men, he wrote President Davis, "have wandered to a distance, feigning sickness, wounds, &c., deceiving the guards and evading the scouts. Many of them will not stop until they reach their distant homes." He called on the president for the strongest measures to correct this evil.

Finally it became clear even to Lee that the Army of Northern Virginia had been fearfully wounded in spirit as well as in body at Sharpsburg. Since early August he had driven his men ruthlessly toward that elusive goal of a decisive victory that might spell Southern independence. Now they could be driven no more. "The whole of our time is taken up by two things, marching and fighting," Brigadier Dorsey Pender of A. P. Hill's division wrote his wife on September 22. "Some of the Army have a fight nearly every day, and the more we fight, the less we like it." The one opinion he had heard about the Maryland invasion, he continued, was "regret at our having gone there." On September 25, outlining his thoughts for a renewed offensive to Mr. Davis, Lee wrote, "I would not hesitate to make it even with our diminished numbers, did the army exhibit its former temper and condition; but, as far as I am able to judge, the hazard would be great and a reverse disastrous. I am, therefore, led to pause."[15]

General McClellan, for his part, was well satisfied to see the Confederates gone, and made no further effort at pursuit. "Our victory was complete," he boasted to Halleck on September 19. "The enemy is driven back into Virginia. Maryland and Pennsylvania are now safe." His role as the Union's messiah was vindicated, his campaign a personal triumph over every imaginable adversity: he had repelled both the massive Rebel army in the field and the veritable army of detractors in the capital. "I feel some little pride in having, with a beaten and demoralized army, defeated Lee so utterly and saved the North so completely," he informed his wife. " . . . I am confident that the poison still rankles in the veins of my enemies at Washington, and that so long as they live it will remain there," he told her, but he was certain he had answered a higher calling: "I have the satisfaction of knowing that

God has, in His mercy, a second time made me the instrument for saving the nation."

His primary concern now was to restore his army to health. It needed time to recover from the fearful shock of Antietam. Shoes and uniforms and equipment of all kinds were required. Depleted regiments had to be brought up to strength, and the numerous new regiments trained. His opponent had forced him into the field before the troops had recovered from their mistreatment at the hands of General Pope, and that could not be allowed to happen again; his grand army must regain its former temper before he could begin to think of embarking on any new campaign. In correspondent Smalley's opinion, "It is to be quiet along the Potomac for some time to come. George, whom Providence helps according to his nature, has got himself on one side of a ditch, which Providence had already made for him, with the enemy on the other, and has no idea of moving."[16]

What had been won and lost on Antietam's bloody field was not so quickly measured as McClellan imagined. Judging those twelve hours of desperate combat on a purely tactical level, for example, the Army of Northern Virginia could justly claim a victory. It had beaten back a foe much superior in manpower and ordnance and inflicted substantially greater casualties than it suffered. (In the campaign as a whole, Confederate losses came to some 14,000, against a Federal total, including the Harper's Ferry captives, of nearly 27,000.) Before the battle General Lee had rated his men the best soldiers in the world, and Antietam gave him no reason to think less of them. From one end of the battlefield to the other, from Mr. Miller's cornfield to Mr. Otto's, they had fought to the limits of human endurance and beyond.

And they were given the leadership their courage deserved. Except for the mix-ups that caused the Sunken Road to be abandoned prematurely, the severest military critic would be hard pressed to find fault with the way the Confederate high command conducted the battle. "Had Lee known all that we know now of the Federal plans and forces," staff officer William Allan, the army's historian, later wrote, "it is difficult to see how he could have been more wisely disposed or more effectually used the means he had at hand." It was said that in later years, of all his battles General Lee took the most pride in Sharpsburg. When it became clear how destructive the loss of Order 191 was to his plan of campaign, he felt that never before or after did his army face greater odds.[17]

Yet for all that, Lee had lost the campaign and made a miscalculation that nearly lost him his army as well. A major reason he stood and fought at Sharpsburg was his measured judgment that he was challenging a timid general heading an army demoralized by past defeats. That judgment was only half right. In fighting courage the Federal soldiers who struggled in the Cornfield or at Bloody Lane or who charged the guns on the Harper's Ferry road proved themselves every bit the equal of the Rebels they faced. It would be the particular tragedy of the men of the Army of the Potomac that (unlike their opponents) they seldom got the generals they deserved. Antietam was a case in point. With conspicuous exceptions — Joe Hooker and Israel Richardson and George Greene among them — that courage was betrayed by their officer corps, most notably by the army commander himself.

On no other Civil War field did a commanding general violate so many of what a Union officer at Antietam called "the established principles of the military art" that a professional soldier was expected to know. General McClellan failed to employ his cavalry either to gather intelligence or to protect the flanks of his army against surprise attack; thus he learned nothing and was surprised. Throughout the day, without exception, he put his troops into action in "driblets," as General Sumner aptly described it, without coordination and without mutual support. He failed to get all his men to the battlefield, and in any case held back fully a third of those who were available to him.

And however poorly some of his lieutenants served him, he shrank from his paramount responsibility — to command. Repeatedly his men fought desperately to the threshold of victory, and repeatedly he let that victory slip away by playing the idle spectator rather than the general commanding; in no instance did he honor that indisputable military maxim to reinforce success. There is no little irony in the coincidence that, like General Lee, he underestimated the Yankee fighting men. "It always seemed to me that McClellan, though no commander ever had the love of his soldiers more, or tried more to spare their lives, never realized the metal that was in his grand Army of the Potomac," a veteran re-

To Nobly Save or Meanly Lose 311

called. "... He never appreciated until too late what manner of people he had with him."[18]

General McClellan entertained no such reservations concerning his spendidly fought battle. Having delivered Maryland and Pennsylvania — and his army — from the untender mercies of the invaders, he was uplifted emotionally in the days immediately following the battle. No doubt he savored a letter of congratulations from his cabinet supporter, Montgomery Blair. "Never in the history of this nation has any man rendered it a more important service," Blair wrote him on September 19, and added that the president had called him aside "& said I rejoice in this success for many public reasons but I am also happy on account of McClellan!" Blair took this as fresh proof of what he had always maintained: "the President is your friend."

Confident he was now acting from a position of strength, McClellan determined to force changes on the administration. "An opportunity has presented itself through the Governor" — presumably he meant one of his mentors, former Ohio governor William Dennison — "... to enable me to take my stand," he wrote his wife on September 20. "I have insisted that Stanton shall be removed & that Halleck shall give way to me as Comdr in Chief. I will not serve under him — for he is an incompetent fool — in no way fit for the important place he holds." He went on to say that the time had come for the country to rally to him "and remove these difficulties from my path. If my countrymen will not open their eyes and assist themselves they must pardon me if I decline longer to pursue the thankless avocation of serving them."[19]

Authentic news of the battle had been slow reaching Washington. McClellan's dispatches, Gideon Welles complained on September 18, "are seldom clear or satisfactory. 'Behaved splendidly,' 'performed handsomely,' but what was accomplished is never told and our anxiety is intense." The first detailed account of the fighting to arrive in the capital, in fact, was furnished by correspondent Smalley. He had ridden through the night to Frederick, where he tried to persuade the telegrapher there to wire his preliminary dispatch to the *Tribune* in New York. The operator had orders to route everything through the War Department, however, and by noon on the day after the battle Stanton and Lincoln finally had some hard news. Determined not to be balked further by the censors, Smalley caught a train to Baltimore and then one to New York, writing his story by the dim light of an oil lamp as the train rolled northward. At 5 A.M. on September 19 he reached the *Tribune* offices, where the printers were standing by, and by midmorning an extra was on the streets. It was the best and most accurate piece of on-the-spot battle reporting of the war, and would be reprinted in hundreds of newspapers across the country and abroad.[20]

News was even slower to reach Richmond. War Department clerk John B. Jones first learned of the battle in Maryland on September 20, from a Philadelphia paper passed through the lines. The Yankees, Jones wrote sarcastically in his diary, claimed a great victory, "having killed and taken 40,000 of our men, made Jackson prisoner, and wounded Longstreet!" Two days later the *Richmond Enquirer* made the news public, calling it "one of the most complete victories that has yet immortalized the Confederate arms." The next day the *Enquirer* announced that Lee "with steady foresight" had withdrawn his army south of the Potomac, "whence he will, of course, project the necessary combinations for again defeating his adversary." The *Charleston Mercury* was not so easily persuaded: recrossing the Potomac was a "movement which, to the unmilitary eye, with no more subtle guide than the map, would certainly resemble a retreat."

Most Southern newspapers, however, described the battle as at worst a draw, with the capture of Harper's Ferry giving General Lee the best of the campaign. The *Petersburg Express* pointed out that although Northerners might "exult, in their crazy fashion, over imaginary successes heralded in the lying dispatches of McClellan and his trumpet-blowers," in fact the Yankees had been taught a lesson and would be well advised "to let Lee and his army alone on this side of the Potomac." There was a hint of sober reality, however, in Richmond's announcement that it was not "deemed advisable" to publish the casualty lists; "persons can obtain information in regard to their relatives in the army by calling at the Army Intelligence office in the Farmer's Bank, opposite the Post Office."[21]

Lee's men were certainly without illusion about their ordeal in the campaign just ended. "The yankees slitely got the best of the fight in Maryland," an artilleryman wrote a friend. "You ought to have seen us Skeedadling across the Potomac River and the yankees close in our rear." "Our Army has shown itself incapable of invasion and we had best stick to the defensive," Dorsey Pender decided, but he added hopefully, "I think if it were hinted around in Yankee land that we would be satisfied with the Potomac as the line that the people would soon bring the government to it." Major Walter H. Taylor of Lee's staff wrote his sister, "Don't let any of your friends sing 'My Maryland' — not 'my Western Maryland' anyhow." He thought Sharpsburg was proof that the men, in spite of exhaustion and short rations, could "contend with and resist three times their own numbers.... We do not claim a victory.... It was not decisive enough for that." The government must recognize the need to reinforce the army substantially if more was wanted of it than it had just demonstrated. "Give us the men and then talk about invading Pennsylvania," Taylor concluded; "... though we have done wonders, we can't perform miracles."[22]

Across the Potomac, in their camps around Sharpsburg, the Federals also talked over what they had been through and read the newspapers and tried to make sense of it all. "You should see my soldiers *now!*" McClellan wrote Ellen three days after the battle. "You never saw anything like their enthusiasm. It surpasses anything you ever imagined & I don't believe that Napoleon even ever received the love & confidence of his men more fully than I do of mine." No doubt such feelings were common. "If our enemy could not whip us at Antietam he never will if our men fight with the same spirit," Alexander Webb of Porter's staff wrote a friend. "And God bless McClellan.... God bless & preserve him. Without His aid we will never succeed & I believe that He is using George B. McClellan as his instrument." A New Yorker in the First Corps admitted that while the Young Napoleon might lack "that lightning rapidity which characterizes the 'Old Napoleon,'" the army feared losing him; "we believe him simply the best general we have got, and do not trust the judgment of old Abe in the selection of a new one."[23]

Other letters, however, suggest a disillusionment with Little Mac's generalship among his officers and men. "Why in the name of heaven McClellan did not let our corps finish up the 'rebs,' and why he did not renew the battle on Thursday, and follow speedily across the river, I can't understand," a man in the Fifth Corps wrote his family. "... I am provoked, perhaps without cause, but I cannot *help feeling* that it prolongs this horrid war." *Tribune* reporter Albert Richardson sensed a similar mood among the men he talked to. "There is great chagrin and disappointment, both in the army and among loyalists here, at the escape of the Rebels across the river," he wrote his managing editor. "... It was one of the supreme moments when by daring something, the destiny of the nation might have been changed.... Had only Hooker been in command — any one, almost, but the Slow Man of the Peninsula! Perhaps I judge unjustly, but I think not." General Meade had the same thought. "I think myself he errs on the side of prudence and caution," he wrote his wife of McClellan, "and that a little more rashness on his part would improve his generalship." A man in the Second Corps aimed his disgust at the entire high command. "It seems that we can't get no Generals to suit us," he complained in a letter home. "They all seem to work against one another. I hope they will all unite and have it settled as soon as possible for I am getting tired of it."[24]

There was full agreement on one point, at least: the sight and smell of the battlefield were enough to destroy anyone's remaining illusions about war as derived from the colored lithographs and the brass bands and the patriotic oratory at recruitment meetings. As a man in Hooker's corps put it, "I feel as if Glory did not count for much...."

"The excitement of battle comes in the day of it, but the horrors of it two or three days after," Samuel Fiske of the 14th Connecticut explained to the people back home in a letter published in a New England newspaper. "Think now of the horrors of such a scene as lies all around us," he wrote of the corpses blackened and bloated in the heat of the sun; "there are hundreds of horses, too, all mangled and putrifying, scattered everywhere! Then there are the broken gun-carriages, the wagons, and thousands of muskets, and all sorts of equipments, and clothing all torn and bloody, and cartridges and cannon-shot, and pieces of shell, the trees torn with shot and scarred with bullets, the farm-houses and barns knocked to pieces and burned down, the crops trampled and wasted, the whole country forlorn and desolate." A diarist in the 9th Pennsylvania found the scene beyond his powers of description: "No tongue can tell, no mind conceive, no pen portray the horrible sights I witnessed this morning." Another man wrote his parents, "We were glad to march over the field at night for we could not see the horrible sights so well. Oh what a smell some of the men vomit as they went along."[25]

A man in one of the new Pennsylvania regiments was assigned to a burial detail, and in a letter home he sketched out the procedure. They advanced across the fields in line-of-battle formation, he wrote, collecting bodies and dragging them to the selected burial site. "When the Pit is dug deep enough the Bodies are placed crosswise and as many as fourty seven in one Grave. After the Union men were all gathered up and buried then we commenced gathering up the Rebs. . . . We seen among the rebels Boys of Sixteen & Fifteen and old Gray headed men. There was not to the best of my knowledge in all that was buried two dressed alike."

Nearly all the corpses were found with pockets turned out, robbed of any valuables, and those Federals who fell behind the Confederate lines had been stripped of their shoes by needy Rebels. General Hancock was seen to gallop into a band of plunderers at the Sunken Road, cursing loudly and threatening them with his pistol as they scattered. But there was evidence of small kindnesses as well. Near the Dunker church the body of Lieutenant Colonel John L. Stetson of Sedgwick's division was found with his name and unit penciled on a scrap of paper pinned to his coat; before he died a Rebel had done him that favor so that he could be identified. Local men and their slaves were hired to haul the dead horses to fields outside town, where they were burned on pyres of fence rails, adding to the malodorous pall that hung over the countryside. "We couldn't eat a good meal," a hired man on the Nicodemus farm recalled, "and we had to shut the house up just as tight as we could of a night to keep out that odor."[26]

The realities of Antietam were brought home to the Northern citizenry more vividly than any previous battle. For the first time, in addition to the casualty lists and the newspaper accounts and the woodcuts in the illustrated weeklies and the soldiers' letters home, there was a new graphic dimension to the actual look of a battlefield. Mathew Brady had sent photographers Alexander Gardner and James F. Gibson to Sharpsburg, and their stark, powerful views of the human wreckage at Bloody Lane and the

Dunker church and along the Hagerstown turnpike were put on display at the Brady gallery in New York in an exhibit called "The Dead of Antietam." "The dead of the battle-field come up to us very rarely, even in dreams," a reporter for the *New York Times* wrote. "We see the list in the morning paper at breakfast, but dismiss its recollection with the coffee.... Mr. Brady has done something to bring home to us the terrible reality and earnestness of war. If he has not brought bodies and laid them in our door-yards and along streets, he has done something very like it."[27]

Numbers of civilians arrived at the battlefield to seek sons and brothers and husbands reported as casualties. Dr. Oliver Wendell Holmes reached Frederick on September 19 and made his way through the backwash of the fighting to try to find his wounded son. "There was something repulsive about the trodden and stained relics of the stale battlefield," he wrote. "It was like the table of some hideous orgy left uncleared, and one turned away disgusted from its broken fragments and muddy heeltaps." He inquired at one field hospital after another. "Many times ... I started as some faint resemblance — the shade of a young man's hair, the outline of his half-turned face — recalled the presence I was in search of." At last he traced young Holmes to Hagerstown and a train about to depart for the North. "In the first car, on the fourth seat to the right, I saw my Captain...." They exchanged quiet greetings, and the doctor observed, "Such are the proprieties of life, ... decently disguising those natural impulses."

When Colonel John B. Gordon of the 6th Alabama, wounded five times at the Sunken Road, was told his wife had come to nurse him, he tried to allay her shock at his appearance by calling out, "Here's your handsome husband; been to an Irish wedding!" Infection threatened the loss of his left arm, Gordon wrote, and the doctors suggested she paint the arm three or four times a day with iodine; "She obeyed the doctors by painting it, I think, three or four hundred times a day." Thanks to his wife's ministrations and his own iron constitution, Gordon would return to the army within three months.

Many quests lacked such happy endings. It was his "sad duty," one searcher wrote his family, to report that William Cullen Robinson of the 83rd New York had died six days after being shot in the head in the struggle for the Cornfield: "I bought a rough coffin

To Nobly Save or Meanly Lose 317

(the best I could get) and washed his face and combed his hair smooth and covered him round with a large clean sheet. And they dug a deep grave on a little knoll on the bank of the Antietam Creek, and I buried him there. I marked the place (which was a conspicious one) by a board neatly made at his head with his initials...." A soldier in the 21st Connecticut, stationed in Washington, got leave to search out the grave of his eighteen-year-old son, killed in the attack on the Burnside Bridge, but he could not find it. "Oh how dreadful was that place to me, where my dear boy had been buried like a beast of the field!" he wrote. He had sworn vengeance, he added bitterly, on "this uncalled for, and worse than hellish, wicked rebellion."[28]

Viewed solely in military terms, then, Antietam was a day of fearful violence beyond anything in the nation's experience, notable above all for its missed opportunities and its hideous memories. Robert E. Lee had taken his army into Maryland to wage the decisive campaign for Southern independence, and he had failed. George McClellan had been granted the certain opportunity to crush the Southern army, and he too had failed. Almost 23,000 men had paid the price of these failures. Fourteen months later, at another little town where the roads came together, thirty-five miles to the north, Abraham Lincoln would find the words to give meaning to the dead and maimed of Gettysburg. On September 22, 1862, he also gave deeper meaning to the terrible struggle along the banks of Antietam Creek. If what he read that day lacked the eloquence of his address at Gettysburg, it was nevertheless a document with a significance even more timeless.

That Monday morning, messengers notified the cabinet to assemble at noon at the White House for a special meeting. The president opened the session on a light note, reading a chapter from a new book by one of his favorite homespun humorists, Artemus Ward. "Read it, and seemed to enjoy it very much — the Heads also (except Stanton)," Secretary Chase remarked in his diary. Taking "a graver tone," Chase wrote, Lincoln then reminded his listeners of the paper on emancipation that he had presented to them two months before, and of the decision to withhold its announcement until the military situation improved. In the midst of the Maryland campaign, he continued, he had made a vow (as Gideon Welles recorded it) "that if God gave us the victory in the approaching battle, he would consider it an indication of Divine Will" to proceed with emancipation. The fight at Sharpsburg did not produce as complete a victory as he would have liked — clearly the president had measured General McClellan's conduct of the battle and found it wanting — but it was enough for his purposes that the Confederate invaders had been turned back. "God had decided this question in favor of the slaves," Welles quoted him as saying. Lincoln then read the draft of his preliminary Emancipation Proclamation.

The paper he began writing in the War Department telegraphers' room back in July and had put in its finished form just the day before was couched in cool legalisms, invoking congressional legislation and presidential war powers, written without rhetorical flourish but containing that singular riveting phrase: unless the states in rebellion returned to the Union within the next hundred days, on January 1, 1863, all persons held in bondage in those states "shall be then, thenceforward, and forever free. . . . " Beyond whatever other purpose, the dead of Antietam had died to make men free.

That was a transcending purpose, a revolution in the affairs of the Republic. As Lincoln would tell the Congress, "The fiery trial through which we pass, will light us down, in honor or dishonor, to the latest generation. . . . In *giving* freedom to the *slave,* we *assure* freedom to the *free* — honorable alike in what we give, and what we preserve. We shall nobly save, or meanly lose, the last, best hope of earth."[29]

The proclamation was released to the newspapers the next day, and 15,000 copies were printed and sent to the various army commands for distribution to the troops. On September 24 Lincoln issued a second proclamation, suspending the writ of habeas corpus as it might apply to persons accused of "discouraging volunteer enlistments, resisting militia drafts, or guilty of any disloyal practice, affording aid and comfort to Rebels. . . . " Much of the public comment, not surprisingly, was divided along partisan lines. Horace Greeley of the *New York Tribune* predicted that emancipation would be "the beginning of the end of the rebellion; the beginning of the new life of the nation." Abolitionist Senator Charles Sumner thought "the skies are brighter and the air is purer, now that slavery has been handed over to judgment." At the other extreme, the Democratic *New York Journal of Commerce* warned the president not to expect "his new policy to be supported by the conservative men of the country, who believe it to be unconstitutional and wrong." The *New York World* took the two proclamations as clear evidence that Lincoln had "swung loose from the constitutional moorings of his inaugural address" and was "adrift on the current of radical fanaticism."[30]

If such reactions were predictable, it was a matter of no small concern in Washington how the emancipation decree would be received in the Army of the Potomac. (Only this most highly politicized of the Union armies seems to have caused any worry.) After all, as long ago as early July General McClellan had warned the president that if the radicals' views on slavery became government policy the men in the ranks would not stand for it and the army would disintegrate. Fitz John Porter, for one, still thought so. Continuing to supply ammunition to the opposition press, he wrote Manton Marble, editor of the anti-administration *New York World*, that the proclamation "was resented in the army, — caused disgust, discontent, and expressions of disloyalty.... All such bulletins tend to prolong the war by rousing the bitter feelings of the South...." While he and the others who had to fight the battles were doing their best to bring the war to an honorable conclusion, Porter said, they were being undermined "by the absurd proclamation of a political coward who ... holds in his hands the lives of thousands and trifles with them."

It was no secret in Washington that talk like this was common enough in the high councils of the Potomac army, and that it was not new. McClellan had shared his convictions of betrayal during the Peninsula campaign with members of his military household as well as with the Democratic party leaders. When the army was at Frederick, Colonel Thomas M. Key of the general's staff had told *Tribune* reporter Nathaniel Paige of the coterie of officers plotting to intimidate the government by force of arms. Now the Washington correspondent for James Gordon Bennett's *New York Herald* was writing his employer, "The sentiment throughout the whole army seems to be in favor of a change of dynasty...." If the attitude of the officers he had talked to was typical, he went on, "there is large promise of a fearful revolution ... that will startle the Country and give us a Military Dictator." He did not feel it necessary to identify that potential dictator.[31]

Whether or not there was real substance behind prediction of this sort, the president was determined to come down hard on it. He soon had his opportunity. One day shortly after Antietam, Major John J. Key of Halleck's staff was discussing the campaign with Major Levi C. Turner of the War Department's judge advocate's office. Turner wondered why McClellan had not "bagged" the Confederate army after the battle on the seventeenth. Key replied (as Turner remembered it), "That is not the game. The object is that neither army shall get much advantage of the other; that both shall be kept in the field till they are exhausted, when we will make a compromise and save slavery." (Major John Key was the brother of Colonel Thomas Key of McClellan's staff, who had heard about that recent plot by army officers to march on the capital; the Key brothers seem to have had an ear for conspiracy theories.) Turner thought the whole business should be investigated, and before long a report of the conversation reached the White House.

Lincoln remarked to his secretary John Hay that if Key had indeed uttered such language, "his head should go off." Hay wondered if this signaled a larger conspiracy centering on McClellan, but the president would say only that the general "was doing nothing to make himself either respected or feared." On September 27 Key and Turner appeared before him. Turner repeated the conversation and Key admitted those were the words he had used. Major John Key was promptly dismissed from the service of the United States. In rejecting his appeal for clemency, Lincoln wrote him that he "had been brought to fear that there was a class of officers in the army, not very inconsiderable in numbers, who were playing a game to not beat the enemy when they could, on some peculiar notion as to the proper way of saving the Union; ... I dismissed you as an example and a warning...." No doubt it was an unfair judgment to pass on the unfortunate Major Key, but the message it conveyed was unmistakable: the commander in chief was telling the officer corps of the Army of the Potomac to toe the mark on matters of loyalty or else.[32]

How deeply this poison had seeped into the ranks of the fighting men was another question. Their response to emancipation, expressed in letters and diaries, ranged as widely as their politics, prejudices, and beliefs. The abolitionist-minded, most commonly found in the New England regiments, welcomed it. "I do not intend to shirk now there is really something to fight for," one of these men wrote; "I mean *Freedom*...." At the other end of the spectrum were those who despised abolitionists and all their works; "... the men are all exasperated against the Tribune and would hang Greeley if they had their way," a spokesman for this group observed. The proclamation, he wrote, "meets with denouncement among the men of the Army. They do not wish to think that they are fighting for Negroes, but to put down the Rebelion." After the South was defeated, he added, would be "time enough to talk about the *dam'd niggers.*"

Regardless of personal feelings about emancipation and the slaves it stood to free, what was missing from these reactions was the wholesale demoralization or the forceful demands for a "change of dynasty" that seemed to preoccupy a number of the army's officers. George Whitman of the 51st New York reflected a common appraisal of the matter in a letter to his mother on September 30: "I see by the papers that Uncle Abe has issued a proclamation.... I dont know what effect it is going to have on the war, but one thing is certain, he has got to lick the south before he can free the niggers." Whitman doubted Southerners could be persuaded before the first of January "that we are bound to lick them, and it would be better for them to behave themselves and keep their slaves.... I dont think the proclamation will do much good."[33]

General McClellan meanwhile was contemplating his future and deciding what public position he should take on the question of emancipation; presumably his mission to save the country gave him that privilege. First he wanted the advice of his political mentors, and on September 26 he addressed a letter to the merchant William H. Aspinwall, one of the leading figures in conservative New York Democratic politics. "I am very anxious to learn," he wrote, "how you and men like you regard the recent Proclamation of the Presdt inaugurating servile war, emancipating the slaves, & at one stroke of the pen changing our free institutions into a despotism — for such I regard as the natural effect of the last proclamation suspending the Habeas Corpus throughout the land." While he waited for wisdom from that quarter, he received some unsolicited advice from another direction.

His one friend in the cabinet, Montgomery Blair, wrote him on September 27 to offer a suggestion. Though a Republican, Blair was a conservative and a border state man and stood alongside the general on many issues. He was moved to this action, he explained, by what he had just heard from the president regarding Major Key, who had been caught saying that at Antietam "the plan was to withhold your resources so that a compromise might be made which would preserve Slavery & the union at the same time." He thought it wise for General McClellan to heed that cautionary tale by quickly declaring himself on the slavery question. While of course the general was above any "partizan calculations" in this matter, Blair continued, he could head off his opponents by stating that "whilst you supposed the object of the war to be the maintainance of the Union, . . . yet the natural result would be the extinction of Slavery. . . . " He concluded his political lecture with an additional bit of advice: "Even if you had the ambitions to be President this would be the best course to adopt, for I can assure you that no appreciable portion of the nation will favor the long continuation of Slavery after this war is over. . . . "

Three days later the head of the Blair clan himself wrote McClellan along the same lines. Francis P. Blair — Old Man Blair, political power broker whose influence dated back to the days of Andrew Jackson — was at pains to point out the military advantages offered by emancipation, for he felt it would force the South to divert manpower to guard against slave insurrections: "The conscripts that face you are to a great extent the very men, who but for the slaves would be their substitutes at home to raise the necessities of life." Only the general and his army could make good this military promise and prevent "great mischief tending probably to incendiary movements in the loyal States." If he would "manifest in every way a fixed purpose to give full effect to the proclamation," Old Man Blair told him, it would give the lie to the radicals "raising the outcry against you. . . . "

The general also solicited guidance from within his military household. One evening late in September he hosted a dinner for

To Nobly Save or Meanly Lose 323

three of his generals he believed had the confidence of the administration: Ambrose Burnside, to whom the president had twice offered the command of the army; Jacob Cox, a former Republican legislator from Ohio; and John Cochrane, a war Democrat from New York. He told them he was being urged by political figures and high-ranking army friends to lead the public fight against emancipation, and since he was certain the army would follow his lead, he wanted their advice about what he should do. His guests were frank. "We pointed out very clearly," Cox wrote, "that any public utterance by him in his official character criticising the civil policy of the administration would be properly regarded as a usurpation." They also told him he was badly misinformed about the army's state of mind; those he had been listening to were his own worst enemies, and none but a corporal's guard would follow him if he sought to place the military above the civil authority. The general supposed they were right. Slavery probably would not survive the war, although he thought the proclamation premature and evidence that the president was under the thumb of radical subverters of the Constitution. He would give the matter more thought.[34]

General McClellan had by now come down abruptly from his emotional peak. Matters had not gone as he hoped. The groundswell of support he expected did not materialize; he complained to his wife that not a word of praise had come from the Washington authorities for his conduct of the great battle. His effort to be rid of his superiors in the capital was not bearing fruit, and they were back at the business of finding fault with everything he did. "Stanton is as great a villain as ever & Halleck as great a fool," he told Ellen, and wondered if he could — or should — remain in command. A debate began with the War Department over his demand for all manner of supplies and equipment he considered essential before he could think about moving the army. Advisers wanted him to acquiesce in the president's proclamations although he believed they spelled the country's ruin. His only solace was his conviction that "the short campaign just terminated will vindicate my professional honor." And on October 1 President Lincoln arrived unexpectedly to see for himself the army and its commanding general. Fitz John Porter warned the *World*'s Manton Marble that such visits "have been always followed by injury. So look out — another proclamation or war order." No doubt McClellan shared that apprehension.[35]

Lincoln remained with the army four days, reviewing troops, touring the recent battlefields, visiting hospitals. The soldiers were amused at the sight of their president on a horse, "an odd figure . . . ," a man wrote, "and the odder for wearing a stovepipe hat that increased his height and angularity." A young Massachusetts private told his parents, "He looks the same as his pictures, though much more careworn; one of his feet is in the grave." General Alpheus Williams had a long talk with Lincoln as they sat at their ease on a pile of logs, and found him "really the most unaffected, simple-minded, honest, and frank man I have ever met." Beyond anything else, however, the president had come to confer with General McClellan. That no third party recorded their conversations is unfortunate, for it appears that each man took away a quite different impression of what had been said.[36]

"I incline to think that the real purpose of his visit is to push me into a premature advance into Virginia," McClellan wrote his wife on October 2, and went on to explain that the army was in no way fit for such a movement. "The President was very kind personally," he told her in summarizing his impressions; "told me he was convinced I was the best general in the country, etc, etc. He was very affable, and I really think he does feel very kindly towards me personally."

As far as the president was concerned, there was considerably more to it than polishing the general's ego with affability and compliments. An old friend, Judge David Davis, visited Lincoln a few weeks later and heard him say that he had tried to make McClellan understand — just as he had tried during the Peninsula campaign — "that he wd be a ruined man if he did not move forward, move rapidly & effectively." Reminiscing to John Hay, Lincoln recalled that "I went up to the field to try to get him to move & came back thinking he would move at once. But when I got home he began to argue why he ought not to move."[37]

A clue to McClellan's continued inability — or unwillingness — to grasp the import of what Lincoln sought to explain to him is contained in a letter the general wrote his wife later that month. He had grown more furious than ever with the administration; he was being bombarded with insults and innuendoes and accusations, he wrote, "from men whom I know to be greatly my inferior socially, intellectually & morally! There never was a truer epithet applied to a certain individual than that of the 'Gorilla.' " General Williams might sit casually on a log pile with the president of the United States and find him unaffected and honest and frank; the Young Napoleon saw only a man quite his inferior in every respect, unworthy of his office, ignorant of the arts of war, and the captive of the despised radicals.

No doubt the president sensed this conceit in his general — and despaired of penetrating it. Early one morning during his visit he and an acquaintance from Illinois, Ozias M. Hatch, walked up to some high ground that overlooked the encampment of a large part of the army. As they gazed at this vast sea of tents spread out below, Lincoln suddenly asked, "Do you know what this is?"

"It is the Army of the Potomac," Hatch replied in some puzzlement.

"So it is called," Lincoln said, "but that is a mistake; it is only McClellan's bodyguard."[38]

A second visitor to McClellan's camp was William Aspinwall. The Democratic political figure was firm in his opinion (McClellan wrote) that he should "submit to the President's proclamation and quietly continue doing my duty as a soldier. I presume he is right...." Consequently, on October 7 he issued a general order to the army regarding the preliminary Emancipation Proclamation, a decision of interest primarily because the general commanding thought the matter required his calming touch. The order was, in effect, a primer on the constitutional doctrine that the military was the servant of the civil government. Whenever discussion of a public measure within the army was "carried at all beyond temperate and respectful expressions of opinion," he explained, the soldier's duty to support his government was threatened by "the spirit of political faction." He pointedly reminded the troops that the remedy for "political errors" was to be found at the ballot box. If this was hardly the affirmation of the emancipation decree the Blairs had urged on him, it did mean that the general's opinion — neither temperate nor respectful — would remain private.[39]

On October 6 McClellan had received a dispatch from Halleck

ordering him, by the direction of the president, to "cross the Potomac and give battle to the enemy. . . . Your army must move now, while the roads are good." Clearly Lincoln believed that to be the import of his recent meeting with the general. It was suggested that he take the "interior line," keeping between Washington and the Confederates, and 30,000 reinforcements were promised him from the capital's garrison. Should he go directly into the Shenandoah after Lee, however — as McClellan had said he might do, and which General Lee devoutly hoped he would try — only half that number of supporting troops would be available. In either case, Mr. Lincoln was "very desirous that your army move as soon as possible."

What followed was reminiscent of the telegraphic duel waged between McClellan and Halleck during the Second Bull Run crisis. There was the same promise of great activity as soon as certain conditions were met, and the same lack of result. Already McClellan had adopted his familiar position that Lee's army was "undoubtedly greatly superior" to his own and that unless he was reinforced "I may have too much on my hands in the next battle." The enemy was a constant threat to invade Northern soil once again. To this he added that he was not receiving the supplies — shoes and clothing and blankets for the men, horses for the cavalry, hospital tents for the ill, and various other items — that were absolutely essential before the army could take a step. Each quartermaster involved issued long communiqués insisting that he was certainly blameless; any problem invariably lay at the other end of the supply pipeline. The bickering grew heated, and sometimes petty. It was suddenly discovered, for example, that the standard allotments of shoe sizes were all wrong, so that a considerable number of men were rattling around in oversize shoes because the average Easterner had smaller feet than the supply people had imagined. A good deal of paperwork was required to straighten that out.[40]

While it was true that there were indeed supply mix-ups and shortages — General Meade wrote his wife on October 20, "I have *hundreds* of men in my command without shoes, going barefooted, and I can't get a shoe for a man or beast" — it was equally true that the Army of the Potomac was notoriously profligate with the supplies it did have, and the more it received, the more it wasted.

To Nobly Save or Meanly Lose

General McClellan's reluctance to move until everything was in place and every last man drilled and equipped to regulation standards was long-standing and well known, and his lieutenants had acquired the same traits. Rufus Ingalls, McClellan's chief quartermaster, admitted to his counterpart in Washington, "I have frequently remarked that an army will never move if it waits until all the different commanders report that they are ready and want no more supplies." The Young Napoleon, in short, was playing his old game again, Washington knew it, and the delay was driving General Halleck, for one, to distraction. "There is an immobility here that exceeds all that any man can conceive of," he wrote a friend. "It requires the lever of Archimedes to move this inert mass. I have tried my best, but without success."[41]

Meanwhile, left undisturbed in its pleasant camps in the Shenandoah, the Army of Northern Virginia rapidly recovered strength and spirit. The ranks were filled out as stragglers were rounded up and conscripts and convalescents forwarded from Richmond. The army's returns for October 10 gave a present-for-duty strength of more than 64,200 men, less than two-thirds the size of the Army of the Potomac but still a doubling of manpower since the day it had left Sharpsburg. The most nagging supply problem continued to be shoes — as late as two months after the battle nearly one man in five in Longstreet's command was still barefooted — but, for a change, food was plentiful. "We are trying to shoe & clothe our men and stretch out the wrinkles from their stomachs caused by their short rations ...," Longstreet wrote General Joseph Johnston on October 5. "We are now beginning to feel like game cocks again," he went on, looking "for the chance to convince the Yankees that Sharpsburg is but a trifle to what they could do."[42]

Confederate morale rose several notches after another Jeb Stuart exploit. Lee had decided there might be profit in an armed reconnaissance to the north, of the sort Stuart had made on the Peninsula in June when he circled the Army of the Potomac. In addition to gathering intelligence, it was hoped he could destroy a key bridge on the rail line running from Pennsylvania to Hagerstown and perhaps collect valuable booty, especially much-needed horses. At dawn on October 10 Stuart's 1,800 picked cavalrymen splashed across the Potomac a few miles upstream from Williamsport and began what proved to be a gaudy adventure.

By nightfall the column had reached Chambersburg, Pennsylvania. "Our people were confounded with astonishment at the brilliant audacity of the rebels penetrating twenty miles in Gen. McClellan's rear," wrote Alexander McClure, newspaper editor and colonel of the small home guard. He thought it best to surrender the town before some of his bewildered militiamen were hurt. The railroad bridge was made of iron and resisted destruction, but the raiders collected hundreds of horses from nearby farms and destroyed a quarter-million dollars' worth of government property — including, in a bit of fine irony, the ammunition from Longstreet's ordnance train that Grimes Davis's Yankee cavalry had captured when they broke out of Harper's Ferry nearly a month before.

Continuing their circle east and south, Stuart's hard-riding troopers evaded the frantic but uncoordinated Federal efforts to trap them and recrossed the Potomac at White's Ford near Leesburg on October 12. At a cost of one man wounded and two captured, they brought with them 1,200 horses liberated from outraged Pennsylvania farmers. Militarily it was a comparatively mild exploit, but it left McClellan looking very foolish, particularly since this was the second time Stuart had ridden completely around his army. "It is humiliating, disgraceful," Gideon Welles wrote angrily in his diary on October 13. "... It is not a pleasant fact to know that we are clothing, mounting and subsisting not only our troops but the Rebels also." He thought McClellan's detractors "will triumph in this evidence of alleged inertness, and imbecility."[43]

As he had done after the Peninsula failure, Abraham Lincoln was laboring to get the war back on track. In the eastern theater, for the first time since the Seven Days, General Lee had lost the strategic initiative, and the president was determined that McClellan should seize it while he had the opportunity. In the West, too, the Confederate tide had receded after reaching as far north as the Ohio River. Two sharp battles fought in northern Mississippi, at the towns of Iuka and Corinth, frustrated Southern hopes of advancing forces in support of the Kentucky invasion. And on October 8 Braxton Bragg's offensive was brought up short at a place called Perryville in central Kentucky. It was a battle badly managed on both sides, but decisive for the campaign. Gen-

To Nobly Save or Meanly Lose

eral Bragg presently concluded that the prudent course was to withdraw into Tennessee, the other Rebel army under Edmund Kirby Smith joined him there, and their dream of carrying the war into the Ohio Valley flickered out. East and West, the great Confederate counteroffensive had failed.

The Union commander in Kentucky, Don Carlos Buell, was content (like McClellan) to let the Rebels withdraw unmolested, apparently well satisfied to see their designs frustrated. Buell was seemingly cast from the same mold as McClellan, displaying the same caution and slowness and the same inability to envision his opponent's problems. In urging Buell to take the offensive after Perryville, Halleck told him that the president "does not understand why we cannot march as the enemy marches, live as he lives and fight as he fights...."[44] General Buell had no answer for that, Lincoln's patience with him was exhausted, and on October 30 he was dismissed.

There remained the problem of the inactive Army of the Potomac. After waiting a week for his order to advance to be obeyed, on October 13 Lincoln composed a long letter to General McClellan. There is about it the sense of one last attempt, of a summoning up of the last reserves of patience toward a general who had turned a blind eye and a deaf ear on all previous attempts to reason with him. "You remember my speaking to you of what I called your over-cautiousness," Lincoln began, referring to their recent conversations at Sharpsburg. "Are you not over-cautious when you assume that you can not do what the enemy is constantly doing? Should you not claim to be at least his equal in prowess, and act upon the claim?" The general had maintained he could not advance without first reconstructing a rail supply line. That "ignores the question of *time*, which can not, and must not be ignored," the president insisted. The Rebels were supporting their army (a very large army, by McClellan's count) far from a railhead; why could not he?

Lincoln went on to apply cool logic to a number of strategic questions. Should Lee again attempt to invade the North, he would leave himself open to an attack on his communications and so be forced to fight at a great disadvantage. If, on the other hand, McClellan advanced into Virginia along a line east of the Blue Ridge, he would be moving on the chord of a circle and the Confederates on its arc. Thus the Federals should reach Richmond first, "unless you admit that he is more than your equal on a march. . . . I would press closely to him, fight him if a favorable opportunity should present, and, at least, try to beat him to Richmond on the inside track. I say 'try'; if we never try, we shall never succeed." Above all, the general must understand that his target was the other man's army. "As we must beat him somewhere, or fail finally, we can do it, if at all, easier near to us, than far away." (One characteristic President Lincoln shared with General Lee was the killer instinct.) He explained the advantages in supply routes and reinforcements if this inside track was adopted, and then returned to his theme that what General Lee demanded of his troops should be no more than what General McClellan demanded of his: "It is all easy if our troops march as well as the enemy; and it is unmanly to say they can not do it."

The president closed by saying his letter was not an order; no doubt he hoped his arguments would persuade on their logic. Soon afterward, McClellan showed the letter to Darius Couch and observed that he did not expect to be in command much longer. "Lincoln is down on me," he said. Couch replied that he detected no ill will in the president's tone. "Yes, Couch, I expect to be relieved from the Army of the Potomac, and to have a command in the West. . . . " He responded to the letter on October 17, promising to give such an advance a "full and respectful consideration . . . the moment my men are shod and my cavalry are sufficiently renovated. . . . " Five more days passed, and on October 22 he notified Washington that he would follow the line the president had recommended — although he would need more cavalry and infantry. On October 25 he raised an entirely new alarm: " . . . a great portion of Bragg's army is probably now at liberty to unite itself with Lee's command." Halleck coldly suggested he not worry about that; after all, he was 20 miles from Lee's army and Bragg was 400 miles distant.[45]

The same day he brought up the specter of Braxton Bragg's army, McClellan forwarded a report by one of his cavalrymen announcing that his mounts were "absolutely broken down from fatigue and want of flesh." At that the president's temper snapped, and he wired back a stinging inquiry: "Will you pardon me for asking what the horses of your army have done since the battle of Antietam that fatigues anything?"

There was a certain injustice to the barb — for one thing, an epidemic of foot-and-mouth disease had spread among the army's horses — and McClellan bristled and launched into a lengthy defense of his cavalry forces, noting especially (if rather unwisely) their recent "remarkable expeditions" in pursuit of Jeb Stuart's raiders.[46] Yet the frustration with the army's inactivity that had triggered Lincoln's outburst entirely escaped the general. Oblivious to any considerations beyond his own narrow and obstinately held concerns, he maintained his glacial pace.

There was a sense of frustration in the army as well as in Washington. S. L. M. Barlow heard from one of his tipsters at McClellan's headquarters that the opinion there was widespread that "had we marched two weeks ago, Mac would today have been General-in-Chief." Lieutenant Whitman wrote his family on October 20, "We ought to have force enough now, to go right ahead and balsmather the secesh ers. I dont like the idea of fighting the same ground over three or four times...." *Tribune* reporter Richardson remarked that he was surprised "at the number of brigade, division, and regimental commanders who are not only anti-McClellan, but swear that the country is dying of McClellan." Richardson had heard from insiders at headquarters, including Colonel Thomas Key and other "echoes" of the general, that "McClellan's heart is not in this movement. He clings to the Peninsula . . . , is in favor of going into winter quarters." But far and away the most common rumor, in the camps and in the country, was that the Young Napoleon's future was most precarious.[47]

The president's mood on the day he wrote his long letter to his recalcitrant general was described by a White House visitor, James S. Wadsworth, Republican candidate for governor of New York. As Wadsworth reported their conversation, Lincoln "seemed to doubt that George would move after all. Said he'd got tired of his excuses, said *he'd remove him at once but for the elections.*" Certainly the fall elections in the Northern states were being taken into account in all of Lincoln's calculations for getting the war moving again.

Joseph Medill of the Republican *Chicago Tribune* wrote a friend on the eve of polling day in the Midwest that his party's prospects were gloomy, and he blamed it on McClellan: "The democracy, taking advantage of the treachery that keeps the army motionless, are fomenting public discontent, and promising a peace if brought into power. The future is dark and dismal. Lincoln issued his proclamation and then set down on his a—s contented. But proclamations like faith without works are dead." Fears were again raised concerning the loyalty of the Old Northwest, the fears the Confederates had hoped to prey upon with their invasions. "My dear friend, *we must have victories* & that *soon*," one of Senator Sumner's correspondents wrote him from Michigan. "... The spirit of the people is sinking under the Seward-McClellan do-nothing policy. Good God! — What are they thinking about to let this beautiful fall pass without fighting...."[48]

Lincoln was put in a dilemma by this sort of political forecasting. To displace McClellan just then was to risk an outpouring of protest at the ballot box by the general's partisans. To keep him in place was to risk the continued stalling of the military machine, encouraging war weariness and a tide of votes against the administration. He had managed to defuse the potentially dangerous threat to his leadership posed by the Northern governors, meeting at Altoona, Pennsylvania, by the announcement of the emancipation decree that seemed to meet their demand for a reinvigorated war effort. But the situation was precarious, and he apparently felt that keeping McClellan in command was the lesser of evils. If he thought the cause would be benefited "by removing General McClellan tomorrow, I would remove him tomorrow," he assured the governors. "I do not believe so today...."

As for the general, he made sure his political views were known regarding at least the gubernatorial race in New York. Republican candidate Wadsworth had served under him as a brigadier in the Potomac army, and McClellan had no use for the man's professed radical convictions. Writing to his friend Barlow, he observed that should the state go Democratic in the coming election, "some of our dear friends in Washn will feel a little crest fallen. I must confess a double motive for desiring the defeat of Wadsworth — I have so thorough a contempt for the man & regard him as such a vile traitorous miscreant that I do not wish to see the great State of N.Y. disgraced by having such a thing at its head."

To Nobly Save or Meanly Lose

In the event, the election results were bad enough for the Republicans, although not as bad as they might have been. Seven states that had voted to send Lincoln to the White House in 1860 went Democratic in the fall of 1862. (One of them was New York, to McClellan's satisfaction.) However, the president's party retained control of both houses of Congress. Equally important, a large majority of the Democratic officials elected at both state and national levels were war Democrats, opposed to those in their party who would seek a compromise peace with the South. Even so, it was considered fortunate that several Republican governors who strongly supported the war effort were not up for re-election that fall. It was a great deal more than fortunate that the elections were not held with Confederate armies on the loose in the Ohio Valley or ranging through Pennsylvania and threatening Northern cities. General McClellan may have been a problem for the administration at the polls, but his soldiers who had forced the Rebel army out of Maryland were a decided asset. Their fight at Antietam had a major impact in the political arena.[49]

Less immediately visible but equally telling was the battle's effect overseas. The first reports of Antietam reached London on September 27 and led the interventionists to pause. From the beginning, no matter how severe the effects of the cotton famine (and these effects were now becoming very severe), Europe's statesmen sought assurance that in taking the side of the Confederacy they would be backing a prospective winner. Now it seemed that the string of Southern victories was at an end. On October 2 British Prime Minister Palmerston wrote Foreign Secretary Russell, the strongest advocate of intervention, that the favorable circumstance for any sort of involvement — the "great success of the South against the North" — was made suddenly less favorable by the news from Maryland. "The whole matter is full of difficulty, and can only be cleared up by some more decided events between the contending armies," he concluded.

By October 22, the day before the cabinet was scheduled to discuss the matter, Palmerston had more information from America and had concluded, he told Russell, "that at present we could take no step nor make any communication of a distinct proposition with any advantage. . . . I am very much come back to our original view of the matter, that we must continue merely to be lookers-on till the war shall have taken a more decided turn." The cabinet discussion was postponed and finally was not held at all. Lord Russell, noted an opponent of intervention with considerable satisfaction, "had thought to make a great deal of his colt by Meddler out of Vanity" only to be shown "that the animal was not fit to start and would not run a yard if he did...."[50]

If Antietam abruptly halted the movement toward foreign intervention, the proclamation on emancipation put the seal on the matter. That was not immediately apparent, however. The initial reaction to the president's act was a torrent of abuse from much of the English press. The august *Times* was more savage in its denunciation than the most unrestrained Southern editor. Lincoln was playing his last frightful card, the *Times* charged, by calling for servile insurrections: "He will appeal to the black blood of the African; he will whisper of the pleasures of spoil and of the gratification of yet fiercer instincts; and when the blood begins to flow and shrieks come piercing through the darkness, Mr. Lincoln will wait till the rising flames tell that all is consummated, and then he will rub his hands and think that revenge is sweet." *Blackwood's Magazine* found the proclamation "monstrous, reckless, devilish," fully justifying the South "in hoisting the black flag, and in proclaiming a war without quarter against the Yankee hosts."

It became evident soon enough that the decree was not in fact the signal for the slaves to rise up and lay waste the South in an orgy of murder and pillage and rapine, and that Yankee and Rebel armies were not descending to barbarism by making war under the black flag. Instead, Europe's statesmen began to grasp a crucial reality of the situation that Abraham Lincoln had recognized almost a year earlier, when he was grappling with the whole slavery question. "I cannot imagine that any European power would dare to recognize and aid the Southern Confederacy," he observed in January 1862, "if it became clear that the Confederacy stands for slavery and the Union for freedom." In making that distinction clear by his proclamation, he made it virtually impossible for any civilized power to enter the conflict on the side of the South. And despite occasional flare-ups in foreign relations, none would attempt to do so. "We must make up our minds to fight our battles ourselves," General Lee had predicted when the war was young, and so it would be. The Confederate States of America would

To Nobly Save or Meanly Lose 335

live or die by its armies, without intervention from overseas.[51]

News of the blows delivered against the Rebels in Maryland cheered Ambassador Adams in London, and on October 17 he wrote, "If General McClellan will only go on and plant a few more of the same kind in his opponent's eyes, I shall be his very humble servant...." On October 26, almost six weeks after Antietam, McClellan announced to Washington that his army was starting to cross the Potomac into Virginia. The war was finally under way again.

Gradually Sharpsburg emptied of troops, and the local citizens began putting their lives back together. Barns and haylofts and corncribs and henhouses had been cleaned out by the army's demands for food and forage. Fences had been carried off for firewood, and people found it hard to tell where one farm ended and the next began. The queerest thing about it, a man remembered, was the quiet the battle had inflicted. There were no roosters left to crow, he said, and hardly any dogs to bark, and the birds did not return until the next spring. "When night come I was so lonesome that I see I didn't know what lonesome was before. It was a curious silent world...."[52]

· EPILOGUE ·

A LAST FAREWELL

On the evening of November 6, 1862, Francis P. Blair paid a call on President Lincoln "in his solitude" at the White House. They talked at length about politics and the case of General McClellan. As Old Man Blair saw it, the peace Democrats in Congress, those "who are in heart on the side of oligarchy & the South," were intent on making the general their candidate for the presidency two years hence. McClellan must be "pushed on in the line he has taken & compelled to make a winter campaign," Blair urged. Should he be successful it would rally the war Democrats to the administration's policy and force the peace advocates to disavow him. If he should "fail as a general," on the other hand, that faction would be discredited along with him. He pointed out the army's devotion to its commander and the difficulty of finding another general "capable of wielding so great a force & to be trusted with working so complicated a machine...." Lincoln kept his own counsel, although he did remark, Blair reported, that he "had tried long enough to bore with an auger too dull to take hold."[1]

The president in fact had already come to a decision concerning McClellan. Some two weeks earlier, when the general finally agreed to adopt Washington's plan for advancing into Virginia to the east of the Blue Ridge, he privately set the Young Napoleon a test. By marching swiftly along that inside track toward Richmond, it was Lincoln's reckoning that he should intercept the Confederate army and bring it to battle at a considerable advantage. If, however, he allowed Lee to get ahead of him — that is, in

A Last Farewell

the metaphor the president favored, if the Rebels in the Shenandoah marched more rapidly on the arc of the circle than the Federals did on the chord — he would be dismissed.

It is hardly credible that Lincoln imagined that General McClellan could meet this test. Certainly nothing in his past record suggested he would rise to the occasion and drive relentlessly against the foe. If he did, that would be all to the good; and whether he did or not, no politically difficult change need be made in the midst of the fall elections. Pragmatism would guide the matter.

In the event, the general remained in character. He would "push forward as rapidly as possible to endeavor to meet the enemy," he assured the president on October 27. The army "shall go forward from day to day as rapidly as possible," he wired on November 1. "The entire army will advance rapidly to-day" he said on November 2. Using pontoon bridges at Harper's Ferry and at Berlin, a few miles downstream, the Army of the Potomac, just over 100,000 strong, required eight full days to cross the Potomac and push its leading columns twenty miles into Virginia. The president later remarked to a newspaperman that after Antietam General Lee had got his entire army across the river into Virginia in a single night.

McClellan's next step was to advance another twenty miles to the vicinity of Warrenton so as to exchange his Harper's Ferry supply route for a safer one linking him to Washington via the Orange and Alexandria and Manassas Gap railroads. Like a man walking a tightrope, he negotiated this passage with the utmost care. As the army pushed southward in short marches, it successively seized the gaps in the Blue Ridge on its right to prevent any surprise Rebel thrust from the Shenandoah against its communications. By November 4 the railroads were secured and the supply-line changeover begun. Substantial reinforcements from Washington reached the field. "We are in the full tide of success, so far as it is or can be successful to advance without a battle," McClellan wrote his wife that night.[2]

If he had a plan for battle, he was keeping it to himself; his dispatches to Washington gave no hint of a plan of any sort. To General Lee, it appeared that the Yankees were going back to John

Pope's line of advance toward Richmond along the line of the Orange and Alexandria, and he acted promptly to be in position to repeat his August tactics against Pope. On October 28, two days after the Federals began crossing the river, he divided his army. Longstreet was ordered to move south and east to the town of Culpeper Court House, astride the railroad. Jackson would remain in the Valley, alert to any opportunity to fall on the enemy's communications. McClellan, Lee remarked, was moving "with more activity than usual."

Longstreet made his sixty-mile march without interference, however, and by November 4 it was known in Washington that his command had reached Culpeper and was squarely between the Army of the Potomac and Richmond. The next day, November 5, Lincoln sent a message of authorization to General Halleck: "By direction of the President, it is ordered that Major General McClellan be relieved from the command of the Army of the Potomac; and that Major General Burnside take the command of that Army."

"I began to fear he was playing false — that he did not want to hurt the enemy," Lincoln later told John Hay in explaining his decision. " ... If he let them get away I would remove him. He did so & I relieved him." In a conversation with the *Tribune*'s Albert Richardson he called the deliberate pace of the army's Potomac crossing "the last grain of sand which broke the camel's back. I relieved McClellan at once." There was in fact considerably more to it than that.[3]

With General McClellan it was always a case of weighing benefits against liabilities, and now the scales no longer balanced in his favor. His notable achievement in organizing and training the army would be his monument, but Antietam was proof that the task was finished. The Yankee fighting men who had checked Lee's invasion did so not because of McClellan but in spite of him. He was not after all the indispensable man; the Army of the Potomac was no longer his army but the country's. Conceivably on another field on another day he might overcome his crippling caution and his distorting self-deceptions and his lack of moral courage in the heat of battle. However that might be, it was no longer possible for the president to indulge him the opportunity.

A Last Farewell

The problem of General McClellan, in short, had grown far larger than simply a question of his military competence. He stood for limited war, compromise peace, a return to the old order of things — all hopes that over the months of fighting had dimmed and faded and at Antietam were finally extinguished. Rejecting the revolutionary turn the war was taking — a change he helped bring about, however unwittingly and unwillingly — he had permitted himself to become the magnet for opposition to the administration and its policies. It was a challenge that could not be ignored.

His demand, delivered "thru certain friends of mine," that Secretary of War Stanton and General-in-Chief Halleck be removed was at the least a violation of his soldier's duty under the articles of war and at worst an attempt at military usurpation. Widespread disaffection was reported in the Potomac army's officer corps, taking its tone from the general commanding, and whether or not there was a clear and present danger involved, Lincoln heard enough to be convinced that it could not be allowed to continue. Nor was there any doubt in the minds of the president and his advisers that the general was deeply and actively involved in opposition politics; he saw it as his calling to save his country from civilian as well as military enemies. It was true enough, as one of McClellan's admirers said, that in the end he was not a Caesar; yet, at this critical turning point in the affairs of a nation at war with itself, neither was he standing aloof.[4]

That McClellan might in fact emulate Caesar and attempt a coup d'état was a matter of grave concern to the administration — or at least to Edwin Stanton — and the whole matter of the change in command was carefully calculated. On the evening of November 6, while Old Man Blair was at the White House outlining the political benefits to be gained by retaining McClellan, Secretary Stanton called in the War Department's adjutant general, Brigadier Catharinus P. Buckingham. Buckingham was instructed to board a special train the next day and proceed to the army's headquarters in the field. Stanton handed him two envelopes and told him to return to his office, read the orders they contained, and then seal them. Before departing on his mission the next morning, he was to report to the secretary's home for final instructions. Buckingham described himself as "thunderstruck" when he read the orders, one set directing McClellan to turn over his command and repair to his home in Trenton, New Jersey, to await further orders, the other assigning the command to Burnside.

Friday, November 7, brought with it the first blast of winter, a heavy snowstorm said to be the worst to strike Virginia in years. It reminded the New Englanders in the army of a typical winter storm back home. Calling at Stanton's house on K Street, General Buckingham was told he had been chosen for his task because of fears that McClellan might not surrender control of the army. "The Secretary had not only no confidence in McClellan's military skill," Buckingham wrote, "but he very much doubted his patriotism, and even loyalty...." McClellan was to understand from the fact the order was being delivered in person by the highest-ranking officer in the War Department that it carried "the full weight of the President's authority." Buckingham was further instructed to go to Burnside first and press him to take the command. If he should refuse, however, Buckingham was to return to Washington without seeing McClellan; Stanton wanted the plan to remain secret until the new man was on the scene and prepared to take over immediately. General McClellan would be allowed no time for any second thoughts.

Buckingham's special train made its slow way in the blinding storm to Manassas Junction, where it was switched from the Orange and Alexandria to the Manassas Gap Railroad running west toward the Blue Ridge. At Salem he left the train and rode on horseback through the snow to Burnside's headquarters. Burnside testified to "my surprise, the shock, &c." when he read his orders. He protested that he did not want the army command and was unqualified for it, and said that twice before he had rejected it for the same reasons. The situation was different now, Buckingham explained, and then played his trump card: McClellan was going to be removed in any case, and if he did not take the command it would go to Joe Hooker. In Burnside's view Hooker was a devious conniver, responsible for his humiliating role as the general without troops at Antietam. After consulting with his staff, Burnside reluctantly accepted the post.

The two men rode back to the special train and proceeded sev-

A Last Farewell

eral miles up the line to the village of Rectortown, where McClellan had his headquarters. It was about 11 P.M. and the general was alone in his tent, writing a letter to his wife. When Buckingham and Burnside arrived he greeted them cordially. There was an exchange of small talk, and then Buckingham handed over the envelope he had brought. It was a painful task, he recalled, but he was glad at least that the matter was not being handled by "an unkind hand and in a mortifying way."

"Of course I was much surprised," McClellan wrote Ellen; "but as I read the order in the presence of Gen. Buckingham I am sure that not the slightest expression of feeling was visible on my face, which he watched closely. They shall not have that triumph. They have made a great mistake. Alas for my poor country!" He added, "Poor Burnside feels dreadfully, almost crazy.... He never showed himself a better man or truer friend than now."

He closed his letter on a reflective note. "I have done the best I could for my country," he thought. That he had made "many mistakes" he did not deny, but he could not see any great blunders, although "no one can judge of himself." That moment of self-doubt soon passed. "Our consolation must be that we have tried to do what was right; if we have failed it was not our fault."[5]

Staff aide David Strother was in Washington when he learned of McClellan's dismissal. "This news shocked and confused me greatly, and put the world at Willard's in a ferment," he wrote in his diary on November 9. People in the capital talked of nothing else. Soliciting the opinion of the man in the street, newspapers reported much debate concerning the president's decision. One man was quoted as saying the change was long overdue; perhaps now the war would be ended "some time within the present century." Another, however, advised the administration to keep McClellan close at hand in the event of "Bull Run Number 3." When the news reached Richmond, editorialists there thought it possible that the general might defy the order and march on Washington at the head of his army and depose Lincoln and the black Republicans. General Lee, who had taken such cruel advantage of his opponent's weaknesses, remarked to Longstreet, "I fear they may continue to make these changes till they find some one whom I don't understand."[6]

At Burnside's request, McClellan agreed to stay on a few days to help with the details of the command changeover and to brief his successor on the tactical situation. It would also give him the opportunity to take ceremonial leave of an army that was (as he told one of his staff) "my army as much as any army ever belonged to the man who created it." He wrote later that he remained only to calm those who favored a descent on the capital to overthrow the government. Certainly he had no objection to confounding his critics with a public demonstration of the Potomac army's loyalty and affection for him.

He dramatized his own feelings in a farewell message printed and distributed to the troops. "In parting from you I cannot express the love and gratitude I bear to you," he told them. "As an army you have grown up under my care.... The battles you have fought under my command will proudly live in our Nation's history. The glory you have achieved, our mutual perils and fatigues, the graves of our comrades fallen in battle and by disease, the broken forms of those whom wounds and sickness have disabled, — the strongest associations which can exist among men, — unite us still by an indissoluble tie. Farewell!"[7]

His emotions were answered in kind on November 10 when the army was turned out corps by corps in a final review to honor him. For the last time the Potomac soldiers in their tens of thousands cheered him to the echo. The drama was intense, catching men up in the moment of it, and was felt most deeply by those Peninsula veterans who had been with him the longest. "I never before had to exercise so much self-control," McClellan wrote to his wife. "The scenes of to-day repay me for all that I have endured."

Men wept unashamedly as he rode past and gazed after him "in mute grief, one may almost say despair," a diarist wrote. "The great army, his creature, have shed more tears to-day than ever before during the eighteen months of their trying experience," a Massachusetts veteran wrote home. "Neither the government nor the country have any idea what a hold little Mac has on our hearts." Brigadier Thomas Meagher had the color-bearers of his Irish Brigade throw down their emerald banners before the general in a flamboyant gesture of devotion and protest; McClellan ordered the colors picked up before he would proceed. "I have this moment returned to my tent after witnessing, with a full

A Last Farewell

heart, a most painful yet noble scene," Meagher wrote S. L. M. Barlow that day. "... Ah! if the gentlemen of the White House could have seen what I saw this morning — could have heard the cheers from those 100,000 soldiers which rent the air and deadened the artillery itself as the parting salute was fired — they would have felt that a mistake or crime has been committed by them, which the Army of the Union will never forgive."[8]

Like that day early in September when McClellan reclaimed the army from General Pope, men remembered his leave-taking as long as they lived. Not everyone was displeased. In some units it was noted that the cheers were perfunctory. Many men in the Ninth Corps were bitter at McClellan's failure to support them at Antietam, and in any case they liked their General Burnside and welcomed his promotion. But even among the doubters there was puzzlement and anger at the change in command in the midst of this new campaign. "We had a rough time last night, as Officers & men had been drinking, to drown grief & the Camp was noisy," Brigadier Marsena Patrick recorded in his diary on November 11; "... in their cups men spoke their minds."[9]

General Meade told his wife he was surprised, "as I thought the storm had blown over.... This removal now proves conclusively that the cause is political, and the date of the order, November 5th (the day after the New York election) confirms it." A Massachusetts colonel agreed, attributing the change to politicians and "the influence they have over the President, who is frightened into doing anything by the late elections." In common with many officers, John Gibbon thought the government had gone mad to act in the midst of an ongoing campaign. Fitz John Porter blamed McClellan's enemies in the War Department, whom he knew to be his enemies as well. "You may soon expect to hear my head is lopped ...," he wrote editor Marble of the *New York World*. He was right. Relieved of duty on November 10, he was tried by court-martial for his alleged disobedience of Pope's orders at Second Bull Run and cashiered.[10]

A good many of the troops credited the radicals with bringing McClellan down. "Well Jim I am so mad that I can hardly write," a man in the First Corps told a friend; "the God-d —— abolitionists of the North have succeeded in their hellish work of removing little Mac. . . . The boys all want to go home." A half-dozen staff officers, stoking their anger with liquor, took revenge on what they considered the mouthpiece of the radicals, Greeley's *New York Tribune*, by assaulting correspondent Albert Richardson. The next day Richardson went about armed with a pistol, but found that the mood had cooled.[11]

The idea that civilians were criticizing the general and passing judgment on his actions was a particular source of irritation to many in the army as well as to General McClellan. Ohioan Thomas Galwey thought any man in the ranks was "at least as well qualified to criticize his movements as the backwoods Yankee pettifoggers who control, in a large degree, the legislature in Washington." Lieutenant Henry Ropes of the 20th Massachusetts decided that McClellan's caution was actually commendable foresight: "The people say the war *must* be finished in 9 months. McClellan lays his plans merely to finish the war, whether 9 months or 9 years are required."[12]

And there was talk, not all of it whiskey-inspired, of marching on Washington. Lieutenant Edgar Newcomb of the 19th Massachusetts expressed a common opinion when he wrote on the day of the final review, "If McClellan wished to establish himself Supreme Dictator to-day, the army in the heat of their resentment of this wrong would be with him." The foreign officers at headquarters wondered, if feelings ran that deep, why the men did not in fact take the government hostage to their demand that the Young Napoleon be reinstated. Colonel Charles Wainwright had an answer: "Doubtless that would have been the way were we French or Germans," he wrote in his diary, "but our people are naturally too law abiding." So in the end all the loose talk and the threats came to nothing. In a last farewell to his staff, McClellan offered a toast to the Potomac army and the day when he would be with it again, and that mild hint was the closest he came to taking matters into his own hands. Secretary Stanton's alarms were unfounded.[13]

The next day, November 11, McClellan boarded the train at Warrenton Junction that would take him out of the war. As it was about to leave, the men in the honor guard drawn up along the tracks broke ranks, uncoupled the car carrying the general, and

A Last Farewell 345

cried out that he must not be allowed to leave. McClellan came out and made a little speech and calmed them, asking their pledge to stand by General Burnside "as you have stood by me, and all will be well." The car was finally recoupled and the train steamed slowly away to the accompaniment of "one long and mournful huzza," with the general standing on the rear platform and calling out, "Good bye, lads."[14]

APPENDIXES
SOURCES AND ACKNOWLEDGMENTS
NOTES
BIBLIOGRAPHY
INDEX

· APPENDIX I ·

THE LOST ORDER

The Lost Order has long been a topic of fascination and debate among students of the Maryland campaign of 1862. Certainly it is a subject that has merited the attention; as General Lee observed after the war, ". . . it is probable that the loss of the dispatch changed the character of the campaign."[1] How the copy of Special Orders No. 191 was lost, how and when it was found, and whether Lee was promptly informed that his entire operational plan was in Federal hands are the chief questions calling for answers.

In the absence of new evidence, it seems unlikely that there will ever be a satisfactory solution to the mystery of how Order 191 was lost. If D. H. Hill is to be believed — and he went to considerable pains to document his defense — the copy of the order addressed to him by adjutant R. H. Chilton never reached anyone at Hill's headquarters with the authority to sign for its receipt, namely Hill or his adjutant, Major J. W. Ratchford. Chilton kept no operational log or journal that would prove that his courier returned with the required evidence of delivery. Nevertheless, as he wrote Jefferson Davis in 1874, "That omission to deliver in his [the courier's] case so important an order w'd have been recollected as entailing the duty to advise its loss, to guard against consequences, and to act as required. . . . But I could not of course say positively that I had sent any particular courier to him [D. H. Hill] after such a lapse of time."[2] The publication in 1886 of the intriguing detail of the three cigars, which might possibly have stimulated memories, unfortunately came too late for Chilton; he had died seven years before. As noted in the text, D. H. Hill's assertion that the order might have reached enemy hands through treachery appears unwarranted, leaving carelessness on the part of a courier or someone on Hill's staff, combined with administrative neglect at Lee's headquarters, as the likeliest explanation.

As to how and when the Lost Order was found by the Federals, General Alpheus Williams's covering note accompanying his transmission of the find to McClellan — which so far as is known is the only contemporaneous reference to the actual discovery — refines minor details of the accepted story.[3] It indicates that on September 13 the find was credited solely to Corporal (not Private) Barton Mitchell, with no mention of Sergeant Bloss; that the order's last stop before reaching McClellan was Twelfth Corps headquarters; and that it arrived in McClellan's hands with its authenticity already vouched for by Williams's aide, Colonel Samuel Pittman.

Williams's note bears no time of transmission, but that McClellan accepted the import of the discovery as early as noon on September 13 is clear from his dispatch to Lincoln, marked "Headquarters, Frederick, September 13, 1862 — 12 m.," in which he wrote, "I have all the plans of the rebels...."[4] (The time designation "12 m." stood in contemporary military parlance for 12 meridian, or noon, not for midnight as has sometimes been stated.) Why McClellan immediately notified the president of his find rather than General Halleck, whom he did not telegraph until eleven that night, may best be explained by his receipt that morning of the two dispatches from Lincoln sent the previous afternoon, the first asking "How does it look now?" and the second detailing the latest intelligence on Jackson's movements.[5] The president, in short, was insisting on some answers, and McClellan was pleased enough to reply with his good news. It may be noted that the general was in error — or dissembling — when he told Halleck that night that the Lost Order had reached him "this evening." He had already, at 3 P.M., put cavalryman Pleasonton to checking the Confederate march routes as spelled out in Order 191.[6]

The final major question concerning the Lost Order is what, if anything, General Lee soon learned about it. It has been widely stated that the Maryland civilian present when McClellan was handed Corporal Mitchell's discovery learned specifically that it was the Confederate operational plan and, through Jeb Stuart, so informed Lee. Since the key piece of documentation on this point, Stuart's dispatch to Lee, is not on the record, other evidence must be sifted. With one exception, this evidence supports the conclusion presented in the text — that the civilian in fact learned only that fresh intelligence of some unspecified sort had made General McClellan suddenly confident and offensive-minded.

The authority for the existence of this amateur civilian spy is General Lee himself. He mentioned him for the first time (so far as the record shows) after the war, in two conversations concerning the Maryland campaign on February 15, 1868, and then in a letter to D. H. Hill six days

The Lost Order

later.[7] It was the discovery of the two memoranda of these 1868 Lee conversations that caused Douglas Southall Freeman to change his view on the Lost Order following the publication of his biography of the general. In 1934, in *R. E. Lee*, Freeman maintained that Lee did not learn until months later that the Federals had found the dispatch; in *Lee's Lieutenants*, in 1943, he described his revised opinion that Lee did indeed learn that fact on September 13 from the Marylander.[8]

Yet when these two conversations, recorded in notes by E. C. Gordon and William Allan, are examined closely, Lee's remarks on the subject are ambiguous; in neither did he state in so many words that the civilian learned that what has handed to McClellan in his presence was a lost copy of Order 191. Colonel Allan reflected these two memoranda accurately when he published the story of the Marylander, stating only that the man "had accidently been present when the order" — an identification Allan, like Lee, supplied from hindsight knowledge — "had been brought to McClellan, and had heard the expressions of gratification that followed, and had learned of the orders then issued. He ... brought this information after night to Stuart, who at once forwarded it to General Lee." Only in the 1868 letter to D. H. Hill was Lee explicit, writing that Stuart "had learned from a citizen of Maryland, that he [McClellan] was in possession of the order directing the movement of our troops."[9]

However, there is substantial evidence that in this instance Lee's memory had failed him. In his letter to President Davis of September 16, 1862, three days after McClellan's discovery, Lee indicated no knowledge of the Lost Order, writing only that "the enemy was advancing more rapidly than was convenient. . . ." He did mention the Lost Order in his official report, written in August 1863 after the find had been made public by the Federals, but not that he had learned about it from the Marylander or from anyone else at the time.[10] Had he been presented with that highly important fact, it is scarcely credible that he would not have revealed it to Longstreet in their conversation on the night of September 13, yet Longstreet makes no mention of it in his postwar writings on the campaign. In fact there is no reference of any kind to the Lost Order in the wartime reports of Longstreet, D. H. Hill, or Stuart, those best positioned to have learned about it. This omission is most significant in Stuart's case. Had the Marylander told him on September 13 that McClellan possessed all the Confederate plans, it seems completely out of character that he would have excluded such a counterintelligence coup from his official report. Finally, there is the unqualified statement on the matter by Charles Marshall, Lee's wartime aide. In an 1867 letter to D. H. Hill, Marshall wrote, "I remember perfectly that until we saw that report [by McClellan] Gen. Lee frequently expressed his inability to understand the sudden change in McClellan's tactics which took place after we left Frederick."[11]

Thus the conclusion seems inescapable that Lee learned from the Maryland civilian only that the Federal army had suddenly become active. Although this was important enough intelligence, in effect it simply confirmed what he had learned earlier that evening from Stuart and D. H. Hill. Not until some months later, after the Federals revealed the story, did he learn the specific reason for that activity — the finding of Order 191.

As noted in the text, it is highly improbable that McClellan or one of his staff was so careless as to reveal a top secret such as this to an unknown civilian, particularly one from a state where loyalties were known to be divided. As important as anything else, however — and the reason the whole question is critical to an understanding of the campaign — is the pattern of Lee's subsequent actions.

Robert E. Lee was a most daring general, but not a foolhardy one. Had he actually known late on September 13 that his opponent possessed a copy of Order 191, it defies belief that he would not have met such an obvious crisis by ordering Longstreet to the rescue with a night march, by ordering D. H. Hill to Turner's Gap that night with every man at his command, by ordering McLaws to take positive and immediate measures to avoid being trapped, or even by taking Longstreet's advice and pulling back out of immediate danger to Sharpsburg. But he issued no such explicit orders; instead, he took the precautions of a general puzzled by the suddenly inexplicable moves of his opponent. And it is equally hard to imagine him taking his defiant stand at Sharpsburg on September 15 and 16 — daring enough as it was — with the knowledge that McClellan then knew the exact dispositions of the still-scattered commands of the Army of Northern Virginia. To be sure, the Young Napoleon managed to throw away the glittering opportunities for total victory offered him by the Lost Order, but Lee was hardly so reckless as to rely on that happening.

There remains Lee's 1868 letter to D. H. Hill. It should be noted that Lee was greatly irritated at an article by Hill on the Lost Order that had just appeared, particularly at Hill's contention that the loss of the order was actually a piece of good fortune for the Confederacy by focusing McClellan's attention on Turner's Gap rather than on the more critically dangerous situation at Harper's Ferry.[12] In his angry and forceful rebuttal of this argument, it seems reasonable to assume that the general unintentionally let the knowledge of events gained through hindsight cloud his memory of the exact contents of Stuart's dispatch reaching him that eventful night almost five and a half years before.

· APPENDIX II ·

BURNSIDE AND HIS BRIDGE

No aspect of the fighting on September 17, 1862, created more controversy than Ambrose Burnside's operations against the Confederate right flank. The primary points of debate centered on the exact nature of Burnside's assignment, and on when and how he attempted to carry it out.

The role intended for the Ninth Corps in McClellan's "design" for the battle remains unclear, but — in common with other disputed points in George McClellan's Civil War career — his earliest statement on the matter is probably the closest to the truth. Less than a month after Antietam, in his preliminary report dated October 15, he wrote that it was his intention to focus the main attack against Lee's left and "at least to create a diversion in favor of the main attack, with the hope of something more by assailing the enemy's right — and, as soon as one or both of the flank movements were fully successful, to attack their center with any reserve I might then have on hand." This idea of mounting a diversion to assist the primary effort against the Confederate northern flank also appears in Jacob Cox's report, written six days after the battle. Cox repeated that understanding in his postwar writings in *Battles and Leaders of the Civil War* and in his memoirs, adding that it was also "the opinion I got from Burnside at the time."[1]

In his preliminary report McClellan went on to say that Burnside "was intrusted with the difficult task of carrying the bridge across the Antietam, near Rohrback's farm, and assaulting the enemy's right, the order having been communicated to him at 10 o'clock a.m." That is also the time of receipt stated in Burnside's September 30 report and repeated in his testimony before the Joint Committee on the Conduct of the War. Cox originally asserted that the order was received "about 9 o'clock," but he observed in his *Battles and Leaders* article that he had not thought to look at his watch and that "the cumulative evidence seems to prove conclusively that the time stated by Burnside, and by McClellan himself in his original report, is correct."[2]

On that point, at least, there is conclusive evidence. Although it did not appear in the volume of the *Official Records* covering the Maryland campaign, the 9:10 A.M. dispatch to Burnside to begin his attack was later published in a supplementary volume. That it *was* the initial order is obvious from its content. Signed by Colonel George D. Ruggles of the headquarters staff, it read: "General Franklin's command is within one mile and a half of here. General McClellan desires you to open your attack. As soon as you shall have uncovered the upper Stone bridge you will be supported, and, if necessary, on your own line of attack. So far all is going well."[3]

Why some forty-five minutes elapsed before the message reached Burnside's headquarters, only two miles from the Pry house as the crow flies, is unclear. In any case, it was in Burnside's hands by ten o'clock (possibly a few minutes earlier), passed on to Cox, and acted upon promptly. In addition, Burnside was assured that once the Ninth Corps was across the creek his offensive would be supported by reserves from the Fifth or Sixth corps advancing on his right across the Middle Bridge on the Boonsboro turnpike.

So far as the historical record is concerned, that would seem to settle the matter, except that General McClellan elected to tamper with the record. When he came to write his *Report*, dated August 4, 1863, detailing his tenure as head of the Army of the Potomac, his situation had changed considerably since he prepared the preliminary report on Antietam. Instead of the acclaimed savior of the Republic, he was now a general dismissed from command and the increasingly visible opponent of the Lincoln administration and its war policies. His performance at Antietam had come under sharp public scrutiny. In commenting on the general's preliminary report, for example, the *New York Tribune*, on April 4, 1863, indicted him for failure to "have destroyed at once the Rebel army and the Rebellion itself." His conduct on September 17, the *Tribune* continued, was "a pitiable confession of irresolution" that "wholly forfeited the regard of that portion of the loyal public, which once trusted him. . . ." Admittedly the Republican *Tribune* had an ax to grind, but then, as would soon be demonstrated, so did General McClellan.

In his *Report*, published by the Government Printing Office in Washington in February 1864 and reprinted later in that election year by a New York publishing house, certain important changes are apparent. Rather than creating a diversion with the Ninth Corps, he maintained

Burnside and His Bridge

that it had been his original plan "as soon as matters looked favorably" on the northern flank "to move the corps of Burnside against the enemy's extreme right, upon the ridge running to the south and rear of Sharpsburg, and having carried their position, to press along the crest towards our right"; and a few pages later he wrote, "The attack on the right was to have been supported by an attack on the left." For whichever of these two purposes Burnside went into action in his enlarged role, there was now an earlier starting time: "At 8 o'clock an order was sent to him by Lieutenant Wilson, topographical engineers, to carry the bridge...."

After expressing disappointment that the bridge was not captured until one o'clock and the offensive not resumed until three in the afternoon, McClellan concluded, "If this important movement had been consummated two hours earlier . . . and turned their right and rear, our victory might thus have been much more decisive." However apt this judgment of events may be, Burnside's delay was extended by at least an hour, thereby transferring the burden of the failure to destroy the Rebel army from the shoulders of the general commanding to those of General Burnside. And by the time the *Report* was published, that argument was lent a certain plausibility by Burnside's dismal record as army commander at the Battle of Fredericksburg.[4]

This rewriting of history continued in *McClellan's Own Story* (1887), in which Burnside, who had died in 1881, became the full-fledged scapegoat. "The ground held by Burnside beyond the bridge," McClellan wrote, "was so strong that he ought to have repulsed the attack and held his own. He never crossed the bridge in person!" — an allegation, it may be noted, that was flatly denied by General Cox. On September 18, McClellan continued, "Burnside told me that his men were so demoralized and so badly beaten the day before that were they attacked they would give way," and that after he was sent Morell's division as reinforcement, Burnside had "withdrawn his own men, his excuse to me being that he could not trust his men on the other side!" (In the margin of his copy of *McClellan's Own Story*, next to these statements, Cox wrote, "I don't believe a word of it" and "Stuff!") Summing up his old friend's conduct at Antietam as "inexcusable" and "pernicious" in its effect on the battle, McClellan wrote, "I cannot, from my long acquaintance with Burnside, believe that he would deliberately lie, but I think that his weak mind was turned; that he was confused in action; and that subsequently he really did not know what had occurred, and was talked by his staff into any belief they chose."[5]

In preparing *McClellan's Own Story* for posthumous publication, McClellan's editor, William C. Prime, included two 1876 letters the general had solicited from Delos B. Sackett, the Army of the Potomac's inspector general at the time of the battle. In these letters Sackett confirmed the state of Burnside's demoralization and also implied that in fact it was he who had delivered the initial message to Burnside to open his attack, "at about nine o'clock on the morning of the battle." McClellan, however, had been selective in using Sackett's recollections, restating in his memoirs that the original attack order left headquarters at 8 A.M. in the care of Lieutenant John M. Wilson. Indeed, Sackett's account is hardly credible in light of his statement that Burnside greeted him with the remark, "... you are the third or fourth one who has been to me this morning with similar orders."[6]

The actual sequence of messengers may be sorted out thus. First, Lieutenant Wilson with the 9:10 order to open the battle on the left, reaching Burnside very close to ten o'clock. Second, two or three unnamed follow-up couriers — " 'What is Burnside about? Why do we not hear from him?' " staff aide David Strother quoted McClellan as asking; "During the morning he sent several messengers to hasten his movements." Third, Colonel Sackett, who probably reached Burnside's headquarters between eleven o'clock and noon. Finally, Colonel Thomas M. Key, one of McClellan's most trusted aides, who made two trips to the left, arriving there about one and two o'clock, respectively, the second time carrying McClellan's order to relieve Burnside if it became necessary.[7]

What makes the exact timing of Burnside's orders to attack the Rohrbach Bridge critical, of course, were the consequences: at 3:30 on the afternoon of September 17 it looked very much as if Lee's right flank would be turned, cutting his line of retreat to the Potomac and putting his army in deadly peril; and at 4:30 the Ninth Corps was itself in retreat. It is hard to imagine A. P. Hill reaching Sharpsburg any earlier than he did; indeed the Light Division's feat was remarkable enough as it was. In an offensive when the saving of an hour or even half an hour might well have changed the course of the battle, Burnside had required five hours to launch his potentially decisive assault. McClellan sought to add substantially to that time span and leave it to history to apportion the blame. "The story of the 8 o'clock order is an instance of the way in which an erroneous memory is based upon the desire to make the facts accord with a theory," Cox wrote.[8]

To be sure, General Burnside's performance at Antietam gave McClellan good reason to write, in a letter to his wife on September 29, "He is very slow; is not fit to command more than a regiment."[9] Yet at the same time, McClellan's catalog of failures is lengthy and manifest. The Ninth Corps made its battle under an unwieldy command structure he imposed on it and without clearly stated objectives. Reconnaissance of the Antietam fords was ineptly performed, and by McClellan's staff rather than by cavalry. No use was made of the potential reinforcement of Couch's division. The decision to open the attack was taken not only inexplicably late but without coordination with the rest of the army. The elementary precaution of guarding the army's left flank with cavalry was ignored, granting Powell Hill the decisive advantages of surprise and position. Finally, the Ninth Corps was denied any support from the more than ample reserve, either to exploit victory or to salvage defeat. Clearly General Burnside failed to rise to the occasion at Antietam; equally clearly, no other Union officer on the field that day was so badly served by the general commanding.

· APPENDIX III ·

THE ARMIES AT ANTIETAM

The following tabulation of the forces present on the Antietam battlefield on September 17–18 is drawn primarily from the tables of organization in the Antietam Battlefield Board's *Atlas of the Battlefield of Antietam*, a compilation directed by Ezra A. Carman. In the notation of officer casualties, (k) stands for killed, (w) for wounded, and (mw) for mortally wounded.

Army of the Potomac
Maj. Gen. George B. McClellan

FIRST CORPS
Maj. Gen. Joseph Hooker (w)
Brig. Gen. George G. Meade

First Division: Brig. Gen. Abner Doubleday
  First Brigade: Col. Walter Phelps, Jr.
    22nd New York   30th New York
    24th New York   84th New York
    2nd United States Sharpshooters
  Second Brigade: Lt. Col. J. William Hofmann
    7th Indiana   95th New York
    76th New York   56th Pennsylvania
  Third Brigade: Brig. Gen. Marsena R. Patrick
    21st New York   35th New York
    23rd New York   80th New York
  Fourth Brigade: Brig. Gen. John Gibbon
    19th Indiana   6th Wisconsin
    2nd Wisconsin   7th Wisconsin

Artillery: Capt. J. Albert Monroe
  New Hampshire Light, 1st Battery   1st Rhode Island Light, Battery D
  1st New York Light, Battery L   4th United States, Battery B

Second Division: Brig. Gen. James B. Ricketts
  First Brigade: Brig. Gen. Abram Duryea

97th New York	105th New York
104th New York	107th Pennsylvania

  Second Brigade: Col. William A. Christian
               Col. Peter Lyle

26th New York	88th Pennsylvania
94th New York	90th Pennsylvania

  Third Brigade: Brig. Gen. George L. Hartsuff (w)
              Col. Richard Coulter

12th Massachussetts	83rd New York
13th Massachusetts	11th Pennsylvania

  Artillery:
    1st Pennsylvania Light, Battery F   Pennsylvania Light, Battery C

Third Division: Brig. Gen. George G. Meade
              Brig. Gen. Truman Seymour
  First Brigade: Brig. Gen. Truman Seymour
             Col. R. Biddle Roberts

1st Pennsylvania	6th Pennsylvania
2nd Pennsylvania	13th Pennsylvania
5th Pennsylvania	

  Second Brigade: Col. Albert L. Magilton

3rd Pennsylvania	7th Pennsylvania
4th Pennsylvania	8th Pennsylvania

  Third Brigade: Lt. Col. Robert Anderson

9th Pennsylvania	11th Pennsylvania
10th Pennsylvania	12th Pennsylvania

  Artillery:
    1st Pennsylvania Light, Battery A   5th United States, Battery C
    1st Pennsylvania Light, Battery B

SECOND CORPS
Maj. Gen. Edwin V. Sumner

First Division: Maj. Gen. Israel B. Richardson (mw)
            Brig. Gen. John C. Caldwell
            Brig. Gen. Winfield S. Hancock
  First Brigade: Brig. Gen. John C. Caldwell

5th New Hampshire	64th New York
7th New York	81st Pennsylvania
61st New York	

Second Brigade: Brig. Gen. Thomas F. Meagher
             Col. John Burke
  63rd New York   88th New York
  69th New York   29th Massachusetts
Third Brigade: Col. John R. Brooke
  2nd Delaware   66th New York
  52nd New York   53rd Pennsylvania
  57th New York
Artillery:
  1st New York Light, Battery B   4th United States, Battery C
  4th United States, Battery A

Second Division: Maj. Gen. John Sedgwick (w)
                 Brig. Gen. Oliver O. Howard
  First Brigade: Brig. Gen. Willis A. Gorman
    15th Massachusetts (1st Co. Massachusetts Sharpshooters, attached)
    1st Minnesota (2nd Co. Minnesota Sharpshooters, attached)
    34th New York   82nd New York
  Second Brigade: Brig. Gen. Oliver O. Howard
                  Col. Joshua T. Owen
                  Col. De Witte C. Baxter
    69th Pennsylvania   72nd Pennsylvania
    71st Pennsylvania   106th Pennsylvania
  Third Brigade: Brig. Gen. N. J. T. Dana (w)
                 Col. Norman J. Hall
    19th Massachusetts   42nd New York
    20th Massachusetts   59th New York
    7th Michigan
  Artillery:
    1st Rhode Island Light, Battery A   1st United States, Battery I

Third Division: Brig. Gen. William H. French
  First Brigade: Brig. Gen. Nathan Kimball
    14th Indiana   132nd Pennsylvania
    8th Ohio   7th West Virginia
  Second Brigade: Col. Dwight Morris
    14th Connecticut   130th Pennsylvania
    108th New York
  Third Brigade: Brig. Gen. Max Weber (w)
                 Col. John W. Andrews
    1st Delaware   4th New York
    5th Maryland
Unattached Artillery:
    1st New York Light, Battery G   1st Rhode Island Light, Battery G
    1st Rhode Island Light, Battery B

FIFTH CORPS
Maj. Gen. Fitz John Porter

First Division: Maj. Gen. George W. Morell
  First Brigade: Col. James Barnes
    2nd Maine   13th New York
    18th Massachusetts   25th New York
    1st Michigan   118th Pennsylvania
    22nd Massachusetts (2nd Co. Massachusetts Sharpshooters, attached)
  Second Brigade: Brig. Gen. Charles Griffin
    2nd District of Columbia   4th Michigan
    9th Massachusetts   14th New York
    32nd Massachusetts   62nd Pennsylvania
  Third Brigade: Col. T. B. W. Stockton
    16th Michigan (Brady's Co. Michigan Sharpshooters, attached)
    20th Maine   44th New York
    12th New York   83rd Pennsylvania
    17th New York
  Sharpshooters:
    1st United States
  Artillery:
    Massachusetts Light, Battery C   5th United States, Battery D
    1st Rhode Island Light, Battery C

Second Division: Brig. Gen. George Sykes
  First Brigade: Lt. Col. Robert C. Buchanan
    3rd United States   12th United States, 2nd Battalion
    4th United States   14th United States, 1st Battalion
    12th United States, 1st Battalion   14th United States, 2nd Battalion
  Second Brigade: Maj. Charles S. Lovell
    1st United States   10th United States
    2nd United States   11th United States
    6th United States   17th United States
  Third Brigade: Col. Gouverneur K. Warren
    5th New York   10th New York
  Artillery:
    1st United States, Battery E   5th United States, Battery I
    1st United States, Battery G   5th United States, Battery K

Third Division: Brig. Gen. Andrew A. Humphreys
  First Brigade: Brig. Gen. Erastus B. Tyler
    91st Pennsylvania   129th Pennsylvania
    126th Pennsylvania   134th Pennsylvania

The Armies at Antietam

    Second Brigade: Col. Peter H. Allabach
        123rd Pennsylvania   133rd Pennsylvania
        131st Pennsylvania   155th Pennsylvania
        Artillery: Captain Lucius N. Robinson
            1st New York Light, Battery C   1st Ohio Light, Battery L
    Artillery Reserve: Lt. Col. William Hays
        1st Battalion, New York Light: New York Light, 5th Battery
            Battery A   1st United States, Battery K
            Battery B   4th United States, Battery G
            Battery C
            Battery D

                    SIXTH CORPS
              Maj. Gen. William B. Franklin

First Division: Maj. Gen. Henry W. Slocum
    First Brigade: Col. Alfred T. A. Torbert
        1st New Jersey   3rd New Jersey
        2nd New Jersey   4th New Jersey
    Second Brigade: Col. Joseph J. Bartlett
        5th Maine   27th New York
        16th New York   96th Pennsylvania
    Third Brigade: Brig. Gen. John Newton
        18th New York   32nd New York
        31st New York   95th Pennsylvania
    Artillery: Capt. Emory Upton
        Maryland Light, Battery A   New Jersey Light, Battery A
        Massachusetts Light, Battery A 2nd United States, Battery D
Second Division: Maj. Gen. William F. Smith
    First Brigade: Brig. Gen. Winfield S. Hancock
               Col. Amasa Cobb
        6th Maine   137th Pennsylvania
        43rd New York   5th Wisconsin
        49th Pennsylvania
    Second Brigade: Brig. Gen. W. T. H. Brooks
        2nd Vermont   5th Vermont
        3rd Vermont   6th Vermont
        4th Vermont
    Third Brigade: Col. William H. Irwin
        7th Maine   49th New York
        20th New York   77th New York
        33rd New York
    Artillery: Capt. Romeyn B. Ayres
        Maryland Light, Battery B   5th United States, Battery F
        New York Light, 1st Battery

First Division, Fourth Corps (attached): Maj. Gen. Darius N. Couch
  First Brigade: Brig. Gen. Charles Devens, Jr.
    7th Massachusetts   36th New York
    10th Massachusetts   2nd Rhode Island
  Second Brigade: Brig. Gen. Albion P. Howe
    62nd New York   102nd Pennsylvania
    93rd Pennsylvania   139th Pennsylvania
    98th Pennsylvania
  Third Brigade: Brig. Gen. John Cochrane
    65th New York   23rd Pennsylvania
    67th New York   61st Pennsylvania
    122nd New York   82nd Pennsylvania
  Artillery:
    1st Pennsylvania Light, Battery C   New York Light, 3rd Battery
    1st Pennsylvania Light, Battery D   2nd United States, Battery G

NINTH CORPS
Maj. Gen. Ambrose E. Burnside
Brig. Gen. Jacob D. Cox

First Division: Brig. Gen. Orlando B. Willcox
  First Brigade: Col. Benjamin C. Christ
    28th Massachusetts   79th New York
    17th Michigan   50th Pennsylvania
  Second Brigade: Col. Thomas Welsh
    8th Michigan   45th Pennsylvania
    46th New York   100th Pennsylvania
  Artillery:
    Massachusetts Light, 8th Battery   2nd United States, Battery E

Second Division: Brig. Gen. Samuel D. Sturgis
  First Brigade: Brig. Gen. James Nagle
    2nd Maryland   9th New Hampshire
    6th New Hampshire   48th Pennsylvania
  Second Brigade: Brig. Gen. Edward Ferrero
    21st Massachusetts   51st New York
    35th Massachusetts   51st Pennsylvania
  Artillery:
    Pennsylvania Light, Battery D   4th United States, Battery E

Third Division: Brig. Gen. Isaac P. Rodman (mw)
            Col. Edward Harland
  First Brigade: Col. Harrison S. Fairchild
    9th New York   103rd New York
    89th New York
  Second Brigade: Col. Edward Harland
    8th Connecticut   16th Connecticut
    11th Connecticut   4th Rhode Island

Artillery:
    5th United States, Battery A

Kanawha Division: Col. Eliakim P. Scammon
  First Brigade: Col. Hugh Ewing
    12th Ohio   30th Ohio
    23rd Ohio
    Artillery: Ohio Light, 1st Battery
    Cavalry: Gilmore's and Harrison's Co's., West Virginia Cavalry
  Second Brigade: Col. George Crook
    11th Ohio   36th Ohio
    28th Ohio
    Artillery: Kentucky Light, Simmonds's Battery
    Cavalry: Schambeck's Co., Chicago Dragoons

Unattached Artillery:
    2nd New York, Battery L   3rd United States, Battery M
    3rd United States, Battery L
Unattached Cavalry:
    6th New York (8 co's.)   Ohio Cavalry, 3rd Independent Co.

TWELFTH CORPS
Maj. Gen. Joseph K. F. Mansfield (mw)
Brig. Gen. Alpheus S. Williams

First Division: Brig. Gen. Alpheus S. Williams
                Brig. Gen. Samuel W. Crawford (w)
                Brig Gen. George H. Gordon
  First Brigade: Brig. Gen. Samuel W. Crawford
                 Col. Joseph F. Knipe
    10th Maine   124th Pennsylvania
    28th New York   125th Pennsylvania
    46th Pennsylvania   128th Pennsylvania
  Third Brigade: Brig. Gen. George H. Gordon
                 Col. Thomas H. Ruger
    27th Indiana   107th New York
    13th New Jersey   3rd Wisconsin
    2nd Massachusetts (Zouaves d'Afrique, attached)

Second Division: Brig. Gen. George S. Greene
  First Brigade: Lt. Col. Hector Tyndale (w)
                 Maj. Orrin J. Crane
    5th Ohio   66th Ohio
    7th Ohio   28th Pennsylvania
  Second Brigade: Col. Henry J. Stainrook
    3rd Maryland   111th Pennsylvania
    102nd New York

Third Brigade: Col. William B. Goodrich (k)
    Lt. Col. Jonathan Austin
  3rd Delaware   78th New York
  60th New York   Purnell (Maryland) Legion

Corps Artillery: Capt. Clermont L. Best
  Maine Light, 4th Battery   Pennsylvania Light, Battery E
  Maine Light, 6th Battery   Pennsylvania Light, Battery F
  1st New York Light, Battery M 4th United States, Battery F
  New York Light, 10th Battery

CAVALRY DIVISION
Brig. Gen. Alfred Pleasonton

First Brigade: Maj. Charles J. Whiting
  5th United States   6th United States
Second Brigade: Col. John F. Farnsworth
  8th Illinois   1st Massachusetts
  3rd Indiana   8th Pennsylvania
Third Brigade: Col. Richard H. Rush
  4th Pennsylvania   6th Pennsylvania
Fourth Brigade: Col. Andrew T. McReynolds
  1st New York   12th Pennsylvania
Fifth Brigade: Col. Benjamin F. Davis
  8th New York   3rd Pennsylvania
Unattached: 15th Pennsylvania (detachment)
Artillery:
  2nd United States, Battery A   2nd United States, Battery M
  2nd United States, Battery B   3rd United States, Battery C
  2nd United States, Battery L   3rd United States, Battery G

Army of Northern Virginia
Gen. Robert E. Lee

LONGSTREET'S CORPS
Maj. Gen. James Longstreet

McLaws's Division: Maj. Gen. Lafayette McLaws
  Kershaw's Brigade: Brig. Gen. Joseph B. Kershaw
    2nd South Carolina   7th South Carolina
    3rd South Carolina   8th South Carolina
  Cobb's Brigade: Lt. Col. C. C. Sanders
                Lt. Col. William MacRae
    16th Georgia   15th North Carolina
    24th Georgia   Cobb's (Georgia) Legion
  Semmes's Brigade: Brig. Gen. Paul J. Semmes
    10th Georgia   15th Virginia
    53rd Georgia   32nd Virginia

Barksdale's Brigade: Brig. Gen. William Barksdale
   13th Mississippi   18th Mississippi
   17th Mississippi   21st Mississippi
Artillery: Col. Henry C. Cabell
   Manly's (North Carolina) Battery   Richmond Howitzers, 1st Co.
   Pulaski (Georgia) Artillery   Troup (Georgia) Artillery
   Richmond (Fayette) Artillery

Anderson's Division: Maj. Gen. Richard H. Anderson (w)
                    Brig. Gen. Roger A. Pryor
  Wilcox's Brigade: Col. Alfred Cumming
                Maj. H. A. Herbert
   8th Alabama   10th Alabama
   9th Alabama   11th Alabama
  Featherston's Brigade: Col. Carnot Posey
   12th Mississippi   19th Mississippi
   16th Mississippi   2nd Mississippi Battalion
  Armistead's Brigade: Brig. Gen. Lewis A. Armistead (w)
                    Col. J. G. Hodges
   9th Virginia   53rd Virginia
   14th Virginia   57th Virginia
   38th Virginia
  Pryor's Brigade: Brig. Gen. Roger A. Pryor
                Col. John C. Hately (w)
   14th Alabama   8th Florida
   2nd Florida   3rd Virginia
   5th Florida
  Mahone's Brigade (attached to Pryor's Brigade): Col. William A. Parham
   6th Virginia   41st Virginia
   12th Virginia   61st Virginia
   16th Virginia
  Wright's Brigade: Brig. Gen. Ambrose R. Wright (w)
                  Col. Robert Jones (w)
                  Col. William Gibson
   44th Alabama   22nd Georgia
   3rd Georgia   48th Georgia
  Artillery: Capt. Cary F. Grimes (k)
          Maj. John S. Saunders
   Donaldsonville (Louisiana) Artillery (Maurin's Battery)
   Huger's (Norfolk) Battery   Grimes's (Portsmouth) Battery
   Moorman's (Lynchburg) Battery

Jones's Division: Brig. Gen. David R. Jones
  Toombs's Brigade: Brig. Gen. Robert Toombs
                  Col. Henry L. Benning
   2nd Georgia   17th Georgia
   15th Georgia   20th Georgia

Drayton's Brigade: Brig. Gen. Thomas F. Drayton
   50th Georgia	15th South Carolina
   51st Georgia	3rd South Carolina Battalion
Pickett's Brigade: Brig. Gen. Richard B. Garnett
   8th Virginia	28th Virginia
   18th Virginia	56th Virginia
   19th Virginia
Kemper's Brigade: Brig. Gen. James L. Kemper
   1st Virginia	17th Virginia
   7th Virginia	24th Virginia
   11th Virginia
Jenkins's Brigade: Col. Joseph Walker
   1st South Carolina (Volunteers)	6th South Carolina
   2nd South Carolina Rifles	4th South Carolina Battalion
   5th South Carolina
   Palmetto (South Carolina) Sharpshooters
Anderson's Brigade: Col. George T. Anderson
   1st Georgia	9th Georgia
   7th Georgia	11th Georgia
   8th Georgia
Artillery:
   Wise (Virginia) Artillery (J. S. Brown's Battery)

Walker's Division: Brig. Gen. John G. Walker
  Walker's Brigade: Col. Van H. Manning (w)
              Col. E. D. Hall
   3rd Arkansas	48th North Carolina
   27th North Carolina	30th Virginia
   46th North Carolina
   Artillery: French's (Stafford) Battery
Ransom's Brigade: Brig. Gen. Robert Ransom, Jr.
   24th North Carolina	35th North Carolina
   25th North Carolina	49th North Carolina
   Artillery: Branch's (Petersburg) Field Artillery

Hood's Division: Brig. Gen. John B. Hood
  Hood's Brigade: Col. William T. Wofford
    18th Georgia	5th Texas
    1st Texas	Hampton (South Carolina) Legion
    4th Texas
  Law's Brigade: Col. Evander M. Law
    4th Alabama	11th Mississippi
    2nd Mississippi	6th North Carolina
  Artillery: Maj. B. W. Frobel
    German (Charleston) Artillery	Rowan (North Carolina) Artillery
    Palmetto (South Carolina) Artillery

The Armies at Antietam

Evans's (Independent) Brigade: Brig. Gen. Nathan G. Evans
                               Col. P. F. Stevens
  17th South Carolina   23rd South Carolina
  18th South Carolina   Holcombe (South Carolina) Legion
  22nd South Carolina
  Artillery: Macbeth (South Carolina) Artillery

Corps Artillery:
  1st Battalion: Col. John B. Walton
    Washington (Louisiana) Artillery, 1st, 2nd, 3rd, 4th Co's.
  2nd Battalion: Col. Stephen D. Lee
    Ashland (Virginia) Artillery   Eubank's (Bath) Battery
    Bedford (Virginia) Artillery   Madison (Louisiana) Light Artillery
    Brooks (South Carolina) Artillery Parker's (Richmond) Battery

JACKSON'S CORPS
Maj. Gen. Thomas J. Jackson

Ewell's Division: Brig. Gen. Alexander R. Lawton (w)
                 Brig. Gen. Jubal A. Early
  Lawton's Brigade: Col. Marcellus Douglass (k)
                  Maj. J. H. Lowe
    13th Georgia   38th Georgia
    26th Georgia   60th Georgia
    31st Georgia   61st Georgia
  Early's Brigade: Brig. Gen. Jubal A. Early
                Col. William Smith (w)
    13th Virginia   49th Virginia
    25th Virginia   52nd Virginia
    31st Virginia   58th Virginia
    44th Virginia
  Trimble's Brigade: Col. James A. Walker (w)
    15th Alabama   21st North Carolina
    12th Georgia   1st North Carolina Battalion
    21st Georgia
  Hays's Brigade: Brig. Gen. Harry T. Hays
    5th Louisiana   8th Louisiana
    6th Louisiana   14th Louisiana
    7th Louisiana
  Artillery: Maj. A. R. Courtney
    Louisiana Guard Artillery (D'Aquin's Battery)
    Staunton (Virginia) Artillery (Balthis's Battery)
    Johnson's (Virginia) Battery

Hill's Light Division: Maj. Gen. A. P. Hill
  Branch's Brigade: Brig. Gen. L. O'Brien Branch (k)
                Col. Thomas H. Lane

7th North Carolina	33rd North Carolina
18th North Carolina	37th North Carolina
28th North Carolina	

  Gregg's Brigade: Brig. Gen. Maxcy Gregg

1st South Carolina (Provisional)	13th South Carolina
1st South Carolina Rifles	14th South Carolina
12th South Carolina	

  Field's Brigade: Col. John M. Brockenbrough

40th Virginia	55th Virginia
47th Virginia	22nd Virginia Battalion

  Archer's Brigade: Brig. Gen. James J. Archer
                Col. Peter Turney

19th Georgia	7th Tennessee
1st Tennessee	14th Tennessee

  Pender's Brigade: Brig. Gen. William D. Pender
                Col. R. H. Brewer

16th North Carolina	34th North Carolina
22nd North Carolina	38th North Carolina

  Artillery: Lt. Col. R. L. Walker
      Fredericksburg (Virginia) Artillery (Braxton's Battery)
      Pee Dee (South Carolina) Artillery (McIntosh's Battery)
      Purcell (Richmond) Artillery (Pegram's Battery)
      Crenshaw's (Richmond) Battery

Jackson's Division: Brig. Gen. John R. Jones (w)
                  Brig. Gen. William E. Starke (k)
                  Col. Andrew J. Grigsby
  Winder's Brigade: Col. Andrew J. Grigsby
                Lt. Col. R. D. Gardner (w)
                Maj. H. J. Williams

4th Virginia	27th Virginia
5th Virginia	33rd Virginia

  Taliaferro's Brigade: Col. James W. Jackson (w)
                Col. James L. Sheffield

47th Alabama	23rd Virginia
48th Alabama	37th Virginia

  Jones's Brigade: Capt. John E. Penn (w)
                Capt. A. C. Page (w)
                Capt. R. W. Withers

21st Virginia	48th Virginia
42nd Virginia	1st Virginia Battalion

Starke's Brigade: Brig. Gen. William E. Starke
              Col. Leroy A. Stafford (w)
              Col. Edmund Pendleton
  1st Louisiana   10th Louisiana
  2nd Louisiana   15th Louisiana
  9th Louisiana   1st Louisiana Battalion
  Artillery: Maj. L. M. Shumaker
    Alleghany (Virginia) Artillery (Carpenter's Battery)
    Danville (Virginia) Artillery (Wooding's Battery)
    Lee (Virginia) Battery (Raine's Battery)
    Rockbridge (Virginia) Artillery (Poague's Battery)
    Brockenbrough's (Maryland) Battery

Hill's Division: Maj. Gen. D. H. Hill
  Ripley's Brigade: Brig. Gen. Roswell S. Ripley (w)
              Col. George Doles
    4th Georgia   1st North Carolina
    44th Georgia   3rd North Carolina
  Rodes's Brigade: Brig. Gen. Robert E. Rodes
    3rd Alabama   12th Alabama
    5th Alabama   26th Alabama
    6th Alabama
  Garland's Brigade: Col. D. K. McRae
    5th North Carolina   20th North Carolina
    12th North Carolina   23rd North Carolina
    13th North Carolina
  Anderson's Brigade: Brig. Gen. George B. Anderson (mw)
              Col. C. C. Tew (k)
              Col. R. T. Bennett
    2nd North Carolina   14th North Carolina
    4th North Carolina   30th North Carolina
  Colquitt's Brigade: Brig. Gen. Alfred H. Colquitt
    13th Alabama   27th Georgia
    6th Georgia   28th Georgia
    23rd Georgia
  Artillery: Maj. C. F. Pierson
    Jones's (Virginia) Battery   Hardaway's (Alabama) Battery
    King William (Virginia) Artillery Jeff Davis (Alabama) Artillery

RESERVE ARTILLERY
Brig. Gen. William N. Pendleton

Cutts's Battalion: Lt. Col. A. S. Cutts
  Blackshears's (Georgia) Battery   Ross's (Georgia) Battery
  Patterson's (Georgia) Battery   Lloyd's (North Carolina) Battery
  Irwin (Georgia) Artillery (Lane's Battery)

Jones's Battalion: Maj. H. P. Jones
    Turner's (Virginia) Battery   Wimbish's (Virginia) Battery
    Orange (Virginia) Artillery (Peyton's Battery)
    Morris (Virginia) Artillery (Page's Battery)
Unattached: Magruder Artillery   Cutshaw's (Virginia) Battery

CAVALRY DIVISION
Maj. Gen. J. E. B. Stuart

Hampton's Brigade: Brig. Gen. Wade Hampton
    1st North Carolina   Cobb's (Georgia) Legion
    2nd South Carolina   Jeff Davis (Mississippi) Legion
Lee's Brigade: Brig. Gen. Fitzhugh Lee
    1st Virginia   5th Virginia
    3rd Virginia   9th Virginia
    4th Virginia
Robertson's Brigade: Col. Thomas T. Munford
    2nd Virginia   12th Virginia
    7th Virginia
Horse Artillery: Maj. John Pelham
    Pelham's (Virginia) Battery   Hart's (South Carolina) Battery
    Chew's (Virginia) Battery

SOURCES AND ACKNOWLEDGMENTS

The late Bruce Catton, with whom I was associated for many years at *American Heritage*, was of inestimable help in the planning of this book. In addition to providing counsel and encouragement, he put at my disposal his extensive notes on the Maryland campaign, including research material collected for his *Centennial History of the Civil War.*

Mr. Catton also provided a suggestion that led me to the discovery of the Antietam Collection at the Dartmouth College Library, a large repository of letters by Antietam veterans, both Union and Confederate, assembled by the 10th Maine's Major John M. Gould. Dennis A. Dinan furnished generous help and hospitality during my investigation of this collection, and I am grateful as well to the Dartmouth Library's archivist, Kenneth C. Cramer.

The most detailed account of the events of September 17, 1862, is contained in the unpublished manuscript on the Maryland campaign by Ezra A. Carman, in the Manuscript Division, Library of Congress. Carman, colonel of the 13th New Jersey at the time of the battle, served on the Antietam Battlefield Board as its "Historical Expert" and was instrumental in the compilation of the authoritative *Atlas of the Battlefield of Antietam.* The situation maps of the battle, prepared by Herbert S. Borst of Mount Kisco, New York, are based on this atlas and on data in the Carman manuscript. Carman's research sources for his study of the campaign included his own extensive correspondence with Antietam veterans, designated Antietam Studies and Antietam Battlefield Board Papers and deposited at the National Archives, as well as the collection of correspondence made available to him by Major Gould and now at the Dartmouth Library. I am greatly indebted to David A. Lilley, Park Historian, Fredericksburg National Military Park, for his unstinting assistance, especially for sharing his expert knowledge of the Carman materials.

Betty J. Otto, Park Historian, Antietam National Battlefield, kindly assisted me during my visits and made available material from the research files at the battlefield. Mike Musick at the National Archives and Paul T. Heffron at the Manuscript Division, Library of Congress, aided my researches at those institutions. Among the holdings at the Library of Congress that relate to the campaign are the George B. McClellan Papers, which include not only the general's Letterbook, containing copies of his wartime letters to Mrs. McClellan, but also many important documents and dispatches from his army headquarters files that were not available to the compilers of the *Official Records.*

Stanley Crane of the Pequot Library, Southport, Connecticut, generously guided me through that library's Civil War resources, especially its extensive collection of regimental histories. Janis Rodman of the Darien, Connecticut, Library was helpful with interlibrary loan requests, and Margaretta Colt of the Military Bookman in New York City located key out-of-print volumes. I am grateful to my editor, Geoffrey C. Ward, for his astute comments on the manuscript and for his valuable suggestions.

NOTES

Published and manuscript materials cited in the Notes by author and short title appear in full in the Bibliography. Reference to material in the *Official Records* (U.S. War Department, *The War of the Rebellion: A Compilation of the Official Records of the Union and Confederate Armies*) is abbreviated *OR;* unless otherwise noted, all references are to Series One. Manuscript citations drawn from the research compiled by E. B. Long, with Barbara Long, for Bruce Catton's *Terrible Swift Sword,* volume II of *The Centennial History of the Civil War,* are designated Long Notes. The designation Nevins Notes refers to material compiled by Allan Nevins and incorporated in the *Centennial History's* research project. (A copy of the research notes for that project has been deposited at the Manuscript Division, Library of Congress, by Doubleday & Company.) Citation of material in the George B. McClellan Papers, Manuscript Division, Library of Congress, is by microfilm reel number. Dates cited or implicit in the text for quoted letters and other documents are not repeated in the Notes.

Prologue. The Last, Best Hope
1. Worthington Chauncey Ford, ed., *A Cycle of Adams Letters, 1861–1865,* I, pp. 177–78.
2. *OR,* XII, Part 2, p. 66; Part 3, pp. 679, 699–700.
3. August 24, 1862, Letterbook, McClellan Papers, Manuscript Division, Library of Congress, microfilm reel 63; Porter to J. C. G. Kennedy, July 17, Fitz John Porter Papers, Massachusetts Historical Society; Herman Haupt, *Reminiscences of General Herman Haupt,* p. 83. A selection of General McClellan's wartime letters to his wife appears in his memoirs, *McClellan's Own Story,* published posthumously in 1887, with various censorious passages (such as this commentary on General Pope) deleted, apparently by William C. Prime, his literary executor. The originals of these letters have not been located, but many of them appear in McClel-

lan's hand and in less censored form in his Letterbook under the heading, "Extracts from letters written to my wife during the war of the Rebellion."
4. George B. McClellan, *Report on the Organization of the Army of the Potomac, and of Its Campaigns in Virginia and Maryland* (Washington, D.C., 1864), p. 171 (the section of McClellan's *Report* covering this period also appears in *OR*, XI, Part 1, pp. 5–105); *OR*, XII, Part 3, p. 691; McClellan, *Report*, p. 174. All citations to McClellan's *Report* herein refer to the Washington edition, published in February 1864 as a congressional document by the Government Printing Office. A second edition, with different pagination, was published later in 1864 by Sheldon & Co., New York.
5. David Homer Bates, *Lincoln in the Telegraph Office*, p. 9; *OR*, XII, Part 3, p. 719.
6. *OR*, XII, Part 3, pp. 709, 710.
7. Louis M. Starr, *Bohemian Brigade: Civil War Newsmen in Action*, pp. 82–83; *OR*, XII, Part 3, p. 706.
8. McClellan, *Report*, p. 175; *OR*, XII, Part 3, p. 722; McClellan, *Report*, pp. 175–76.
9. Hill to S. H. Gay, August 30, S. H. Gay Papers, Columbia University Library, quoted in Starr, *Bohemian Brigade*, p. 151; September 1, John Hay, *Lincoln and the Civil War in the Diaries and Letters of John Hay*, ed. Tyler Dennett, p. 45. McClellan's use of the offending phrase probably represented more thoughtlessness than calculation. It was a figure of speech he favored and applied to many situations.
10. George Templeton Strong, *The Diary of George Templeton Strong: The Civil War, 1860–1865*, eds. Allan Nevins and Milton H. Thomas, p. 249; Salmon P. Chase, *Inside Lincoln's Cabinet: The Civil War Diaries of Salmon P. Chase*, ed. David Donald, p. 116.
11. *OR*, XII, Part 3, pp. 733, 723–24.
12. John Sedgwick, *Correspondence of John Sedgwick, Major General*, II, pp. 78–79; *OR*, XII, Part 3, p. 747; McClellan, *Report*, p. 180.
13. *OR*, XII, Part 3, p. 739; George C. Gorham, *Life and Public Services of Edwin M. Stanton* (Boston: Houghton Mifflin, 1899), II, pp. 38–39; Chase, *Diaries*, p. 116.
14. *OR*, XII, Part 3, p. 741; Strong, *Diary*, p. 249.
15. Margaret Leech, *Reveille in Washington, 1860–1865*, pp. 188–89; Haupt, *Reminiscences*, pp. 116–18; Charles F. Walcott, "The Battle of Chantilly," *The Virginia Campaign of 1862 Under General Pope*, ed. Theodore F. Dwight, Papers of the Military Historical Society of Massachusetts, II (Boston 1895) p. 144.
16. *OR*, XII, Part 2, p. 79; Horace H. Thomas, "What I Saw Under a Flag of Truce," *Military Essays and Recollections*, Illinois Commandery of the Military Order of the Loyal Legion of the United States, I (Chicago, 1891–92), p. 243.
17. September 1, Hay, *Diaries and Letters*, pp. 45–46; Elizabeth Lindsay Lomax, *Leaves from an Old Washington Diary, 1854–1863*, ed. Lindsay Lomax Wood (New York: Dutton, 1943), p. 211.
18. Allan Nevins, *The War for the Union*, II: *War Becomes Revolution, 1862–1863*, p. 184.

19. OR, XII, Part 2, p. 80; McClellan, Report, p. 181; OR, XII, Part 3, p. 773; McClellan, Report, p. 182.
20. Hill to S. H. Gay, Gay Papers, Columbia University Library, quoted in Starr, Bohemian Brigade, p. 132; Leech, Reveille in Washington, p. 192.
21. Letterbook, McClellan Papers, reel 63.
22. Stanton Papers, Manuscript Division, Library of Congress, quoted in Roy P. Basler, ed., The Collected Works of Abraham Lincoln, V, p. 486n.; Gideon Welles, Diary of Gideon Welles, ed. Howard K. Beale, I, pp. 101–2.
23. OR, XII, Part 2, pp. 82–83.
24. McClellan, Report, p. 183; Hay, Diaries and Letters, p. 46; OR, XII, Part 3, pp. 787–88, 798.
25. OR, XII, Part 3, pp. 796–97; George B. McClellan, McClellan's Own Story, pp. 535, 566.
26. Leech, Reveille in Washington, p. 193.
27. Welles, Diary, I, pp. 104–5; Chase, Diaries, pp. 119–20; Hay, Diaries and Letters, p. 47; Benjamin P. Thomas and Harold M. Hyman, Stanton: The Life and Times of Lincoln's Secretary of War (New York: Knopf, 1962), p. 221.
28. Jacob D. Cox, Military Reminiscences of the Civil War, I, p. 243; Abner R. Small, The Road to Richmond: The Civil War Memoirs of Major Abner R. Small of the 16th Maine Volunteers, ed. Harold A. Small (Berkeley: University of California Press, 1939), p. 43.
29. Cox, Military Reminiscences, I, p. 245; Rufus R. Dawes, Service with the Sixth Wisconsin Volunteers, pp. 75–76; Battles and Leaders of the Civil War, eds. Robert U. Johnson and Clarence C. Buel, II, pp. 490, 550.
30. OR, XIX, Part 2, p. 169.

Chapter 1. The Limits of Limited War

1. July 30, August 9, November—, 1861, McClellan, Story, pp. 83, 85, 177. The general's messianic vision is examined in James B. Fry, "McClellan and His Mission," Century, XLVIII (October 1894), pp. 931–46.
2. July 25, 1861, OR, II, pp. 196–97; November—, 1861, Hay, Diaries and Letters, p. 33.
3. Nathaniel Hawthorne, "Chiefly About War Matters," Atlantic Monthly, X (July 1862), quoted in Jack Lindeman, ed., The Conflict of Convictions: American Writers Report the Civil War, p. 165; March 14, 1862, quoted in Frank Moore, ed., The Rebellion Record: A Diary of American Events, IV, Documents, p. 307.
4. July 30, 1861, McClellan, Story, p. 83; Edward Bates, The Diary of Edward Bates, 1859–1866, ed. Howard K. Beale (Washington, D.C.: Government Printing Office, 1933), p. 194.
5. These statements, and others like them in this period, may be found in McClellan, Story, pp. 168–77 passim, and in the general's Letterbook, McClellan Papers, reel 63.
6. John D. Billings, Hardtack and Coffee: The Unwritten Story of Army Life, p. 276.
7. McClellan, Report, pp. 6–9 (the pre-Peninsula campaign portion of the Report is also in OR, V, pp. 1–66); McClellan, Story, p. 177. The term "inoffensive defensive" is General Jacob Cox's, one of the marginal comments Cox penciled

into his copy of *McClellan's Own Story*. The copy is in the Oberlin College Library.
8. William Swinton, *Campaigns of the Army of the Potomac*, p. 72. Pinkerton's methods are summarized in Bruce Catton, *The Centennial History of the Civil War*, II: *Terrible Swift Sword*, pp. 270–71. A sampling of his reports is in *OR*, XI, Part 1, pp. 264–72. A discussion of intelligence-gathering may be found in Edwin C. Fishel, "The Mythology of Civil War Intelligence," in John T. Hubbell, ed., *Battles Lost and Won: Essays from Civil War History* (Westport, Conn.: Greenwood Press, 1975), pp. 83–106.
9. Allan Nevins, *The War for the Union*, I: *The Improvised War, 1861–1862*, p. 301; *Harper's Weekly*, August 24, 1861.
10. James Russell Lowell, "General McClellan's Report," *Political Essays* (Boston, 1899), quoted in Lindeman, *Conflict of Convictions*, p. 169.
11. Joseph L. Harsh, "On the McClellan-Go-Round," in Hubbell, *Battles Lost and Won*, p. 71.
12. S. L. M. Barlow Papers, Huntington Library (Long Notes); May 26, 1861, *OR*, II, p. 197; July 11, 1862, *OR*, XI, Part 3, p. 316.
13. Basler, *Works of Lincoln*, V, p. 49.
14. Edward Dicey, *Spectator of America*, ed. Herbert Mitgang (Chicago: Quadrangle, 1971; originally published in 1863 as *Six Months in the Federal States*), p. 249.
15. Richard Henry Boker, January 1862, quoted in Richard B. Harwell, ed., *The Union Reader*, pp. 98–99.
16. *Report of the Joint Committee on the Conduct of the War*, I, pp. 129–30.
17. Nevins, *Improvised War*, p. 405; Swinton, *Army of the Potomac*, p. 80.
18. McClellan, *Report*, p. 42.
19. May 18, 1862, *OR*, XIX, Part 2, p. 725; Charles A. Dana, *Recollections of the Civil War: With the Leaders at Washington and in the Field in the Sixties* (New York: D. Appleton, 1898), pp. 4–5.
20. McClellan, *Report*, p. 52; Helen Nicolay, *Lincoln's Secretary: A Biography of John G. Nicolay* (New York: Longmans, Green, 1949), pp. 142–43; Jacob W. Schuckers, *The Life and Public Services of Salmon Portland Chase* (New York: D. Appleton, 1874), p. 446.
21. McClellan, *Report*, pp. 56–57; March 16, 1862, Barlow Papers, Huntington Library (Long Notes).
22. McClellan, *Story*, pp. 195–96.
23. April 1, McClellan, *Story*, p. 306; Barlow Papers, Huntington Library (Long Notes); *OR*, XI, Part 3, pp. 60–61.
24. McClellan, *Report*, pp. 75, 79; McClellan's decisions at Yorktown are examined in Catton, *Terrible Swift Sword*, pp. 272–77.
25. Basler, *Works of Lincoln*, V, p. 185; April 11, McClellan, *Story*, p. 310; April 14, Barlow Papers, Huntington Library (Long Notes).
26. Hay, *Diaries and Letters*, p. 40; McClellan, *Report*, pp. 94–95, 121; Lowell, "General McClellan's Report," quoted in Lindeman, *Conflict of Convictions*, pp. 169–70.
27. McClellan, *Report*, p. 132; July 20, McClellan, *Story*, p. 452; Bates, *Lincoln in the Telegraph Office*, pp. 108–9; July 13, Letterbook, McClellan Papers, reel 63.
28. *OR*, XII, Part 3, p. 299; July 7, Letterbook, McClellan Papers,

Notes to Chapter 1

reel 63; August 1, Ford, *A Cycle of Adams Letters*, I, p. 173.
29. July 15 and 30 (to Barlow), McClellan Papers, reel 29; July 19 (to Aspinwall), McClellan, *Story*, pp. 451–52; Porter to Marble, June 20, Manton Marble Papers, Manuscript Division, Library of Congress (Nevins Notes).
30. McClellan, *Story*, pp. 487–89; July 17, Letterbook, McClellan Papers, reel 63. The general's Harrison's Landing letter did in fact serve as a political document, appearing as a broadside titled "McClellan's Platform" during his Democratic campaign for the presidency in 1864.
31. July 11 and 29 (to Mrs. McClellan), Letterbook, McClellan Papers, reel 63; July 8 (anonymous letters), McClellan Papers, reel 48.
32. November 28, 1861, quoted in Belle Becker Sideman and Lillian Friedman, eds., *Europe Looks at the Civil War*, p. 100.
33. Frank Lawrence Owsley, *King Cotton Diplomacy: Foreign Relations of the Confederate States of America*, p. 142; Ephraim Douglass Adams, *Great Britain and the American Civil War*, II, p. 19; Owsley, *King Cotton Diplomacy*, p. 323.
34. August 2, 1862, Adams, *Britain and the Civil War*, II, p. 35.
35. D. P. Crook, *The North, the South, and the Powers, 1861–1865*, p. 136; Cobden to Sumner, July 11, *American Historical Review*, II, no. 2 (January 1897), p. 307, quoted in Crook, *The North, the South, and the Powers*, p. 205; Cobden to John Bigelow, December 1861, Bigelow, *Retrospections of an Active Life* (New York, 1909), quoted in Sideman and Friedman, *Europe Looks at the Civil War*, p. 91.
36. Crook, *The North, the South, and the Powers*, p. 221; Adams, *Britain and the Civil War*, II, p. 37.
37. Douglas Southall Freeman, *Lee's Lieutenants*, II, p. 144; Basler, *Works of Lincoln*, V, pp. 292 (June 28), 350 (July 31), 346 (July 28); Michael C. C. Adams, *Our Masters the Rebels: A Speculation on Union Military Failure in the East, 1861–1865*, p. 109.
38. Charles Sumner, *The Works of Charles Sumner* (Boston: Lee & Shepard, 1872), VI, p. 215; Basler, *Works of Lincoln*, V, pp. 160, 318; August 24, William T. Sherman Papers, Manuscript Division, Library of Congress, quoted in George Winston Smith and Charles Judah, eds., *Life in the North During the Civil War*, p. 99.
39. Bates, *Lincoln in the Telegraph Office*, pp. 138–40; Welles, *Diary*, I, pp. 70–71; Chase Papers, Historical Society of Pennsylvania, quoted in Hans L. Trefousse, *The Radical Republicans: Lincoln's Vanguard for Racial Justice*, p. 224n.
40. Basler, *Works of Lincoln*, V, pp. 336–37; John G. Nicolay and John Hay, *Abraham Lincoln: A History*, VI, pp. 125–30; Francis B. Carpenter, *Six Months at the White House with Abraham Lincoln* (Boston: Hurd & Houghton, 1866), p. 22.
41. McClellan, *Report*, pp. 154, 156.
42. Trefousse, *Radical Republicans*, p. 198; September 3, Welles, *Diary*, I, p. 107; July 27, Letterbook, McClellan Papers, reel 63; McClellan, *Story*, p. 464.
43. September 3, Wilder Dwight, *Life and Letters of Wilder Dwight, Lieutenant Colonel, 2nd Massachusetts Infantry*, p. 285.
44. September 14 and 17, Spencer Walpole, *The Life of Lord John*

Russell (London, 1889), II, pp. 360–61, quoted in Henry Steele Commager, ed., *The Blue and the Gray*, p. 540.

Chapter 2. Confederate Tide

1. Thomas L. Connelly, *The Marble Man: Robert E. Lee and His Image in American Society* (New York: Knopf, 1977), p. 194.
2. Owsley, *King Cotton Diplomacy*, p. 16.
3. December 29, 1861, R. E. Lee Papers, Duke University Library, quoted in Catton, *Terrible Swift Sword*, p. 116.
4. John Letcher, "Official Correspondence," *Southern Historical Society Papers*, I (June 1876), p. 462.
5. Walter Clark, ed., *Histories of the Several Regiments and Battalions from North Carolina*, I, p. 221.
6. Charles B. Marshall, *An Aide-de-Camp of Lee* (Boston: Little, Brown, 1927), p. 32; Emory M. Thomas, *The Confederate Nation, 1861–1865*, pp. 152–55.
7. Dunbar Rowland, ed., *Jefferson Davis, Constitutionalist: His Letters, Papers and Speeches*, V, pp. 198–202.
8. Alexander Hunter, *Johnny Reb and Billy Yank* (New York: Neale, 1905), pp. 155, 158.
9. Rowland, *Jefferson Davis*, V, p. 246; June 4, 1862, *OR*, XI, Part 3, p. 355.
10. E. P. Alexander, *Military Memoirs of a Confederate*, pp. 110–11.
11. *OR*, XI, Part 3, pp. 456, 233.
12. *OR*, XI, Part 2, p. 497.
13. *Dispatch* and *Whig* quoted in Douglas Southall Freeman, *R. E. Lee, A Biography*, II, pp. 244–45; Mallory Papers, Southern Historical Collection, University of North Carolina, quoted in Catton, *Terrible Swift Sword*, p. 339; Freeman, *Lee's Lieutenants*, I, p. 656n.
14. J. Cutler Andrews, *The South Reports the Civil War*, p. 181.
15. C. Vann Woodward, ed., *Mary Chesnut's Civil War*, p. 361; Henry Kyd Douglas, *I Rode With Stonewall*, p. 57; Robert Stiles, *Four Years Under Marse Robert* (New York: Neale, 1903), pp. 245–46; Austin C. Stearns, *Three Years With Company K*, ed. Arthur A. Kent, p. 93.
16. Woodward, *Mary Chesnut's Civil War*, p. 410.
17. General Jacob Cox wrote that after the war Pope told him these notorious orders were drafted by Secretary of War Stanton to condemn by implication McClellan's excessive caution and his "overtenderness toward rebel sympathizers and their property." Be that as it may, Pope issued the orders in his own name. Cox, *Military Reminiscences*, I, pp. 222–23.
18. *OR*, Series Four, II, p. 34.
19. Owsley, *King Cotton Diplomacy*, p. 136; Norman A. Graebner, "Northern Diplomacy and European Neutrality," in David Donald, ed., *Why the North Won the Civil War* (Baton Rouge: Louisiana State University Press, 1960), p. 60.
20. Adams, *Britain and the Civil War*, II, p. 29.
21. *OR*, XII, Part 3, p. 919.
22. September 2, J. N. Shealy Collection, Louisiana State University, quoted in Frank E. Vandiver, *Mighty Stonewall*, p. 372; Alexander Hunter, "A High Private's Account of the Battle of Sharpsburg," Part 1, *Southern Historical Society Papers*, X (1882), p. 505; [John Hampden Chamberlayne], "Narrative of a

Rebel Lieutenant," Moore, *Rebellion Record*, V, Documents, p. 404.
23. Lee's dispatches to Davis concerning the Maryland invasion are in *OR*, XIX, Part 2, pp. 590–603 passim.
24. The notes of these postwar conversations, in the William Allan Papers, Southern Historical Collection, University of North Carolina, are printed in Freeman, *Lee's Lieutenants*, II, pp. 716–21.
25. *Battles and Leaders*, II, pp. 605–6.
26. Rowland, *Jefferson Davis*, V, pp. 338–39.
27. D. Augustus Dickert, *History of Kershaw's Brigade*, p. 143.
28. Hunter, "A High Private's Account," Part 1, p. 507.
29. *Charleston Daily Courier*, September 11, quoted in Andrews, *The South Reports*, p. 204; September 3, James W. Shinn, "Recollections of the Late War," Augustus Osborne Papers, Southern Historical Collection, University of North Carolina, copy at Antietam National Battlefield; *Battles and Leaders*, II, p. 621.
30. *OR*, XIX, Part 2, p. 592; Freeman, *Lee's Lieutenants*, II, p. 149.
31. September 30, Joseph Clay Stiles Papers, Huntington Library (Nevins Notes); Clark, *North Carolina Regiments*, II, p. 296; Freeman, *Lee's Lieutenants*, II, p. 152.
32. G. Moxley Sorrel, *Recollections of a Confederate Staff Officer*, pp. 96–97; Douglas, *I Rode With Stonewall*, p. 148.
33. September 6, Shinn, "Recollections of the Late War"; William A. Johnson, "Barbara Frietchie," *The National Tribune Scrapbook*, No. 1, p. 4.
34. *Battles and Leaders*, I, p. 238; Heros Von Borcke, *Memoirs of the Confederate War for Independence*, I, p. 185.
35. *Southern Illustrated News*, September 20, quoted in Richard B. Harwell, ed. *The Confederate Reader*, p. 133.

Chapter 3. Will Send You Trophies
1. September 3 and 7, Strong, *Diary*, pp. 251–52, 253; September 6, McClellan Papers, reel 48; Henry J. Spooner, "The Maryland Campaign with the Fourth Rhode Island," *Personal Narratives of the Events of the War of the Rebellion*, p. 3.
2. J. Cutler Andrews, *The North Reports the Civil War*, pp. 269–70; Nevins, *War Becomes Revolution*, p. 216.
3. September 3, Alfred Davenport, 5th New York, Lydia Minturn Post, *Soldiers' Letters from Camp, Battle-field and Prison*, p. 154; Sedgwick, *Correspondence*, II, p. 80; September 6, William T. Lusk, *War Letters of William Thompson Lusk* (New York: privately printed, 1911), p. 189.
4. September 6, McClellan Papers, reel 48; Stanton Papers and Trumbull Papers, Manuscript Division, Library of Congress, quoted in Wood Gray, *The Hidden Civil War: The Story of the Copperheads* (New York: Viking, 1942), pp. 101–2.
5. September 2?, Basler, *Works of Lincoln*, V, p. 404.
6. McClellan, *Story*, p. 567; Letterbook, McClellan Papers, reel 63.
7. Starr, *Bohemian Brigade*, p. 135; Elizabeth Lindsay Lomax, *Leaves from an Old Washington Diary, 1854–1863*, ed. Lindsay Lomax Wood (New York: Dutton, 1943), p. 213.

8. McClellan told this tale to Henry Kyd Douglas in 1885 (Douglas, *I Rode With Stonewall*, p. 177) and repeated it in *McClellan's Own Story*, p. 551, and in *Battles and Leaders*, II, p. 552.
9. *Report of the Joint Committee*, I, pp. 451, 453; Welles, *Diary*, I, p. 116.
10. *OR*, XIX, Part 2, p. 182; McClellan Papers, reel 31; McClellan, *Story*, p. 567.
11. Pope to Richard Yates, September 21, John Pope Papers, Chicago Historical Society (Long Notes); Hay, *Diaries and Letters*, p. 47.
12. *Report of the Joint Committee*, I, p. 650.
13. Andrews, *The North Reports*, p. 705; September 5, Hay, *Diaries and Letters*, p. 47.
14. *OR*, XIX, Part 2, pp. 197–98; W. A. Croffut and John M. Morris, *The Military and Civil History of Connecticut During the War of 1861–65*, p. 260.
15. September 5, Hay, *Diaries and Letters*, p. 47.
16. September 7, Dwight, *Life and Letters*, p. 287; September 9, Alpheus S. Williams, *From the Cannon's Mouth: The Civil War Letters of General Alpheus S. Williams*, ed. Milo M. Quaife, p. 111; September 2, Charles S. Wainwright, *A Diary of Battle: The Personal Journals of Colonel Charles S. Wainwright, 1861–1865*, ed. Allan Nevins, p. 90.
17. September 5, McClellan, *Story*, p. 567; *Chicago Tribune*, September 9, quoted in Andrews, *The North Reports*, p. 698n.
18. McClellan, *Story*, p. 551; Welles, *Diary*, I, p. 115.
19. Leighton Parks, "What a Boy Saw of the Civil War," *Century*, LXX, no. 2 (1905), p. 258; *Harper's Weekly*, September 27.
20. George W. Shreve, "Reminiscences of the History of the Stuart Horse Artillery, C.S.A.," Virginia State Library (Long Notes); J. R. Boulware diary, September 12, Virginia State Library (Long Notes); Hunter, "A High Private's Account," Part 1, pp. 511–12.
21. September 7, Shinn, "Recollections of the Late War"; Johnson, "Barbara Frietchie," pp. 4–5; *OR*, XIX, Part 2, p. 596; Richard R. Duncan, "Marylanders and the Invasion of 1862," in Hubbell, *Battles Lost and Won*, pp. 188–89.
22. Duncan, "Marylanders and the Invasion of 1862," pp. 183–88; Lewis H. Steiner, *Report of Lewis H. Steiner, M.D., ... Containing a Diary Kept During the Rebel Occupation of Frederick, Md.*, in Harwell, *Union Reader*, pp. 159–62; "Kate" to "Minnie," September 13, *Southern Historical Society Papers*, X (1882), p. 509.
23. Duncan, "Marylanders and the Invasion of 1862," p. 188; *OR*, XIX, Part 2, p. 602; Steiner, *Report*, pp. 164, 166–67.
24. *OR*, XIX, Part 1, p. 1011; William D. Pender, *The General to His Lady: The Civil War Letters of William Dorsey Pender to Fanny Pender*, ed. William W. Hassler, p. 173.
25. Douglas, *I Rode With Stonewall*, p. 150; W. W. Blackford, *War Years with Jeb Stuart*, pp. 141–42; Borcke, *Memoirs*, I, pp. 193–98.
26. McClellan, *Story*, p. 550; D. H. Strother, *A Virginia Yankee in the Civil War: The Diaries of David Hunter Strother*, ed. Cecil D. Eby, Jr., p. 121; *OR*, XIX, Part 2, p. 189.
27. *OR*, XIX, Part 1, p. 523.

28. *Battles and Leaders*, II, pp. 606, 663.
29. *OR*, XIX, Part 2, pp. 603-4.
30. Steiner, *Report*, pp. 168-70; J. R. Boulware dairy, September 10, Virginia State Library (Long Notes); William M. Owen, *In Camp and Battle with the Washington Artillery of New Orleans*, pp. 133-34; Johnson, "Barbara Frietchie," pp. 19-20.
31. George O. Seilheimer, "The Historical Basis of Whittier's 'Barbara Frietchie,'" *Battles and Leaders*, II, pp. 618-19; Steiner, *Report*, p. 167; *Richmond Examiner*, quoted in Harwell, *Union Reader*, p. 158.
32. *Richmond Dispatch*, September 13, quoted in James V. Murfin, *The Gleam of Bayonets: The Battle of Antietam and the Maryland Campaign of 1862*, p. 112; Charles R. Anderson and Aubrey H. Starke, eds., *Centennial Edition of the Works of Sidney Lanier* (Baltimore: Johns Hopkins University Press, 1945), VII, p. 61.
33. *OR*, LI, Part 1, p. 819; Douglas, *I Rode With Stonewall*, pp. 155-58.
34. William Allan Papers, Southern Historical Collection, University of North Carolina, quoted in Freeman, *Lee's Lieutenants*, II, p. 721.
35. *Mobile Daily Advertiser and Register*, September 25, quoted in Andrews, *The South Reports*, p. 207; J. R. Boulware diary, September 11, Virginia State Library (Long Notes).
36. Duncan, "Marylanders and the Invasion of 1862," p. 189; Owen, *In Camp and Battle*, pp. 135-36; *OR*, XIX, Part 2, pp. 604-5.
37. John B. Jones, *A Rebel War Clerk's Diary*, ed. Earl Schenck Miers, p. 97; September 7, 11, and 13, Strong, *Diary*, pp. 253-55; Andrews, *The North Reports*, p. 271.
38. *OR*, XIX, Part 2, p. 602; Duncan, "Marylanders and the Invasion of 1862," pp. 190-91; *OR*, XIX, Part 2, pp. 230-31, 250, 278.
39. *OR*, XIX, Part 2, p. 273; A. K. McClure, "Recollections of Antietam," Antietam National Battlefield. Governor Curtin's telegrams and their replies through September 10 are in *OR*, XIX, Part 2, pp. 203-249 passim.
40. May 6, August 22, and September 12, 1862, Letterbook, McClellan Papers, reel 63.
41. Francis W. Palfrey, *The Antietam and Fredericksburg*, p. 7; *OR*, XIX, Part 2, pp. 264-65.
42. McClellan Papers, reel 29; *OR*, XII, Part 3, p. 710.
43. The various Federal messages concerning intelligence matters in this period are in *OR*, XIX, Part 2, pp. 193-230 passim. Numerous intelligence dispatches from General Pleasonton and others, not included in the *Official Records*, are in the McClellan Papers, reel 31.
44. McClellan to Halleck, September 8 and 9, *OR*, XIX, Part 2, pp. 211, 219; to Mrs. McClellan, Letterbook, McClellan Papers, reel 63; Strother, *A Virginia Yankee*, p. 103.
45. *OR*, XIX, Part 2, pp. 254-55.
46. *OR*, XIX, Part 2, p. 254; Part 1, p. 758; Part 2, pp. 280-81.
47. September 11, Shinn, "Recollections of the Late War"; Steiner, *Report*, p. 167.
48. John M. Gould, *History of the First — Tenth — Twenty-ninth Maine Regiment*, p. 222; Edwin E. Marvin, *The Fifth Regiment, Connecticut Volunteers* (Hartford: Wiley, Waterman & Eaton, 1889), p. 236; Thomas W. Hyde, *Follow-*

ing the Greek Cross or, Memories of the Sixth Army Corps, p. 90.
49. Gould, History of the 10th Maine, p. 223; Robert G. Carter, Four Brothers in Blue, p. 106.
50. September 13, Strong, Diary, p. 255; Samuel Fiske, Mr. Dunn Browne's Experiences in the Army, p. 42; OR, XIX, Part 2, pp. 226–27.
51. McClellan, Story, p. 570; Strother, A Virginia Yankee, p. 105. The dispatches cited for September 11–12 are in OR, XIX, Part 2, pp. 266–74 passim.
52. Battles and Leaders, II, pp. 583–84; Steiner, Report, p. 173.
53. Steiner, Report, p. 173; David L. Thompson Collection, Pound Ridge, N.Y., copy at Antietam National Battlefield; September 18, Edgar M. Newcomb, A. B. Weymouth, ed., A Memorial Sketch of Lieut. Edgar M. Newcomb of the Nineteenth Mass. Vols., p. 89.
54. Hay Papers, Illinois State Historical Library, and Washington Capitol, March 21, 1880, quoted in Nevins, War Becomes Revolution, p. 231n.
55. The Lost Order (as it soon came to be known) and General Williams's covering note to McClellan concerning it are in the McClellan Papers, reel 31; the order is reproduced in McClellan, Story, p. 573. McClellan's reaction to the order is cited in Freeman, Lee's Lieutenants, II, p. 718. Williams's note seems to be the only contemporary reference to the actual finding of Order 191. The discovery was later described by Colonel Silas Colgrove in Battles and Leaders, II, p. 603; by John M. Bloss in "Antietam and the Lost Dispatch," War Talks in Kansas, Kansas Commandery of the Military Order of the Loyal Legion of the United States, I, pp. 84–88; and by Richard Carroll Datzman in "Who Found Lee's Lost Order?" (1973), copy at Antietam National Battlefield. See also the discussion in Appendix I.
56. McClellan Papers, reel 31; OR, XIX, Part 2, pp. 270, 281.

Chapter 4. Fire on the Mountain
1. Report of the Joint Committee, I, p. 439, D. H. Hill stated his case in "The Lost Dispatch" in his magazine The Land We Love, IV (February 1868), pp. 270–84, and in "The Lost Dispatch," Southern Historical Society Papers, XIII (1885), pp. 420–23. Chilton's defense is in his letter to Jefferson Davis, December 8, 1874, Rowland, Jefferson Davis, VII, pp. 412–13. The matter of the Lost Order is examined in detail in Appendix I.
2. John Gibbon, Personal Recollections of the Civil War, p. 73.
3. Battles and Leaders, II, pp. 560, 584.
4. The Army of the Potomac's table of organization for this campaign listed Couch's force separately, as the First Division, Fourth Corps. However, for all practical purposes it was attached to Franklin's Sixth Corps and will be so considered here. After Antietam, on September 26, the attachment was formalized, Couch's command becoming the Third Division of the Sixth Corps.
5. OR, XIX, Part 2, pp. 287, 281; McClellan, Report, p. 199 (the portion of the Report covering the Maryland campaign is also in OR, XIX, Part 1, pp. 36–94).
6. OR, LI, Part 1, p. 829; McClellan, Report, p. 195; Freeman, Lee's Lieutenants, II, p. 171.

Notes to Chapter 4

7. McClellan, *Report*, pp. 191–92, *OR*, LI, Part 1, pp. 826–27 (it is unclear whether Franklin's instructions were contained in one dispatch or two; if the latter, both were marked 6:20 P.M.); August 22, 1862, Letterbook, McClellan Papers, reel 63; McClellan, *Report*, p. 195.
8. *OR*, XIX, Part 2, p. 282.
9. Nathaniel Hawthorne, "Chiefly About War Matters," *Atlantic Monthly*, X (July 1862), quoted in Lindeman, *Conflict of Convictions*, p. 82; Strother, *A Virginia Yankee*, p. 4.
10. R. H. Beatie, Jr., *Road to Manassas* (New York: Cooper Square, 1961), pp. 80, 213; *OR*, XIX, Part 1, pp. 632, 697, 592.
11. The fight for Maryland Heights is described in detail in the voluminous testimony taken by the Harper's Ferry court of inquiry, published in *OR*, XIX, Part 1, pp. 549–803. Particularly useful is the account by Lieutenant S. A. Barras, adjutant of the 126th New York, pp. 672–82. The description of the routed men is on p. 707. Ford's dispatch to Miles, and Miles's response, are on pp. 760 and 712, respectively. Miles's instructions to Captain Russell are on p. 720. The court censured Colonel Miles posthumously, and on its recommendation Colonel Ford and an officer of the 126th New York were cashiered. The testimony suggests that Ford was caught between a stronger enemy and an erratic, fuzzy-minded superior and deserved a better fate.
12. *OR*, XIX, Part 2, p. 606.
13. *OR*, XIX, Part 1, p. 817; Freeman, *Lee's Lieutenants*, II, p. 171.
14. The experience of the civilian visitor to McClellan's headquarters is described in two memoranda of conversations with Lee, February 15, 1868, William Allan Papers, Southern Historical Collection, University of North Carolina, quoted in Freeman, *Lee's Lieutenants*, II, pp. 716–21; and in William Allan, *The Army of Northern Virginia in 1862*, p. 345. See Appendix I for a discussion of the interpretation presented here. The time that Stuart's dispatch reached Lee is examined in Freeman, *Lee's Lieutenants*, II, pp. 722–23, although possibly it did not arrive until about midnight. See Hal Bridges, "A Lee Letter on the 'Lost Dispatch' and the Maryland Campaign of 1862," *Virginia Magazine of History*, LXVI (April 1958), p. 165.
15. *Battles and Leaders*, II, pp. 665–66.
16. *OR*, XIX, Part 2, p. 607; Part 1, p. 951; *Battles and Leaders*, II, p. 560; James E. B. Stuart Papers, Huntington Library, quoted in Hal Bridges, *Lee's Maverick General: Daniel Harvey Hill*, p. 104.
17. *Battles and Leaders*, II, p. 564.
18. McClellan, *Report*, p. 195; *Battles and Leaders*, II, pp. 585–86.
19. Accounts by D. H. Hill and Cox, *Battles and Leaders*, II, pp. 536–66, 586–87; *OR*, XIX, Part 2, p. 464; T. Harry Williams, *Hayes of the Twenty-Third: The Civil War Volunteer Officer*, p. 137.
20. Clark, *North Carolina Regiments*, II, p. 116; *Battles and Leaders*, II, pp. 566, 587; Cox, *Military Reminiscences*, I, p. 286.
21. McClellan, *Story*, p. 571; *OR*, XIX, Part 1, pp. 720–22; McClellan, *Report*, p. 191; Strother, *A Virginia Yankee*, p. 106.
22. Charles F. Walcott, *History of the Twenty-First Regiment Massachusetts Volunteers*, p. 188; *Battles and Leaders*, II, p. 586.

The approximate starting time for Willcox's division is extrapolated from Sturgis's statement that it took his division two and a half hours to reach Cox's position. *OR*, XIX, Part 1, p. 443.
23. *Battles and Leaders*, II, p. 569; Clark, *North Carolina Regiments*, I, p. 166; Oliver C. Bosbyshell, ed., *Pennsylvania at Antietam*, p. 53; *OR*, XIX, Part 1, pp. 428–29, 437; September 26, William Brearly, 17th Michigan, Detroit Public Library, quoted in Bell Irvin Wiley, *The Life of Billy Yank*, p. 84.
24. J. B. Polley, *Hood's Texas Brigade* (New York: Neale, 1910), p. 114; J. B. Hood, *Advance and Retreat*, p. 39; *Battles and Leaders*, II, p. 551.
25. *Battles and Leaders*, II, pp. 558, 573–74; Stearns, *Three Years with Company K*, pp. 119–20.
26. J. Harrison Mills, *Chronicles of the Twenty-first Regiment, New York State Volunteers* (Buffalo: J. M. Layton, 1867), p. 237.
27. *OR*, XIX, Part 1, pp. 1033–36; *Battles and Leaders*, II, pp. 572–73; *OR*, XIX, Part 1, p. 894.
28. McClellan Papers, reel 31; *OR*, XIX, Part 1, p. 262; A. P. Smith, *History of the Seventy-sixth Regiment New York Volunteers* (Cortland, N.Y.: Truair, Smith & Miles, 1867), p. 153; *OR*, XIX, Part 1, pp. 222, 1036.
29. *Charleston Daily Courier*, September 29, quoted in Andrews, *The South Reports*, p. 208; George W. Smalley, *Anglo-American Memories* (New York, 1911), p. 140, quoted in Andrews, *The North Reports*, pp. 273–74.
30. *OR*, XIX, Part 1, p. 442; D. H. Strother, "Personal Recollections of the War by a Virginian, Antietam," *Harper's New Monthly Magazine*, XXXVI (February 1868), p. 278; *Battles and Leaders*, II, p. 558; David L. Thompson Collection, Pound Ridge, N.Y., copy at Antietam National Battlefield.
31. Gibbon, *Personal Recollections*, pp. 38, 93; *Battles and Leaders*, II, p. 580.
32. *OR*, XIX, Part 1, p. 250; March 1, 1863, Rufus Dawes Papers, Rufus D. Beach Collection, Evanston, Ill. (Long Notes); James H. Wilson, *Under the Old Flag*, I, pp. 105–6.
33. *OR*, XIX, Part 1, p. 187; Freeman, *Lee's Lieutenants*, II, p. 183 (Confederate casualties were not separately reported, and this figure is an approximation); *OR*, XIX, Part 2, p. 289.
34. Jennings C. Wise, *The Long Arm of Lee: The History of the Artillery of the Army of Northern Virginia*, pp. 291–92; *OR*, XIX, Part 1, pp. 767, 954, 913, 854.
35. *OR*, XIX, Part 1, pp. 913, 954; William H. Nichols, "The Siege and Capture of Harper's Ferry by the Confederates, September 1862," *Personal Narratives of the Events of the War of the Rebellion*, p. 31; James H. Clark, *The Iron Hearted Regiment: The 115th Regiment N.Y. Vols.* (Albany: J. Munsell, 1865), p. 16.
36. *OR*, XIX, Part 1, p. 854; *Report of the Joint Committee*, I, pp. 625–26; McClellan, *Report*, p. 194; *OR*, XIX, Part 1, p. 384.
37. *Battles and Leaders*, II, p. 595; *OR*, XIX, Part 1, pp. 826–27; George M. Neese, *Three Years in the Confederate Horse Artillery* (New York: Neale, 1911). This Confederate strength figure, like others for the day, can only be estimated. Munford thought the 6th and 12th Virginia had a total

of 300 men. The 10th Georgia engaged 173. The strength of the 16th Virginia and of Munford's two cavalry regiments is unknown. Howell Cobb estimated the Confederate total for the Crampton's Gap fighting (including his own brigade of 1,310 infantry) at 2,200, but gave no breakdown. *OR*, XIX, Part 1, pp. 826, 861, 870.

38. McClellan, *Report*, p. 192; McClellan Papers, reel 32.
39. *OR*, XIX, Part 1, p. 394; Letters of John F. Sale, Virginia State Library (Long Notes).
40. *OR*, XIX, Part 1, pp. 826–27, 854–55; Freeman, *Lee's Lieutenants*, II, p. 191.
41. *Battles and Leaders*, II, p. 594; *OR*, XIX, Part 1, pp. 388, 183, 375.

Chapter 5. We Will Make Our Stand

1. *OR*, LI, Part 2, pp. 618–19; *OR*, XIX, Part 1, p. 951; Part 2, p. 608; Part 1, p. 830.
2. *OR*, XIX, Part 1, p. 818; Part 2, p. 305. Accounts by participants in Colonel Davis's breakout include William M. Luff, "March of the Cavalry from Harper's Ferry, September 14, 1862," *Military Essays and Recollections*, Illinois Commandery of the Military Order of the Loyal Legion of the United States, II; and Henry Norton, *History of the Eighth New York Volunteer Cavalry* (Norwich, N.Y.: Chenango Printing Co., 1889). John W. Mies examined the incident in "Breakout at Harper's Ferry," *Civil War History*, II, no. 2 (June 1956), pp. 13–28.
3. George Baylor, *Bull Run to Bull Run: or, Four Years in the Army of Northern Virginia* (Richmond: Johnson Publishing Co., 1900), p. 73; *OR*, XIX, Part 1, p. 539; Douglas, *I Rode With Stonewall*, p. 162; Blackford, *War Years with Jeb Stuart*, p. 146. Figures on prisoners, captured materiel, and casualties are derived from *OR*, XIX, Part 1, pp. 549, 860–61, 955.
4. *OR*, XIX, Part 1, p. 951; Dickert, *Kershaw's Brigade*, p. 150; Clark, *North Carolina Regiments*, II, p. 30; Borcke, *Memoirs*, I, p. 222; Douglas, *I Rode With Stonewall*, p. 163; *New York Times*, September 18, quoted in Moore, *Rebellion Record*, V, Documents, pp. 447–48.
5. McClellan, *Report*, pp. 193, 194; *OR*, LI, Part 1, p. 836.
6. *OR*, XIX, Part 1, p. 855; Blackford, *War Years with Jeb Stuart*, p. 145; McClellan, *Report*, p. 194; *OR*, XIX, Part 2, p. 296.
7. September 15, Benjamin Hirst, Charles D. Page, *History of the Fourteenth Regiment, Connecticut Vol. Infantry* (Meriden, Conn.: Horton Printing Co., 1906), pp. 27–28; September 21, George W. Whitman, *Civil War Letters of George Washington Whitman*, ed. Jerome M. Loving, p. 67; Hilbert Thompson diary, Manuscript Division, Library of Congress (Long Notes); Walcott, *History of the 21st Massachusetts*, p. 194.
8. McClellan Papers, reel 31; Benjamin F. Cook, *History of the Twelfth Massachusetts Volunteers*, p. 70.
9. *OR*, XIX, Part 2, p. 294; McClellan Papers, reel 31; McClellan, *Story*, p. 612; McClellan, *Report*, p. 199; Welles, *Diary*, I, p. 130.
10. McClellan Papers, reel 32.
11. Bosbyshell, *Pennsylvania at Antietam*, p. 173; Dawes, *Service with the 6th Wisconsin*, p. 86; H.

R. Dunham diary, 19th Massachusetts, Fred Scheller Collection, quoted in John W. Schildt, *Drums Along the Antietam*, p. 190.
12. Cox, *Military Reminiscences*, I, pp. 298–300; McClellan, *Report*, p. 200.
13. *OR*, LI, Part 1, p. 836.
14. Owen, *In Camp and Battle*, p. 138; *Battles and Leaders*, II, p. 611; W. H. Morgan, *Personal Reminiscences of the War of 1861-65* (Lynchburg, Va., 1911), p. 141, quoted in Freeman, *R. E. Lee*, II, p. 378. Lee's strength at Sharpsburg on September 15 is derived from Ezra A. Carman, "History of the Antietam Campaign," Manuscript Division, Library of Congress.
15. *OR*, XIX, Part 2, p. 597.
16. Samuel McD. Tate, 6th North Carolina, Antietam Collection, Dartmouth College Library; Hunter, "A High Private's Account," Part 2, p. 11; Clifton Johnson, *Battleground Adventures: The Stories of Dwellers on the Scenes of Conflict*, p. 119; Ben Milliken, 27th Georgia, Antietam Studies, National Archives.
17. Barlow Papers, Huntington Library (Long Notes); *OR*, XIX, Part 2, p. 307; *OR*, LI, Part 1, p. 839.
18. McClellan, *Report*, p. 201; Owen, *In Camp and Battle*, p. 139. See Note 31 below for the calculation of McClellan's effective strength.
19. *OR*, XIX, Part 2, p. 311.
20. Charles Cormier, 1st Louisiana, Louisiana Historical Association (Long Notes); *OR*, XIX, Part 1, p. 955.
21. Douglas, *I Rode With Stonewall*, p. 166; William H. Andrews, 1st Georgia, "Recollections," Washington County Free Library, Hagerstown, Md., copy at Antietam National Battlefield.
22. *OR*, XIX, Part 2, p. 310; McClellan, *Report*, p. 187; Strong, *Diary*, p. 258; Andrews, *The North Reports*, p. 257.
23. August 22, Basler, *Works of Lincoln*, V, p. 388.
24. *London Times*, September 16, quoted in Owsley, *King Cotton Diplomacy*, pp. 192–93; September 17, Spencer Walpole, *The Life of Lord John Russell* (London, 1889), II, p. 361, quoted in Commager, *The Blue and the Gray*, p. 540.
25. Schildt, *Drums Along the Antietam*, p. 22.
26. *New York Tribune*, September 19; *Battles and Leaders*, II, p. 631.
27. Strother, "Personal Recollections," p. 281. The general's explanations of his plan of battle are in *OR*, XIX, Part 1, p. 30; McClellan, *Report*, pp. 201–2; McClellan, *Story*, pp. 588–90.
28. McClellan, *Story*, p. 586; *Battles and Leaders*, II, pp. 631–32.
29. May 6, 1862, Letterbook, McClellan Papers, reel 63; *OR*, XIX, Part 1, p. 217.
30. The revolutionary tactical effect of the rifled musket is examined in Grady McWhiney and Perry D. Jamieson, *Attack and Die: Civil War Military Tactics and the Southern Heritage* (University: University of Alabama Press, 1982), especially ch. 4.
31. Albert D. Richardson, *The Secret Service, the Field, the Dungeon, and the Escape*, p. 279. Federal roster strengths are from McClellan, *Report*, p. 214, and "Memorandum Showing the Strength of the Army of the Potomac at the Battle of Antietam," McClellan Papers, reel 32. The investigation of fighting-line strength in Car-

man, "History of the Antietam Campaign," Library of Congress, reveals a wide disparity among the various Federal corps. The First Corps put only 64 percent of its roster strength on the firing line at Antietam, while the figure for the Ninth Corps was 91 percent. Franklin described the effective strength of his Sixth Corps in *Battles and Leaders,* II, pp. 595–96. The divisions of Morell, Sykes, and Couch are estimated at 80 percent of their roster totals. The figure for Humphreys's Fifth Corps division is in his September 17 dispatch, McClellan Papers, reel 32.

32. *Report of the Joint Committee,* I, pp. 581–82 (Hooker), 369 (Sumner), 441 (McClellan); Strother, *A Virginia Yankee,* p. 112; September 28, Alexander S. Webb Papers, Historical Manuscripts Division, Yale University Library (Long Notes); George W. Smalley, "Antietam," *New York Tribune,* September 19 (Smalley's account of the battle is printed in Moore, *Rebellion Record,* V, Documents, pp. 466–72).

33. McClellan Papers, reel 32.

34. Freeman, *Lee's Lieutenants,* II, p. 149. In his official report (*OR,* XIX, Part 1, p. 151), Lee gave his strength at Antietam as "less than 40,000 men." Shortly after the battle he told a military visitor, Colonel Garnet Wolseley of the British army, that at no time on September 17 did he have more than 35,000 men engaged; presumably he did not include Stuart's cavalry in that figure. Wolseley, "A Month's Visit to the Confederate Headquarters," *Blackwood's Magazine,* XCIII (January–June 1863), p. 18. The fullest investigation of the matter, in Carman, "History of the Antietam Campaign," gives Lee a total effective strength of just over 38,000, including A. P. Hill's five brigades that reached Sharpsburg on September 17.

35. *New York Tribune,* September 19; Starr, *Bohemian Brigade,* p. 140.

36. *OR,* XIX, Part 1, p. 475; J. Porter Howard, 111th Pennsylvania, Antietam Collection, Dartmouth.

37. *Battles and Leaders,* II, p. 660; Robert M. Mackall, Pelham's Battery, Antietam Studies, National Archives; September 22, Williams, *From the Cannon's Mouth,* p. 125.

38. September 18, George I. Fenno, 107th New York, Post, *Soldiers' Letters,* p. 161; Oliver Wendell Holmes, Jr., *Touched With Fire: Civil War Letters and Diary of Oliver Wendell Holmes, Jr.,* ed. Mark DeWolfe Howe (Cambridge, Mass.: Harvard University Press, 1946), pp. 54–55.

Chapter 6. To the Dunker Church

1. The most exhaustive study of the Battle of Antietam is Ezra A. Carman, "History of the Antietam Campaign," Library of Congress. The *Atlas of the Battlefield of Antietam* contains fourteen highly detailed situation maps prepared by the Antietam Battlefield Board. Figures given for troops engaged are derived primarily from Carman's researches.

2. William L. DeRosset, 3rd North Carolina, Antietam Collection, Dartmouth; Swinton, *Army of the Potomac,* p. 211.

3. Blackford, *War Years with Jeb Stuart,* pp. 150–51.

4. *OR,* XIX, Part 1, p. 976.

5. John L. Delancey, 107th Pennsylvania, Antietam Collection, Dartmouth. In his report (*OR,*

XIX, Part 1, p. 218) General Hooker dramatized these opening moments of the battle, writing that he discovered "a heavy force of the enemy" standing at arms in the Cornfield by the flashes of sunlight reflecting from their bayonets, and ordered half a dozen batteries to rake the field with canister. "Every stalk of corn in the northern and greater part of the field was cut as closely as could have been done with a knife," he wrote, "and the slain lay in rows...." No doubt the general confused this incident with a later phase of the battle, for just then there were no Confederates in the Cornfield except the few skirmishers at its southern edge.

6. Henry J. Shaefer, 107th Pennsylvania, Antietam Battlefield Board Papers, National Archives.

7. John L. Delancey, 107th Pennsylvania, Antietam Collection, Dartmouth. Casualty figures for September 17 are derived from the various reports and tables in *OR*, XIX, Part 1; William F. Fox, *Regimental Losses in the American Civil War, 1861–1865*; Thomas L. Livermore, *Numbers and Losses in the Civil War in America, 1861–1865*; and Carman, "History of the Antietam Campaign."

8. John D. Vautier, 88th Pennsylvania, W. H. Holstead, 26th New York, Antietam Collection, Dartmouth.

9. William Todd, ed., *History of the Ninth Regiment, New York State Militia* (83rd New York Volunteers), p. 198; September 24, Prince A. Dunton, 13th Massachusetts, Antietam National Battlefield.

10. Richard Taylor, *Destruction and Reconstruction* (New York: D. Appleton, 1879), p. 49

11. Louise Hall Tharp, 'The Song That Wrote Itself,' *American Heritage*, VIII, no 1 (December 1956), pp. 10–13, 100–101; Cook, *History of the 12th Massachusetts*, p. 73.

12. George Kimball, Lewis Reed, 12th Massachusetts, Antietam Collection, Dartmouth; Stearns, *Three Years with Company K*, p. 28.

13. A. J. Sellers, 90th Pennsylvania, Antietam Studies, National Archives. Possibly the 12th Massachusetts casualty rate was even higher. George Kimball, in *Annual Circular of the Secretary of the 12th Massachusetts Association* (Boston, 1897), states that only nine of the regiment's ten companies were in action and that losses were 222 of 262, or 85 percent.

14. Wise, *Long Arm of Lee*, p. 289; *OR*, XIX, Part 1, pp. 194, 846; Alexander, *Military Memoirs*, p. 247.

15. *New York Tribune*, September 19; September 12, Letterbook, McClellan Papers, reel 63; Cook, *History of the 12th Massachusetts*, p. 72.

16. Dawes, *Service with the 6th Wisconsin*, p. 88; September 18, Lyman C. Holford diary, Manuscript Division, Library of Congress (Long Notes); James M. Garnett, Winder's brigade, Antietam Studies, National Archives.

17. Dawes, *Service with the 6th Wisconsin*, pp. 90–91; *Charleston Daily Courier*, September 29, quoted in Moore, *Rebellion Record*, V, Documents, p. 472.

18. R. P. Jennings, 23rd Virginia, Antietam Studies, National Ar-

Notes to Chapter 6

chives; William H. Humphrey, 2nd U.S. Sharpshooters, Antietam Collection, Dartmouth.
19. Oliver T. Reilly, *The Battlefield of Antietam*, p. 26; Strother, "Personal Recollections," p. 282; William Child, *A History of the Fifth Regiment New Hampshire Volunteers*, p. 120. In reporting McClellan's remark, Colonel Edward Cross of the 5th New Hampshire timed it at about 8 A.M., but the context of events suggests that the message was received an hour earlier.
20. *OR*, XIX, Part 1, pp. 909, 981; William W. Hassler, *A. P. Hill: Lee's Forgotten General*, p. 104.
21. Freeman, *Lee's Lieutenants*, II, p. 206; Woodward, *Mary Chesnut's Civil War*, p. 441; William E. Barry, 4th Texas, Antietam Collection, Dartmouth.
22. Dawes, *Service with the 6th Wisconsin*, p. 91; April 26, 1863, Rufus Dawes Papers, Rufus D. Beach Collection, Evanston, Ill. (Long Notes); Susan P. Lee, *Memoirs of W. N. Pendleton* (Philadelphia, 1893), p. 216, quoted in Freeman, *Lee's Lieutenants*, II, p. 208; Hood, *Advance and Retreat*, p. 44.
23. James Thompson, Pennsylvania Light Artillery, Antietam Collection, Dartmouth; Samuel W. Moore diary, 90th Pennsylvania, Antietam National Battlefield; Stearns, *Three Years with Company K*, p. 129; William M. Robbins, 4th Alabama, Antietam Collection, Dartmouth.
24. *New York Tribune*, September 19; Frank Holsinger, "How Does One Feel Under Fire?" *War Talks in Kansas*, Kansas Commandery of the Military Order of the Loyal Legion of the United States (Kansas City, Mo., 1906), I,

p. 301; *OR*, XIX, Part 1, pp. 229, 931.
25. Gibbon, *Personal Recollections*, pp. 83–84; William H. Humphrey, 2nd U.S. Sharpshooters, Antietam Collection, Dartmouth.
26. James S. Johnston, "A Reminiscence of Sharpsburg," *Southern Historical Society Papers*, VIII (1880), p. 528; *Report of the Joint Committee*, I, p. 368; Henry A. V. Post, 2nd U.S. Sharpshooters, Antietam Collection, Dartmouth.
27. J. Porter Howard, 111th Pennsylvania, Antietam Collection, Dartmouth; Dwight, *Life and Letters*, p. 292; Miles C. Huyette, "Reminiscences of a Private," *The National Tribune Scrapbook*, No. 1, p. 86; unidentified, 102nd New York, Antietam Collection, Dartmouth.
28. September 22, Williams, *From the Cannon's Mouth*, p. 126; John M. Gould, *Joseph K. F. Mansfield: A Narrative of Events Connected with His Mortal Wounding at Antietam*, p. 11.
29. Gould, *Mansfield*, pp. 15–17; James Fowler, E. J. Libby, 10th Maine, Antietam Collection, Dartmouth.
30. Bosbyshell, *Pennsylvania at Antietam*, pp. 149–150; Hugh A. Jameson, 28th New York, Antietam Collection, Dartmouth; *OR*, XIX, Part 1, p. 493.
31. September 22, Williams, *From the Cannon's Mouth*, p. 126; Calvin Leach diary, Southern Historical Collection, University of North Carolina, quoted in Bridges, *Daniel Harvey Hill*, p. 126; William L. DeRosset, 3rd North Carolina, Antietam Collection, Dartmouth; Datzman, "Who Found Lee's Lost Order?"

32. B. H. Witcher, 6th Georgia, Antietam Collection, Dartmouth; *New York Tribune*, September 19 (Smalley mistakenly attributed this stand to Hartsuff's brigade of the First Corps); September 22, Williams, *From the Cannon's Mouth*, p. 127; William L. DeRosset, 3rd North Carolina, Antietam Collection, Dartmouth; Edwin Weller, *A Civil War Courtship: The Letters of Edwin Weller from Antietam to Atlanta*, ed. William Walton (Garden City, N.Y.: Doubleday, 1980), p. 20.

33. *OR*, XIX, Part 1, p. 1023; Francis W. Palfrey, "The Battle of Antietam," *Campaigns in Virginia, Maryland and Pennsylvania, 1862–1863*, p. 16; J. M. Smither, 5th Texas, Antietam Collection, Dartmouth.

34. Eugene Powell, 66th Ohio, B. H. Witcher, 6th Georgia, Antietam Collection, Dartmouth.

35. Unidentified, 102nd New York, Antietam Collection, Dartmouth.

36. *OR*, XIX, Part 1, p. 218; September 19, Frank A. Haskell Papers, State Historical Society of Wisconsin (Long Notes); Blackford, *War Years with Jeb Stuart*, p. 150.

37. Freeman, *Lee's Lieutenants*, II, p. 209; Jed Hotchkiss, "Virginia," *Confederate Military History* (Atlanta: Confederate Publishing Co., 1899), III, p. 352.

38. *Report of the Joint Committee*, I, p. 582; McClellan Papers, reel 32.

Chapter 7. A Savage Continual Thunder

1. David Lavender, *Bent's Fort* (Garden City, N.Y.: Doubleday, 1954), pp. 319–20; *Report of the Joint Committee*, I, p. 366.

2. John C. Ropes, *The Story of the Civil War*, II: *The Campaigns of 1862*, p. 359; P. A. Hanaford, *The Young Captain: A Memorial to Capt. Richard C. Derby, Fifteenth Reg. Mass. Volunteers, Who Fell at Antietam* (Boston, 1865), p. 168.

3. *Report of the Joint Committee*, I, p. 368; George F. Noyes, *The Bivouac and the Battlefield, or Campaign Sketches in Virginia and Maryland*, p. 196.

4. Wilson, *Under the Old Flag*, I, pp. 105–6; September 22, Williams, *From the Cannon's Mouth*, p. 127; J. Albert Monroe, "Battery D, First Rhode Island Light Artillery, at the Battle of Antietam," *Personal Narratives of the Events of the War of the Rebellion*, pp. 25–27.

5. Lafayette McLaws, Antietam Studies, National Archives.

6. *Report of the Joint Committee*, I, pp. 581, 368; September 24, Williams, *From the Cannon's Mouth*, p. 135.

7. *OR*, LI, Part 1, p. 842; Palfrey, *Antietam and Fredericksburg*, p. 84.

8. Abner Doubleday to Samuel P. Bates, October 19, 1875, Bates Collection, Pennsylvania Historical and Museum Commission (Long Notes).

9. Strother, *A Virginia Yankee*, p. 124; Palfrey, *Antietam and Fredericksburg*, p. 84; Carman, "History of the Antietam Campaign," ch. 17, p. 26.

10. *OR*, XIX, Part 1, p. 492.

11. Thomas Francis Galwey, *The Valiant Hours*, ed. W. S. Nye, p. 173; *OR*, XIX, Part 1, p. 492; William H. Andrews, Washington County Free Library, Hagerstown, Md., copy at Antietam National Battlefield.

12. Huyette, "Reminiscences of a Private," p. 87; Catherine S.

Notes to Chapter 7

Crary, ed., *Dear Belle: Letters from a Cadet and Officer to His Sweetheart, 1858–1865*, p. 152.
13. George A. Bruce, *The Twentieth Regiment of Massachusetts Volunteer Infantry*, p. 169; Joseph R. C. Ward, *History of the One Hundred and Sixth Regiment Pennsylvania Volunteers, 1861–1865* (Philadelphia: F. McManus, 1906), p. 104.
14. October 27, Jonathan Peacock, 59th New York, M. M. McClure Collection, Shoreville, Ind., copy at Antietam National Battlefield.
15. Palfrey, *Antietam and Fredericksburg*, p. 87; September 22, Williams, *From the Cannon's Mouth*, p. 128; Carman, "History of the Antietam Campaign," ch. 17, p. 45.
16. Catherine Drinker Bowen, *Yankee From Olympus: Justice Holmes and His Family* (Boston: Little, Brown, 1944), p. 168; Bruce, *The 20th Massachusetts*, p. 169; Weymouth, *Memorial Sketch of Lt. Newcomb*, p. 90.
17. March 1, 1863, Rufus Dawes Papers, Rufus D. Beach Collection, Evanston, Ill. (Long Notes); Rufus Dawes, 6th Wisconsin, Antietam Studies, National Archives.
18. Norwood P. Hollowell, "Remarks Written for My Children," quoted in Schildt, *Drums Along the Antietam*, p. 181.
19. McClellan Papers, reel 32; *OR*, XIX, Part 1, p. 134. Casualties in the Confederate brigades of Early, Barksdale, and Semmes in this action totaled 804. Losses in the commands of Grigsby, Kershaw, and G. T. Anderson are unknown, but their engagement was brief and their losses comparatively light.
20. Carman, "History of the Antietam Campaign," ch. 17, pp. 67–68; Clark, *North Carolina Regiments*, II, p. 606; V, p. 76.
21. Charles R. Mudge, *In Memoriam: Charles Redington Mudge, Lieut.-Col. Second Mass. Infantry* (Cambridge, Mass., 1863), p. 20; *OR*, XIX, Part 1, p. 500; Dwight, *Life and Letters*, p. 293.
22. *Charleston Daily Courier*, September 29, quoted in Moore, *Rebellion Record*, V, Documents, p. 473; William H. Andrews, 1st Georgia, Washington County Free Library, Hagerstown, Md., copy at Antietam National Battlefield; Johnathan P. Stowe diary, 15th Massachusetts, Antietam National Battlefield.
23. *OR*, XIX, Part 1, pp. 915, 506; Charles E. Smith, 102nd New York, Antietam Collection, Dartmouth.
24. *OR*, XIX, Part 1, pp. 857–58, 1030; *Battles and Leaders*, II, pp. 676–77; A. L. Long, *Memoirs of Robert E. Lee* (New York: J. M. Stoddart, 1886), p. 222.
25. Strother, "Personal Recollections," p. 282.
26. *OR*, LI, Part 1, p. 844.
27. John B. Gordon, *Reminiscences of the Civil War*, p. 84; *Battles and Leaders*, II, p. 671.
28. *OR*, XIX, Part 1, pp. 871, 324, 1023; Gordon, *Reminiscences*, p. 85.
29. 5th Maryland, Antietam Studies, National Archives; Clark, *North Carolina Regiments*, II, p. 500; Gordon, *Reminiscences*, p. 87.
30. Fiske, *Mr. Dunn Browne's Experiences*, pp. 47–49; Bosbyshell, *Pennsylvania at Antietam*, pp. 163–64.
31. Galwey, *Valiant Hours*, pp. 40, 42; Frederick L. Hitchcock, *War From the Inside*, pp. 56–57; Bosbyshell, *Pennsylvania at Antietam*, p. 191.
32. Bradley T. Johnson, "The First

Maryland Campaign," *Southern Historical Society Papers*, XII (1884), p. 531; Richardson, *The Secret Service*, p. 284; Charles F. Johnson diary, Minnesota Historical Society, quoted in Wiley, *Billy Yank*, p. 78.

33. *OR*, XIX, Part 1, p. 1026; Alex C. Chisholm, 9th Alabama, Antietam Collection, Dartmouth; Gordon, *Reminiscences*, p. 90.
34. Thomas L. Livermore, *Days and Events, 1860–1865*, p. 133.
35. *OR*, XIX, Part 1, pp. 294–95; D. P. Conyngham, *The Irish Brigade and its Campaigns* (Boston: P. Donahoe, 1869), pp. 305–6.
36. Strother, *A Virginia Yankee*, p. 113; Hitchcock, *War from the Inside*, pp. 63–64; Andrews, *The North Reports*, p. 284; Billings, *Hardtack and Coffee*, p. 144. In the margin of his personal copy of *McClellan's Own Story* (Oberlin College Library), where Meagher's role in the battle is described, General Cox wrote, "Commonly reported *drunk*."
37. *OR*, XIX, Part 1, p. 1037; R. T. Bennett, 14th North Carolina, Antietam Studies, National Archives.
38. Livermore, *Days and Events*, p. 137. In his account Livermore diplomatically deleted Caldwell's name, but the context of events makes it clear that general was the subject of Richardson's ire. When Caldwell as senior officer took over the division after Richardson's wounding, McClellan was quick to replace him, reaching into another corps for General Hancock.
39. William H. Osborne, *The History of the Twenty-Ninth Regiment of Massachusetts Volunteer Infantry* (Boston: A. J. Wright, 1877), p. 187; September 17, Shinn, "Recollections of the Late War"; *OR*, XIX, Part 1, p. 1048; *Savannah Republican*, quoted in Moore, *Rebellion Record*, VI, Incidents, p. 19; Alex C. Chisholm, 9th Alabama, Antietam Collection, Dartmouth.

40. *OR*, XIX, Part 1, pp. 1037–38.
41. *Battles and Leaders*, II, p. 684; Strother, *A Virginia Yankee*, p. 110.
42. Livermore, *Days and Events*, p. 140; *OR*, XIX, Part 1, p. 335.
43. Cooke Family Papers, Virginia State Historical Society, quoted in Freeman, *Lee's Lieutenants*, II, p. 145.
44. Carman, "History of the Antietam Campaign," ch. 19, p. 10; Clark, *North Carolina Regiments*, II, p. 436.
45. September 22, Williams, *From the Cannon's Mouth*, p. 129.
46. Clark, *North Carolina Regiments*, II, p. 436; Sorrel, *Recollections of a Confederate Staff Officer*, p. 114.
47. Hyde, *Following the Greek Cross*, p. 97.
48. Sorrel, *Recollections of a Confederate Staff Officer*, pp. 112–13; Alex C. Chisholm, 9th Alabama, Antietam Collection, Dartmouth.
49. Child, *History of the 5th New Hampshire*, p. 123; Livermore, *Days and Events*, pp. 140–41.
50. *OR*, XIX, Part 1, p. 1024; *Battles and Leaders*, II, p. 669; Clark, *North Carolina Regiments*, II, p. 436.
51. *OR*, XIX, Part 1, pp. 343–44. In his report (*OR*, XIX, Part 1, p. 206) Brigadier Henry J. Hunt, McClellan's chief of artillery, said that the request for a rifled battery came not from Richardson but from his successor, Hancock, and that he could dispatch only Graham's battery of

smoothbores. From Graham's report cited here, however, it seems clear that Richardson was still on the field when that battery arrived.

Chapter 8. The Spires of Sharpsburg
1. Eugene Carter, 8th U.S. Infantry, Carter, *Four Brothers in Blue*, p. 107; September 17, Shinn, "Recollections of the Late War."
2. McClellan Papers, reel 32. The dispatch as sent is in *OR*, XIX, Part 2, p. 312.
3. W. F. Smith Papers, Walter Wilgus Collection, Arlington, Va. (Long Notes); Benjamin F. Clarkson, 49th Pennsylvania, *Hagerstown* (Md.) *Weekly Globe*, June 1, 1922, Antietam National Battlefield.
4. As no report by General Couch is on record, his movements are extrapolated from the reports of generals Franklin and Smith (*OR*, XIX, Part 1, pp. 376, 402) and from Ezra Carman's researches. It seems clear that had Couch been so ordered — or had he exercised the same initiative that A. P. Hill displayed — he could have reached the field in support of Burnside by midafternoon after a total march no greater than the distance covered by Hill's Light Division. General Cox made this point in *Battles and Leaders*, II, pp. 657–58.
5. *OR*, LI, Part 1, p. 843.
6. Croffut and Morris, *Military History of Connecticut*, p. 295; *History of the Thirty-Fifth Regiment Massachusetts Volunteers, 1862–1865* (Boston: Mills, Knight & Co., 1884), p. 44; Walcott, *History of the 21st Massachusetts*, p. 198.
7. Palfrey, *Antietam and Fredericksburg*, p. 117; *OR*, XIX, Part 2, pp. 308, 314; Cox, *Military Reminiscences*, I, pp. 380–81; Carman, "History of the Antietam Campaign," ch. 21, p. 11.
8. *Battles and Leaders*, II, p. 650. Some Confederate accounts maintained that Antietam Creek was in fact quite shallow and easily waded. In his report (*OR*, LI, Part 1, p. 162) Colonel Benning described it as "not more than knee-deep" in most places. Kyd Douglas, who grew up in nearby Shepherdstown, wrote, "Go look at it and tell me if you don't think Burnside and his corps might have executed a hop, skip and jump and landed on the other side" (*I Rode With Stonewall*, p. 172). This may have been true in some places and in some seasons, but numerous Federals of the Ninth Corps who actually waded the creek that day testified that even at the fords the water came up to their waists or chests.
9. *Battles and Leaders*, II, p. 648; *OR*, LI, Part 1, p. 844. The controversy regarding this and subsequent dispatches to Burnside is examined in Appendix II.
10. *OR*, XIX, Part 1, p. 31; September 28, Webb Papers, Historical Manuscripts Division, Yale University Library (Long Notes).
11. Croffut and Morris, *Military History of Connecticut*, pp. 265–66.
12. Carman, "History of the Antietam Campaign," ch. 21, pp. 25–26.
13. James I. Robertson, Jr., "A Federal Surgeon at Sharpsburg," *Civil War History*, VI, no. 2 (June 1960), p. 141.
14. McClellan Papers, reel 32; Sackett to McClellan, February 20, 1876, McClellan, *Story*, p. 609.
15. September 21, Whitman, *Civil*

War Letters, p. 67; Thomas H. Parker, *History of the 51st Regiment of Pennsylvania Volunteers*, pp. 232–35; *OR*, LI, Part 1, p. 163.
16. Strother, "Personal Recollections," p. 284; McClellan, *Report*, p. 209; William F. Biddle, *United Service Magazine* (May 1894).
17. William A. Frassanito, *Antietam: The Photographic Legacy of America's Bloodiest Day*, p. 195; Johnson, *Battlefield Adventures*, p. 115; Theodore Gerrish, *Army Life: A Private's Reminiscences of the Civil War* (Portland, Me.: Hoyt, Fogg & Donham, 1882), p. 31; Strother, *A Virginia Yankee*, p. 111; *OR*, XIX, Part 1, p. 344; Schildt, *Drums Along the Antietam*, pp. 130–31.
18. Clark, *North Carolina Regiments*, II, p. 437; Alex C. Chisholm, 9th Alabama, James Fowler, 10th Maine, Antietam Collection, Dartmouth.
19. Strother, *A Virginia Yankee*, p. 111; Wainwright, *A Diary of Battle*, p. 103; McClellan, *Report*, p. 207; *OR*, XIX, Part 1, p. 339.
20. McClellan to Pleasonton, 11:45 A.M., Alfred Pleasonton Papers, private collection (Long Notes); Pleasonton to Randolph Marcy, 2:30 P.M., McClellan Papers, reel 32; Marcy to Pleasonton 3:30 P.M., *OR*, LI, Part 1, p. 845.
21. Charles Francis Adams, Jr., *Autobiography* (Boston: Houghton Mifflin, 1916), pp. 152–53.
22. *Battles and Leaders*, II, p. 597; Francis A. Walker, *History of the Second Army Corps*, p. 117; Wilson, *Under the Old Flag*, I, pp. 113–14; McClellan, *Report*, p. 208; *Report of the Joint Committee*, I, p. 627. Accounts differ as to the time of McClellan's visit to Sumner's headquarters. The best evidence suggests that he left the Pry house sometime after two o'clock and had returned by about four.
23. George W. Smalley, "Chapters in Journalism," *Harper's New Monthly Magazine*, LXXXIX (August 1894), pp. 428–29; Wilson, *Under the Old Flag*, I, p. 116. In recording this conversation, Smalley did not identify Wilson by name. Wilson revealed his role in his memoirs written eighteen years later.
24. G. F. R. Henderson, *Stonewall Jackson and the American Civil War*, p. 536; *Battles and Leaders*, II, p. 679; R. E. Lee, Jr., *Recollections and Letters of General Robert E. Lee* (New York: Doubleday, Page, 1904), p. 78; Clark, *North Carolina Regiments*, II, pp. 604, 607; IV, p. 78.
25. Strother, *A Virginia Yankee*, p. 111.
26. McClellan, *Story*, pp. 86–87; Thomas M. Anderson, 12th U.S. Infantry, Antietam Battlefield Board Papers, National Archives.
27. September 26, Detroit Public Library, quoted in Wiley, *Billy Yank*, pp. 78, 84.
28. William H. Palmer, 1st Virginia, Hugh R. Garden, Garden's Battery, Antietam Studies, National Archives; Johnson, *Battlefield Adventures*, p. 122.
29. Matthew J. Graham, 9th New York, Antietam Studies, National Archives; Matthew J. Graham, *The Ninth Regiment New York Volunteers (Hawkins' Zouaves)*, pp. 248–49.
30. *Battles and Leaders*, II, pp. 661–62; Graham, *9th New York*, p. 295; D. G. McIntosh, McIntosh's Battery, Antietam Studies, National Archives.
31. Hunter, "A High Private's Account," Part 2, p. 18; John E. Dooley, *John Dooley, Confeder-*

Notes to Chapter 8

ate Soldier: His War Journal, ed. Joseph T. Durkin, p. 48.
32. Johnson, Battlefield Adventures, pp. 111, 120–21; J. R. Boulware diary, September 17, Virginia State Library (Long Notes); Strother, A Virginia Yankee, p. 114.
33. Clark, North Carolina Regiments, I, p. 575.
34. OR, XIX, Part 1, p. 138.
35. OR, XIX, Part 1, p. 453; J. L. Napier, McIntosh's Battery, Alexander C. Haskell, Gregg's brigade, Antietam Studies, National Archives; Croffut and Morris, Military History of Connecticut, p. 272.
36. Croffut and Morris, Military History of Connecticut, pp. 226, 271; Louise Haskell Daly, Alexander Cheves Haskell (Norwood, Mass., 1934), p. 82, quoted in Freeman, Lee's Lieutenants, II, pp. 223–24; OR, XIX, Part 1, pp. 456–57; J. F. J. Caldwell, The History of [Gregg's] Brigade of South Carolinians, p. 46.
37. OR, XIX, Part 1, pp. 892, 468; Freeman, Lee's Lieutenants, II, p. 218.
38. OR, XIX, Part 1, p. 436; Bosbyshell, Pennsylvania at Antietam, p. 227; September 21, Whitman, Civil War Letters, p. 68.
39. OR, XIX, Part 1, p. 1010.
40. New York Tribune, September 19. Smalley's account of these conversations is supported by a 4:30 P.M. message to Pleasonton from Porter's aide, Major C. J. Kirkland: "Gen. Porter has sent off as much of his infantry as he can spare.... The infantry he has is the *only* infantry the General in Chief has now to rely on in reserve." Pleasonton Papers, private collection (Long Notes).
41. OR, XIX, Part 1, p. 339.
42. OR, XIX, Part 1, p. 412; Hyde, Following the Greek Cross, pp. 100–104.
43. Boston Journal, September 20, quoted in Emmet Crozier, Yankee Reporters, 1861–65 (New York: Oxford, 1956), p. 269; September 20, Crary, Dear Belle, pp. 155–56; Douglas, I Rode With Stonewall, p. 174.
44. "Memoirs of William Gates LaDuc," p. 2, Huntington Library (Long Notes).
45. Federal casualties at Antietam are tabulated in OR, XIX, Part 1, pp. 189–200. Confederate casualty returns are incomplete — a partial summary for the Maryland campaign is in OR, XIX, Part 1, pp. 810–13 — and the estimate here, as well as the numbers engaged on both sides, is derived primarily from Carman, "History of the Antietam Campaign," especially ch. 23. Carman considered McClellan's claim (Report, p. 212) that "about 2,-700" Confederate dead were buried on the field of battle as too high. Evidence of the probable undercount in the final death toll is the notation on an undated tabulation of captured Confederate wounded (McClellan Papers, reel 32) that "160 died in hospital."
46. Battles and Leaders, II, p. 671; Owen, In Camp and Battle, p. 157. In R. E. Lee, II, p. 404n, Douglas Southall Freeman rejected Stephen D. Lee's more dramatic account of this meeting as recorded in Confederate Military History (Atlanta: Confederate Publishing Co., 1899), III, pp. 356–57. Colonel Lee termed it a council of war and reported that Longstreet, D. H. Hill, and Jackson all recommended an immediate withdrawal. Seeing this account in manuscript in 1896, Ezra Carman queried Longstreet,

who replied on February 11, 1897, "Not one word was mentioned referring to withdrawal from our position.... If there was a council of war or anything that could be so called I failed to hear of it...." *Battles and Leaders* "Extra Illustrated," VIII, Huntington Library (Long Notes).
47. Johnson, *Battlefield Adventures*, p. 111.

Chapter 9. To Nobly Save or Meanly Lose

1. *New York Tribune*, September 19; Strother, "Personal Recollections," p. 285.
2. *OR*, XIX, Part 2, p. 322; McClellan Papers, reel 32; McClellan, *Story*, p. 612; *OR*, XIX, Part 1, p. 32; *New York Tribune*, September 29.
3. McClellan, *Report*, p. 211; *OR*, XIX, Part 2, p. 349. In testimony before a congressional committee in March 1863, McClellan claimed this First Corps field return showed only "about 3,500 men." *Report of the Joint Committee*, I, p. 441.
4. *Report of the Joint Committee*, I, p. 642; Sackett to McClellan, March 9, 1876, McClellan, *Story*, p. 610; marginal comment in General Cox's copy of *McClellan's Own Story*, Oberlin College Library.
5. McClellan, *Report*, p. 212; *OR*, LI, Part 1, p. 844. Estimates for effective strength in these Fifth and Sixth corps divisions are calculated on the basis of 20 percent noncombatants.
6. Humphreys to McClellan, 7:15 P.M., September 17, McClellan Papers, reel 32; *OR*, XIX, Part 1, p. 32. Humphreys's adventures with his new division are described in *OR*, XIX, Part 1, pp. 368–74, and in reports by his brigade commanders, *OR*, LI, Part 1, p. 157.
7. McClellan Papers, reel 32; McClellan, *Report*, p. 211.
8. *OR*, XIX, Part 1, p. 151.
9. Alex C. Chisholm, 9th Alabama, Antietam Collection, Dartmouth; September 18, Shinn, "Recollections of the Late War"; Calvin Leach diary, Southern Historical Collection, University of North Carolina, quoted in Bridges, *Daniel Harvey Hill*, p. 126; September 20, Tully McCrae, Crary, *Dear Belle*, p. 156.
10. Strother, *A Virginia Yankee*, p. 113.
11. George I. Fenno, 107th New York, Post, *Soldiers' Letters*, pp. 160–61; H. F. Young, 7th Wisconsin, State Historical Society of Wisconsin, copy at Antietam National Battlefield; A. M. Erskine, Texas Brigade, Erskine Papers, University of Texas, quoted in Bell Irvin Wiley, *The Life of Johnny Reb*, p. 213.
12. *Mobile Daily Advertiser and Register*, October 2, quoted in Andrews, *The South Reports*, p. 212; *Battles and Leaders*, II, p. 691; Schildt, *Drums Along the Antietam*, pp. 150, 195; Duncan, "Marylanders and the Invasion of 1862," p. 195; Strong, *Diary*, p. 261.
13. Palfrey, *Antietam and Fredericksburg*, p. 119; *Mobile Daily Advertiser and Register*, October 2, quoted in Andrews, *The South Reports*, p. 212; Lafayette McLaws to Lida Perry, March 28, 1893, Simon Gratz Autograph Collection, Historical Society of Pennsylvania (Long Notes); *OR*, LI, Part 1, pp. 848, 849; McClellan Papers, reel 32.

Notes to Chapter 9

14. *OR*, XIX, Part 1, pp. 204, 348.
15. Jones to unknown, September 20, *Battles and Leaders* "Extra Illustrated," VIII, Huntington Library (Long Notes); *OR*, XIX, Part 2, p. 627; September 22, Pender, *The General to His Lady*, p. 175; *OR*, XIX, Part 2, p. 627.
16. *OR*, XIX, Part 2, p. 330; September 20 and 22, McClellan, *Story*, pp. 613–15; S. H. Gay to Adams Hill, September 25, Gay Papers, Columbia University Library, quoted in Andrews, *The North Reports*, p. 316.
17. Allan, *Army of Northern Virginia*, p. 441; Freeman, *R. E. Lee*, II, p. 409.
18. Palfrey, *Antietam and Fredericksburg*, p. 134; Hyde, *Following the Greek Cross*, p. 46.
19. McClellan Papers, reel 48; Letterbook, reel 63. That Dennison was McClellan's message-bearer may be surmised from Cox, *Military Reminiscences*, I, p. 356.
20. Welles, *Diary*, I, p. 140; Smalley, "Chapters in Journalism," pp. 429–30; Andrews, *The North Reports*, pp. 282, 700.
21. Jones, *A Rebel War Clerk's Diary*, p. 98; *Richmond Enquirer*, September 22, and *Charleston Mercury*, September 23, quoted in Freeman, *Lee's Lieutenants*, II, p. 236; *Richmond Enquirer*, September 23, quoted in Moore, *Rebellion Record*, V, Documents, p. 476; *Petersburg Express*, September 23, quoted in Murfin, *Gleam of Bayonets*, p. 307; *Richmond Enquirer*, September 30, quoted in Andrews, *The South Reports*, p. 212n.
22. September 26, John S. Sawyers, Rockbridge Artillery, McAllister Papers, Duke University Library, quoted in Robertson, *Stonewall Brigade*, p. 161; September 22, Pender, *The General to His Lady*, p. 175; September 21, Walter H. Taylor Papers, quoted in Freeman, *R. E. Lee*, II, p. 409.
23. September 20, Letterbook, McClellan Papers, reel 63; September 28, Webb Papers, Historical Manuscripts Division, Yale University Library (Long Notes); September 28, William T. Lusk, *War Letters of William Thompson Lusk* (New York: privately printed, 1911), p. 214.
24. September 23, Walter Carter, 22nd Massachusetts, Carter, *Four Brothers in Blue*, pp. 131–32; Richardson to S. H. Gay, September 19, Gay Papers, Columbia University Library (Nevins Notes); October 12, George G. Meade, *The Life and Letters of George Gordon Meade*, I, p. 319; October 6, Jacob Fryberger, 57th New York, Antietam National Battlefield.
25. Todd, *History of the [83rd] New York*, p. 198; Fiske, *Mr. Dunn Browne's Experiences*, pp. 49–50; John Taggert diary, September 20, Pennsylvania Historical and Museum Commission (Long Notes); September 23, Cyrus R. Stone, Minnesota Historical Society, quoted in Wiley, *Billy Yank*, p. 83.
26. October 11, John W. Weiser, 130th Pennsylvania, Frederick S. Weiser Collection, Gettysburg, Pa., copy at Antietam National Battlefield; W. F. Smith Papers, Walter Wilgus Collection, Arlington, Va. (Long Notes); Newton M. Curtis, *From Bull Run to Chancellorsville: The Story of the Sixteenth New York Infantry* (New York: Putnam's, 1906), p. 196; Johnson, *Battlefield Adventures*, p. 101.
27. *New York Times*, October 20,

quoted in Frassanito, *Antietam: The Photographic Legacy,* pp. 15–16.
28. Oliver Wendell Holmes, "My Hunt After 'The Captain,'" *Atlantic Monthly,* X (December 1862), pp. 738–64; Gordon, *Reminiscences,* pp. 88–91; September 28, James Weeks Collection, Birmingham, Mich., quoted in Schildt, *Drums Along the Antietam,* p. 231; Alvin Flint, 21st Connecticut, *Hartford Courant,* October 29, quoted in Frassanito, *Antietam: The Photographic Legacy,* pp. 234–35.
29. Chase, *Diaries,* pp. 149–50; Welles, *Diary,* I, p. 143; December 1, Basler, *Works of Lincoln,* V, p. 537.
30. Basler, *Works of Lincoln,* V, p. 437; *New York Tribune* (September 23 and October 7), *New York Journal of Commerce* (reprinted in *Richmond Examiner* October 16), *New York World* (September 24) — all quoted in John Hope Franklin, *The Emancipation Proclamation,* pp. 62, 61, 66, 67.
31. Porter to Marble, September 30, Marble Papers, Manuscript Division, Library of Congress (Nevins Notes); L. A. Whiteley to Bennett, September 24, James Gordon Bennett Papers, Manuscript Division, Library of Congress, quoted in Smith and Judah, *Life in the North,* p. 91.
32. Basler, *Works of Lincoln,* V, pp. 442, 508; Hay, *Diaries and Letters,* p. 51.
33. March 29, 1863, Urich N. Parmelee, Parmelee Papers, Duke University Library, quoted in Wiley, *Billy Yank,* pp. 41–42; July 12 and September 26, 1862, Alfred Davenport, 5th New York, New-York Historical Society, quoted in Wiley, *Billy Yank,* p. 42; Whitman, *Civil War Letters,* p. 71.
34. McClellan to Aspinwall, *Battles and Leaders* "Extra Illustrated," VIII, Huntington Library (Long Notes); Blair letters, McClellan Papers, reel 32; Cox, *Military Reminiscences,* I, p. 360.
35. September 22 and 25, Letterbook, McClellan Papers, reel 63; September 30, Marble Papers, Manuscript Division, Library of Congress (Nevins Notes).
36. Abner R. Small, *The Road to Richmond: The Civil War Memoirs of Major Abner R. Small of the 16th Maine Volunteers,* ed. Harold A. Small (Berkeley: University of California Press, 1939), p. 51; October 3, Robert Carter, 22nd Massachusetts, Carter, *Four Brothers in Blue,* p. 137; October 5, Williams, *From the Cannon's Mouth,* p. 136.
37. October 2 and 5, McClellan, *Story,* pp. 654, 655; Davis to Leonard Swett, November 26, David Davis Papers, Illinois State Historical Library (Long Notes); September 28, 1864, Hay, *Diaries and Letters,* p. 218. In *McClellan's Own Story* the general claimed that during this visit Lincoln "wished me to continue my preparations for a new campaign, not to stir an inch until fully ready, and when ready to do what I thought best" (p. 628). Considering the contemporary evidence, that is a highly unlikely statement of the president's views, reflecting instead McClellan's flexible memory as often demonstrated in his memoirs.
38. Oct. — , Letterbook, McClellan Papers, reel 63; Nicolay and Hay, *Lincoln,* VI, p. 175.
39. October 5, McClellan, *Story,* p. 655; *OR,* XIX, Part 2, pp. 395–96.

40. McClellan, *Report*, pp. 219, 218; *OR*, XIX, Part 2, p. 505.
41. Meade, *Life and Letters*, I, p. 320; Ingalls to Montgomery Meigs, October 26, *OR*, XIX, Part 2, pp. 492-93; Halleck to H. R. Gamble, October 30, *OR*, Series Three, II, pp. 703-4.
42. *OR*, XIX, Part 2, pp. 410, 660, 718; Longstreet Papers, Duke University Library (Long Notes).
43. A. K. McClure, "The Invasion of Pennsylvania," quoted in Moore, *Rebellion Record*, VI, Documents, p. 1; Welles, *Diary*, I, p. 169.
44. *OR*, XVI, Part 2, pp. 626-27.
45. Basler, *Works of Lincoln*, V, pp. 460-61; *Battles and Leaders*, III, pp. 105-6; *OR*, XIX, Part 1, p. 16; Part 2, p. 464; McClellan, *Report*, pp. 232, 233. It is worth noting that McClellan did not include Lincoln's perceptive letter of October 13 among the documents printed in his official report.
46. *OR*, XIX, Part 2, pp. 484-85.
47. Unknown writer, October 28, Barlow Papers, Huntington Library (Long Notes); Whitman, *Civil War Letters*, p. 72; Richardson to S. H. Gay, October 22 and 31, Gay Papers, Columbia University Library (Nevins Notes).
48. Adams Hill to S. H. Gay, October 13, Gay Papers, Columbia University Library, quoted in Starr, *Bohemian Brigade*, p. 152; Medill to O. M. Hatch, October 13, Hatch Papers, Illinois State Historical Library (Nevins Notes); Jacob M. Howard to Sumner, October 31, Sumner Papers, Harvard College Library, quoted in Smith and Judah, *Life in the North*, pp. 91-92.
49. Nicolay and Hay, *Lincoln*, VI, p. 167; October 17, McClellan Papers, reel 33; Christopher Dell, *Lincoln and the War Democrats*, p. 181.
50. Palmerston to Russell, October 2 and 22, Russell Papers, Public Record Office, London; Earl of Clarendon to George Cornwall Lewis, October 26, H. E. Maxwell, ed., *Clarendon* (London, 1913), II, p. 265 — all quoted in Adams, *Britain and the Civil War*, II, pp. 43-44, 54-55, 59.
51. *London Times*, October 7, and *Blackwood's Magazine*, November 1862, quoted in Commager, *The Blue and the Gray*, pp. 546, 548; Carl Schurz, *The Reminiscences of Carl Schurz* (New York: McClure Co., 1907-8), II, p. 309; December 29, 1861, R. E. Lee Papers, Duke University Library, quoted in Catton, *Terrible Swift Sword*, p. 116.
52. Ford, *A Cycle of Adams Letters*, I, p. 192; Johnson, *Battlefield Adventures*, p. 103.

Epilogue. A Last Farewell

1. Francis P. Blair to Montgomery Blair, November 7, Blair Family Papers, Manuscript Division, Library of Congress (Long Notes).
2. September 28, 1864, Hay, *Diaries and Letters*, pp. 218-19; *OR*, XIX, Part 2, pp. 497, 523, 531; Richardson, *The Secret Service*, p. 324; McClellan, *Story*, p. 659.
3. *OR*, XIX, Part 2, pp. 685-86, 697; Basler, *Works of Lincoln*, V, p. 485; September 28, 1864, Hay, *Diaries and Letters*, pp. 218-19; Richardson, *The Secret Service*, p. 324.
4. September 20, Letterbook, McClellan Papers, reel 63; *History of the Corn Exchange Regiment, 118th Pennsylvania Volunteers*, p. 108.

5. C. P. Buckingham, *Chicago Tribune*, September 4, 1875, quoted in Comte de Paris, *History of the Civil War in America*, II, pp. 555–57n; *OR*, XIX, Part 2, pp. 545–46; *Report of the Joint Committee*, I, p. 650; November 7, Letterbook, McClellan Papers, reel 63.
6. Strother, *A Virginia Yankee*, p. 127; Leech, *Reveille in Washington*, p. 222; Freeman, *Lee's Lieutenants*, II, p. 313; *Battles and Leaders*, III, p. 70.
7. Wilson, *Under the Old Flag*, I, p. 122; McClellan, *Story*, p. 652; McClellan Papers, reel 48. McClellan's farewell address is quoted here from the printed broadside distributed to the troops, which the general preserved in his papers. As it appears in *McClellan's Own Story*, p. 653, and in *OR*, XIX, Part 2, p. 551, however, there is an additional, statesman-like closing sentence: "We shall ever be comrades in supporting the Constitution of our country and the nationality of its people." Whether this was omitted inadvertently in the printing of the broadside or added later "for the record" is unclear.
8. McClellan, *Story*, p. 661; Wainwright, *A Diary of Battle*, p. 125; Weymouth, *Memorial Sketch of Lt. Newcomb*, p. 93; *History of the Corn Exchange Regiment*, p. 107; Barlow Papers, Huntington Library (Long Notes).
9. William Todd, *The Seventy-ninth Highlanders, New York Volunteers* (Albany: Brandon, Barton & Co., 1886), p. 245; Marsena Patrick, *Inside Lincoln's Army: The Diary of Marsena Rudolph Patrick, Provost Marshal General, Army of the Potomac*, ed. David S. Sparks, p. 174.
10. November 8, Meade, *Life and Letters*, I, p. 325; November 9, Archibald Hopkins, "Letters from the Civil War Front," *The Military Engineer*, XX, no. 112 (July–August 1928) (Long Notes); November 9, Gibbon, *Personal Recollections*, p. 96; November 9, Marble Papers, Manuscript Division, Library of Congress (Nevins Notes).
11. November 9, George W. Salter, John Hay Library, Brown University (Long Notes); Richardson to S. H. Gay, November 20, Gay Papers, Columbia University Library (Nevins Notes).
12. November 9 (misdated November 7), Galwey, *Valiant Hours*, p. 53; November 19, Henry Ropes, 20th Massachusetts, Boston Public Library (Long Notes).
13. November 10, Weymouth, *Memorial Sketch of Lt. Newcomb*, p. 94; November 10, Wainwright, *A Diary of Battle*, pp. 125–26; November 10, Eugene Carter, 8th U.S. Infantry, Carter, *Four Brothers in Blue*, p. 161.
14. George Ticknor Curtis, *McClellan's Last Service to the Republic* (New York: D. Appleton, 1886), pp. 81–83; November 16, Robert E. Jameson Papers, Manuscript Division, Library of Congress (Long Notes).

Appendix I. The Lost Order

1. Freeman, *Lee's Lieutenants*, II, p. 721.
2. December 8, 1874, Rowland, *Jefferson Davis*, VII, pp. 412–13.
3. McClellan Papers, reel 31.
4. *OR*, XIX, Part 2, p. 281.
5. McClellan Papers, reel 31; *OR*, XIX, Part 2, p. 270.
6. *OR*, XIX, Part 2, pp. 281–82; *OR*, LI, Part 1, p. 829.
7. William Allan Papers, Southern Historical Collection, University

Notes to Appendix II

of North Carolina, quoted in Freeman, *Lee's Lieutenants*, II, pp. 716–21; Hal Bridges, "A Lee Letter on the 'Lost Dispatch' and the Maryland Campaign of 1862," *Virginia Magazine of History*, LXVI (April 1958), pp. 161–66.

8. Freeman, *R. E. Lee*, II, p. 369n.; Freeman, *Lee's Lieutenants*, II, Appendix I.
9. Allan, *Army of Northern Virginia*, p. 345; Bridges, "A Lee Letter," p. 165.
10. *OR*, XIX, Part 1, pp. 140, 146.
11. November 11, 1867, D. H. Hill Papers, Virginia State Library (Long Notes).
12. D. H. Hill, "The Lost Dispatch," *The Land We Love*, IV (February 1868), pp. 270–84.

Appendix II. Burnside and His Bridge

1. *OR*, XIX, Part 1, pp. 30, 426; *Battles and Leaders*, II, p. 657; Cox, *Military Reminiscences*, I, p. 307.
2. *OR*, XIX, Part 1, pp. 31, 419; *Report of the Joint Committee*, I, p. 640; *Battles and Leaders*, II, p. 649n.
3. *OR*, LI, Part 1, p. 844.
4. McClellan, *Report*, pp. 201, 208, 209.
5. McClellan, *Story*, pp. 604, 607, 608; *Battles and Leaders*, II, p. 653. Cox's copy of *McClellan's Own Story* is in the Oberlin College Library.
6. Sackett to McClellan, February 20 and March 9, 1876, McClellan, *Story*, pp. 609–11.
7. Strother, "Personal Recollections," p. 283; William F. Biddle, *United Service Magazine* (May 1894).
8. *Battles and Leaders*, II, p. 649n.
9. McClellan, *Story*, p. 616.

BIBLIOGRAPHY

Manuscript Collections

Antietam Battlefield Board Papers. Record Group 92, Series 707. National Archives, Washington, D.C.
Antietam Collection. Dartmouth College Library, Hanover, N.H.
Antietam National Battlefield, Sharpsburg, Md.:
   William H. Andrews. "Recollections" (copy). Washington County Free Library, Hagerstown, Md.
   Richard Carroll Datzman. "Who Found Lee's Lost Order?" (1973).
   A. K. McClure. "Recollections of Antietam."
   Samuel W. Moore diary.
   Jonathan P. Stowe diary.
Antietam Studies. Record Group 94. National Archives.
Ezra A. Carman Papers. "History of the Antietam Campaign." Manuscript Division, Library of Congress, Washington, D.C.
George B. McClellan Papers. Manuscript Division, Library of Congress.
James W. Shinn. "Recollections of the Late War." Augustus Osborne Papers. Southern Historical Collection, University of North Carolina, Chapel Hill, N.C.

Manuscript collections excerpted in the Long and Nevins research notes, *Centennial History of the Civil War*, of particular relevance to the period of the Antietam campaign:

William Allan Papers. Southern Historical Collection, University of North Carolina.
S. L. M. Barlow Papers. Huntington Library, San Marino, Calif.
J. R. Boulware diary. Virginia State Museum, Richmond, Va.
S. H. Gay Papers. Columbia University Library, New York, N.Y.

Manton Marble Papers. Manuscript Division, Library of Congress.
Alexander S. Webb Papers. Historical Manuscripts Division, Yale University Library, New Haven, Conn.

Books and Articles

Adams, Ephraim Douglass. *Great Britain and the American Civil War.* 2 vols. London: Longmans, Green, 1925.
Adams, Michael C. C. *Our Masters the Rebels: A Speculation on Union Military Failure in the East, 1861–1865.* Cambridge, Mass.: Harvard University Press, 1978.
Alexander, E. P. *Military Memoirs of a Confederate.* New York: Scribner's, 1907.
Allan, William. *The Army of Northern Virginia in 1862.* Boston: Houghton Mifflin, 1892.
Allan, William. "First Maryland Campaign." *Southern Historical Society Papers,* XIV (1886), pp. 102–18.
Allan, William. "Strategy of the Campaign of Sharpsburg or Antietam." *Campaigns in Virginia, Maryland and Pennsylvania, 1862–1863,* Papers of the Military Historical Society of Massachusetts, III, Boston, 1903.
Andrews, J. Cutler. *The North Reports the Civil War.* Pittsburgh: University of Pittsburgh Press, 1955.
Andrews, J. Cutler. *The South Reports the Civil War.* Princeton: Princeton University Press, 1970.
Antietam Battlefield Board. *Atlas of the Battlefield of Antietam.* Washington, D.C.: War Department, Chief of Engineers, 1904, 1908.
Basler, Roy P., ed. *The Collected Works of Abraham Lincoln.* 9 vols. New Brunswick, N.J.: Rutgers University Press, 1953–55.
Bates, David Homer. *Lincoln in the Telegraph Office.* New York: Century, 1907.
Battles and Leaders of the Civil War. Eds. Robert U. Johnson and Clarence C. Buel. 4 vols. New York: Century, 1887–88.
Billings, John D. *Hardtack and Coffee: The Unwritten Story of Army Life.* 1887; Chicago: R. R. Donnelley, 1960.
Blackford, W. W. *War Years with Jeb Stuart.* New York: Scribner's, 1945.
Bloss, John M. "Antietam and the Lost Dispatch." *War Talks in Kansas,* Kansas Commandery of the Military Order of the Loyal Legion of the United States, I, Kansas City, Mo., 1906.
Borcke, Heros Von. *Memoirs of the Confederate War for Independence.* 2 vols. 1866; New York: Peter Smith, 1938.

Bosbyshell, Oliver C., ed. *Pennsylvania at Antietam.* Harrisburg: Antietam Battlefield Memorial Commission, 1906.

Bridges, Hal. "A Lee Letter on the 'Lost Dispatch' and the Maryland Campaign of 1862." *Virginia Magazine of History,* LXVI (April 1958), pp. 161-66.

Bridges, Hal. *Lee's Maverick General: Daniel Harvey Hill.* New York: McGraw-Hill, 1961.

Bruce, George A. *The Twentieth Regiment of Massachusetts Volunteer Infantry, 1861-1865.* Boston: Houghton Mifflin, 1906.

Caldwell, J. F. J. *The History of [Gregg's] Brigade of South Carolinians.* Philadelphia: King & Baird, 1866.

Carter, Robert G. *Four Brothers in Blue.* Washington, D.C.: Gibson Press, 1913.

Catton, Bruce. *Mr. Lincoln's Army.* Garden City, N.Y.: Doubleday, 1954.

Catton, Bruce. *The Centennial History of the Civil War, II: Terrible Swift Sword.* Garden City, N.Y.: Doubleday, 1963.

Chambers, Lenoir. *Stonewall Jackson.* 2 vols. New York: Morrow, 1959.

Chase, Salmon P. *Inside Lincoln's Cabinet: The Civil War Diaries of Salmon P. Chase.* Ed. David Donald. New York: Longmans, Green, 1954.

Child, William. *A History of the Fifth Regiment New Hampshire Volunteers, in the American Civil War, 1861-1865.* Bristol, N.H.: R. W. Musgrove, 1893.

Clark, Walter, ed. *Histories of the Several Regiments and Battalions from North Carolina in the Great War, 1861-'65.* 5 vols. Raleigh: State of North Carolina, 1901.

Commager, Henry Steele, ed. *The Blue and the Gray.* Indianapolis: Bobbs-Merrill, 1950.

Cook, Benjamin F. *History of the Twelfth Massachusetts Volunteers.* Boston: privately printed, 1882.

Cox, Jacob D. *Military Reminiscences of the Civil War.* 2 vols. New York: Scribner's, 1900.

Crary, Catherine S., ed. *Dear Belle: Letters from a Cadet and Officer to His Sweetheart, 1858-1865.* Middletown, Conn.: Wesleyan University Press, 1965.

Croffut, W. A., and John M. Morris. *The Military and Civil History of Connecticut During the War of 1861-65.* New York: Ledyard Bill, 1868.

Crook, D. P. *The North, the South, and the Powers, 1861-1865.* New York: Wiley, 1974.

Davis, Charles E. *Three Years in the Army: The Story of the Thirteenth Massachusetts Volunteers.* Boston: Estes & Lauriat, 1894.

Davis, George B. "The Antietam Campaign." *Campaigns in Virginia, Maryland and Pennsylvania, 1862–1863*, Papers of the Military Historical Society of Massachusetts, III, Boston, 1903.
Dawes, Rufus R. *Service with the Sixth Wisconsin Volunteers.* Marietta, Ohio: Alderman & Sons, 1890.
Dell, Christopher. *Lincoln and the War Democrats.* Rutherford, N.J.: Fairleigh Dickinson University Press, 1975.
Dickert, D. Augustus. *History of Kershaw's Brigade.* Newberry, S.C.: E. H. Aull Co., 1899.
Dooley, John E. *John Dooley, Confederate Soldier: His War Journal.* Ed. Joseph T. Durkin. Washington, D. C.: Georgetown University Press, 1945.
Douglas, Henry Kyd. *I Rode With Stonewall.* Chapel Hill: University of North Carolina Press, 1940.
Duncan, Richard R. "Marylanders and the Invasion of 1862," in John T. Hubbell, ed., *Battles Lost and Won: Essays from Civil War History.* Westport, Conn.: Greenwood Press, 1975.
Dwight, Wilder. *Life and Letters of Wilder Dwight, Lieutenant Colonel, 2nd Massachusetts Infantry.* Boston: Ticknor & Fields, 1868.
Fiske, Samuel. *Mr. Dunn Browne's Experiences in the Army.* Boston: Nichols & Noyes, 1866.
Ford, Worthington Chauncey, ed. *A Cycle of Adams Letters, 1861–1865.* 2 vols. Boston: Houghton Mifflin, 1920.
Fox, William F. *Regimental Losses in the American Civil War, 1861–1865.* Albany: Albany Publishing Co., 1889.
Franklin, John Hope. *The Emancipation Proclamation.* Garden City, N.Y.: Doubleday, 1963.
Frassanito, William A. *Antietam: The Photographic Legacy of America's Bloodiest Day.* New York: Scribner's, 1978.
Freeman, Douglas Southall. *Lee's Lieutenants.* 3 vols. New York: Scribner's, 1942–44.
Freeman, Douglas Southall. *R. E. Lee, A Biography.* 4 vols. New York: Scribner's, 1934–35.
Galwey, Thomas Francis. *The Valiant Hours.* Ed. W. S. Nye. Harrisburg: Stackpole, 1961.
Gibbon, John. *Personal Recollections of the Civil War.* New York: Putnam's, 1928.
Gordon, John B. *Reminiscences of the Civil War.* New York: Scribner's, 1903.
Gould, John M. *History of the First — Tenth — Twenty-ninth Maine Regiment.* Portland, Me.: Stephen Berry, 1871.

Bibliography 409

Gould, John M. *Joseph K. F. Mansfield: A Narrative of Events Connected with His Mortal Wounding at Antietam.* Portland, Me., 1895.

Graham, Matthew J. *The Ninth Regiment New York Volunteers (Hawkins' Zouaves).* New York: Coby & Co., 1900.

Harsh, Joseph L. "On the McClellan-Go-Round," in John T. Hubbell, ed., *Battles Lost and Won: Essays from Civil War History.* Westport, Conn.: Greenwood Press, 1975.

Harwell, Richard B., ed. *The Confederate Reader.* New York: Longmans, Green, 1957.

Harwell, Richard B., ed. *The Union Reader.* New York: Longmans, Green, 1958.

Hassler, Warren W., Jr. *General George B. McClellan: Shield of the Union.* Baton Rouge: Louisiana State University Press, 1957.

Hassler, William W. *A. P. Hill: Lee's Forgotten General.* Richmond: Garrett & Massie, 1957.

Haupt, Herman. *Reminiscences of General Herman Haupt.* Milwaukee: Wright & Joys, 1901.

Hay, John. *Lincoln and the Civil War in the Diaries and Letters of John Hay.* Ed. Tyler Dennett. New York: Dodd, Mead, 1939.

Henderson, G. F. R. *Stonewall Jackson and the American Civil War.* 1898; New York: Longmans, Green, 1936.

Hendrick, Burton J. *Lincoln's War Cabinet.* Boston: Little, Brown, 1946.

Hesseltine, William B. *Lincoln and the War Governors.* New York: Knopf, 1948.

Heysinger, Isaac W. *Antietam and the Maryland and Virginia Campaigns of 1862.* New York: Neale, 1912.

History of the Corn Exchange Regiment, 118th Pennsylvania Volunteers. Philadelphia: J. L. Smith, 1888.

Hitchcock, Frederick L. *War from the Inside.* Philadelphia: Lippincott, 1904.

Hood, J. B. *Advance and Retreat.* New Orleans: privately printed, 1880.

Hunter, Alexander. "A High Private's Account of the Battle of Sharpsburg." *Southern Historical Society Papers,* Part 1, X (1882), pp. 503-12; Part 2, XI (1883), pp. 10-21.

Huyette, Miles C. "Reminiscences of a Private." *The National Tribune Scrap Book,* No. 1. Washington, D.C.: National Tribune, c. 1909.

Hyde, Thomas W. *Following the Greek Cross or, Memories of the Sixth Army Corps.* Boston: Houghton Mifflin, 1894.

Johnson, Bradley T. "The First Maryland Campaign." *Southern Historical Society Papers,* XII (1884), pp. 500-37.

Johnson, Clifton. *Battlefield Adventures: The Stories of Dwellers on the Scenes of Conflict in Some of the Most Notable Battles of the Civil War.* Boston: Houghton Mifflin, 1915.
Johnson, William A. "Barbara Frietchie." *The National Tribune Scrap Book*, No. 1. Washington, D.C.: National Tribune, c. 1909.
Jones, John B. *A Rebel War Clerk's Diary.* Ed. Earl Schenck Miers. New York: Sagamore Press, 1958.
Leech, Margaret. *Reveille in Washington, 1860–1865.* New York: Harper, 1941.
Lilley, David A. "The Antietam Battlefield Board and Its Atlas: or The Genesis of the Carman-Cope Maps." *Lincoln Herald*, LXXXII, no. 2 (Summer 1980), pp. 380–87.
Lindeman, Jack, ed. *The Conflict of Convictions: American Writers Report the Civil War.* Philadelphia: Chilton, 1968.
Livermore, Thomas L. *Days and Events, 1860–1865.* Boston: Houghton Mifflin, 1920.
Livermore, Thomas L. *Numbers and Losses in the Civil War in America, 1861–1865.* 2nd ed. Boston: Houghton Mifflin, 1902.
Longstreet, James. *From Manassas to Appomattox.* Philadelphia: Lippincott, 1896.
Luff, William M. "March of the Cavalry from Harper's Ferry, September 14, 1862." *Military Essays and Recollections*, Illinois Commandery of the Military Order of the Loyal Legion of the United States, II, Chicago, 1894.
McClellan, George B. *McClellan's Own Story.* New York: Webster, 1887.
McClellan, George B. *Report on the Organization of the Army of the Potomac, and of Its Campaigns in Virginia and Maryland.* Washington, D.C.: Government Printing Office, 1864.
McClellan, H. B. *I Rode with Jeb Stuart: The Life and Campaigns of Major General J. E. B. Stuart.* Boston: Houghton Mifflin, 1885.
Meade, George G. *The Life and Letters of George Gordon Meade.* 2 vols. New York: Scribner's, 1913.
Michie, Peter S. *General George Brinton McClellan.* New York: D. Appleton, 1901.
Mies, John W. "Breakout at Harper's Ferry." *Civil War History*, II, no. 2 (June 1956), pp. 13–28.
Monroe, J. Albert. "Battery D, First Rhode Island Light Artillery, at the Battle of Antietam, September 17, 1862." *Personal Narratives of the Events of the War of the Rebellion*, Rhode Island Soldiers and Sailors Historical Society, Third Series, no. 16, Providence, 1886.
Moore, Frank, ed. *The Rebellion Record: A Diary of American Events.* 11

Bibliography

vols. and supplement. New York: Putnam's, 1861–63; Van Nostrand, 1864–68.

Murfin, James V. *The Gleam of Bayonets: The Battle of Antietam and the Maryland Campaign of 1862.* New York: Yoseloff, 1965.

Myers, William Starr. *A Study in Personality: General George Brinton McClellan.* New York: D. Appleton-Century, 1934.

Naisawald, L. Van Loan. *Grape and Canister: The Story of the Field Artillery of the Army of the Potomac, 1861–1865.* New York: Oxford, 1960.

Nevins, Allan. *The War for the Union,* I: *The Improvised War, 1861–1862.* New York: Scribner's, 1959.

Nevins, Allan. *The War for the Union,* II: *War Becomes Revolution, 1862–1863.* New York: Scribner's, 1960.

Nichols, William H. "The Siege and Capture of Harper's Ferry by the Confederates, September, 1862." *Personal Narratives of the Events of the War of the Rebellion,* Rhode Island Soldiers and Sailors Historical Society, Fourth Series, no. 2, Providence, 1889.

Nicolay, John G., and John Hay. *Abraham Lincoln: A History.* 10 vols. New York: Century, 1890.

Noyes, George F. *The Bivouac and the Battlefield, or Campaign Sketches in Virginia and Maryland.* New York: Harper, 1863.

Owen, William M. *In Camp and Battle with the Washington Artillery of New Orleans.* Boston: Ticknor & Fields, 1885.

Owsley, Frank Lawrence. *King Cotton Diplomacy: Foreign Relations of the Confederate States of America.* 2nd ed. Chicago: University of Chicago Press, 1959.

Palfrey, Francis W. *The Antietam and Fredericksburg.* New York: Scribner's, 1882.

Palfrey, Francis W. "The Battle of Antietam." *Campaigns in Virginia, Maryland and Pennsylvania, 1862–1863,* Papers of the Military Historical Society of Massachusetts, III, Boston, 1903.

Paris, Louis, Comte de. *History of the Civil War in America.* 4 vols. Philadelphia: Porter & Coates, 1875–88.

Parker, Thomas H. *History of the 51st Regiment of Pennsylvania Volunteers.* Philadelphia: King & Baird, 1869.

Patrick, Marsena. *Inside Lincoln's Army: The Diary of Marsena Rudolph Patrick, Provost Marshal General, Army of the Potomac.* Ed. David S. Sparks. New York: Yoseloff, 1964.

Pender, William D. *The General to His Lady: The Civil War Letters of William Dorsey Pender to Fanny Pender.* Ed. William W. Hassler. Chapel Hill: University of North Carolina Press, 1965.

Post, Lydia Minturn. *Soldiers' Letters from Camp, Battle-field and Prison.* New York: Bunce & Huntington, 1865.
Reilly, Oliver T. *The Battlefield of Antietam.* Hagerstown, Md.: Hagerstown Printing Co., 1906.
Report of the Joint Committee on the Conduct of the War. 3 vols. Washington, D.C.: Government Printing Office, 1863.
Richardson, Albert D. *The Secret Service, the Field, the Dungeon, and the Escape.* Hartford: American Publishing Co., 1865.
Robertson, James I., Jr. "A Federal Surgeon at Sharpsburg." *Civil War History*, VI, no. 2 (June 1960), pp. 134–51.
Robertson, James I., Jr. *The Stonewall Brigade.* Baton Rouge: Louisiana State University Press, 1963.
Ropes, John C. "General McClellan." *Critical Sketches of Some of the Federal and Confederate Commanders,* Papers of the Military Historical Society of Massachusetts, X, Boston, 1895.
Ropes, John C. *The Story of the Civil War, II: The Campaigns of 1862.* New York: Putnam's, 1905.
Rowland, Dunbar, ed. *Jefferson Davis, Constitutionalist: His Letters, Papers and Speeches.* 10 vols. Jackson: Mississippi Department of Archives and History, 1923.
Schenck, Martin. "Burnside's Bridge." *Civil War History*, II, no. 4 (December 1956), pp. 5–19.
Schildt, John W. *Drums Along the Antietam.* Parsons, W. Va.: McClain Printing Co., 1972.
Sedgwick, John. *Correspondence of John Sedgwick, Major General.* 2 vols. New York: privately printed, 1903.
Sheppard, Eric W. *The Campaign in Virginia and Maryland, June 26 to Sept. 20, 1862.* New York: Macmillan, 1911.
Sideman, Belle Becker, and Lillian Friedman, eds. *Europe Looks at the Civil War.* New York: Orion Press, 1960.
Smalley, George W. "Antietam." *New York Tribune*, September 19, 1862, in Moore, *Rebellion Record*, V, Documents, pp. 466–72.
Smalley, George W. "Chapters in Journalism." *Harper's New Monthly Magazine*, LXXXIX (August 1894), pp. 426–35.
Smith, George Winston, and Charles Judah, eds. *Life in the North During the Civil War: A Source History.* Albuquerque: University of New Mexico Press, 1966.
Sorrel, G. Moxley. *Recollections of a Confederate Staff Officer.* New York: Neale, 1905.
Spooner, Henry J. "The Maryland Campaign with the Fourth Rhode Island." *Personal Narratives of the Events of the War of the Rebellion,*

Bibliography

Rhode Island Soldiers and Sailors Historical Society, Sixth Series, no. 5, Providence, 1903.
Stackpole, Edward J. *From Cedar Mountain to Antietam.* Harrisburg: Stackpole, 1959.
Starr, Louis M. *Bohemian Brigade: Civil War Newsmen in Action.* New York: Knopf, 1954.
Stearns, Austin C. *Three Years with Company K.* Ed. Arthur A. Kent. Cranbury, N.J.: Fairleigh Dickinson University Press, 1976.
Steiner, Lewis H. *Report of Lewis H. Steiner, M.D., . . . Containing a Diary Kept During the Rebel Occupation of Frederick, Md.* 1862; reprinted in Harwell, *The Union Reader,* pp. 158–74.
Stine, J. H. *History of the Army of the Potomac.* Philadelphia: Rogers Printing Co., 1892.
Strong, George Templeton. *The Diary of George Templeton Strong: The Civil War, 1860–1865.* Eds. Allan Nevins and Milton H. Thomas. New York: Macmillan, 1952.
Strother, D. H. "Personal Recollections of the War by a Virginian, Antietam." *Harper's New Monthly Magazine,* XXXVI (February 1868), pp. 275–91.
Strother, D. H. *A Virginia Yankee in the Civil War: The Diaries of David Hunter Strother.* Ed. Cecil D. Eby, Jr. Chapel Hill: University of North Carolina Press, 1961.
Sumner, George C. "Recollections of Service in Battery D., First Rhode Island Light Artillery." *Personal Narratives of the Events of the War of the Rebellion,* Rhode Island Soldiers and Sailors Historical Society, Fourth Series, no. 11, Providence, 1891.
Sumner, Samuel S. "The Antietam Campaign." *Civil War and Miscellaneous Papers,* Papers of the Military Historical Society of Massachusetts, XIV, Boston, 1913.
Swinton, William. *Campaigns of the Army of the Potomac.* New York: Charles B. Richardson, 1886.
Thomas, Emory M. *The Confederate Nation, 1861–1865.* New York: Harper & Row, 1979.
Todd, William, ed. *History of the Ninth Regiment, New York State Militia* (83rd New York Volunteers). New York: privately printed, 1889.
Trefousse, Hans L. *The Radical Republicans: Lincoln's Vanguard for Racial Justice.* New York: Knopf, 1969.
Trobriand, Régis de. *Four Years with the Army of the Potomac.* Boston: Ticknor & Co., 1889.
U.S. War Department. *The War of the Rebellion: A Compilation of the Official Records of the Union and Confederate Armies.* 128 parts in

70 vols. and atlas. Washington D.C.: Government Printing Office, 1880–1901.
Vandiver, Frank E. *Mighty Stonewall.* New York: McGraw-Hill, 1957.
Vandiver, Frank E. *Their Tattered Flags: The Epic of the Confederacy.* New York: Harper & Row, 1970.
Wainwright, Charles S. *A Diary of Battle: The Personal Journals of Colonel Charles S. Wainwright, 1861–1865.* Ed. Allan Nevins. New York: Harcourt, Brace & World, 1962.
Walcott, Charles F. *History of the Twenty-First Regiment Massachusetts Volunteers in the War for the Preservation of the Union, 1861–1865.* Boston: Houghton Mifflin, 1882.
Walker, Francis A. *History of the Second Army Corps.* New York: Scribner's, 1886.
Welles, Gideon. *Diary of Gideon Welles.* Ed. Howard K. Beale. 3 vols. New York: Norton, 1960.
Weymouth, A. B., ed. *A Memorial Sketch of Lieut. Edgar M. Newcomb of the Nineteenth Mass. Vols.* Malden, Mass., 1883.
Whitman, George W. *Civil War Letters of George Washington Whitman.* Ed. Jerome M. Loving. Durham, N.C.: Duke University Press, 1975.
Wiley, Bell Irvin. *The Life of Billy Yank.* Indianapolis: Bobbs-Merrill, 1952.
Wiley, Bell Irvin. *The Life of Johnny Reb.* Indianapolis: Bobbs-Merrill, 1943.
Williams, Alpheus S. *From the Cannon's Mouth: The Civil War Letters of General Alpheus S. Williams.* Ed. Milo M. Quaife. Detroit: Wayne State University Press, 1959.
Williams, Kenneth P. *Lincoln Finds a General: A Military Study of the Civil War.* 5 vols. New York: Macmillan, 1949–59.
Williams, T. Harry. *Hayes of the Twenty-Third: The Civil War Volunteer Officer.* New York: Knopf, 1965.
Williams, T. Harry. *Lincoln and His Generals.* New York: Knopf, 1952.
Williams, T. Harry. *Lincoln and the Radicals.* Madison: University of Wisconsin Press, 1941.
Wilson, James H. *Under the Old Flag.* 2 vols. New York: D. Appleton, 1912.
Wise, Jennings C. *The Long Arm of Lee: The History of the Artillery of the Army of Northern Virginia.* 1915; New York: Oxford, 1959.
Woodward, C. Vann, ed. *Mary Chesnut's Civil War.* New Haven: Yale University Press, 1981.

INDEX

abolitionists, 26, 37, 42–43, 58, 343–44
Adams, Charles Francis, 1, 36, 40, 41, 335
Adams, Lt. Charles Francis, Jr., 1–2, 13, 271
Albany Evening Journal, 42
Alexander, Maj. E. Porter, 53–54
Alexander, Peter W., 93, 96–97, 305, 306
Alexandria, Va., 3, 4, 7, 10, 12, 117
Allan, Col. William, 67, 309, 351
Altoona governors' conference, 166, 332
Anderson, Brig. Gen. George B., 134; Antietam, 236, 238, 239, 241, 243, 245–46; wounded, 242
Anderson, Col. George T., 134; Antietam, 195, 220, 224, 225, 231, 252, 260
Anderson, Maj. Gen. Richard H., 90, 115, 116, 118, 120, 160, 165, 174; Antietam, 195, 240, 241, 242, 244, 245, 251, 262, 269; wounded, 241
Anderson, Lt. Col. Robert, 201
Andrew, John A., 166
Andrews, Sgt. William, 225
Annandale, Va., 8
Antietam, battle of, xi–xii; news of, 311–12; military judgment re, 317; effect of, on elections, 333; effect of, on Europe's support of Confederacy, 333–35
Antietam battlefield, 168–69, 180–82, 202, 213, 260–61, 314–16; Cemetery Hill, 260, 277, 279, 280–81; Cornfield, 180, 181, 182, 185–90, 192–94, 198–202, 205–6, 207–9, 210–11, 213, 218, 223, 234; East Woods, 180, 181, 184–85, 187, 189–90, 198–99, 201, 205, 209, 210, 213, 234; North Woods, 185, 191, 229; Sunken Road (Bloody Lane), 180, 236–47, 251–54, 257, 292–93, 309; West Woods, 180, 181, 182, 190–91, 193–95, 202, 207, 213, 219, 223–29, 231–32, 234, 240, 248–49, 271, 276
Antietam Creek, 158, 159, 160, 168, 169, 175, 261, 395; fords, 172, 175, 218, 259, 261, 262, 263–64, 267, 356–57, 395
Archer, Brig. Gen. James J., 289
Army of Northern Virginia, 50–51, 63; strength, 51, 69, 70–71, 102–3, 118, 161, 174, 175–76, 304, 389; conscripts in, 51–52, 59, 131, 154, 178, 209, 210; Peninsula cam-

Army of Northern Virginia (cont'd)
paign, 52–57; command structure, 55–56; morale, 55, 63, 86–87, 307–8; character of, 56, 57–58, 71; cavalry, 57, 83, 88, 103, 146, 148, 175, 327–28; condition of, 63, 70–71, 83–84, 85–86, 161–62, 164, 175, 327; supply lines, 64, 66, 83, 126; Maryland campaign, 65–66, 69–73, 74, 76, 77, 82–100, 149, 150; diet, 70, 84, 162, 177; foraging, 70, 84, 162; straggling, 70–71, 175–76, 252, 284–85, 286, 307–8; artillery, at Antietam, 182, 187, 188, 189, 190–91, 208–9, 211, 225, 228–29, 240, 275, 280, 287, 290; general-officer casualties at Antietam, 290; condition of, after Antietam, 303–5; return to Virginia, 306, 307–8; leadership of, 309–10; returning to strength, 327–28.

Units of: Stonewall Brigade, 153, 194; Texas Brigade, 57, 135, 197–201; Hampton's Legion, 197, 200; 4th Alabama, 197, 199, 205, 211; 6th Alabama, 139, 246; 9th Alabama, 241; 12th Alabama, 137; 3rd Arkansas, 248–50; 1st Georgia, 225; 2nd Georgia, 260; 6th Georgia, 208, 211; 12th Georgia, 186; 18th Georgia, 197, 200; 20th Georgia, 260; 21st Georgia, 186, 199, 205, 211; 27th Georgia, 162; 50th Georgia, 261, 264; 1st Louisiana, 194–95; Louisiana Tigers, 188–89, 190, 194; 2nd Mississippi, 197; 11th Mississippi, 197; 16th Mississippi, 244; 18th Mississippi, 88, 306; 1st North Carolina, 207–8; 2nd North Carolina, 246; 3rd North Carolina, 208–9; 4th North Carolina, 245; 5th North Carolina, 209, 210; 6th North Carolina, 197; 12th North Carolina, 131; 14th North Carolina, 246; 21st North Carolina, 186; 27th North Carolina, 248–50; 30th North Carolina, 238; 35th North Carolina, 275; 48th North Carolina, 274, 291; 49th North Carolina, 248–49; 1st South Carolina, 289; 1st Texas, 201; 4th Texas, 200; 5th Texas, 199, 205, 209, 210, 211; 1st Virginia, 284; 17th Virginia, 283; 23rd Virginia, 194; 30th Virginia, 232; *see also* division and brigade commanders, by name

Army of the Potomac, 4–18, 20–21, 30–39, 310; merged with Army of Virginia, 2, 3, 80; morale, 14–15, 16, 68, 79–80, 81, 111, 158–59; straggling, 108–9, 202, 300, 302; Peninsula campaign, 28, 29, 31–37, 41, 45–46, 52–56, 57, 58, 61, 160; new troops in, 65, 80, 134–35, 203, 204–5, 206–7, 215, 230, 238–40, 249, 287–88, 290, 301–2; strength, 102–3, 117, 163, 173, 300–303, 388–89; command structure, 101–2, 170–71; cavalry, 103, 157, 172, 175, 263–64, 271, 276, 330–31; disaffection in, 111, 319–20, 321, 339; reconnaissance, 172, 174–75, 259–60, 263–64, 356–57; artillery, at Antietam, 184, 185–86, 190–91, 192, 194, 198, 200–201, 208–9, 225–26, 240–41, 249, 253–54, 280, 290; general-officer casualties at Antietam, 287; condition of, after Antietam, 304–6, 309; leadership of, 310–11, 356–57; reaction to Emancipation Proclamation, 319–21; wasted supplies, 326–27; Lincoln visits, after Antietam, 323–24, 325; crosses Potomac into Virginia, 337–38; McClellan's dismissal from command, 336–45.

Units of: First Corps, 102, 129, 136–37, 139, 141, 156, 159, 170, 171, 173, 176, 180–82, 184–202,

Index 417

Army of the Potomac (cont'd)
204, 206, 207, 214–15, 219, 220, 229, 254, 258, 272, 273, 274, 291, 296, 300, 389; Second Corps, 4, 102, 156, 159, 173, 195, 216, 217–18, 221–30, 234, 235, 237–54, 257, 272, 273, 296, 300; Fifth Corps, 102, 106, 156, 170, 172, 173, 221, 256, 270, 273, 279–80, 289, 291, 296, 301, 307; Sixth Corps, 4, 102, 117, 119–20, 145–49, 154–56, 160, 171–72, 173, 235, 251, 256, 271, 273, 292, 293, 296, 301, 384; Ninth Corps, 102, 110, 117, 119, 129–36, 139–41, 145, 156, 170, 171, 172, 173, 195, 221, 235, 258–68, 276–92, 296, 300, 303, 353–57, 389; Twelfth Corps, 102, 112, 156, 171, 172, 173, 177, 181, 190, 195, 199, 202–15, 216, 219, 220, 224, 229, 230–32, 248–49, 272, 273, 296, 300, 350; Kanawha Division, 110, 117, 125, 129–32, 262, 276, 289; Black hat Brigade, 141–42, 192–94, 219, 229; Irish Brigade, 242–44, 245, 247, 342; Philadelphia Brigade, 226; Purnell Legion, 249; 8th Connecticut, 264, 286–87; 11th Connecticut, 262–63; 14th Connecticut, 238–39; 16th Connecticut, 80, 286, 287–89; 1st Delaware, 237–38; 14th Indiana, 239–40, 250; 19th Indiana, 141–42, 193; 27th Indiana, 112, 207–9; 7th Maine, 293; 10th Maine, 205–6; 2nd Maryland, 264–65; 5th Maryland, 237–38; 2nd Massachusetts, 207–9, 230–31; 12th Massachusetts, 188–90, 390; 15th Massachusetts, 227–28; 19th Massachusetts, 228; 20th Massachusetts, 227, 228; 29th Massachusetts, 243, 245; 35th Massachusetts, 290; 7th Michigan, 224, 225, 226; 17th Michigan, 134–35, 280; 1st Minnesota, 222, 223; 5th New Hampshire, 251–52; 6th New Hampshire, 264–65; 9th New Hampshire, 140; 4th New Jersey, 149; 13th New Jersey, 230–31, 248–49; 4th New York, 237–38; 9th New York, 136, 281–84; 12th New York (militia), 89; 21st New York, 137; 28th New York, 207; 34th New York, 224, 225, 226; 42nd New York, 227; 46th New York, 140; 51st New York, 265–66, 290; 59th New York, 227–28; 61st New York, 247; 63rd New York, 242–43; 64th New York, 247; 69th New York, 242–43; 76th New York, 139; 79th New York, 279; 83rd New York, 188; 84th New York, 193–94; 88th New York, 242–43; 89th New York, 141; 102nd New York, 213, 232; 107th New York, 139; 108th New York, 238–39; 126th New York, 123, 131, 225; 7th Ohio, 232; 8th Ohio, 239–40, 250; 23rd Ohio, 131; 32nd Ohio, 89, 124; 60th Ohio, 89; 66th Ohio, 211; 13th Pennsylvania, 184–85; 28th Pennsylvania, 203, 210–11; 45th Pennsylvania, 134–35; 51st Pennsylvania, 265–66, 267; 90th Pennsylvania, 190, 198–99; 107th Pennsylvania, 185, 187; 118th Pennsylvania, 108, 307; 124th Pennsylvania, 204–5; 125th Pennsylvania, 205, 215, 219, 224–25, 229; 128th Pennsylvania, 206–7; 130th Pennsylvania, 238–39, 250; 132nd Pennsylvania, 239–40; 4th Rhode Island, 286, 287–89; 7th West Virginia, 239–40; 2nd Wisconsin, 141–42, 193–94; 3rd Wisconsin, 207–9; 6th Wisconsin, 141–42, 192–93; 7th Wisconsin, 141–42, 193; *see also* division and brigade commanders, by name

Army of Virginia, 2–13, 15–17, 61–62, 80, 102, 173
artillery. *See* Army of Northern Virginia; Army of the Potomac
Aspinwall, William H., 25, 37, 321–22, 325

Bagley, George W., 56
Baltimore, Md., 6, 66, 68, 82, 88, 99–100, 104
Baltimore and Ohio Railroad, 29, 67, 89
Banks, Maj. Gen. Nathaniel P., 102, 203, 272
"Barbara Frietchie" (Whittier), 93
Barksdale, Brig. Gen. William, 95, 123–24, 225, 226
Barlow, Col. Francis C., 243, 244, 247, 250, 252
Barlow, S.L.M., 25, 30, 32, 33, 37, 331, 332, 343
Barnes, Lt. Col. Joseph H., 245
Barton, Clara, 305–6
Bates, Edward, 9, 13, 21
"Battle Hymn of the Republic, The" (Howe), 189
Battles and Leaders of the Civil War, 353
Belmont, August, 25, 42
Bennett, James Gordon, 25, 319
Bennett, Col. R. T., 243, 244, 245
Benning, Col. Henry L., 260, 266–67, 395
Berlin, Md., 337
Blackford, Lt. Col. William, 184, 213–14
Blackwood's Magazine (England), 334
Blair, Francis P., 322, 336, 339
Blair, Montgomery, 14, 45, 311, 322
Blakeslee, Lt. B. G., 288
blockade, 43, 60, 76
Bloody Lane. *See* Antietam battlefield: Sunken Road
Bloss, Sgt. John M., 112, 208, 350

Bolivar Heights (Va.), 90, 91, 124, 143, 144, 153
Bonaparte, Napoleon Joseph Charles Paul, Prince Napoleon, 23–24
Bondurant, Capt. J. W., 130–31
Boonsboro, Md., 91, 94, 96, 109, 116, 118, 119, 128, 129, 154, 159
Boonsboro turnpike, 159, 161, 168, 169, 261, 270, 277
Borcke, Maj. Heros Von, 73, 154
border states, 26, 43, 45
Boteler's Ford, 168, 174, 175, 276, 277, 285, 292, 305, 306
Boulware, Capt. J. R., 84, 92, 96, 284
Brady, Mathew B., 30, 315–16
Bragg, Gen. Braxton, 63, 65, 69, 104, 165, 328–29, 330
Branch, Brig. Gen. L. O'Brien, 289, 290
Brearley, Pvt. William, 280
Brooke, Col. John R., 242
Brown, John, 152, 188
Brownsville, Md., 146
Brownsville Gap (Md.), 145, 146
Brownsville Gap road, 146, 147
Buckeystown, Md., 85, 117
Buckingham, Brig. Gen. Catharinus P., 339–41
Buell, Maj. Gen. Don Carlos, 329
Bull Run, First, battle, 8, 12, 19, 21, 52, 56, 62, 64
Bull run, Second, campaign, 1–14, 47, 61–62, 63, 166–67, 203, 259; battle, 9–12, 14, 16, 47, 62, 64, 69, 74, 79, 81, 103, 117, 133, 192, 259
Burkittsville, Md., 145
Burnside, Maj. Gen. Ambrose E., 3, 8, 102, 110, 170, 282; declines command of Army of the Potomac, 78–79, 323, 340; Turner's Gap, 133, 141, 142, 143; and McClellan, 170–71, 259, 268; Antietam, 170–71, 172, 173, 195, 218, 221, 235, 256, 258–59, 261, 263,

Index

Burnside, Maj. Gen. Ambrose E. (cont'd) 265, 267, 268, 271, 276, 277, 279, 280, 286, 290–92, 296, 300, 303, 353–57; replaces McClellan as head of Army of the Potomac, 338, 340–41, 343, 345
Burnside Bridge. *See* Rohrbach Bridge

cabinet (the), 13–14, 16; and Emancipation Proclamation, 44–45, 317–18
Caldwell, Brig. Gen. John C., 242, 243, 244–45, 247, 394
Cameron, Simon, 28
Campbell, Pvt. William, 250
Carman, Col. Ezra A., xii, 230, 248, 373
Carter, Hill, 25
casualties, 10, 52–53, 55, 64, 69; Turner's Gap, 143; Crampton's Gap, 149; Harper's Ferry, 153; Antietam, 294, 296, 317, 397; Maryland campaign, 309
Catoctin Mountain (Md.), 82, 117, 125
cavalry. *See* Army of Northern Virginia; Army of the Potomac
Cemetery Hill. *See* Antietam battlefield
censorship. *See* press: censorship of
Centreville, Va., 10, 11, 12, 30
Chamberlayne, Lt. John, 63
Chambersburg, Pa., 96, 97, 328
Chambersburg raid, 327–28, 331
Chandler, Zachariah, 75–76
Chantilly, Va., 15, 64, 69
Charleston Mercury, 312
Chase, Salmon P., 8, 9, 13–14, 16, 27–28, 29; and slavery issue, 44, 45; and Emancipation Proclamation, 317–18
Chesapeake and Ohio Canal, 29, 73, 95, 167

Chesnut, Mary Boykin, 56, 58, 197
Chicago Tribune, 81
Chickahominy River, 216
Chilton, Col. R. H., 91, 112, 113, 114–15, 116, 349
Chisholm, Capt. Alex, 304
Christ, Col. Benjamin C., 279, 280, 281
Christian, Col. William A., 187–88, 190, 198
Cincinnati, Ohio, 63, 74, 165
Civil War, xi–xii, 52–53, 74–76; politics of, 24–27, 29, 36–38, 166, 319–21, 332–33, 343; threat of foreign intervention in, 39–41, 50, 59–61, 166–67; changing character of, 41–44, 48, 318, 339; cost of, 76
civilians, 3, 10, 12, 77; reception of Confederate soldiers, 70, 85, 94–95, 96–97; reception of Union soldiers, 108–9, 111; in Sharpsburg, 162, 167, 184, 269, 281, 284–85, 296, 297, 306, 315, 316–17, 335
Clark, Adj. Walter, 230
Cobb, Brig. Gen. Howell, 59, 92–93, 236, 242, 248, 250; Crampton's Gap, 145, 147, 148–49
Cobden, Richard, 41
Cochrane, Brig. Gen. John, 323
Coffin, Charles C., 246, 293
Colgrove, Col. Silas, 112, 113
Colquitt, Brig. Gen. Alfred H.: Turner's Gap, 128, 129, 132, 142; Antietam, 208, 210–11, 214, 236
Confederacy: King Cotton theory, 50, 59–60; and European intervention, 50, 59–61, 166–67, 333–35; conscription in, 51–52, 59; military strategy of, 58–59, 65–66, 68–69; financial structure of, 59
Congress, Confederate, 51–52
Congress, U.S., 43–44, 58, 333; *see also* Joint Committee of the Conduct of the war

conscription, Confederate, 51–52, 59
Cooke, Col. John R., 248, 249–51, 252, 253
Cooke, Brig. Gen. Philip St. George, 248
Corinth, Miss., 328
Cornfield. *See* Antietam battlefield
cotton: King Cotton theory, 50, 59–60
cotton famine (Europe), 40–41, 50, 59–60, 166, 333
Couch, Maj. Gen. Darius N., 102, 117, 257, 296, 301, 330, 357, 395; Crampton's Gap, 120, 145, 147, 155
Coulter, Col. Richard, 187, 188, 189, 190, 192
Cox, Brig. Gen. Jacob D., 17, 110, 117, 125, 169, 258, 323; Turner's Gap, 129–30, 132, 133, 134, 140; Antietam, 171, 173, 258–60, 261, 263, 265–66, 268, 276, 277, 289, 290, 300, 303, 353–54, 355
Crampton's Gap (Md.), 119, 120, 121, 128, 145, 146, 154, 170, 301; battle of, 145–49, 152, 156, 163, 220, 242, 271
Crampton's Gap road, 146, 147
Crane, Maj. Orrin J., 232
Crawford, Brig. Gen. Samuel W., 204–5, 206, 215, 224
Crome, Lt. George, 131
Crook, Col. George, 130, 131, 262, 263, 267, 277
Cross, Col. Edward E., 243, 251–52
Culpeper Court House, Va., 338
Cumberland Valley (Md.), 82–83, 126
Cumberland Valley Railroad, 97
Cumming, Col. Alfred, 241, 244
Curtin, Andrew G., 100–101, 104, 109, 118, 137, 152, 164, 165, 166, 206, 239
Curtis, Brig. Gen. Samuel R., 31
Custer, Capt. George Armstrong, 157, 158, 160

Dana, Charles A., 28
Dana, Brig. Gen. N.J.T., 222, 224, 226, 227
Davis, Col. Benjamin Franklin, 151–52, 153, 328
Davis, Judge David, 324
Davis, Jefferson, 20, 34, 49, 50, 52, 53, 64–65, 66, 67, 79, 161; war objectives of, 68–69
Davis, Varina Howell, 53
Dawes, Maj. Rufus R., 142, 159, 193, 198
"Dead of Antietam, The" (exhibit), 316
De Fontaine, Felix G., 70, 93, 139–40, 194
Delancey, Pvt. John, 187
Democratic party, 25, 26, 333, 336
Dennison, William, 311
Derby, Capt. Richard C., 217, 228
Dicey, Edward, 26
Dimon, Dr. Theodore, 264
Dingle, Maj. J. H., 200
Dooley, Pvt. John, 284
Doubleday, Brig. Gen. Abner, 181, 182, 185, 190, 191, 193, 194, 202, 214, 272
Douglas, Col. Henry Kyd, 94–95, 153, 164, 294, 395
Douglass, Col. Marcellus, 186, 189
Drayton, Brig. Gen. Thomas F., 134, 277, 283, 284
Dudley, Thomas H., 40
Dunker church, 180, 181, 182, 190, 214–15, 224–25, 232, 247–48, 251, 316
Duryea, Brig. Gen. Abram, 185–87, 190, 193
Duryea, Lt. Col. Jacob, 264–65
Dwight, Lt. Col. Wilder, 47, 81, 203–4, 231

Eakle, Martin, 269
Early, Brig. Gen. Jubal A., 214, 219–20, 224, 225, 226

Index

East Woods. *See* Antietam battlefield
Eckert, Maj. Thomas T., 44
elections, 66, 69, 332–33, 343
Elk Mountain (Md.), 82, 95, 144
emancipation and Emancipation Proclamation, 26, 38, 43, 44–45, 48, 166, 317–19, 325; Army of the Potomac's reaction to, 319–21; McClellan's reaction to, 321–24, 325; effect of, on European support for Confederacy, 334–35
Europe: potential intervention in Civil War, xi, 39–41, 50, 59–61, 166–67; effect of cotton famine on, 40–41, 50, 59–60, 166, 333; effect of Antietam on support for Confederacy, 333–34; effect of Emancipation Proclamation on support for Confederacy, 334–35
Ewell, Maj. Gen. Richard S., 56, 181
Ewing, Col. Hugh, 277, 289

Fair Oaks, Va., 34, 53, 216
Fairchild, Col. Harrison S., 281–82, 286–87, 289
Fairfax Station, Va., 10
Faithful, Capt. William T., 85
Falmouth, Va., 3, 8, 282
Featherston, Brig. Gen. Winfield S., 241–42, 244, 245
Ferrero, Brig. Gen. Edward, 265–66
field hospitals, 274, 294, 305–6
Fiske, Capt. Samuel ("Dunn Browne"), 109, 238–39, 314
Forbes, Edwin, 99
Ford, Col. Thomas H., 123–24, 385
foreign intervention, threat of, xi, 39–41, 50, 59–61, 166–67
Fort Donelson, Tenn., 31
Fort Henry, Tenn., 31
Fort Monroe, Va., 31, 62
Fort Sumter, S.C., 20, 50
Fox's Gap (Md.), 128, 129, 130, 132, 134, 135, 156, 157, 208, 209, 262, 280

France, 39, 40
Frankfort, Ky., 165
Franklin, Maj. Gen. William B., 4, 5–6, 7, 8–9, 10–11; Maryland campaign, 102, 117, 170; Crampton's Gap, 119–20, 121, 145–49, 152, 154–56, 160, 162, 163, 170, 271, 301; Antietam, 171–72, 173, 235, 257, 271, 272–73, 296, 301, 303, 307
Frederick, Md., 82, 83, 105, 106, 125; occupied by Army of Northern Virginia, 85–88, 92–93, 104; occupied by Army of the Potomac, 110–12
Freeman, Douglas Southall: *Lee's Lieutenants*, 351; *R. E. Lee*, 351
Frémont, Maj. Gen. John C., 26
French, Brig. Gen. William H., 218, 221, 230, 235–37, 238, 240, 241, 243, 246, 247, 253, 256, 261
Frietchie, Barbara, 93
Frosttown, Md., 136
Furlough and Bounty Act (1861), 51

Galwey, Sgt. Thomas, 240, 344
Garber, Lt. A. W., 182
Garden, Capt. Hugh R., 280
Gardner, Alexander, 315–16
Garland, Brig. Gen. Samuel, 128, 129, 130–32, 137, 209–210, 211, 236; death of, 131, 140, 157, 208, 209
Garnett, Brig. Gen. Richard B., 277
Gettysburg, Pa., 104, 110, 317
Gibbon, Brig. Gen. John, 115, 141, 343; Turner's Gap, 141–42, 229, 242; Antietam, 191, 192–94, 200–201, 207, 219, 229
Gibson, James F., 315–16
Gordon, E. C., 351
Gordon, Brig. Gen. George H., 207, 208, 210, 219

Gordon, Col. John B., 139, 235, 237, 238, 316; wounded, 242, 246
Gorman, Brig. Gen. Willis A., 222, 223–24, 226, 229
Gould, Maj. John M., xii, 108, 373
Graham, Capt. James A., 250
Graham, Capt. William M., 253, 254, 269, 394–95
Grant, Brig. Gen. Ulysses S., 31
Great Britain: threat of intervention, 39–41, 50, 59–60, 166–67, 333–35; effect of cotton famine on, 40–41, 59–60, 166, 333; effect of Antietam on support for Confederacy, 333–34; effect of Emancipation Proclamation on support for Confederacy, 334–35
Greeley, Horace, 166, 318, 344
Greene, Lt. Dana, 210
Greene, Brig. Gen. George Sears, 210–11, 213, 214, 219, 231–32, 235, 240, 248–49, 310
Greene, Nathanael, 210
Gregg, Brig. Gen. Maxcy, 288–89
Grigsby, Col. Andrew J., 153, 193, 194, 220, 223–24
Griswold, Capt. John, 262
Groveton, Va., 141

habeus corpus, proclamation suspending, 318, 319, 321–22
Hagerstown, Md., 83, 91, 96, 97, 109, 116, 118, 125, 327; Ladies Union Relief Association, 306
Hagerstown turnpike, 168, 175, 176, 177, 180, 181, 190, 192, 194, 200, 213, 223, 230, 316
Hall, Col. Norman J., 223
Halleck, Maj. Gen. Henry W., 3–4, 7, 99, 166, 329; appointed general-in-chief, 39; and McClellan, 4–5, 311, 323, 339; and withdrawal from Peninsula, 5, 45–46, 61; and Second Bull Run campaign, 3–8, 11–14; and McClellan's reappointment to command, 15, 77–78; and Maryland campaign, 18, 77, 101; and defense of Harper's Ferry, 88–89, 121, 122; and defense of Washington, 104, 106, 109, 116, 165; actions after Antietam, 325–26, 327, 330; and McClellan's dismissal, 338; McClellan's dispatches to, Maryland campaign, 104–6, 158, 162, 255–56, 299, 308, 350
Hammond, James H., 50
Hampton, Brig. Gen. Wade, 110–11
Hancock, Brig. Gen. Winfield Scott, 257, 303, 315
Harland, Col. Edward, 281–82, 286–87, 289
Harman, Maj. John A., 73
Harper's Ferry, Va., xii, 29, 30, 65, 83, 164, 175, 195, 257, 285, 290, 337; Confederate attack and siege, 88–92, 94–95, 106, 109–10, 116, 117, 118, 119, 121–24, 125, 126, 128, 143–44, 145, 146, 150–54, 155, 156, 161, 162, 164, 166, 174, 220, 285, 296, 312, 352, 385
Harper's Ferry road, 109, 116, 168, 277, 283, 285, 287
Harper's Weekly, 24, 83, 99
Harrisburg, Pa., 67, 97, 110
Harrison's Landing, Va., 36, 37, 38, 45, 46, 61
Hartranft, Col. John F., 266
Hartsuff, Brig. Gen. George L., 187, 188, 192, 194
Hatch, Brig. Gen. John P., 17, 136, 137, 139, 181
Hatch, Ozias M., 325
Haupt, Col. Herman, 3–4, 5, 10, 12
Hauser's Ridge, 214, 223, 227, 229, 232
Hawthorne, Nathaniel, 21, 121
Hay, John, 8, 11, 14, 16, 34, 79, 320, 324, 338
Hayes, Lt. Col. Rutherford B., 131
Hays, Brig. Gen. Harry T., 188

Index

Higgins, Col. Jacob, 224-25
Hill, Adams S., 8, 13
Hill, Maj. Gen. Ambrose Powell, 57, 58, 71, 307; Maryland campaign, 103-4; Harper's Ferry, 94, 153-54, 165, 174; Antietam, 176, 195, 197, 257, 276, 277, 285-87, 289-90, 291, 296, 356-57, 395
Hill, Maj. Gen. Daniel Harvey, 57, 58, 69, 141, 162, 219; Maryland campaign, 95, 96, 107, 116, 117, 118, 119, 120, 125, 145, 150, 151; and Lost Order, 92, 112, 114-15, 349, 350-52; Turner's Gap, 126, 128-29, 132-34, 136, 140, 142-43, 147, 258; Antietam, 182, 205, 208, 211, 235-37, 239-42, 248, 251-52, 274, 292, 304, 397
Holmes, Oliver Wendell, 294, 316
Holmes, Capt. Oliver Wendell, Jr., 179, 228, 294, 316
Holmes, Lt. Col. William R., 267
Hood, Brig. Gen. John Bell, 57, 71-72, 197; Turner's Gap, 135, 140; Antietam, 176, 177, 181, 182, 197-98, 199, 201, 202, 205, 206, 211, 213, 214, 218, 276
Hood, Pvt. William, 275
Hooker, Maj. Gen. Joseph, 79, 81, 191, 303, 340; Maryland campaign, 101, 102, 110, 118-19, 157, 160; Turner's Gap, 129, 133, 135, 136, 139; Antietam, 170, 171, 172, 173, 176-77, 180-81, 182, 185, 190, 191, 195, 197, 199, 201-3, 204, 207, 213, 214-15, 216, 218, 219, 220, 229, 273-74, 296, 310, 390; wounded, 215, 221
Howard, Brig. Gen. Oliver Otis, 222-23, 224, 226-27
Howe, Julia Ward, 189
Humphreys, Brig. Andrew A., 257-58, 301-2
Hunter, Pvt. Alexander, 53, 63, 70, 84, 283
Hyde, Maj. Thomas W., 108, 293

Ingalls, Lt. Col. Rufus, 327
intelligence, Federal, 23-24, 30, 32-34, 45-46, 54, 74-75, 100, 103-7, 116, 118, 157-58, 160
Irwin, Col. William H., 250, 256, 293, 296
Iuka, Miss., 328
Ives, Col. Joseph, 53, 54, 61

Jackson, Maj. Gen. Thomas J., 19, 56, 73, 87-88, 161, 188, 338; generalship, 55, 56-57, 70, 71, 164; Shenandoah Valley campaign, 34-35, 39, 54, 55, 89, 192, 203, 239; Seven Days' battles, 35, 55; Second Bull Run campaign, 7, 9, 11, 47, 61-62, 141; Maryland campaign, 71-73, 74, 85-86, 87-88, 103-4, 105, 107, 109, 112, 113, 118; Harper's Ferry, 90-92, 94-95, 116, 122, 124, 126, 143-44, 150, 152-54, 160; Antietam, 164-65, 173, 174, 175, 177, 181-82, 191, 201-2, 213-14, 219, 224, 226, 234, 240, 274-76, 397
James River, 31, 35, 46
Jefferson, Md., 145
Jenkins, Brig. Gen. Micah, 277, 281
Jennings, Capt. R.P., 194
Johnson, Lt. William, 72-73, 85, 92
Johnston, Gen. Joseph E., 23, 28, 30, 34, 54, 327
Joint Committee on the Conduct of the War, 27, 78, 79, 114, 174, 300, 353
Jones, Brig. Gen. David R., 260, 276-77, 285, 292
Jones, John B., 97, 312
Jones, Brig. Gen. John R., 181-82, 191, 307-8

Keedysville, Md., 159, 164, 169, 302
Kelton, Col. J. C., 2, 13, 15
Kemper, Brig. Gen. James L., 277, 283, 284
Kentucky, 26, 63, 65, 69, 328-29

Kernstown, Va., 239
Kershaw, Brig. Gen. Joseph B., 95, 123–24, 225, 226, 231
Key, Maj. John J., 320, 322
Key, Col. Thomas M., 111, 267–68, 319, 320, 331, 356
Kimball, Lt. Col. Edgar A., 282
Kimball, Brig. Gen. Nathan, 239–40, 250
King, Charles E., 269
Kingsbury, Col. Henry W., 262–63
Knipe, Col. Joseph F., 207
Kop, Capt. Peter, 112, 208

LaDuc, Capt. William G., 294
Lanier, Sidney, 94
Law, Col. Evander M., 197, 198, 199–200, 205, 213, 223
Lawton, Brig. Gen. Alexander R., 181, 182, 186, 188, 194, 197, 201–2
Leach, Pvt. Calvin, 207–8
Lee, Brig. Gen. Fitzhugh, 175
Lee, Gen. Robert E., xi, 34, 49–52, 61, 334; background, 49, 53; and conscription, 51–52; generalship, 34, 53–54, 55–56, 57–58, 61–62, 87, 91, 120, 220, 232, 234, 309–10, 330; and McClellan, 34, 51, 54, 66, 68, 91, 96, 110, 121, 160–61, 163, 234, 270, 303–4, 310, 341; and Shenandoah Valley campaign, 34, 54; Seven Days' battles, 35, 53–55; Second Bull Run campaign, 7, 47, 61–62, 234; plan for Maryland campaign, 63–69, 79, 81, 82–83, 96, 167, 317; Maryland campaign, 69–72, 77, 85, 86–88, 94, 96–97, 99–100, 150–51, 310, 317; injury to, 72, 87, 135, 214, 285; Harper's Ferry, 90–91, 116, 124–28; and Lost Order, 90–91, 104, 112, 115, 125–26, 349, 350–52; Turner's Gap, 126, 128, 135, 143, 157–58, 159, 352; decision to fight at Antietam, 160–62, 164–65, 173, 174–76, 310, 352;
Antietam, 173, 176, 195, 214, 220, 230, 232, 234, 235–36, 260, 274–75, 276, 284–85, 296–97, 309–10, 317, 397–98; return to Virginia, 303–4, 307; actions after Antietam, 307–8, 327, 328, 337–38
Lee, Capt. Robert E., Jr., 275
Lee, Col. Stephen D., 182, 184, 185, 187–88, 190–91, 208, 211, 214, 232, 397
Leesburg, Va., 69–70, 328
Leslie's Illustrated, 99
Letcher, John, 51
Libby, Sgt. E. J., 206
Lightfoot, Lt. Col. J. N., 246
Lincoln, Abraham, xi–xii, 11, 165, 234, 311; war policies, 25–26, 37, 41–43, 76–77; management of war, 5, 7–8, 13, 14, 27–28, 33, 38–39, 75–76, 102, 104, 106, 110, 113, 158, 206, 313, 319, 328–32, 336–37; and McClellan, 7–8, 16, 20, 22, 27, 29, 30–31, 32, 33, 36, 37–38, 47, 80, 106, 163, 318, 320, 324–25, 329–31; visits to Army of the Potomac, 37, 323–25, 326, 329, 400; and slavery and emancipation, 42–44, 166, 334; Emancipation Proclamation, 44–45, 48, 317–18, 334; offers Burnside army command, 78–79, 170, 323, 338; and McClellan's reappointment to command, 15, 16–17, 78–79; habeas corpus proclamation, 318, 319, 321–22; and loyalty of officer corps, 320, 339; and McClellan's dismissal, 330, 331, 332, 336–37, 338–39, 340; Gettysburg Address, 317
Line, George, farm, 177
Livermore, Lt. Thomas L, 244–45, 247, 251–52
Lomax, Elizabeth Lindsay, 77
Long, Col. Armistead L., 217
Longstreet, Maj. Gen. James, 55, 57, 58, 61, 72, 112, 327, 338, 351;

Index

Longstreet, Maj. Gen. James (cont'd)
Seven Days' battles, 55–56; Second Bull Run campaign, 62; Maryland campaign, 87, 90, 95–96, 116, 117–18, 120, 125–26, 150, 152; Turner's Gap, 126, 134, 137, 143; Antietam, 151, 160, 164–65, 175, 214, 236, 239, 247–48, 249, 251–53, 277, 297, 352, 397–98

Lost Order (Special Orders No. 191), 90, 91–92, 104, 112–13, 114–21, 160, 163, 208, 298, 310, 349–52

Loudoun Heights (Va.), 90, 95, 116, 124, 143, 144, 152

Lowell, James Russell, 24, 34

Lusk, Capt. William T., 75

Lyle, Col. Peter, 190

McClellan, Ellen Marcy: General McClellan's letters to, 3, 13, 15, 19, 21, 22, 23, 33, 35, 36, 38, 47, 77, 78, 81, 102, 105, 109, 120, 132, 158, 162, 171, 299, 308–9, 313, 323, 324–25, 337, 341, 342

McClellan, Maj. Gen. George B., xi, xii, 3, 4, 188–89, 279, 312; background, 20, 49; character, 19–20, 22–24, 32, 77, 120–21, 174, 303, 308–9, 338, 341; political views, 24–25, 36–38, 45, 48, 79, 319, 321–23, 332–33, 339; management of military intelligence, 23–24, 32–33, 46, 103–7, 118, 172, 174, 263–64; estimates of enemy strength, 6, 23–24, 30, 32–34, 45, 54, 74–75, 101, 103–7, 109, 117, 118, 160, 163–64, 174, 217, 256, 326; and army organization, 20–21, 79–81, 101–2, 103, 108–9, 160, 170–71, 192, 338; generalship, 6, 20, 30, 32–36, 47, 53–55, 62, 68, 91, 101–2, 107, 120–21, 118–21, 136, 149, 157, 163, 172, 217–18, 234–35, 255–57, 270, 272–73, 292, 296, 298–99, 303, 310–11, 313–14, 320, 338–39, 342–44, 354–57; and Lincoln, 7–8, 16, 20, 22, 27, 29, 30–31, 32, 33, 36, 37–38, 47, 80, 106, 163, 318, 320, 324–25, 329–31; and Stanton, 6–7, 8, 9, 11, 13, 16–17, 28, 36, 311, 323, 339–40, 380; and Halleck, 4–5, 311, 323, 339; western Virginia campaign, 20, 25, 48; as general-in-chief, 20–23, 27–31; illness of, 27–28, 102; Peninsula campaign, 2, 5, 28–29, 31–38, 41, 45–46, 51, 52–55, 57, 58, 61, 117, 160, 163, 319; and Second Bull Run campaign, 2, 4–15, 16–17, 62, 81, 117; reappointment to command, 15–17, 77–78, 79; Maryland campaign, 77–78, 81–82, 88, 91, 101–13, 115–17, 150, 298, 308–9, 317; Harper's Ferry, 88–89, 109–10, 119, 121, 122, 133, 153, 154; and Lost Order, 113–21, 125, 126, 128, 163, 298, 350–52; Turner's Gap, 118–19, 129, 132, 135–36, 140, 142, 143, 149, 157–59, 160; Crampton's Gap, 119–20, 146, 147, 154–55; decision to fight at Antietam, 159–61, 162–64, 167; plan for Antietam, 169–74, 176–77, 181, 256, 273, 353–55; Antietam, 181, 190, 195, 202, 215, 216–18, 220, 222, 234–35, 246–47, 253, 255–57, 258–59, 261–62, 263–64, 265, 267–68, 269–74, 280, 286, 290–92, 296, 298–304, 306–7; actions after Antietam, 309, 311, 320, 324–27, 328, 329–31, 332; and Emancipation Proclamation, 321–23, 325; begins Virginia campaign, 335, 337–38, 343; dismissal from command, 331–32, 336–37, 338–45, 402; report on Antietam, 169, 261, 299, 302, 353–54; official report, 28, 163, 169, 299, 354–55; *McClel-*

McClellan, Maj. Gen. George B. (cont'd)
  Ian's Own Story, 355; dispatches to Halleck, Maryland campaign, 104–6, 158, 162, 255–56, 299, 308, 350; letters to wife: see McClellan, Ellen Marcy
"McClellan's Platform" (broadside), 379
McClure, Alexander K., 101, 328
McCrea, Lt. Tully, 225–26
McDowell, Maj. Gen. Irvin, 1, 2, 17, 33, 81, 102, 170, 192
McGee, Capt. James, 243
McGuire, Dr. Hunter, 274
McIntosh, Capt. D. G., 287
McKinley, Sgt. William, 131
McLaws, Maj. Gen. Lafayette, 69, 115, 118; Harper's Ferry, 90, 95, 116, 119, 120, 124–25, 126, 143, 144–45, 152, 160, 165, 174, 220; Crampton's Gap, 145, 148, 150–51, 152, 155–56, 220, 352; Antietam, 195, 214, 220, 224–26, 228, 232, 234, 236, 242, 248, 262
McMaster, Col. F. W., 279
McRae, Col. D. K., 208, 209
MacRae, Lt. Col. William, 250
Magruder, Maj. Gen. John B., 33, 35, 56
Mallory, Stephen R., 55
Malvern Hill, Va., 55
Manassas Gap Railroad, 337, 340
Manassas Junction, Va., 2–3, 4, 5, 8, 28, 30, 62, 340
Manning, Col. Van H., 232
Mansfield, Maj. Gen. Joseph K. F., 102, 112, 203, 303; Antietam, 171, 172, 173, 177, 181, 195, 199, 202, 203–5, 216, 296; death of, 206, 207, 215
Marble, Manton, 37, 319, 323, 343
Marcy, Brig. Gen. Randolph B., 137, 139
Marshall, Col. Charles, 52, 351–52

Martinsburg, Va., 65, 83, 88–89, 91, 94, 118, 307
Maryland, 26, 82–83, 84–85
Maryland Heights (Md.), 90, 95, 116, 119, 122–24, 126, 128, 133, 143, 144, 145, 148, 151, 152, 153, 220, 257
Mason, James M., 39–40, 50
Matthews, Capt. Ezra W., 185, 188
Meade, Brig. Gen. George G., 314, 326, 343; Turner's Gap, 136–37, 139; Antietam, 176, 181, 184, 197, 199, 201, 202, 207, 272, 291, 300, 303
Meagher, Brig. Gen. Thomas F., 242–45, 246, 342–43, 394
Medill, Joseph, 331–32
Merrimack (warship), 31, 210
Middle Bridge (Antietam Creek), 169, 261, 268, 270, 277, 280, 292, 301, 354
Middletown, Md., 117, 120, 125
Miles, Col. Dixon S., 89–90, 94, 106, 116, 119, 122–24, 133, 143, 151, 152, 153, 385
Miller, David R., farm, 181, 182, 185, 192–93, 194, 200, 204, 208, 213, 214, 218, 219, 229, 235
Miller, Capt. M. B., 251
Milliken, Capt. Ben, 162
Missouri, 26
Mitchell, Cpl. Barton W., 112, 115, 208, 350
Monitor (warship), 31, 210
Monocacy River, 95, 105
Moor, Col. Augustus, 110–11, 130
Morell, Maj. Gen. George W., 218, 268, 355
Morris, Col. Dwight, 238, 239
Mumma, Samuel, farm, 167, 182, 184–85, 198, 199, 202, 205, 208, 212, 213, 237, 238, 248, 250, 301
Munford, Col. Thomas T., 145, 146, 147, 148, 175
Munfordville, Ky., 165

Index

Nagle, Brig. Gen. James, 264
Napoleon III of France (Louis Napoleon), 40
Nashville, Tenn., 31
National Road, 83, 91, 95, 97, 116, 117, 128, 135, 156, 168
New Orleans, La., 31, 38, 76
New York Herald, 25, 75
New York Journal of Commerce, 75, 319
New York Times, 154
New York Tribune, 74–75, 312, 344, 354
New York World, 25, 37, 319, 343
Newcomb, Lt. Edgar, 344
Nicodemus farm, 184, 229, 315
Nicodemus Hill, 175, 182, 190–91, 201, 214, 223, 291, 303
Norfolk, Va., 62
North Woods. *See* Antietam battlefield
Noyes, Capt. George F., 218

Old Hagerstown Road, 128–29, 136
Old Sharpsburg Road, 128, 130, 136, 156
Orange and Alexandria Railroad, 2–3, 337, 338, 340
Otto, John, farm, 167, 277, 281, 282, 286, 288–89
Owen, Lt. William M., 92, 97

Paige, Nathaniel, 111, 319
Palfrey, Lt. Col. Francis W., 222, 223
Palmer, Capt. William J., 164
Palmerston, Viscount Henry John Temple, 40, 47, 60, 167, 333–34
Parham, Col. William A., 146, 148, 242
Parker, Col. F. M., 238
Parmelee, Lt. Lewis C., 194–95
Patrick, Brig. Gen. Marsena R., 192, 193, 200, 219, 343

peace movement, Union, 26, 69, 332–33, 336
Pelham, Maj. John, 177–78, 182, 223, 229
Pender, Brig. Gen. William Dorsey, 87, 308, 313
Peninsula campaign, 2, 28–29, 31–38, 41, 45–46, 51, 52–55, 57, 58, 61, 160, 216
Pennsylvania, 66, 67, 87, 100–101, 110
Pennsylvania Railroad, 67
Perryville, Ky., 328
Petersburg, Va., 46
Petersburg Express, 312
Phelps, Col. Walter, Jr., 192, 193
Philadelphia, Pa., 68, 97, 100
Pinkerton, Allan, 23, 24, 30, 34, 46, 54, 103
Piper, Henry, farm, 241, 244, 245, 247, 251–52, 292–93
Pittman, Col. Samuel E., 112–13, 350
Pleasant Valley (Md.), 82, 95, 119, 146, 149, 154–56, 168, 171, 173, 235, 256, 257, 296, 301
Pleasonton, Brig. Gen. Alfred, 103–7, 117, 118, 129, 130, 172, 175, 270–71, 276, 292, 350
Poague, Capt. William P., 275, 291
Poffenberger, Alfred, farm, 224, 226
Poffenberger, Joseph, farm, 176, 181, 185, 187, 219, 291, 301
Poffenberger, Sam, farm, 306
Poland, Capt. John S., 279–80
Pope, Maj. Gen. John, 39, 58–59, 65, 380; Army of Virginia, 1, 2, 39, 46, 80, 81, 173, 309, 337–38; Second Bull Run campaign, 2–15, 16, 17, 47, 61–62, 63, 74, 76, 103, 133, 172, 259, 270; dismissal from command, 78
Porter, Maj. Gen. Fitz John, 3, 25, 37, 79, 105, 115, 259, 319, 323–24, 343; Second Bull Run campaign,

Porter, Maj. Gen. Fitz John (cont'd)
3, 8, 14–15, 79; Maryland campaign, 102, 106, 117, 159, 170, 257, 307; Antietam, 172, 173, 195, 217, 221, 256, 270, 272, 273, 291–92, 296, 301, 303
Posey, Col. Carnot, 242, 244, 245
Potomac River, 18, 21, 22, 64, 69, 72–73, 77, 89, 116, 167–68, 175, 309; *see also* Boteler's Ford
Potter, Col. Robert B., 266
Powell, Lt. Col. Eugene, 211
press, 11–12, 25, 36, 54, 69, 74–75, 77, 93–94, 97, 99, 315, 319, 341; censorship of, 7, 13, 74, 99, 166, 311–12
Prime, William C., 355, 375
Pry, Philip, farm, 195, 217, 218, 246, 253, 255, 256, 267, 269, 272, 290, 354
Pry, Samuel, 169, 171
Pryor, Brig. Gen. Roger A., 242, 244, 245

Quantrell, Mary, 93
Quince, Lt. William, 51

Ramsay, Lt. John, 285
Randolph, George W., 59
Ransom, Col. Matthew W., 248–49, 251
Ransom, Brig. Gen. Robert, Jr., 230
Rappahannock River, 30, 62, 64
Ratchford, Maj. J. W., 349
Rectortown, Va., 341
Red Hill, 269, 286
Reed, Cpl. Lewis, 189
Reno, Maj. Gen. Jesse L., 102, 118–19, 133; Turner's Gap, 129, 130, 133, 139, 140, 143; death of, 140, 171, 266
Republican party, 26, 43–44, 333; radical wing, 26, 27, 75–76, 166
Reynolds, Brig. Gen. John F., 101, 137

Richardson, Albert D., 99, 172, 241, 314, 331, 338, 343–44
Richardson, Maj. Gen. Israel B., 159, 242; Antietam, 218, 235, 240, 242–43, 244–45, 247, 253–54, 310; mortally wounded, 254, 255, 257, 303
Richmond, Va., 2, 24, 31, 34–35, 52–53, 58, 65
Richmond Dispatch, 55, 94
Richmond Enquirer, 312
Richmond Examiner, 93
Richmond Whig, 55
Ricketts, Brig. Gen. James B., 136, 181, 185, 187, 190, 198–99, 202, 221
Ripley, Brig. Gen. Roswell, S., 134, 205, 206–8, 211, 214
Robinson, Pvt. William Cullen, 316–17
Rockville, Md., 102
Rodes, Brig. Gen. Robert E.: Turner's Gap, 134, 137, 236; Antietam, 236, 238, 239, 244, 246, 249–50, 252
Rodman, Brig. Gen. Isaac P.: Turner's Gap, 133, 139; Antietam, 262, 263–64, 267, 276, 277, 281, 286–87, 300; death of, 287
Rohrbach, Henry, farm, 167, 258, 261, 263, 353
Rohrbach, Bridge (Burnside Bridge), 169, 171, 172, 175, 195, 218, 235, 258, 259, 260–61, 262–68, 276, 290, 292, 353–56
Rohrbach Bridge road, 260, 279
Rohrersville, Md., 146, 155
Ropes, Lt. Henry, 344
Rosser, Col. Thomas, 128, 130
Roulette, William, farm, 237
Ruffin, Col. Thomas, 131
Ruggles, Col. George D., 354
Russell, Capt. Charles H., 124, 132–33
Russell, Lord John, 41, 47–48, 167, 333–34

Index

Sackett, Col. Delos B., 265, 300, 355–56
Sale, Pvt. John, 148
Salem, Va., 340
San Jacinto (warship), 39
Scammon, Col. Eliakim P., 130, 131, 132, 262
Schell, Frank H., 99
Scott, Lt. Gen. Winfield, 22, 49
Second Confiscation Act (1862), 44, 58
Sedgwick, Maj. Gen. John, 9, 75, 99, 222, 242; Antietam, 218, 221–22, 224, 225, 226, 227, 229–30, 235, 240, 248, 249, 270, 272, 275; wounded, 227
Semmes, Brig. Gen. Paul J., 226, 228–29
Seven Days' battles, 35–36, 42, 46, 54–55, 57, 61, 62, 160
Seward, William H., 14, 40–41, 81, 332; and Emancipation Proclamation, 44, 45
Seymour, Brig. Gen. Truman, 184, 185, 186
Sharpe, Horatio, 167
Sharpsburg, Md., xi, xii, 94, 126, 159, 160, 161, 163, 167–68, 175, 281, 284–85, 298, 335
Shenandoah River, 89, 116
Shenandoah Valley, 29, 64, 65, 66, 83, 168, 307, 326, 327; campaign, 34–35, 39, 54, 55, 89, 192, 203, 239
Shepherdstown, Va., 94, 168, 305
Sherman, John, 43
Sherman, Maj. Gen. William T., 43
Sherrick, Joseph, farm, 279, 280
Sherrill, Col. Eliakim, 123
Shinn, Sgt. James W., 70, 72, 85, 245
Sickles, Brig. Gen. Daniel E., 23
slavery issue, 25–26, 38, 42–45, 58, 59, 166, 334; *see also* emancipation and Emancipation Proclamation

Slidell, John, 39–40, 50, 60–61
Slocum, Maj. Gen. Henry W., 146, 147–48, 149, 155, 156, 256, 257, 271
Smalley, George W., 99, 140, 176, 191, 199, 208, 273–74, 291, 298, 309, 311–12
Smith, Caleb B., 13
Smith, Maj. Gen. Edmund Kirby, 63, 69, 87, 329
Smith, Maj. Gen. William F., 146, 147, 148, 149, 155, 156, 251, 256
Smoketown, Md., 182
Smoketown road, 182, 184, 186, 211, 213
Snavely's Ford, 263–64, 267
Solomon's Gap (Md.), 95, 122
Sorrel, Maj. Moxley, 250
South Mountain (Md.), xii, 82–83, 90, 91, 119, 125, 126, 128, 129, 149, 150, 158, 170, 258, 298; *see also* Crampton's Gap; Turner's Gap
Southern Illustrated News, 73
Special Orders No. 191. *See* Lost Order
Springfield Republican, 109
Stainrook, Col. Henry J., 211, 214
Stamp, Sgt. Charlie, 139
Stanton, Edwin M., 5, 6, 10, 15–16, 28–29, 32, 35–36, 76, 152, 166, 259, 302; and McClellan, 6–7, 8, 9, 11, 13, 16–17, 28, 36, 311, 323, 339–40, 380
Starke, Brig. Gen. William E., 191, 193, 194, 195, 200, 202; death of, 194
Stearns, Cpl. Austin C., 136
Steiner, Dr. Lewis H., 85–87, 92, 93, 107, 110, 111
Stetson, Lt. Col. John J., 315
Stevens, Thaddeus, 101
Stewart, Lt. James, 200
Stiles, Rev. Joseph C., 71
Strong, George Templeton, 8, 10, 74, 99, 108, 166, 306

Strother, Lt. Col. David Hunter, 105, 110, 121, 170, 173–74, 195, 234, 244, 247, 267, 269, 270, 276, 298–99, 304–5, 341, 356

Stuart, Maj. Gen. J.E.B., 57, 112, 152, 248; Maryland campaign, 77, 82, 88, 103, 107, 116, ,117, 119, 125, 126, 128, 145, 148–49, 152, 162; and Lost Order, 350, 351, 352; Antietam, 175, 177–78, 182, 187, 190–91, 201, 213, 228–29, 274–76, 291, 296; Chambersburg raid, 327–28, 331

Sturgis, Brig. Gen. Samuel D., 3–4, 12; Turner's Gap, 133, 139, 140; Antietam, 262, 264–65, 267, 268, 276, 290

Sumner, Charles, 41, 42, 43, 318–19

Sumner, Maj. Gen. Edwin V., 102, 216; Second Bull Run campaign, 4, 6, 7, 9, 10–11; Maryland campaign, 102, 118, 170; Antietam, 171, 172, 173, 195, 215, 216–17, 218, 220–23, 226–28, 229, 230, 234, 235, 237, 240, 248, 256, 270, 271–73, 274, 296, 303, 307, 310

Sumner, Capt. Samuel S., 217

Sunken Road. *See* Antietam battlefield

Susquehanna River, 67

Sykes, Brig. Gen. George, 118–19, 156, 159, 270, 279–80, 292

"Tardy George" (poem), 27

Taylor, Maj. Walter H., 313

Tennessee, 63

Thomas, Brig. Gen. George H., 31

Thompson, Pvt. David L., 111, 136, 141, 282

Thompson, Capt. James, 185–86, 188, 189, 198

Times (London), 41, 60, 334

Tompkins, Capt. John A., 231, 232, 239, 253

Toombs, Brig. Gen. Robert, 58, 261, 262, 267, 277, 285, 287, 289

Trent, (ship), 39, 50

Trimble, Brig. Gen. Isaac R., 184, 185, 186

Trumbull, Lyman, 76

Turner, Maj. Levi C., 320

Turner's Gap (Md.), 83, 91, 116, 117, 119; battle of, 128–43, 149, 157, 163, 170, 176, 192, 229, 236, 273, 352

Tyndale, Lt. Col. Hector, 210–211, 214

Union: restoration of, as war aim, 24–27, 42, 166; peace movement in, 26, 69, 332–33, 336

Upper Bridge (Antietam Creek), 169, 171, 176, 218

Urbana, Md., 88

U.S. Sanitary Commission, 85, 108, 166, 306

Virginia, 62, 65

Wachusett (ship), 16

Wade, Benjamin F., 27, 46, 78, 79

Wadsworth, Brig. Gen. James S., 23, 331, 332

Wainwright, Col. Charles S., 270, 344

Wait, Pvt. Thomas, 206

Walcott, Capt. Charles E., 11

Walker, Col. James A., 184–85, 186

Walker, Brig. Gen. John G., 67–68, 69; Harper's Ferry, 90, 95, 116, 118, 124, 143, 144, 160, 174; Antietam, 164, 214, 230, 232, 248, 260, 274–75

Walker, Col. Joseph, 277, 281

war correspondents, 36, 74–75, 93, 96, 99, 154, 191, 311–12; *see also* press

War Department (Confederate), 53, 94

War Department (U.S.), 2, 5, 15, 77, 78, 104, 106, 311, 323; news cen-

Index

War Department (U.S.) (*cont'd*)
   sorship by, 7, 13, 74, 99, 166, 311–12
Ward, Artemus, 317
Warrenton, Va., 337
Warrenton Junction, Va., 344
Washington, D.C., 1, 7, 68, 88; defense of, 1, 2, 4, 6, 7, 12, 13, 15–16, 20–21, 22, 29, 31, 32, 33, 34, 45–46, 64, 80, 102, 104, 106, 109, 165
Waud, Alfred, 83, 99
Webb, Col. Alexander S., 174, 313
Weber, Brig. Gen. Max, 237, 238, 239
Webster, Daniel, 188
Webster, Col. Fletcher, 188, 189
Welles, Gideon, 9, 14, 16, 44, 46–47, 78, 82, 158, 311, 317, 328
Welsh, Col. Thomas, 279, 281
western Virginia campaign, 20, 25, 49, 258
West Woods. *See* Antietam battlefield
White, Capt. Elijah V., 104–5
White, Brig. Gen. Julius, 94, 121–22, 153
White's Ford, Va., 72–73, 82, 328
Whitman, Lt. George Washington, 156, 265, 266, 290, 321, 331
Whittier, John Greenleaf, 93

Wilcox, Brig. Gen. Cadmus M., 241
Wilkes, Capt. Charles, 39–40, 50
Willcox, Brig. Gen. Orlando B.:
   Turner's Gap, 133, 134–35; Antietam, 262, 268, 276, 277, 279, 281, 286, 289
Williams, Brig. Gen. Alpheus S., 81, 324, 325; Maryland campaign, 102, 118; and Lost Order, 112–13, 350; Antietam, 178, 204–5, 207, 208–9, 215, 219, 221, 227, 230, 249, 272
Williamsport, Md., 94, 110, 113, 152, 168, 169, 307, 327
Wilson, Lt. James, 272, 273–74
Wilson, Lt. John M., 261, 355, 356
Winchester, Va., 65, 83, 305, 307
Wise, Daniel, farm, 132, 140, 157
Witcher, Pvt. B. H., 211
Wofford, Col. William T., 197, 198, 200, 205
Woodruff, Lt. George A., 225–26
Wool, Maj. Gen. John E., 89, 90, 100, 104, 118, 143
Wright, Brig. Gen. Ambrose R., 241, 242, 243, 244, 245

York River, 31
Yorktown, Va., 32–34, 160

Zacharias, Rev. Daniel, 87